STEVEN JENKINS

CHEESE
PRIMER

STEVEN JENKINS
CHEESE PRIMER

WORKMAN PUBLISHING
NEW YORK

DEDICATION

This book is for my wife and partner of fifteen years,
Michelle Sims, and for my children, Lily Olive
Jenkins and Maxwell Mayer Jenkins.

Library of Congress Cataloging-in-Publication Data
Jenkins, Steven (Steven W.)
Steven Jenkins cheese primer
p. cm.
Includes index.
ISBN 0-89480-762-5 (pbk.)
1. Cheese. I. Title.
TX382.J46 1996 641.3'73—dc20
93-23175 CIP

Front cover photographs by Elizabeth Watts
Back cover photographs by Michael Harris

Workman books are available at special discounts when purchased
in bulk for premiums and sales promotions as well as for fund-rais-
ing or educational use. Special editions or book excerpts can also
be created to specification. For details, contact the Special Sales
Director at the address below.

Workman Publishing Company, Inc.
708 Broadway
New York, New York 10003-9555

Manufactured in the United States of America

First printing September 1996

10 9 8 7 6 5 4 3 2 1

Acknowledgments

verything I am I owe to my mom and dad, Cissie and Bill Jenkins. My sisters, Perry Cizek and Julie Hathaway, have been a lifelong source of inspiration.

My wife Michelle's mom and dad have made me feel like a member of their family, and their support through some lean years made all the difference. Thanks Mary Lou and Dr. Murry Sims.

I thank heartily Suzanne Rafer of Workman, the editor of so many books I consider the treasures of my library. Thanks, too, to publisher, Peter Workman and my agent, Susan Bergholz. A true friend and catalyst to the realization of all this material has been my copy editor Joni Miller. Barbara Raives and Mardee Haidin Regan were indispensable. I love you both and miss the time we spent together. At Workman, I'd also like to thank Andrea Glickson, Bert Snyder, Paul Gamarello, Sheilah Scully, and Arlene Lee. Thanks forever to the owners of Fairway Market in New York. David Sneddon, Harold Seybert, and Howard Glickberg are the greatest food retailers I've ever met, and they shared with me everything they know about the business.

It was Joel Dean and Giorgio DeLuca who lit a fire under me in 1977. Their contribution to the way Americans now perceive food has been immeasurable.

I am deeply grateful to Henry Kaplan, Gene Kaplan, and Bob Bruno of De Choix Specialty Foods Company of Woodside, New York, for their generous support in turning over their amazing warehouse to us to do with as we saw fit.

I have such fondness for the cheese importers with whom I have worked for so many years. Thank you for your professionalism and dedication: John Ciano, Ben Moskowitz, Joe Moskowitz, Herb Boden, Fred Chesman, Jean-Paul Grasmuck, Tom Slattery, Shelli Morton, Carol Goodrich, Walter Salidor, Jack Gasser, Margaret Gasser, Don Epstein, Bob Giambalvo, Dick Rogers, Michael Trullinger, and Angela Zamboni.

I have been tremendously influenced by a number of people in and out of the food business. My deep, eternal gratitude is extended to them: Lucian Todaro, owner of

Bel Canto Foods and Todaro Brothers; Miles and Lillian Cahn, owners of The Coach Farm; Gerd Stern and Sarah Stern, owners of Infood/Galilee; Jack Ceglic, a founder of Dean & DeLuca; sculptor August Christian; attorneys Margo Levine and Robert Cantor; psychologists Annabella Bushra and Peter Abrons (the Magnificent Abo); financial consultant Michael Kelly; playwright Margaret Dulaney Balitsaris and musician Matthew Balitsaris; writer James Mellgren; and entrepreneur Jay Magazine.

The American cheesemongers and cheesemakers that I have been closest to over the years have been responsible for much of the success I have enjoyed. I thank them heartily and pledge my undying respect and support: Rob Kaufelt, owner of Murray's Cheese Shop in Greenwich Village; Michel Lemmerling, owner of Bon Appetit in Princeton, New Jersey; Peter Moen, president of Grafton Village Cheese Company; Randolph Hodgson, owner of Neal's Yard Dairy in London; Brian McCabe, owner of Cote and Company in Doylestown, Pennsylvania; David and Bill Sunceri, owners of The Pennsylvania Macaroni Company in Pittsburgh; David Grotenstein; Peter Beattie; Kevin Rock; Howard Dorman; Sally and Roger Jackson; Jacques Williams; Liz and Tom Parnell; Letty and Bob Kilmoyer; Olga Dominguez; Avanelle and Randy Rivera; Ignazio Vella; Ari Weinzweig; Franklin Peluso; Bill Wallace; Greg Sava; Frank Meilak; Mary Keehn; Judy Schad; Cindy Major; Kent Smith; and John Strober.

I am especially grateful to the writers and editors in our industry who are enlightened about cheese and give it the respect it deserves. They have served to elevate its entire realm for those of us in America who either missed it or never knew it existed. Bless you Regina Schrambling, Cara Da Silva, Francine Maroukian, Florence Fabricant, Susan Orlean, Nancy Verde Barr, Zanne Stewart, Edward Behr, Ruth Reichl, Ed Levine, Julia Della Croce, Lorna Sass, Suzanne Hamlin, Corby Kummer, Nancy Harmon Jenkins, Mark Bittman, Marie Simmons, Patricia Wells, Maria Guarnaschelli, Paula Wolfert, and Mimi Sheraton. I celebrate the life of Richard Sax.

I owe a special thanks to the following: Tom Jordan, Richard MacKenzie, Arlene Wanderman, Deeann Jones, Dr. Daniel Sims, writer and raconteur extraordinaire from Lancashire Gary Regan, marketing genius Tim Metzger, Leslie Sims, Jay Rosengarten, wine prophet Stephen Tanzer, David Sims, Dr. Luc Lemmerling, Jeff Hellerbach, Harvey Rosenblum, Harold Hochman, Gino Roselli, Fedele Bruno, Bill Holland of the John Volpi Company, Dan Dahl, architects Warren Ashworth and Larry Bogdanow, Mitchel London, Fern

Berman, Gisella Isadori, winemaker Dr. Max Lake of Hunter Valley, New South Wales, Don Schoenholt, Paul La Pietra, Roberto and Rodolfo Ramirez, Takis Petrakos, Joanne Wynkoop, Terence Brennan, Tony Fortuna, Lex Alexander, Carmine Dellaporta, Ted Koryn, Steve Paverman, Pino Luongo. Monica Lavery Andrew Balducci, Darien Phillips. Greg Drescher, John Greeley, Sara Baer-Sinnot, Mildred Berman, Liz Castledine, Tim Lang, Jonathan Malbin, Dun Gifford, Philippa Goodrick, Marion Nestle, Fred Plotkin, Michael Romano, Bill Wallace, Hilary Waeson, Sandra and Greg Ray, Anna Herman, and Constantine Karvonides.

Thanks also to the people of The Oldways Preservation and Exchange Trust of Cambridge, Massachusetts for allowing me to participate in their crucial endeavor. Tirelessly and without profit, they have created a truly global forum in which to communicate the importance of preserving traditional recipes, the old ways of cooking, respect for regional integrity, and the importance of promoting artisanal food producers. They understand that cheese is good for you.

Finally, thanks to The American Cheese Society, The Switzerland Cheese Association, The Comté Cheese Association, Foods and Wines from Spain, and The International Olive Oil Council.

Contents

ITALY

181

THE BRITISH ISLES

291

SPAIN

325

U.S.A.

363

THE GREAT CHEESES
Ready Reference

473

An at-a-glance buying guide for the world's finest cheeses.

SAY
CHEESE!

Growing up on American home cooking in Columbia, Missouri, my early acquaintance with cheese was as limited as the next person's. I ate grilled cheese sandwiches, macaroni and cheese, and cheeseburgers made with processed "American" cheese, pizza blanketed with plenty of factory-made Mozzarella, and spaghetti liberally sprinkled with "Parmesan" shaken from a cardboard container. I relished the usual teenage quantities of Velveeta cut from a plastic-wrapped loaf in a box and Cheez Whiz spooned up from a glass jar. I didn't know much about food back then, but I did know I was destined to leave my hometown and head for New York City in 1973 to realize my dream of becoming an actor. Like most struggling actors, I nearly starved. When I fell into a job at a cheese shop on Madison Avenue that was part of a small chain, I remember thinking how good it would be to receive a steady paycheck.

It was in 1977, the beginning of the "gourmet" food shop onslaught that Leo Kauffer of A. & A. Richter Foods, who was the professor emeritus of Manhattan's fancy food world, gave me the break of a lifetime, sending me to see Joel Dean and Giorgio DeLuca. I became their first employee, and that summer, the legendary Dean & Deluca, a specialty food shop opened in New York.

Although it's hard to imagine now, when Dean & DeLuca opened there were virtually no great, authentic European cheeses available in the U.S., and though more and more Americans were traveling abroad, few had tasted, let alone

Steve Jenkins, cheesemonger.

developed an appreciation for fine cheese. Aside from domestic cheeses at the local supermarket, even the most sophisticated cooks and eaters rarely encountered much beyond Gruyère, Brie, Roquefort, Havarti, Feta, Emmental, and the occasional wheel of Stilton. A scant six years earlier Alice Waters had first entranced diners at Chez Panisse in Berkeley, serving French-style goat cheese with greens, but chèvre was not yet in our national food vocabulary. At the store I liberated the cheeses from the confines of refrigerator cases, crowded the counters with them, and liberally offered tastes. I lured customers with massive displays of the few decent cheeses we were able to obtain, integrating them with Joel Dean's sophisticated array of kitchenwares. Baskets overflowed with what passed for Camembert; bowls were filled with excellent authentic Ricotta and Mozzarella from Little Italy's Alleva Dairy; platters were heaped with baked farmer's cheeses from Ben's Cheese Shop on Houston Street. I built pillars and pyramids of cheese atop the counter using hundred of pounds of rock-hard, aged orange Goudas. I used slabs of Carrara marble and wooden cutting boards to display Bries and heaped Pillivuyt porcelain soufflé dishes with fresh goat cheeses sprinkled with herbs and drizzled with olive oil. For shoppers, the sensory experience was electrifying.

An American in Paris

By early 1979 the store was receiving enormous amounts of publicity, but we still sorely lacked the great cheeses mentioned in Waverley Root's books and M.F.K. Fisher's essays. That winter I went to Paris for the first time. I walked the city, absorbing the style and literally gobbling up the contents of the great cheese shops. After being initially staggered by the quality of "real" cheeses and admiring the manner in which they were merchandised, the fun really began—I paid my first visit to the Rungis wholesale market just south of Paris.

The Rungis market consists of huge airplane hangar–like buildings with specialized sectors for meats, poultry, and fish, for flowers, and, of course, for dairy products. I just followed the signs that read "Produits Lait, Beurre, Fromages."

Tools of the cheese trade: To cut a whole Parmigiano-Reggiano, the tough rind is scored around the cheese's circumference with a hooked knife (left), then the exterior is pierced with a sharp stiletto (center). Finally, the short, broad-bladed knife (top) is used to twist and split.

Arriving as early as 2:00 A.M., cheese buyers from around the world converge on the vast, colorful Rungis wholesale market located in a suburb of Paris. They pick and choose from literally miles of artisanal and factory-made cheeses displayed by négociants *(wholesale merchants) in the area of the market that features dairy products.*

On my first visit, as I hurried into the first cathedral-high cheese building, my jaw dropped. Stretching before me was box after box of every type of French cheese stacked in rows outside each *négociant's* stall. Buyers walked down the center aisle periodically stopping to deal with suppliers as they sought a certain type of cheese of a certain quality at a favorable price. The market is open daily, except for Sundays, and most of the buyers and sellers have known each other for years. The first day I just walked the aisles, taking notes on specific brands and their sellers. These *négociants,* who are wholesale middlemen buy the cheeses from the producers and sell them directly to shops, restaurants, export/import consolidators, and to each other. (Then as now, rather than assume the risks of being my own importer, I worked with several agents who had offices and warehouses at Rungis.)

On my return to New York City, my shipments from Rungis began to arrive—cheese the likes of which had never been tasted in New York before. Real Brie from Brie, not the nonsense that comes from just any cheese factory in France (usually Lorraine), and real Camembert from Normandy. Our goat cheeses from small, traditional, family-run companies were a special source of pride. I stocked French chèvres made the traditional way, from fresh raw milk—not the mutant stuff made from frozen curds and powdered milk.

After that first trip to Paris

when I "looted" Rungis, I began my travels in earnest. I found that I had a passion for maps, obsessed with visiting each cheese-producing district in order to understand the terrain and pastureland. I traveled extensively throughout the cheese-producing regions of France, Switzerland, and Italy before canvassing Spain and England.

Moving On

I eventually left Dean & DeLuca for other cheese counters, most especially at Fairway Market and Balducci's in New York. Along the way, I was awarded membership in France's 800-year-old Guilde de St. Uguzon, which is essential if you want to call yourself a *maître-fromager,* or master cheesemonger. And I was inducted into the cheese world's honorary Chevalier du Taste-Fromage. In my 20 years at the counter I

Medals awarded by the Compagnons de St. Uguzon (shown) and Confrérie des Chevaliers du Taste-Fromage de France represent the highest honors awarded to a master cheesemonger.

have seen interest in real cheese grow. I've observed more and more customers returning from European visits with the desire to re-create that cheese experience on home ground. The positive aspect of this interest is that it encourages retailers to expand their cheese counters. The down side is that most Americans are being sold unexceptional imported cheeses that they should ignore. This primer will acquaint you with delicious real cheeses and it will also point out the cheeses or brands to ignore.

Many people are concerned about fat and cholesterol in their diets. My theory is that you have to eat, and if you're going to eat, you might as well enjoy quality food. Cheese is a proud representative of our common food heritage, and despite the attention it has received in this era of deprivation chic, you've probably decided not to give it up altogether or you wouldn't have bought this book. I doubt you'll eat cheese three times a day—or even once a day—but when you do indulge, it should be with a cheese that is worthy of your discriminating taste.

For those of us who take eating, particularly cheese eating, seriously, information is ammunition in the battle against tastelessness. Of course, this doesn't mean we should reject truly subtle flavors, but it does mean we can and must rally against mass-produced, pasteurized, imitative dairy substances that masquerade as cheese. Time is running out. All too soon the great cheeses will disappear—each year there are fewer and fewer of the fine dairy products that have been around for centuries. As a devoted cheese advocate, I want to do everything in my power to help prolong the centuries-old traditions that are fast succumbing to technology.

Above all, I continue to place a premium on the nurturing of artisans, whether it be in the form of proffering advice or by exercising my buying power to support their noble efforts. The American artisans in particular are of paramount interest to me as part of the effort we should all be involved in to forestall the distinct possibility that in all of our lifetimes everything is going to taste the same.

About This Book

My intention is to arm you with information about cheese that will pique your interest, steer you in the right direction, and, ultimately, enable you to ignore the ordinary and zero in on the extraordinary. My approach is a very personal one—I'll tell you about the cheeses I adore as well as some that I don't. I'm opinionated about flavor and pull no punches. I have enormous respect for cheeses that are unchanging and true to their region; I am less enamored of cheeses that have become mass-produced, tasteless dairy products, cheeses that are not original and that stress

THE GEOGRAPHY OF CHEESE

The maps provided in the primer are cheese-friendly ones, intended to help establish a sense of place and geographical perspective for the cheeses discussed. Like the special wine and cheese maps used by travelers in France, they occasionally include historic as well as contemporary information. In a country with a past as rich and complex as France's, for instance, where hundreds of cheeses are made, the ebb and flow of ancient customs and cultures, as well as changing borders, give special relevance to each cheese's origins. Over time, in France, Italy, Spain, and the British Isles, borders have expanded and contracted, for one reason or another, and the configuration and names of regions and subregions have fluctuated. The maps reflect some of these variables, with an eye to clarifying the context within which cheeses are made.

At Fairway Market in Manhattan, the author's informal handmade signs provide customers with each cheese's "biography" as well as its price per pound.

visible style over palatable substance.

This is by no means an attempt to itemize and define the entire world of cheese. I have chosen instead to focus on a combination of the cheeses you are likely to come in contact with here in the United States, and the many irresistible cheeses you should seek out when traveling abroad. Always the emphasis is on cheeses that have enjoyed a long, grand tradition of hands-on attention.

The book begins with chapters that are meant to acquaint you with cheese in general, to familiarize you with cheese terminology, to explain how cheese is made, plus how to store it, serve it, cook it, and, above all, enjoy it.

The heart and soul of the book is a country-by-country and region-by-region description of the really worthwhile cheeses—ones available here plus the gems that aren't—accompanied by information on selecting and serving each cheese.

I stress the importance of France, Italy, and Switzerland because I believe that the world's finest cheeses are made in those countries. I am also a great admirer of the classic "farmhouse" cheeses and the rustic cheeses of Spain.

The chapter on the U.S. explains the way our national dairy industry markets cheeses. It also stresses the talents and products of our rapidly improving artisanal cheesemakers, and to this end, you'll find a lengthy list of mostly small-scale, artisanal cheesemakers whose products would have made Thomas Jefferson, America's gourmand President, proud.

The chapter "A Mixed Plate" explores the cheeses of Scandinavia, the Netherlands, Belgium, Germany and Austria, the Balkan countries, and Canada. There is no question that these countries produce and export tremendous quantities of cheese—some admirable, but some merely lesser-copies of the great cheeses that are made elsewhere.

Finally, there is a useful, quick-reference section that includes at-a-glance buying information for what I consider the world's finest cheeses. Of course, I hope you'll find every page of the primer interesting, but cheese shoppers in a hurry might want to refer to these cheese profiles, which consist of an alphabetical listing with information on origin, characteristics, fat content, best brands, appropriate wines to serve alongside each and notations about related cheeses. This section will allow you to buy on the run, then enjoy reading the more in-depth discussions at your leisure.

I have written this book because so few people have access to serious cheesemongers. It seems ironic to me that at a time when so many food lovers are curious about cheese, there are so few knowledgeable retailers to introduce consumers to the world's finest, and to advise and guide them in selecting the most enticing examples.

As I travel across America vis-iting cheese stores, specialty food shops, and cheese departments in supermarkets, I frequently see people buying cheeses that are not worthy of anyone's attention or appetite, certainly not yours. If you are interested in cheese, I intend to save you time and money as well as to open the doors wide on the world of cheese, adding a new dimension to your taste and table.

Today, after four years of criss-crossing the country helping design and establish specialty food shops from top to bottom, I am once again a partner at Fairway, this time overseeing not one but two burgeoning cheese departments that feature a selection none of us would have imagined possible a decade ago. Eating cheese in America has transited from the fondue fad of the 1950s to Julia Child's demystification of quiche Lorraine in the 1960s to the rise of celebrity chefs in the 1970s and 1980s to a new era of sophistication and appreciation that encompasses both the bounty of farmers' markets and the uniqueness of the finest American and European cheeses.

CHEESE PRECEPTS

My feelings about cheese have evolved over the last two decades, but if at the outset someone had shared with me these honest, unequivocal constants, my own cheese learning curve might well have been shorter.

I firmly believe that raw-milk cheeses taste better than cheeses made from pasteurized milk. But the USFDA forbids the importation of raw-milk cheeses aged less than 60 days, which means that it is illegal to sell all but the world's longer-aged raw-milk cheeses in the United States. No Brie, no Camembert, no Epoisses, no *fermier* chèvre—none of the great, unctuous cheeses are legally available in the U.S. Consequently, our frame of reference for understanding and choosing cheeses is skewed. But what's worse is that these venerable cheeses have been "replaced" by pretenders—inauthentic imposters bearing their names.

In addition, the notion of any given cheese's best time of year has become obfuscated by science and the incredibly efficient and sensible procedures by dairymen, dairy farmers, and cheesemakers. In all but a few cases, seasonality is no longer as important as it was 30 or 40 years ago, and even I find myself confused from time to time about the few authentically seasonal cheeses that remain.

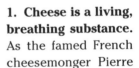

While a few of these precepts fly in the face of convention, they are no less true than the others, which are borne out by centuries of cheese tradition.

1. Cheese is a living, breathing substance. As the famed French cheesemonger Pierre Androuët once observed, it is the soul of the soil. Cheese is the purest and most romantic link between humans and the earth.

2. Find yourself an impassioned cheesemonger, or encourage and nurture a receptive retailer.

3. While you can't judge a book by its cover, you can judge a cheese by its exterior (the rind or crust). Up with natural rinds, buffed, brushed, washed, or cloth-covered. Down with plastic, paraffin (wax), and paint.

4. The younger the cheese, the less flavor it will have. Most cheeses taste best when they've been aged past their bland youth, and before they've reached their sharp maturity. Fresh cheeses are generally not very interesting, and overly sharp aged cheeses have been reduced to the status of a condiment.

Cabrales

Emmental (front) and Keen's Cheddar (rear)

5. Cheese should be cut fresh for you. Avoid any that has already been cut or grated, plastic-wrapped, weighed, and priced.

6. The edibility of a cheese's rind is a matter of taste and common sense. For example, the rind of Stilton is obviously inedible, while that of Reblochon is a matter of personal preference. Unless you like the flavor of mold, it is advisable to trim it away. Similarly, most washed, buffed, brushed, or natural rinds are not only unclean, they are probably also bitter and gritty. Soft-ripened rinds are usually eaten,

though it is certainly considered acceptable to trim them away.

7. Cheese is best stored in the refrigerator as close to the bottom of the appliance as possible—the vegetable compartment is ideal. Wrap it in aluminum foil, waxed paper, or plastic wrap. Wrapped this way, the cheese will be able to breathe and further develop without drying out. Cheeses of various types need not be segregated. They may share space inside the compartment.

8. The harder the cheese, the longer it will stay fresh (up to a month) in the vegetable compartment of the refrigerator.

(continued)

Semisoft cheeses will usually be fine for several weeks. Cut pieces of soft cheeses will last for less than two weeks.

Vacherin Fribourgeois (left) and Appenzeller (right)

9. Cheese suffers enormously from being frozen, so simply get the notion out of your head.

10. Cheese must be brought to room temperature before it is served. Cold cheese has very little flavor and an unnatural texture. Leave the cheese wrapped while it is warming up. Depending on the temperature of the room, this should take no more than an hour.

11. When serving two or more cheeses, select cheeses of divergent milks (cow, sheep, goat), textures, and flavor intensities, without regard for shape, color, or origin. Variety bestows upon each cheese the respect for its singularity that it deserves.

12. Serious cheese requires serious bread. Serious bread is handmade bread, the kind of artisanal loaf where the crust is as important as (if not more than) the inside. Crackers are suitable for ordinary cheeses.

13. Choosing wine to serve with cheese is not something you need to get all worked up about. Cheese is partnered best with wine produced near the cheese's home. For instance, serve Sancerre wines with Crottin de Chavignol, or Chianti with Pecorino Toscano. What matters is that neither overwhelms the other.

14. A great cheese will make an average wine seem greater than it is and an average cheese will drag down a great wine.

Gaperon

15. In recipes, cheese should be incorporated toward the end. If it is meant to be melted, low heat is recommended; for browning, the cheese should be shredded or grated, and broiled very briefly.

16. A proper fondue is a wonderful thing; you've simply forgotten (see page 276).

About Cheese

Cheese can be made from the milk of any mammal. The best, tastiest cheeses are made from fresh, raw milk—just as it comes from the animal, alive and vibrant with living organisms which are, unfortunately, very perishable and open to contamination.

When French microbiologist Louis Pasteur took the danger out of fresh milk with his invention of the pasteurization process, it was a great day for humankind, but a sad one for many of the world's great cheeses.

Milk and Pasteurization

Pasteurization of milk can be accomplished in many ways, using various combinations of time and temperature: From a cheese lover's (or cheesemaker's) standpoint, some are "good," but most of the most popular methods are

Scientist Louis Pasteur's research revealed that heat kills germs, a finding that opened the door to the process called pasteurization. Although many cheeses are made from pasteurized milk, the most delicious are made from raw milk.

"bad." In the basic, "good" way, milk is heated to 144°F (62°C) and held at that temperature for 30 minutes; most of the time this temperature, if carefully maintained, is low enough not to result in milk that has a "cooked" flavor. This cooked flavor is apparent in finished cheeses made from milk pasteurized in the "bad" way—especially in fresh (unaged) cheeses that rely heavily on the high quality of the milk used to make them.

In the basic "bad" way to pasteurization, the milk is heated to 160°F (71°C) and held there for 15 seconds; yes, it's much faster (and therefore more economical, and hence, more popular) but this temperature alters the flavor of the milk, adding a perceptible cooked flavor to cheeses made from it.

The makeup of milk varies with the animal, and the variations are what make sheep cheese and goat cheese different from cow's-milk cheeses. On the average, cow's milk consists of (by weight) about 87% water, 3½% protein, 3¾% fat, almost 5% lactose (milk sugar), along with water-soluble vitamins, such as A, B complex, and D, and minerals, including calcium and phosphorus. It is the protein and the lactose that are key in cheesemaking; most of the vitamins and minerals that are present in the milk remain with the cheese during the cheesemaking process. Fat is important to an individual cheese's character, but is less important overall, since cheese can be made from milk that is full fat or reduced fat, or from skim milk that has virtually no fat at all.

Milk protein consists of about 82% casein, the form of the protein that is capable of coagulation into curds, and 18% whey, the liquid component. To make cheese from milk two things must happen: The lactose must be coaxed into converting into lactic acid, which is lower in acidity, and an acid or rennin (the active enzyme in rennet), must be added to trigger the clumping together of the casein molecules. When that happens, the whey is drawn off (or in a few special cases, made into cheese) and you're on your way to cheese.

How Cheese Is Made

It is easier to understand the process of making cheese when you realize that cheesemaking is a series of stages of controlled spoilage. Whether the cheesemaking operation is large or small, the process remains basically the same.

First, you need milk. A big operation sends out its tanker trucks to gather the milk; small-scale cheesemakers collect it from their own animals—usually, cows, sheep, or goats—or buy milk from nearby farms. It is of the utmost importance that the milk stay clean, untainted, and in good condition until the cheesemaking process begins.

The best-tasting cheeses are made from unpasteurized (raw) milk. Unfortunately, from the perspective of flavor, the majority of cheeses today are made from pasteurized milk, milk which has been heated above 100°F, resulting in the neutralization of most of the flavor constituents. It is easier, and therefore more profitable, to make cheese out of pasteurized milk. And it is also easier for the cheesemaker to control what happens during the "controlled spoilage" process that is cheesemaking.

Cheesemaking requires three very basic stages, which are unvarying for all but the unripened (fresh) cheeses such as Ricotta or Petit Suisse (they skip Stage 3). Stage 1 is producing curd, Stage 2 is concentrating curd, and Stage 3 is ripening curd.

MILK INTO CHEESE

Here are some basic calculations:

1 cow = 8 to 20 quarts (8 to 20 l) of milk per day

1 goat = 3 to 4.5 quarts (3 to 4.5 l) of milk per day

1 sheep = about 1 quart (1 l) of milk per day

2 quarts (2 l) milk = 8 ounces (250 g) Camembert

16 quarts (16 l) milk = 5 pounds (2½ k) Brie

1,250 quarts (1,250 l) milk = 220 pounds (110 k) Emmental

Stage 1

The goal is to produce curds from the protein component of the milk. This requires three steps.

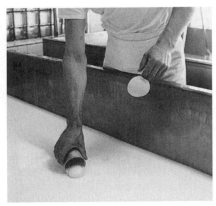

When the starter culture is added to warmed milk, it jump-starts the coagulation or curdling process. Next rennet is stirred into the milk and begins working on the milk protein (casein), turning it into curd.

Step 1: The milk for the day's cheesemaking is "pooled" (put in one receptacle) and warmed. A starter culture, usually containing *Streptococci* and *Lactobacilli,* is added to the milk. The starter is necessary to change the lactose (milk sugar—the only carbohydrate in milk) into lactic acid, a process that equalizes the pH (acidity level) so the milk protein (casein) will coagulate, forming curds when rennet is added.

Step 2: When the pH is at the proper level, rennet is stirred into the milk. The chief enzyme of rennet is rennin, which causes the individual cells of the casein to clump together. It's important to note that the rennet does not kill the starter; it works alongside it. The starter remains active in the cheese, ready to contribute a great deal later during the ripening process, including affecting the cheese's finished flavor.

Depending on the kind of cheese being made, the rennet liquid has been extracted from the lining of the appropriate animal's stomach chamber. There is calf rennet for cow's-milk cheeses (though there are a few rare cow's-milk cheese recipes that call for kid rennet), kid rennet for goat cheeses, and lamb rennet for sheep cheeses. (It is possible to make cheese without rennet, but it takes a long time and you wouldn't want to eat it.) Animal rennet is not as frequently used as it once was. These days most cheesemakers, even artisanal ones, are using highly concentrated exam-

ples of vegetable rennet that have been organically derived from plant material. French Saint-André, as well as many English farmhouse Cheddars and Spanish cheeses, which were formerly made with animal rennet, are now made with vegetable rennet; so are some Dutch-made diet cheeses, whose labels, unlike those of the other cheeses mentioned, clearly state they are made with vegetable rennet.

The cheese industry overall has only just begun to promote cheeses made with this rennet to the burgeoning vegetarian market. Although the conventional wisdom has always been that the flavor, color, and texture of a cheese is significantly affected by the rennet type used, opinions about this may be changing as breakthroughs are made in vegetable rennet research. In the past, old-style vegetable rennets lacked sufficient strength to curdle the quantities of milk used in wide-scale cheese production. The newer, improved, concentrated formulations are making it nearly as potent as animal versions, so it is becoming a more practical option. But old habits die hard, so at least in the near term you can still expect to see most cheeses made with animal rennet.

Step 3: The curd mixture is allowed to set anywhere from 30 minutes to two hours, until a soft, jellied mass forms. The ambient temperature at this

Once curd reaches a custard-like consistency, the cheesemaker uses a harp, an implement strung with taut metal wires, to cut it into small pieces and encourage the release of whey. This French cheesemaker is cutting curd for Comté.

stage will affect the finished cheese: For a soft cheese, the temperature is surprisingly low; for firm cheese, the temperature is in the medium range; for semihard cheeses, you want a rubbery curd, and, therefore, a higher temperature is needed to set the curd.

Stage 2

The goal of this stage is to concentrate the curd. The methods of doing this—cutting, cooking, pressing, milling, salting, etc.—may vary with the cheese being made.

Step 1: First, the curds are cut up to expel the whey (a cloudy liquid like milky water) that is trapped in the jellied network. The size of the curds determines the finished texture of a cheese. Curd size may be fine, medium, or coarse, depending upon the texture called for in the recipe of that particular cheese (fine-cut for a hard cheese, coarse-cut for a soft one). The finer the curd, the more whey released, resulting in a firmer, drier cheese with a "tight" texture. The larger the curd, the softer (usually) the cheese. In fact, many of my favorite cheeses are the result of little or no cutting at all—cheeses such as traditional French chèvre and Camembert, and the majority of American artisanal goat's-milk and sheep's-milk cheeses.

Step 2: The next step for some cheeses is called cheddaring, a method of treating curd to achieve

COLORING AGENTS

For many cheeses, coloring agents, usually an organic orange dye, are added to the milk along with the starter. Some traditional cheeses once had a natural orange hue caused by the vitamin D that cows ingested from grazing on green plants. But winter milk comes from cows that are fed silage, and the cheeses that result from this milk are white. This variation persuaded cheesemakers to color their cheeses so that they would look uniformly "healthy." The earliest coloring agents were carrot juice and marigold petals. Today, as they have for at least a century, cheesemakers add color by using annatto bark and berries.

English cheesemakers are doing increasingly more alarming things with coloring agents, such as tinting new cheeses with fruit and berry extracts. American companies, too, have shown no shame about the dyes in their flavored cold-pack cheeses. Granted, many of these dyes are organic, but do we really need green cheeses (from spinach and parsley), red cheeses (from strawberries), and purple and orange cheeses ("port wine" Cheddar)?

The texture of Cheddar and some similar firm cheeses is the result of a procedure called cheddaring, in which thick slabs of curd are repeatedly stacked and turned to expel the maximum amount of whey.

a particular texture in the finished cheese. In this process, used only for Cheddars or Cheddar-type (Colby, Cantal, Cheshire) cheeses, the curds are piled on top of each other, cut up, pressed together, and then piled up again. This action allows a large amount of whey to be expelled, resulting in a very fine-textured, dry, semifirm cheese (once the curds have been passed through a grinder or "mill" to mince them into extremely fine pieces before they are pressed into molds).

For other cheeses, ones which will be firmer textured and aged longer, the next step is to reheat the curds, or to "cook" them, as cheese-makers would say, while they are being agitated. Heating the curd and shaking it causes the protein clumps to fuse into tiny filaments, thus changing the texture of the curd. Not all cheeses call for cooked curds, although quite a few do. The curds for some are cooked only briefly (Fontina) at temperatures

After cut curd has drained sufficiently, it is salted. At this American factory, salt is hand-sprinkled over Cheddar curd. The salt contributes to flavor and also slows down bacterial activity on the rind that might cause spoilage.

between 104°F to 120°F (40°C to 48°C), but more are the result of longer cooked curd (French and Swiss Emmental-type cheeses and Gruyère) heated at 120°F (48°C) or more. At this point, the pressure, heat, and acidity level of the mixture have combined to produce a curd of tender strings. For Italian Mozzarella and Provolone, which are in the category of *pasta filata* (spun or stretched curd) cheeses, the process ends here, with a batch of rubbery curd that can be stretched or molded into any shape. Blue cheeses (French Roquefort, Italian

Each cheese type acquires its distinctive taste, aroma, and texture during the ripening or curing stage, which takes place in an environment in which the temperature and level of humidity are carefully controlled.

Gorgonzola), on the other hand, are not cooked because this would make the texture so tight (no holes or fissures) that air could not be introduced to promote the blueing.

Step 3: The salting stage, which follows cooking, also varies with the cheese. Salt dehydrates and slows, or controls, ripening rates, retarding the action of the starter bacteria so that a cheese can be aged for a longer period to achieve the desired flavor and texture. Without salting, cheeses would very quickly become over-ripe and spoilage would set in.

There are four methods of salting a cheese. The salt can be added directly to the curd, by machine or by hand (as is done with Cheddar). Or the cheeses can be allowed to float in a brine bath for a few hours, the way Emmental is handled. These giant Emmentals, which may weigh over 200 pounds (100 k), are left to bob around in brine for 15 minutes to an hour until the desired degree of saltiness is reached. The third method is to rub the surface of the cheese with salt granules, which is done with Parmigiano-Reggiano, Roquefort, and most of the English cheeses. This method produces a hard, dry rind that allows the cheese to ripen from the inside out, producing a big-flavored, hard cheese. The fourth method is to rub or "wash" the cheese with a brine-soaked cloth, as is done with Livarot, Taleggio, and Mahón.

At this point, many cheeses are put into a mold and pressed to further remove the whey and to give the cheese its shape. Not all cheeses are pressed. For example, in traditional French chèvre-making, the goat's-milk curd is hand-ladled into small colander-like molds, and gravity works to extract the whey. These molds determine the shape of the final product—a neatly formed little cheese. Larger-size cow's-milk cheeses and almost all of the sheep's-milk cheeses are packed into hoop-type molds and then pressed. The harder a cheese is pressed, the firmer the final product will be.

Stage 3

The goal of this stage is to ripen the prepared cheese and treat it as needed to produce a cheese that is of an age, texture, flavor, aroma, and appearance true to its type. The ripening stage is a continuation of the controlled spoilage cycle; it is vital that during this cycle some of the components of the milk—protein, fat, and carbohydrate—break down into simpler, smaller molecules through natural chemical changes to a degree that will result in a balance of flavors in the finished cheese. The breakdown of these molecules is all-important in the flavor-creating process.

Ripening (also referred to as curing or aging) is the cheesemaker's chance to help nature turn that cheese into the best it can be. Lacking a cool, moist cave in which temperature and humidity are constant, cheeses are ripened in storage rooms in which these two factors can be controlled. Of course, different cheeses require different temperatures and humidity levels. Temperatures are usually relatively low, with humidity in the high range

A STIRRING NOTE

In Roquefort, France, *Penicillium roqueforti* is derived from the mold spores formed on specially baked loaves of rye bread, which are allowed to harden and become moldy. The loaves are then dried and crumbled and the mold is combined with the curd. One of my favorite Roquefort makers, Gabriel Coulet, whose rare cheeses I was the first to bring to America, may be the only one left who still folds these spores into the curd by hand.

(about 95%) for soft cheeses and lower (around 80%) for hard cheeses. The humidity prevents the surface of the cheese from drying and ripening too fast and keeps the cultures of the starter bacteria alive.

Soft cheeses, like Brie, ripen quickly, so they are ripened at lower temperatures. Most hard cheeses take longer because they ripen from the inside out, due to the action of the starter cultures throughout the interior of the cheese; their exteriors are occasionally washed, regularly brushed, and turned at intervals during the ripening process. Since butterfat seeps downward, turning the cheese allows the butterfat to redistribute itself through new areas of the interior of the cheese.

During the ripening stage, a number of natural components of the cheese are triggered to play their role in the cheese's final character. Some of them occur naturally; others are the result of a cheese's treatment at this stage of its development. For example, *Propionibacter shermanii*, a strain of bacterium that is included in the Emmental starter, ultimately produces the "eyes," or holes, that are its hallmark. These particular bacteria live on lactic acid, and as they consume it, they give off carbon dioxide, which in turn, produces the bubbles of gas that create the eyes.

Similarly, the starter for Roquefort cheese contains a bacterium, *Penicillium roqueforti,* originally found in a moldy loaf of bread accidentally left in the caves of Roquefort. When the cheese is pierced with metal skewers (a process called needling), oxygen is introduced to the interior, which feeds the bacteria, and in time, at specific temperatures and humidity levels, the bacteria produce blue veins in the paste (interior) of the cheese.

Brie and Camembert ripen from the outside in, rather than the inside out, thanks to *Penicillium candidum* or *Penicillium camemberti,* which is added to the starter. These bacteria act to produce a soft,

Two famous, pungent washed-rind classics: Name-controlled Pont l'Evêque and Livarot.

bloomy crust on the outside of the immature cheese, then continue working from the outside in to ripen it. Mass-produced Brie is literally treated to a shower of chemically produced *Penicillium candidum* by a worker who wears a big tank on his back and sprays a liquid form of the bacteria onto the cheeses through a hose. The bacteria slowly penetrate the interior, turning it from a chalky, crumbly, bland cheese into a soft, nearly liquid wonder. A soft-ripening cheese of this type is always shaped into thin, flattish disks or squares to provide a large surface area to be coated with the bloomy crust. French Chaource and Coulommiers, which like Brie and Camembert are soft-ripened cheeses, are molded into thicker shapes. Because they are thick, they ripen unevenly, which means that they become runny beneath their bloomy crust but their centers are firm and chalky. The French call this characteristic chalky center the *l'âme,* or "soul" of the cheese. They are no less delicious than Brie or Camembert—they are simply another style of soft-ripened cheese.

There is another category of cheeses—my favorite—that is ripened in a different way. These cheeses are soft and their rinds are "washed" or rubbed or brushed periodically during their ripening time with a liquid such as brine (salt and water), wine, beer, *eau-de-vie*, or simply water, and the liquid acts as food for the myriad surface bacteria that ultimately give this style of cheese its distinctive flavor and very pronounced (smelly) aroma. In France, the cheesemaking term for such cheeses is *lavée* (washed). Among the most well-known washed-rind cheeses are French Langres, Epoisses, Munster, Pont-l'Evèque, Livarot, and Italian Taleggio.

Parmigiano-Reggiano is an example of a cooked, pressed cheese.

Cheese Classifications

A cheese can be classified in many ways: by the process or recipe used to make it, by the type of milk used, solely by its texture, by the appearance of its rind, and in other ways—it's impossible to choose the classification method that works best and has the fewest exceptions. Based on the recipes used by some cheesemakers, it is not unusual for a cheese—a soft-ripened one that is also blue-veined, for instance—to belong to more than one family. For simplicity's sake, I've chosen to classify cheeses by family, grouping together those which share primary characteristics and are related by their finished appearance, texture, and level of flavor.

Fresh cheeses are essentially uncooked and unripened (or slightly ripened) curd that may or may not have been drained of its whey. (Ricotta is undrained, while cream cheese is a drained example.) Usually very moist and mild, their flavor is characterized by a pleasant tartness. Some are molded, while others are simply scooped from a container. Examples include farmers cheese, cottage cheese, French *fromage blanc* and unaged *fromage de chèvre,* and Italian Mascarpone.

Soft-ripened or bloomy rind cheeses, which have a semisoft consistency, have been surface ripened—either sprayed or exposed to molds so that they ripen from the rind inward. Their crusts are thin, white, and velvety ("bloomy"). Examples include French Brie, Camembert, and triple-crèmes such as Gratte-Paille and Pierre Robert, as well as Italian Paglia-style and Toma cheeses.

Washed-rind cheeses, whose rinds are usually orange-hued, have been rubbed or washed (sometimes immersed) during the ripening process with a solution of brine, wine,

A NOTE ON VISITING CHEESEMAKERS

Local, traditional cheesemakers are far more common in Europe—especially in Italy and France—than in the U.S., though we're getting increasingly better. One way to track them down is to scrutinize the label of a cheese you've especially enjoyed. The label will give you the name of the city, town, or hamlet where the cheese was made, which you can then pinpoint with the help of a detailed road map. Many times the label will even supply a phone number. If not, it should be easy enough to obtain the number if you have the location. Cheesemakers, although among the nicest, most gracious people alive, may have too much going on to be able to afford the time for a visit. Therefore, don't show up unannounced—it is always polite and prudent to telephone

At Sweet Home Farms, milk for the cheeses made by Alyce Birchenough (shown here) and Doug Wolbert comes from the couple's own Guernsey cattle and Nubian goats. The photographs on the walls of their farm's small retail store provide visitors with behind-the-scenes glimpses of how cheese is made.

and schedule your visit first.

Another way to locate regional cheesemakers is to visit the local tourist bureau in the principal town of the region, or, in the U.S., the state. If it is an area known for its cheeses (and probably even if it isn't), you can be sure they will be able to give you information on visiting local producers. The drawback is that you will doubtless be led to the most commercial of the lot. Persist. Seek out the small producer, the artisan. You might stumble across a likely candidate while driving or hiking around, or perhaps the concierge at your hotel or the neighborhood shopkeeper might have a suggestion. When you do find a serious cheesemaker, your visit will no doubt be a memorably illuminating and delicious experience.

beer or grape brandy to promote a desirable exterior mold that is instrumental in creating the cheese's characteristically pronounced flavor. Examples include French Epoisses, Livarot, and Font-l'Evêque, Italian Taleggio, Spanish Mahón, and most Trappist or monastery-style cheeses.

Natural-rind cheeses have self-formed rinds; no microflora or molds and no washing are used to create their thin exteriors. They are denser in texture than other cheeses and usually aged longer. Examples include English Stilton, Lancashire, French Cantal, *fromage de chèvre,* Mimolette, Tomme de Savoie, and Spanish Roncal.

Blue-veined cheeses, which are marbled with a bluish-green mold, reveal visible mold cultures within their interiors. Examples include American Maytag Blue, English Stilton, French Roquefort, Italian Gorgonzola, and Spanish Cabrales.

Uncooked, pressed cheeses, which are made from curd that has not been heated (or "cooked") to solidify it, are pressed to complete the drainage of whey and to achieve a specific, firm texture. Examples include English Cheddar, French Morbier and Tomme de Savoie, Italian Montasio, and Spanish Manchego.

A **cooked, pressed cheese** is made from curd that has been heated (or "cooked") before pressing.

Examples include Dutch Gouda, English Cheshire, French Cantal and Gruyère, Italian Parmigiano-Reggiano, Swiss Appenzeller, and French and Swiss Emmental.

Process(ed) cheese is a cheese by-product made from a combination of natural cheese, vegetable-based gums, dyes, emulsifiers, and stabilizers. Blandly uniform in flavor, it has a smooth or spreadable consistency and a long shelf life. Examples include American Cheese, "imitation" cheese and cheese "spreads," as well as imported examples such as French Gourmandise, La Vache Qui Rit, and Rambol.

Cheeses and Their Seasons

M ost of the important cheeses have a season—not only a time when it is best to make them, but also a time that they are best eaten. This has to do with the pasturage, which is the vegetation that a cow, goat, or sheep is grazing on at the time of milking. There are some excellent winter cheeses—for example, Vacherin Mont d'Or, made from the milk of animals that have grazed on cold-weather fodder. However, the best vegetation an animal can eat comes right out of the ground rather than out of a bucket, as is the case with winter fodder. For this

Dairy farmer Ellie Barton of Caprielli Farm tends her mixed herd of 200 goats in northern Vermont, supplying milk to the nearby Vermont Butter & Cheese Company. Once goats freshen (give birth), they supply milk for ten months, at an average rate of about one gallon per day.

reason the richest milk comes from animals grazing in September and August (and a bit less so in July and June), when the grasses are their most lush. (When I say grasses, I am including clover, flowers, herbs, mosses, berries, wild onions— everything that a dairy animal eats. These foods enhance the flavor and quality of the milk as well as its butterfat content.)

How long the cheese is aged after the milk is given depends on the desired flavor and consistency of the cheese. A firm cheese, aged longer, is usually better in the winter because it will have been made from May milk. A fresh, young, soft cheese will be best in the late summer or early fall.

Because goat cheeses are made when the milk is fresh and the cheeses are not aged very long, they are splendid all summer and fall. The French have always looked eagerly for the goat cheeses that appear in spring because their flavor reflects the first growth of the new grass. If a fresh goat cheese is aged for a month or two, by September or

October it will be absolutely terrific, still young yet piquant (not creamy).

Now, say a cow in Switzerland or France is eating wonderful August Alpine pasturage. Gruyère, Reblochon, Morbier, and some other Alpine cheeses are made from this milk. According to each cheese's recipe, it must be aged (ripened or cured) for a certain period of time. In the case of French Morbier, the cheese needs about three months of aging before it will be at its most delicious—so for Morbier, which has been made from August, September, and/or October milk, November or December is the *plus bonne époque.* For Gruyère or Comté it takes longer—four or five months. January and February will be the best time to buy those cheeses.

Real Brie and real Camembert (made from unpasteurized cow's milk) take only one or two months to ripen, so they'll be great in September and October. Of course, you can buy these cheeses—and others—in December, January, or February. They will still be good, but just not *as* good because the cattle

THE DAIRY CASE

Milk is a dairy product that contains water, milk solids, and fat. In fresh milk, cream rises to the top naturally, or it can be separated out using centrifugal force. Cream is composed of milk's larger fat globules, which float because they are heavier than water. From cream, we derive butter, which occurs when cream is agitated, shaken, churned, or beaten, causing the fat globules to fuse—clump together—leaving behind buttermilk, a watery substance that is the liquid component of the churning process. Buttermilk is practically fat-free, and when bacteria are introduced either deliberately or by chance, the mixture becomes more acidic as it sours and thickens into soft, fresh clumps. At that point, it becomes the familiar drink butter-milk, a tart-tasting, nutritious, low-fat dairy product.

Yogurt, sour cream, and crème fraîche are all forms of fresh milk in which bacteria have acted on the lactose to produce lactic acid. Depending on the particular bacteria involved, the milk develops into different dairy products, each with its own characteristics—tangy and thickened, bland and very thick, tangy-sweet and moderately thickened. Old-fashioned homemade unrenneted cottage cheese, which curdles and thickens from increased lactic acid, is also a member of this group; renneted cottage cheese, the store-bought type, is a true cheese. Other soured milk products that are technically dairy products, not cheeses, include quark, kefir, and labneh.

will have been fed with fodder. The same is true for goats—winter pastures simply don't provide the same flavor to the milk.

Other cheeses are less seasonal in quality. Parmigiano-Reggiano, for example, is made 12 months a year. Some people feel it will be better made from July and August milk than from March milk, but this is difficult to judge. It is simply a matter of taste.

American Cheddars are the same all year round—it doesn't matter when you buy them. They are made on such a grand scale that there is no chance for seasonal virtue to be a factor.

Large-scale cheese producers send stainless-steel tankers to dairies to collect milk. The milk is "pooled" or poured into special cheese vats and heated to the specific temperature required for the type of cheese being made.

THE BASICS OF BUTTERFAT

Although cheese does contain plenty of fat, there are a number of misperceptions about what type and how much is present. When a cheese is said to be 50% butterfat, most consumers believe this means that one-half of the cheese is fat, which is actually not the case. Fat content information on virtually all imported cheese labels is calculated based on the percentage of solids in the cheese, all liquids excluded. On average, most cheeses are between 50% to 70% water, depending on the type of cheese, and the rest is protein and other dry solids. Since all cheeses are in a constant state of increasing dessication, or "drying out," manufacturers cannot accurately state the exact percentage of fat.

On the labels of U.S.-made cheeses, this percentage is more accurately referred to as "in dry matter," or IDM, while on French cheeses it is called *matière grasse*, or *m.g.*, which, once again, is how virtually all imported cheese labels state their case. To use this information to determine the actual butterfat content of an imported cheese, divide the percentage of milk solids and fat (m.g.) by two. A cheese whose label shows 45% m.g. contains about 22.5% fat overall. Approximately 60% of the fat is saturated, 40% is unsaturated.

Density makes a difference. Due to their higher moisture content, soft cheeses such as Brie are actually lower in butterfat than either semisoft cheeses like Gouda or Fontina d'Aosta or hard ones like Cheddar or Parmigiano-Reggiano. On average, most cheeses, including Provolone and Roquefort, and French or Swiss Emmental, are 40% to 45% butterfat (m.g.). When a cheese reaches between 60% to 74% butterfat (m.g.) content, it is called a double-crème, a classification that includes Gratte-Paille or extra-cream Gouda. Triple-crèmes, a category of cheeses with 75% (m.g.) butterfat or higher, include Brillat-Savarin, Explorateur, and Saint-André.

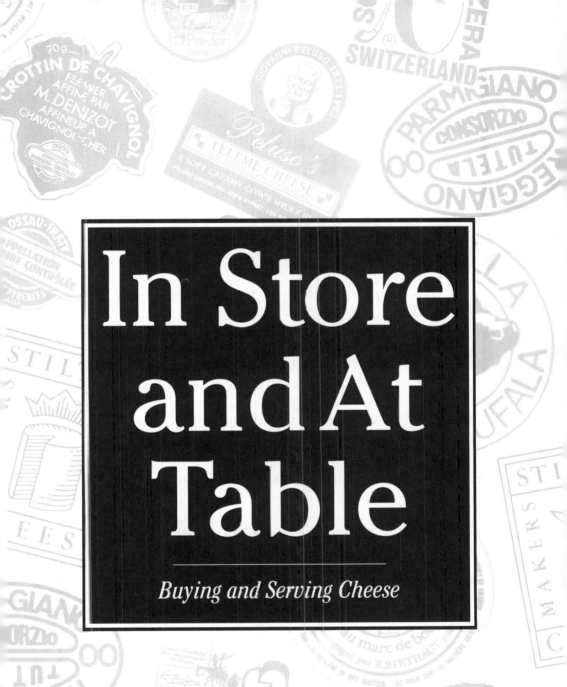

In Store and At Table

Buying and Serving Cheese

When it comes to buying cheese, the biggest favor you can do yourself is to find a reliable, impassioned cheesemonger and benefit from his or her knowledge each time you go shopping for cheese. Profit in a practical way from your passion—take your time, linger over the signs and descriptions, ponder the overview of the selection. Each visit should expose your palate to a new taste, suggest a new way of serving cheese, and inspire your quest for the best.

Most cheeses have a label of some kind so that buyers can be sure of their authenticity, although it's not always visible to the customer since so many shops display cheeses already cut, wrapped, weighed, and priced. If you can see the whole, uncut cheese with its label, look for the name of the cheese, its maker, and the town and region where it was made. These days the phrases *fabriqué en France* or *hecho en España* are not enough. In order to discern if a cheese is the real thing, you need more specific information about its exact place of origin.

Check to determine from which type or types of milk a

An appetizing display makes decision making tougher.

The basics of cheese shopping are the same regardless of where you live. Always taste before buying. Remember that cheeses with natural, rustic rinds are the most flavorful and that a fresh-cut cheese always tastes better than a pre-cut, plastic-wrapped one.

cheese was made. Be sure the cheese looks fresh. Bear in mind, of course, that artisanal cheeses are usually much scruffier on the outside than factory-made ones. For once in your shopping life this is likely to be a good rather than a bad sign because choosing a cheese is one of the few times you should judge a book by its cover. The more rustic the rind and the more natural the color, the more memorable the cheese is likely to be. The interior of the cheese must be free of mold (unless it's a blue cheese). without cracks or visible discoloration such as reddening or grayishness.

Always taste cheese before making a purchase. Although it is very likely to have been under

KEY WORDS AT THE CHEESE COUNTER

Cow
vache (French)
vacca or *mucca* (Italian)
vaca (Spanish)

Sheep
brebis (French)
pecora (Italian)
oveja (Spanish)

Goat
chèvre (French)
capra (Italian)
cabra (Spanish)

*Never commit yourself to a
cheese without having
first examined it.*

T. S. Eliot

refrigeration and you'll be tasting it cold—a disadvantage since cold mutes the taste—you should still be able to determine if it is too strong or sharp, too mild, or has a flavor you will enjoy.

Though saying so makes me feel like a traitor to my business as a retailer, say it I must: It is best not to buy big hunks of cheese unless you serve it frequently. However, if you're so far away from your best cheese source that you have to buy big pieces rather than modest amounts that can be polished off in one or two sittings, it is vital that

you know how to wrap and store cheese properly.

First, cut off only as much cheese as you are going to use at one time. Rewrap the big piece and put it away immediately. (Don't bring the whole piece to room temperature and then take some off before you put it back in the refrigerator.) When wrapping it, the main thing is to be sure the cheese is kept covered and moist, still able to breathe, but without breathing so much that it dries out and cracks. To accomplish this, wrap the cheese tightly in aluminum foil, waxed paper, or plastic wrap. (If the cheese weighs more than 3 pounds (1½ k), first wrap it in damp cheesecloth or other cloth and then in foil.)

Though at one time I railed against it, my feelings about plastic wrap have tempered over time, as the quality and consistency of this

Although in France you are more likely to be served cheese as a separate course at the dinner table, this restaurant in Bordeaux sets out an amazing buffet-style array for patrons to savor. Featured are local chèvres in a variety of shapes.

WRAP UP

Cheesemongers often use bakery paper, the same very thin, fragile squares of paper used in pastry shops to pick up breads and pastries. A common brand is Sav-a-Wrap. It is used primarily to protect small goat's-milk cheeses and extra-cream cheeses which do not have any wrapping of their own. The paper helps prevent too rapid oxidation while the cheeses age and it is also used to "seal" the surfaces of cheeses once they've been cut for a customer.

irreplaceable kitchen material have improved. While I once loathed allowing a petroleum product to touch any food—and certainly not my hallowed cheeses—I now discover that after all my ranting and raving about it, plastic wrap really does a pretty good job. I must offer one caveat, however: If the plastic wrap is in contact with rind or interior of the cheese for too long (more than a week) the cheese begins to suffer; it suffocates, becomes slimy-rinded, discolored, and certainly less than it should be, or was the week before. But guess what? Had you used aluminum foil, cheesecloth, waxed paper, or a combination of all three, you would have fared no better. The rule of thumb is that harder cheeses will last better and longer than softer ones, with semisoft (or semifirm) cheeses falling somewhere in between.

For traditional French *fromage de chèvre*—and this includes goat's-milk cheeses made in any country—I strongly recommend that you reject plastic wrap, opting instead for waxed paper, aluminum foil, or a glass or plastic container with a tight-fitting lid. The reason is that whole, uncut cheeses bought young (a few days old) have a lot of life left in them. They can be brought to a desired stage of ripeness—from very fresh to up to two months from the time you bought them. Plastic wrap prevents air from circulating, and for chèvres, stasis is actually rapid decomposition. In order to forestall this, they must be allowed to breathe and very slowly oxidize. Plastic wrap brings out all the negative qualities of goat's-milk products.

Whether you use aluminum foil, waxed paper, or plastic wrap, be aware that once you've unwrapped a cheese stored in the refrigerator, the wrapping should be discarded and the cheese should be put in a new wrapping. Reused materials won't reseal properly.

How to Eat Cheese

Once you've bought a perfectly ripe, peak-of-the season cheese, what's the best way to enjoy it?

In France, often one, two, or three—rarely more—cheeses are offered as a separate course at dinner. An individual serving is cut from the

I am grateful to have learned young that cheese has an important place in a menu. It isn't something to serve with apple pie, and it isn't something to cut into nasty little cubes and serve with crackers. Early in life I learned to see the beauty of great slabs or rounds of cheese on the table, and I still respond to the sight of a well-stocked cheese tray properly presented.

James Beard,
Delights and Prejudices

larger piece, and then put on the diner's plate, and eaten with a knife and fork. This cheese course is meant to be eaten accompanied by bread and any dinner wine that remains from the main course, or perhaps with a special dessert wine.

In Italy, cheese is often eaten as part of a meal with some form of *salumi* (cured pork products) and fruit or vegetables, olives, nuts, bread, and wine. It is also frequently served as an appetizer before an evening meal. However, there is an argument in favor of offering cheese after a meal rather than before, as cheese is very filling and may dissipate the enjoyment of the course or courses that follow.

Nevertheless, the enjoyment of cheese need not be relegated to the end of a fancy multi-course meal. If you are like me, at that point you barely have room for dessert, much less anything as filling as cheese. What's more, after all the various flavors afforded by the previous courses, the flavor of a fine cheese may seem to pale.

Fine cheeses come into their own when treated as a main course, and what could be a better time

than at lunch to really appreciate their merits? *Casse-croûte* is the term the French sometimes use to refer to a snack or unfussy light lunch, one that often features cheese as its main component. Two people can share three cheeses accompanied by bread and fruit, raw vegetables, and/or a salad with a delicious vinaigrette—a far more enjoyable experience than any hamburger or sandwich will provide. (I adore a lunch of wine, cheese, and a salad, but some people quarrel with the presence of wine and vinegar in such close proximity. Beer and iced tea are also good with a salad dressed with vinaigrette, although I would draw the line at pairing water and cheese, as this invites indigestion.)

For me, lunch is the time I most enjoy a fresh goat's-milk cheese, perhaps sprinkled with a pinch of dried thyme or a few cracked peppercorns and drizzled with a bit of extra-virgin olive oil. Add a handful of good Gaeta or Niçoise olives, a hunk of bread, and a glass of simple wine for a most satisfying interlude. Or choose fresh Mozzarella with a ripe tomato or a roasted sweet pepper. Or a piece of Roquefort or Gor-

CRISPY FRICO

Makes approximately 15 to 20 wafers

According to Carol Field, author of *Italy in Small Bites*, these crispy, lacy cheese wafers are so delicious that in the Friuli region they are described as *frico fa respirare i morti*—so tasty they can make the dead breathe again. Although they can be eaten warm from the pan, my version is at its best when allowed to cool and become crunchy. Serve *frico* as a savory nibble with chilled white wine or with a tossed green salad.

1 pound (500 g) aged Montasio, Asiago, or Parmigiano-Reggiano
1 to 2 teaspoons extra-virgin olive oil or melted unsalted butter

1. Grate the cheese and set aside.

2. Brush a thin film of olive oil or butter over the bottom of a large nonstick skillet. Set the skillet over medium-low heat.

3. For each wafer, sprinkle 1½ to 2 tablespoons of grated cheese into the skillet to form a 2- to 3-inch round. The skillet will hold about 4 to 5 wafers per batch. Cook until the cheese melts completely and the edges turn crisp and golden, 3 to 4 minutes. While each round of cheese cooks, press down on it occasionally with a spatula to make sure it remains flat. The cheese will bubble and spread before turning crunchy. Gently turn each round over with a spatula and continue cooking for another minute, or until light-golden brown.

4. Remove the wafers from the skillet, set them on a paper towel, and blot lightly with another towel to remove excess oil. For fancier-looking wafers, shape warm-from-the-pan *frico* over an inverted glass or measuring cup or drape over the handle of a wooden spoon, then blot with a paper towel to remove excess oil. Allow to cool to room temperature before serving.

gonzola with a glass of sweet Barsac and some good bread.

Breakfast is another excellent time to enjoy cheese, especially fresh cheeses such as unaged chèvre or Robiola Piemonte, along with muffins, croissants, or toast. Omelets, scrambled eggs, or frittatas are splendid when the eggs are combined with goat cheese, Gruyère, Parmigiano-Reggiano, or any fine cheese you happen to have in the house. My young son Max's favorite breakfast is bread, butter or olive oil, and grated Parmesan, grilled in the toaster oven.

Cheese can make the difference between slim pickings and gracious hospitality when unexpected visitors arrive on your doorstep. What could be faster, simpler, and more satisfying than setting out a bowl of olives, a bottle of wine, and some bread and cheese?

The Art of Serving Cheese

Always serve cheese at room temperature, not cold from the refrigerator. In order to ensure the emergence of its full flavor, always take the cheese out of the refrigerator early enough for it to come to room temperature. Depending on the hardness of the cheese, this could take about an hour in cool weather, or in hot weather, as little as 30 minutes. Hard cheeses take longer to come to room temperature than soft ones. When you take it out, leave the cheese wrapped so that the exposed surfaces don't dry out. Just before you're ready to serve the cheese, unwrap it and throw the wrapping away. Never use the same wrapping twice—it won't reseal properly.

For serving, I like to present each cheese on a small wooden cutting board, piece of marble, or plate, rather than forcing two, three, or four cheeses to share one big platter. If you put them all together, soft cheeses may run into each other; also, the aromas intermingle and it's hard to differentiate between them. What's more, big plates often aren't completely flat, and cheese must lie flat in order to be easily cut. That's why I prefer flat, sturdy, individual cutting boards rather than plates, which tend to be tippy. If you don't have small cutting boards

Professionals use enormous double-handled knives like this one for cutting into large wheels of firm cheeses. For home use, forget about cheese planes and other special instruments—all you need is a good, sharp utility or chef's knife.

THE FROMAGE FORMULA: HOW TO BUY CHEESE FOR A CROWD

To determine how much cheese you'll need for a party, answer the following questions:

1. How many people? Count each adult as one, each child as one-half. Multiply the total number by 3.5 (105 g), which is the rule-of-thumb number of ounces (grams) per individual that I have found works best. (This figure can be adjusted up or down, taking into account several other factors mentioned below.) To determine the amount of cheese you need to buy, divide the total by 16 (ounces in 1 pound; 500 g) and round up.

2. What time of day are you serving and for how long? Noon until 3:00 P.M. is a hungry time of day; even more so is the period from 5:00 P.M. to 8:00 P.M. For these times I usually figure 4 ounces (125 g) per person unless the answer to question three proves significant.

3. What other food will be served and in what quantity? If a wide variety of other foods will be offered, you'll want to lower the 3.5 ounce (105 g) standard by ½ ounce to 1 ounce (15 to 30 g), allowing 2.5 to 3 ounces (75 to 90 g) per person.

4. There is no need to serve more than three or four types of cheese. Indeed, serving more would be disrespectful since it makes it very difficult to focus on the merits of any one cheese long enough to make tasting it a meaningful experience. Also bear in mind the more cheeses you serve, the smaller the quantity of each will be required.

Of course, there's always the possibility that two people who take an instant liking to the same cheese will focus on it, thereby depriving other guests of the opportunity to taste it. Buying a bit extra can't hurt.

or marble slabs, then use a big cutting board and keep the cheeses as far away from each other as possible.

It's best—although I confess to occasionally breaking this rule—to have a separate knife for each cheese. The radical me suggests you gather up all the specialized cheese tools you have in the house and throw them away. Those ridiculous Scandinavian cheese planes—toss them out. They are as injurious to cheese, and just as insulting, as the Stilton "scoop" tool. How on earth can you rewrap the concave husk that remains? Cheese planes, while seemingly novel in design and a cinch to use, are in reality wasteful (they create great valleys in the cheese's face) and in many cases flimsy and/or shoddy in manufacture. However, they can be useful at a retail cheese counter for trimming away dryness and/or discoloration. The other cutesy cheese tools with decorative handles and the like are not so good either. They are invariably flimsy and dangerously dull.

To cut any cheese properly—hard or soft—use a good chef's knife (a good all-purpose utility knife). To cut soft, fresh cheeses such as chèvre cleanly, use a length of tautly stretched dental floss.

Creating a Cheese Board or Cheese Plate

The path to cheese appreciation lies on the palate and at the table. Sampling a single cheese can be illuminating, but tasting two or three in a convivial social setting can be both educational and indulgent, whether you create an informal cheese board or a more refined presentation called a cheese plate.

A cheese board is an assemblage of three or four cheeses laid out in large pieces (sometimes whole cheeses) on a platter, a board, or a flat piece of marble or granite set in the center of a table so that it can be approached from all angles. Although a perfectly acceptable means of serving cheese, it is also the height of informality. Everyone hacks away at the cheeses with whatever

implements have been provided. But with just a little more effort, the enjoyment of a cheese sampling can be elevated to a more civilized endeavor that I call the cheese plate. It's a stylish way of providing each guest with their own personal array of cheeses to savor as they sit at a table rather than hovering above a cheese board with a paper napkin clutched in one hand and a knife in the other.

A cheese plate consists of anywhere from one to three or four well-chosen cheeses arranged in small portions on large, individual plates set out on the table along with a regular place setting (table knife, fork, spoon, and a cloth napkin). Basic accompaniments such as a good, crusty bread (served warmed in a cloth-covered basket) and a compatible beverage, usually wine, are also arranged on the table. The cheeses should be chosen to represent a balanced spectrum of cheese types and textures (ripened, unripened, washed rind, blue, hard, soft, semisoft), levels of flavor intensity (strong, gentle, sharp), and milk types (cow, sheep, goat). Country of origin may also influence the choices if you've decided it would be intriguing to create a sampling from a single spot, such as all English cheeses or only Italian ones.

Each cheese is cut into a portion size that reflects how the cheese plate fits into the scheme of your entertaining or dining plans. If it is meant to be served as an appetizer, a three-cheese plate should feature 1-ounce (30 g) chunks or slivers. If the plate is meant to be hearty and filling, offer 2- to 2½-

You can never go wrong with an authentic crisp-crusted handmade rustic loaf or baguette as a perfect companion for any cheese.

ounce (60 to 75 g) portions. Arrange the cheese portions equidistant from one another and close to the outer rim of a large dinner plate. Then in between them, arrange the accompaniments—whole or sliced fresh fruit, dried or fresh berries, paper-thin slices of cured meat, a thin slice of fruit paste, some glistening olives, or a scattering of toasted nuts.

Cheese boards or plates, such as the following suggestions, offer a unique opportunity to combine enjoyment with enlightenment. Tell your guests the name, type, and origin of each cheese you're serving and in which order it's best to sample them—beginning with mild cheeses and progressing to strong-tasting ones. Of course, guests should feel free to taste in whatever order they wish, but a little advice and information may be welcomed by less knowledgeable cheese-eaters.

AN ECLECTIC MIX

An eclectic exploration that includes a unique "blue"-rinded American chèvre, a venerable English classic, and a delectable French favorite.

The Cheeses
- Westfield Farm Hubbardston Blue (U.S.; Massachusetts)
- Abbey Farm Cheshire (England)
- Saint-Nectaire (France)

The Accompaniments
Slices of ripe Comice pear and crisp, spicy Macoun apple; toasted black walnuts and pecans; crusty, whole-grain bread

The Wine
Oregon Pinot Noir

A TASTE OF ITALY

Here is a taste of the Italian cheese-making tradition, from the south to the north.

The Cheeses
- Mozzarella *di bufala*
- Aged Pecorino Toscano
- Taleggio

The Accompaniments
Thick-cut slices of Italian *sopressata;* roasted sweet red peppers; assorted olives; *mostarda di Cremona;* thick slices of Tuscan-style bread

The Wine
Chianti *riserva*

SPANISH FAVORITES

An introduction to Spain's reigning cheeses.

The Cheeses
- Cabrales
- Roncal
- Mahón

The Accompaniments
Thick slices of *chorizo;* thin-sliced smoked or *serrano* ham; dried or fresh figs; toasted almonds; marinated olives with lemon zest and garlic; walnut bread

The Wine
Spanish Rioja

An ideal choice for summertime entertaining on the patio, this tasting of diverse Italian cheeses includes (left) aged Pecorino Toscano, Mozzarella di bufala (rear), and Taleggio (front). Each offers a different level of flavor intensity, so begin with the milder Mozzarella, then progress to the nutty, olivey Pecorino, and taste the more intense Taleggio last.

The perfect cheese board for a wintry afternoon showcases a trio of American Treasures: (from left to right) Grafton Cheddar produced in Vermont, Maytag Blue made in Iowa, and Vella Dry Jack from California. Each is assertively flavored and full of character. In addition to the serving suggestions below, consider pairing them with dried fruits, nuts, and a bottle of Merlot.

A FRENCH SELECTION

A triumvirate of regional French classics.

The Cheeses
- Crottin de Chavignol
- Fourme d'Ambert
- Pyrénées *brebis,* such as Etorki or Prince de Claverolle

The Accompaniments
Sweet peppers, radishes, and celery stalks; lightly steamed green beans; rustic farmhouse-style bread with unsalted butter

The Wine
White Sancerre (chilled in a Champagne bucket)

REAL AMERICAN CHEESE

A flight of America's foremost artisanal cheeses.

The Cheeses
- Maytag Blue (Iowa)
- Vella Dry Jack (California)
- Grafton Cheddar (Vermont)

The Accompaniments
Medjool dates; honeydew melon wedges; paper-thin slices of domestic or Italian prosciutto; chutney; crusty sourdough bread

The Wine
Zinfandel

The forthright and at the same time subtle flavor of cheese stimulates the taste buds and readies them for wine. Wine, in turn, permits cheese to attain unimaginable heights of flavor. These twin fruits of the earth were made for one another.

Pierre Androuët,
The Complete Encyclopedia of French Cheese

Cheeseboard Accompaniments

Bread and Crackers

Fine cheese calls for handmade, crusty, ungussied-up bread. Its simple goodness makes it a perfect companion. However, some flavored breads enhance the cheese-tasting experience, when the primary flavors complement one another. For example, since I love the flavor of nuts and goat cheese together, I often serve chèvre with a walnut-studded loaf of whole-wheat bread. Olive bread is particularly good with any sheep's-milk cheese. A crusty *baguette* or sourdough loaf is an ideal foil for unctuous, soft-ripened cheeses such as Italian Toma Carmagnola or French Gratte-Paille and for aromatic, washed-rind cheeses such as French Livarot or Spanish Mahón. The earthiness of whole-grain and multigrain breads complements English farmhouse cheeses. In general I don't approve of crackers with cheese, but if you must succumb to crunch, look for crisp, plain, flatbread-style crackers.

Wine

Choosing the proper wines to go with specific cheeses is not the mind-bending mystery you might imagine. Cheese is partnered best with wine produced near the cheese's home. For instance, serve Sancerre wines with Crottin de Chavignol, Chianti with Pecorino Toscano, or a strong Spanish Rioja with Cabrales.

If you're serving a range of cheeses, you should offer a range of wines. What matters most is that neither overwhelms the other. A balance of flavor intensity is the key. It's also worth remembering that a great cheese will make an average wine seem greater than it is and an average cheese will drag down a great wine.

Cured meats, such as chorizo *and* jámon serrano, *should always be served at room temperature when accompanying cheese.*

LEFTOVER CHEESE

Never discard those little leftover bits and pieces of cheese lurking in your refrigerator. The tag ends of Brie, Cheddar, farmer cheese, chèvre, Roquefort, Mozzarella, and scores of other cheeses can be quickly transformed into a tasty mixture which the thrifty French call *fromage fort* ("strong cheese"). Seasoned with fresh garlic and a few splashes of wine, it makes an assertively flavored topping for toast or thick slices of crusty country bread and tastes best when briefly melted under the broiler.

To make *fromage fort,* gather together 1 pound of leftover cheese (3 kinds is enough, 6 or 7 will be even better). Trim off any mold or very dried out parts from the surface. Toss 3 or 4 peeled cloves of garlic into a food processor and process for several seconds until coarsely chopped. Add the cheese to the garlic along with ½ cup dry white wine and at least 1 teaspoon of freshly ground black pepper. Process until the mixture becomes soft and creamy, about 30 seconds. Remove the mixture from processor and transfer it to a crock or bowl. Cover tightly with plastic wrap and refrigerate.

Meats

Cured meats are very compatible with cheese. Serve Italian *prosciutto di Parma,* with its soft texture and stunning flavor, or a tasty American-made prosciutto. Another good choice is paper-thin slices of subtly flavored *Bündnerfleisch,* a traditional air-dried beef from Switzerland. Burgundy-colored *jamón serrano,* the extraordinarily flavorful and sweet marbled ham of Spain, complements sheep's-milk cheeses. Like the cheese they accompany, the meats should be served at room temperature.

Fruit

Fruit has long been the stereotype accompaniment for cheese, but frankly, on the whole, I find it the least inspired of all possibilities. If I do choose fruit to accompany cheese, it is going to be so seasonal, so achingly sweet, so crisp or pudding-soft, so aromatic and full of juice, so just-harvested that leaves or vines are still attached. If I'm not convinced that the fresh fruit available to me is going to provoke that kind of response, I'll look elsewhere for something worthy of being served with cheese. For example, dried fruit—the best of which are Medjool dates, Mission or Turkish figs, cranberries, cherries, raisins, prunes from Agen in southwest France, and the yellow French plums called *mirabelles*—are all sublime with most cheeses.

Olives

Another of my favorite accompaniments is olives, washed of their brine and dressed as is customary for their particular type and region of origin. Among the possibilities are purple Gaeta olives with lemon zest, crushed garlic, and extra-virgin olive oil or Moroccan olives with fresh rosemary, crushed garlic, and extra-virgin olive oil. Table olives come into their own when served with sheep's- and goat's-milk cheeses. And indeed, their origins are closely linked—practically all such cheeses are made with the milk of animals who graze in pastures surrounded by, or actually among, olive groves.

Nuts

Though the idea may be new to many food lovers, nuts are delicious with many cheeses. Almonds, which happen to be indigenous to regions known for their sheep's- and goat's-milk cheeses, are wholly compatible with these cheeses. This is especially true if the almonds are toasted. And toasted hazelnuts and black walnuts are both great with all cheeses.

Chutneys and Fruit Pastes

Serving chutney with cheese is one of my latest passions. The match is such a natural one that I'm a little shocked it has taken me this long to recognize it. This condiment, made with an abundance of fruit, vinegar sugar, and spices, goes with many cheeses, though I most enjoy it with English farmhouse cheeses. Their sturdy, dry, somewhat crumbly textures and rustic, rather muted flavors are delightfully complemented by the

spicy sweetness of a chutney. (Make an English Cheddar and Major Grey chutney sandwich on whole-wheat bread if you don't believe me.) Sharp American Cheddars, such as Vermont-made Grafton Village Cheddar, are another good match.

Traditional French-style chèvres, too, can be served with chutney. Choose a slightly firm chèvre that has been allowed to ripen for a week or so and is not too moist. Il Mongetto, a family-operated farm turned artisanal food producer in Italy's Piedmont, makes a chutney called *mostarda di uva*, which combines Barolo grape must, hazelnuts, quinces, apricots, and mustard seed. It is absolutely stunning served with Fontina d'Aosta or Major Farm's Vermont Shepherd Cheese.

Fruit pastes, another unusual accompaniment, are simultaneously primitive and elegant served in tandem with peasanty cheeses such as Italian Fiore Sardo, English Wensley-

dale, and Spanish Roncal. One to look for at specialty food stores is *membrillo* from Catalonia, a sweet quince specialty of ancient origin. Serve it cut into thin slices.

Cooking with Cheese

Although the best way to savor cheese is on its own, plain and simple, cheese is also an indispensable ingredient in a wide range of famous regional specialties, including fondue (Switzerland) and Welsh rabbit (or rarebit, as it is often called in the British Isles); as an ingredient in casseroles and sauces; and melted as a topping for a wide array of main dishes. Here are a few tips that are worth remembering.

Regardless of whether it is added to a dish cooked on top of the stove, in the oven, or in a microwave, cheese is best incorporated into recipes that call for "low and slow" cooking. When exposed to high heat or overcooking, virtually all types of cheese, especially firm cheeses with relatively low moisture content, will seize up, becoming stringy and tough as their protein and fat content form a rubbery mass. When microwaving dishes that call for cheese, also follow the low and slow rule, being sure to stir and rotate the dish often. When used as a topping for a hot dish, add cheese during the last 5 to 10 minutes of the cooking time.

Shredded or grated cheese is easier to incorporate into cooking than slices or chunks; the smaller bits melt more quickly and blend together with other ingredients more readily. When cheese is grated or shredded, its weight does not change but its volume increases because it has been "inflated" with air. Grated cheese doubles in volume. A 4-ounce (125 g) chunk of firm-textured cheese will yield enough grated (not tamped or packed down) to fill a 1-cup or 8-ounce (250 g) measure. If the cheese has been shredded rather than grated, it will be a bit coarser and yield slightly more.

MY FAVORITE CHEESES

I so often refer to this or that cheese as being one of the world's greatest that my colleagues constantly rib me about my ever-lengthening list. Forget about a measly top 10—here are my 36 favorites in alphabetical order. These are the cheeses that, standing on their own, accompanied only by a glass of wine and some good, crusty bread, astound and delight me. They command and earn my complete attention and respect.

My favorites never cease to please me, though just because they're on my list you should not assume they're immutably superior to many other cheeses deserving of praise and allegiance. My favorites are authentic, the real thing, palpably linked to the milks from which they are made and to their geographic origins. To taste them is to appreciate the link that must take place for a cheese to achieve greatness—a concomitance of soil and herbage, beast and human, climate and the passage of time.

- **Afuega l'Pitu**
  Asturias, Spain

Afuega l'Pitu

- **Appleby's Cheshire**
  Cheshire, England

- **Beaufort**
  Savoie, France

- **Brie de Meaux au lait cru**
  Ile-de-France, France

Brie de Meaux

- **Brindamour**
  Corsica, France

- **Cabrales**
  Asturias, Spain

- **Coach Farm Green Peppercorn Pyramid**
  New York, U.S.

- **Comté**
  Franche-Comté, France

- **Croghan**
  County Wexford, Ireland

- **Crottin de Chavignol**
  Berry, France

- **Epoisses de Bourgogne**
  Burgundy, France

Crottin de Chavignol

- **Fontina d'Aosta**
  Aosta, Italy

- **Gorgonzola**
  Lombardy, Italy

- **Gubbeen**
  County Cork, Ireland

- **Hubbardston Blue**
  Massachusetts, U.S.

Gorgonzola

- **Keen's Cheddar**
  Somerset, England

- **Kirkham's Farmhouse Lancashire**
  Lancashire, England

- **Laguiole**
  Rouergue, France

- **Langres**
  Champagne, Burgundy, France

- **Major Farm Vermont Shepherd Cheese**
  Vermont, U.S.

- **Mendip**
  Somerset, England

- **Milleens**
  County Cork, Ireland

- **Montgomery's Cheddar**
  Somerset, England

- **Munster**
  Alsace, France

- **Parmigiano-Reggiano**
  Emilia-Romagna, Italy

- **Pecorino dell'Umbria** and **Pecorino Toscano**
  Umbria, Tuscany, Italy

- **Peluso's Teleme**
  California, U.S.

- **Pico Chèvre *au lait cru***
  Périgord, France

- **Reblochon**
  Savoie, France

- **Saint-Marcellin**
  Dauphiné, France

- **Sally Jackson's Sheep Cheese**
  Washington, U.S.

- **Taleggio**
  Lombardy, Italy

Taleggio

- **Tomme d'Arles;** also called **Poivre d'Ane**
  Provence, France

- **Vacherin du Haut-Doubs**
  Franche-Comté, France; **Vacherin Mont d'Or**
  Vaud, Switzerland

- **Vella Bear Flag Dry Jack**
  California, U.S.

- **Véritable Camembert de Normandie *au lait cru***
  Normandy, France

Munster

France

France, for me, is a glorious wonder. But what astounds me most—French history, custom, and style aside—are the cheeses. I have worked with French cheeses virtually every day for the last 20 years. I coddle and caress them, occasionally inadvertently abuse them, but mostly, I am in awe of them. The range of types, sizes, shapes, and flavors is unparalleled.

No other country even comes close to the scope of France's majestic array. Countless of its many cheeses remain constant after hundreds and hundreds of years. Many more have spawned imitations worldwide. All of them were originally created as a means of preserving extra milk for future nourishment, sustenance, and survival. Today, great quantities of French cheeses are being sent to every corner of the earth. What was once a purely local foodstuff has achieved universal status, a distinction few other agricultural by-products can match, certainly not on this scale.

How many French cheeses are there? Despite the fact that the late French president Charles de Gaulle once only half-jokingly observed in a speech back in the 1950s that "Nobody can simply bring together a country that has 265 kinds of cheese," the total is said to be around 650. But many of those 650 are really the same cheese with a different name and made in a different locale. I feel comfortable telling you that I could serve you a different French cheese every day for a year.

Whatever the actual number (and it changes as old cheeses die out and new ones are created), the thing to remember is that France—a country the size of Texas—produces *hundreds* of cheeses. And instead of numbers, it is more relevant, and important, to concentrate on flavor, style (the recipe), and origin in order to appreciate each particular cheese, and how it fits into the body of the larger context of all French cheeses.

To grasp a topic as diverse and regionally specific as French cheeses,

France

it helps to look at a map of France. For now, ignore the dizzying 95 political departments (*départements*) which roughly correspond to American counties, and focus instead on the 21 classical regions of France, designations that may be thought of as similar to our states. Most of these regions will already be familiar and significant to you (Burgundy, Normandy, Provence, for example). Some are major cheese-producing areas, while others have no real importance in terms of cheesemaking.

But it's not absolutely necessary to have a geographic grasp of France to enjoy its cheeses. With the aid of this primer it will be rela-

tively simple for you to literally (and figuratively) taste your way from region to region, cheese by cheese, becoming acquainted with the seemingly inexhaustible array of French cheeses which I know will bring you endless pleasure.

When you begin to match cheeses with their areas of production, you'll discover that certain types or styles of cheese tend to cluster in specific regions (though there are exceptions to every rule). For nearly every province of France has not only its own identity, its own place in France's long and fascinating history, its special style of cooking, its most coveted variety of

France, a country the size of Texas, produces an astonishing array of hundreds of different cheeses.

fruit or vegetable, fish or game, but also its own cheese or cheeses. Sheep's-milk cheeses, for example, are found throughout the Pyrénées, France's southern border with Spain, running west to east, from the Atlantic Ocean to the Mediterranean. Goat's-milk cheeses, though made throughout France, are predominantly found in the west-central area, whereas blue cheeses are largely produced in the center and south-central regions.

Not all of France's classical regions are home to a major or even a minor cheese. Therefore, I have grouped certain areas together based on similar geography, history, and cheese types, creating 13 "cheese regions." Bear in mind that in some respects the cheeses of France are confounding: For every rule, I find there is an exception. And despite the French *appellation d'origine contrôlée* (A.O.C.) system of legally protecting how certain cheeses are made, the authentic and the traditional are often under siege from the new and inauthentic. For every perfect, farm-made (*fermier*) or small producer (*fruitière* or *crémier*) cheese, there is a factory (*laitier*) knockoff backed by marketing efforts that may well push the really delicious original cheese into obscurity. For every authentic, artisanal cheese made with unpasteurized milk, another less flavorful one made with pasteurized milk waits in the wings.

Some of France's finest cheeses are not available to us here in the U.S.—those which are made from raw milk and aged less than 60 days are barred from the United States by USFDA regulations put into effect as a measure meant to guard against listeriosis, a virulent bacterial disease. But regulations change and you never know when a one-time outlaw will become a much-welcomed guest. Of course, when you're traveling in France, there are no restrictions.

The truth about cheese is: The best cheeses are artisanal, made by real people who lavish a heritage of hands-on attention to their cheese-making craft. And nowhere is this tribute to tradition more evident than in the flavors of French-made cheeses. They are a revelation in a bite—a marriage of humankind and nature well worth your time and attention.

"*Let these words of warning provoke you into probing markets and good shops during your travels for the genuine articles which persist there. You will find splendid and unusual cheeses made by farmers and artisans, cheeses which owe their virtues to devotion to local tradition and high standards, with the natural use of raw milk.*"

Patrick Rance,
The French Cheese Book

APPELLATION D'ORIGINE CONTROLEE (A.O.C.)— THE NAME-CONTROLLED CHEESES OF FRANCE

Although for many years the French wisely and prudently took legal steps to protect their national treasures, it was not until 1979 and 1980 that France began to grant formal name-controlled status to its cheeses. To date, just 32 French cheeses have met the legal requirements necessary to receive this important distinction, which is aimed at keeping the quality of these cheeses unassailably high and, by extension, honoring the traditions of their production.

Makers entitled to use the A.O.C. designation for their cheese must be in compliance with legal stipulations regarding how and where the cheese is made. The following areas are defined by law for each cheese:

1. The breed of sheep, goats, or cows from which the milk is derived.
2. The area where the milk comes from and the area where the cheese is made.
3. The cheesemaking process or technique (including aging).

4. The composition of the cheese (fat content, type of milk, rind, etc.).
5. The cheese's physical characteristics (size, shape, weight).
6. Specific attributes of the cheese (including color, flavor, aroma).

Although the name-controlled cheeses of France sport an emblem on their label stating they are *appellation d'origine contrôlée,* this is not an absolute guarantee that each cheese is perfect. The quality of a name-controlled cheese may vary from maker to maker, from batch to batch, and may also reflect the time of year it was made and the duration of its ripening.

The following is a complete list of the name-controlled cheeses of France, their places of origin, and an idea of their availability in the U.S. Of the cheeses unavailable in the U.S., some are illegal to export to this country because they are made from raw milk and aged less than 60 days. Others are rare even in France and simply don't make their way here.

Abondance: Savoie; available, though rare

Beaufort: Savoie; available, spotty

Bleu d'Auvergne: Auvergne; widely available

Bleu de Gex-Haut-Jura (includes Bleu de Gex and Bleu de Septmoncel): Franche-Comté; available, though rare

Bleu des Causses: Rouergue; available, though rare

Brie de Meaux: Ile-de-France; available (pasteurized), though rare

***Brie de Melun:** Ile-de-France; available, though rare

***Camembert de Normandie:** Normandy; not available

Chabichou du Poitou: Poitou; available, though rare (look for Le Chevrot made in same region)

Chaource: Champagne; available (pasteurized)

Comté: Franche-Comté; widely available

Crottin de Chavignol: Berry; available

***Epoisses de Bourgogne:** Burgundy; not available

Fourme d'Ambert: Auvergne; widely available

Fourme du Cantal (also called Cantal or Cantal de Salers): Auvergne; widely available

***Langres:** Champagne; not available

Laguiole: Rouergue; available, though very rare

Livarot: Normandy; available (pasteurized)

Maroilles: Picardy; available, though rare

Munster: Alsace; available (pasteurized)

Neufchâtel: Normandy; available, though very rare

Ossau-Iraty Brebis Pyrénées: Pyrénées; available

***Picodon de l'Ardèche** (Languedoc) and **Picodon de la Drôme** (Dauphiné): not available

Pont-l'Evêque: Normandy; available (pasteurized)

Pouligny-Saint-Pierre: Berry; available

Reblochon: Savoie; available, though rare

Roquefort: Rouergue; widely available

Saint-Nectaire: Auvergne; widely available

Sainte-Maure de Touraine: Touraine; available, spotty

Salers: Auvergne; available, though very rare

Selles-sur-Cher: Berry; available, spotty

***Vacherin du Haut-Doubs** (also called **Vacherin Mont d'Or**): Franche-Comté, not available

*Raw-milk cheese, aged less than 60 days illegal for export to U.S. due to USFDA regulations. Sometimes pasteurized versions available.

NORMANDY AND BRITTANY

(Normandie and Bretagne)

NORMANDY

Normandy is a large area in France that is known throughout the world for the high quality of its dairy products. Its heart is lush, rolling farmland, while its northern English Channel beaches are dotted with busy, tourist-filled, commercial port cities. The soil along the coastline is rich, and cows and sheep graze right up to the bluffs that overlook the sea. The vegetation in the area has a high sodium content and the pastures of the Cotentin peninsula are referred to as the *prés-salé,* meaning "salty fields." The animals that these pastures nourish make for extraordinarily delicious meat, and not surprisingly, cheese. Farther inland, the soil, which is black and even more fertile, also provides vegetation for the cattle and is a rich growing medium for the orchards and kitchen gardens of the farms and small villages that are the essence of Normandy and its brilliant cuisine.

Five *départements* make up Normandy: Seine-Maritime, Eure, Calvados, Manche, and Orne. All but Orne border the English Channel. This coastline changes from chalky cliffs in the east to the low, sandy beaches of D-Day fame; then the granite peninsula becomes that rocky coastline associated with Brittany—like our state of Maine— with a predominance of apples, plenty

Typically Norman: the half-timbered facade of a crémerie *(cheese shop).*

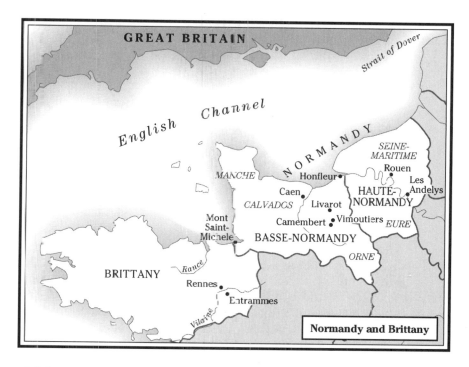

Normandy and Brittany

of fish, cows, and horses. Norman cattle are such prodigious grazers and deliverers of milk that it is no wonder they are world-renowned. A single cow can eat 65 pounds (32½ k) of grass each day while giving 30 quarts (30 l) of milk.

There is a perfect marriage between Normandy's cheeses—the good strong, *real* Camembert de Normandie, or the even stronger Pont-l'Evêque, or Livarot—and the marvelous ciders (*cidres*) of the area. These ciders vary in alcohol content—from the effervescent, soft ciders with low alcohol levels of about 2% to the hard (fermented) ciders whose alcohol levels may be as high as 5½%. Another traditional companion is Normandy's famous brandy, Calvados, which is distilled from cider apples and is around 40% alcohol. (Calvados is named for the

galleon, *El Calvador,* which sank off this coast at the time of the Spanish Armada in the sixteenth century.) Cider and Calvados are the preferred drinks with Norman cheeses. The local breads that accompany the cheeses are notable, made with the hard water that seeps through the mineral-rich, fertile aquifers and with fine, durum wheat grown in the southern sector of Normandy, which is called Basse-Normandie.

The cuisine of Normandy makes generous use of dairy products, such as butter, crème fraîche, and eggs, not only in the region's famous apple-based desserts but also in seafood and meat dishes. It is very rich eating, hardly health food, and a far cry from Mediterranean fare, which favors olive oil and vegetables. In this marvelous haven for big eaters, those seeking low-fat cuisine will be challenged to fit tastes of this region's best flavors and ingredients into their diets. When I'm in Normandy, I savor it all—in reasonable quantities.

The Cheeses

The three most important cheeses of Normandy—Camembert de Normandie, Livarot, and Pont-l'Evêque—originally came from the Pays d'Auge, an historic name for an area within that modern-day region. Each of these A.O.C. cheeses is made from cow's milk. Real Livarot and Pont-l'Evêque will have the *appellation d'origine contrôlée* stamp on the box and paper wrapper. Real Camembert de Normandie will also have a V.C.N. (Véritable Camembert de Normandie) stamp. If there is no stamp, you can assume it is Camembert-*style* cheese, not *true* Camembert, regardless of whether it is made from pasteurized or unpasteurized milk. Unfortunately, in the United States you cannot legally purchase raw (unpasteurized) cow's milk Camembert that has been aged for less than 60 days. Since the best raw-milk Camemberts are aged for just 16 days or so and *must* be eaten *à point* ("just right") at about one month old, Americans will never know the joy of eating real Camembert unless they travel to France. The pasteurized versions of Normandy's trio of great cheeses can be found everywhere in the U.S.

CAMEMBERT DE NORMANDIE

Any cheese can call itself Camembert if it takes on the configuration of a cow's-milk, soft-ripened, 8-ounce (250 g) disk, but real Camembert, Véritable Camembert de Normandie, is made only in the five *départements* that make up the region. Strangely enough, the cheese is not made in Camembert—a rather nondescript village—itself.

On the label of Camembert de Normandie (kam-um-BARE-duh-nor-mahn-DEE) you will be told that it is handmade, *moulé à la louche* (hand-ladled). The milk usually comes from many small herds and the cheese is always made from raw cow's milk—*au lait cru*. The paste will be straw-colored and the white, bloomy rind will take on a reddish mottling as it begins to ripen. Many cheese experts warn that any tiny holes in the interior paste are evidence of misfermentation. Though possible, I never have found this to be a negative in terms of flavor.

DON'T BELIEVE A WORD

Perhaps you've heard about Camembert's being invented by a certain Marie Harel? Nonsense. This myth was born in 1926, when an American doctor approached the mayor of Vimoutiers. He told the mayor that he had been prescribing Camembert to many of his patients to treat various stomach ailments. This "prescription" was such a success that the former sufferers wanted to express their regard for the cheese's inventor by erecting a statue of him or her. The mayor, recognizing a good thing, came up with Marie Harel's name in a Norman archive dated 1859, which stated that in 1791 Camembert was first made on Marie Harel's farm.

It is probably more accurately reported in the Vimoutiers

In 1928, residents of Vimoutiers dedicated a statue of Marie Harel.

parish archives that in 1680 Camembert was already highly regarded: "A very good cheese, well-suited to aid digestion after a meal washed down with good wines." Waverley Root, author of *The Food of France,* the book from which I culled this information, believed that at that time Camembert was probably a blue cheese and acquired its present characteristics long after Marie Harel was dead.

The verifiable hero behind Camembert is a man named Ridel. In 1890 he invented the wafer-thin, round wooden boxes that all Camemberts are packaged in, thus allowing for transportation worldwide. Without it, a cheese of Camembert's fragility would certainly lose its shape or be damaged.

A real Camembert is a thing to worship—it is a full-flavored cheese at once garlicky truffly, mushroomy, and slightly salty, with an underlying flavor of nuts and wood. There are not many sources left that still produce an excellent Camembert. But there are dozens of large, mass-production factories spewing out millions of pieces of so-called Camembert every year, and alas, people buy it and eat it and think of it as Véritable Camembert de Normandie. But it is not the real McCoy.

The name Camembert is not origin-controlled, and as a result, many cheesemakers from locales outside of Normandy make their living producing so-called Camembert. There is Camembert made in Denmark, Germany, and the U.S. (California, Ohio, Texas). The fear is that it would adversely affect the sales of mass-produced Camembert if the Normans were able to origin-control it, though I doubt this would happen. The industry is a juggernaut. Real Camembert takes time, expertise, and special milk.

A PAIR OF CAMEMBERT RIPENESS TESTS

When shopping for Camembert you want to make sure that it is neither too firm (not ripe enough) nor too soft (overripe). To choose a perfect Camembert, use either of the following ripeness tests—the first is the one I use, the second is from a well-known French winemaker.

- Make a loose fist. Then gently press the fleshy area between your index finger and your thumb—it should yield to the touch like bread dough. That's the feel of a perfectly ripe Camembert.

- Put your left index finger on your eye and your right index finger on the cheese ... if they sort of feel the same, the cheese is ready.

Only 6% of all Camembert made in France is A.O.C.

When you're in France, look first for the finest real Camembert, which is made by Moulin de Carel. If for some reason it is unavailable, look for the following brands, all of which are quite good: Artisan Fromager, Etendard, Grand Béron, Henri Voy's Camembert de Paris, Isigny Sainte-Mère, La Ferme d'Antignac, Lanquetôt, and Réo.

Choosing and Serving Camembert

Unfortunately, the vast majority of French Camembert brands available in the U.S. are not worthy of your attention since they are made with pasteurized milk. The few reasonably good ones are relatively rare and must be sought out with vigilance. French-made brands of non-A.O.C. Camembert to look for include Lescure, Isigny Sainte-Mère, and Vallée. Ironically, the cheeses available to us in the U.S. that are closest in flavor to real Camembert are Italian Toma di Carmagnola, Toma della Valcuvia, and the Paglia-style cheeses (see page 197), all of which are vastly superior to French-made pasteurized Camembert. Roucoulons (roo-koo-LAWN), a French soft-ripened cow's-milk cheese from Franche-Comté, is also close in taste, as is American-made Blythedale Farm Camembert from Vermont (page 422).

If you can gracefully get away with it, I recommend that you slightly open a Camembert's paper

RIND AND ALL

You can, if you want, eat the rind on Brie and Camembert. Many people do. (French *maître-fromager* Pierre Androuët would never, while English cheese expert Patrick Rance would never not. I do both.) But you probably won't want to eat the rind on Pont-l'Évêque and Livarot because it is often gritty and bitter. The rind of real Camembert and Brie often can be bitter and ammoniated, while the rinds of factory-made Bries and Camemberts are like the cheese itself—rather flavorless.

wrap for a furtive peek at the rind to determine ripeness. If it is ugly-looking and smells ammoniacal, it is overripe. If you come home with an overripe cheese, take it back to the merchant (along with dated proof-of-purchase receipt) and request an exchange or a refund.

Camembert is fine to serve anytime and it marries well with most fruit. Match Camembert with any Gamay or Pinot Noir red.

LIVAROT

All production of Livarot (LEE-vah-roe) is legally limited to the area around the town of Vimoutiers in the *département* of Calvados, and the valley of the Viette river. The vil-

lage of Camembert is also here. Livarot is about six miles downstream (north), where the Viette becomes the Vie. Lisieux, an important cheese- and dairy-production center, is another ten miles north. Livarot, which dates from the thirteenth century, is one of the oldest of all French cheeses, in good company with only three others: Roquefort (eleventh century), Maroilles (seventh to tenth century), and Cantal (pre-tenth century).

Livarot that has aged for two months has a soft, straw-colored paste and a good, strong, beefy, slightly salty, beery, nutty flavor. It hasn't gained much popularity in the United States because it's a terrifically smelly washed-rind cheese. If Livarot were left to ripen naturally it would have a bloomy rind—like Camembert. Instead, it is washed with a brine that causes the exterior of the cheese to ferment and darken to orange, encouraging another specific mold growth and an odor that contributes to a much more pronounced flavor than Camembert. (For more about washed-rind cheeses, see page 83.)

There are always five bands of narrow red raffia wrapped latitudinally around this partially skimmed cow's milk cheese before it is wrapped in orange paper. (This originally served a practical purpose—to keep it from losing its shape when it was removed from its mold.) Since these bands echo the military stripes on the sleeves of a French colonel, Livarot was nicknamed "the colonel" about 200 years ago.

Livarot is sometimes paired

with Calvados, the apple brandy native to the region, although apple ciders, both alcoholic and nonalcoholic, are much more agreeable, it seems to me. It also teams well with any sappy, well-knit, big red wine, and I have often enjoyed it with English ale, Irish stout, or one of the winey Belgian beers. Like Camembert, disks of Livarot are always shipped in a flimsy wooden box, although retailers sometimes remove it and sell less than a whole cheese. Traditional-size Livarots weigh about a pound (500 g), though some makers offer half sizes and larger disks. In the U.S. both the Graindorge and Levasseur brands of pasteurized Livarot are excellent.

Choosing and Serving Livarot

Livarot is one of those touchy, temperamental cheeses that seems to know how good it is.

When it is too young, it is chalky, tart, and lifeless, not unlike underripe Brie and Camembert. Livarot that is too young is rarely a problem in the U.S.; overripeness is much more likely to occur. This famous cheese is still relatively unknown here, and the cheese merchants who do handle it often don't sell it fast enough. Smell the cheese: If it is "high"—ammoniacal or sharply barnyardy—don't buy it. Like its brother Camembert and not-too-distant cousin Brie, in its final stage of ripeness, it is positively putrid.

Livarot is wonderfully smelly during its short but glorious ripe life—don't worry, you'll know the difference between smelly and putrid. Livarot comes wrapped in waxed, orange-colored paper inside its box and it must entirely fill the box. If the paper is wrinkled at all and the cheese sunken or shrunken, it is dying or dead. If the cheese is too firm to the touch, it is too young; however, it is advisable and prudent to purchase Livarot in this state: Leave it whole, in the box, wrapped in its paper, and allow it to ripen in the vegetable compartment of the refrigerator.

An unripe Livarot should not take more than a week to reach the desired ripeness. Use the soft-to-the-touch test: The

Thick disks of wonderfully pungent Livarot are wrapped in orange paper and tucked into thin wooden boxes.

cheese should feel as yielding as the flesh between the base of your thumb and forefinger when your hand is lightly clenched.

Livarot is at once a peasant and a noble. It is a joy for lunch or as a snack with fruit and bread and a potent red wine, apple cider, beer, or Calvados. It is perfect at the end of an evening meal. Apples and pears are a perfect match with Livarot because their juicy crispness contrasts nicely with its warm, salty beefiness. As for wine, I tend to enjoy most the spiciness of a Châteauneuf-du-Pape with the corresponding spiciness of a perfectly ripe Livarot. Big reds, such as Burgundy or Bordeaux, are also a good match.

Little seaside villages dot Normandy's Côte Fleurie ("flowered coast"). At the pretty port of Honfleur, slope-roofed stone houses overlook the 17th-century harbor.

PONT-L'EVEQUE

Pont-l'Evêque (PAWHN-leh-VECK), which has as long a history as Livarot, is named for the town (and the bridge) at l'Evêque, and is made mostly in the Pays d'Auge. Pont-l'Evêque is square in shape, a bit smaller than a Livarot but larger than a Camembert, and is ripened for 1 to 1½ months—only half as long as Livarot. Whole-milk Pont-l'Evêque is also higher in fat content, about 50% *matières grasses* (butterfat), compared to Livarot, made with partially skimmed milk, at 40% to 45% *m.g.* The standard square cheese, made in 8-ounce and 13-ounce sizes (250 g and 390 g) is about half again as big as

Camembert, and is a "brushed," washed-rind cheese—its surface has been washed or rubbed with a brine solution. (For more about washed- and brushed-rind cheeses, see page 83.) Pont-l'Evêque has the texture and all of the nuances of Camembert but with a much more pronounced beefiness of flavor and an intensity level somewhere between Camembert and Livarot.

Pont-l'Evêque is easy to recognize. In addition to its square shape, the top rind is crosshatched by the mesh the cheese sits on while it's draining. It is always packed in a wooden container, and beside the standard sizes, it is also available in 5-pound (2 k) *pavés* and a smaller 6-ounce (170 g) size.

PURE ENJOYMENT

Real Pont-l'Evêque, Livarot, and Camembert are at once majestic and staple. They appear on the tables of Normandy as prominently as do apples, butter, and cream. They may be eaten before or as dessert or instead of a cooked meal, in the form of a *casse-croûte des fermiers*—a farmer's snack. These cheeses do not traditionally figure in the cooking of the region, although today they are added to cheese crêpes and salads. But most often they're eaten as a separate course with baguettes or the crusty breads of the region and are also terrific served after, not with, fruit.

Choosing and Serving Pont-l'Evêque

In America, the possibility of finding a healthy Pont-l'Evêque is fraught with the likelihood of overripeness. Because it is less familiar than Camembert or Brie, it tends to sit around longer at the cheese counter. "Dead" Pont-l'Evêque has a decidedly unhealthy odor. It will have sunken into its box, and upon closer inspection, will be noticeably slimy, if it has not already passed this stage into one of complete desiccation.

A ripe, healthy Pont-l'Evêque will be fat in its fragile wooden box, with a pleasantly barnyardy aroma. The crosshatch-impressed rind will be beige to red-colored, bumpy, and dry.

This is a cheese worthy of attention at the end of any meal or at any time of day. Like Livarot, Pont-

There are great small producers of A.O.C. Pont-l'Evêque throughout the Pays d'Auge area and the same two large-scale producers of Livarot, Graindorge, and Levasseur also make the only two pasteurized brands you can find in the U.S. When you are in France, try the Pont-l'Evêque from Lepeudry brand, Bisson et fils, Lanquetôt, and La Varinière.

After Roquefort, Brie, and Camembert, Pont-L'Evêque is the most popular cheese in France.

l'Evêque is a natural partner to the ciders of Normandy. In addition, it is great with beer or red wine, especially full-bodied reds with big noses. Crisp (not creamy) pears such as Bosc are a tasty accompaniment, since they counter the creamy texture of the cheese; crisp, spicy sweet apples such as Macouns are also good.

BRILLAT-SAVARIN

B etween the two wars, Normandy became the home of a great triple-crème cheese called Brillat-Savarin (bree-YAH sah-vah-RAN), a name given the cheese by Henri Androuët whose son, Pierre, has continued to build upon the family's reputation as *maître-fromager par excellence* (see box, page 78). The original Brillat-Savarin, author of the oft-quoted phrase, "Tell me what you eat and I will tell you what you are," was a writer, statesman, and gastronome born in Belley in the Eresse region near Burgundy. He fed France during Napoleon I's reign and lived in Virginia for a time. (His book, *The Physiology of Taste,* which was translated by an idol of mine, M.F.K. Fisher, is one of the most dog-eared books in my library. If you haven't already, you must read it.)

Brillat-Savarin is a cheese "confection" that has hot, rich cream added to its milk to achieve a butterfat content (*matière grasse*) above 75%. Brillat can't be too young (air transport is a must with

Buttery Brillat-Savarin, a famous triple-crème, is named for the illustrious French gastronome, Anthelme Brillat-Savarin.

this cheese). It certainly is permissible for the cheese to be a bit "seasoned," not really aged, but allowed to pass that stage where it resembles a curd more than a cheese and to the point where it "blondes up," or becomes a smooth, suspended paste, too rich to run or even bulge. At this point it becomes what it is—a thick "confection-sauce," if you will, for fruit.

Although Brillat-Savarin is not difficult to import, few American cheese shops carry it these days. Brillador, one of three brands of Brillat-Savarin exported to America, is produced by Soulié, from down near Toulouse. It is rather one-dimensional—much like eating a stick of butter. Another, called Pansy and produced in massive quantities by a company called Pansey (with an "e"), is wrapped in plastic and individually packed in garish boxes. It is made from pasteurized milk and is intended for supermarket cheese departments. It is no better or worse than the Soulié examples—both brands are acceptable, but characterless. The one Brillat-Savarin I can recommend bears a label saying La Ferme Imports, and stating that it was selected by Pierre Androuët (whose famous cheese business in Paris is now owned by a French conglomerate). Each cheese is sold in a round wooden box bearing his logo. This is true Brillat-Savarin and offers all the joys of a well-made, small-production triple-crème cheese. It is quite expensive and scarce, as its U.S. distribution is spotty.

Choosing and Serving Brillat-Savarin

The only brand of Brillat-Savarin readily available to us in the U.S. is the previously mentioned Brilla-dor. Weighing in at just over a pound (500 g), it should be eaten as young as possible, though I have a slight preference for the soft-ripened version over the chalky *frais* (fresh) variety, which is little more than a shaped, cream-added curd. Avoid

NEUFCHATEL

Neufchâtel is greatly misunder-stood in the United States. This very pleasant, creamy, name-controlled Norman cheese with a *croûte fleurie* (mold-ripened rind) is available in France in a variety of shapes and sizes, including small hearts, and from several makers. I occasionally carry it at my cheese counters, but the pas-teurized examples that are legal for export to the U.S. are rather uninteresting. Here's where the misunderstanding comes in.

Some of America's largest dairy concerns produce a richer, softer, cream cheese-like sub-stance they have chosen to call Neufchâtel. As a result, customers appear at my counters request-ing Neufchâtel cheese, probably because they are trying to follow

some ill-begotten recipe that calls for it. So, you say, why not carry it? Because this so-called Neufchâtel is nothing but pro-cessed cheese thickened with xanthan and carrageenan gums. It's not really Neufchâtel at all.

If you have a recipe that calls for Neufchâtel, regard it with a jaundiced eye. If you insist on following through, substitute a good-quality, gum-free cream cheese. If you are one of my customers, you will be packed off with Ben's Fresh Cream Cheese from my dear friend Jonah Friedman, the owner of Ben's Cheese Shop on East Hous-ton Street in Manhattan. It's made from fresh cream and *no gums!* Search out an equivalent in your area.

any Brillador that shows a split rind, any sagging, or liquefaction—all are evidence of overripeness.

Caterers and many of my customers find this cheese to be an impressive offering—elegant and memorable, a cheese that evokes ooohs and aaahs. Brillat is meant for dessert, a cheese crying out for the sweetest, most delectable, in-season fruits such as peaches, raspberries, apricots, and strawberries, and exotics such as cherimoya, passion fruit, guava, and atemoya. Personally, I prefer my cheese to be less showy, less machine-made, less creamy, and more piquant, but whatever makes you happy is good. Serve Brillat-Savarin with a good Champagne or try it with a *cava,* the wonderfully refreshing sparkling wine from just outside Barcelona.

PETIT-SUISSE

For all intents and purposes, Petit-Suisse (PEH-tee-SWEES), like Brillat-Savarin, is history. It still exists but the original method of manufacture and sweetly lactic flavor have mostly disappeared. Although it was the first double-crème, for the past 20 years it has been a cheese created through the use of centrifugal force to achieve its texture and flavor, rather than renneting. The result: no flavor, no texture, no right to have the name Petit-Suisse.

I sell little plastic six-packs of Petit-Suisse, with each individual 2-inch-high cylindrical cheese weighing just 1 ounce (30 g). And though

LES CREMES DE LA CREME

The lushest, butteriest, and most luxurious of all French cheeses—made by adding extra cream to the fresh curd used to make soft-ripened cheeses—are double-crèmes (DOO-bull-KREMS) and triple-crèmes (TREE-pull-KREMS). By law, double-crèmes must contain 60% to 74% butterfat, while the even richer triple-crèmes are required to have 75% or more butterfat. The first double-crème, Petit-Suisse, was created in Normandy in 1850 by a short, Swiss-born cheesemaker whose name is lost in the mists of time but whose diminutive stature is forever immortalized as the cheese's name. The first triple-crème, called Le Magnum, was made by the Dubuc family in Normandy about 75 years later and later evolved into Brillat-Savarin, the most famous contemporary triple-crème.

I rail against the methods used to make them, they really are quite pleasant, particularly with berries or melon or with baked potatoes. I also sell them with various real French fruit compotes added. My problem, I suppose, is that for those of us who remember, Petit-Suisse is not what it once was. But, then, who or what among us is?

Bretons produce 20% of France's milk, yet eat more fish than fromage!

BRITTANY

The cheeses made in Brittany are among the least important in this book. Yet I adore this region and its history—physically it is so like our state of Maine, so possessed by the sea and seafood, by ships and by weather. Settled by Gaelic Celts fleeing invading Angles and Saxons, Brittany still embraces the people and ancient traditions from across the channel in England more than it does the rest of France.

Ironically, from a cheese point of view, this is great dairy territory that produces only blah, commercial-tasting cheeses. One has to wonder where the cheesemaking tradition went awry in this region that raises 20% of France's cattle and produces 20% of its milk and 33% of its butter, to say nothing of mountains of crème fraîche.

Even the briefest examination of Brittany's cheeses suggests that Bretons would rather eat fish than cheese. And there is some historical precedent for this observation from a government bureaucrat who, in 1801, reported back to Napoleon about Brittany that: "They consume salted pork, pressed sardines, milk dishes, and butter. They do not know about cheese." Enough said.

The Cheeses

Brittany's cheese production consists of two of the most plastic, unillustrious, though very popular, cheeses in France—Port-Salut (PORE-sah-LOO) and Saint-Paulin (SAN-paw-LAN). To locate these boring cow's-milk cheeses, you need look no farther than any supermarket in the world. There you will find Port-Salut, a cheese with a proud past

Brittany is France's maritime province.

and uninspiring present, and Saint-Paulin, its mutant kin and the only European cheese perhaps less memorable than Port-Salut.

Port-Salut's history is more interesting than its taste. Originally named Port-du-Salut after the abbey of Notre Dame du Port-du-Salut at Entrammes, it was first made in the mid-1800s by Trappist monks, only for consumption at the monastery. But in 1873 a visit to Paris by the head of the abbey resulted in an advantageous distribution agreement with a Parisian cheese seller. A year later sales of this flat, cylindrical cheese were brisk enough to warrant the monks registering Port-du-Salut as a trade name to guard against imitations. Unfazed imitators quickly began

calling their version Saint-Paulin.

In the 1950s, the cheese began its descent into mediocrity when the monks struck several deals with outside parties, a circumstance that eventually led to the sale of the trade name. The monks no longer make Port-Salut. Today it is produced by SAFR, a big dairy company in eastern Lorraine. Port-Salut is a thick, dyed-orange disk with a flabby, glistening interior and stupefyingly bland flavor. Each rubbery wheel weighs about 4 pounds (2 k).

There are virtually no differences between Port-Salut and Saint-Paulin. Saint-Paulin is made in the same configuration as Port-Salut and is just as banal. A vaguely Trappist-style cheese, about all I can say is that t is slightly smelly.

DIVINE CURD

Historically, Christian religious orders were the source of many of the original European cheeses and wines. This certainly makes sense since many monasteries and nunneries prided themselves on their hospitality, and the high quality of the food and wine served was enjoyed not only by the monks and nuns, but also by visitors.

The cheeses made by these religious orders, most of which were founded in France, Belgium, and Switzerland, share a basic recipe and milk type; they are semisoft, cow's-milk cheeses

Pungent washed-rind cheeses have been made in monasteries since at least the 7th century.

made from uncooked curd and with washed rinds. Each has a pronounced flavor and considerable aroma. One of the most famous examples of this genre is Munster, which takes its name from an old form of the word monastery. As a result of their tremendous popularity, today many monastery or Trappist cheeses—again, French Munster, for example—are produced in vast quantities in factories owned by companies not affiliated with any religious order. Monastery-style copycat cheeses are everywhere (each with a religious-sounding name, of course), but they are consistently flavorless. You'll certainly want to avoid Austrian Sebastian and Trappist, and German Bruder Basil. The best, such as Belgian Chimay (she-MAY) and French Pierre-Qui-Vire (pee-AIR-kee-veer), however, are still completely artisanal, but unfortunately are not exported to the U.S. as yet with any frequency. Below is a list of the best-known monastery and Trappist cheeses, the area where they are made, and their availability in the U.S. Those marked with an asterisk I consider to be the finest. For the most part, you will have to visit their country of origin to taste them.

*Boulette d'Avesnes: France (Le Nord); rare

Bricquebec: France (Alsace); rare

Bruder Basil: Germany; widely available

Campénéac: France (Brittany); rare

Chambarand: France (Dauphiné); rare

Chimay: Belgium; rare

Cîteaux: France (Burgundy); rare

Echourgnac: France (Périgord); rare

Entrammes: France (Maine); rare

*Epoisses: France (Burgundy); not available

Esrom: Denmark; widely available

*Herve: Belgium; rare

Laval: France (Maine); rare

Limburger: Belgium; rare

Limburger: Germany; available, spotty

*Livarot: France (Alsace); available, spotty

Maredsous: Belgium; rare

*Maroilles: France (Le Nord); rare

Mondseer: Austria; widely available

Mont-des-Cats: France (Le Nord); rare

*Munster: France (Alsace); available, spotty

Nantais: France (Brittany); rare

Oka: Canada (Quebec); available, spotty

*Pavé d'Auges: France (Normandy); rare

*Pavé de Moyaux: France (Normandy); rare

*Pierre-Qui-Vire: France (Burgundy); rare

*Pont-l'Evêque: France (Normandy); available, spotty

Port-Salut: France (Lorraine); widely available

Providence: France (Normandy); rare

Saint Michael: Austria; widely available

*Saint-Nectaire: France (Auvergne); widely available

Saint-Paulin (also Abbey, a brand of Saint-Paulin): France (all regions); widely available

Sebastian: Austria; widely available

*Tamié: France (Savoie); rare

*Tête de Moine: Switzerland (Bern); available, spotty

Trappist: Austria; widely available

Trappiste de Melleray: France (Brittany); rare

Véritable Trappe: France (Maine); rare

THE NORTH: FLANDERS, ARTOIS, AND PICARDY

(Flandres, Artois, and Picardie)

Flanders, Artois, and Picardy are the classical names for this northern, flat, English-Channel-and-Belgium-bound region that boasts little gastronomic import (beyond great fish) or export. Textiles and metallurgy are the area's main industries. The political *départements* of these classical regions are Nord and Pas-de-Calais (Flanders and landlocked Artois), and Somme, Aisne, and Oise (Picardy), which are named after rivers. Picardy has been part of France since 1477, Artois since 1559, and Flanders since 1668.

The Cheeses

The cheeses of the region are rather coarse and unrefined (Maroilles, Gris de Lille, Boulette d'Avesnes) or completely derivative of the cheeses of the nearby Netherlands. (Mimolette, for example, is a French copy of Edam.) In terms of cheese, *le Nord,* as the French refer to this region, must be consid-

As is traditional in France, sharp-eyed shoppers forage for the finest on market day.

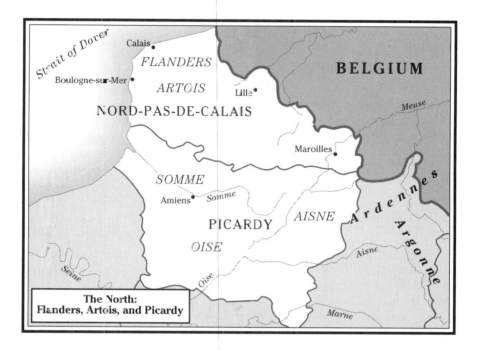

The North:
Flanders, Artois, and Picardy

ered Maroilles country. Maroilles, created in a monastery sometime between the seventh and tenth centuries, is France's strongest smelling and tasting cheese. Until a hundred or so years ago, it was also one cf France's most important. Its low price and assertive flavor served to satisfy many a laborer: a few thin slices—crust and all—placed between two hunks of bread made for a very economical lunch. Hence its popularity.

These regions are famous for smelly, cow's-milk, washed-rind cheeses, made from practically identical recipes and similarly aged. They are largish, salty cheeses with strong odors that go well with beer. They weigh about a pound (500 g), are shaped into a square (like a Pont-l'Evêque), but are thicker. They are of a semisoft, almost bulging, Brie-like texture and offer a smooth,

subtle yet sharp attack on the tongue, as opposed to crumbly, sharp cheeses that signal their taste sensations in a more straightforward manner. When overripe, they taste terrible. Indeed, even on the young side, these cheeses are overpowering for Americans' taste—even mine.

GRIS DE LILLE AND MAROILLES

Gris de Lille (GREE-duh-leel), made in Flanders, is nicknamed *le puant* (the stinker). You will see it only rarely in the United States—I used to sell a few of them, but never enough to warrant their constant presence.

Gris de Lille is identical to the most important cheese of the region, Maroilles (mah-WAHL), named after an ancient abbey in the Ardennes forest. It is a powerfully odoriferous name-controlled cheese that many cheese lovers consider delicious. Also identical to Maroilles in terms of recipe are a number of cheeses made in nearby small towns located within the A.O.C. boundaries specified for Maroilles (see box).

Choosing and Serving Gris de Lille and Maroilles

Do not purchase Gris de Lille- or Maroilles-type cheeses unless you are allowed to open the box, pull back the waxed paper overwrap a bit, and give the rind a peek and a sniff. Since such a small amount of Maroilles and Gris de Lille makes the journey to the U.S., what does get here is very likely to be overripe. The box and the label will survive in pristine shape, but the cheese inside may be hideous. Avoid any with an overpowering, unpleasant odor. The cheese will be shrunken, hard, and dried out, and its appearance will be a dead (literally) giveaway as well: The crust will be dark brown, graying, and crumbly. Look for a healthy crust—smooth, rich, and reddish-creamy brown—and an aroma that smells of cheese, not manure.

Serve these cheeses with all kinds of fruit (their salinity counterbalances ripe fruit, cutting the sweetness) and rye or pumpernickel bread. Make a sandwich from thin strips of one of these cheeses and add just a smear of Dijon mus-

THE MANY SIZES OF MAROILLES

Maroilles is sold in a wide variety of sizes, each with a name for that particular size prominently displayed on the top of the cheese's square wooden box. Look for:

- **Rollot** (round or heart shaped): 5½ to 7 ounces (165 to 210 g)
- **Quart:** 6½ ounces (195 g)
- **Demi-baguette:** 8 ounces (250 g)
- **Mignon:** 12 ounces (375 g)
- **Baguette Laonnaise:** 1 pound (500 g)
- **Sorbais:** 1¼ pounds (625 g)
- **Gros:** 1½ pounds (750 g)

A statue of Joan of Arc in Reims commemorates her role in persuading the Dauphin to march on Reims, where he was crowned King Charles VII in 1429.

tard. You can leave the rind on, but this is a matter of taste.

To me, the saltiness of these cheeses makes them appropriate with beer, but they also marry well with strong red wines.

BOULETTE D'AVESNES AND DAUPHIN

You may come across a cheese called Boulette d'Avesnes (boo-LETT-dah-VANE), named for the town of Avesnes in the extreme southeastern part of Flanders. This cheese is popularly referred to as *le suppositoire du diable*—it's spicy. Boulette d'Avesnes is a small, soft-textured, 7- to 9-ounce (210 to 270 g) cone of cheese, made from raw cow's milk that's been mixed with paprika, parsley, tarragon, crushed pepper, and cloves. (In the old days it was made from scraps of Maroilles.) The whole cheese—flecked with these flavorings and washed with beer—becomes very strong after aging for several weeks. Brash and aggressive, it has an enticing, roughneck appeal that matches up marvelously with crusty bread and cold ale.

The exact same cheese is also

made in the shape of a porpoise or dolphin. Called Dauphin (doh-FAN), it was originally created to commemorate the Dauphin of France, the disinherited Charles VII who persecuted Joan of Arc. Typically, Dauphin weighs slightly more than Boulette d'Avesnes; the paprika-dusted rinds of both cheeses are very red.

Miners in this region make their own *boulettes* of a sort by kneading Maroilles with gin or beer and parsley, tarragon, and pepper, potting it, and letting it sit for a few days to get really nasty. It is called *fromage fort de Bethune.* It's coarse and unrefined, but fun.

Choosing and Serving Boulette d'Avesnes and Dauphin

You can have confidence in Boulette d'Avesnes or Dauphin when the patina of its paprika-covered rind is dry and healthy-looking and the aroma is clean, spicy, and cheesy. A shriveling, slimy rind and/or an overpowering odor mean this rare cheese is dead. This is the perfect cocktail or snack cheese, one as good with beer and crackers as it is with a rough red wine and rustic bread. Cold gin is often recommended with Boulette. I find the cheese too spicy to serve for a dinner course.

MIMOLETTE

The other cheeses of *le Nord* are mostly derivatives of Dutch, Belgian, and British cheeses, the most popular of which is Mimolette (mee-moh-LETT), a copy of Edam. This is the cheese the guidebooks to France urge visitors to try, assuming that most French cheeses will be too strong for outsiders—which is, of course, ludicrous. Except for its color, Mimolette is one of the blandest cheeses you'll ever taste—though one particular aged version is passably tasty. It is almost spherical in shape, although a bit flattened on the top and bottom (looks a lot like a cantaloupe), and weighs 7 to 8 pounds (3 to 4 k). Its texture is very waxy, as is its flavor.

I have to remind myself I'm eating cheese when I ponder the flavor of Mimolette. Every cheese book I've read includes the baffling statement that Mimolette was Charles de Gaulle's favorite cheese, so let this book be no exception.

*There were cheeses
from the North,
There were cheeses
from the South.
There were dozens
of ones which
Melted in the mouth.*

T. A. Layton

(I wonder if this tidbit is meant to elevate or condemn the poor cheese. I choose to believe that, though a great leader, General de Gaulle must not have been much of a judge of his country's provender, certainly not of its cheese.)

Mimolette s also made in Normandy and in the Netherlands. The name is derived from its texture— *demi-molle,* not quite soft. The Isigny-Sainte-Mère cheese company of Normandy, makers of excellent Camembert and superb butter and crème fraîche, produces an aged Mimolette that, though expensive, has a bit of flavor. It tastes a little like a slightly smoky, two-year-old American Cheddar.

Mimolette is a great cheese to look at and a winner with cheese-eating neophytes. Many people simply prefer substantial, weighty cheeses that treat the palate gently.

Choosing and Serving Mimolette

Not much can go wrong with this simplest of cheeses. Mimolette's mild chewiness and imposing shape, color, and heft fit the bill nicely where a sharp Cheddar or Parmesan might be just too strong. Avoid dryness and mold. The best examples are aged (12 to 18 months) ones produced in Normandy (not the North) by Besnier, Isigny-Sainte-Mère, or Valco. Mimolette is best eaten as a snack with fruit, bread, crackers, and beer or wine. Its shredding and melting qualities are the same as Cheddar, though it is firmer and denser. It could be substituted for mild Cheddar whenever desired, though it doubtless will be more expensive.

Similar to Dutch Edam, mild-tasting Mimolette is said to have been Charles de-Gaulle's favorite cheese.

CHAMPAGNE AND ILE-DE-FRANCE

CHAMPAGNE

Neither *La* Champagne, the region, nor *Le* Champagne, the wine, need much introduction. Champagne, the region, has figured prominently throughout the prehistory and history of France. Today, Champagne consists of four political *départements:* Ardennes, Aube, Marne, and Haute-Marne. Champagne's name is derived from the Roman *campania,* meaning "flat fields," and indeed, though those fields roll, most of Champagne is flat. The area between Burgundy and Belgium is called *Champagne pouilleuse*—"poor" Champagne; the chalky plain is *Champagne humide*—"damp" Champagne—and is an area of more fertile, clay soil that nourishes the vineyards, the most northerly in all of France.

The production of cheese in Champagne is both factory-made and artisanal; it is the artisanal, and only the artisanal, that I feel is worthy of mention.

The Cheeses

CHAOURCE

The Champagne region is famous for one cheese, and it is quite special. Chaource (shah-OORSE), named after the town of the same name, is a rich and creamy cheese with slightly more butterfat than Brie.

Classic Chaource is a soft-ripened, raw cow's milk cheese with a white, bloomy rind. You can find it

Sumptuous and creamy, aged Chaource is similar to Brie and Camembert.

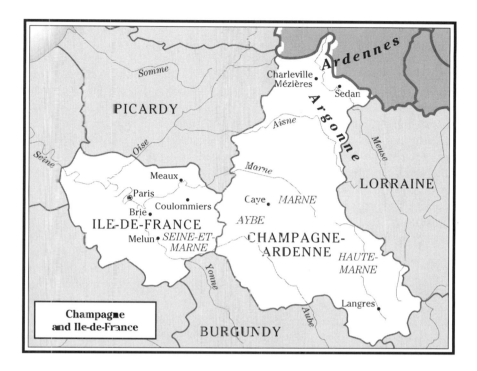

Champagne and Ile-de-France

in every good French *fromagerie* in 1-pound (500 g) or 8-ounce (250 g) short (3 to 4 inches high), fat drum shapes, 3 to 4 inches in diameter. Chaource can be eaten at any stage: very young, when it's rather flaky, very white, bland, and chalky-tasting; aged a bit, when it's creamy and runny around the edges; or fully ripe, when the thickish white crust shows faint, reddish mottling and the cheese is soft, nutty, sharp, and runny throughout. I prefer it in its aged form—when it is a bit straw-colored and tastes like icing without the sugar, or like a salty Mascarpone.

At its ripest stage, the texture of Chaource is like butter, yet it is not oily like butter. It is still very much like a cheese—quite creamy and mildly acidic and rich.

Choosing and Serving Chaource

Chaource is delicious in several stages of ripeness. The flavor of this creamy, soft-ripened cow's-milk cheese will intensify, growing with age from mild to piercingly sharp. But take care to avoid over-ripeness—a sagging, too runny appearance. When shopping for Chaource in France, look for the Hugerot or Rouzaire brands. In the U.S., the only available version is a very good pasteurized one by Lincet. All except *fermier* examples are loosely wrapped in plastic to keep this exceptionally runny cheese from losing its shape.

Begin your day or end a meal with Chaource. It makes an enjoyable breakfast cheese with pastry, croissants, toast, or muffins. Later on, luxuriate in its richness as a dessert cheese, where it is a perfect foil to the sweetest fruits. It is delicious with berries and, not surprisingly, Champagne. Just as Livarot and Pont-l'Evêque were created to go with the ciders of Normandy, Chaource is meant to go with Champagne's great sparkling wines. Chaource is too sumptuous for snacks and too creamy for a salad course.

LANGRES

L angres (LAHNG-gruh), made in the area surrounding the village of Langres, is a special favorite of mine, one of the great washed-rind, unpasteurized cheeses. Very similar to the sublime name-controlled Epoisses de Bourgogne (page 105), Langres is a small 6-ounce (180 g) to 1½-pound (750 g) drum with a concave top especially designed to be filled, traditionally, with Chablis, *marc*, brandy, or Champagne. Then, when the cheese is cut, it bathes the paste with the spirit. For the most part the shape has outlived the practice, I'm happy to report, since this hugely flavorful cheese needn't

be bathed in spirits in order to enjoy its rich flavor.

Langres looks very appealing with its little concave top and red-orange rind. Then it hits you with the pronounced smelly aroma characteristic of all washed-rind, full-fat cheeses. Langres is excruciatingly delicious—it just shocks your tongue with its intense, spicy, creamy flavor.

I brought Langres (and Epoisses) to the U.S. some years ago, but these days, due to USFDA regulations banning raw-milk cheeses aged less than 60 days, I can no longer do so. It is our loss. You'll have to seek out this memorable cheese in France where the versions to look out for are made by Germain and Schertenleib.

Choosing and Serving Langres

W hen shopping for Langres note that the rind should be a shiny red-orange and look moist, not sodden; eating this rind is a matter of taste. The interior should be blond or pale-straw in color. The aroma of Langres is irresistible, undeniably barnyardy but not overpoweringly so—more a healthy, outdoorsy earthiness.

As is the case with Epoisses, Langres is a superb after-dinner cheese. Try it with a Rhône red accompanied by a few tiny dried mirabelle plums from Burgundy or some of the famous prunes from Agen in southwest France.

ILE-DE-FRANCE

Brie is the classical name of a region—politically known as the Seine-et-Marne (for the two rivers)—within the Ile-de-France, which is essentially the greater Paris area. Brie consists of many small suburban centers to the south and east of Paris, and much of its population commutes to work in the city.

The history of Brie is voluminous and dates by legend to the fifth century, although this can't be authenticated. *Le* Brie (the cheese) was made even way back then in *La* Brie (the classical region). Charlemagne is said to have first tasted—and loved—Brie as early as 774. Until the Franco-Prussian War of 1870, the plains of Brie were all dairy pastureland. However, the war caused widespread destruction, from which the region's dairy business never fully recovered. The land fell to industrial ownership and the focus shifted from small

BELLISSIMA BRIE

Heretical as it may sound, there is evidence that the Italians make better Brie than the French (given, of course, that authentic raw-milk Brie and Camembert are unavailable to us in the U.S.). Superior examples of commandingly good, soft-ripened cow's-milk cheeses are to be found among the Toma and Paglia-style cheeses made in Piedmont and Lombardy. Consider them under-appreciated treasures and make their acquaintance soon.

Toma Carmagnola (TOH-mah-kar-mon-YOH-lah) from Piedmont and Toma della Valcuvia (TOH-mah-deh-lah-val-koo-VEE-yah) from Lombardy are plump, thickish, 8- to 12-ounce (250 to 375 g) disks of cheese with a straw-colored interior and a beige-mottled bloomy rind. When properly ripened, their white truffle-like taste and mushroomy aroma promise an experience every bit as refined as that of any real French Brie or Camembert. (For more about Toma, see page 197.)

Paglia-style (PAHL-yah) cheeses are soft, flat, 6- to 8-ounce (180 to 250 g), paper-wrapped disks of cheese made primarily in Piedmont. Their peak-of-perfection flavor and aroma are reminiscent of mushrooms, wild onions, and garlic. Nearly every major producer in this region makes a Paglia-style cheese and each calls it something slightly different. Look for Pagliola (pahl-YOH-lah) made by Mauri, Paglierino (pahl-yer-REE-noh) made by Quaglia, and Paglietta (pahl-yet-tah) made by Cademartori. (For more about Paglia-style cheeses, also see page 197.)

farms and cheesemaking to more commercial agricultural pursuits.

By 1914, there were half as many cattle as there had been 50 years earlier, and most of these were being raised for beef, not dairy. It was 1929 before the region managed to recover from the effects of World War I, and cheese production was slow to revive. It took until 1953 to equal 1929's output. By this time industrialization was rampant in the area, and those pastures not used for corn and sugar beets fell victim to urban sprawl. It was around this time that Brie became a factory cheese, as did Camembert, in Normandy. Factories sprang up all over the Ile-de-France and Champagne, and to this day the overwhelming percentage of cheese calling itself Brie is not only completely characterless, it is not even made there. Most of it comes from factories in Lorraine.

The Cheeses

I t is important to note that the numerous villages of the Seine-et-Marne and Ile-de-France

produce many different styles of Brie. As a rule, cheeses are named after the town nearest to where they are made.

BRIE DE MEAUX, BRIE DE MELUN, COULOMMIERS

Most famous of all is the big, 5-pound (2½ k) Brie de Meaux (BREE-duh-MOH), from a town just east of Paris that produces one of the two name-controlled Bries. When you find cheese that claims to be Brie de Meaux, be sure to read the label carefully. Out of its box, real Brie de Meaux (which can be made from unpasteurized *or* pasteurized milk) will have a foil label affixed to the center of the wheel that states "Appellation d'Origine Contrôlée" and will also state whether or not the cheese is *au lait cru* (raw milk) and/or *moulé à la louche* (hand-ladled). If the A.O.C. designation is not in evidence, it is a pasteurized imitator made outside the A.O.C. area, but the name Brie de Meaux will be on it as a brand name. Without the A.O.C. designation, whether made with raw or pasteurized milk, the cheese is not real Brie de Meaux! It is a French-made "Brie" that only approximates real Brie in shape and texture. Pack-

To identify an authentic, name-controlled Brie de Meaux, look for the appellation d'origine contrôlée designation on the label.

WHEN IN CHAMPAGNE AND ILE-DE-FRANCE (BRIE)

Some cheeses to search out when visiting the area include:

- **Boursault** (boor-SO): Made in Brie; a soft, thin-crusted triple-crème that is produced in 8-ounce (250 g) drums, was invented in 1953 by Henri Boursault. The company is now owned by Boursin. Gold-label, raw-milk Boursault is excellent. The silver-label version is surprisingly good, though made from pasteurized milk and a bit commercial-tasting. Since 1993 it has become increasingly available in the U.S.

- **Ervy-le-Châtel** (AIR-vee-luh-shah-TELL): Made in the Champagne district, this is identical to Chaource except it is always made from raw milk. When visiting France, seek out the *fermier,* or artisanal versions, which are never exported.

- **Fontainebleau** (fone-tan-BLOE): A beaten mixture of cow's-milk fromage blanc and crème fraîche or cream, which is sold in France in plastic containers or in bulk, usually topped with a piece of mesh, plastic, or cheesecloth. There is some commercial production from the Seine-et-Marne area, but most is made in individual cheese shops.

- **Pierre Robert** (pee-AIR-roe-BAIR): A soft-ripened triple-crème made from pasteurized cow's milk by Robert Rouzaire. Its name harkens back to antiquity when the area where it is made was a dukedom called Brie-Comte-Robert. Pierre refers to a limestone outcropping that is a regional landmark. Practically identical to double-crème Gratte-Paille, Pierre Roberts are disks about 1½ inches thick and 6 inches in diameter; they weigh about 1 pound (500 g).

aged in a wooden box with a predominantly blue label featuring a picture of the famous cathedral at Meaux, this copycat is imported by the Anco Foods Company of New Jersey.

Brie de Melun (BREE-duh-meh-LOON), the other name-controlled Brie, is a bit more rustic, a bit less perfect, and slightly smaller than the benchmark Brie de Meaux. Made only in raw-milk versions, it is not exported. Brie de Melun Frais is a variation, a completely unripe Brie with no rind on it at all, that's eaten fresh. It is very interesting, very milky, very fresh tasting, and with an airy, whipped texture that is light on the

THE KING OF CHEESES

In 1815, at the conclusion of the Napoleonic Wars, the Congress of Vienna was held to discuss the reorganization of the states of Europe. The diplomats dined nonstop at scores of ceremonial dinners, and as one might expect, grew a bit bored. To liven things up, French statesman Talleyrand produced a wheel of Brie de Meaux at one of the dinners and an informal competition among the nations took place, each vying for "best cheese in the world" status. Brie, the winner, was "crowned" *le roi du fromage.*

tongue—very much worth trying when you're in the area.

Coulommiers (koo-LOAM-yay) is as much an ancient and true Brie as Brie de Meaux and Brie de Melun, but it does not have A.O.C. status. Though the differences may seem minor to us, the reason for this is that there is no standard recipe or uniform size agreed upon by its various makers. This absence of standardization prevents it from qualifying for name-controlled protection and is also the reason it cannot officially be called Brie. It takes its name from the town of Coulommiers where it was first made. Like Brie

and Camembert, over 90% of the cheeses labeled Coulommiers that are available in the U.S. are not the real McCoy. These cheeses are thicker than other Bries (about 2 inches) or Camemberts, and often do not ripen all the way through; a thin, chalky line will remain in the center. (This is perfectly all right as long as the line is thin and the cheese is not too underripe.) Lincet makes a decent version of Coulommiers in the village of Gaye near Coulommiers; it is called, not surprisingly, Coulommiers de Gaye (koo-LOAM-yay-duh-GAY).

For many years I have been dealing with Robert Rouzaire, whose firm is in the town of Tournan, near Meaux. He jobs out production, gathers cheeses from small producers, and then puts his own label on them. His justifiably famous signature Coulommiers is named Le Fougéru (luh-foo-ZHAIR-roo), or "the one with the fern on it." Its flavor is extraordinary. He places a fern or bracken (*fougère,* in French)—the kind you find in the woods all over France—on his

The full flavor of Coulommiers includes hints of mushroom, truffle, and garlic.

Coulommiers to set it apart from all the others. It's a 1½-pound (750 g) wheel that is made from raw milk for European consumption. For a while, years ago, I could import this cheese, but not anymore. Mr. Rouzaire makes a pasteurized version of Le Fougéru for export to the U.S., and though it's not what it used to be, it can be very good when properly ripened and not too salty. If you come upon Le Fougéru in good condition jump on it. It makes a gorgeous party cheese. Its fern-bedecked top is a lovely, rustic throwback to the era when there were no machine-made Brie cheeses. (I don't recommend eating the fern—remove it before serving.)

Cheese affineur *Claudine Rouzaire with racks of ripening Coulommiers.*

Choosing and Serving Brie

When choosing Brie or any soft-ripened cheese, it is critical that you guard against over- or underripeness. Overripe Brie will be excessively runny, the rind falling completely away from the oozing cheese, and will have an ammoniacal odor. Oddly enough, sometimes "dead" Brie just hardens and becomes totally solid.

Underripe Brie will have a thick, white, chalky interior. Remember, once a wheel of Brie is cut, the ripening process is finished. Don't buy a piece of underripe Brie and expect to be able to ripen it and eat it in a week or two; it will simply get old, hard, and dry. If you can't find real Brie or Brie-style cheese in good condition, opt instead for Italian Toma from the Piedmont or Lombardy regions or any of the Italian Paglia-style cheeses from Piedmont. Avoid all of the phony, factory-made Brie and Camembert such as the President brand line of cheeses as well as faux versions called Valembert, Belle des Champs, Delice, Revidoux, Supreme, and any other factory-made cheeses.

When buying authentic, name-controlled Brie, look for a beige-mottled rind, and an interior that bulges rather than runs. If you've found a runny true Brie, it very likely may be overripe and too strong. Runny pasteurized Brie is another story: When a blander, factory-made Brie is runny, it is universally considered "ready." Remember: Real Brie should bulge—just slightly "flow" at most. Taste it before you make a decision.

Real Brie is a celebration and should be served with reverence—any time of the day. Give it your full attention and a big red wine.

ABOUT BRIE AND CAMEMBERT

The names "Brie" and "Camembert" are not protected by law (which accounts for their counterfeit proliferation), but Véritable Camembert de Normandie (the label clearly states V.C.N. *and* A.O.C.), Brie de Meaux, and Brie de Melun (their labels clearly state A.O.C.), are protected.

Even though real Brie and real Camembert come from completely different regions, they frequently are grouped together as a single type. And though few cheese experts point this out, real Brie and real Camembert taste identical. If you were to taste them blindfolded you would not be able to distinguish between them. They are made from the exact same recipe, and the areas they come from have similar topography.

The same criteria apply to real Brie as to real Camembert, but their sizes are different. Brie is made in 1-, 2-, 3-, and 6-pound (500 g to 3 k) wheels, whereas Camembert is always an 8-ounce (250 g) disk. Both cheeses are essentially the same thickness—about 1 inch. The dissimilarity of their sizes doesn't make any difference in the taste; they both ripen naturally, from the outside in, and since they're both the same thickness, they can ripen only so far, regardless of their diameter.

In the U.S., people think that Brie and Camembert are good only if they are runny—like melted Mozzarella on American-style pizza. But that's not the way real Brie and Camembert are supposed to be eaten. When ripe, they are creamy and at their peak of flavor just before they lapse into "runny." Runniness is a sign the cheese is overripe. Ideally, a ripe Brie or Camembert should bulge, not run.

Over the last 30 years we cheesemongers have had to endure an appalling travesty: Vast amounts of Brie and Camembert produced from milk that is so violently overpasteurized (rendering it "dead"), that the standing of these great real cheeses has become diminished and undermined. Without question, you can taste the difference between scalded-tasting, violently pasteurized milk that has been subjected to high temperatures for a short time and gently pasteurized milk that has been heated over a longer period at lower temperatures. Factory (*laitier*) production has resulted in thousands and thousands of tons of so-called Brie (or Brie *laitier*) and Camembert (or Camembert *laitier*) that is nothing but texture—little flavor whatsoever is involved. Any textural appeal is primarily the result of the tremendous amount of cream added to these cheeses— their labels often state 60% butterfat. Real Brie and Camembert, made with raw milk, will taste simultaneously fried-eggy, garlicky, nutty, truffle-like, and mushroomy; they'll melt on your tongue with a sensuous feel unmatched by the mass-produced stuff.

Not so many years ago, I managed to bring in any Camembert and Brie I wanted—six award-winning brands of Camembert and real Brie from several villages. All that ended in 1985 when the USFDA began requiring all raw-milk cheeses to be aged for at least 60 days before export.

At this writing, there are some French-made Brie/Camembert-style cheeses available in the U.S. that I can strongly recommend. In fact, I so heartily endorse them that I challenge any other example of soft-ripened cheese made with pasteurized milk to surpass them in terms of flavor, texture, and overall quality. I say "at this writing," because we never know when U.S. Customs or the USFDA might ban their importation. To add to these problems, cheese companies seem to have a habit of going out of business or being swallowed up by a larger competitor, and often the cheese is altered for the worse, its name is changed, or its production is curtailed altogether. Nonetheless, if you want to enjoy serious, Brie-style, soft-ripened, cow's-milk cheese made from milk that has been only very gently pasteurized, try any of the following examples, all of which are carried in specialty cheese shops:

- **Le Briardin** (bree-ar-DAN): Made by Lincet in Lorraine; available in 2- or 4-pound (1 or 2 k) sizes from which wedges are cut and sold; distinguished by its raw milk flavor.
- **Roucoulons** (roo-koo-LAWN): Made by Milleret in Franche-Comté; an 8-ounce (250 g) disk made by a small, good company in the Franche-Comté region.
- **Brie de Meaux:** Made by Rouzaire in Ile-de-France; a 6-pound (3 k) wheel of a well-made, pasteurized version of the "prince of cheeses"—not to be confused with the audaciously titled Brie de Meaux trademarked by the Anco Foods Company of New Jersey. Look for the A.O.C. insignia.

Also look for other perfectly acceptable pasteurized Bries (Brie *laitier*) made by the Fromageries Ermitage, Fromageries Henri Hutin, and Fromageries Vitelloise.

GRATTE-PAILLE

Robert Rouzaire, maker of Le Fougéru (page 72), is also responsible for the greatest double-crème of all: Gratte-Paille (GROTT-PIE). Rouzaire had it created to his specifications and named it himself; roughly translated the name means "straw-hugger" because the cheese sits on straw mats to dry and ripen. My English friend Patrick Rance (who, along with Rouzaire and America's Gerd Stern, is one of the world's greatest cheesemen), told me that *gratte paille* is a nickname for the town of Meaux. It seems the historic brick-walled lanes were so narrow that hay wagons passing through town left wisps of straw stuck to the walls.

Gratte-Paille weighs about 12 ounces (375 g) and is a rectangular brick, 3 inches high and 5 inches long, of raw cow's-milk cheese—it is

EXCUSEZ-MOI!

When French and Italian cheese companies transliterate their own languages, the results can be quite interesting. The label on Le Fougéru, Rouzaire's brand, used to read: "This crud [sic] is from the finest milk soley [sic] from the cow's [sic] of the Brie region." It has since been corrected.

a wipeout at 70% butterfat. It's so special because it tastes of raw milk, pasture, grass, and soil—not of neutral-flavored, oily, rich, smooth butterfat as do many other pasteurized triple-crème dessert cheeses from France. The Gratte-Paille exported to the U.S. are now pasteurized, though apparently very gently, for they still retain an unmistakable raw-milk quality.

Choosing and Serving Gratte-Paille

Avoid any Gratte-Paille that appears "wrinkled" or striated with brown—it is too old and will be sharp and salty. Choose those that are plump and white, with beige mottling; the rind is edible. Rouzaire, the only maker of Gratte-Paille, makes an unpasteurized version for sale in France and a

The ultimate double-crème: hand-molded Rouzaire Gratte-Paille.

pasteurized version for export. Serve them for dessert with sweet fruits and Champagne or a sweet dessert wine such as Sauternes or Barsac.

EXPLORATEUR

A t first glance it seems odd that the label on Explorateur (explore-ah-TOOR) bears the picture of a space rocket. However, knowing that this well-crafted cheese was first developed by its sole maker Fromagerie du Petit-Morin during the early days of the Sputnik satellites in the 1950s helps to put things in place. It was then that the classification of triple-crème was created and defined as any cheese richer than 75% butterfat.

And, in fact, Explorateur is 75% butterfat This heightened level is achieved by adding cream to milk to make it even richer than a double-crème cheese, such as Gratte-Paille.

Explorateur is made in three sizes: 8-ounce (250 g) barrels, 14-ounce (420 g) disks, and 4-pound (2 k) wheels. It's a lovely cheese, although I prefer the small-production triple-crèmes in Robert Rouzaire's line—Pierre Robert, Grand Mogol, and Jean Grogne. They have more flavor because of their milk quality and gentle pasteurization, and are usually less salty. But Explorateur is a well-made, less expensive cheese that is still worth buying.

Choosing and Serving Explorateur and Other Triple-Crème Cheeses

T he perfect stage for any triple-crème cheese is a matter of personal taste. While half again as rich as Brie, triple-crèmes are soft-ripening cheeses since beneath their bloomy, white, Brie-like crust the buttery cheese will ripen from the outside in. Young triple-crèmes will be whitish and chalky, a state that's not completely undesirable. In cheeses as rich as Explorateur, this young stage can be quite delectable—moist and flavorful, and not at all chalky. As a triple-crème ripens, its crust becomes beige-brown and mottled and its interior a glistening white-gold. Its flavor will intensify and it will become a more substantial cheese. This is the stage I recommend.

Avoid overripe triple-crèmes which sag and exhibit a predominance of brownish-reddish mottling on their rinds. They will have a bitter, salty, "commercial" flavor and ammoniacal aroma.

Triple-crèmes make dazzling party fare served with berries or tropical fruits and Champagne. They are also a worthy choice to end a light supper, with fruits as a counterpoint to the creamy texture. Or you might want to do what Parisians do: Turn baguettes into *tartines* by slathering split bread halves with a favorite triple-crème, rind and all.

THE CHEESE SHOPS OF PARIS

The neighborhoods of Paris are dotted with scores of *fromageries* (cheese shops), each showcasing an enviable assortment of the finest cheeses. The most dedicated *fromagers* age the cheeses in special cellars below their tiny shops, skillfully assessing the moment when each is *à point,* or "just right." Many of these shops also have small, casual dining rooms or adjacent restaurants that offer a *dégustation* (tasting) of cheese, either in the form of a cheese platter with six or seven examples to explore or a more elaborate sampling served in courses.

Androuët, 41 Rue d'Amsterdam: Paris's most famous *fromagerie* was founded in 1909 by Henri Androuët. His son, *maître-fromager extraordinaire* Pierre, carried on the legacy until selling the shop a few years ago to the conglomerate that operates Air France. Now in his eighties, Pierre has been the director of our master cheesemongers' guild, the 700-year-old Confrérie des Compagnons de Saint-Uguzon, for as long as I've been a member. His mission in life has been to support French cheesemaking artisans and preserve what he considers to be an irreplaceable facet of France's heritage. In 1973, a translation of his pioneering book, *The Complete Encyclopedia of French Cheese,* helped ignite interest in fine French cheeses in America. Still a cheese-lover's mecca, the shop is now run by Pierre's assistant. In the peach-walled dining room upstairs, the menu lists numerous tastings of cheeses presented as they should be—in ascending degree of flavor intensity. The *pièce de résistance* is the *ronde des plateaux,* an extravagant multi-

course *dégustation* of well over 60 cheeses.

Barthélémy, 51 Rue de Grenelle: In Roland Barthélémy's shop an amazing 240 varieties of cheese vie for attention in 30 feet of retail sales space; the rest of the space is used for the ripening (*affinage*) of cheeses. Don't miss the shop's specialty, a ball of chèvre that has been rolled in kirsch-marinated raisins.

Marie-Anne Cantin, 12 Rue du Champ-de-Mars: Second generation *fromager* Marie-Anne (she is the daughter of noted *fromager* Christian Cantin) and her husband, Antoine Dias, run one of Paris's most delightful *fromageries,* offering more than 100 cheese varieties. Two aging cellars—a humid one for cow's-milk cheeses, a drier one for goat's-milk cheeses—ensure the cheeses are ripened to perfection.

Owner Marie-Anne Cantin surveys the scene at her fromagerie.

La Ferme St.-Hubert, 21 Rue Vignon: Owner Henri Voy opened his little shop around the corner from Fauchon, Paris's most famous specialty food shop, in 1977. More than 100 varieties of cheese are featured, most ripened in Voy's cellars below the store. With his son Antoine, Voy also runs a casual, 32-seat country-style restaurant next door which specializes in mini-*dégustations.* Among the offerings you'll find are raclette and Roquefort Napoleons. Don't miss an opportunity to sample the goat's-milk butter that accompanies the bread.

La Maison du Bon Fromage, 35 Rue du Marché Saint-Honoré: This tiny *fromagerie* owned by Michèle and Alain Eletufe features more than 200 cheeses, including aged Brillat-Savarin and an impressive selection of chèvres.

Other fromageries: Alain Dubois (80 Rue de Tocqueville); Alléosse (13 Rue de Lévis, in the middle of the lively Rue de Lévis market); Chez Tachon (38 Rue de Richelieu, near the Louvre); Christian Cantin (2 Rue de Lourmel); Creplet-Brussol (17 Place de la Madeleine, near Fauchon and Hédiard); Durand (147 Rue Saint-Martin); Fromagerie de Montmartre (9 Rue du Poteau); Guy Genève (16 Rue de Dufresnoy); Jean Carmes et Fils (24 Rue de Levis); La Ferme Sainte-Suzanne (4 Rue des Fossés Saint-Jacques); Lillo (35 Rue des Belles-Feuilles, near the Place Victor-Hugo).

ALSACE AND
LORRAINE

Alsace and Lorraine are situated in the extreme northeastern part of France that borders on Luxembourg, Germany, and Switzerland. Alsace is to Alsace-Lorraine what Massachusetts is to New England—a small part of the whole, but better known, more frequently traveled, and, arguably, a distillation of cultures. It is adjacent to Germany, and indeed, the region has been shuttled back and forth over the centuries from the Teutonic-Germanic political organization, to the Austro-Hungarian, to the French, until at the end of World War I it became, and has remained (despite Nazi Germany's attempt to annex it during World War II), a part of France.

The southeastern part of Lorraine, which sprawls into Alsace, is the political *département* of Vosges. The tree-laden mountains that rise slowly from west to east drop precipitously to the plain of Alsace. And what a gorgeous region it is! From the west the deciduous fir trees appear to rise from the hills in steel-blue waves, and in the autumn they burn electric with color. From atop the southern Vosges mountains you can look east into Germany's Black Forest, and south into the Jura Alps. The Rhine acts as a natural border between France and Germany. The French build their houses away from the flood banks

A full range of the region's famous white wines, including Gewürztraminer and Riesling, is served at small, informal wine bars throughout Alsace.

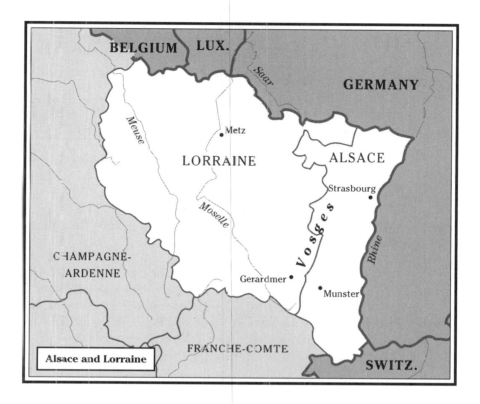

of the river; opposite them, the Germans are right at the edge of the deeper eastern shore.

The milk that comes from the cows that feed on the lush, green pastures of Alsace is extraordinarily rich and very, very delicious. The cheese made from it has been famous for centuries. Visiting Alsace fills you with a sense of well-being and wonder: well-being at the beauty and order, and wonder at the relationship between people and foodstuffs, and how that relationship has remained unchanged for centuries. The abundance and variety of edibles and potables is staggering.

Most of the region's alcohol distillers, breweries, and vintners are located in Alsace. Alsace is justly famous for its powerful, clear fruit brandies called *eaux-de-vie.* Besides the kirsch made from the region's bounty of cherries, comes pear brandy, as well as *eau-de-vie* from blueberries, strawberries, raspberries, and many obscure fruits. I am amazed at the quantity of fruit required to produce *eau-de-vie*—about 50 pounds (25 k) to make one liter of brandy.

Many of the wonderful restaurants in the area use the local provender exclusively. *Choucroute garnie,* the delectable sauerkraut and cured-pork dish, is featured on virtually every menu in Alsace, as are various freshwater fish and eels. There are terrific desserts and some very spicy wines, and of course, the famous Alsatian beers. But perhaps Alsatian *foie gras* is the greatest source of regional pride. Strasbourg, the capital of Alsace, lends its name to the region's goose liver, practically all of which is processed and exported. A spirited and intense rivalry exists between the Alsatian *foie gras* producers and those of Périgord and Gascony. The truth is, Europewide, Alsatian *foie gras* is held in much higher esteem than the *foie gras* of Périgord or Gascony for reasons of longevity. Commercial quantities of *foie gras* have been produced in Alsace for a much longer time. Qualitatively, though, the produce is on an equal footing.

The Cheeses

MUNSTER

Alsace is known for one cheese—Munster (moon-STAIR or MUNster)—and though it has several local names and identities, it is just about the only regional cheese you'll find in this area. Géromé (ZHAIR-oh-MAY), a very well-known cheese from Lorraine, is identical to Munster, though slightly larger in size. Géromé is a corruption of the name of the village, Gérardmer, while Munster takes its name from

French and German influences converge in canal-dotted Strasbourg, the capital of Alsace.

the French village of Munster, a corruption of an ancient reference to the word "monastery."

Don't make the mistake of confusing French Munster with German Münster, a rather boring, dissimilar cheese, whose only kinship to the French cheese is that both are made from cow's milk and both are smelly. The French name-controlled Munster is the great one. Its flavor is at once piercingly sharp, beefy

and nutty. The sharpness belies the texture of the cheese and is not what one expects from such a creamy consistency. Odd as it may sound, I always think of fried eggs when I eat Munster.

Munster has a very pronounced, powerful aroma, and I have never figured out how it is that a food that smells like rotting fruits and vegetables and barnyard animals can evoke hunger pangs in me.

BATHING BEAUTIES

Many of Europe's most assertively flavored and highly aromatic cheeses, including French Munster, Livarot, Maroilles, and Pont-l'Evêque, Belgian Maredsous and Limburger, Italian Taleggio, and Swiss Tête de Moine, have washed rinds. These cheeses are washed or "rubbed" by hand with a cloth moistened by a brine solution of rock salt and water. This solution inhibits the growth of mold while encouraging the growth of bacteria instrumental to giving the cheese a strong flavor and smell.

Brine is not the only liquid used; depending on the cheese, it may have been washed with wine, beer, brandy, *eau-de-vie*, or cider. The liquid feeds certain bacteria causing them to multiply, and the characteristic strong aroma and distinctively pronounced flavor of washed-rind cheeses are the result of the

fecundity of this bacterial growth. In addition to provoking flavor, the wash is instrumental in the formation of the cheese's rind—as the liquid seeps into the cheese's interior, the salt remains on the surface helping to keep it from drying out.

Some washed-rind cheeses, such as Pont-l'Evêque, occasionally have also had their rinds brushed, or dry-salted, a technique that involves coarse salt being applied, or "brushed," on the exterior of the newly formed cheese either by hand or with a brush. Salting a cheese's surface in this fashion is a way of drawing the moisture out so that it can properly ripen. In addition, the dry crust or rind formed by the salt protects the interior from intrusions of unwanted bacteria, allowing the cheese to breathe while it ripens.

Strong-flavored Gérômé from Lorraine is Alsatian Munster's identical twin.

But I, along with many others, am a great appreciator of the earthy smell that is associated with certain cheeses. Munster is smelly due to its washed rind (see Bathing Beauties, page 83).

At about 7 inches in diameter and about 1¼ inches thick, when it comes out of its draining mold, Munster is perfectly white and odorless, and at this stage, gloppy dollops of this *fromage frais* can be served as an appetizer, with cream and sugar. It is not at all like the cheese that it will become a month later, when its flavor has ripened to excruciatingly delicious and its aroma to full-blown smelliness. It truly is a major cheese.

Munster usually comes in a 1¼-pound (about 625 g) size, packaged in a wooden box. But, now it is also available in unboxed 1-pound (500 g) and 8-ounce (250 g) disks. With re-

gard to the smaller cheeses, it's important to note that you cannot expect from them the same texture or full flavor characteristic of the larger ones.

Choosing and Serving Munster

The only great Munster comes from France's Alsace region—not Germany, not Denmark, and not Wisconsin. (These cheeses are called Muenster or Münster and are not even vaguely related to Munster.) When choosing this remarkable cheese, you want it to be either young or ripe, but not too old. Young Munster will be firm with a smooth, dry, russet-colored rind. Its interior will be white and chalky. Ripe Munster will have a

Forget about bland imitators from other countries, French Munster from Alsace is a triumph of cheesemaking.

EATING IN ALSACE-LORRAINE

If you are fortunate enough to be planning a trip to France that includes Alsace-Lorraine, here are a few restaurants worth seeking out.

Maison Grojean in Commercy (Meuse): The most famous baker of madeleines in France.

Restaurant La Grange du Paysan in Hinsingen (Bas-Rhin, halfway between Metz and Strasbourg—way out in the middle of the country): This is a splendid, traditional, Alsatian country-style restaurant. You can buy ham, cheese, and other charcuterie to take away.

Restaurant Les Alisiers (named for a local wild berry) in Lapoutroie (Haut-Rhin): High in the Vosges mountains, here you'll find unequaled authentic, regional home cooking.

Also in Lapoutroie is **Jacques Haxaire**, who buys fine, farm-made Munsters and ripens them to perfection. His business makes him a *maître-affineur.*

Just outside of Lapoutroie (eastern exit off the N415) is **Gilbert Miclo Distillerie**. Stop for the finest *eaux-de-vie,* including Alisier, a local wild berry prized for its bitter almond flavor.

Restaurant Hostellerie du Cerf in Marlenheim (Bas-Rhin): Fabulous, family-run hotel and restaurant with a beautiful outdoor stone courtyard. The hôtelier is the *père,* Robert Husser, the imaginative chef is *fils* Michel.

Auberge de l'Ill in Illhaeusern: One of only 21 *Michelin* three-star restaurants, this is a "destination" restaurant you cannot miss. While expensive, you'll never forget your experience there. Be sure to reserve well in advance. The Alsace region gets its name from the Ill river. "Illsass" in dialect, means the country of the Ill, which runs parallel to the Rhine.

---

more developed aroma, a darker crust, and a more viscous, straw-colored interior. Both stages are delicious. I prefer the ripe stage, when both the flavor and the aroma have ascended to their zenith—perhaps the biggest flavor of any cheese. The edibility of the rind is a matter of taste.

If Munster is too old, its rind will be a dull, drab, khaki color and probably cracked and slimy. Its interior will be oozy, runny, and reddish. Its aroma will not be a healthy, barnyardy perfume but an overpowering horsiness, like a stable that hasn't been mucked out in months.

Munster is a joy at the end of

WHEN IN ALSACE-LORRAINE

The following cheeses are not yet available in the U.S., but are worth seeking out when traveling in Alsace-Lorraine:

- **Trappiste d'Oelenberg** (trappeest-DOE-len-burg): A raw cow's-milk Port-Salut.
- **Emmental Français Ermitage Vosges** (emm-awn-TAHL-frahn-SAY air-mee-tahzh-VOZHE): An excellent raw cow's milk Emmental.
- **Bargkass** (bairg-KAHSS): A hard cheese made on several Munster farms for local consumption. My guess is that this cheese inspired the creation of Le Brouère.

a meal, whether with the salad course, or better yet, with the season's sweetest fruits—cherries, pears, plums, peaches. Perversely, I enjoy seeing it served at parties and gatherings where, to the uninitiated, its penetrating aroma is startling to say the least.

Alsatians eat Munster with at least one meal every day—usually at midday. It is often served with fruit, and always with wine, such as a spicy Alsatian Gewürztraminer, or beer. It is brilliant with Alsace's great beers and fantastic local rye breads. Curiously, I suppose because of their Germanic heritage, Alsatians seem to prefer Munster with caraway, cumin, fennel, or anise seeds somehow insinuated into the taste experience—if not into the bread, then directly into or onto the cheese. The licorice taste of the anise or fennel gives the cheese an even bigger presence, an even bigger bite. These seeds are ubiquitous; you rarely see the cheese without them.

LE BROUERE

Le Brouère (luh-broo-AIR) is a recent (first made only a decade ago) Alsatian cheese that is an imitation of a very ancient French Gruyère that comes from the neighboring region of Jura just to the south. Le Brouère is being made by one of the biggest, oldest makers of Munster in Alsace, a company called Ermitage.

Le Brouère is the Alsatian dialect for the French word *bruyère,* meaning "heath" or "heather," a marvelously romantic term that conjures up Hardy-Brönte-Lawrencian English images of sloping pastures, alternately dotted with trees and wildflowers, lush with grass and wild leeks and clover for the cows to graze on. Instead, this is the Vosges—heath after heath of fabulously unspoiled pastureland in the northwestern part of Alsace.

Le Brouère is a thick, hardish,

buttery, nutty, sweet-tasting, Comté-type cheese with a unique and quite beautiful appearance. Each cheese is numbered and signed and carries a distinguishing characteristic: its rind. The oakwood hoop that goes around the cheese to keep it in shape after it has been formed is hand-carved in deep relief with alternating fir trees and grouse (both hallmarks of the Vosges). When the mold is removed, the edges of the rind bear a beautiful bas-relief design of fir trees and big grouse that are about the size of your palm. Each 14- to 20-pound (7 to 10 k) wheel-shaped or ovoid disk is 4 inches thick and between 10 and 20 inches in diameter.

Choosing and Serving Le Brouère

Since Le Brouère is made by only one Alsatian producer, selecting a perfect cheese is a simple matter. You need only determine that it is not too old. Healthy Le Brouère will have a milk chocolate–brown rind and bright yellow interior. Neither should appear dull or faded, nor should the crust be cracked or splintered. Shop at a busy cheese store with frequent turnover. Over-ripe Le Brouère may have a slimy rind, a gray-white gooey rind, or a rind that is dried and cracked. Serve Le Brouère with fruit, nuts, and light red wines. Shredded or grated, its melting capacity is excellent for soups and gratins.

OTHER ALSATIAN CHEESES

All other Alsatian cheeses resemble Munster.

Chaumes (SHOHM): a very popular and much exported Munster-type cheese, named for the high pastures of the Vosges mountains, yet it is made in the Périgord region of southwest France. Chaumes is a mass-produced, factory cheese with the merest hint of the piercing, raw, nutty flavor of Munster. It's not bad, but it has neither the power nor the rusticity of true Munster.

Lingot d'Or (LANGO-DORE): also similar to Munster; from Contrexéville, a famous Vosges mountain town known for its mineral water, cherries and other fruits, and good restaurants. Lingot d'Or means "brick of gold" or "gold bar," and that is exactly what it looks like. It is an exquisite washed-rind cheese whose flavor, like Munster, reminds me of fried eggs.

THE LOIRE RIVER'S VALLEYS AND TRIBUTARIES

T he cheeses of the Loire and its tributaries are from the region called Berry and the classical regions known as Poitou, Touraine, Charente, Orléanais, Anjou, Maine, and the Nantes area. They are almost exclusively made from goat's milk and include such famous name-controlled chèvres as Crottin de Chavignol, Pouligny-Saint-Pierre, Sainte-Maure de Touraine, and Selles-sur-Cher. Farms and factories throughout this part of France turn out a staggering variety of chèvre (goat cheese). Some are made the traditional way, by hand; others are made in factories, chiefly located in Poitou and Charente, using modern equipment and frozen curd. But with a few exceptions, the most desirable chèvre *fermier* comes from Berry.

Berry is a large area south of the Loire River that encompasses most of the political *départements* of Indre and Cher. When something is referred to as being from Berry, it is called Berrichon, a very pretty word that you'll see often in history books and cookbooks, on maps, and in magazines. The region includes the valleys of three of the Loire's four major tributaries: the Cher, which is the easternmost; the Indre; and the Creuse. The Creuse, a tributary of a tributary,

France's most exquisite raw-milk chèvres are made by hand on small farms throughout Berry. Along country roads, farmers post hand-painted signs like this amusing one to alert travelers that cheese can be purchased at the source.

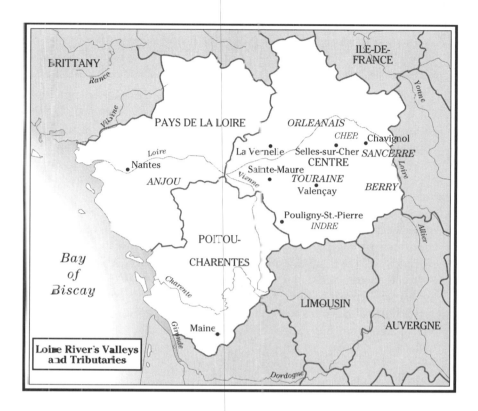

runs into a more important river, the Vienne, in neighboring Poitou. All of these tributaries of the Loire have their sources high in the Massif Central, the rugged Auvergnat mountains in the center of France.

Berry is famous for its production of goat cheeses from numerous small herds of goats that average just 40 heads per farm. It is lush and beautiful pastureland, so lush that it belies the myth that goats are always pastured on land with inferior vegetation. Because of this lush pasturage, the goats' milk is exceptionally rich and the cheese it produces is especially delicious, incorporating subtle nuances of clover, herbs, pine, walnuts, and pepper. Many farms surrounding the little villages have been making their own styles of goat's-milk cheese for hundreds of years.

Big-city French people who frequently buy specific shapes of chèvre, and have access to a vast choice, often opt for a cheese made by a specific cheesemaker: for instance, pyramid-shaped Valençay by Jacquin, log-shaped Sainte-Maure by Couturier (Couturier is actually in Pouligny, just outside Sainte-Maure), tiny cork-shaped *bouchon* by Anjouin, and little barrels of Chavignol by Chamaillard. A limited, but well-chosen selection of good French goat cheeses are available in the U.S. at most serious cheese shops.

NOTES ON CHEVRE

Since all French goat cheeses are made from a similar recipe, certain generalizations and basics apply to chèvres as a group. A goat cheese has no specific stage of perfection as does a Camembert or Brie. The ideal point of ripeness is completely a matter of personal taste. In France, most cheesemongers sell a chèvre unripened and customers ripen it at home. In the U.S., consumers are likely to expect to buy chèvre at the point of ripeness they prefer; as a general rule, Americans are unaccustomed to ripening their own cheeses at home. Personally, I regard fresh, moist, creamy, mild, snowy-white goat cheeses as rather innocuous. And I don't particularly care for them when they are hard, flinty, and strong. Between these two points are several markedly different stages and only you can decide for yourself which you enjoy most.

Use your common sense when buying cheese. Real goat cheese is made by ladling curd, very gently, by hand, into molds that have holes in them, like colanders, so that the whey will drip out and the curd will take on the shape of the mold. The classic French goat cheese is so special because the human touch involved in its process encourages the real, natural flavor to emerge. If the cheese is encased in fancy, too-modern packaging and has a gaudy, costly label, it is nearly always the product of a commercial plant and should be passed up in favor of some more artisanal example.

When shopping for chèvre, avoid buying cheeses that show slimy rinds or are too hard and dried out unless, of course, you know that you like them that way. Both of these conditions foretell a strong goatiness. I happen to find that unpleasant in a cheese and you may also feel that way. However, do not be concerned about any blue mold you see on the rind of goat cheeses. Mottled blue mold (called *fleurs de bleu*) will be omnipresent except when a goat cheese is very young and fresh. The rinds of goat cheeses are natural and commonly will sport this type of mold growth. If it bothers you, scrape it off or simply avoid eating the rind. Even ashed goat cheeses will show a little blue. Again, this is completely natural and even desirable.

At any age, goat cheeses are versatile in terms of how and when to serve them. Any time of day—including breakfast—is a grand time. They are as wonderful warmed, with a salad course, as they are served at room temperature after dinner with fruit.

The Cheeses

SELLES-SUR-CHER

The town of Selles-sur-Cher (SELL-sir-SHAIR) in Orléanais is famous for an A.O.C. goat cheese named (naturally) for the town itself. The finest examples of this cheese, however, are actually made across the Cher River in Berry. It has the configuration of a hockey puck (a shape referred to as a *rond*), is about 1 inch thick, 3 inches in diameter and weighs 4 to 6 ounces (125 to 180 g). Like many other French goat cheeses, it is usually ashed. This "cindering" or ashing practice originated many years ago in an attempt to dry the outside of the cheese by covering it with the remains of burned birch bark. The ash coating also encourages the interior cheese to ripen, and creates definition and visual contrast between the bright white interior and the stark black rind. Ashing soon became fashionable, and people began to look for other goat cheeses that were ashed as a sign of beauty, quality, expertise, and regionality.

Today, commercial mix is used. Made from cauterized milk combined with salt and wood ash, it is completely clean and sterile, odorless and tasteless, and if the cheese is young and fresh, it is perfectly acceptable and customary to consume it. If the cheese is an older one, you may wish to remove the rind. Cindering is a treatment given to almost all goat cheeses of the Loire Valley—Sainte-Maure de Touraine, Valençay, Pouligny-Saint-Pierre—but it is not a necessity, more a nod to tradition. All these chèvres, except Selles-sur-Cher, can be found uncindered. For Selles-sur-Cher, ash is definitive.

Choosing and Serving Selles-sur-Cher

In the U.S., it is rare to see any Selles-sur-Cher other than the Jacquin brand, although occasionally you will see Anjouin. Both are excellent. This chèvre is almost always an ashed, stark black. Look for those that are most flawlessly black or with a touch of blue mold. They are sold whole, so it is doubtful you will be offered a taste. Fear not—they are uniformly delicious.

Selles-sur-Cher marries well with all sweet fruits, and is particularly good with citrus and melon. I like to serve it with wine—preferably a white Sancerre.

LUNCHING *CHEZ* JACQUIN

One fine spring day several years ago I was in the Loire Valley at a hamlet near the River Cher. This hamlet, La Vernelle, is just outside Selles-sur-Cher, a village in the Loir-et-Cher *département*. It is here that Pierre Jacquin, and most of the members of his family, make perfect goat cheeses.

I was sitting at the family table with Pierre and his wife, son, daughter, and son-in-law and we were eating his cheese and bread and drinking his wine, a Bourgeuil that he bought by the barrel. They had what I considered was a well-ripened Valençay on the table and they were cutting it with a butter knife, eating it rind and all. I was astounded. I thought surely the artisans who make the cheese would trim away the rind. But they were eating it, so I did too, and I discovered the unfinicky pleasure of enjoying the whole cheese.

The rind was beige with a few spots of blue mold and I found that it was not only pleasant to feel the texture of the rind mixed up with the paste of the cheese, but that it also added a nuance of flavor that I had never before experienced. The Jacquins told me that, had it been too blue, they would have trimmed the rind away. I realized that I'd been a bit prissy about it all this time. It changed my attitude and I grew a little bit as a cheeseman with that experience.

VALENCAY

Farther up the Cher river, about 10 miles from Selles in Berry, is the famous little town of Valençay, where Talleyrand used to entertain Napoléon on his estate, Château de Valençay. The story told to me by Valençay cheesemaker Pierre Jacquin is that during the period that Napoléon was infatuated with his campaign in Egypt, Talleyrand had a goat cheese made for him in the shape of a pyramid. When the campaign turned into a debacle, Talleyrand had the cheese's peaked top flattened so that the sight of a pyramid wouldn't upset Napoléon and spoil his visits to Valençay.

Valençay (VAL-awn-SAY) cheeses weigh about 8 ounces (250 g), and the best ones, of course, are not pasteurized. Even cheese experts whom I respect contend that you can't tell the difference between pasteurized and unpasteurized goat's milk, but I disagree. There's a depth of flavor to cheeses made from unpasteurized milk that, to me, is immediately apparent, particularly after they've been allowed to age for a few weeks. But for a cheesemaker, pasteurization has its advantages. It is a less troublesome and capricious cheesemaking process, and poses less of a hassle with export regulations.

There are still, though, in the area around Valençay and Selles-sur-Cher, a considerable number of small producers who continue to produce *fromage de chèvre fermier*—farm-made, unpasteurized goat's-milk cheese—and it's great goat cheese. Around nearly every bend of the many small highways you will be greeted by hand-printed signs, attached to trees, proclaiming *"chèvre fermier ici."*

Valençay and the A.O.C. chèvres—Crottin de Chavignol, Pouligny-Saint-Pierre, Selles-sur-Cher, Sainte-Maure de Touraine—legally can be sold after only eight days in their molds. I sell mine between three and eight weeks old.

Choosing and Serving Valençay

Avoid any Valençay showing *peau de crapaud,* or "toad's skin," a rippling, warty, loose, thick rind—a sign that the cheese has suffered from storage and/or handling abuse at high temperatures. Avoid any that are rock hard or cracked or wrapped in plastic. Valençay starts out very moist, as do all traditional chèvres, and it evolves its own rind that will show considerable mold growth—again, this is natural and desirable. Simply cut out quarter-sections from the truncated pyramid and trim away the rind, if desired. Choose the cheese that is at the stage of ripeness you like best. If you've chosen a young cheese with ash,

The peacock in the foreground near the statue is not the only exotic presence at this Valençay château. Llamas and flamingos also roam the vast, neatly manicured grounds.

Fromages de chèvre *are created in every shape imaginable, from pyramids, bells, and buttons to thimbles, corks, and hexagons. Often they are dusted with spices or sprinkled with herbs or ash.*

you need not remove it—the ash is tasteless and good for you.

If you intend to keep the whole cheese or a part of it for any length of time, store it toward the top of your refrigerator (where it is less cold), loosely wrapped in flimsy bakery or pastry paper or a paper towel. Waxed paper is not bad, but avoid aluminum foil and plastic wrap— foil gets too cold and plastic wrap suffocates the cheese.

Serve Valençay anytime—for breakfast with toast, pastry, and juice or coffee; for lunch with fruit or raw vegetables, white wine, and bread; at dinner with the salad course, or for dessert with fruit. Crumble it over baked potatoes or cooked vegetables. Age it until it is hard and grate it onto pasta or salads. Add crumbled young Valençay to omelettes.

PUR CHEVRE

*P*ur chèvre *is* a description often found on the labels of chèvres. It is a guarantee that the cheese is made only from 100% ("pure") goat's milk.

CHEVRE SHAPES

It is the visual effect of French chèvres that so captivates me. Some have "official" names (Chabichou, Selles-sur-Cher, Valençay) but most are known by their shapes. The range of shapes is enormous—from the little beads of chèvre threaded on a string to the faceted diamonds that look like gems. What follows is only a sampling of the creativity of French chèvre-makers. Some shapes are unique to one maker, others are produced by numerous makers. Nearly all are made by hand-ladling the curd into plastic molds.

Besace (beggar's purse): Périgord; Besace Desport

Bicorne (two horns): Périgord; François Desport

Bondon (bung): Angoumois; Le Petit Bondon; numerous makers

Bouchon (cork): Poitou, Angoumois, Limousin; Bouchon d'Anjou; numerous makers

Boulette or **Boule** (ball): Picardy; numerous makers

Bouton (button): Burgundy; numerous makers

Brique (brick): Savoie; B. du Forez

Brochette (skewered lumps): Quercy, Périgord; Pelardons; Bernard Screda and other makers

Bûche (log): Touraine, Sainte-Maure; numerous makers

Carré (square): all regions; numerous makers

Cerise (cherry): Berry; Cerise Soreda

Clochette (little bell): Berry, Poitou; Chaput, Couturier, and other makers

Crottin (horse turd): Berry; Crottin de Chavignol; numerous makers

Coeur (heart): Berry; Coeur de Chèvre; numerous makers

Figue (fig): Périgord; Figue Soreda

Fleur (flower, petaled round): Périgord; Fleur Verte; numerous makers

Lingot (bar): Poitou, Touraine, Berry; Lingot Cendre; numerous makers

Médaillon (medallion): Quercy; Rocamadour; numerous makers

Pavé (square or hexagonal paving stone): Berry; Jacquin and other makers

Pavé Amalthée (hexagonal paving stone): Poitou; Chef-Boutonne

Pyramide (pyramid): Berry; Valençay, Pouligny; numerous makers

Quatre Feuille (four-leaf clover): Périgord; François Desport

Rond (round, hockey puck): Berry; Selles-sur-Cher; numerous makers

Taupinière (molehill): Périgord; numerous makers

SAINTE-MAURE DE TOURAINE

Twenty-five miles south of Tours, the Vienne, Creuse, and Indre Rivers meander through fertile alluvial soil. The Vienne passes near a little town called Sainte-Maure, the pretty name of an obscure female saint.

Sainte-Maure is famous for its log-shaped goat cheeses—cheeses from 5 to 8 inches long and about as big around or slightly bigger than an A-OK circle, made by joining a thumb and index finger. Their weight varies, according to the maker, from 11 to 14 ounces (330 to 420 g). The characteristic feature of name-controlled Sainte-Maure de Touraine (SAHNT-MORE-duh-ter-RAN) is that it always has a piece of straw or a stick stuck through it from end to end, which prevents it from falling to pieces when it is in its fragile young state. Sometimes the cheeses are ashed black, which has no effect on the flavor whether the cheese is young and soft or aged and dry.

Choosing and Serving Sainte-Maure de Touraine

Sainte-Maure de Touraine can be clearly identified by the foil or paper label which is affixed to each log. Virtually all will be pierced end to end by a piece of straw, a stick, or a dowel, in the tradition of this cheese. The stage of ripeness or flavor development is, of course, a matter of personal taste. I prefer Sainte-Maure de Touraine at the state where its rind is noticeably advanced and it has attained some blue mold growth. Avoid any that are mushy or ammoniacal, evidence of mishandling and/or overripeness. Choose this chèvre ashed or not ashed—there is no flavor difference whatsoever.

Sainte-Maure de Touraine is name-controlled and the A.O.C. insignia will always appear on its label. In the U.S., look for A.O.C. cheeses from Courthial Père et Fils, Couturier, or Jacquin. But bear in mind that there are dozens of absolutely first-class non-A.O.C. versions of this

PHEEW!

Male goats (bucks) are understandably repellent. They urinate all over themselves in an attempt to make their presence known to the rutting females (does). It is standard practice for dairy goat farmers to keep the bucks far away from the females, particularly during the milking process, which occurs twice a day—before dawn and late in the afternoon. If the procedure at the farm where they're kept is not strict about this, the milk will very likely be too goaty.

cheese made outside of the legal area and these are simply called Sainte-Maure. Among the excellent non-A.C.C. versions are Saint-Christophe-en-Bazelle made by Anjouin in Berry and those made in Périgord by Jacquin or Desport. In the U.S., look for non-A.O.C. Sainte-Maures made by Coopérative Sèvre-et-Belle Jacquin, and Desport.

Serve Sainte-Maure as you would any other fine chèvre—with fruit or salad, a crusty bread, and local wines such as Chenin Rouge or a *pétillant* (still young and slightly bubbly) Vouvray. If the cheese is advanced in age, I recommend the region's red Bourgueil. Saumur and Champigny whites are also a good match.

wildflowers. There were no billboards, no newfangled buildings, no auto dealerships, just a classic little farm town, where everything, though centuries old, was immaculate and lived-in—and you knew it would still be there tomorrow. Pouligny-Saint-Pierre (POO-leen-yee-SAHN-pee-AIR), the piquant, name-controlled cheese from this town is a truncated pyramid, like the Valençay, but taller, about 4 inches high and weighing about 9 ounces (270 g).

Tournon-Saint-Martin and Tournon-Saint-Pierre are neighboring villages known for their pyramidal chèvres, which are identical to Pouligny-Saint-Pierre.

POULIGNY-SAINT-PIERRE

In terms of goat cheese, the Indre *département*'s Creuse River is most famous for a town called Pouligny-Saint-Pierre. It is a little farm town that 400 years ago became known for a goat cheese (as did its neighbors, Tournon-Saint-Pierre and Tournon-Saint-Martin), that endures to this day. I was there one June and everywhere I looked I saw warblers, thrushes, hummingbirds, bees, and

Choosing and Serving Pouligny-Saint-Pierre

In America, one of the only available original Pouligny-Saint-Pierres is from Couturier, a company that has become an aggressive manufacturer of goat cheeses for export. Most of their Pouligny made for export is unaged and plastic-wrapped, a far cry from their handmade, unwrapped, traditional line. The traditional line sports red-and-gold-foil, banner-like labels and are the

cheeses to seek out. They will have the full, round, rich flavor that I demand from French chèvres. If these Poulignys have aged to a pleasing beige color dotted with blue mold (if not completely covered by it), and are not moist and slimy, but are a bit dry, yet still yielding to the touch, they will be delicious. If they are pure white, they have definitely been sent over by jet container and will be very good, although too young for my taste. Pouligny are also delicious, and considerably stronger, when rock hard, dry and flinty in texture (aged for 8 to 12 weeks).

The plastic-wrapped examples of Pouligny-Saint-Pierre will have a blue and silver foil label encircling their pyramid tops. They are rather characterless and have no rind at all, since they have not had enough time to form their own. They usually are touched with a bit of blue mold nourished by trapped moisture. Although blue mold is not undesirable (in fact, it is inevitable) on the unwrapped, traditional cheeses, the plastic-wrapped cheeses with mold are simply not fresh. There is a difference. These plastic-wrapped cheeses are made from frozen curd, an unfortunate practice of the big, year-round producers. If you can't find Couturier's red and gold foiled cheeses, opt instead for one such as La Pointe de Bique by Jacquin.

As with most French cheeses, serve Pouligny for dessert with any fruit, crusty bread, and a red or white wine. Pouligny is classically and advantageously married to Chenin Blanc and Sauvignon Blanc as well as the white Burgundy, Mercurey, although I enjoy it with many red wines. It is also delicious served with a salad course.

CROTTIN DE CHAVIGNOL

As the Loire stretches upstream, east and then south, to the middle of France, you come upon the area of Sancerre in Berry, midway between Tours and Dijon. Sancerre is most famous for its wine, which is very dry (eternally described as "flinty") and predominantly white (though red and even pink Sancerres are available). These wines are perfectly structured to complement the area's name controlled goat cheese—Crottin

These little barrels of name-controlled Crottin de Chavignol are among the tastiest, most popular chèvres in France.

Historic chateaux and ancient cathedrals line the banks of the Loire. St. Martin's Church and the Cathedral of St Gratien create Tours' skyline

de Chavignol (crow-TAN duh shah-veen-YOLE)—named after a hamlet just outside of Sancerre. If you're driving fast—whoosh—there goes Chavignol! But this area's cheese bears the name of that town, because for centuries, goat herds have pastured near there. The word *crottin* refers, literally, to a piece of horse or mule dung! Figuratively, it refers to the shape of the cheese—to this day I find t remarkable that a cheese would be named that. Each of these little 2- to 3-ounce (60 to 90 g) cheeses is 1½ inches high and 2 inches in diameter. They should be as sweet and white, moist and mild as any young goat cheese from other regions; if aged too long, they become brown, hard, and strong. Locals often select *crottins* (the cheese!) when they are quite aged—at least two months old—and have acquired a dark brown crust.

Like any goat cheese, if you allow it to age too long, or if it comes from milk that got too near the bucks, or was simply from an off batch, it is likely to be very goaty and unpleasant tasting—acrid and sharp. Some food books urge you to avoid Crottin de Chavignol—I'm sure that's because they looked up the word *crottin* and couldn't associate it with anything edible. Or perhaps the only examples of *crottin* that these writers came upon were aged to the maximum. If you purchase a well-made Crottin de Chavignol, it will doubtless be delicious. And it will have none of that unpleasant pronounced goatiness.

ROASTED GARLIC CROTTINS

Delicious! Each diner slips the cloves of roasted garlic from their skin and mashes them gently with a fork as a spread on crusty bread accompanied by *crottins*.

Preheat the oven to 350°F (180°C). Allowing 1 whole head of garlic per person, remove the white, papery skin from each head, but do not peel or separate the cloves. Wrap each head of garlic in aluminum foil. Place on a baking sheet or in a roasting pan. Bake until the cloves are very soft, about 1 hour. Remove the garlic from the oven. Let it cool for about 10 minutes. Flatten each head a little with the heel of your hand, so that the cloves will easily slip out of their skins. Serve while still hot.

Choosing and Serving Crottin de Chavignol

Although name-controlled Crottin de Chavignol is made only in the hamlet of Chavignol, some excellent *crottins de chèvre*, which share the same characteristics, are made in other villages in Berry, as well as in other regions of France. In fact, most other *crottins*—including Jacquin Crottin—are actually better than the single authentic A.O.C. Chavignol example, which is factory made and sold under the Denizot brand. Certainly avoid any *crottins* that are wrapped in plastic. Do, though, seek out the Jacquin, Desport, and Soreda cheeses, as well as those made by Bougon in Poitou. (Jacquin is located in Berry, but not within the name-controlled area of Chavignol. Desport and Soreda are in Périgord, not too far away, and they are uniformly excellent.)

Choose Crottins de Chavignol and non-A.O.C. *crottins* that are neither too fresh and white, nor too brown and hard. Look for beige examples, even ones touched with blue mold. Even with mold, the entire cheese is perfectly acceptable.

Serve *crottins*

The finest examples of Crottin de Chavignol are made by hand on farms. When shopping, look for the word fermier *on labels.*

anytime, but preferably for dessert with sweet fruit and crusty bread. They make excellent appetizers as well, especially served with Niçoise olives and rustic bread. My wife and I adore these little cheeses halved horizontally and well heated, adorning the top of individual plates of greens. They are also perfect as a first course with roasted garlic (see Roasted Garlic Crottins, opposite). Crottin de Chavignol and other *crottins* are a natural match with Sancerre wines, either white or, if you can find it, red. Any light, fruity red, such as Beaujolais Fleurie or Juliénas, would also be a very good choice.

OTHER CHEESES OF THE LOIRE

West of the prime goat cheese–producing area of Berry, an array of big commercial cheese plants produce huge amounts of completely unspecial goat cheese made by mixing frozen curd with powdered milk. Water is added to yield a wet, grainy mixture that is then extruded from a machine. Miraculously, this slumgullion is turned into "cheese." When the cheese has been put into molds to attain the desired shapes, it is sprayed with *Penicillium* so that it will grow a *croûte fleurie*, a flowery crust, that will help it to ripen. As a final insult, it is wrapped in plastic.

These industrially made goat cheeses are really no more important to a serious cheese eater than processed American cheese, which is, incidentally, made in much the same way. I don't have much to say that's good about these huge factories that grind out goat cheese, except that if you're craving goat cheese, it's better to find a passable factory-made chèvre than nothing at all.

On the other hand, there *are* big companies that produce some decent examples of French goat cheese. They are, to name a few, Saint-Saviol, Saint-Loup, Ligeuil, Bougon, La-Mothe-Saint-Heray, Triballat, Soulié, and Lezay.

My particular congratulations go to a rather large, commercial producer of goat cheeses, Coopérative Sèvre-et-Belle in Poitou. Their wide array of chèvres includes a Sainte-Maure-style and a drum-shaped, 7-ounce (210 g) Chabichou-style called Le Chevrot. I never have tasted better goat cheese—both are sublime.

WHEN IN THE LOIRE VALLEY

The larger-than-life splendor of the châteaux nestled along the banks of the Loire is simply breathtaking. Built in 1501 by François I as a hunting lodge, the massive 440-room Château de Chambord's distinguishing feature is the 365 graceful chimneys rising from its roof.

The following Loire Valley cheeses are worth seeking out on a visit to this area:

- **Bondaroy au Foin** (bone-dah-WAH-oh-FWA): raw cow's milk, *fermier;* various makers in Orléanais; 8-ounce (250 g) disks of Camembert-like cheese with wisps of very fine green or blond hay sticking to the exterior (it is ripened in boxes of hay); widely available commercial versions such as Olivet or Pithiviers au Foin are not as good as Bondaroy.

- **Chabichou du Poitou** (SHAH-bee-shew-due-pwah-TOO): A.O.C.; chèvre *fermier;* diminutive 6-ounce (180 g) cylinders produced by numerous makers throughout Poitou; quite often made by cheese shop owners and farmers who sell it directly to their customers (you'll often see hand-written signs posted near roads proclaiming this cheese for sale at a nearby farm). Look for examples made by La Chevrerie Authon, which also makes raw-milk chèvres such as Aperi, Bigoton, *crottin,*

Saint-Maure, and Croque-Chèvre (spiked with little *eau-de-vie*-soaked dried mirabelle plums); all excellent.

- **Graçay** (grah-SAY): Ashed chèvre; disks; similar to Selles-sur-Cher but slightly larger; various makers in Berry; all excellent.

- **La Pointe de Bique** (lah-PWAHNT-duh-BEEK): Chèvre; "nanny goat's horn"; made in Berry; brand name of Jacquin's version of Pouligny-Saint-Pierre; excellent.

- **Le Cornilly** (kor-nee-YEE): Chèvre; brand name of Jacquin's (Berry) version of Chabichou; very good when about one month old.

- **Le Gien** (luh-zhee-AW): Chèvre; truncated 7-ounce (210 g) raw goat's milk cones made in Orléanais; ashed or wrapped in chestnut leaves; excellent.

- **Le Petit Billy** (luh-PEH-tee-bee-YEE): Chèvre; named for the village of Billy in Berry, where it is made by An-

jouin: essentially an unashed Selles-sur-Cher; excellent.

- **Levroux** (leh-VROO): Chèvre; pyramid-shaped; various makers in Berry; identical to Valençay; excellent.

- **Pavé** (pah-VAY): Chèvre; square shape; numerous makers; look for 8-ounce (250 g) versions with fresh herbs by Desport (Périgord); 2-pound (1 k) ashed versions by Soreda (Périgord); both excellent.

- **St.-Christophe-en-Bazelle** (SANT-kree-STOFE-awn-bah-ZELL): Chèvre; made by Anjouin (Berry); made in the style of Sainte-Maure de Touraine; excellent.

- **Tomme** (TUM): Chèvre, 2- to 3-pound (1 to 1½ k) wheels from which wedges are cut; numerous producers throughout Loire Valley; Jacquin makes a beauty called Tomme Jacquin; also look for Tomme de Chèvre by Sèvre-et-Belle (Poitou) and Chèvrechard's Tomme de Ma Grand-Mère (Poitou).

BURGUNDY

(Bourgogne)

Modern Burgundy more or less starts southeast of Paris around Auxerre, and finishes up a little below Mâcon. In between are the Morvan forest, rivers, valleys, and fields that, to me, are the visual epitome of France. The terrain is at once rocky and fertile. The trees are old, huge, and gorgeous. Burgundy seems to roll. The Côte d'Or is a big, undulating bank that rolls down eastward to a plain. It's the soil and the vines that grow on these banks that make the great Burgundy wines what they are. The land continues in a southerly trajectory all the way down to where the appellation Burgundy melds in and out of the Langres plateau and becomes fuzzy—it's not really Burgundy anymore but becomes Chalonnais, Mâconnais (the Ain *département* famous for its Bresse poultry and Bleu de Bresse cheese), and Beaujolais.

There are few lakes to speak of in Burgundy, but there are beautiful, peaceful little rivers with willow-lined banks. You can hire a barge and float dreamily down the Burgundy canals and tributaries of the Rhône. The light is very soft and the water is smooth, deep, cold, and green, and the tiny freshwater fish that come from these rivers are delicious fried up Loire River–style and heaped in great mounds on plates. The people here do love oil-and-vinegar-marinated, grilled eel, and they make a delicious white wine stew called *pochouse* with river fish caught in the area.

The forest of Morvan is formidable—a county-size area, remote,

The famous vineyards at Château du Clos-de-Vougeot, once owned by the monks of Cîteaux.

and unspoiled. It is truly lovely, not as mystical as the densely forested Vosges region, or the area around Grenoble that is all mountains and magic, but it's very accessible, businesslike, rural farm country with some great houses that have been responsible for wines forever and ever.

The Cheeses

EPOISSES DE BOURGOGNE

One of the great Burgundian cheeses made from unpasteurized cow's milk—and one of my favorite cheeses in the world—is name-controlled Epoisses de Bourgogne (ay-PWOSS-duh-boor-GOYNE), made in the little hole-in-the-road town of Epoisses, a few miles north of the Langres plateau.

Very similar to Langres (page 68), though flatter and more disk-shaped (about an inch thick and 4 inches in diameter), each 9-ounce (270 g) cheese packs a powerhouse of rich flavor and aroma because as it ripens the rind of Epoisses is washed daily with *marc de Bourgogne*, a local *eau-de-vie*. Beneath the smooth, reddish-brown rind lies a creamy, blond interior that exudes a delightfully smelly, barnyardy aroma typical of only the most alluring washed-rind, full-fat cheeses.

I brought Epoisses (and Langres) to the U.S. some years ago, but these days due to USFDA regulations banning raw-milk cheeses aged less than 60 days, I can no longer stock the authentic A.O.C. version of this sublime cheese. You'll have to seek it out in France, where real Epoisses is available all over Paris, Burgundy, and in the area of the Saône River just to the west. But beware! There are a few brands that audaciously call them-

selves Epoisses but are not. The Epoisses you want is either the one made by Robert Berthaut or the staggeringly delicious Epoisses-type Ami du Chambertin, made in Brochon near the famous wine village of Gevrey-Chambertin. Avoid the flavorless so-called Epoisses made by Auxon (Fromagerie de l'Armançon), Renard, and Lincet (Saligny d'Or).

Choosing and Serving Epoisses de Bourgogne

There is considerable *fermier* (farm-made) production of Epoisses available at markets throughout Burgundy. Choose only those cheeses that fill their wooden boxes and/or haven't shrunk from desiccation. The rind should look moist, not sodden, and be a russet ranging anywhere from a healthy orange to *café-au-lait* brown; eating the rind is a matter of personal taste. Should you have the opportunity to see the interior (unlikely, since they are rarely sold in halves), it should be a creamy-blond, almost straw color. If the paste bulges or runs, it is approaching (or already is) overripe.

The aroma of Epoisses is undeniably barnyardy but it should not be an overpoweringly dirty one—more a healthy, outdoorsy earthiness. There is no mistaking the difference between a good, strong cheese *aroma* and a bad, strong cheese *odor*. You will find the aroma of Epoisses tantalizing, I assure you.

Epoisses is a superb after-dinner cheese, one that can elegantly top off even the most memorable meal. It is a majestic cheese meant to go with the biggest red wine you can muster, preferably a Burgundy. Try serving Epoisses with handfuls of tiny dried mirabelle plums or Medjool dates, both of which are a good match for strong cheeses. As for bread, any type is fine as long as it is rustic and crusty.

Grape pickers (vendangeurs) harvesting the bounty of Burgundy's legendary vineyards.

CÎTEAUX AND PIERRE-QUI-VIRE

One of Burgundy's oldest cheeses is a raw cow's milk Trappist cheese from the Abbaye de Notre Dame de Cîteaux near Losne. It has been made for longer than records have been kept by the Cistercian monks of the area. Though many people say Cîteaux (SEE-TOH) resembles Munster, I don't agree, although another Burgundian cheese that does is named Pierre-Qui-Vire (pee-AIR-key-VEER). This Trappist cheese is made by the monks at the Abbaye Sainte-Marie de la Pierre-Qui-Vire. Cîteaux is not as rich as Munster; it is firmer and glossier, but not nearly as flavorful. It is also compared to Reblochon, though, again, I disagree. The Cîteaux are bigger around and they're neither as buttery and bulging nor as delicate and delicious as Reblochon. Cîteaux and Pierre-Qui-Vire are both disks, Cîteaux weighing 3 pounds (1½ k) and Pierre-Qui-Vire about 1 pound (500 g). Both are a creamy brown on the outside with a beige interior.

WHEN IN BURGUNDY

In addition to Epoisses, seek out some of the other terrific Burgundian cheeses not exported to the U.S.

- **Aisy Cendré** (eh-ZEE-sawn-DRAY): Raw cow's milk; 8-ounce (250 g) disks ripened in wood ash (*sarments*) made by Berthaut of Epoisses fame; excellent.
- **Bouton-de-Culotte** (boo-TAW-duh-koo-LOTE); also called **Chèvreton de Mâcon** (shev-reh-TAW-duh-mah-KAW): *Chèvre fermier;* tiny, 1-ounce (30 g) goat cheeses from Mâcon, usually sold hard and dry. The nuttiest, chewiest cheeses I can think of.
- **Charollais** (sha-roll-LAY) or **Charolles** (sha-ROLL): *Chèvre fermier;* 5- to 8-ounce (150 to 250 g) cylinders, sold at markets from fresh to very aged; often excellent.
- **Claque-Bitou:** (CLOCK-bee-TOO): *Chèvre fermier;* fresh, very goaty-tasting curd blended with garlic and *fines herbes;* sold during the summer and fall at markets in the Côte d'Or.
- **Gadin** (gah-DAH) or **Bouchons** (boo-SHAW): Pellet-like, cow's-milk cheeses that taste of black walnuts. They're usually packed in stacks of three, bound by a rubber band, and are sold rather dry and hard.

Sometimes they are marinated in olive oil and sold in jars containing two to four stacks.

- **La Perrière d'Epoisses** (lah-PAIR-ee-AIR-day-PWOSS): Raw cow's milk; larger version of excellent Epoisses.
- **Les Laumes** (lay-LOME): Cow's milk; factory-made; about 2 pounds (1 k); once similar in flavor to Epoisses, but now a milder semisoft cheese.
- **Lormes** (LORM); also called **Le Fin Morvan** (luh-FAM-mor-VON): Raw cow's milk; 8-ounce (250 g) disks; very tasty soft cheese, aged for just a few weeks.
- **Pourly** (pore-LEE): 12-ounce (375 g) flat-bottomed, soft, snow-ball-like domes of chèvre with crinkly crust; excellent nutty flavor.
- **Saint-Florentin** *fermier* (SAHNT-floor-awn-TAN-fair-mee-AY): Raw cow's milk; 1 pound (500 g) drums; very soft, washed rind, full flavored; similar in style to Chaource; creamy and rich. Look also for very good non-*fermier,* factory-made examples.
- **Soumaintrain** *fermier* (soo-man-TRAN-fair-mee-AY): Raw cow's milk: 8-ounce (250 g) disks; washed-rind, soft double-crème with medium to strong flavor; has the taste and texture of a triple-crème; excellent.

Barges drift along the rivers and canals of Burgundy.

Choosing and Serving Cîteaux and Pierre-Qui-Vire

Choose Cîteaux or Pierre-Qui-Vire as you would any semisoft cheese. Make sure it looks healthy and taste it before you buy it. Semisofts are nearly foolproof—difficult for even the most inept merchant to abuse. Any American merchant who stocks it doubtless knows what he or she is doing. Failing Cîteaux or Pierre-Qui-Vire, I half-heartedly recommend Canadian Oka, which is very similar, though getting blander year by year.

Serve Trappist cheeses with luncheon fare rather than at the end of a more substantial meal. They marry well with any charcuterie, including pâtés, rillettes, and ham, and with any fruit and good bread. Wine choices are open—I recommend a light and fruity red—and beer is also good with these cheeses.

BLEU DE BRESSE

There is a cheese in Burgundy (actually in Bresse, which sprawls into the *départements* of Ain, Saône-et-Loire, and Jura, a little south and east of Burgundy, but for our purposes it can be grouped with Burgundy) called Bleu de Bresse (BLUH-duh-BRESS). It was created in 1950, solely to compete with Italian Gorgonzola. To my mind, it doesn't succeed, although you can get some good examples. Whereas Gorgonzola could stand alone sans its blue veins—that is, as a semisoft cheese with a great

THE TRUTH ABOUT MONTRACHET

Back in the 1970s, real Burgundian Montrachet (moan-rah-SHAY), an unripened goat's-milk cheese made with fresh milk at Laiterie Saint-Gengoux-le-National (about 17 miles from the village of Montrachet), and Bucheron (boo-share-OH), a goatier-tasting ripened chèvre made by Saint-Saviol in Poitou using powdered milk and frozen curd, were the first French chèvres to be exported to the U.S. Both were—and still are—highly commercial mass-produced cheeses. For the past 25 years or so these 11-ounce (330 g) logs of chèvre have been stocked in virtually every American and French cheese department.

In particular, Montrachet, which developed enormous cachet, became synonymous with all goat's-milk cheeses in the minds of Americans, and even now it is common to see it specifically called for by name in recipes that could be made with any number of other fresh (unripened) goat's-milk cheeses. Although it is only a borrowed generic name (it is also the name of a famous wine) used to elevate the status of Burgundy's various log-shaped, unripened chèvres, Montrachet became so imprinted on the minds of American food journalists and consumers as the name of a single cheese, that it has become one for all intents and purposes.

Considering the wealth of goat's-milk cheeses there, Montrachet is not held in particularly high esteem in France, where it sells well, but is dismissed by serious cheese lovers as a rather uninteresting, commercially produced cheese used as a staple ingredient by caterers. As a nation, the French prefer ripened or semi-ripened chèvres over fresh, unaged ones and I am in complete agreement with them. While there is nothing inherently wrong with fresh chèvre, I believe that the glory of *fromage de chèvre* is revealed only after it has aged for a month or so and its flavor has had time to evolve and grow more complex.

When shopping for Montrachet, look for the original fresh-milk versions, which are made at Saint-Gengoux-le-National and Savigny-sur-Grosne. Avoid date-stamped, plastic-packaged versions and any not-so-fresh-cheese; it will be mushy, wet, bitter, and decidedly unpleasant.

My best advice is to bypass Montrachet altogether and opt instead for other chèvres.

raw flavor not unlike Taleggio—Bleu de Bresse without its blueing would be exactly like *pasteurized* Brie—one-dimensional, buttery, and blah. They are made in a variety of foil-wrapped sizes: 4-pound (2 k) wheels, 3 inches thick; 3-pound (1½ k) cylinders, and 8-ounce (250 g) small medallions (or disks), each with a white, fuzzy *Penicillium candidum* crust.

I think it noteworthy that the French, who are so ethnocentric, have imitated the Italians here in such a straightforwardly commercial manner. Bleu de Bresse does have some merit, and in fact, has become so successful, that Griège, one of the two French companies that make it, has built a plant in the U.S. (Here, by law, the U.S.-made version is called Bresse Bleu.) The French-made Pipo 'Crem brand Bleu de Bresse is very, very good. U.S.-made Bresse Bleu is cheaper—deservedly so, as it is rather bland.

Choosing and Serving Bleu de Bresse

Bleu de Bresse is too young if the white, bloomy rind is flawlessly white and perhaps a bit chalky; better the rind shows a bit of gray to beige mottling and the interior bulges a bit, but not too much. This cheese can be easily overripened. Avoid it if it is runny or has a cracked rind or grayish interior. A pronounced ammoniacal smell also indicates overripeness.

Bleu de Bresse is an excellent snack or lunch cheese with pears, grapes, apples, crackers, or fresh bread, and light, fruity red wines. It works nicely as a dessert cheese and is delicious melted on toast, and in pasta dishes, gratins, and soufflés.

FRANCHE-COMTE

In general, mountain people are known for their rugged individuality, a tenacious desire to maintain links to their pasts and customs, and a fierce resistance to change and modernism. The men and women of Franche-Comté who raise dairy cows and make cheese are no exception. Their *pays* stretches from the low, eastern edge of Burgundy, through the foothills of the Jura Alps to the Alps along the Swiss border. If natural beauty and serious cheese are your passions, Franche-Comté is a glorious area in which to pursue them. In fact, the land rises so steadily and steeply, were it not for the considerable plateaus, heaths, and high mountain pastures, one would believe the old Comtois joke about their Montbéliard cattle having been bred to have two short legs and two long in order to keep their balance.

The name Franche-Comté dates back to 1366, a time when Europe was comprised of kingdoms, not countries. Today, the classical region of Franche-Comté includes three political *départements:* the Jura, the Doubs, and the Haute-Saône.

The Cheeses

....

COMTE (GRUYERE DE COMTE)

The full name for Comté (cone-TAY), French Gruyère, is Gruyère de Comté (grew-YAIR or gree-AIR-duh-cone-TAY). Franche-Comté is adjacent to Switzerland just above Haute-Savoie and south of the Vos-

Limitless pasturage for Montébeliard cattle covers much of Franche-Comté.

ges in the Alsace region. The original Gruyère was neither Swiss nor French (see box, page 115). But as the French became more and more nationalistic, and perhaps increasingly ethnocentric, they wanted their cheese to have its own identity. After all, it *was* somewhat different from the Swiss Gruyère: Occasionally, it had pea- or cherry-size holes (eyes), it was a bit more straw-colored, a bit firmer, and the favor was more nutlike. Rather than call it French Gruyère, they began referring to it as Comté, or at the very least as Gruyère de Comté.

I find that Swiss Gruyère is a little granular and tastes a bit waxy, with some bite, whereas French Gruyère de Comté has more of an oily sweetness to it. I prefer the nuttier, toffee-tasting French variety, although both are great cheeses.

The real difference between Swiss Gruyère and French Comté is: The Swiss allow their cheeses to go to market after only three months, whereas Comté is rarely aged for less than six months and often it is aged as long as a year.

Comté is used frequently in the cooking of the region and throughout France, appearing in quiches, onion soup—of course—and numerous tarts, onion gratins, and potato gratins. It is also considered an essential table cheese for eating out of hand or to finish a meal.

All French Comté is name-controlled and excellent. The "least best" example is that from the lowlands of Comté, because the milk used to make it just cannot approach the quality of high Alpine pasture Franche-Comté milk. The grading of Comté before its release is stringent and only excellent cheeses which have earned 14 (or more) out of 20 points on the grading scale are allowed to have their rinds stamped in green with the cheese name and the image of a bell. To identify the best you must taste; two good brands are Arnaud and Jura-Gruyère. There are no Comté factories; there are about 300 small dairies (*fruitières*) that turn out an average of only six to seven cheeses a day. These are then sold to companies that age (*affiner*) them following rules established by the *fruitières.* These *affineurs* (some of whom also make cheese) sell the cheeses they have ripened to retailers and exporters. Some Savoie-based producer/*affineurs,* namely Perrin and Delean, make fine mountain cheese similar to Comté but are primarily known for their indigenous Reblochon and Tomme de Savoie. Reybier, located in the Jura, is another firm with a reputation for distributing fine-quality Comté as well as other great cheeses of Franche-Comté and Savoie.

Wheels of Comté average 75 to 80 pounds (37½ to 40 k) each and are

only about 4 inches thick, whereas French Emmental, a regional kinsman, can be as much as 10 inches thick. The Comtés have parallel, flat faces, whereas Emmentals are great, convex, rounded balloons like inner tubes without the hole. Comtés are more than 3 feet in diameter with a beautiful brown, pebbled rind, and always a striking paper label.

Choosing and Serving Comté (Gruyère de Comté)

It's hard to come home with a less than perfect piece of Comté, one of the most enjoyable, versatile cheeses imaginable. Avoid any batch that is moldy or dried out, and don't let your cheesemonger sell you a hunk that has a disproportionate amount of rind.

It is preferable to have a piece of Comté cut for you rather than to purchase it pre-cut and pre-wrapped. (The cheese will have lost its perfume and some of its life, even if it was cut and wrapped only a day earlier.) Here is the only advisory needed: Don't buy old stock. The cheese should be a yellowish-ivory color inside, and the gray-brown pebbled rind should be uniform and intact, not cracked. Avoid any batch that shows more than one-half inch of darkness between

THE ORIGINS OF "GRUYERE"

The word "Gruyère" has at its root a great deal more than Gruyères, a town in Switzerland's canton of Fribourg.

A thousand years ago, when Charlemagne's Holy Roman Empire included all of what is now France, Switzerland, and parts of Germany, the forests were called *gruyères*. His men sold wood to the cheesemakers (who "invented" the cheeses we know as Comté and Gruyère), so that they could fire their kettles to cook curd. They paid for the wood with cheeses, and the name for the forests eventually took on a double meaning, becoming the name of the cheese as well.

So you see, it is primarily through Swiss marketing prowess that Switzerland has assumed title to the name of Gruyère. Indeed, there are a number of places in France that have names similar to that of Gruyères in Fribourg.

mainly for rind if your piece is surrounded on three sides. Don't be bothered by the horizontal fissures (*lènures*) in the cheese's interior near the rind. These are natural and are always found in Comté.

Use Comté anytime, any way— melt it, cube it, julienne it. However you treat it, know that Comté is a classic, all-purpose winner—as appropriate with salami and bread for lunch as it is as an elegant afterdinner treat with fruit and any wine of your choosing.

Comté is superb as a snack— try it grated or thinly sliced on bread, toasted, and topped off with a twist of freshly ground black pepper. It is also excellent as a salad cheese— diced into the salad or served on the side.

EMMENTAL

Like French Comté and Swiss Gruyère, both French and Swiss Emmental (EM-awn-TAHL) have been made for over a thousand years and they are among the world's most recognizable cheeses. (For complete information about Swiss Emmental, see page 271.) Each is Paul Bunyanesque in scale: French Emmental is made in huge, convex, 175- to 220-pound (about 87½ to 110 k) wheels, 6 to 12 inches thick, 40 to 44 inches in diameter. With its straw-colored rind and pronounced buttery, nutty, fruity taste and smooth-as-satin mouthfeel, French Emmental is a formidable *fromage,* its light-straw colored in-

the interior cheese and the outer crust—an indication of excessive drying. Don't let the purveyor cut you a piece too close to the side rind: Either insist on a piece closer to the center of the wheel or buy a long *tranche* (s ab). You are paying terior liberally dotted with a well-spaced proliferation of walnut-size holes.

Although both French and Swiss Emmental are made with partially skimmed unpasteurized cow's milk, I would say that generally the French version tastes somewhat stronger than the Swiss—even in its young stage it is fruitier and nuttier, a deeper color, and more visually striking due to its dramatically bulbous shape. Although the Swiss and French recipes are identical, in France, Emmental is marketed in a choice of ages: young, for cooking or fondue; middle-aged, a bit more flavorful, for eating or fondue; and extra-aged, sharp, for cooking (soups, gratins) and eating.

French Emmental is always an excellent choice, but it irritates me that I have to retail it for considerably more money than the Swiss Emmental. This marketing problem is a direct reflection of supply-and-demand—the demand for French Emmental, not only in France, but throughout Europe, is such that the French don't really need to export it.

Choosing and Serving Emmental

First and foremost, be sure you are being sold authentic French Emmental, not one of the more common, garden-variety imitators made with pasteurized milk which fall dismally short on all levels. The finest French Emmental, which is made with rich, Alpine milk, will exhibit the identifier "Emmental Français Grand Cru" imprinted in red on its rind. You will be able

With a sweeping gesture, this cheese shop clerk cuts into a wedge of Comté with a wire cutter.

THE HOLE TRUTH

Emmental, the massive mountain cheese from France and Switzerland, is imitated by cheesemakers all over the world. Indeed, Emmental is so famous that whenever artists and illustrators need to paint or draw a cheese, they unfailingly show one with a few holes—just to make sure we get the point! But the truth is that most cheeses don't have holes. Those that do get them as a result of the gas (usually CO_2), given off by natural, harmless bacteria introduced into the milk early in the cheesemaking process, which adds acidity and facilitates curdling. Holes may also be the result of bacteria that are naturally present in raw milk. Sometimes the gas is an indication that a run (batch) of cheese has gone bad. Whether holes, or "eyes," are considered desirable or a defect depends on the type of cheese. French cheesemakers classify holes according to their size, for example:

Hole Size	Name	Cheese
Tiny	*Les yeux de perdrix* (partridge eyes)	Tomme de Savoie Various cow's-milk Pyrénées cheeses Véritable Camembert de Normandie (occasionally)
Small	*Petit pois* (little peas)	Comté Mimolette (occasionally) Morbier (occasionally)
Medium	*Cerises* (cherries)	Comté
Large	*Noix* (walnuts)	Emmental

to tell the difference visually in other ways as well: French Emmental is extraordinarily convex—as though it had been overinflated to the point of bursting. Avoid any that looks dry—the eyes in French Emmental will "cry" when exposed to the air, weeping glorious tears of somewhat diluted butterfat.

Emmental is a perfect anytime cheese, though I find it a bit bland served after a meal. It is better as a snack cheese, sliced for sandwiches, or diced into salads. It melts beautifully if you don't mind a slightly

Milk for making Comté and other cheeses is carried from the dairy to cheesemaking facilities in stainless-steel bidons.

ropey melt. It is one of the classic choices for fondue. At parties and buffets, it makes a dramatic visual display that is mouthwateringly enticing when a huge prow of it is allowed to loom over a table laden with food. Pair it with light, fruity red wines or light, spicy white ones. Wrap Emmental in waxed paper or aluminum foil, and store it in the vegetable compartment of the refrigerator.

MORBIER

One of the political *départements* in the foothills of the Jura mountains is called Doubs, after the river that meanders down from its source in the mountains. The Doubs region is best known for its rare, strong, dry, sherry-like yellow wine called *vin jaune,* used both for cooking and as a dessert wine. From this region also comes Morbier (MORE-bee-yay), a special semisoft cow's-milk cheese that's as old as Comté and named for a little farm town called Morbier.

Morbier is very striking to look at for it was traditionally two cheeses: one made from the morning milk and one from the evening milk, which were separated by a layer of ash. Long ago, when the cheesemaker's day was finishing up, there would be leftover curd, not enough to make another huge Gruyère de Comté, but enough for a smaller, softer cheese. The cheesemaker would press leftover evening curd into a mold. Next he would rub his hands on the blackened outside surface of the copper pot used for cooking the curd and spread this ash on the top to protect the cheese from drying out (and perhaps to keep the flies away). The next day he would press leftover morning curd on top of the ash.

Nowadays, the cheese is made from a single milking, and commercial ash is used to maintain a traditional appeal; as far as I know, just two farms continue to make it the old-fashioned way.

Some of the Morbier made today is excellent. This is a semisoft cheese, not strong but not mild either. It has no eye structure and is similar to Fontina d'Aosta and Vacherin Fribourgeois (see pages 191 and 287). It is a platter-size (10 to 18 inches in diameter) wheel, from 13 to 16 pounds (6½ to 8 k). It has an appealing, complex flavor that is full of nuts and fruit along with a distinct taste of hard-boiled egg and veal sautéed in butter. The aroma is like fresh hay or new-mown grass. The problem is that what is available to us often is made from pasteurized milk by cheesemakers not even in Franche-Comté. It is much cheaper, and as you would expect, quite bland. It in no way resembles true Morbier except for the thin layer of ash in the middle.

Happily, in a few small creameries and on some farms, cheesemakers still make Morbier in small batches from raw milk, and the interesting thing is that you can actually taste the difference between the morning and evening versions. The evening milk may be fruitier or more pronounced than the other; there should be a fleeting, subtle difference in the flavor of a milk coming from a cow that has been standing or lying motionless through the night and is milked in the morning, as compared with the milk from a cow that has been active throughout the day—grazing, walking, moving, and ruminating in the field.

Choosing and Serving Morbier

The creamy-brown crust on Morbier must be dry and smooth; avoid this cheese if the crust is slimy, cracked, or has a profusion of tiny white dots—all are evidence of staleness. The interior should be a nice, healthy-looking, almost glossy, yellowish-ivory color. The horizontal dark line of ash separating the halves should be bold and evident. If it isn't, the cheese is probably one of the several Morbier impostors—not overtly bad, just bland. Try to read the top label, although it may be obscured by age or it may be missing. If you see the label, look for a Franche-Comté/Jura or Doubs origin and the fact that it was made from raw milk (*au lait cru*). Morbier made in factories in the Auvergne and even Poitou is trucked to Franche-Comté to age in caves where it is shamelessly labeled Morbier. Close inspection of the cheese's label will reveal this. If it's phony Morbier, the label will read "Fabriqué en Poitou" or "Fabriqué en Auvergne."

Morbier is a cheese that makes me want to take it outside—way outside, as far from the city as I can get. It marries well with ham on a sandwich, or as I prefer it, with a well-made *saucisson*-type salami (coarse, all-pork, spiked with pepper or garlic, perhaps blended with

Raw-milk Morbier is the most seductive of all semisoft cheeses. Inside its creamy brown rind, the glossy, yellowish-ivory paste reveals a thin, horizontal layer of dark ash.

crushed walnuts or red wine), a fresh country-style bread, and any good wine—my preference is a light, fruity red.

Morbier also melts beautifully, and is a very decent salad-course cheese.

VACHERIN DU HAUT-DOUBS (VACHERIN MONT D'OR)

High in the département of Doubs, cheese-makers and their livestock often live under one roof.

Vacherin du Haut-Doubs (vash-er-ANN-doo-oh-DOO) is a name-controlled cow's milk cheese which is also called Vacherin Mont d'Or (vasher-ANN-moan-DOR). (A nearly identical cheese, also called Vacherin Mont d'Or, is one of Switzerland's most famous cheeses; see page 287.) Vacherin certainly ranks as one of the world's most delicious cheeses and I am one of its biggest fans. It is also one of the most unique. What makes it unique is that unlike most of the other major cheeses of the world, which achieve their depth of flavor from spring and summer milk (considered the creamiest and most desirable), Vacherin is made in the autumn and winter (from August 15th through March 31st) from the milk of cows fed on cold-weather vegetation such as hay and silage, plus grain. Vacherin's appearance is also unique—each wheel is banded with a strip of resinous, aromatic bark

before it is packed in a lidded wooden box.

Though both the French and the Swiss have been making Vacherin Mont d'Or since the eighteenth century, practically all of the Mont d'Or, or "golden mountain," that lies in the Alps between the two countries and from which the cheese takes its name lies in France. Historically, both countries called their cheese Vacherin Mont d'Or until 1973 when, to the outrage of the French, the Swiss quietly arranged to commandeer exclusive legal rights to the name. Curiously, the French responded to this semantic takeover with uncharacteristic restraint and the result is that today French Vacherin Mont d'Or is either labeled "Le Mont d'Or" or "Vacherin du Haut-Doubs" (the name under which "real" Vacherin is now designated as A.O.C.) The Haut-Doubs appellation is particularly ridiculous since the French have been making this cheese for decades, even before the *département* of Haut-Doubs was created, but it is nonetheless the name-controlled designation. Even more outrageous is the fact that by 1983 the Swiss chose to begin using pasteurized instead of raw milk for their cheese in an attempt to rein in the capriciousness of Vacherin's recipe. The result, as is occasionally the case with pasteurized-milk cheeses, was a serious outbreak of listeriosis (poisoning from a rare, virulent bacteria). In the end the problem was traced directly to the pasteurized Swiss cheese, but for quite some time French-made raw-milk Vacherin bore the brunt of the blame for this catastrophe. The result in France

was a few years of disastrously slow sales since all of Europe was too scared to eat it. Demand declined dramatically until the truth about the listeriosis outbreak was laid squarely to rest at the door of Swiss cheesemakers. Unfortunately, another consequence of the Swiss problem was that the USFDA prohibited export of all French raw-milk Vacherin regardless of how long it had been aged, to the U.S.

Despite Vacherin's convoluted recent history, its origins are straightforward: It was initially created as a result of the climate in Franche-Comté, the coldest region in France, where winter temperatures fall well below zero for most

The great cheeses of Franche-Comté (clockwise from the left, rear): Bleu de Gex, Morbier (under the Gex), Comté, Edel de Cléron (an excellent faux Vacherin), and Vacherin Haute-Rive (the real thing).

FINE FAUX VACHERINS

Several relatively new cheeses made with Vacherin du Haut-Doubs as their model must be considered flat-out triumphs and they are readily available in the U.S. They are identical in oozy texture to the real, raw-milk French-made cheeses.

The Perrin company's excellent Edel de Cléron (AY-del-duh-kleh-RAW) is made in Franche-Comté from gently pasteurized cow's milk. Available all year round, it comes banded with the traditional strip of aromatic bark, and its presence at my cheese counters has relieved my anguish over my inability to offer raw-milk versions to discerning customers. Edel de Cléron is also marketed with a different label and sold under the name Ecorcé de Sapin (ay-kor-SAY-duh-sah-PAN), which means "barked with spruce." The other fabulous fake, made by Prédor, is called Tourrée de l'Aubier (ter-RAY-duh-lo-bee-YAY). The name roughly translates as "anthem to the dawn," and this cheese, too, is made in Franche-Comté in the exact configuration of authentic Vacherin. A third, similar but not quite as delicious version of traditional Vacherin, called Tavaillon, is made by Girod (Savoie).

of the season. Two hundred years ago these cold winters made daily delivery of milk to the local Comté-making cooperatives unthinkable. So a smaller cheese was made at home, one so creamy it had to be eaten with a spoon. And so it would not crack and collapse at its runny peak of ripeness, its perimeter was wrapped with pliant strips of bark for support.

Before a luscious 5- to 7-pound (2½ to 3½ k) 1¼-inch-thick, 9- to 12-inch-diameter disk of Vacherin is put into its wood-chip box to age today, the young cheese is banded with a strip of Norwegian spruce bark (occasionally fir or pine bark). This bark further flavors the cheese, giving the rind, and eventually the cheese, a balsamy, woodsy, piney redolence evocative of aromatic, fresh-cut wood.

When a Vacherin is ripe, it has a thick, reddish-brown rind that ripples like waves. The cheese is ready to eat when it is so runny that you must remove the top rind and eat the cheese with a spoon—the French word is *coulant* (running). Ripe Vacherin literally flows and has a strong barnyardy aroma. If it isn't oozing, it isn't quite ready to eat. Occasionally, it will be slightly cracked, but not too much so or you can be sure it will be overripe. The cheese's interior is a glistening beige rather than white, and the flavor is absolutely extraordinary—there is no cheese like it.

Choosing and Serving Vacherin du Haut-Doubs/ Vacherin Mont d'Or

Purchase Vacherin when the velvety, reddish-brown rind is rippled or wavy, and if you're buying a wedge from a wheel, taste it. It shouldn't be too strongly flavored and its interior color should be beige without reddening. If you have purchased a wedge, make sure the cheesemonger wraps it up very tightly lest all the cheese seep out from the rind and stick to the wrapping material. When shopping in Europe, where you will have a choice between French and Swiss Vacherin, opt for the French cheese, which has more depth of flavor. Look for examples made by the Badoz family in Pontarlier (Franche-Comté); these are very fine tasting.

Serve Vacherin du Haut-Doubs as a dessert with the finest, sweetest fruit you can find and accompany it with a Beaujolais or Chardonnay. And don't hesitate to serve it by itself on a plate—it should be so runny that you'll be able to eat it with a spoon.

BLEU DE GEX-HAUT-JURA

Bleu de Gex and Bleu de Septmoncel

Bleu de Gex (BLUH-duh-JECKS) and Bleu de Septmoncel (BLUH-duh-SET-moan-sell) are two name-

Cows graze serenely in a pasture near a chapel in Pontarlier, where Vacherin is made.

Whether it be the high mountains and alpine meadows where shepherds go about their age-old tasks of heating milk in great copper cauldrons over open wood fires and pressing curds by hand, or the dim caves hewn out of living rock, where young cheeses ripen for months and even years, through cheese we experience the joy of being in communion with nature in all its purity and serenity.

Pierre Androuët,
The Complete Encyclopedia of French Cheese

controlled blues grouped together under the A.O.C. designation of Bleu de Gex-Haut-Jura. They are among the few surviving raw cow's milk blue cheeses of the world—besides Bleu des Causses and the occasional small producer of Fourme d'Ambert. Both are unique blues in terms of their configuration; only softer, sharper Gorgonzola shares their flat, wheel shape.

What makes the cheese so special is that, owing to the prowess of the few remaining Franche-Comté master cheesemakers, even without the delicious flavor of the blue, this cheese would still be a winner—a scrumptious convergence of faint salinity paired with overtones of fruit and nuts. The blue adds a certain snap and is less piercing than other blues. It is aged from one to three months; the younger cheeses are markedly milder than those with longer age.

Gex's counterpart, the more obscure and therefore rarer Bleu de Septmoncel, is from a neighboring town. Contrary to what you may read elsewhere, Septmoncel is *not* a mixture of cow's and goat's milks. It is identical to Bleu de Gex in the way that Fourme de Montbrison is neighbor to and identical to Fourme d'Ambert, or that Munster and Géromé are one and the same.

Gex and Septmoncel, like so many related cheeses, are becoming even more identical with each passing year. No longer do they exhibit the eccentric quirks they did as recently as 20 years ago. They used to blue-out naturally, the result of a happenstance I find joyous.

Expert Patrick Rance, the savior of English cheese and a French cheese master, taught me that Gex's and Septmoncel's blue (a light, sky-blue, sometimes purplish) was once exclusively the result of a fungal bloom found on two species of wild Alpine violets. The violets were eaten by Montbéliard cattle and the fungus found its way to their mammary glands. Its presence in the cheeses was responsible for the blue of both Gex and Septmoncel. (Today, the cows still munch on violets, but the curd is given a dose of factory-made *Penicillium roqueforti,* the same bacteria added to less distinguished brands of Roquefort. Given how strict the French A.O.C. cheesemaking guidelines are for many other cheeses, it strikes me as a bit inconsistent that they do not insist that Gex's and Septmoncel's blueing be the result of natural, air-borne bacteria and plant-based enzymes. Though both Bleu de Gex-Haut-Jura cheeses are usually excellent, one can still imagine how much greater they once were.

Choosing and Serving Bleu de Gex and Bleu de Septmoncel

Beware of a cracked or slimy rind—it should be dry and slightly rough to the touch—and watch out for a graying interior. Good, healthy 12- to 14-pound (6 to 7 k) wheels of Gex or Septmoncel will sport a yellowish ivory interior with blue veining that looks like marble and a rind that is dry, pebbled, and grayish-beige. Both cheeses

Fromage et pain est

médecin au sain.

Bread and cheese is

medicine for the well.

French proverb

are comparatively mild blues with a subtly beefy, fruity flavor that is gently saline. They shouldn't taste overly sharp.

Gex and Septmoncel are superb snack or lunchtime cheeses. They are also fine at the end of a meal, and can be paired extraordinarily well with other, more assertive types of cheese. Like most blues, they are superb with salad, on the side or crumbled up and added to the greens. Thanks to their creamy rather than crumbly textures, Gex or Septmoncel can be planed into sheets or cigarette shapes for melting or garnishing.

These blue cheeses are nice suited to the wines of the Viognier grape, including the Rhône's rare, famous white Condrieu. Pair them also with Château Grillet, the famous white Graves from Bordeaux or Burgundy's Meursault.

SAVOIE AND HAUTE-SAVOIE

Just to the south of Geneva, France and Switzerland physically overlap, and a finger of Switzerland sneaks itself between the Jura mountains of Franche-Comté and the area known as Savoie. Lake Geneva—Lac Léman to the Swiss—hooks down from the northeast and is surrounded on three sides by France. At the southern tip of Lake Geneva is the city of Geneva. You can head east from there and be in France again. (To confuse matters even more, the Geneva airport is actually located in France, not Switzerland.)

In the heart of the Savoie is the *département* of Haute-Savoie, a mountainous region that enjoys a wealth of lush pastureland. Here is valley after valley interlaced with winding roads that make it take forever to get anywhere. It is a beautiful, towering area, too vertical for towns and people but not for the dairy cattle of the region. Despite the elevation, the summers are quite warm; the winters, though, are severe with deep, deep snow. This is a place I would love to live as a hermit, hanging out in the woods and watching the seasons come and go. During cold weather the cattle are housed in sheds in the lowland pastures and are fed silage, which doesn't produce the quality milk that Savoie cheeses require. In fact, from November through February, little cheese is made that will bear a Savoie or Haute-Savoie imprimatur. Instead, at this time of year plenty

Savoie's storybook geography: Towering mountain peaks preside over countless tiny villages nestled in valleys lush with pasturage. This one is near Chamonix.

Savoie and Haute-Savoie

of cheeses come out of the aging rooms, making winter a grand time for eating Savoie cheeses. Reblochon and Tomme Savoie, made from peak-of-summer milk, emerge from their ripening caves. Beaufort, with up to two years' aging time, also makes an appearance.

During the spring and summer, vegetables are plentiful at local farmer's markets throughout the Savoie. Fennel, radishes, garlic, cabbage, carrots, and turnips abound. All are heavily perfumed with the region's black soil, which is glacially rich in minerals. The grass is so green and the air so clear all summer, particularly in August, that you will never see lusher color. The butter, eggs, and bread of the region are sublime. The people of the region drink a great deal of fresh milk, which is unusual—milk is not usually the French beverage of choice. But in Savoie milk reigns. The wines are minor but good and mostly white. With the Burgundy and Rhône vineyards so nearby, their availability is widespread.

Savoie is so beautiful it hurts. The way the sun filters down through the pine, spruce, oak, maple, and fir trees, the way it reflects its light off the grassy pastures, you feel as

FRANCE'S VENICE

Annecy is an immaculate, precious little town at the western tip of Lac d'Annecy, not far from the most remote parts of Haute-Savoie, just south of Lake Geneva. Annecy is a not-to-be missed treat, if you're traveling from France to Switzerland or France to Italy. It's a wonderfully unspoiled region, the only intrusion being the occasional ski lift. Tourists come to the region in the summertime because there are so many pretty streams to swim in and Lac d'Annecy is great for both fishing and boating.

The magic of Annecy is its charming flower-lined canals.

Annecy is France's own miniature Venice—canals run throughout the town—except the water in Annecy is sparkling clean. In the spring, summer, and fall, the outdoor market in the rue Sainte-Claire offers perfect fruits, vegetables, cheeses, and game—all sold against the gorgeous natural backdrop of a big sky and the crystal-clear water that meanders through the town. In the summer the breathtaking profusion of flowers is equaled only by the scores of admiring visitors.

All around Annecy are the towering mountains behind the lake, and if you can get in a car and get up to them, there are some compelling little villages—most with a lovely little inn and a fantastic place to eat.

In Annecy you must stop at the Auberge de Savoie; stay the night and most certainly dine there. Every regional foodstuff is represented on the menu. I was served *écureuil* (squirrel pâté) once, and I followed it with a kind of *daube* of young wild boar (*marcassin*), which had a flavor different from mature boar in much the same way that lamb tastes different from mutton. As you may guess from my Savoie fervor, this meal was extraordinary.

though you have found a home. You want to gather together the people you love most and start a commune. It's a magical and thrilling place.

Three of the greatest cheeses in the world come from Savoie and Haute-Savoie regions—Beaufort, Tomme de Savoie, and Reblochon. All three are quite different from each other, but all are raw cow's milk cheeses. In areas as mountainous as these, it is necessary to identify certain valleys and mountains so as to differentiate between specific pasturages and thereby pinpoint the best cheeses. For the best Reblochon, we look for cheeses from the Aravis mountain chain; for Tomme de Savoie, look to Les Beauges and Les Bellevilles as well as the valleys of Haute-Tarentaise and Maurienne. Beaufort is best from the area around the town of Beaufort as well as from the area around the mountain Madeleine.

The Cheeses

....

BEAUFORT

Beaufort is a tiny farm town in the *département* of Haute-Savoie where you have to drive around the cows that wander in the streets. Actually, it's hardly a town at all, but more a marketplace for the area's cattle dealers and breeders. It is in an extremely remote part of Haute-Savoie, but because of my respect for the cheese, I felt I

had to go there to commune with Beaufort's namesake. I drove miles out of the way to get there—not exactly punishing duty since the journey is beautiful.

Name-controlled Beaufort (bo-FORE) is a massive cheese, a creamy, white, raw cow's milk cheese, much like Swiss Gruyère. It weighs about 80 pounds (40 k) and is about as big around as a Gruyère but almost twice as thick, say about 8 inches, with a beige rind. It has a higher butterfat content and a creamier texture than Gruyère or Comté. It is most sought after in its *d'alpage* (pasture) version (Beaufort d'Alpage), which is made from milk given by Tarentaise cattle that have been grazing on summer grasses, herbs, and flowers at elevations over 6,000 feet (2,000 m). The milk from the height of summer—late August—is much richer, and naturally, the cheese is better. The sweetness and the lush aroma of the grass, herbs, flowers, and clover comes through, as does a distinct, omnipresent nuttiness not apparent in other-season Beaufort. These days, almost all the Beaufort I see is Beaufort d'Alpage. Some producers may be slightly stretching the meaning of *alpage,* for I must say that I have tasted more than a few examples that, while very good, I would certainly not characterize as extraordinary, and certainly not worth their high price. Nonetheless, Beaufort is considered the prince of Gruyères—superior to French Comté and Swiss Gruyère. I'll leave the final analysis to you. Taste and judge for yourself.

Beaufort figures into much of

the cooking of Savoie—in the soups of the region, the fondues and gratins made with the wonderful Dauphinoise-style potatoes, as well as in the famous *omelette à la savoyarde* (made with shredded Beaufort and chervil).

Choosing and Serving Beaufort

Beaufort is relatively rare in the U.S., sold almost exclusively at specialty food shops, where it is among the more expensive offerings. If you see it, make sure it's healthy—not dried out, cracked, or graying. The interior should be a buttery ivory color; don't worry about the horizontal fissures (*lènures*); it's vertical cracks due to desiccation that are worrisome. (These allow mold to enter and tell you that this Beaufort has been in stock too long.)

Beaufort should have a creamy, firm texture, no granularity, and an excellent, mild, fruity, sweet flavor. It is a terrific melter (ideal for fondue), good as a snack cheese with *saucission sec* (dry salami) and/or fruit, and as an after-dinner cheese with the finest bread, a red Rhône wine, and fresh fruit. Beaufort is also good cubed or shredded into salads. There's a famous *salade de Gruyère* that is simply cubes of Beaufort with walnuts and *laitue*— a green similar to Boston lettuce— dressed with a walnut oil vinaigrette. Marvelous! Beaufort is compatible with all big red wines.

Interestingly, it is a cheese that brings out the best in less costly, less complex reds such as Côtes-du-Rhône and everyday Bordeaux.

TOMME DE SAVOIE

Tomme de Savoie (TUM-duh-sav-WAH) is an honest, unpretentious cheese—I feel incomplete unless I have a really good batch of it on hand for people who want some good cheese. Tommes are 3½- to 12-pound (1¾ to 6 k) disks of raw

TOMME TERMINOLOGY

While the ancient word *tomme, tome,* or *toma* has at its Alpine roots the meaning, roughly, of "hunk," "round," or "piece," what it really is meant to suggest is that the cheese is *not* the produce of one specific herd. *Tomme* implies the cheese is the product of milk gathered from several or perhaps even numerous herds, specifically from animals pastured within that particular region or area. Thus, the cheese has been made by a professional, experienced cheesemaker, not a farmer, and therefore, the cheese is much more likely to be well made.

cow's-milk cheese, about 2 inches thick and 8 inches in diameter, that are as cheeselike visually as cheese can be. Tomme de Savoie has a beautifully rustic, gray-brown, fuzzy, obviously inedible thick crust. The disks are packed like motion picture film canisters in wooden crates especially made to hold them. The outsides of these crates are stenciled with little information except for the cheese's name and a number that denotes the fat content—from 20% to 40% butterfat. Amazingly, the 20% and 30% examples manage to retain that grand Savoie flavor unlike any other reduced-fat cheese—a far cry from those plastic and rubber "diet" cheeses found in American supermarkets. This is a testament to the quality found in Savoie tradition: its cattle, pasturage, milk, and cheesemakers.

Tomme de Savoie has always meant to me the simplest, most peasant-like cheese, all complexity reduced to its common denominator—the most accessible cheese taste experience in the world. It is a cheese completely unrefined and perfectly delicious. Beware—there are many brands of look-alike Tomme de Savoie. If you're getting the real thing, it will proclaim its Savoie origin (*fabriqué en Savoie*) on the paper label and its rustic-looking crust will ensure that the cheese has been aged for at least six months. If it's a smooth clean crust, it's not real Tomme de Savoie.

Ersatz Tomme de Savoie, made in the Auvergne or Poitou region from pasteurized milk, and then shipped to Savoie to be aged for a while, has no flavor (the label will read *affiné en Savoie*). Real Tomme de Savoie has an unmistakable raw flavor—beefy, hazelnutty, slightly saline, milky. It is beige to straw-colored with tiny holes all through it, though occasionally the paste will be smooth.

Genuine versus fake: The label of a real Tomme de Savoie (left) will indicate that it is made in Savoie from raw milk (au lait cru); a faux, pasteurized version (right), made in Poitou or Auvergne, will indicate only that it has been aged (affiné) in Savoie.

Choosing and Serving Tomme de Savoie

Your goal should be to find real Tomme de Savoie, not a look-alike. To do so, you must read the label affixed to the surface of the cheese. Although to date it has not been a "stock" item at any of the big American imported cheese wholesalers, I adore this cheese and so provide it for my customers. When purchasing, watch out for the usual things that can be wrong with any fine cheese due to over-age—cracks, dryness, interior reddening.

Serve Tomme any time you want the most basic, perfect, peasanty, cheese to enjoy with *charcuterie,* fruit, bread, and wine. It is a joy. It marries exceedingly well with picnic fare—salami (*saucisson sec*), ham, pâtés (particularly liver-stoked types), in conjunction with juicy peaches and plums, and light red wines, such as those from neighboring Beaujolais and, across the border, Italy's Piedmont. Most white wines will do, too, as Tomme de Savoie is not a strong cheese.

REBLOCHON

The third cheese in the Savoie trilogy that includes Beaufort and Tomme de Savoie is name-controlled Reblochon (ruh-bloe-SHAW). The name Reblochon may have come from several possible sources: One theory is that a rough translation of the word means "to milk again." Another, my favorite, is that in Savoyard patois *reblessa* means "to steal, swipe, or engage in some sort of thievery" (which is apt, considering the origins of this cheese). And that leads to the Reblochon story.

In the old days taxes were paid according to the amount of milk each Savoyarde farmer could deliver to his clients. With the taxman literally looming over his shoulder, a farmer would finish the milking as though his herd had been milked

RARE RACLETTE

In the eastern part of France (Poitou, Vendée, Charente), a handful of chèvre makers produce Raclette cheeses made from local goat's milk. The cheeses, which weigh 13 to 17 pounds (6½ to 8½ k) and are 3 inches thick and 17 inches in diameter, are identical in size and recipe to the cow's-milk Raclette cheeses made in the French provinces of Savoie and Franche-Comté (see page 135) and in the canton of Valais in Switzerland. In fact, once they are ready for aging, these *Raclette pur chèvre* are trucked to Franche-Comté, where they are ripened in caves for a few months, before they are marketed as *Tomme de chèvre pour raclettes.* They are excellent as a table cheese and, of course, as a melting cheese for raclette.

dry. In reality, the cows had plenty of milk left. The tax collector would go away happy and the farmer return and milk the cow again. This second milking was found to provide a much richer milk than the first milking. The tradition was that the farmer's wife (it is unique to Reblochon that these cheeses have always been made by women) would then make a special cheese out of this higher-in-butterfat milk, for consumption by the family. Thus was invented a new cheese: a 1-pound (500 g) disk, 1 inch thick and 5½ inches in diameter, which was ripened more quickly by brine-washing the rind and curing it at a higher temperature. Reblochon was a cheese the farmer and his family intended to enjoy rather than derive income from, and thus a long ripening process was not desirable. The result was a creamy, unctuous, al-

most Brie-textured cheese, but with a bone-colored rather than straw-colored hue, and the flavor, augmented by its washed rind process, deliciously smelly. When I taste Reblochon, I am reminded of a rare filet mignon that melts in your mouth with a decidedly pleasant, balsamy quality, and a hazelnut butteriness.

Until recently, as a raw-milk cheese aged less than 60 days, Reblochon, which is aged for between 50 and 55 days, was not legally allowed in the United States. But a few U.S. importers are instructing their French suppliers to age their cheeses a few extra days to meet USFDA requirements. As a result, Reblochon is occasionally available in the U.S. This A.O.C. cheese is one of my favorites. You must seek it out when you are in France.

Velvety Reblochon is always tucked between two paper-thin disks of wood before it is wrapped in paper. This paper wrap will also tell you if it's real Reblochon or not—look

A Savoie sampler (from left to right): a large half-disk of Tomme de Montagne, Tomme de Savoie, Perrin's diminutive Tomme de Yenne, and wrapped and unwrapped Reblochon.

for the words Haute-Savoie or village identities such as Thônes, La Clusaz, or Le Grand-Bornand. Regional identifiers will include Haute-Tarantaise and Aravis, the chain of Savoie mountains in which much Reblochon is made. The terms *fermier, moulé à la main* (milk ladled by hand), and *au lait cru* are also dead giveaways of authenticity and they promise bliss.

Choosing and Serving Reblochon

Consider only 1-pound (500 g) sizes of Reblochon. Avoid half-sizes, as they are sure to be from a mass-producer. Some cheesemongers will allow you to purchase this cheese by the half. This will afford you the advantage of tasting before you buy. Make sure the café au lait–colored rind is smooth and dry, without cracks or sliminess. The interior should be ivory in color. Reblochon will be smelly but pleasantly so. Avoid Reblochon that has been wrapped in plastic.

I most enjoy this cheese outdoors, with a fruity red wine, a thick-crusted peasant bread, a coarse *saucisson sec* (dry salami), and fruit. My hope is that the USFDA will change its regulations and this joy of Savoie will again honor us with its presence.

BEAUMONT

Another cheese no longer to be found in the United States is a very well made, oversize Reblochon named Beaumont (bo-MAWH), after the town nearest its area of production. This is a cheese trademarked by Girod, the producers. It weighs about 3½ pounds (1¾ k), and is 1½ to 2 inches thick and about 8 inches in diameter. Lately it has been disallowed for export because it is not made with pasteurized milk. Even if it is no more than a bulk version of Reblochon, it is a very worthy, serious cheese and deserves to be mentioned. Indeed, Girod also makes fine Reblochon under the name Beulet.

Although a commercial outfit, Girod is an excellent company that distributes Comté and Tomme de Savoie from independent cheesemakers. They are committed to unassailable quality; look for their cheeses and try them for yourself.

Choosing and Serving Beaumont

Beaumont should have a healthy, outdoors, noticeably barnyardy aroma (as do Reblochon and Munster), not a rancid, mangy stench. Avoid any that smells like manure as opposed to the way it is supposed to smell—as though you were distantly downwind from a farm or ranch. Avoid any with a cracked rind or graying interior; the interior should be between ivory and straw in color. The flavor should be pronounced, but not strong.

Serve Beaumont with fruit and light, fruity red wine (a Rhône, for instance), at the end of a meal. It is wonderful melted on crusty bread and delicious in omelets. Beaumont is also a fine luncheon cheese with fruit, bread, and smoked ham.

WHEN IN SAVOIE

The following Savoie cheeses are well worth seeking out on a visit to this region. Next to impossible to locate in the U.S., they are difficult to find even in Paris *fromageries.*

- **Abondance** (ah-bone-DAH-NCE) also called **Tomme d'Abondance** (tum-DAH-bone-DAHNCE): An extraordinary, name-controlled cheese, made from partially skimmed raw cow's milk, that deserves 10 points on a 10-point scale. Made in large wheels, most weighing from 15 to 20 pounds (7½ to 10 k), it is similar in taste to Comté—firm, nutty, and sweet, with a gloriously ripe, almost funky fruitiness—although more complex and buttery. It is a great melting cheese often substituted for French or Swiss Raclette.

- **Persillé des Aravis** (pair-see-YAY-daze-ar-ah-VEE): A raw goat's milk (sometimes mixed with cow's milk) blue cheese that is firm-textured, chewy, and complex in flavor.

- **Raclette** (rack-LETT): It will surprise most people to learn that raclette, the dish, is as adored in the eastern part of France (Savoie, Franche-Comté) as it is in Switzerland. A succulent version of this cow's-milk cheese, quite a bit softer in texture than Swiss Raclette cheeses made in the canton of Valais, is produced in small quantities in Savoie and Franche-Comté (it is nearly identical to Morbier). Some versions are excellent, but not all are of top quality. The labels of the best examples will say *au lait cru* and indicate "Fabriqué en Savoie" (or Franche-Comté). Avoid ones that specify *pasteurisé* or "Fabriqué en Poitou" or Charente, Angoumois, or Normandie; though aged, they are flavorless.

- **Tamié** (TAH-mee-yay): A Trappist cheese, similar to Reblochon, with a pudding-soft texture, off-white interior, and a thin, cappuccino-colored rind. The raw cow's milk flavor of this 1-pound (500 g) cheese abounds with fruitiness and nuttiness.

- **Tavaillon** (tah-vah-YONE): Another extraordinary cheese produced by Girod in Beaumont. Like Vacherin Mont d'Or, it is ringed by the bark of an indigenous tree we know as larch. This bark, which is boiled before being wrapped around the circumference of the 3-pound (1½ k) cheese, contributes its fascinating, balsamy essence. To me, this raw cow's milk wonder tastes like a cross between Reblochon and Vacherin Mont d'Or. And that's not a bad place to be!

PERIGORD AND QUERCY

(Aquitaine)

During Roman times Aquitaine was a huge province, a sprawl of land that included Périgord and Quercy, Gascony to the south, the Rouergue to the east, and reached as far north as Angoulême in Angoumois and Limoges in Limousin. Today Aquitaine is part of the *département* of Gironde, which also includes Bordeaux. The Périgord and Quercy regions are sort of "Aquitaine Central," and it is there that some fine goat's-milk cheeses are made.

Périgord got its name from its pre-Roman inhabitants, the Petrocores. Quercy comes from the Latin *quercus,* for oak, since Quercy is home to the famed Limousin oak trees, which also grow around Limoges, to the north. Barrels made from this special oak are much sought after, used to age and impart their unique flavor and qualities to all types of wines and spirits in France and elsewhere.

While Quercy, Limousin, and Angoumois are of nominal importance to us in terms of cheeses we can buy in the U.S., all three areas have considerable output of *fermier* and *artisanale* goat's-milk cheeses. Some of these can be found at *fromageries* across France, but most are consumed in the same area where they are made—sold at village markets and cheese shops, and featured on the cheese trolleys of almost all the local restaurants.

Périgord and all that surrounds

Horses, reindeer, bulls, and bison frolic on the walls of the ancient caves of Lascaux in Périgord.

it is extraordinarily rich in reasons to visit. Its prehistoric treasures are well known—especially the caves at Lascaux, where ancient images of man and beast have astounded us since their discovery in 1940. Unfortunately the caves are no longer open to the public for fear that our very breath will lead to the further decomposition of these remarkable images.

The food of Périgord, too, is enough to make you want to live there. First, Périgord is contiguous with Bordeaux—less than an hour's drive away—and Bordeaux wines rule the region. And while the great ones are expensive anywhere, a dizzying selection of the near greats are at hand at considerably lower prices than in Paris or large American cities. Périgord is justly proud of its place in gastronomy. Besides the famous black truffles and *foie gras,* there are remarkable hams, walnuts, walnut oil, and freshwater fish and crayfish.

The Cheeses of Périgord

There are two cheesemakers in Périgord who specialize in goat cheese: Bernard Soreda and François Desport. Both men are highly esteemed and respected throughout France. Bernard Soreda is famous for his fancy, colorful little chèvres that are sweet, nutty, creamy, and

NOT WORTH THE PRICE

A few Périgord chèvre makers, including Bernard Soreda, augment their line by infusing chopped black truffles into the curd of some of their cheeses. This is a commercial convention, a nod to Périgord's tourist industry; the truffles add nothing but cost to the chèvre; they have no flavor, having come, packed in brine, from cans.

The nose knows. Périgord's pricey, pungent fresh truffles are called "black diamonds."

is probable the truffles came from another European country where they doubtless left their flavor. Canned or jarred truffles serve only as an effort to fill a recipe requirement when fresh truffles are unavailable. However, the truffled cheeses found in Italy's Piedmont and Umbria regions, where fresh white and black truffles impart their

These days, Pèrigord is practically truffled out, and it enormous flavor, are absolutely sublime.

rustic—never salty, never goaty, and always as pure as can be. He is a master cheesemaker who enjoys the trompe-l'oeil effect of crafting his cheeses into things they are not.

Soreda puts four or five little disks on a stick and calls it a "brochette." His *taupinières* are "molehills," perfectly hemispherical, 7-ounce (210 g) herbed, spiced, or ashed chèvres perched on flawless chestnut leaves. Soreda also makes a classic *tomme,* a 2-pound (1 k) disk, wrapped in chestnut leaves, as well as tiny little balls of goat cheese that weigh about half

an ounce (15 g) each. These he arranges in four neat rows nestled into a protective straw mat; he covers one row with chopped dill, another with paprika, the third with black ash, and the fourth row he leaves unembellished. They look like a nest of multicolored quail's eggs. They're perfect.

Soreda creates even more endearing cheeses than these. For example, he offers *cerises* (cherries)—tiny rounds of goat cheese coated with cherry-red paprika with a fresh pine needle stuck into the tops. The first time I saw them, I thought they were real fruit. When they arrive fresh, the chestnut leaf these cheeses sit on is vividly colored, having been plucked from its tree the very day the cheese was turned out of its mold. As they ripen, the leaf dries out and begins to turn brown. In France, you can always judge the age of the cheese by the color of the leaf—it's a perfect presentation. But in the U.S. the USFLA has cracked down, saying, "No more cheese on leaves. The leaf might be dirty." So those sent to the U.S. come on paper leaves instead.

Soreda's farm-style operation is in Beaumont-en-Périgord, a tiny spot on the road near the bustling town of Périgueux. About 15 miles north of there, in a town called Nontron, you'll find François Desport. Desport's signature cheese shape is called a *berace*, which means "beggar's purse." Picture the child who runs away from home and puts a change of clothes and an apple or pear in a cloth and ties it to the end of a stick like a hobo. That's the shape of Desport's goat cheese beggar's purses.

The cheese is made by taking a fist-size hunk of drained curd, packing it by hand like a snowball, placing it in a piece of cheesecloth, tightly twisting the gathered ends together, then loosening them to release a wrinkled little fig-shape ball with the suggestion of a pointed top. Then it is sprinkled with ash or herbs or left natural, and as with Bernard Soreda's *taupinières* and little barrel-shaped *chabis,* it is usually placed on an oak or chestnut leaf. It's a stunning goat cheese to

look at, and it can be eaten right away—fresh and sweet and mild— or aged under climate-controlled conditions for a week or two, until it is buff-colored, less creamy, and develops a more piquant flavor.

The aging process for these cheeses, which are sold at specialty food shops in the U.S., can be accomplished in your refrigerator. Avoid plastic wrap, and instead, loosely shroud the chèvre in the flimsiest paper you can find. (I use thin leaves of the unwaxed paper found in bakeries and paper shops and at some cheese counters, but you can also use cheesecloth.) Depending on the age of the cheese when you buy it, leave it to ripen in the vegetable compartment of your refrigerator for three weeks to two months. The length of time depends on personal taste.

In the countryside, a hand-painted sign advises: "Buy directly from the farm."

A BED OF STRAW

In the U.S., too many merchants put cheese on a metal shelf in the store, or wrap it in plastic, or put it in a cardboard box.

In France, the serious cheeses are put on mats that are woven from beautiful blond-gold straw that has been sewn together. This allows air to pass beneath the cheese (through the straw) and keeps it from getting mushy, so that the bottom stays as fresh and firm as the top and sides.

Another Desport creation is his *bicorne* (two-horns)—a cheese that is twisted a bit differently in its cheesecloth so that it forms two horns. This cheese, too, is placed on an oak (or paper) leaf. Desport is also responsible for the popular French goat cheese, Tomme Fleur Verte (TUM-FLUR-VAIRT). Desport's Tomme Fleur Verte is a 5-pound (2½ k), 3-inch-thick, 9-inch-diameter, scallop-sectioned wheel of chèvre that is covered with fresh savory and tarragon, and a little bit of dried thyme, which give it a lovely salad-green color. All in all, it's a rich, flaky—very expensive—"cake" of goat cheese.

Desport's Cabécou (dialect for "little goat" and pronounced CAB-bay-koo) is a 1-ounce (30 g) button, wrapped in chestnut leaves and pinned with a wooden toothpick. In France, you can gauge the cheese's ripeness by the color of the leaf as it fades from green to brown with age. When the leaf begins to lose its chlorophyll, the little chèvre inside is generally very creamy, rather than dry, since the leaves cause the cheese to retain moisture. The chèvre's color will have changed from white to beige and the flavor will be truly delicious—intensely nutty and fruity. Cabécou are lovely and elegant served one per person with the salad course.

My newest Périgord chèvre producer is Picandine in Saint-Astier. Their cheeses are flawless and presented in the typically fancy, pleasing idiom. Look for the buff-colored, custard-soft Pico, 6-ounce (180 g) disks in little wooden boxes. Their flavor is the very essence of nutty—an altogether perfect cheese that is a joy to me and my customers.

The Cheeses of Quercy

ROCAMADOUR

Though the goat cheeses of Quercy are splendid, only one—Rocamadour (ROH-cah-mah-dore)—is famous. For all intents and purposes, it's a Cabécou, named after the nearest town, an ancient village built into the side of a mountain. This part of Quercy is physically dramatic—rather like our South-

Each tiny button of Rocamadour, a nutty-tasting chèvre, is a mere quarter inch thick. These labels are shown actual size.

west, rocky and somewhat barren. It is a popular hiking and camping area, and were it not for Rocamadour's touristy overkill (souvenir shops and fast-food outlets line the village's main street), it would be completely charming.

Each small disk of this raw goat's milk cheese weighs about an ounce (30 g), and is only 2 inches in diameter and ¼ inch thick. Although they are available young, Rocamadour are at their best after two to three weeks of ripening, and will have a soft, dry, beige crust with grid marks from the mesh surfaces they are placed on as they mature. The unctuous interior is agreeably nutty tasting with a peppery bite (young cheeses are soft and sweet-tasting). As Rocamadour fully matures, it becomes darker inside and out, turning brown and chewy, with an intensely goaty flavor. When shopping for this cheese, look for examples made by Fromagerie Artisanale de Roc-Amadour (the label identifies the cheese as Le Roc-Amadour).

So Cute

C abécou s a dialect word from Languedoc that refers to a "little goat" or a little goat cheese. They come from numerous farms and small cheesemakers in many locales all over west and southwest France, particularly from Quercy and Angoumois. They are always tiny disks or buttons of various sizes and configurations and are found at many ages— from very white, soft, and mild to very brown, hard, and strong. Their color, which ranges from light to dark, is a good indication of how far their flavor has developed. I find them almost always palatable, if not delightful, up to the point at which they are offensively goaty smelling and tasting. Rare in the U.S., they are sold in France by the tiny unit, so you will probably be unable to taste before purchasing. No matter—use your good goat cheese instinct. Serve as you would any other goat cheese. If young, they are perfect for heating and placing atop a serving of chilled salad greens or nestled in a baked potato.

AUVERGNE AND ROUERGUE (THE CAUSSES)

AUVERGNE is the classical name for a region a little bit south and east of the geographical center of France. Politically, it includes most of three *départements*—the Puy-de-Dôme, Cantal, Haute-Loire—and part of two more, Aveyron and Allier. Maps also refer to the Auvergne as the Massif Central, a name that sort of lumps the many separate mountain ranges into one identifiable unit.

The area is known for its good skiing, for its extreme remoteness, and for its people—in many ways the French equivalent of hillbillies of the Ozark Mountains of Arkansas and Missouri near where I grew up. They have a particular sartorial style, and strictly Auvergnat speech patterns and dialect. And naturally, their cuisine is distinctly regional. Many of the physical trappings are worn for effect—authentic regionalism melded with self-promotion, which translate into tourism revenue. But I believe they deserve everything they gain, for the Auvergne is the source of the most stunning array of cheeses in the world.

Cantal and other specialties are for sale at the Auvergne region's own shop in Paris.

Four great rivers are born in the Auvergne—the Loire, the Cher, the Dordogne, and the Lot. The fertile areas of the region are not easily accessible, separated by the rugged mountain ranges that make up the Massif Central. But such great quantities of fruit and vegetables come from there that the Auvergne has its own special-interest group with an office in Paris, a testimony to the hard work and skill of these farmers.

The Cheeses

SAINT-NECTAIRE

In the north of the Auvergne, near the lovely skiing capital of Mont-Dore in the highest part of the mountains, is a town called Saint-Nectaire. It was named for a member of the leading family of this area in the seventeenth century whose name was then spelled Sennecterre. Today, it is a decent-size farm town known for an A.O.C. cheese that predates its own name. It became famous for its cheeses around the same time as the town was incorporated, the cheese having been presented to Louis XIV. Apparently, he loved it.

The best Saint-Nectaire (SAN-neck-TARE) is made on farms from raw cow's milk. We cannot legally import these name-controlled cheeses to the U.S. because of USFDA aging requirements for raw-milk cheeses. (They must be aged for 60 days or longer.) But though I confess to worshipping the joys of Saint-Nectaire *fermier* (farm-made), there are some excellent, non-*fermier* examples available. These cheeses are made by a few specific small producers who somehow manage to deliver that inimitable fresh, grassy aroma and flavor characteristic of *fermier* cheeses. The finest small producer of Saint-Nectaire is, in my opinion, Babut. Two firms tie for a very close second place: Allayrangue and Prugne. If other brands are all you can find, however, go ahead and give them a try. They will be decent enough and will give you an idea of the taste of the real thing. But be warned: Mass-produced, pasteurized Saint-Nectaire is bland and banal with one exception. The only factory-made brand that is acceptable is Roussel, which has a full round flavor that reminds me of black walnuts.

Saint-Nectaire is made in 3½-pound (1¾ k) disks, 1½ inches thick, 8 inches in diameter. It is an unsalty cheese with a fruity flavor and the buttery texture of beef tenderloin. The rind will harbor up to four separate strains of bacteria, each adding its own color and aroma and causing the cheese to ripen according to age-old specifications. It may sound peculiar, but I often smell lettuce in the rind of a Saint-Nectaire. These bacteria are not only desirable, they are anticipated. Unfortunately, most factory-made Saint-Nectaire is ripened in such clinical facilities that these molds are unable to contribute their desirable essences.

In France, *fermier* Saint-Nectaire cheeses bear an oval green stamp on their rinds (though it often is obscured by mold growth). All other Saint-Nectaire (from small producers and factories) bears a square green stamp. The interior of the cheese will be ivory- to straw-colored with an occasional errant "eye" or tiny hole structure. Often there will be no holes at all. Either way, they don't suggest any qualitative difference.

Saint-Nectaire is best in the summer and autumn, as its ripening period of two months means that the high mountain pastures of spring and summer with their lush flowers, herbs, and grasses would have contributed their essences to the milk. It is this highly flavorful milk that results in the best cheese.

Until 1964 all Saint-Nectaire was fermier, *made on farms from raw milk. Today there are some fine examples from small producers, but avoid factory-made versions.*

Choosing and Serving Saint-Nectaire

A void any wheel of Saint-Nectaire that has a cracked or slimy rind and/or a bulging or reddening interior. The rind should be smooth and reddish in color. (This rind is inedible, as are all natural, brushed rinds.) Saint-Nectaire's aroma should be earthy and grassy, never sharp and unpleasant. The flavor should be mild and fruity.

Serve Saint-Nectaire anytime you want to enjoy a creamy, tasty, semisoft cow's-milk cheese. You can pair it with just about anything—fruits, raw vegetables, olives, ham or salami, nuts, dried fruit, bread, or crackers.

Saint-Nectaire has too much flavor to be enjoyed with a simple white wine, lest the wine be overwhelmed. It is better with good Rhône reds, not-too-expensive Saint-Emilions and Médocs, a Beaujolais, or a Chianti. But the best wine for it is Chanturgue, a big, beefy red from the Auvergne.

milk *(gape)*, from which it was once made. Buttermilk is very low in fat, and indeed, before World War II farm-made, low-fat Gaperons were plentiful. Today, there are not only fewer farms but hardly any small-scale butter producers, and cheese production has been taken over by commercial cheesemakers who prefer to make Gaperon from partially skimmed cow's milk. (With the current level of interest in "diet" cheeses, unless I miss my guess, I fully expect to see real buttermilk Gaperons back on the market any day now.)

Gaperon is not a subtle cheese. It is spiked—liberally—with chunks of garlic and cracked peppercorns. Garlic has always been an important cash crop in the Auvergne, and certainly the cuisine reeks of it (doubtless the reason I love it so). Apart from the garlic and pepper, the flavor of the cheese itself is slightly salty, buttery, and not unlike a good Brie or Camembert. Young (underripe) Gaperon is mar-

GAPERON

G aperon (gah-PAIR-ohn) is a cheese that has been known in the Auvergne for at least 1,200 years. Its name is derived from the Auvergnat dialect word for butter-

Buttery Gaperon's Brie-like taste, powerfully augmented by chunks of garlic and bits of cracked black peppercorns, is best savored with a robust red, such as Côtes-du-Rhône.

In the old days, so the Auvergnat legend goes, when a young man returned home from military service, he would seek a wife. He would walk down the country lanes, observing the Gaperons drying on farmhouse windowsills. The young man would know that the number of cheeses being made within was directly related to the size of this farmer's herd—a clear indication of his wealth, and hence of the desirability of his daughters!

kedly tart and chalky-tasting, whereas those cheeses that have been allowed to age to perfection are pillow-soft, straw-colored, and bulging, if not slightly oozing. It is at this stage that I consider this cheese most enjoyable.

The shape of Gaperon is unusual and, I think, highly appealing: a flat-bottomed ball, about the size of a baseball. They weigh about 12 ounces (375 g).

For the last two decades, Garmy, the major producer of Gaperon, has been inoculating its cheeses with a strain of *Penicillium candidum* in order to produce the fuzzy white rind we associate with Brie and Camembert. This allows the cheese to ripen more conventionally, from the outside in. In the old days a natural crust formed on the outside as the cheeses dried, and often this dry-

ing was facilitated by hanging the cheeses in bunches over wood fires. Certainly, the woodsmoke played a role in the cheese's overall flavor.

Gaperons are bound up with raffia or yellow ribbon, and unless the fuzzy rind has overgrown it, you will find the cheese's label either on the top or the bottom.

Choosing and Serving Gaperon

Gaperon is one of those cheeses where "just right" is a matter of personal taste. It can be eaten at any stage: Young ones will feel firm and are chalky-whitish inside. Ripened Gaperon is soft and glisteningly gold and oozy inside. I like this stage because the flavor is strong enough to stand up to the cheese's usually liberal apportionment of garlic and pepper.

Ripened further, the cheese eventually becomes dry and firm, as it was when it was a young cheese, and is protected by a fuzzy crust. If very ripe, they will once again become soft and runny. Gaperon is a unique exception to a general rule about cheese: Practically all flavored cheeses are augmented in an attempt to obfuscate their blandness. This one is far from bland.

Gaperon is a pleasantly tender, tangy treat. At my house we make a meal of it with a salad, bread, and wine; we also put it in omelets. But our favorite preparation is to combine it with potatoes and bacon and fry the whole in butter, like a sort of pancake (see recipe, facing page).

THE JENKINS FAMILY'S GAPERON AND POTATO GRATIN

Makes 4 main course servings, serves 6 to 8 as a side dish

2 pounds (1 k) potatoes, peeled
¼ pound (125 g) Italian pancetta
(salt-cured, unsmoked Italian
bacon) or American bacon,
thickly sliced, rind trimmed
2 cloves garlic, peeled
3 tablespoons extra-virgin olive
oil
¾ pound (375 g) Gaperon
(approximately 1 whole
cheese)
Salt and freshly ground black
pepper to taste

1. Cut the potatoes into ¼-inch-thick rounds, and set them aside in cold water to prevent discoloration. Cut the pancetta or bacon into long narrow strips. Crush the garlic clove with the flat side of a kitchen knife.

2. Combine the pancetta, garlic, and olive oil in a large skillet and sauté over low heat until the pancetta is nicely browned.

3. While the pancetta is cooking, cut the cheese into ¼-inch slices.

4. When the pancetta is browned remove it from the skillet and set aside to drain on paper towels. Remove the garlic and discard it. Turn the heat up to medium-high. Adding about 10 potato slices at a time, sauté the potatoes in the skillet, allowing each batch to brown slightly before turning them and adding another layer of potatoes. As the potatoes cook, push them aside to make room for the additional slices. Continue sautéing until all of the potatoes have been added to the skillet and are thoroughly browned, crisp, and cooked through.

5. Sprinkle the pancetta over the potatoes and flip the potatoes over one last time. Season to taste with salt and pepper. (Remember, the pancetta and cheese will contribute salt to the dish, so go lightly.) Cover the potatoes with overlapping slices of cheese, evenly arranging them to cover the entire surface of the potatoes. Cover the skillet with a tight-fitting lid. Count to 10 slowly, then turn off the heat. Keeping the skillet covered, wait—using all your reserves of self-control—for 1 full minute. Then uncover the skillet and serve immediately.

Gaperon is most enjoyable as a luncheon or snack cheese with light, fruity wines or beer, crackers or crusty bread, and makes a perfect accompaniment to crudités. It works beautifully as a cocktail cheese, too; its garlic and pepper flavors stand up boldly to mixed drinks as well as to olives or spicier fare. In fact, Gaperon is one of the few cheeses I recommend as an appetizer, because its flavor is stimulating to the appetite, assuming one refrains from gorging on it.

FOURME D'AMBERT

Fourme d'Ambert (FORM-dom-BAIR) takes its name from the wooden mold or form traditionally used to shape the cheese into its cylindrical shape about 8 inches high and 4 to 5 inches in diameter. Originally, the milk for Fourme d'Ambert came from pastures around the town of Ambert. Today, though, the cheese is made in factories in several locations within the Auvergne region, but miles from these original pastures.

Fourme d'Ambert is an ancient cow's-milk blue cheese, one first made long before the English Stilton that it resembles visually and in terms of recipe and flavor. Fourme is not as crumbly as Stilton—unlike Stilton, it is a pressed cheese. If it has been well made, it

is sharp and mellow at the same time, not salty, with a big perfume of fruit and wood. And it is smaller—5 pounds (2½ k) compared to 14- to 16-pound (7 to 8 k) cylinders of Stilton. If we had before us prime examples of a fine Stilton and a Fourme d'Ambert, I would challenge you to tell me that the Stilton has the depth of flavor of the Fourme. When I hear Stilton-lovers raving about their favorite cheese, I like to provide tastes of each in order to give this creamier, moister French treasure its due.

As with Saint-Nectaire, there are great examples of Fourme d'Ambert and there are the ordinary, mass-produced examples, which still are rather good—far better than most blue cheeses made in Scandinavia or the United States. It is a sumptuous cheese, a good old trencherman's mouthful of blue

Although it is not as well known as other blues such as Roquefort, Gorgonzola, or Stilton, Fourme d'Ambert is one of the world's finest cheeses.

cheese—not nearly as sharp as Danish Blue, not smelly like Gorgonzola, and not wet and sticky like Roquefort, which you often can eat only in little bits because it is so sharp. Fourme d'Ambert is simply one of the world's finest cheeses.

The gray-brown crust of Fourme d'Ambert is rough and inedible. The cheese is white to straw-colored. and should be very evenly speckled throughout with a definite blue, a decidedly navy blue color, rather than what the French call *persillé* (parsley), or a greenish-blue, as is found in some examples of Roquefort. In reality, the color of the blue in a blue cheese will darken with exposure to air, often in minutes, right before your eyes.

Fourme is very pretty (the pale, marble-like interior is a lovely contrast to the dark, rustic rind), not too hard, creamy but firm, and worthy of its distinction as one of France's 32 name-controlled cheeses.

Choosing and Serving Fourme d'Ambert

Avoid any batch of Fourme d'Ambert that has dried out. any that has obviously not sold quickly enough to retain its freshness (crucial with all cheeses), and any that shows a cracked rind or graying interior. Avoid Fourme that doesn't show liberal interior blueing and is mostly ivory- or straw-

JUST AS GOOD

The twin to Fourme d'Ambert is Fourme de Montbrison, an identical cheese from a neighboring village, but not produced much anymore because it has been superseded by the other's reputation. The makers fetch a better price by calling their cheese d'Ambert instead of Montbrison; that which remains, though, is identical to d'Ambert and equally wonderful.

colored rather than one that is visually arresting because of its blue. This pale variety is factory-made Fourme, mass-produced with little human attention. Also avoid any that is bitter-tasting or has a granular texture.

Fourme is excellent for lunch with bread and fruit, after dinner, and definitely at buffets. It is a marvelous cheese in a salad—either "pebbled" with a tiny melon-baller, or finely diced. There is nothing tastier than a very good apple with Fourme; the crispness of the apple contrasts perfectly with the smoothness of the cheese. By the same token, the creamy pears of the Auvergne, and our own Comice, go very well with Fourme and offer a completely different taste experience. At home, my wife, Michelle, and I have been known to toss Fourme d'Ambert with pasta. We also enjoy tiny balls of Fourme sur-rounding a 6-ounce (180 g) cylinder of fresh chèvre.

This cheese calls for a big red wine, but doesn't demand a *great* red—very often the flavor of a lesser-quality wine is enhanced by the flavor of a cheese. Bordeaux and Burgundy are frequent com-panions, as are my chosen few—the Rhônes, Châteauneuf-du-Pape, Saint-Joseph, Côtes-du-Rhône, and Gigondas. I wouldn't recommend beer with this cheese, because I don't like blue cheeses with beer. I find that it obfuscates the complex

VISITING THE AUVERGNE

I urge you to go to the Auvergne because it's still unspoiled—remote and wild. I've been there only in the bad weather of the wintery months and still I was captivated by its purity and beauty. Lately, too, its fine regional rest-aurants have come into their own.

Restaurant Michel Bras in Laguiole (Aveyron): Michel Bras, the famous owner/chef, was trained by his mother, not by a master chef.

Restaurant Jean-Yves Bath in Clermont-Ferrand Puy-de-Dôme.

Restaurant Auberge Fleurie in Montsalvy (Cantal): A classic inn with a motherly chef/owner who will prepare whatever is fresh that day. Simple, friendly, fun, memorable.

La Maison des Fromages (cheese museum) in Egliseneuve-d'Entraigues (Puy-de-Dôme): Don't miss it. It contains more than you'll ever want to know about the making of cheese.

flavor of a good blue, giving it an almost bitter sensation.

CANTAL AND SALERS

Name-controlled Cantal (kahn-TAHL), also called Cantal de Salers (kahn-TAHL-duh-sah-LAIR) or Fourme du Cantal (FORM-doo-kahn-TAHL), is named for the Cantal Mountains in Auvergne. Cantal and Salers (sah-LAIR), which is also called Fourme du Salers (FORM-doo-sah-LAIR), its nearly identical name-controlled counterpart, are among the world's oldest cheeses—Pliny the Elder wrote about them 2,000 years ago. As tall as a fireplug, but much bigger around, Cantal and Salers are both huge beer keg-size cow's-milk cheeses weighing around 80 pounds (40 k). Both of these semi-firm cheeses have a moist beige paste and a smooth, dry, grayish-brown rind. Today, Cantal is ubiquitous, as a result of being mass-produced in vast quantities from pasteurized milk in factories centered around Aurillac in the lowlands. The factory-made examples are mild-flavored with a hint of tangy butteriness. Raw-milk Cantal, which is

sharper and has greater depth of flavor, is relatively rare.

Salers, however, has remained an artisanal cheese, made from raw milk in mountain *burons* (stone huts). Named for the famous cheese-making, dairy, and cattle center in the Cantal area of Auvergne, and for Auvergne's famous chestnut-colored Salers cattle that provide the milk from which it is made, the cheese is infinitely more authentic and rustic, and its fuller taste is evocative of flowers and herbs.

Cantal and Salers are often compared to Cheddar—an error, in my judgment. Though they are big cheeses and a little bit sharp with buttery overtones, their recipe is different; their texture is not nearly as dense as Cheddar. With the exception of farmhouse Cheddar from Somerset, the milk used for most Cheddars doesn't compare to the quality of the milk from the few Salers cattle that remain. Even the least-good factory-produced Cantal possesses considerable merit, having far better flavor than common-

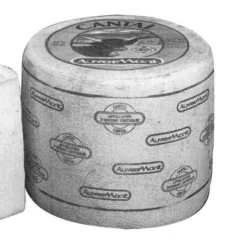

Mild, buttery-flavored Cantal has been made since antiquity.

place American and English factory-made Cheddars.

Choosing and Serving Cantal and Salers

Look for Cantal and Salers that have a smooth, dry rind with hardly any cracks and a beige- to straw-colored paste with no mold streaks or graying. The inedible crust of the cheeses has a tendency to crack, allowing mold to develop in the cheese. The French call this condition *fleurs de bleu* and just keep eating. I recommend that you trim it off—although it's certainly not going to hurt you.

Make sure your cheesemonger cuts Cantal or Salers correctly. I often see Cantal in particular cut so that many portions have a disproportionate amount of rind, that is, a piece cut too close to the outside of the form. You needn't pay for an excess of it. If your cheesemonger markets it properly, he or she will show an entire form but with an enormous wedge removed from it. This effect is irresistible—like a mountain with a huge chunk taken away. Avoid Cantal or Salers that tastes at all bitter—it simply is not fresh and has been in the store too long. The flavor should be mild, but with a lingering, slightly acidic finish. All brands of Cantal and Salers are excellent, but I don't recommend the small 20-pound (10 k) drums of factory-made Cantalet, which are made from pasteurized milk.

Cantal and Salers are a delight for lunch or as a snack. They are delicious planed off in thin slices onto bread with lettuce and ham, or just by themselves in a sandwich with sweet butter. I love to serve these cheeses at midafternoon in their singular glory with fruit—pears, apples, grapes—crusty bread, and a simple red wine. I often enjoy Cantal or Salers cubed into salads with crumbled walnuts. They also melt nicely, though not with the quality of texture and flavor of Comté or Swiss Gruyère (or Beaufort or Swiss Raclette from the canton of Valais). Cantal and Salers are also fine after-dinner cheeses, especially served with a robust Madiran.

ALIGOT

The fresh (unripened) curds of Cantal or Salers are called *aligot* (or *tomme fraîche*) and are used in one of the signature dishes—also called *aligot*—of the Auvergne. It's a mixture of mashed potatoes, garlic, bacon, and Cantal curd that is baked in the oven. There is a great Auvergnat restaurant in Paris, the Ambassade d'Auvergne, on the Rue du Grenier–Saint-Lazare in the third *arrondissement.* You can bet that *aligot* will be available along with those neighbors of the Auvergne, Madiran and Cahors wine, and, of course, all the cheeses of the Auvergne.

ROUERGUE (THE CAUSSES)

Traveling south from mountainous, wooded Auvergne you will find yourself in Rouergue, the birthplace of Roquefort. The sprawling expanses of the Rouergue region and of the prime cheese-producing area called the Causses (a sub-region of Languedoc) encompass a series of flat, high, rocky plateaus given dramatic dynamics by cliffs and gorges. For eons this has been quintessential sheep pasturage, though to a lesser extent cattle also graze here.

The Lacaune sheep that inhabit this austere landscape are able to weather the seasonal extremes well and remain in their pastures all year round. (This contradicts the tales about their fragility—some owners don't consider them hardy. In fact, it is said, they never sleep outside!) The sky and horizon open up to reveal a broad plain stretching far to the south toward the Pyrénées, east to the Rhône, and west toward Gascony.

Parts of Rouergue are lovely—rolling and grassy, with intermittent swaths of forest—but much of it, especially the Causses in the eastern part, is monotonous, severe, foreboding, and windy. Here, I am reminded

A view from the caves of Cambalou: The serpentine village of Roquefort-sur-Soulzon clings to the sides of the famous honeycomb grottoes where this famous cheese acquires its unique flavor.

of Spain's La Mancha. Huge tracts of Rouergue have been rendered off limits by the French government, which uses them for weapons testing and as military training sites. The dramatic, noisy appearance in the sky of French-made Mirage jet fighter-bombers is commonplace. Toulouse, to the south, is the largest city for miles in any direction.

Though workmanlike and rather severe (it reminds me a bit of Poitier in Poitou), I rather like Toulouse, and I love tooling around rural Rouergue fueled by copious quantities of cassoulet, the famous slow-cooked casserole composed of various combinations of beans, garlic, confit of goose or duck, sausages, and various meats.

The Cheeses

....

ROQUEFORT

Roquefort (roke-FORE) must be the most intensely flavored cheese of all, though Spanish Cabrales is a close second. I cannot think of any other food that possesses such complexity of flavor. Its ancient roots lie in the Rouergue, an area of southern France, where its production predates recorded history.

The creation of Roquefort is not complicated, though great pains are taken to ensure its quality. Besides protecting the cheese, The Roquefort Association, Inc., has made great strides in the past century, perfecting techniques for artificial insemination of sheep, providing a specific chemical-free diet, and improving the milking process and the milk's quality. In addition, it acts as the cheese's guardian against name infringement, and most importantly, keeps the price of the cheese high enough to provide a living for all those involved in the business of making Roquefort.

Choosing and Serving Roquefort

All Roquefort is good—some is just saltier than others. My favorite brands—and this is subjec-

THE FAMOUS CAVES OF CAMBALOU

The limestone *caves* of Cambalou, near the town of Roquefort-sur-Soulzon, are the locus of the world's most famous cheese. Every square inch of the mile and a half of cellars below the limestone plateau have been turned into a geological corporate headquarters for Roquefort, a business never more prosperous than it is today.

At some points there are 11 separate levels, each given to a specific function. At the top are offices and loading docks. The lower levels are the famous ripening rooms, the vaulted *caves* that have the *fleurines,* the currents of air that pass through the rock fissures and allow the *caves* to breathe. The natural presence of this constant flow of air maintains the damp, cool atmosphere that encourages the growth of mold that transform simple sheep's milk into Roquefort.

tive—are Le Papillon, Gabriel Coulet (the only maker who still adds the mold by hand), Carles, and Cons ans-Crouzat. If you cannot read the maker's name on the foil, at least try to find the red sheep seal that only real Roquefort is permitted to bear. Taste as many Roqueforts as you can before selecting your own favorites. Buy Roquefort at a shop where a considerable amount of cheese goes out the door—you don't want to purchase any that has been in the store too long.

Roquefort should be crumbly, but cohesive; it should hold together and not fall apart under its own weight. It should be ivory-colored, not yellowish, and the veins of green-blue mold should be profuse and extensive, reaching right to the outside edge of the cheese. Roquefort has no rind, so everything within the foil wrap can be eaten, though the exterior will be salty. There should be little or no moisture or mold on the surface. If the choice at hand is insufferably salty, reject it.

I have never cottoned to the practice of blending Roquefort into a dressing for salad. For this purpose, any blue cheese, such as Danish Blue, will do, and at one-third to

Heavenry, strong-flavored blues such as classic Roquefort (always made from raw sheep's milk) or the less well known Bleu des Causses (made from raw cow's milk), are marbled with bluish-green mold. Rindless, soft, and a bit crumbly, they are always wrapped in foil.

MAKING ROQUEFORT

The making of Roquefort cheese begins with the careful shipping of sheep's milk to the various *laiteries* (cheese-making facilities) in the area—not in tanker trucks but in trucks bearing *bidons,* stainless steel churn-shaped, 40-liter milk containers. (Tankers bounce the milk around too much, which breaks up the fat globules in sheep's milk.) On arrival, the whole milk is tested and filtered into water-jacketed stainless-steel vats. This milk is never pasteurized or homogenized. Next, it is usually renneted with the Roquefort region's scarce and costly lambs' rennet (although at least one maker uses calf's rennet) at about 85°F (29°C), and left undisturbed for about two hours. The resulting

In cool vaulted ripening rooms, carved into the limestone caves of Cambalou, air currents called fleurines encourage the growth of Penicillium roqueforti, the mold responsible for Roquefort's characteristic green-blue veining and deep flavor.

curd is then cut into small cubes, stirred to expel more whey, and lifted onto pieces of cloth lying on wicker grids, where even more whey can seep out.

Next, the curds are hand ladled into draining molds, and it is at this point that the special mold, *Penicillium roqueforti,* is added. Some cheesemakers add the mold by hand, some by machine; each cheesemaker has his own formula, method, and point at which the mold is added, but the result is the same.

To obtain this mold, the cheesemakers buy rye grown in the nearby area of Lévézou, and have huge, oval, 10- to 20-pound (5 to 10 k) loaves of rye bread made from it. The loaves are baked until the crusts are almost black. Then they are set aside to rot—literally, the moist bread in the interior becomes host to the essential mold spores. After a month or two, the loaves are split and the mold is dried, ground, and sifted before being combined with the curd.

Once the mold is added, the cheeses, still in their cylindrical draining molds, go into a room where they are turned frequently for about a week. They are then removed from their molds and marked with a date and vat number. At this point the cheeses have lost about 4 ounces (125 g) of their original weight. Roquefort starts out at about 7 pounds (3½ k). Ultimately, these cheeses will weigh 5½ to 6½ pounds (2¾ to 3¼ k), and will be about 4 inches high and 8 inches in diameter. They are stored at 50°F (10°C) and 98% humidity until the twice-weekly trucks arrive to transport them to the nearby caves of Cambalou, where the alchemy begins.

Upon arrival in the drafty, damp, well-ordered caves, the cheeses are salted and pierced to allow carbon dioxide to escape

Dry salted wheels of Roquefort are pierced with long needles to promote blueing. Then the young cheeses are placed with great care on moistened antique oak planks where they will ripen for at least three months.

and moist oxygen to enter and encourage the growth of the mold. After a short period most of the salt is brushed off, and the cheeses are scraped and placed on 15- to 20-foot-long moist oak planks. Some of these planks are 180 years old, and they are crucial to the process: They exude into the cheese a sort of intensified atmosphere of temperature and humidity.

Cheeses rest on these planks to ripen for a minimum of three months. After this ripening period they are actually ready to be eaten, but they won't be released onto the market immediately. Instead, they are stored elsewhere, but still *en cave,* until the market calls for them—as little as another three months or even up to a year. I feel that any cheese that sits at near-freezing temperatures in complete humidity for too long is not going to benefit. The delay robs the cheese of a considerable amount of aroma, texture, and flavor. The brands that are stored for a shorter time are the ones I seek out.

one-fourth of the price. The deep, full, spicy, round flavor of Roquefort is denigrated when used in this way. It deserves solo billing *alongside* a salad; then, both tastes are elevated, rather than diminished.

Roquefort provides a royal finish to a meal. If you don't choose a sweet dessert wine, I recommend the big reds. As a bonus, Roquefort has the property of making less-expensive wines taste like they cost more. I have paired Roquefort with Sauternes, Bordeaux's famous, sweet white wine, and I recommend it without reservation. A less expensive Château Suduiraut will please you, I promise, just as much as a Château d'Yquem, and you won't have to sell the car to afford it.

LAGUIOLE

A bit farther south of the Cantal Mountains is another range of the Massif Central from which hails a cheese that looks almost exactly like Cantal and Salers (see page 151) but with a straighter, less barrel-shape form. Laguiole (lah-YOLE or lie-YULL) is one of my favorite cheeses, magnificent in both flavor and size. It is called either Laguiole or Laguiole-Aubrac (lah-YOLE or lie-YULL-oh-BROCK) after two tiny towns about 30 miles apart (which actually lie within the classical region called Rouergue). Rare Salers and Aubrac cattle graze the pastures between the two towns.

The difference between Cantal and Laguiole is that the comparatively tiny production of the latter is never pasteurized and is aged longer. Therefore it is a bit firmer, a bit tighter in texture, and has much more presence—a sharp, bursting tang that some people just don't appreciate. I find it a remarkable achievement that cattle and man can produce something that tastes so good and gives the additional bonus of hints of mountain gentian, fennel, and thyme. Laguiole is a very rare cheese—it's even hard to find in Paris—but a few of us dedicated U.S. cheesemongers always keep it in stock. The name is stamped in red all over the dry, grayish-brown rind, much the same way "Parmigiano Reggiano" (without a hyphen) is always burned into the rind of that cheese. The straw-colored interior is crumbly but very moist. Laguiole is made in 70- to 80-pound (35 to 40 k) barrel shapes that are as high as they are wide (about 16 inches).

Choosing and Serving Laguiole

Watch that the flavor of the Laguiole you're considering buying is not so pronounced that it's unpleasant; it can become overly strong. Though it breaks my heart to admit it, I've thrown away a lot of Laguiole. If it stings your tongue or has a bitter flavor, it isn't good. If it's too soft or is off-color, with whitish patches, then don't fool yourself: The cheese is dead.

Don't let a cracked rind bother you too much when considering Laguiole, or its neighbor Cantal. This is natural, as this very heavy, moist cheese must settle and dry out a bit during its life in transit. Nor should a bit of interior mold be of too much concern. Though I am leery of any cheese bearing unintentional mold, with Laguiole and Cantal it is often present. Simply trim it away. As with all cheeses, taste first; don't reject it because of a little show of blue mold. The cheese just may be delicious.

Laguiole is a dream anytime—with pears, apples, crusty bread, coarse *saucisson sec* (dry salami), prosciutto, or smoked ham. I enjoy it with strong, sappy red wines such as Côtes-du-Rhône and Hermitage.

BLEU DES CAUSSES AND BLEU D' AUVERGNE

Bleu des Causses (bluh-duh-KOSE) and Bleu d'Auvergne

The great cheeses of Auvergne and Rouergue: foil-wrapped Fourme d'Ambert (left) and Bleu d'Auvergne (front), a giant wedge of Laguiole (far right), an unwrapped wheel of Saint-Nectaire (right front). A small dome of raffia-tied Gaperon rests near a steel tool used to test cheeses for ripeness.

BLUEPRINT

In the aftermath of World War II, at a time when blue cheeses such as French Roquefort and English Stilton were in great demand and short supply, Danish cheesemakers seized the moment to create a new blue. Using Bleu d'Auvergne and Bleu des Causses as models, they began making a cheese that we know today as Danish Blue.

Danish Blue is made with big machinery and modern technology. It is a flawless blue cheese but comparatively uninteresting and one dimensional, with a predominant flavor of salt.

Bleu d'Auvergne and Bleu des Causses, particularly Bleu des Causses, have a fuller, more complex flavor, and rarely are oversalted.

In the Auvergne cheeses you can taste the grass and milk, as well as the cheese and its blue; you are aware of clover, wild onions, wildflowers, grass, and nuts, in addition to other undertones frequently found in handmade cheeses—fruit, wood, and occasionally a hint of woodsmoke. These are simply more flavorful cheeses than Danish Blue.

(bluh-doe-VAIRN), two very important French cheeses, are, like Fourme d'Ambert, name-controlled blue cheeses. Bleu des Causses, made in 5- to 5½-pound (2½ to 2¾ k) wheels, is from Rouergue, a small area that is contiguous to Auvergne. Bleu des Causses is always unpasteurized and therefore has a bit more complex and interesting flavor than Bleu d'Auvergne, which is always pasteurized. The texture is creamier than Bleu d'Auvergne although the recipe is the same; the difference is in the quality of the milk. The chalky, barren Causses hills, just south of the Cantal mountains in southern Auvergne, are a desolate, nearly treeless area—territory for goats and, primarily, sheep. But there are a few folds in the hills where the more fertile valleys support the famous cattle that provide milk for this centuries-old cheese.

Causses cattle are superior milkers, meaning they yield more milk per pound—even more than Auvergne cattle, which is saying a lot. This is odd because the diet of the Causses is much less rich than the rest of the Auvergne. Causses cattle really have to move around and work at grazing to get their fill, the reason, I believe, for their milk's high fluid-to-butterfat ratio. This is in contrast to the Auvergne cow, which merely needs to stand and pivot in order to graze on the lush grasses surrounding her.

The domain of Bleu d'Auvergne encompasses the entire area of the

Auvergne, where this classic cheese has been made without major changes for centuries. Bleu d'Auvergne made in 6-pound (3 k) wheels that are 4 inches high, 8 inches in diameter, is your "basic blue," not at all a complicated cheese. It is rather sharp, with a grand rustic flavor, always of high quality, and suitable for any blue cheese recipe.

You won't have much trouble finding Bleu d'Auvergne because it's made by volume producers who supply supermarkets in France, Europe, and the United States. Bleu des Causses, on the other hand, is made by only a very few small producers and is quite rare. Only the most dedicated cheesemongers will endeavor to provide it for their customers.

You may have heard of Bleu de Laqueuille (bluh-duh-lah-KAY-yuh). Laqueuille is an Auvergne town where, in about 1840, a cheese was developed that rivaled the popularity of Bleu d'Auvergne. An almost negligible amount is made today by artisans; virtually all is now industrialized and identical to, and in fact sold as, Bleu d'Auvergne.

Choosing and Serving Bleu des Causses and Bleu d'Auvergne

The foil wrappers on Bleu des Causses and Bleu d'Auvergne obscure the salty rinds, but the interior (bone-white for Bleu des Causses, beige for Bleu d'Auvergne), should be liberally and evenly blued, with no evidence of reddening or browning. The cheese should not have an overly strong, piercing flavor nor an overbearing odor. There should be no cracks in the rind, though this is obviously hard to detect, and the cheese should not be mushy-soft.

Bleu des Causses and Bleu d'Auvergne are perfect as snack cheeses. They are also fine salad cheeses—on the side, in the salad, or incorporated into a vinaigrette. But their truest glory is as after-dinner or dessert cheeses. Blues this flavorful practically demand the sweetness and moisture of fruit, or a sweet or fortified wine.

DAUPHINE AND PROVENCE

Dauphiné is an enormous region bounded by Burgundy and Savoie to the north, and the Rhône valley on the west, which becomes mountainous almost immediately as you meander east into the foothills of the French Alps all the way to the Italian border. To the south—past Montélimar, Nyons, famous for olives and olive oil, and the village of Apt, where some marvelous freshwater fishing can be enjoyed—lies Provence. It was Gigues V, a local feudal lord–cum–king, who first rather mysteriously adopted the dolphin (*dauphin*) as his official title, incorporating its image onto his coat of arms early in the twelfth century. In 1349, King Philippe VI bought the territory and as part of the deal promised to allow all future heirs to the French throne to bear the title Dauphin until they assumed the throne. In 1560, Dauphiné officially became part of France, and after the Revolution it was divided into the *départements* of Isère, Hautes-Alpes, and Drôme.

Provence is a series of undulating folds that start at Montélimar—it is there that you suddenly realize you're in Provence. It feels different for some inexplicable reason—perhaps it's the fleeting whiffs of thyme and rosemary infusing the air. You don't really say, "I smell herbs in the air," but subconsciously your nose tells you they're there. Or maybe it's the light—so vivid, so stark, so startlingly strong. And

The fragrance of fresh-picked wild herbs permeates the air of Aix-en-Provence on market day. All the ingredients for creating the famous herbes de Provence *mixture are for sale, including thyme, marjoram, rosemary, basil, oregano, lavender, and savory.*

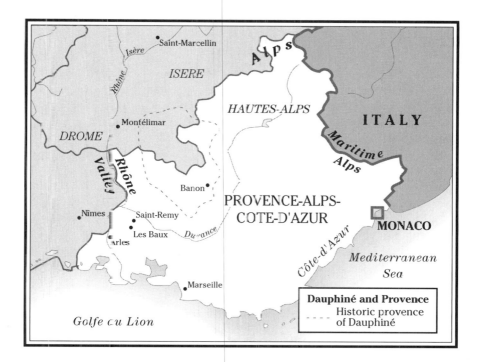

Map legend:
Dauphiné and Provence
——— Historic provence
- - - - of Dauphiné

the countryside looks different—rocky, scrubby, and foreboding, yet strangely welcoming.

The largest mountain in Provence is Mont Ventoux, just north of Montagne du Lubéron. It appears as an oversize hump in a very bumpy landscape, yet is formidable and rugged, with snow visible year round. Ventoux implies windy (*vent* means "wind"), and the wind rushes down the Rhône valley and funnels into the tributary valleys formed by the folds of these mountains before the land tapers off into the Mediterranean. This wind is called Le Mistral, and it begins in late autumn and is pretty much incessant until March or April, when the weather becomes seasonally warm again.

Provence is first of all a land of food. I'll allow that its writers and historic places are second and third, but first and foremost, this is a land of food and wine. The majority of traditional cheeses produced here are decidedly noncommercial, made by farmers, many of whom keep goats and sheep. This is the reason we see virtually no Provençal cheese in the U.S. save the Picodon and Banon from Royannais, the largest commercial producer.

As you move farther south down the Rhône Valley you're surrounded by fields and orchards of melons, apricots, peaches, and the fabulous nectarine that grows there, the *brugnon,* one of the most delicious fruits you'll ever taste. Bonne Maman preserves, and several other brands that are exported to the U.S. are made from fruits grown by the local farmers.

Then there is the Mediterranean. Beyond the glitz and commerciality, expensive hotels, and tourists, there is indeed an absolutely beautiful coastline. Here the cuisine remains essentially Provençal, but seafood predominates. For me, the allure of the coast lies in the herbs, garlic, and olive oil that flavor the many types of fish and other sea creatures that the Mediterranean continues to offer up. It's paradise—every inch of this Riviera, from Banyuls to La Spezia.

West of Marseilles lie the lagoons, which have been taken over by oil refineries. You can see the huge tankers gliding into the bays to release the crude oil that they've brought from the Middle East. These lagoons are the beginning of the Camargue, at the marshy mouth of the Rhône. It is similar to New Orleans, where the Mississippi branches out into marshy levees in its quest to deliver its water to the sea. But whereas the Mississippi has its origin in a Minnesota lake, the origin of the Rhône is high up in the Swiss Alps. The Camargue is humid and damp, completely unlike the rest of Provence.

The Camargue is a nature lover's paradise. There are countless species of birds in the area— thrushes, warblers, egrets, and herons—in addition to semi-wild bulls and semi-wild horses, and a profusion of game. It's really quite desolate, still inhabited by a few itinerant Gypsies—you almost think you're in Spain, not France.

Just above the Camargue are Nîmes, Saint-Rémy, Les Baux, and Arles, with its remarkable Roman theater. I love Arles's tiny, ancient, sycamore-crowded old square and the great little Nord Pinus hotel. Arles features a huge, bustling, weekly farmers' market all spring, summer, and fall. The dramatic side effect to the agribusiness of Provence and all its productivity are the farmers' markets which pop up for a good part of the year in nearly every village. They operate on a rotating basis like a Gypsy road show. Citizens of the larger villages know that starting in early spring through October their "market day" will be, for example, Saturday. On that day, usually in the cramped and crowded town square, there is a colorful riot of edibles and potables. Every regional fruit, cheese, vegetable, animal, and fish is sold from stalls and

Olive vendors at a Provençal market tempt shoppers with pots of tapenade and tubs of Niçoise, Nyons, and Picholine olives, perfect for serving with cheese.

tables, truck beds and display counters that also feature home-sewn dresses, baked pies, and whittled flutes. There are housewares and smocks and clogs, farm implements and fishing equipment, even candlemakers and basketweavers—not just food. There is really nothing more fun in the world.

The Cheeses

BANON AND SAINT-MARCELLIN

Banon (BAN-awh), a northern Provençal goat's-milk or cow's-milk cheese named after the market town of Banon, is a 3½- to 5-ounce (105 to 150 g), 3-inch-wide round that is usually wrapped in a chestnut or grape leaf that has been dipped in white wine, *eau-de-vie,* or *marc,* then tied with ribbon or raffia. The leaves that cover the cheese allow it to ripen and develop a pronounced fruity, winey flavor. Many factory-made Banons, however, are not leaf-wrapped; instead, their bare surfaces are sprinkled with flavorings such as curry powder, savory, or dill.

Saint-Marcellin (SAN-mar-sell-AN), Banon's cousin, is made a bit farther north of Provence in the Dauphiné region. Saint-Marcellin is a 3-ounce (90 g) disk of cheese that, like Banon, is sometimes wrapped in chestnut leaves, dipped in spirits, and tied with raffia or ribbon. The two cheeses were once identical, made primarily from either goat's or sheep's milk; nowadays, though, virtually all Saint-Marcellin is made from cow's milk, whereas Banon is just as likely to be made from goat's milk as from cow's milk.

Both cheeses are at their best after they've ripened for a few weeks. Eaten young, when the leaf-wrapping is still green, the cheese is crumbly (*friable*) and tart, sort of like a young white wine that could use more aging. But when allowed to ripen, the leaves begin to darken, often growing sodden from released whey, and the cheese inside will begin to liquify and develop a pronounced fruity, winey, nutty, very woodsy flavor that is quite alluring.

Choosing and Serving Banon and Saint-Marcellin

In France, young Banon and Saint-Marcellin will sport fresh-looking, green leaves. At this stage the cheese inside the leaves will be chalky, sour, and acidic. It's better to buy them when the leaves have turned a darker green or brown and the interior may be touched with a hint of blue mold. At this stage, the cheese will be creamy and have developed its characteristic nutty flavor.

Although leaf-wrapped examples of Saint-Marcellin are good, the very best of them are not leaf-wrapped and will be labeled *crèmier* (made in a small dairy) and *affiné* (ripened). They are one of the most staggeringly delicious cheeses I've tasted in all my experience. Their intensely nutty (imagine black walnuts) and rustic flavor combined with an unctuous texture represent to me the very essence of France and French cheese. When I am able to bring these to my cheese counters in the U.S., they are often so creamy and so fragile that they must be lovingly removed from their wooden boxes one at a time with a spatula.

These cheeses are a delight as an appetizer with olives and coarse salami (*saucisson sec*). They are also superb with the salad course or as dessert cheeses with peak-of-perfection summer fruits and sweet dessert wines or whatever you drink with dinner. The important

Banon and Saint-Marcellin are often wrapped in chestnut leaves. This maker's factory lies at the edge of a chestnut forest.

thing to remember about the Banon and Saint-Marcellin available in the U.S. is to remove their protective plastic wrapper immediately. Then, if you intend to hold on to the cheese for a week or two in order to bring it to a certain stage of ripeness, I recommend rolling it loosely in waxed paper or aluminum foil about the size of a piece of stationery. Fold the corners under gently and store it in the vegetable compartment of the refrigerator.

PICODON DE LA DROME AND PICODON DE L'ARDECHE

Picodon de la Drôme (pee-koh-DAW-duh-lah-DROHM) is a little 3- to 4-ounce (90 to 125 g) disk of name-controlled goat cheese from the east side of the Rhône Valley in Provence and Dauphiné. It shares its A.O.C. designation with Picodon de l'Ardèche (pee-koh-DAW-duh-lar-DESH), an identical chèvre made on the west side of the valley in Languedoc. There are several stories about how Picodon got its name. The most likely version suggests that Picodon is a variation of the French verb *piquer,* which means "to prick" or "sting." In the old days, farm-made Picodon cheeses were pricked with holes, then set to marinate in earthenware or sandstone pots filled with *eau-de-vie,* brandy, or wine. As time went by, the cheeses

A RUSTIC RHONE CHEVRE

Pelardon de Cevennes (peh-lar-DAW-dah-seh-VEN) is a diminutive, rustic goat's-milk cheese made in the rough, remote, and ultra-rural area north and west of Provence on the other side of the Rhône. There goat cheeses are called Pelardon, local dialect for "pieces." Wonderfully flavorful, the little cheeses' configuration falls somewhere between Picodon and Cabécou—thick, irregular coins about the size of a U.S. silver dollar.

absorbed the flavorful liquid, taking on a quite sharp, fermented, alcoholic taste and aroma. Artisanal versions of Picodon de la Drôme and Picodon de l'Ardèche are still made this way in small batches by numerous farm families throughout northern Provence, Dauphiné, and Languedoc. Some residents of these areas also buy young Picodon, which they prefer to marinate at home either in the spirits traditionally used or in glass jars with olive oil and herbs.

The flavor of Picodon is pure poetry and it can be eaten at varying ages, depending on how you prefer it: young, sweet, creamy, and mild with an aftertaste of rosemary and butter, or aged, crackling hard, nutty-sharp, and balsamy.

As is so often the case with venerable name-controlled cheeses, there are inauthentic imitators. Farther north in the Drôme-Isère area of Dauphiné, a few big factories mass-produce a characterless cheese that they call Picodon. Theirs, however, are made from cow's milk rather than goat's milk, and are embellished with a fancy foil label. Unfortunately, authentic Picodon rarely, if ever, makes its way to the U.S.

Choosing and Serving Picodon de la Drôme and Picodon de l'Ardèche

Should you by some slim happenstance have the good fortune to be offered a Picodon from Provence, Dauphiné, or Languedoc, use your goat cheese-buyer instincts in making a choice. You will find the cheeses sold in all stages of ripeness, from soft and creamy to firm and rather dry. Unmarinated Picodons are nutty and mild, with a soft, creamy interior. Those that have undergone the traditional soaking in spirits will have a dark, golden crust and a marvelously intense nutty, balsamy flavor.

Serve Picodon as you would any other goat cheese—with sweet fruit, crusty bread, and any dry white wine. Côtes-du-Rhône and Côtes-de-Provence are also good matches.

THE WESTERN PYRENEES: BASQUE COUNTRY AND BEARN

(Pays Basque and Béarn)

T he Pyrénées, which stretch from the Atlantic to the Mediterranean, form the natural border, a historically impenetrable one, that separates France from Spain. Within this scant 240 miles are 11 provinces further jumbled by four *départements*. Without question the physical impenetrability and inaccessibility of the Pyrénées has allowed the Basque people, their language, and their cheeses to withstand outside pressure to become assimilated. The people of this region and their cheeses are neither French nor Spanish—they are, simply, Basque. Cheesemaking in this area is concentrated within the western quarter in the region known as Béarn, and within Béarn, primarily in its western portion, the Basque Country (Pays Basque).

The Western Pyrénées, called Pyrénées Atlantique by the French, are not like any mountains I've ever seen. They're certainly not like the Alps, which soar and are craggy,

The hills are alive with sheep in the rugged Pyrénées, where their milk has been used to make cheese for thousands of years.

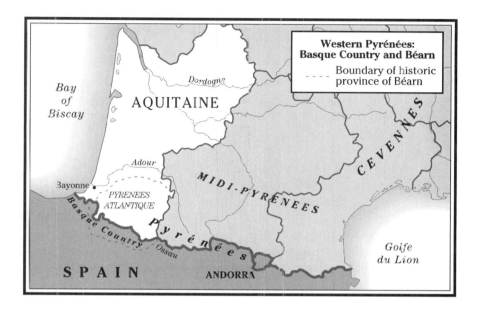

Western Pyrénées:
Basque Country and Béarn
---- Boundary of historic
province of Béarn

Bay of Biscay

Dordogne

AQUITAINE

CEVENNES

Adour

Bayonne

PYRENEES
ATLANTIQUE

MIDI-PYRENEES

Pyrénées

Basque Country

Ossau

SPAIN

ANDORRA

Golfe du Lion

like mountains are expected to be. The Pyrénées are every bit as dramatic and gorgeous, but what sets them apart is that they rise and fall with much more dignity and regularity than wilder ranges, which appear to have been impulsively thrust up from out of the ground. Much of the Pyrénées is rounded and mound-like. And these curves, in contrast to the sharp angles usually associated with mountains, suffuse this landscape with a tangible serenity. Eons upon eons of grazing sheep and cattle have worn down each slope and rounded each summit to a nub (though some remoter areas are still spiked with tracts of virgin pine and hardwood forest). And though they are rounded, these mountains soar, then plunge downward a thousand, two thousand, sometimes even three thousand feet to a valley, a ravine with a stream coursing through, or a river banked by huge trees. Much of this terrain is too steep for humans to negotiate, but not for sheep. One can see them as thousands of grazing white dots in the distance.

The Cheeses

When you read about which cheeses are the world's oldest—English Cheshire, French Cantal, Livarot, Maroilles, and Roquefort—be aware that none of them can be said to predate the sheep's-milk cheeses of the Pyrénées. The Basques insist they have remained unchanged for 4,000 years and this is undisputed. Though cow's-milk cheeses are produced here, first and foremost this is sheep's milk territory, and the cheeses made from this milk are an

A PRECIOUS MEMORY

One of the greatest times of my life was in 1980, when I made a trip to Paris to do some business in the Rungis wholesale market. This was my third or fourth trip, and I was beginning to feel my oats, pounding away at making a reputation as a cheesemonger.

I wrapped up my business in Paris and then drove down through the Loire Valley visiting a few of the chèvre makers from whom I had been buying cheese. I continued south and west into the Périgord region and visited two small goat cheese producers, passed through the tourist trap that is Rocamadour, and pushed all the way down to Toulouse and beyond to the Pyrénées. At that time, I found the Pyrénées the most beautiful place I had ever been— all those shimmering, rounded, green humps of mountains that have been grazed over for centuries stunned me. You could see forever. The rarefied light that

seemed so golden down in that part of France made everything glow. I was traveling by myself and it was a real adventure to be so completely alone.

Because there were no guardrails on the mountain roads, my knuckles were white from holding so tightly to the steering wheel. I stopped the car often and stood on the shoulder of the road gazing almost straight down the grassy slope of the mountain, whose sides swooped and ended about a mile down in a gully, and then started right back up again. At one point, having crossed into Spain, I was so dazzled by the beauty that I again stopped the car, got out, and rested beside a rushing mountain stream. A chestnut mare with her foal appeared beside me, having stepped out of the woods as though she wanted to share with me her joy in her newborn daughter. It was miraculous and holy and I will never forget it.

integral part of Basque culture and cuisine. In Euskari, the Basque language, Basques refer to their sheep's-milk cheeses as *ardi-gasna* (AR-dee-GAHZ-nah), dialect for "our cheese" or "local cheese." The French call them *brebis* (breh-BEE), which means "sheep," or *fromage de brebis*. These cheeses, which are

absolutely among the most delicious in the world, are oily, olivey, nutty, fruity, and firm-textured, with little or no hole structure.

All *brebis* are essentially made from the same recipe using identical techniques; they look alike as well. Typically, they have a beautiful brownish, buffed rind and are big, 8-pound (4 k) wheels with rounded edges, though they can be as small as 3 pounds (1½ k) or as large as 11 pounds (5½ k). They are the classic shape you think of when you think of cheese, the same shape as a Dutch Gouda. Most are named for their village of origin.

Brebis Pyrénées doesn't appear often in the area's cooking because it's primarily eaten by itself, rather than used as an ingredient. It's often served accompanied by a good *saucisson sec* from the neighboring Landes region or some of the fabulous ham from Bayonne that is smoked or air-cured like Spanish *serrano* ham. (The area around Bayonne and Orthez is famous for its hams and the very simple, rustic red wines that go so well with them.)

OSSAU-IRATY BREBIS PYRENEES

The A.O.C. for Pyrénées raw sheep's milk cheese was granted in 1980 and protected under the name of Ossau-Iraty Brebis Pyrénées, which is shortened in common usage to Ossau-Iraty (OH-soh-ear-ah-TEE). Ossau is a river and a valley in Béarn. The name Iraty has been given to many things, including a river; an ancient, sprawling forest; several remote mountain villages in France; and even a village in nearby Spain. The geographic area for making the A.O.C. cheeses

PYRENEES COW'S-MILK CHEESES

Although the most important cheeses made in the Western Pyrénées are made from sheep's milk, there has always been considerable cow's-milk cheese production. Pasteurized, factory-made export versions (often spiked with green peppercorns), which are made in lowland factories on the northern Pyrénées plain as well as in the Auvergne region, are widely available in American cheese shops and supermarkets. Their rinds are either painted black or covered with black paraffin and the labels usually read, "Fromage de Pyrénées fabriqué avec lait de vache." Semisoft and vapid with virtually no discernible flavor, they offer the same meager level of taste as Danish Havarti. The most commonly available examples are Doux de Montagne, St. Albray, Lou Palou, and Le Capitoul, none of which I recommend. However, Le Somport, made from unpasteurized milk, is quite tasty and worth buying if you can find some.

encompasses all of the Basque Country and all of Béarn, plus a bit of neighboring Bigorre in the *département* of Haute-Pyrénées.

Somewhat confusingly, the name Ossau-Iraty (which, as it happens, you will rarely see on a cheese, though the A.O.C. symbol will appear) actually applies to more than one *brebis Pyrénées* made in the A.O.C.-designated areas. In addition to Ossau-Iraty, the A.O.C. applies to Abbaye de Bellocq (AB-BAY-duh-bel-AWK), which is made at a Benedictine monastery; Etcheria (etch-eh-REE-ah) and Larceveau (larse-VOH) made by Pyrénéfrom; Laruns (la-ROON), and Matocq (mah-TOKE).

The cheeses are made from late December (around Christmastime), when the ewes have just begun giving birth to their lambs, until mid-July, when they are once again impregnated by the rams and both milking and cheesemaking cease. The *brebis* are made in *fruitières,* small village cooperatives that are similar to the privately owned *fruitières* in Comté. From June to September, the flocks transhumance to high pastures, some by hoof, others transported in multi-deck trailers towed by trucks. The transhumance gives the lowland pastures a rest from incessant grazing, allowing the farmers to build up a reserve of fodder for the winter months. While in the high pastures, the shepherds live and make a few cheeses (even after

mid-July) in ancient stone huts called *kaiolars.* Much of this delectable, though scarce, summer cheese is marketed as Arneguy (ar-NEH-ghee), named for one of the main villages where it is sold.

The recipe for making Ossau-Iraty and other *brebis* is simple. Finely cut curd is pressed in plastic molds, which are vertically stacked to press the curd and expel the whey. Following a two-hour brine bath, the cheeses are placed in cold rooms (the more artisanal cheesemakers put them in special caves), where they will initially be turned and hand-rubbed with salt, and then later rubbed at varying intervals with a brine-soaked cloth over a period of around four months. The final cheese will be oily with butterfat, firm yet supple, with an extraordinary, almost taffy-like mouthfeel. The flavor is indescribable. It is neither meaty, fruity, yeasty, nor vegetal; if Comté had a lactic, nutty edge to it, it would taste like *brebis*. Non-A.O.C. factory-made cheeses, such as Etorki and Prince de Claverolle, are vacuum-packed and held at very low temperatures in order to arrest their development altogether. This is done so that the company that makes them can stockpile cheeses to better respond to market demand. Despite this unnatural method of aging, these cheeses actually taste very good and they retail for about half of what you would pay for A.O.C. versions.

Choosing and Serving Ossau-Iraty Brebis Pyrénées

Any Pyrénées cheese made with sheep's milk will be excellent, regardless of whether or not it qualifies for an A.O.C. designation. What you want to stay away from, however, are the black-paraffin-rinded cow's-milk cheeses which look, except for their rind, identical to *brebis*. Avoid any Ossau-Iraty or other *brebis* that is cracked inside or outside, is graying, or has butterfat pooling inside its wrapper. (Often a cheese in this condition will taste absolutely fine but won't last in

Proud Basque cheesemongers with their display of fromage de brebis.

your refrigerator—it must be consumed very quickly.) Also watch out for any cut pieces that show a profusion of tiny, white granules. This is a sign of abuse—too long a stay at room temperature.

All A.O.C. Ossau-Iraty will be splendid—fruity, nutty, and olivey—but, unfortunately, they rarely make it to the U.S. Non-A.O.C. *brebis* are more likely to be available in the U.S. and all are excellent. Look for Esbareich (eh-bah-RESH), Etorki (eh-tor-KEE), Onetik (oh-neh-TEEK), Prince de Claverolle (PRANZ-duh-CLAH-vair-ROLL), Prince de Navarre (PRANZ-duh-nah-VAR), and Yolo (Yoh-loh).

As a buffet or picnic cheese serve *brebis* with raw vegetables, sweet peppers, hot pickled chiles, olives, prosciutto, and salami. *Brebis* makes an excellent luncheon cheese slivered and tossed with ripe tomatoes, olive oil, and plenty of freshly ground black pepper. At my house we like to serve it with hot salsa and red wine or cocktails. And all Pyrénées cheeses taste terrific with apples and pears.

FOR WHOM THE BELL TOLLS

Sheep, cattle, and goats throughout the Pyrénées are adorned with tinkling bells (*clarines*). Each animal's bell produces a unique tone and pitch exclusive to that particular animal, a sort of audible "fingerprint." As a result, when strays wander off, keen-eared shepherds can identify not only where the animal is but also which one has strayed based on the sound of its unique bell.

CORSICA

(Corse)

T he best discoveries are often accidental. Take the day in 1978 that I unwittingly and happily encountered Brindamour for the first time. I was in Paris strolling around the Ile-Saint-Louis and went into a little cheese shop to see what they had. I saw this bristly little pillow about the size of a half-pint of raspberries. It was the undersung Corsican cheese called either Brindamour (*brin d'amour,* which means "a bit of love") or Fleur du Maquis ("the flower of the maquis"). *Brin* also means "sprig," which is a reference to the sprigs of herbs on the cheese's surface. This sheep's-milk cheese is thickly coated with rosemary, thyme, savory, coriander seeds, and juniper berries and often garnished with a few tiny red chile peppers for color.

Corsica's *maquis* (its brambly underbrush) covers much of the island—its ravines and gullies, its outback, its scruffy inland. Wild herbs and flowers, juniper and other shrubs grow in profusion throughout the *maquis,* all of which imbue the milk used for Corsican cheeses with an unequaled bouquet. Hunters bring home wild boar, squirrels, and rabbits, which Corsican cooks roast perfectly over a wood fire. The romantic *maquis* is terrain where outlaws once hid. Of course, nowadays this is no longer true, but the *maquis* is still undeniably romantic, mysterious, and untamed. And Corsica itself is stunning, even awe-inspiring, in its physical beauty.

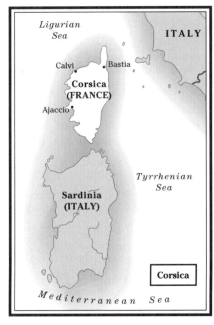

Ligurian Sea

ITALY

Calvi • Bastia

Corsica (FRANCE)

Ajaccio •

Tyrrhenian Sea

Sardinia (ITALY)

Corsica

Mediterranean Sea

Perched atop a craggy peak, Corsica's largest inland city, Corte, rises above a tangle of maquis the island's famous untamed brambly underbrush.

The Cheeses

....

The Corsican cheese industry is made up of virtually all small producers. Several of the larger concerns buy cheese from the smaller cheesemakers in order to have enough product to truck to the Rungis wholesale market on the outskirts of Paris. Commercial Corsican cheese is usually made from unpasturized sheep's milk, and only very rarely from goat's milk, although some sources may claim otherwise. It is sold in a variety of ages, though most people prefer to buy it as a young fresh cheese.

BRINDAMOUR

Also Called Brin d'Amour or Fleur du Maquis

Cheesemakers cover Brindamour or Brin d'Amour (BRAN-dah-MORE), or Fleur du Maquis (FLUR-doo-MAH-KEY) with a mantle of dried, green herbs, as much to make it beautiful as to flavor it. The silvery-green, needle-shaped leaves of rosemary that bristle on its surface make the cheese resemble a porcupine. Each 1¼- to 1¾-pound (625 to 875 g), 4- to 5-inch, pillow-shaped square of this sheep's-milk cheese is about 2 inches thick. If

S'il qui mange
du fromage, s'il ne
le fait, il enrage.

He who does not eat

cheese will go mad.

French proverb

the cheese is young, when cut it will look like ice cream, snow-white with the creamy, soft, moist texture that is the nature of fresh sheep's- or goat's-milk cheese. The flavor will be sweet and gentle, rich and creamy, but extremely herby. Those herbs on the surface aren't just there for show; they assertively contribute their flavors to the cheese.

Brindamour is sold in a range of ages. Young—a week or two old—it is soft and moist with a gentle flavor. At a month or two of age, the paste will have turned bone-white and almost runny, and the flavor will have evolved to encompass a predominantly nutty, olivey sheep's-milk taste that is not as aggressively sheepy as you might expect. (Goat's-milk versions, too, become more flavorful with age, but will not be overly strong. They are more elastic and less crumbly than traditional French chèvre, and have a more subtle goat's-milk flavor.) Brindamour is a sturdy cheese, but even if it has been roughly treated in transit or in the store, it will invariably still be delicious. Aged properly, its flavor will go above and beyond the obvious herbiness, developing nuances of hazelnuts and fruit, along with a hint of olives.

Theoretically, a Brind-amour's rind is edible, but for all practical purposes I consider it inedible since the herbs become dry

A cheese for herb lovers. The surface of these delectable Brindamours bristles with such aromatic herbs as rosemary, thyme, and savory.

Corsican Brindamour is also called Fleur
du Maquis, "flower of the maquis."

and bitter as time goes by. With age, mold growth encompasses the herbs and it begins to resemble the *maquis*. Scrape or cut it away. Exotic and rustic, this is a stunning cheese, visually and on the palate. It's a cheese that serves as a reminder that Corsica is more French than Italian. Certainly I know of no similar Italian cheese.

Choosing and Serving Brindamour

Brindamour is sold in a wide range of ages from a week or two old up to a month or two old. The age at which it tastes best is strictly a matter of personal taste. (In contrast to soft-ripened cheeses such as Brie or Camembert, there is no particular stage at which a simple, whey-drained curd cheese like Brindamour is considered 'ripe.") Brindamour is as satisfying young and fresh as it is aged.

(Young cheeses are air-freighted to the U.S.) As with Banon's leaves, the cheese's age is given away by the appearance of its cloak of herbs. If the dried herbs have lost their greenish color and faded to brown, you can be sure the sheep's-milk cheese lurking inside will have begun the transformation into a runnier, more mature cheese. Past that stage (heading toward two months old), it loses its moisture and becomes firm. At this point the flavor will be extremely concentrated. but not sheepy—a highly desirable state.

I like Brindamour at any stage of ripeness. It is a novel and exciting cheese, one I serve when company comes because it is such a conversation piece. Its straightforward, unsophisticated qualities make it perfect as a snack or lunchtime cheese, and it also makes a good accompaniment to a salad course. Avoid fruit with Brindamour, as its herbiness marries better with savory flavors—olives, tomatoes, peppers, and the like.

WHEN IN CORSICA

Visitors to Corsica are most likely to arrive on the port side of Bastia, the island's lively yet unspoiled largest city. On a clear day you can actually see the hills of Tuscany in Italy from the top of the town's 16th-century citadel.

Brindamour is, of course, not the only Corsican cheese, although it is quite likely to be the only one you will be able to locate in the U.S. This is our loss because Corsica's simple, rustic sheep's-milk cheeses are remarkably delicious. If you are visiting Corsica, these will be of interest.

• **Venaco** (veh-NAH-coh): A 1-pound (500 g) thickish square of cheese that is similar in taste and texture to Pecorino Toscano. It comes from near Venaco, a town in the center of Corsica, and although more closely related to Brindamour, it is a longer-aged, raw sheep's milk cheese (sometimes made with a mixture of sheep's and goat's milk). The mixed milk examples will bear labels that say "lait au mélange." Venaco is a rustic cheese that offers up the flavors of nuts, herbs, berries, olives, woodsmoke, and hard-boiled eggs. It has a strong, fermented smell, the result of its natural rind having been brine-washed at intervals during the three to four months it ripens in local caves. Corsicans mash it ut and marinate it in a robust local red wine or grate it and combine it with fruity olive oil, fresh herbs, and garlic as a topping for thick slices of toasted bread.

- **Niolo** (nee-YOH-loh); also called **Niulincu** (nyew-LEEN-kew): An alluring, strong-flavored, washed-rind cheese similar in size and shape (a round-edged square) to Brindamour, though without herbs. Although it is sold in various stages of ripeness, Niolo is most often aged four to six months, at which point the cappuccino-brown rind still bears the marks of the basket in which it was molded. The inner paste will be white, firm, and melt-in-your-mouth buttery with a rather sharp and powerful but scrumptious spiciness (look for hints of thyme, honeysuckle, rosemary, juniper, savory, and coriander).

- **Fium'orbu** (few-MORE-boo): A smaller, 10- to 12-ounce (300 to 375 g) version of Venaco and Niolo that is made in disks.

- **Asco** (AHSS-koh): Nearly identical to Venaco, Niolo, and Fium'orbu, but round rather than a round-edged square. Corsica's central plateau which is drained by two rivers, the Golo and Asco, is the area where Golo, Asco, and Niolo are made.

- **Golo** (GOH-loh): A semihard to hard, golden-colored, brushed-rind sheep's-milk cheese made in a creamery owned by the huge Roquefort company called Société B. Slightly smaller than most *brebis Pyrénées*, each Golo weighs around 6 pounds (3 k) and is a 5-inch-thick, straight-sided wheel about 8 inches in diameter. Generally aged from three to six months, it is an admirable, rather sharp and nutty cheese suitable for eating or grating. Golo also has a historic link to Roquefort. From the late 1800s until the early 1980s, when the Rouergue region (where Roquefort is made) finally developed a self-sufficient supply of sheep's milk for all the Roquefort made there, Corsican cheesemakers created sheep's-milk cheeses specifically for the Roquefort cheesemakers and shipped them to the mainland, where they were trucked to the caves at Roquefort, injected with blue mold, and set to age. Due to the A.O.C. laws controlling Roquefort-making, Corsica is no longer allowed to supply cheeses to the Roquefort cheesemakers, so the cheese, called Golo, has now developed a reputation of its own.

- **U Macchione** (OO-mah-key-YOH-neh): The brand name of a raw sheep's milk cheese in the same style (herb-covered) and shape as Brindamour. Each soft cheese is thickly coated with rosemary, thyme, and savory.

Italy

I got my first taste of Italy on a crisp October day back in 1979, when my wife, Michelle, her sister Leslie, and I drove from Haute-Savoie in the French Alps, through the tunnel under Mont Blanc (Monte Bianco, to Italians), and into the valleys of Aosta. The trees were green and sun-dappled on the Savoie side, but leafless on the gray, windy, and cold Aosta side. I had come to arrange for the first-ever shipments to

the U.S. of Fontina d'Aosta, one of the world's greatest cheeses. At the time, I was aware of only a handful of other Italian cheeses. I stocked Parmigiano-Reggiano, Gorgonzola, Pecorino Romano, and Provolone—but that was about it. I had no idea of the magnificent cheeses I was about to discover. It had never occurred to me that France did not have a monopoly on cheese.

When most people think of Italian cheeses, what comes to mind is either very soft, moist, bland Mozzarella (usually melted on a pizza), or sharp, oily Provolone on a deli sandwich, or something craggy and geolithic, like shards of hard, crumbly, granular Parmigiano-Reggiano or Pecorino Romano. It's a mental image of Italian cheeses

Discerning shoppers poke, pinch, and sniff as they select the best at an outdoor market. This cheese seller has used a short-bladed knife called a coltello per Parmigiano *to pry apart chunks of Italy's most famous cheese.*

that rarely includes a middle ground. Unless you've traveled extensively in Italy or are very well acquainted with Italian cuisine, your image of its cheeses very likely doesn't include the Brie-like, bloomy-rinded Paglia-style and Toma cheeses of Piedmont with their irresistible truffle-like taste, Lombardy's oozy, glistening, indigo-streaked Gorgonzola or pungent Taleggio with its crust the color of crème caramel.

To appreciate Italian cheeses, it helps to understand both the geography and the culture of the country in the totality of their charming, sometimes confusing, dis-parity. Italy, like France, is an amalgam of fascinating, secretive, insular regions, each with distinctive terrain and foods. But when it comes to their cheese, no one is more adulatory and protective than the Italians, who are, I must add, equally dismissive about all cheese that is not Italian. I have heard Italian cheesemakers say that the best French cheese made is Normandy butter!

When I go into a good cheese shop in Bordeaux or Paris or Lyon, I find there cheeses from all of the regions of France. Not so in Italy. The situation is completely different. If you're in Abruzzi in the town of Pescara on the Adriatic and visit a *latteria* (dairy store) to buy cheese, you won't find any Taleggio from Lombardy, nor are you going to find any Robiola from Piedmont. What you find is the cheese that the people in the Pescara area make and eat—Provolone, Mozzarella, Caciocavallo, and some hard *pecorino* (sheep's-milk cheese). Italy is not

as blatantly nationalistic as France. Italians are regionally, rather than nationalistically, chauvinistic. In Italy, you're not so much an Italian as you are a Tuscan or a Sicilian or a Roman. And when you're in those specific regions, that's the provender you're offered, not the specialties of other regions of Italy. Of course, there are some exceptions, but overall the norm is one of re-

The hard, grainy-textured (grana) *grating cheeses such as Parmigiano-Reggiano and Grana Padano are an integral part of Italy's culinary tradition. At the cheese shop, wedges with the least amount of rind are the best value.*

> *"With this or that cheese, whole villages have
> expressed themselves through the centuries. Cheese is the
> visiting card the past generations present [to] their
> grand- and great-grandchildren, the family book in which
> the ancestors' memories are kept. To recognize a
> denomination of origin means to grant the people of
> the area a patent of nobility."*
>
> **The DOC Cheeses of Italy:**
> **A Great Heritage**

gional exclusivity and insularity carried to the highest degree.

You may be surprised to discover that while France exports a far greater variety of cheeses to the U.S., Italy exports three times more cheese to us than does France. (Enormous quantities of Parmigiano-Reggiano, Grana Padano, Romano, and Gorgonzola make up the bulk of these exports. Curiously enough, despite its wider range of cheeses, France mostly exports Brie to the U.S.)

Italy's cheeses are as ancient as any in the world. In 25 B.C., Marcus Apicius wrote extensively about cheese and the important part it played in the diet of Roman soldiers. Italian cheesemakers make cheese in every conceivable style and then some. Southern Italy's Mozzarella and Provolone are *pasta filata* (pulled or stretched curd) cheeses, created with a cheesemaking technique that is uniquely Italian. The *grana*-style cheese, of which Parmigiano-Reggiano is the most important and famous, are so semi-

nally significant to the Italian table that they spawned a culinary style typified by pasta tossed with sauce and sprinkled with grated cheese.

Piedmont and Lombardy make a staggering array of cheeses, a lineup so vast that if Italy were composed of only these two northern regions, Italy would still rank as one of the world's cheese-producing behemoths. But add Emilia-Romagna's Parmigiano-Reggiano (in my opinion, the world's greatest cheese), Tuscany's Pecorino Toscano, Lazio's Pecorino Romano, and Campania's Mozzarella *di bufala,* and suddenly France no longer seems unrivaled as the center of the cheese-producing universe.

Let's take a look, bearing in mind that although cheese is made in every region of Italy, not every region's cheeses warrant our scrutiny here. Some areas are not specifically covered, among them Alto Adige, Abruzzi, Calabria, and Basilicata, because for the most part the cheeses they make are more traditional to neighboring regions.

DENOMINAZIONE DI ORIGINE CONTROLLATA (D.O.C.)— THE NAME-CONTROLLED CHEESES OF ITALY

In 1955, Italy enacted D.O.C. laws to safeguard the names, origins, and characteristics of certain Italian cheeses. To date, only 26 of them are under the protection of the D.O.C. A permanent commission in the Ministry of Agriculture and Forests officially designates the specific production areas of D.O.C. cheeses, and also works with a government-sanctioned consortium of cheesemakers to standardize the production methods as well as the physical characteristics of each cheese. These efforts help preserve, now and for posterity, the cheesemaking tradition of each and encourage consumer confidence.

The ministry authorizes individual consortiums to strictly regulate their own production methods. Producers who sell cheeses not made within the guidelines are subject to fines and/or legal actions. The descriptions of the milk type, the cheesemaking processes, and physical characteristics, as well as the composition and special attributes for each of the cheeses, are set forth by presidential decree which has become law.

Though the name-controlled cheeses of Italy bear their D.O.C. designation on the label or wrapper or have it imprinted on their rind, this is not an absolute guarantee that each cheese is perfect. In much the same way that wines vary from vintage to vintage or hams differ from one season to another, the quality of a name-controlled cheese may vary from maker to maker, from batch to batch, and may also reflect the time of the year it was made and the duration of its ripening.

Some of these D.O.C. cheeses occupy an important place in Italy's culinary heritage. However, others are less significant than their name-controlled status might lead you to believe. For example, Canestrato Pugliese, a hard sheep's-milk cheese (*pecorino*) from Apulia, is rarely found even in the region where it is produced. But it is similar to other, more widely available *pecorinos*, including Pecorino Romano, Sicilian Incanestrato, and Pecorino Sardo, which you will be able to find in well-stocked American cheese shops.

The following is a complete list of the D.O.C. cheeses of Italy, their places of origin, and an idea of their availability in the U.S. Bear in mind that this list is subject to change as additional cheeses are granted coveted D.O.C. status by the Italian government.

Asiago: Veneto, Friuli–Venezia Giulia; available

Bra: Piedmont; available, though rare

Caciocavallo: Apulia, Basilicata, Calabria, Campania; available, though rare

Canestrato Pugliese: Apulia; not available (rare even in Italy outside of its region of origin)

Casciotta d'Urbino: The Marches; not available (rare even in Italy outside of its region of origin)

Castelmagno: Piedmont; not available (rare even in Italy outside of its region of origin)

Fiore Sardo: Sardinia; available, though rare

Fontina d'Aosta: Piedmont (Aosta); widely available

Formai de Mut: Lombardy; a raw cow's milk cheese in the style of Fontina d'Aosta; not available (rare even in Italy outside of its region of origin; made

in very limited quantities in the high pastures of Alta Valle Brembana and the province of Bergamo in Lombardy)

Gorgonzola: Lombardy; widely available

Grana Padano: Emilia-Romagna, Lombardy, Veneto; widely available

Montasio: Friuli–Venezia Giulia; available, spotty

Mozzarella di bufala: Campania; available, spotty

Murazzano: Piedmont; available, though rare

Parmigiano-Reggiano: Emilia-Romagna; widely available

Pecorino Romano: Lazio, Sardinia; widely available

Pecorino Sardo: Sardinia; available, though rare

Pecorino Siciliano: Sicily; available, though rare

Pecorino Toscano: Tuscany; available, though spotty

Pressato: Veneto; not available

Provolone: all regions; widely available

Ragusano: Sicily; available, though rare

Raschera: Lombardy, Emilia-Romagna; not available (rare even in Italy outside its region of origin)

Robiola di Roccaverano: Piedmont; available, though rare

Taleggio: Lombardy; widely available

Toma: Piedmont; rare

PIEDMONT

(Piemonte)

Piemonte, meaning "foot of the mountains," is an apt name for this fabulous, sprawling northwestern corner of Italy. Its northern border with Switzerland and its western one with France reach high into the Alps, surely the most dramatic mountains in the world. The spiny, ridge-backed Apennine range forms the mountainous southern border that separates Piedmont from Liguria and the Italian Riviera.

In between is Turin (Torino), the cosmopolitan, industrially driven capital (think Fiat, Pirelli), a city filled with wine and chocolate, cheese and bread, fruits and vegetables. Through the ages, Piedmont, more so even than Lombardy and Tuscany, has been self-sufficient as regards food-stuffs and the general economy. The Piedmontese are at home and content in their own land; emigration has never been a factor. While Italians from less prosperous regions have resettled in countries throughout the world, those born in Piedmont seem quite satisfied to stay there. Indeed, Italians from southern regions—Calabria, Basili-cata, and Sicily—have been drawn to Piedmont, and today make up a considerable portion of its work force.

The extreme northwestern corner of Piedmont itself is the au-tonomous region of Aosta, some-times referred to as the Valle d'Aosta.

Just south of Turin is an area called the Langhe. Here are the

Piedmont and Valle d'Aosta

The local latteria *specializes in dairy products, including cow's-milk cheeses. This one also sells cured pork products (*salumi*) and sandwiches (*panini*).*

vineyards that figure so importantly in the production of my favorite "big" Italian red wines—Barolo and Barbaresco—which go so well with full-flavored cheeses. Also in the area are Asti, known for its *spumante* (sparkling) wines, and Alessandria, a city built on rice growing—Arborio, vialone, nano, carnaroli, grains as different from Chinese or Carolina rice as boiled ham is from *prosciutto di Parma.* Alba and Bra are towns below Turin, situated in the heart of Piedmont's agricultural breadbasket. Piedmont is home to winemakers and cheesemakers, truffle hunters and mushroom growers, as well as a grand concentration of lesser-known foodstuff artisans and scores of farmers who grow apples, pears, and peaches in their or-

chards and harvest peppers, beans, and lettuces from their fields. Piedmont is world-renowned for the *tartufi bianchi* (white truffles) found in its soil. The white truffles of Alba are *the* white truffles, just as the black truffles of Périgord are *the* black truffles. As if white truffles, porcini mushrooms, Arborio rice, extraordinary *salumi* (cured pork products), and magnificent cheeses weren't enough, Piedmont is also famous for its production of vermouth and pasta (*agnolotti, tagliarini*), and for great dishes such as *brassato di manzo* (stews of chicken or beef in red wine), and *zabaglione* (the rich dessert made from eggs, sugar, and Marsala wine). It is in Piedmont that you'll often find the cardoon, a prehistoric-looking, celery-like vegetable that

BAGNA CAUDA PIEMONTESE

Makes about 4 servings

If you've never tasted *bagna cauda,* you're in for a treat as you dunk crisp raw vegetables into this warm, flavored olive oil "bath." In fact, this appetizer takes its name from *bagno caldo,* Italian for "hot bath." Like so many other sublime regional specialties, this one is only as good as its ingredients, so you'll want to use the best quality olive oil for it. Although it is not traditional, when I make this at home I like to add a few flakes of hot red pepper and a few twists of freshly ground black pepper.

Use a fondue pot or chafing dish to keep the *bagna cauda* warm at the table—along with a wide, artistically arranged array of raw vegetables for dipping into the heavenly mixture. The vegetables to be dunked are limited only by your imagination and might include: cucumbers, celery, radishes, cherry tomatoes, carrots, spinach, bell peppers, scallions, mushrooms, asparagus, zucchini, radicchio, and cardoon, if you can find it. Serve accompanied by good crusty bread to catch the drippings.

⅔ cup (150 ml) olive oil
2 to 3 tablespoons unsalted butter
3 teaspoons finely minced garlic
1 tin (2 ounces; 60 g) anchovy fillets, drained and cut into small pieces
Raw vegetables for dunking, cut into manageable sticks or slices
Crusty bread, cut into small chunks or slices

1. Combine the olive oil and butter in a medium-size saucepan over low heat. When the butter has melted, add the garlic and sauté it briefly (do not let it brown), stirring constantly with a wooden spoon.

2. Add the anchovies, mashing them with the back of the spoon to help them dissolve into the hot oil. As soon as the anchovies have fallen apart, transfer the mixture to a fondue pot, chafing dish, or other serving dish that can be kept warmed at the table. Serve with your choice of vegetables and plenty of crusty bread.

accompanies an authentic *bagna cauda piemontese* and is so delicious with white truffle-infused *fonduta piemontese. Grissini* (breadsticks) are native to this area— available in a riot of sizes, lengths, flavorings, and colorful wrappings. (Once you compare honest, fresh, nutty, crisp Piedmontese breadsticks to the stale ones you've been confronted with all your life, you'll appreciate what all the fuss is about.)

Here, too, is where *carpaccio* or *carne cruda* (raw beef) is so loved. The paper-thin slices of beef are drizzled with extra-virgin olive oil and strewn with shards of Parmigiano-Reggiano and perhaps a few porcini or shavings of *tartufi bianchi*—a staggering combination.

It would be as impossible to choose my favorite Piedmont cheese as to select my favorite Piedmont recipe. What makes this area's food so appealing to me is that like so much regional French food, it is rustic, bold, and ungussied-up, using only seasonal local ingredients. If the components aren't fresh, the dish isn't made at all. It is a philosophy of cooking and eating that rewards both the palate and the spirit.

The Cheeses

FONTINA D'AOSTA

As I noted earlier, the first time I visited Italy was in early winter. I had driven from the Haute-Savoie in France's Jura mountains and into the Valle d'Aosta. I was reeling from the late autumn beauty of France, where the countryside was still verdant, pastures still grassy, and the colorful, changing leaves still on the trees. When I came out of the tunnel under Mont Blanc and into Italy, I was struck by how different the countryside was. In almost every direction there were grape-vines running vertically up the mountainsides, but the overall effect was one of a brown and barren land. Where were the lush pastures for the dairy cows? How could there be enough milk to produce the only real Fontina, the great, centuries-old cheese named after the nearby village of Fontinaz and the towering peak Mont Fontin? I was perplexed.

My journey to Aosta had a single purpose: to determine whether or not I could get my hands on enough authentic, name-controlled Fontina d'Aosta (fawn-TEE-nah-DAOW-stah) to sell in the United States. For some unknown reason, at that time (around 1979), real Fontina d'Aosta was not available here. Certainly, Fontina was a legal-for-import cheese because its ripening time of about four months more than fulfilled our USFDA requirement of 60 days of aging for raw-milk cheeses. And demand was high—it seemed as if every sixth person who came to my counter asked for Fontina. I don't think a single one of them knew that what I had to offer was only a Fontina-*style* cheese, not the *real* cheese. I was determined to get my hands on the real thing.

True Fontina d'Aosta is the classic, semifirm Italian cheese that is made in large, 17- to 22-pound (8½ to 11 k) wheels, about 4 inches thick and 18 inches in diameter. It has the abundant flavor typical of cheeses made from high-quality, raw cow's milk. Real Fontina, unlike its many imitators, will somehow yield the flavor of grass, nuts, and fruit, as well as the herby, balsamy quality you sense when you smell rich pasture soil. Real Fontina is firm and supple, not flabby, shiny, and bulgy like faux Fontina, and its flavor is immediately fuller and grander than those cheeses that pretend to be what they are not.

Virtually all of the big commercial cheese companies in northern Italy produce a Fontina-type cheese with a name similar to Fontina—Fontinella or Fontella or Fontal. Authentic Fontina d'Aosta has a mark on it that is unmistakable: Stenciled in purple on one side of the cheese will be a large circle with a mountain in the center of it and the word "Fontina" printed across the mountain.

My trip to Piedmont ensured a constant supply of real Fontina at my counters in New York City. Over the last decade, its price has risen steadily, but nonetheless it remains a crucial cheese to me, one I am rarely out of. These days, you will be able to find real Fontina d'Aosta in any shop that is serious about cheese. The consortium for Fontina is so protective of the cheese's quality and so strict about its clearly defined domain that the demand for true Fontina is very strong—and so its price is high.

Exported Fontina-type cheeses by Galbani (Lombardy), Mauri (Lombardy), and Carmagnola (Piedmont) are very decent—far better than Scandinavian-made, so-called Fontina—and they are readily available in the U.S. The red paraffin-rinded, skimmed-milk cheeses that are

The finest Fontina is made from the milk of cows that graze high in the mountains.

called Fontina and sold in almost every U.S. supermarket may be pleasantly edible cheeses, but they do not come close in any way to true Fontina d'Aosta's texture, flavor, or aroma. French Fontal, from the Ain River area, is decent, but not anywhere near the cheese true Fontina is.

Choosing and Serving Fontina d'Aosta

All authentic Fontina d'Aosta is packed with a paper label that identifies it as real Fontina. Lacking that (peeled off or otherwise missing), look for the purple tattoo of a mountain peak on the top surface with the word "Fontina." Once you've gotten that far, and just as importantly, make sure the cheese has not been around too long. Old Fontina is quite disagreeable. It will show a cracked or slimy rind, a graying interior, and will have a decidedly unpleasant flavor and odor. It is as simple to determine healthy Fontina as it is fresh fish; you'll know practically by looking. It doesn't hurt, however, to request a taste. Fresh, healthy Fontina will be mildly fruity and nutty in flavor and aroma.

Fontina is another of the "perfect anytime" cheeses, one of my favorite cheeses. It is splendid at lunch with ham, salami, or pâté, some bread, fruit, and a glass of wine. Because Fontina enjoys such a great reputation as a cooking cheese, it is often underappreciated as an eating cheese. This is a cheese noble enough to appear at the end of any meal, accompanied by whatever fruits you enjoy, plus, of course, crusty bread and your favorite red wine, preferably something big, Italian, and somewhat tannic, such as Barolo or Barbaresco.

Fontina's most famous role is in *fonduta*, a dish that takes its name from *fondere*, "to melt." *Fonduta* is an Italian specialty that is similar to Swiss and French white wine- or kirsch-infused fondues, but the classic *fonduta piemontese* goes a giant step further; it combines Fontina with butter, eggs, and Alba's prized white truffles, resulting in a much richer dish, with greater depth of flavor. While Swiss and French cheese fondues are eaten from a communal fondue pot (cubes of bread impaled on long-handled forks are swirled in the mixture), *fonduta* is whipped and then poured onto individual plates over rice, potatoes boiled in their skins, or polenta, the classic cornmeal mush of Italy. Cooked and raw

vegetables are often served with *fonduta,* and one of the most popular accompaniments is the cardoon, the same artichoke cousin that the Piedmontese enjoy with *bagna cauda.*

Since Fontina is a superb melter, do not hesitate to incorporate it into your cooking. My family particularly enjoys *tramezzini,* small, triangular-shaped, triple-decker sandwiches, made with smoked ham, Fontina, and butter, pressed in a hot griddle or waffle iron until the bread toasts and the cheese melts.

ROBIOLA PIEMONTE

R obiola Piemonte (roh-bee-OH-lah-pyeh-MAWN-teh) is the generic name of a group of snowy-white Piedmont cheeses made with pasteurized or unpasteurized sheep's, cow's, or goat's milk, or any mixture of the three.

Moist, tangy Robiola Osella is an excellent factory-made Robiola Piemonte. Serve it at breakfast time.

It is a traditional style of fresh, rindless, cream-added cheese that is usually allowed to ripen for a week to develop a sweeter flavor and a creamier, more luxurious texture than other styles of fresh cheese, and should not be confused with Robiola Lombardia, a group of entirely different Taleggio-type, washed-rind cheeses (see page 205). These Robiolas are usually sold in 6- to 14-ounce (180 to 420 g) paper-wrapped cubes or disks. The most famous are the name-controlled duo—Robiola di Roccaverano (roka-vehr-AH-noh), made from goat's milk or a combination of milks, and the longer-aged Murazzano (moor-ah-TZAH-noh), made from sheep's milk.

The most com-

monly available Robiola in Italy and the U.S. is made by Osella and is called Annabella La Morbida ("the moist one"). It is usually packed six pieces to the plastic tray and sold individually, by weight or by the piece. Very white and moist, it's like eating ice cream that has a lingering tanginess. Both Annabella and Robiola Osella (identical cheeses from the same maker, each with a different logo) are excellent examples of factory-made Robiola Piemonte.

Although Robiola Piemonte is consumed today as a fresh cheese

that is white inside and out, its name comes from the Latin *rubere,* a reference to the reddening of the cheese's exterior as it oxidizes after the initial ripening period. For a special treat, you might want to allow the cheese to age in its wrapper in the vegetable drawer of the refrigerator for a week or two, until its edible exterior reddens. The cheese will be slightly crumbly, with a more pronounced, fruitier flavor.

Robiola di Roccaverano is made in the village of Roccaverano

Pasteurized examples of rare robiolas are sometimes available in the U.S.

and is well known throughout Piedmont and respected by serious cheese lovers all over Italy. It is primarily made from gently pasteurized goat's milk, although a combination of milks (goat, cow, and sheep) is increasingly being used. The difference between the pure goat's milk versions and mixed milk ones is virtually indiscernible.

Robiola di Roccaverano are irregular, disk-like mounds of unripened cheese that are the whitest of whites, moist with sweet whey, and always wrapped in waxed paper with the maker's name emblazoned on it. Like all Robiola Piemonte, their texture is less frothy than the tradi-

RARE ROBIOLAS

When visiting Piedmont, seek out the following rare Robiola Piemonte:

- **del Bek:** (Piedmont dialect for "goat"): made from goat's milk
- **Caramagna:** made from cow's milk
- **Bossolasco:** made from cow's milk
- **Cocconato:** made from cow's milk
- **delle Langhe:** made from cow's and sheep's milk
- **Monferrato:** made from cow's milk

tional French chèvre they resemble and closer to American cream cheese. They weigh from 9 to 12 ounces (270 to 375 g). Allowed to age for two or more weeks in the refrigerator, they become less moist, slightly reddened, and more pronounced in flavor—more intensely nutty and slightly, but pleasantly, bitter—a sensation that might seem jarring at first. But I find this flavor one that marries quite well with sweet breakfast pastries, such as muffins or babka, as well as with good bread or brioche, and almost any fruit. In Piedmont homes, this cheese is frequently treated to a sprinkling of crushed black peppercorns and herbs (mint, rosemary, or thyme), a variation to be savored at lunch or dinner, accompanied by a crusty bread.

Murazzano is a favorite of mine, and though expensive, I hope you come across it either in the U.S. or in Italy. Its small commercial producer, cryptically called CO.ZO.A.L., is quite happy to report that the demand is considerably greater than the supply of this name-controlled delicacy. Longer aged than other Robiolas, Murazzano is sold in 9- to 12-ounce (270 to 375 g) flat disks, and is made from unpasteurized sheep's milk. When I receive my air-freight shipments of Murazzano, I age the cheeses further in my ripening room, anxiously waiting until they develop a rough, dark beige to golden-brown crust and a straw-colored interior. The edible crust becomes chewy and intensely nutty, while the maturing interior becomes semifirm and a bit leathery, similar to the texture of a dried apricot. The flavor is subdued but full, slightly garlicky and mushroomy with undertones of grilled meat. Murazzano is marvelous served with garlicky, oven-baked Ligurian black olives (*taggiasche*) and warm, whole-grain bread. The wine of choice should be a robust Piedmont red.

Choosing and Serving Robiola Piemonte

Avoid any Robiola Piemonte that appears dry in its plastic, six-pack container (you can purchase them singly). If you have the opportunity to handle them, peek under their wrappers and avoid buying any that have developed a beige skin. This is a cheese that at your first encounter should be moist, soft, pristinely white, and sweet; it should never taste bitter. Get to know Robiola as a fresh (unripened) cheese before you graduate to savoring aged ones.

Serve Robiola Piemonte with preserves, compotes, fruit salads, pastries, or raw vegetables for any occasion—breakfast or luncheon, buffets, snacks, or dessert. Blend it with other ingredients such as smoked salmon, scallions, capers, garlic, anchovies, or herbs and serve it as a dip or spread. Add it to omelets, use it as a filling for ravioli or tortellini, or layer it in a *torta* with other ingredients.

CAPRINI AND FAGOTTINI

Fresh little cheeses similar to Robiola Piemonte are called Caprini (kah-PREE-nee), or "little goats" (*capra* means "goat"). Caprini once were made *only* from goat's milk, but, unfortunately, there are no longer commercial quantities of goat's milk in Piedmont.

LITTLE SPARKS

Caprini, packed in their little Styrofoam boxes, always remind me of Fourth of July fireworks. They look just like the little geometric shapes wrapped with brightly colored paper that you knew were going to go "Bang!" or "Zoom!" Now that I'm older, I'm happier to eat little Caprini "firecrackers" than to set off real ones.

Today they may be made from pasteurized goat's milk (green wrapper) or cow's milk (blue wrapper); their flavors are really not all that different. These small cheeses are usually shipped and displayed for sale in Styrofoam boxes of seven; each individual Caprini is a 2-ounce (60 g), paper-wrapped, 4-inch-long cylinder that is open at both ends. The Piedmontese refer to curd that is this fresh, creamy, frothy, and sweet tasting as *il fiore di latte*—"the flower of the milk."

Piedmont also produces Fagottini (fah-goh-TEE-nee), meaning "little bundles," fresh goat cheeses weighing

1½ ounces (45 g), that are very similar to Caprini. A dollop of pasteurized goat's milk curd—fresh, sweet, anc white—is placed in the center of a small square of paper and the encs are gathered together and tied up with a little strip of raffia. They are utterly charming to look at and taste quite good. The name Fagottini is also given to a soft-ripened, paper-wrapped goat's-milk Toma cheese from Lombardy. Both are delicious.

Choosing and Serving Caprini and Fagottini

Avoid any Caprini or Fagottini that show blue mold or have wrinkled paper, obvious signs of having been in the store too long. Caprini wrappers always say *degustare con olio e pepe,* a reminder to put a little freshly ground black pepper and a little bit of olive oil on it—an estimable suggestion for both Caprini and Fagottini. They are then ready to eat with bread and raw vegetables. I like mine with rye or pumpernickel and an assortment of raw celery, radishes, carrots, endive, and scallions. Before serving Fagottini, untie the raffia bow, open the bundle, remove the cheese, and set it on a plate, or simply spread it on slices of bread.

As with Robiola or any other fresh cheese, the flavor of Caprini and Fagottini is sweet, tart, and creamy. Both cheeses also do an admirable job of enhancing the flavor of fruits; go for the sweetest ones in season—peaches, plums, or nectarines.

PAGLIA-STYLE CHEESES AND TOMA

Paglia-style (PAHL-yah) cheeses and Toma (TOH-mah) are unique among Italian cheeses in that these names signify a style or type rather than an individual cheese name. Think of them as overall designations for two similar types of cheese that originated in Piedmont but are also made in Lombardy. Each style is inextricably linked to its past—so closely linked, in fact, that over the years the names have come to be used as overall identifications for all cheeses in each of these groups.

Paglia-style cheeses take their name from *paglia,* the Italian word for "straw." Many years ago these soft-ripened, gently pasteurized cow's-milk cheeses were aged in piles of loose hay, and it is from this

WHEN IN PIEDMONT

On your next visit to Piedmont, search out the following cheeses.

• **Bra** (BRAH): 12-pound (6 k) wheels of name-controlled raw cow's-milk cheese, 4 inches thick and 15 inches in diameter, named for a village near Alba. Bra cheeses range from soft, mild, and bone-colored (aged for about six months), to firm, flinty-textured, piquant, and straw-colored (aged for one to two years). The rather inedible natural rind is grayish and buffed. This cheese has never been exported to any great degree due to its relatively limited production. One of my importers brings it in now and again, and when he does, I buy it. I like it very much. It reminds me of English Caerphilly.

• **Castagneto** (kah-stah-NYEH-toh): 8-ounce (250 g) disks of fresh goat's milk cheese, 1 inch thick and 4 inches in diameter, named for the paper chestnut leaves used to wrap them. Despite the dearth of goat's milk in Piedmont, this cheese's maker, Merlo, unabashedly copies the French goat's- and cow's-milk cheeses from just across the border in the Savoie and Dauphiné. Their Castagnetos are made the same way, and they are marvelous. (The Merlo company also makes a good, firm sheep cheese in the Pyrénées configuration. It is rather unimaginatively named La Cheso, dialect for "the cheese." Like other Pyrénées cheeses, it is a firm, oily, olivey, very nutty, peasant-style treat—uncomplicated but genuinely scrumptious.)

• **Castelmagno** (kah-stel-MAHN-yoh): 12-pound (6 k), 8-inch-high cylinders of name-controlled raw cow's-milk cheese, Castelmagno is the elusive superstar of Piedmont cheese, so rare and so expensive that you're unlikely to have an opportunity to taste it except on a visit to Piedmont. Sometimes made with a small percentage of sheep's or goat's milk, or a combination of the two,

ancient practice that their name is derived. Every producer in Piedmont and Lombardy features a Paglia-style cheese and calls it something different—Paglietta, Paglierina, Pagliola, for example. The specific brand name doesn't matter; what's important is that all such names are indicative of a style of Piedmont cheese, which is usually made in 6- to 8-ounce (180 g to 250 g) disks, ½ inch thick and 4 to 5 inches in diameter. Cheeses made in the Paglia style are soft and straw-colored, similar to Brie or Camembert, and like Brie and Camembert, their fin-it is a pressed curd cheese with a buff-colored natural, brushed rind and a slightly dry, flaky, yellowish interior. The flavor is relatively mild, slightly tart, and intensely nutty, reminding me of French Laguiole or En-

Patiently waiting to be served at the counter is a shared experience for shoppers in all countries.

glish Caerphilly. One of Piedmont's most remarkable cheeses.

• **Tomini** (toh-MEE-nee): 4-ounce (125 g) disks of fresh cow's-milk (or goat's, or a combination of the two) cheese sold by the piece out of large, bulbous, wide-mouthed jars (*bombati*), in which they are marinated in olive oil flavored with pepper and herbs, or garlic and hot peppers. Tomini are meant to be served with antipasto foods—salami, roasted peppers, olives, raw vegetables. They are quite soft, and while the cheeses themselves are very mild, their seasoned olive oil accompani-ment is often quite piquant, particularly when hot peppers are involved. I offer them at my counters, although they are not widely available in the U.S.

Slather Tomini directly onto slabs of bread and eat as an open-faced sandwich right along with the rest of the antipasto fare. I particularly enjoy placing pieces of Tomini on a slice of crusty, coarse, Tuscan style bread, drizzling the whole thing with an herby, spicy olive oil marinade, and placing it under the broiler for a minute or two. Now that's what I call a grilled cheese sandwich!

ished flavor is truffly, garlicky, wild oniony, mushroomy, and nutty.

Paglia-style cheeses once wore wisps of fresh hay on their natural rinds. This sweet, grassy hay was the same hay fed to the cattle that produced the milk for the cheeses. Its further contribution was that the cheese absorbed the pleasant aroma of the hay. In the commercial cheesemaking world of today, both practices have disappeared. There are doubtless a few *fattorie* (farms) in Piedmont that still turn out Paglia-style cheeses in this manner, but they don't get out of the area, not even to Turin or Milan, and certainly not to the U.S. Now, like Brie and Camembert, they wear bloomy rinds of *Penicillium candidum.* Regardless, some quite delicious examples of commercially produced Paglia-style cheeses are available to us in the U.S. Look for those made by Cademartori, Carmagnola, Lodigiani, Mauri, Oreglia, or Quaglia.

The Italian word *toma,* like the French Dauphinoise/Savoyard word *tomme* or *tome,* is used in a broad sense to describe a round piece of a specific cheese from a specific area. As is also the case with *tomme,* the Toma cheeses are not the result of milk from a single herd (i.e., one farmer's cheese), but rather are the product of several herds pastured within the regional confines of a given area, in this case, Piedmont. This is milk with regional integrity as opposed to milk trucked in from

A ROLL IN THE HAY

In the old days, Piedmont cheesemakers would take a full-fat cream curd—no fat skimmed, no cream added— flatten the curd into a 5-inch-wide pancake, insert it into a pile of hay, and stow the hay in a ripening cellar. The damp warmth and weight of the hay would encourage the cheese to ripen into a true Paglia-style cheese, Italy's answer to France's Brie and Camembert.

another part of Italy. *Toma* also implies that the cheese is made by a true cheesemaking specialist, rather than a farmer with a surplus of milk, who might not necessarily be adept at cheesemaking.

More often than not, Toma cheeses are terrific. Whether from Piedmont (where most originate) or Lombardy (where they also are made), Toma cheeses are 8- to 12-ounce (250 to 375 g), roundish disks made from soft-ripened, very gently pasteurized cow's milk. Their flavor, texture, and appearance are exactly like the Paglia-style cheeses, except Tomas are plump and thickish, whereas the Paglias are quite flat. Like the Paglia cheeses, Toma is paper-wrapped and the flavor is reminiscent of white truffles, a presence owing, no doubt, to the soil and grass of Piedmont. You might also taste hints of wild porcini mushrooms. Italians don't literally flavor their cheeses with porcini; they are content to allow this essence of Piedmont to insinuate itself— just another example of cheesemaking prowess rather than dairy technology.

One more crowning point—the Toma cheeses I am able to import from Italy for my cheese counters are actually vastly superior to any of the Brie or Camembert that is exported by France. Indeed, whenever I am asked to recommend a Camembert (the second most popular cheese in the world), I inevitably offer my customer a Paglia-type or Toma cheese. You owe it to yourself to become acquainted with these vastly underappreciated treasures.

THE LITTLE PIGS OF PIEDMONT

All around Alba, Cuneo, Bra, Asti, and the Monferrato hills, ferreting out wild mushrooms is a regional, indeed a national, passion. Fresh and dried, these porcini, which are part of a larger group of wild mushrooms collectively known as *Boletus edulis,* figure prominently in the cuisine of Piedmont. Though this mushroom grows all over the world, the most delicious are picked in the forests and fields of Piedmont.

Years ago, before fences and highways, Italian farmers allowed their pigs to run wild all summer, foraging in the forests, gorging on acorns, and in general fattening themselves up, oblivious to the inevitable denouement. In the fall, the farmers crashed through the woods, rounding up the pigs in preparation for slaughter. A major bonus of this roundup was the simultaneous seasonal appearance of the *Boletus edulis.* Thus, the farmer gathered not just big, fat, real pigs, but also the "little pigs" (porcini) from the forest floor as well. Hence, the name has endured.

Choosing and Serving Paglia-Style Cheeses and Toma

As with Brie and Camembert, Paglia and Toma cheeses should be beige-mottled and yielding to the touch, with a mushroomy, garlicky aroma. The rind is edible and consuming it is a matter of taste. Avoid any cheeses that are ammoniated, cracked, and/or runny; also come back in a few days for any that are too white and firm at the moment, or buy them knowing you'll need to allow them to ripen in their paper in the vegetable compartment of your refrigerator.

Both of these cheeses are full of seemingly unpasteurized flavor and deserve big red wines, preferably those from Piedmont—Barolo, Barbaresco, Barbera, Gattinara, Ghemme, or Spanna. Soft-ripened cheeses such as these cry out for sweet fruit and crusty bread, whether served as a light lunch or at the end of a meal.

When shopping in Italy or the U.S., look for Pagliola, the Mauri family's brand of Paglia cheeses. For Toma in Italy or the U.S., seek out Toma Carmagnola (from Carmagnola, a town just south of Turin that has a marvelous namesake commercial cheese factory), and Toma della Valcuvia, made by Lodigiani in northern Lombardy.

LOMBARDY

(Lombardie)

The first time I went to Milan, the hub of Lombardy, was in 1979. At that point I had been a New Yorker for six years, and Milan's busy, business-like, crowded, stylish, dirty, and gray New York–like style made me feel truly at home there. I loved it—still do. I knew it would be a perfect, efficient spot to consolidate cheeses from all over Italy, and I was right. Those that require air-shipment for super freshness because they're highly perishable can be flown directly to New York. Those that can stand up to a 10- to 14-day ocean crossing in the hold of a ship or in a deck-level container can travel by refrigerated truck from Milan to Le Havre, France, in one day.

It was in Milan that I found the Peck store, La Casa del Formaggio (see page 212), and was able to locate the Lombardy, Piedmont, and Tuscan cheeses that had never before been sold in the U.S. With a nod to Emilia-Romagna's priceless Parmigiano-Reggiano tradition, I consider Lombardy to be Italy's most important cheese region by far. It not only produces enormous amounts of its regional specialties, Taleggio, Gorgonzola, Stracchino, and Mascarpone, it is also a primary producer of Grana Padano and Provolone.

This fertile region's "cash cows" (as it were) are Gorgonzola, Mascarpone, and Grana Padano, all produced from excellent lowland milk that is transformed into cheese in the modern plants of central Lombardy. The best milk, though, is from the high

Inviting window displays only hint at the treasures inside Italy's most famous cheese shop.

pastures of the Valtellina in northern Lombardy. There, too, one finds the scenic beauty that makes Lombardy a major tourist destination. This is lake country, and each of these lakes has a river running south out of it. The rivers supply power to lowland factories as well as water to the many farms lying in the fertile Po Valley's lowland plains. The rich nutrient-packed milk is used for the manufacture of Lombardy's Taleggio and Taleggio-type cheeses as well as for some production of Gorgonzola. The companies that make the best Lombardy cheeses are situated up in these highlands, nearest the source of their milk supply.

The Cheeses

TALEGGIO

Name-controlled Taleggio (tah-LEDGE-oh) is much like a big Pont-l'Evêque: It is an 8-inch square, about 2 inches thick, and weighs about 5 pounds (2½ k). Usually made from raw cow's milk, it has a washed rind and an off-white, slightly yellowish paste. It can be—indeed, usually is—sublime and it is one of my favorite cheeses. Taleggio ranges in flavor from tart and salty in its

Taleggio, the most refined of all Italian cheeses, deserves to be better known. Italian cooks like to use a few thin slices to garnish polenta.

the virtues of Lombardy's unspoiled high pastureland. Offering a wealth of slightly salty, nutty, meaty flavor, it beckons you to cut off just one more morsel. Moderation is particularly challenging for me when a Taleggio is sitting in front of me.

Real Taleggio has a specific mark imprinted on the top of the rind that proves it to be a bona fide example: Look for four circles embossed into the rind with a different design in the middle of each circle.

Exquisite, rare, Taleggio di Monte (mountain Taleggio), made by hand from raw cow's milk in the Valtellina, an enormous valley at the foot of the Alps, is worth seeking out if you visit northern Lombardy.

youth to rich, buttery, and beefy with nuances of fruits and nuts in aged versions. Excellent Taleggio comes from a number of commercial cheesemakers: Cademartori, Acquistapace, Oreum, Buonacasa, Mauri, and Lodigiani are my favorites. Not-so-good Taleggio is made by big cheese companies in the south of Lombardy. I urge you to avoid the vapid examples that are produced by the dairy giants, Colombo and Galbani.

What separates Taleggio from other cheeses of its type is that it is still largely a northern Italian secret. Only lately has it begun to receive the attention it deserves outside the country. The best commercially available Taleggio is still made in comparatively small batches from unpasteurized or gently pasteurized Valtellina milk of remarkable quality. The resulting cheese is very sophisticated, with great depth of flavor. It is fancy, regal, a decidedly unpeasant-like cheese, reflecting

Choosing and Serving Taleggio

Ripe Taleggio will be not quite runny inside, but sort of bulgy—soft enough to cut with a dull butter knife, and perhaps a bit liquid nearest the rind. The reddish-brown crust should be dry but uncracked. The flavor of the cheese should be full yet gentle, with no more than a tinge of saltiness. If your Taleggio is chalky or firm, and more white than bone-colored, it is underripe and probably arrived here by air. It will merely taste tart, with no meaty nuttiness. (Air-shipping is fine; it ensures freshness, but it carries with it the possibility that an unskilled cheesemonger will not have allowed the cheese to ripen sufficiently. Air-shipping also tacks on at least $2 per pound to the price.) Like any other cheese, once cut, it won't ripen any further, so you are simply out of luck.

Taleggio comes wrapped in several layers of paper stamped with the maker's name. If the Taleggio is fully ripe, this paper can be next to impossible to remove or scrape away. Simply ignore it or rub it off and go on to enjoy one of the world's greatest cheeses.

Traditionally, Taleggio is not used in cooking, although recently a number of inventive young American chefs have discovered it. Now it is showing up in salads, melted in sauces, and cubed in stuffings.

You may serve Taleggio any time you desire a creamy, substantial, full-flavored, luxurious cow's-milk cheese. In Italy, polenta is often served topped with a few thin slices of the cheese. Fruit, crusty bread, and a big red wine, preferably Italian, are good companions. And of course, Taleggio is scrumptious just as it is.

ROBIOLA LOMBARDIA

Robiola Lombardia (roh-bee-OH-lah-lom-bar-DEE-ah) is the generic name of a group of Lombardy cheeses that are essentially diminutive Taleggios. (Don't confuse Robiola Lombardia with Robiola Piemonte, which is a group of fresh, rindless cheeses made in Piedmont.) Many Valtellina producers make Robiola Lombardia and give them fancy names—Tartufella and Baitella made by Cademartori; La Baita made by Lodigiani; d'Artavaggio and Maurella made by Mauri; and Merlo's Antica Cascina. Uniformly excellent, these petite Taleggios vary in size from 6 ounces (180 g) to 1½ pounds (750 g), and come in a variety of shapes including rectangles, cubes, half-moons, and disks. They will always be paper- or foil-wrapped and often the label will give only the brand name without stating the cheese is Robiola Lombardia. Under their wrappers, they will look like any washed-rind, cow's-milk cheese, displaying a rough, reddish-brown crust that is neither too slimy nor too dry. Their flavor and aroma should be exactly like that of Taleggio—meaty, nutty, and slightly saline, with nuances of fruit and a very cheesy aroma.

FORMAGGIO DOLCE DA TAVOLA

Maurella

EMILIO MAURI S.P.A.
PASTURO (VALSASSINA)

Robiola Lombardia are simply small Taleggios, though you might never figure this out from reading some labels. Mauri, a large manufacturer, calls its version Maurella.

Choosing and Serving Robiola Lombardia

Avoid any Robiola Lombardia that has a rancid, mangy odor. Welcome a pronounced cheesy aroma. Avoid any that are cracked outside or graying inside; the color of the interior should be off-white to faintly yellowish. Some growth of blue mold on the rind is perfectly acceptable. The flavor should be full and pronounced, but not sharp or strong (signs of overripeness).

Serve this cheese at the end of a meal with fruit, big red wines, and crusty bread. For lunch or supper, pair it with salami, prosciutto, or smoked ham, fruit, wine, and bread.

GORGONZOLA

Lombardy's most famous cheese is undoubtedly name-controlled Gorgonzola (gor-gohn-ZOH-lah). Its history is entangled with that of its kinsman Stracchino (see page 210), the two cheeses having been the product of "tired" (*stracca*) cattle milked during their long spring and autumn treks to and from seasonal pastures. In fact, in Italy, Gorgonzola is more formally referred to as Stracchino di Gorgonzola. It was near this town (now a city) south of Milan that the herdsmen and their cattle stopped to rest. As a result, this area was flooded with milk twice a year, and since the quantity of milk far exceeded what the residents could possibly drink, it was used to make cheese.

Before the second half of the nineteenth century, when Gorgonzola was first exported, it was the creation of small-production artisans. The curd from the evening milking was suspended in cloth to allow the whey to drip off, as well as to cool, settle, and ripen overnight. The next day the nearly drained curd was placed in a mold of wooden rings and subsequently covered with the still-warm curd from that morning's milking. This "layering" process, which is similar to that used in the making of France's Morbier but without a layer of ash, is still used to make Gorgonzola today.

Gorgonzola is made in two versions: dolce (sweet) and naturale (sharp). Soft, mild dolce (lower left), aged for three months, is more readily available than extra-aged naturale, which is firmer and stronger flavored.

Originally the blueing of Gorgonzola occurred naturally. The instigator was a mold that lurked on the walls of the damp, drafty Valsassina *casere* (caves). This *Penicillium* was found to grow not just upon but also inside, the cheeses that were placed there, forming greenish-blue striations that Italians call *erborinato,* Lombard dialect for "parsley." The process evolved over many years, as the recipe for Gorgonzola was altered and tailored to encourage this miraculous event, which resulted in remarkably delicious cheese.

These days the demand for Gorgonzola has propelled its production into the modern age of cheesemaking No longer can the cheeses be allowed the luxury of languor, of lying about in caves for a year or more, awaiting sufficient inner mold to develop. Instead, for the last 40 years the cheeses have been pierced with copper or stainless-steel needles (the material has no special significance—they could be made from nearly anything), and the resulting fissures allow oxygen to enter and nourish a commercially manufactured mold-producing bacteria called *Penicillium gorgonzola.* In fact, virtually all commercial blue cheeses are made in this way. These bacteria are mixed into the curd early in the cheesemaking process and the piercing markedly speeds up the blueing, thereby shortening the initial aging cycle to three months "in cave," though most are aged for a total of six months. But don't worry—even the best Gorgonzolas I have tasted have been pierced. It is my opinion that al-most all Gorgonzola is so good, I can't imagine that it ever was better. It is one of my favorite cheeses.

Much has been made about Gorgonzola being sweet (*dolce*) or sharp (variously called *naturale, piccante, di monte,* or *stagionato*). In fact, the cheese is marketed in two styles: *dolce,* which is the definitive, familiar Gorgonzola, a soft, mild, and smelly blue cheese, and *naturale,* or aged Gorgonzola, which is firmer and more assertive. The exteriors of both types are washed with brine during the ripening process. And it is the resulting surface bacteria that creates Gorgonzola's powerful, cheesy aroma.

Gorgonzola *dolce* (DOLE-cheh) is released from its cave in the shape and size of a large, 18- to 26-pound (9 to 13 k) hatbox, about 9

THE BLUES BROTHERS

History shows us that both the development of Gorgonzola making and the growing market for this cheese were occurring at about the same pace, though on a much smaller scale, as the development of France's Roquefort, a blue cheese made from sheep's milk. Though both are interior-mold cheeses, they are quite different. Sheep's-milk Roquefort is crumbly and salty, while cow's-milk Gorgonzola is creamy and almost sweet with a spicy, earthy flavor.

LA DOLCE GORGONZOLA

In Italy and in England, you will hear of Dolcelatte, a brand name for a Gorgonzola *dolce* manufactured and distributed by the Galbani company. Dolcelatte (Italian for "sweet milk") is made from the curd of one milking rather than the traditional two, and is no better, nor less fine, than any other example. It is, however, marketed extremely young, or "underripe," compared to other Gorgonzolas, and has become a huge success with a public that finds the Gorgonzola some of us adore to be too strong. Dolcelatte is not yet distributed in the U.S., though I won't be surprised to find it available sometime soon. I'm in no hurry to see this happen since I vastly prefer the standard Gorgonzola.

minum foil to keep air away from the exposed surfaces. (This is not a necessary procedure for hard cheeses because their thick, dry rinds sufficiently protect the interior cheese from the air.) Gorgonzola *dolce*'s rind has been washed frequently with a brine solution during its three-month-long aging period, and is relatively fragile and thin, thus the need for the protective foil wrapping.

Each producer or brand-name marketer has its own color and trademark design for the foil wrapping—blue and silver, or red and gold, for example. They are quite eye-catching and rather pretty. (The foil should be removed before serving the cheese.) Some producers further split the halves into quarters and eighths, which are also foil-wrapped. The danger of this practice is that the many exposed faces of the cheese release butterfat, which seeps against the foil and beneath the cheese, and much of the cheese's flavor and texture are lost. What is left behind is mostly the sharpness of the blue-green mold striations. Whenever possible, try to buy Gorgonzola from large half-wheels.

Each young, sweet Gorgonzola *dolce* has the potential to become aged Gorgonzola *naturale*. Aged Gorgonzola is intensely delicious. Each 14- to 18-pound (7 to 9 k) wheel comes wrapped in foil even though its rind is considerably thicker and drier than young Gorgonzola, the result of repeated brine washings during its year or more in the caves. The interior of an aged Gorgonzola will be markedly whiter, and have bluer striations, than Gor-

inches tall and 12 to 14 inches in diameter. (I use the term "hatbox" to describe the shape and size of any cheese that falls between that of a cookie tin or snare drum and a fireplug or barrel!) Most producers split these forms horizontally in order to make the cheese a more accessible size for the retailer (a soft cheese as big as a whole Gorgonzola is just too difficult to handle). After splitting, the two wheels are wrapped in thin sheets of alu-

Pigeons and pedestrians share the elegant Vittorio Emanuele Galleria, the hub of Milan. A statue of Leonardo da Vinci can be seen at the back.

gonzola *dolce,* which tends toward a yellowish-ivory paste and greenish-blue mold striations.

In Milan, where Peck, Italy's most famous food emporium, dazzles the senses at each of its six locations, their La Casa del Formaggio, on the Via Speronari, creates a Gorgonzola-based specialty that is thoroughly excessive, unique, and delicious. A Gorgonzola *naturale* is split horizontally into 1-inch-thick layers and reassembled with 2-inch-thick alternating layers of fresh, soft, sweet, platinum-blond Mascarpone, a "cheese" made from whey-drained heavy cream (see page 215). The finished product, called Zola Crema, is as theatrical as it is delicious—a taste of gastronomic hedonism (For more on Peck, see page 212.) Several of the larger

Lombardy cheese companies perform much the same trick, though they use soft Gorgonzola *dolce,* and wrap their rectangular blocks of cheese in gaudy-colored foil.

Other types of Gorgonzola you may encounter in Italy include Gorgonzola *bianco* (bee-AHN-ko) or *pannerone* (pan-eh-ROH-neh), both of which are similar to Stracchino. Mild and tart, these soft cheeses lack the greenish-blue striations typical of Gorgonzola, and their flavor is subsequently less exciting.

Choosing and Serving Gorgonzola

Since Gorgonzola comes in a large wheel, you'll probably have an opportunity to check out a large interior portion of the cheese you're thinking about buying. If the cheese is bulging and/or straining against the retailer's plastic wrap, be wary—it's likely to be overripe. To be sure you're getting fresh Gorgonzola, avoid any that shows pinkish, brownish, or grayish interior discoloration—a form of oxidized rancidity that's literally a "dead" giveaway. Also avoid any that is loose-textured or too crumbly and shows excessive pooling of butterfat. Don't misunderstand—Gorgonzola should be moist, but if it weeps or pools, this is evidence that the cheese has been refrigerated too long, or even worse, has been frozen. Freezing, of course, drastically alters the texture and flavor of any soft cheese. A healthy Gorgonzola should be a vivid, glistening ivory-to-straw color, set against liberal striations of greenish-blue mold.

There are a number of excellent brands of Gorgonzola to choose from in the U.S. and Italy. Look for Galbani, Klin, Lodigiani, or Mauri.

Gorgonzola is marvelous anytime with fruit and red wines such as Chianti Riserva or Barolo, or spicy, sweet white dessert wines such as Marsala or the rare Picolit. It is also a superb cheese for salad—on the side, scooped into little balls, or diced—or blended into a vinaigrette. Gorgonzola is also a primary ingredient in numerous recipes for stuffed chicken or veal, pasta sauces, pastries, pizza, and some delightful desserts involving pears and figs.

STRACCHINO

Also Called Stracchino di Crescenza

The root word of Stracchino (strah-KEE-noh) is *stracca,* meaning "tired" or "soft." The centuries-old story of Stracchino, or Crescenza (kreh-SHEN-tsah), is a tale of the transhumance. It tells of herds of cattle that were taken in the autumn from the high Alps in northern Lombardy to the lowlands of southern Lombardy, where they would spend the winter grazing on pasture stubble augmented with fodder. In the springtime, the cattle journeyed back to the summer pastures. Of course, along the way, they needed to be milked. At least a few of these stopping points were

A CHEESE MENAGERIE

Scamorza (skah-MOOR-tsah), a *pasta filata* cow's-milk cheese similar to Mozzarella, though a bit drier and chewier, is produced in both Lombardy and southern Italy (see page 249). In Lombardy, where most Scamorza is made, cheesemakers stretch and carve hand-kneaded plain or smoked balls of this firm, piquant cheese, transforming them into a veritable menagerie of shapes that children find especially delightful. The shapes reflect holidays and seasons—Easter lambs in the spring, for example, or donkeys, chickens, and ducks around Christmastime. Pigs are popular year-round, but I have also seen owls, eagles, alligators, whales, and dolphins, each weighing from 8 to 12 ounces (250 to 375 g).

near the town of Gorgonzola. The milk gathered at these milkings became the cheese that evolved into Stracchino and later also into Gorgonzola. These tired cattle, it seemed, gave extra-good milk, thus the cheesemakers became aware that the physical exertion stimulates a cow's mammolactation to such a degree that her milk is measurably higher in butterfat.

Stracchino is sold in 2-inch-thick loaves or slabs weighing 4 to 8 ounces (125 to 250 g) or 2 to 3 pounds (1 to 1½ k), which are double-wrapped in waxed paper, with the outer layer displaying the maker's logo. Young Stracchino's very thin, smooth, almost invisible bone-white rind harbors a unique tart, white paste that is quite soft. Once the Stracchino has ripened, the rind will be beige, dry, and show a light dusting of *Penicillium candidum* mold, and the white paste will be oozy and satiny. The tart fruity flavor of ripened Stracchino becomes more pronounced in older cheeses—it is very much an acquired taste, one that cries out for the company of berries, pears, peaches, and plums.

Most commercial cheesemakers now market their Stracchino as Crescenza or Stracchino di Crescenza, names they find more appetizing and attractive. Though some cheese experts maintain that Crescenza and Stracchino are different, I absolutely disagree. I've watched both being made, I've talked to the cheesemakers, and I am convinced that they are indeed the same cheese.

Choosing and Serving Stracchino

Stracchino is good both young, when its paste is foam-rubber soft, and older, when its interior glistens and oozes. However, its flavor will be more piquant and fruitier in the ripe state. Avoid any examples that show signs of pink on the rind or interior, an indicator that the cheese is rancid.

Stracchino is a marvelous breakfast and lunch cheese with fruit, brioche, muffins, toast, or croissants. Italians enjoy it with *mostarda di Cremona,* the sweet-spicy, chutney-like, dried fruit and mustard oil condiment from Cremona. Stracchino is also appropriate as a dessert cheese, especially teamed with one or two other cheeses. Its tart, almost uncheese-like flavor provides an illuminating bridge between the other cheeses.

Luxurious soft cheeses from Lombardy (left to right): a torta di mascarpone with layers of fresh basil, a small tub of Mascarpone, and thick little loaves of tart, fruity Stracchino.

VISITING LA CASA DEL FORMAGGIO

One day during my first trip to Italy, I was walking down the Via Speronari in Milan when I came across the most extraordinary cheese store I had ever seen. Peck's La Casa del Formaggio is one of six specialty food stores founded in 1883 by a Czech immigrant named Franz Peck. The empire has expanded considerably since then, especially under the current ownership of the Stoppani brothers.

One of the stores is a grandiose prepared-food shop; one sells spit-roasted meats, pizzas, and roasted vegetables; one is a wine shop; another is a huge restaurant. Yet another store specializes in pork products—a *salumeria*—and then there is La Casa del Formaggio. Visually stunning, it offers as many as 600 Italian cheeses. Don't let this number throw you. Most are variations of the same cheeses we discuss here, but by different makers. The ceiling is festooned with clusters of Gravina, a cheese (not sold in the U.S.) that is like Provolone but from a specific area east of Rome. The clusters look like giant bunches of balloon-size, ovoid, beige grapes, each one weighing 15 pounds (7½ k), with a dozen or so to the "bunch." They are festooned with oak leaves and, because of the

temperature near the ceiling, they glisten from the warm, liquefying butterfat in them. (Obviously they have to be changed every day or at least every week, otherwise all the butterfat would drip out, leaving a desiccated husk of a cheese.)

On the highest wooden shelves circling the room—and the room is big, easily around 2,000 square feet—are striking half-moons of hand-split Parmesan, sitting cheek by jowl. They, at least, are wrapped in plastic so they won't dry out. But down on the selling floor, all around the room at eye level, are half-moons, wedges, triangles, and whole wheels of Parmesan that aren't wrapped. All of them are wide open because they will be sold by the end of the day. I know—I've spent days in there!

In this one place I was able to learn about, sample, and arrange for U.S. import virtually all of the generic, original, regional, pure, and venerated cheeses of Italy—in one fell swoop. I had known these cheeses existed, but at Peck I was able to gather together all the brands I wanted, in all the styles and shapes, because they were all right there in front of me.

From the Stoppani brothers I was able to get the names and addresses of the artisans who make the best Mozzarella *di bufala* so that I could bring it to America. I wanted to import Mascarpone, but I was told that because of its extreme perishability it couldn't be done, which turned out to be balderdash. (I must admit, though, that in the beginning I was so careful with these rare cheeses you'd have thought I was transporting donor organs.) I also began to import fresh Ricotta made from sheep's milk, and a lovely array of the rare goat's-milk cheeses from Piedmont. It was all right there, so I scooped it up and sent it across the ocean. The perishable treasures went by air. The harder, sturdier cheeses like Fontina d'Aosta, Gravina, Asiago *d'allevo,* and mountain Gorgonzola journeyed to the U.S. aboard container ships.

Upon my return to New York City, these cheeses began to arrive and *boom,* they all began to fly off my cheese counters. I received several types and styles of Robiola cheeses and the great brands (Mauri, Oreum) of Taleggio. I offered the Toma and Paglia-style cheeses, three versions of Pecorino Toscano, Caprini, sheep's- and goat's-milk Ricotta, Mozzarella *di bufala,* Mascarpone, and handmade *torte di mascarpone.* I had it all—as my customers discovered to their great delight. Since then, my cheese counters have continued to expand and reflect the glorious panoply of Italian cheeses. My customers have grown more knowledgeable. And the efforts of importers and retailers, food writers and chefs, have also contributed to making these once hard-to-find Italian cheeses almost commonplace in the U.S. Today Mascarpone, Taleggio, Fontina d'Aosta, and scores of other Italian cheeses can now be readily found in countless specialty food shops, and even in some supermarkets.

With more than 600 cheeses on display, Peck's La Casa del Formaggio on the Via Speronari in Milan is paradise for cheese lovers. Some of the same cheeses are also sold at a Peck outpost in Tokyo.

RICOTTA

Some of the big Lombardy cheese producers, who make a wide range of commercial cheeses, truck in enormous quantities of goat's and sheep's milk from the south. After cheese is made, the whey, a by-product of cheesemaking, is used to create Ricotta (ree-COH-tah), which is actually a dairy product rather than a cheese. *Ricotta* means "recooked," and this dairy product was originally made in Rome from whey that was a by-product of Romano cheesemaking. Whey was, and still is, a problem. It is not disposable, because it fouls up sewers and rivers by increasing the growth of algae, which then deplete the water's oxygen supply, eventually killing the fish. Only in the last hundred years was it discovered that this limpid, low-fat, nutritious liquid could be turned into a "cheese." When protein-rich whey is subjected to heat, the casein particles fuse together and create a new curd that, when drained, becomes snowy-white Ricotta.

Italian Ricotta is primarily made from the whey of sheep's milk or water buffalo milk, though occasionally goat's or cow's milk whey is used. American Ricotta is usually made from cow's milk whey and is quite different in taste and texture from the Italian type. Both types are low in sodium and fat, but the Italian product has a mild, sweet, nutty flavor and a rather dry texture. It not only complements and heightens the flavor of other foods, but also

For la dolce vita, *bouquets of fresh flowers are essential.*

adds its pillowy texture as well. Much blander American Ricotta is sweeter, considerably moister, and is more neutral as an ingredient in cooking. Either type of Ricotta can be eaten as is, like cottage cheese, but they are more commonly used in pasta dishes and desserts.

Choosing and Serving Ricotta

If you discover that your cheese shop has a stock of imported Italian Ricotta, my advice is for you to jump all over it. It will likely be fresh, because none but the ardent specialist who cares about it will have gotten it in the first place. In Italy and in the U.S., Italian-made Ricotta is sold by weight, wrapped in paper. If possible, taste before buying. Avoid any that feels prickly on the tongue and tastes sharp and fruity—dead giveaways that it is no longer fresh. Take it home and eat it as is, with fruits or vegetables, or even better, incorporate it into your favorite pasta recipe. Whether made from goat's, sheep's, or cow's milk, and no matter what brand, it will be fantastic. A variation, Italian buffalo-milk Ricotta, is one of the finest things I've ever tasted. I stock it at my counters when it's available.

MASCARPONE

Also Called Mascherpone

It is thought by some that the name Mascarpone or Mascherpone (both pronounced mahs-kar-POE-neh) dates from the sixteenth

THE RAREST MASCARPONE

Perhaps the rarest and most intriguing Mascarpone is that made from water buffalo cream. Unavailable in the U.S., Mascarpone *di bufala* is made in very small quantities in Campania and has a more nutty and elemental flavor than cow's milk versions. If you find yourself around Naples on a visit to Italy, seek it out for a memorable taste experience.

century, when, it is said, a visiting Spanish official remarked to its maker that it was *mas que bueno,* "better than good." Others believe that, around the same time, its name was derived from a salted, alpine Ricotta called Mascherpin. But my most reliable sources tell me the name Mascarpone has at its root the Italian verb *mascherare,* to "dress up" or "camouflage," no doubt referring to the dressing-up treatment undergone by the cream it is made from. Perhaps, though, the dressing-up is the reward received by anything Mascarpone accompanies.

Mascarpone is made from the cream of cow's milk. Like Ricotta, it is more a dairy product than a cheese (no starter or rennet is used in its production). Mascarpone doesn't involve curds at all.

Your very first taste of Mascarpone is a sensation that lingers—you'll never forget it. Pale blond, it is smooth, soft, and sweet, with an extremely high butterfat content of 70% to 75%, which is as high as it can be without becoming butter. When cream is churned, the butterfat globules clump together and the result is pure butter. Mascarpone is different: With the help of citric acid, the heavy cream is merely relieved of its moisture by being set to drain through a finely woven cloth. The result is similar to buttercream cake icing or English clotted cream. Its flavor is sweet because of the high lactose content in the solid mass. The soluble sodium exits with the liquid, and it is this lack of sodium that is responsible for Mascarpone's high perishability. Until

WHEN IN LOMBARDY

When traveling, be on the lookout for:

• **Bitto** (BEE-toe): Raw cow's milk combined with a small percentage of goat's milk; from northern Lombardy. This is a local cheese used primarily in cooking when cheeses such as Parmesan or Gruyère are called for (its flavor falls nicely between the two). It is made in 14- to 22-pound (5 to 11 k) wheels, 7 to 9 inches thick, 18 to 24 inches in diameter, and aged from 40 days to three years. The rind is natural, straw-colored, blotched with mold owing to aging (grayish); the paste is bone- to straw-colored, according to age. The flavor is mild and toffee-like, reflecting its mixed milk origins.

Bitto is made only in summer when cattle are taken to the *alpeggi,* the high alpine pastures. This terrific cheese, on the order of French Beaufort, is usually not exported.

• **Formagella** (for-mah-JELL-ah), or **Formagetta** (for-mah-JEH-tah): Pasteurized cow's-milk cheese principally from Lombardy, but also made in Piedmont, Veneto, the Marches, and Umbria. Sometimes goat's and/or sheep's milk is added. Fresh (aged only three weeks to two months), mild, and lactic-sweet, these cheeses are quadrangular in shape, 4 to 5 inches high, 6 to 7 inches in diameter, and weigh from 1 to 4½ pounds (500 g to 2¼ k). Very soft, supple, and white, this rindless cheese is eaten for breakfast, lunch, and as a snack, with nuts and fruit. It's exported, but not widely available.

• **Quartirolo** (kwar-tee-ROLL-oh): Pasteurized cow's-milk cheese— essentially an unripened Taleggio. The white, dry crust is edible, the soft, white inner paste is mild, buttery, and sweet. The cheeses are wrapped in flimsy paper (to protect the crust) with a brand-emblazoned paper overwrap.

This is a cheese I find to be uninteresting, except for the origin of its name: It was once made only in the autumn after the fourth (*quart*) cutting of the hay. The hay of late September and early October is particularly sweet and perfumy, hence the milk given by the cattle who consumed this hay was considered extra-special.

Today the cheese has become highly commercial and is made year-round from milk of ordinary quality. Exported, but not widely available.

Rich, richer, richest. Sweet, unctuous Mascarpone, which is made from cream, tastes very much like buttercream icing.

not so very long ago it was always made "in store" and sold directly from the muslin draining bags. Today Mascarpone has become so popular that it is now usually supplied by cheese companies.

The special qualities of Mascarpone as an ingredient add lushness and luster to a number of Italian specialties, both sweet and savory. It is the principal ingredient in *tiramisù* (dialect meaning "pick-me-up"), a famous dessert from northern Italy that has become popular in the U.S. Classic *tiramisù* combines Strega liqueur, ladyfingers soaked in espresso, egg yolks, sugar, cocoa, and Mascarpone. Another favorite Lombardy dessert is *zuccotto,* a sort of pound cake with grappa and Mascarpone that's shaped like a large dome.

In neighboring Friuli–Venezia Giulia, Mascarpone is sometimes mixed with anchovies, mustard, and herbs to create a savory mixture to spread on bread. In most households, though, it is enjoyed as is, sprinkled with sugar, cocoa, finely ground coffee beans, or grated chocolate. It is also a delicious companion to strawberries and raspberries.

Mascarpone reaches new heights in a Lombardy specialty called *torta di mascarpone* (literally, "cheesecake"), combined with other ingredients and cheeses. The earliest one I remember eating in the U.S. (it still is available) is the Galbani company's delicious Torta San Gaudenzio, named after a village near their plant in Novara, west of Milan. Torta San Gaudenzio is simply alternating layers of Gorgonzola *dolce* and Mascarpone. It is also made with fresh basil leaves placed on each layer. This cheese confection makes a remarkably good sauce for pasta—simply toss either version of Torta San Gaudenzio with just-cooked, hot pasta and serve without further embellishment.

At Peck's La Casa del Formaggio in Milan (see page 212), a stunning array of *torte di mascarpone* are featured. Among the temptations are Zola Crema (see page 209), *torta di basilico* (layers of fresh basil leaves, Robiola cheese, pliant, unaged Parmigiano-Reggiano, olive oil, pine nuts, and Mascarpone), *torta de salmone affumicato* (smoked salmon), *torta di tartufi bianchi* (costly white truffles), and others made with everything from sweet peppers and garlic to figs and almonds.

Choosing and Serving Mascarpone

Taste, taste, taste—it is the only way to select your dollops or containers of Mascarpone. Mascarpone should be sweet and smooth with no lumps—period—no saltiness, no bitterness. If it is sealed in an 8-ounce (250 g) or 1-pound (500 g) container, check the date on the top or bottom. These containers do work miraculously well at preserving freshness, but don't buy one if the date is too close to expiration. In any case, you should never attempt to store Mascarpone for more than a few days. Enjoy it with fruit salads, atop a wedge of chocolate torte, added to pasta sauces, incorporated in desserts, or slathered on breakfast pastries and sprinkled with cocoa or cinnamon.

Perhaps the most agreeable way to enjoy Mascarpone is as a simple, rustic dessert. Combine a selection of whole, very sweet fruits in a bowl of crushed ice. Mound Mascarpone in a separate bowl. Encourage your guests to choose their own fruit and then spoon dollops of Mascarpone on their plates to eat with the fruit. Accompany with a sparkling wine or a sweet dessert wine such as Marsala or Picolit.

Italian Mascarpone, which is similar to French crème fraîche, can be eaten as is or combined with other cheeses, such as rich, blue-veined Gorgonzola dolce.

BEL PAESE

Bel Paese (BEL-pah-EH-zeh), which means "beautiful country," is one of Italy's best-known cheeses, though it surely doesn't deserve the distinction. This soft, high-fat cow's-milk cheese is immensely popular because it is very mild (read bland), with little or no aroma. The rind is coated with a thin layer of paraffin and it is marketed in plastic-wrapped wedges. It is produced south of Milan in Lombardy in a large factory owned by the Galbani company. Galbani invented this brand-name cheese in 1929 to appeal to customers who preferred a soft, mild-flavored cheese. Virtually nobody dislikes it. In short, it is a cheese for people who don't like cheese. Bel Paese often insinuates itself into recipes where melted cheese is desired but no flavor is required, and it is agreeable to many people when served on antipasto platters. I am baffled that so many *sophisticated* chefs, both in Italy and the U.S., choose to use it as an ingredient, especially in ravioli. Bel Paese is so popular and mainstream that it is now made in the U.S. I stock neither the Italian nor the American versions and I don't recommend it to my customers under any circumstances for any purpose.

FRIULI–VENEZIA GIULIA AND THE VENETO

Although Friuli–Venezia Giulia, also known as Friuli-Udine, is the least fertile and least agriculturally developed region in northern Italy, it is a pretty area, well worth visiting. And it contributes two of the most important Italian foodstuffs in all of Italian gastronomy—Italy's best polenta, made from fine, white maize flour, and *prosciutto di San Daniele,* as prized (and certainly rarer) than the very best hams from Langhirano, Parma, and Carpegna (the Marches). If you are familiar only with American-style cured ham or U.S.-made prosciutto, you simply cannot conceive of how remarkable true Italian prosciutto can be. It is at once sweet, sweetly aromatic, fruity, nutty—almost like candy—but with an aftertaste that anoints the palate like cream. Less important, but no less cherished by the Friulani, are their cheeses, the most famous of which—Asiago and Montasio—are both name-controlled.

In addition to the polenta, prosciutto, and cheeses of Friuli, I urge you to seek out the coffee beans that are blended and roasted there. The beans from two brands—Illy (Trieste) and Udinese (Pordenone)—are *arabica* types (the most prized coffees) of mostly South American origin, but the blending and roasting (over beechwood fire for the Udinese) and patented, vacuum-packing (Illy), are strictly Italian in

Friuli–Venezia Giulia and the Veneto

Groceries to go: A floating fruit and vegetable barge bobs quietly on the water of a canal in Venice, where streets are for pedestrians.

style and execution. They belong in a place above all of the other coffees of Italian blending and roasting, though I'd never turn down a cup of Danesi, Kimbo, Lavazza, Mauro, or Saquella, each an excellent coffee from a famous, long-established Italian coffee specialist.

The borders of three regions—Friuli, the Veneto, and Alto Adige—converge in the northern reaches of the Padana plain in a verdant sweep of lush pasturage near the village of Asiago in the Veneto. The Veneto is a huge region whose sprawling territory encompasses Venice in the east on the Adriatic and Verona in the west. In between lies the vast expanse of the plain, a richly agricultural area that includes the delta of the river Po and the famous Italian cities of Treviso (famed for radicchio), Padua (one of the areas where Parmigiano-Reggiano's less

noble cousin, Grana Padano, is made), and Vicenza (famed for its asparagus).

Though countless cheeses are made in Friuli–Venezia Giulia and neighboring Veneto, the two most distinctive, honest, and straightforward examples, each with a long history and name-controlled status, are the Veneto's Asiago and Friuli's Montasio.

The Cheeses

ASIAGO

The village of Asiago (ah-zee-AH-goh) in northern Veneto gives its name to a handsome, though less than captivating, cow's-milk cheese of name-controlled production. The large, thick wheels weigh 18 to 24 pounds (9 to 12 k), and are 7 to 9 inches high, 14 to 16 inches in diameter. There are two distinctive types of Asiago: Asiago *d'allevo* (dah-LEH-voh), which is available in the U.S., and Asiago *pressato* (preh-SAH-toh), which is not exported.

Asiago *d'allevo,* the more traditional of the two, is produced in small batches from partially skimmed raw cow's milk at traditional cheesemaking facilities located near the Dolomite mountains. Its color is a light beige, both inside and out, with considerable small-hole distribution throughout. Its flavor is mild and lactic, utterly devoid of rusticity. Its texture is firm and supple, making it an easy cheese to cut, shave, or shred (it melts nicely). Asiago *d'allevo* is marketed in three distinct stages of ripeness: Fresh (*fresco*), aged two to three months; medium-ripe (*mez-*

zano), aged three to five months; and slow-ripened (*vecchio*), aged nine months or longer. The aged Asiagos have a very dry, grayish rind and an interior paste that ranges from bone to amber in color. Their textures run the gamut from as soft as Danish Havarti to flinty hard and prone to break into shards, particularly when cut with a classic Parmesan wedge (the tool used in Italy for all hard cheeses). Chewier than *mezzano, vecchio* is slightly sharper and similar in taste to Swiss Sbrinz—sort of butterscotchy, but without the bite one expects from an aged cheese.

Asiago *pressato,* a blander, sweeter, more commercial Asiago made from pasteurized whole milk, is an "industrial" cheese produced in large quantities in factories located in the lowlands of the Po valley near Treviso. It is milder in

Name-controlled Asiago from Veneto (left) and name-controlled Montasio (right) from Friuli–Venezia. Similar in taste and texture is Umbriaco (perched atop the Asiago) from Lombardy, which has a wine-washed rind.

flavor more rubbery in texture, and higher in fat than Asiago _d'allevo._ _Pressato,_ which is aged only briefly, takes its name from the process of pressing the cheeses in order to speed up their ripening, a method that is also used in the U.S. for Colby. It is the same size and shape as _d'allevo,_ but taller. _Pressato_ is not exported.

Choosing and Serving Asiago

A s.ago of any age is rarely sold in bad condition as it is difficult to abuse. Just use your common sense; take a good look at it and, of course, taste it first. Asiago is the perfect snack or lunchtime cheese to accompany hand-hewn slices of salami, crusty bread, and any light, fruity red wine, such as Grave del Friuli or Dolcetto d'Alba. Asiago is used often in Friulani cuisine—grated for pasta, gratins, and soups, cubed in salads, and eaten by itself. The aged _vecchio_-type is excellent as a table cheese and well suited for use in cooking. _Fresco_ is strictly an eating cheese—try it in sandwiches and salads.

MONTASIO

High in the Alps of Friuli–Venezia Giulia, adjacent to the Asiago cheese-producing area, there is a pasture-terraced mountain called Montasio. In the thirteenth century

MONTASIO'S TWIN

If you visit Friuli–Venezia Giulia, keep an eye out for a cheese called Carnia (KAR-nee-yah), made either with whole raw cow's milk or a combination of partially skimmed raw cow's milk augmented with sheep's milk. La Carnia is the most verdant, mountainous part of Friuli–Venezia Giulia, an area often referred to as Alpi Carniche. Carnia, which is not exported, is identical to the more famous name-controlled Montasio.

these pastures were the property of a monastery that became famous for a firm, aged yet mild, partially skimmed, raw cow's-milk cheese named Montasio (mohn-TAH-zee-yoh), for the mountain. In the intervening centuries this cheese has become one of the agricultural pillars of the region's economy and was awarded D.O.C. status in 1986. At that time legal geographic boundaries were established for the production of the cheese and the milk used in its making. All of Friuli–Venezia Giulia and parts of Veneto are Montasio's domain. To give you an idea of just how important D.O.C. status is to an Italian cheese, it took a thirty-year effort on the part of Friulani farmers and cheesemakers to earn this valuable distinction.

Montasio is made in 15- to 23-pound (7½ to 11½ k) wheels, about 3

When shopping for Montasio, look for this D.O.C. symbol, a guarantee of authenticity.

inches thick, 12 to 14 inches in diameter. It is nearly identical in style and flavor to Asiago *d'allevo,* though its size is slightly smaller and the mountain milk it is made with is a bit higher in butterfat, which adds greater richness and depth to its slightly butterscotchy flavor. Inside Montasio's grayish-beige brushed rind the beige-colored paste is dot-

ted throughout with small, irregularly shaped holes. In Italy, Montasio is available aged four months for use as a table cheese and in a two-year-old version intended for grating. The examples we have access to in the U.S. have generally been aged for around nine months and are best as eating cheeses.

Choosing and Serving Montasio

Montasio is a very sturdy cheese that, like Asiago, is hard to abuse. Before purchasing, check for old age, which will be evidenced by excessive dryness, a cracked rind, a gray or darkening amber interior, and an overall lifeless quality.

Montasio is a subtle, butter-

Mouthwatering arrays of salumi *(cured pork) and cheese are commonplace throughout Italy. Prosciutto from Parma is famous, but the more exquisite, rare, and prized one is* prosciutto di San Daniele, *the specialty here in Friuli–Venezia Giulia.*

Time has stood still in the charming mountain villages of Carnia, the Alpine region of Friuli. The area's namesake cheese is identical to Montasio.

scotch- or toffee-tasting cheese with a subdued earthy quality that reflects its raw milk origins and nicely complements other foods. Its fine, rustic flavor can easily be overshadowed if it is served with other cheeses that have bigger personalities, but when Montasio is allowed to speak its mind without interruption you will find it most agreeable. Most often eaten at table, this cheese has a special affinity to pears. I can think of no snack more delectable than a hunk of Montasio accompanied by ripe pears, ruby-red slices of *prosciutto di San Daniele,* good crusty bread, and a bottle of one of Friuli's undersung Grave del Friuli wines made from Merlot, Cabernet, or Pinot Nero grapes. Montasio also finds its way into the kitchen, and is used in pastas, salads, gratins, vegetable dishes, and broths.

EMILIA-ROMAGNA

Emilia-Romagna is Italy's most important food region and the birthplace of the world's greatest cheese, Parmigiano-Reggiano. The wheat grown in Emilia-Romagna makes the area, along with Abruzzi, Italy's number-one pasta region, and the bread made from this wheat is inextricably linked to the glory of this region's cuisine. Thanks to the extremely fertile alluvial soil, the quality and quantity of vegetables and fruit that grow there lead all the other regions of Italy. Tomatoes abound (some for eating, others for canning and concentrating), sugar beets, table grapes, rice, corn (for meal and livestock feed—Italians don't eat corn as such), asparagus, zucchini, and wonderful fruit have given rise to an entire industry based on canning and preserving. The cherries of Vignola are world famous. *Prosciutto di Parma,* cured, not smoked, is deserving of every accolade it has ever been given, and Emilia-Romagna is its home.

Emilia-Romagna is divided into eight provinces, each about the size of Rhode Island. Just hearing a few of their names is a lesson in the history of this region: Ferrara and its Este-family dynasty of 350 years; Ravenna and its expatriate Roman emperors and Byzantine rulers. Bologna, the capital of Emilia-Romagna, has been called "La Grossa" ("the fat one") since the early Middle Ages, a testimony less to its waistline than to its bank account larded with proceeds from the region's rich provender. What Modena lacks in military and artistic history, it compensates for gastronomically. Sausages reign in

The elegant city of Parma is famous for Parmigiano-Reggiano, violets, and prosciutto di Parma

this area, chiefly *zampone,* a practically religious rite of seasoned, chopped pork stuffed into the skin of a pig's foot, boiled, and served with beans or lentils and mashed potatoes.

Balsamic vinegar, which Giorgio DeLuca and I first brought to the United States in 1977 and offered at Dean & DeLuca, originated in Modena, and even today almost every home there is the repository of a family vinegar works. *Aceto balsamico,* which predates the eleventh century, is made from the boiled-down must, not wine, of Trebbiano or other grapes. After it ferments and turns to vinegar with the encouragement of a vinegar "mother" that coats the insides of the barrels, it undergoes the ag-

ing process that accounts for its flavor—and fame. This flavor is a result of the vinegar being transferred over the years from kegs of oak to successively smaller kegs made of mulberry, chestnut, cherry, and ash, each wood contributing its unique fragrances to the liquid.

On the Emilian Way (the Roman highway that bisects the region) is Reggio. Reggio and Parma are two of the eight provinces of Emilia-Romagna. Parma, which means "shield," was founded by Marcus Aemilius Lepidus as a sort of guard town against enemies marching toward Rome. It bears the same name as the fast, rough, and turbulent river below the city. Reggio is more properly called Reggio nell'Emilia, Reggio d'Emilia, or just Reggio Emilia.

Big is beautiful: An average-size wheel of Parmigiano-Reggiano weighs 66 pounds (33 k).

The Cheeses

PARMIGIANO-REGGIANO

The strictly delineated D.O.C. region for Parmigiano-Reggiano (par-mee-JAH-noh-reh-JAH-noh) production is as closely guarded as are wine appellations. Parmigiano-Reggiano can be made only in its *zona tipica,* the provinces of Parma, Reggio Emilia, and Modena in their entirety, the portion of Bologna on the left bank of the River Reno, and the portion of Mantua, in Lombardy, on the right bank of the River Po. By law, Parmigiano-Reggiano can be made only between about April 15 and November 11. This practice ensures that the milk comes from cattle pastured on the zone's fresh grass, rather than on silage or fodder from other locations.

Wheels of Parmesan are required to weigh at least 66 pounds (33 k), with a maximum weight of 88 pounds (44 k). The cheeses must be aged for no less than 14 months, but most are aged for about two years, at which time they can fetch a higher price. The interior of young Parmesan is a yellowish-white, while the paste of older, more desirable examples is straw-colored with a more splintery texture. Along with the words "Parmigiano-Reggiano," the date of the cheese's making is usually stamped on the burnished, golden rind, as are the nearly undecipher-

It is in Reggio that Parmigiano-Reggiano originated.

Cheese is, by far, Reggio's most important industry, but as with Parma, it is an industry linked to the region's others. The cattle that are nourished here on the rich pasturage produce extraordinary milk, some of the best in Italy. This pasturage is so infinitely lush there is even fodder left over for export to other parts of the country. The whey, a by-product of cheesemaking, is used to nourish the region's world-famous hogs. Parma ham is practically as famous as Parmigiano-Reggiano, a fact that fails to credit the many towns within the provinces that are actually responsible for the hams and cheeses that have made Parma famous. In fact, no cheese is made in Parma, though it is the center of commerce. The best cheeses are made in Reggio, the best hams near Langhirano.

able code numbers that tell exactly which *partita* (season's production) and *casello* (a small building where cheese is made) it came from. Even older Parmesan is much in demand. Three-year-old Parmigiano-Reggiano is referred to as *stravecchio* (extra-aged or "very old"); at four it is known as *stravecchione*. At these ages the cheeses will have a deeper golden color, set off by tiny, white, glinting specks that are in no way a defect—they're delicious. My very knowledgeable friend, wine-authority Barbara Ensrud, describes them as "crystalline and crunchy, yet remarkably, they melt in your mouth."

Parmesan is a *grana* (a "grainy"-textured or "granular" cheese), a reference to its finished texture. A *grana* is a hard cheese that when grated will result in fine grains or flakes (depending on the size of the holes in the grater). For pasta, I prefer coarse grated; other times, such as for soup, I think a very fine, powdery texture is desirable. There are many *grana* cheeses made in many towns across northern Italy, but they are not Parmigiano-Reggiano Parmesan is different because of its milk, the care and expertise expended in making it, and the length of its aging period.

Parmesan has enormous flavor As a table cheese, it will melt in your mouth, lozenge-like, creating a thick, delicious, piquant paste. In cooking, this huge flavor disperses and unites with other ingredients to raise their presence and heighten their impact. The flavor can be described as spicy, like cinnamon or nutmeg; salty, like the liquor accompanying an oyster; sweet, like ginger cookies; and nutty, like black walnuts—all at the same time. That is what makes it such a fantastic cheese.

Choosing and Serving Parmigiano-Reggiano

As every other cheese in the world comes after Parmesan, it is important that you know how to buy the real thing. To determine the cheese's authenticity, examine the rind for the words "Parmigiano-Reggiano," which are stamped very closely together all over the side of the cheese. The plant code number and the date of production will also be branded somewhere on the

All Parmigiano-Reggiano is excellent, but many connoisseurs consider Rocca to be the best. This metal emblem is affixed to its rind.

How Parmigiano-Reggiano Is Made

The milk for Parmigiano-Reggiano arrives daily from neighboring farms to the *caselli*—the unimposing, surprisingly small buildings where the cheese is made. Two separate milkings are used for every batch of cheese: the evening milk is poured out into wide trays to rest overnight; the morning milk is turned into curd after it has rested for about an hour. (When the two milkings are combined, most of the naturally accumulated cream is skimmed off and then trucked elsewhere for transformation into butter and other dairy products.)

Next, the morning and evening milkings are combined in huge copper caldrons, the "starter" whey is added, and the fermentation begins. This starter comes from the cheesemaking process of the previous batch. It is whey in which the lactic acid presence is high enough to start the fermentation process in a new batch of milk. This action, along with the heat from the caldron (about 90°F; 32°C), touches off the renneting, which coagulates the milk rapidly, within about 15 minutes. The resulting curd is called *cagliata*. At this point, the separation of the curd from the liquid whey begins. The curd is turned, broken, and cut up with a tool known as a *spino* (thorn brush), until the particles are tiny—about the size of lentils. This thorough cutting action releases so much whey that the resulting cheese is sure to be a hard one.

Next, the curds are "cooked," actually heated slowly to about 112°F (50°C). Once the curd reaches this temperature, the heat is very quickly raised to 131°F (55°C), and is then abruptly turned

cheese, though in most instances you are not likely to see this information since it is unlikely you'll be viewing a whole, uncut cheese. That aside, make sure the cheese is fresh, not dried out from abuse or just plain old. If the cheese is dried out, it will be rock hard and have a white patina.

Avoid any Parmigiano-Reggiano that has been cut and left wrapped in plastic for more than a few days. If this is the case, the wrap will very likely be cloudy and loose with broken crumbs rattling around inside. If possible, have your purveyor cut a piece from the wheel of Parmesan while you are standing at the counter. Try to avoid paying for excess of rind. (The rind, which strictly speaking is inedible, is good as a flavoring agent in minestrone off. This action causes the fine-grained curd particles to mass at the bottom of the caldron, where they are allowed to rest for about 30 minutes. Next the curd is lifted with a wooden paddle and placed in a large piece of cloth, made from hemp grown in the region. The bulging bag is then placed in a *fascera,* the wooden mold that gives the Parmesan its shape, and the curd is gently pressed to expel any remaining whey. It is at this point that the cheese is stenciled with the name "Parmigiano-Reggiano" at close intervals all the way around its side. (This practice began in 1964, when the cheesemakers' union decided to put an end to the rampant imitation, substitution, and misrepresentation of their pride and joy.)

For the next few days, each cheese is turned frequently back and forth, from its flat top to its flat bottom, and is left in the wooden mold to prevent the shape from becoming distorted. Then it is removed from its mold and given a sea-salt brine bath for about three weeks. This bath toughens the rind, making it possible for the cheese to be aged for a long time. Despite the lengthy brine bath, the interior cheese remains relatively low in sodium (in fact, no salt is added to the curd).

After the brine bath the cheeses are given a brief exposure to the sun and are then taken to the *cascina* (climate-controlled warehouses) and arranged on wooden shelves that soar to the lofty ceilings. There they begin the first stage of their aging. The cheeses are classified by *partita* (batch or "crop" from one season's cheesemaking), and the long aging process begins, during which the cheeses are regularly turned and brushed clean.

and other soups, but not at the price you're paying for this very expensive cheese.) Too much rind would be in excess of 10 percent of the weight of the cheese sold to you. After you've purchased Parmesan a dozen or so times, you'll know by sight when you are being sold a fair piece. Never buy pre-grated Parmesan, and don't have it grated for you. The flavor of Parmesan dissipates so rapidly when grated that it's simply folly to grate it in advance. Grate this miraculous cheese yourself, as you need it, always allowing the cheese to reach room temperature before grating.

In many cheese shops you will be charged a hefty premium for Rocca brand Parmigiano-Reggiano, which many cheesemongers consider the finest. My feeling is that all

THE PARMIGIANO WEDGE

As you might expect of a revered cheese that is a daily staple for so many, Parmigiano-Reggiano has inspired the manufacture of cutlery specifically designed for cutting this magnificent cheese. Three knob-handled cutting tools are used by professionals to cut Parmesan. The first is designed to score the tough rind of the cheese. This scorer has a lip, or hook-shaped blade, which is dragged forcefully across the surface and sides of a whole Parmesan (or large wedge), creating a narrow furrow. This furrow is subsequently pierced with a knob-handled stiletto at 3- or 4-inch intervals to a depth of 4 or 5 inches. Longer than the other tools (the one I use is 7 inches long), and possessing dull edges but a very sharp point, this menacing-looking utensil is designed to pierce rather than cut the cheese. Once the scored furrow has been sufficiently pierced, the third tool comes into play. It is one that many nonprofessionals use at home. It is pointed, but broader and shorter than the stiletto, and is used to pry apart the cheese into whatever size and shape has been scored and furrowed. One twists the knob handle while simultaneously rocking the tool from side to side. This may sound difficult, but it is not, particularly when you are simply "downsizing" a precious kilo of Parmigiano at home.

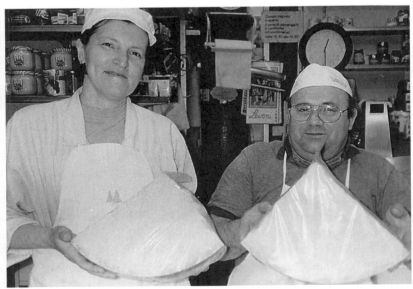

Parmigiano-Reggiano is of very high quality and no brand is worth singling out in terms of taste. Most American "Parmesan," on the other hand, tastes like sawdust. And both the Argentine Reggianito (REH-jah-NEE-toe) "Parmesan" and the Uruguayan "Parmesan" are too salty for my taste.

If you use Parmesan as often as my family does, you have two ways of ensuring that it is always fresh and on hand. The first is to buy it frequently. If this is not feasible, your option is to know how to properly store a large piece. Always lop off only as much as you're going to use at one time. Then moisten a piece of cheesecloth or other cloth—even a paper towel will do—and wrap it around the large hunk. (If you've heard anything about vinegar-dampened cloths, forget it—unless you want your cheese to smell and taste like vinegar.) Then, wrap the whole thing in aluminum foil (aluminum foil is not completely airtight so it won't suffocate the cheese). Store it in the vegetable compartment of the refrigerator. Never bemoan any surface mold on Parmesan. Merely scrape it away, and don't buy quite so much next time.

It is not widely known that Parmesan is a relatively low-fat cheese—made from partially skimmed milk, its fat content varies from 28% to 32%—and this advantage is amplified even further when it is grated. Grated cheese is really more air than substance and the fact that Parmesan is so intensely flavored means a little goes a long way (allow 1 ounce of cheese per serving of pasta).

Parmesan is a superb eating cheese. It is marvelous as a first course with fresh figs, melon, or any fruit. It marries beautifully with carpaccio or prosciutto drizzled with extra-virgin olive oil. It is wonderful slivered over an arugula salad dressed with a mild vinaigrette. If you want to serve Parmesan with fruit for dessert, don't hesitate to partner it with any dessert wine, such as Malvasia, Picolit (rare), Moscato, or Vin Santo. I prefer it with the big Italian reds: Chianti Riserva, Brunello di Montalcino, Barolo, Barbaresco, and Barbera. Or pair it with the wonderful, less expensive Italian reds like Salice Salentino, Bardolino, Valpolicella, or Montepulciano d'Abruzzo.

GRANA PADANO

Name-controlled Grana Padano (GRAH-nah pah-DAH-noh), a *grana* cheese, is made throughout Emilia-Romagna, in cities such as Asti, Bologna, Ferrara, and Piacenza; in the Padua area of the Veneto, between Verona and Venice; and throughout Lombardy (Brescia, Milan) and Piedmont (Cuneo, Novara, Turin). Grana Padano (*padano* meaning "of the Po River") is much less expensive than Parmesan, aged for only about six months, unlike the 14 months (minimum) to four years of Parmesan, and its flavor is that of a very muted Parmesan. The milk used to make Grana Padano can come from anywhere, there is no specific, legally

GREAT FOR GRATING

In my home we are far more likely to grate cheese than to slice it, dice it, or serve it whole. One reason is that we eat a lot of pasta. And while I certainly consider Parmigiano-Reggiano the *ne plus ultra* of grating cheeses, a number of other hard cheeses can be similarly used. Be sure to let the cheese come to room temperature.

- **Aged Gouda** (The Netherlands; cow's milk): Amber-colored and perfumey; combine with mashed potatoes, sprinkle over green salads, grate on buttered bread and broil until browned for an upper-crust variation on the tried and true grilled cheese sandwich.
- **Dry Jack** (U.S.; cow's milk): A unique, original American cheese with depth of flavor nearly rivaling that of Parmigiano-Reggiano.

I like to use a mandoline to make heaping piles of feather-light, translucent wafers of this cheese to serve with melon or alongside a dry Andalusian sherry or a special bottle of red wine. For a superb yet simple hors d'oeuvre, toss warm toasted almonds with grated or "wafered" Dry Jack.

- **Fiore Sardo** (Italy; sheep's milk): Milder than Pecorino Romano; sprinkle over pasta, egg dishes, or cooked vegetables; add to take-out pizza for extra flavor.
- **Grana Padano** (Italy; cow's milk): Milder and considerably less costly than Parmigiano-Reggiano. A serviceable grating cheese.
- **Idiazábal** (Spain; sheep's milk): Similar to Roncal, though usually smoked; splendidly nutty, buttery flavor. Adds appeal and

---

defined area as is the case with Parmesan. In addition, this straw-colored cheese can be made year-round, not just during a specific regulated season. It is made in 80-pound (40 k) convex-sided, flat-topped drums, about 9 to 10 inches

thick, 15 to 16 inches in diameter. When buying an Italian grating cheese, look at the rind. If it doesn't have "Parmigiano-Reggiano" printed in vertical letters all over, but has the same shape, size, and colors as Parmigiano-Reggiano, you're probably being offered Grana Padano, and you should be charged accordingly—half to two-thirds the price of Parmigiano-Reggiano.

I have tasted much excellent Grana Padano. But even a perfect example of this golden-colored cheese simply does not have the ebullient flavor and/or distinctive depth of flavor to egg or rice dishes, potato or pork dishes.

- **Leyden, Aged Leyden** (The Netherlands; cow's milk): Flavored with caraway and/or cumin seeds, both types of Leyden add spice and interest to baked onions or baked stuffed tomatoes, potato or leek gratins. For an unusual use, set out a bowl of grated Leyden to accompany chili or soup.
- **Manchego** (Spain; sheep's milk): Grate Spain's most popular cheese over baked vegetable dishes; tastiest in tandem with squash, beans, tomatoes, or onions.
- **Pecorino Romano** (Italy; sheep's milk): The classic grating cheese of southern Italy; sharp-as-the-devil with a pronounced aroma. Grate over pasta, vegetables.
- **Pepato** (Italy; sheep's milk): An interesting, unusual choice; rather sheepy tasting, with black peppercorns strewn throughout.

Use in any dish that calls for Pecorino Romano. Grate over toasted rounds of bread anointed with olive oil; sprinkle over corn on the cob or baked potatoes.

- **Roncal** (Spain; sheep's milk): Less sharp, more nutty flavor than Pecorino Romano; use whenever a mild grating cheese is called for; ideal cheese for egg and potato dishes.
- **Sapsago;** also called **Glarner Schabzieger** (Switzerland; cow's milk): An acquired taste; strong-flavored, fat-free "novelty" cheese with sharply herby and lettuce-like flavor. Grate over hot noodles, green salads, or mix with sour cream or yogurt for a dip.
- **Sbrinz** (Switzerland; cow's milk): Butterscotchy flavor; a bit milder and less salty than Parmigiano-Reggiano. Sprinkle over hot popcorn or melt under the broiler for the ultimate cheese toast.

texture of an equally perfect Parmigiano-Reggiano. Grana Padano is an acceptable substitute for Parmigiano-Reggiano only if the latter is unavailable.

Choosing and Serving Grana Padano

When purchasing Grana Padano look for examples that are fresh and not dried out. If the cheese is rock hard and exhibits a white patina on the paste, it is old. Look for a golden interior with no obvious cracks or dryness.

In comparison to Parmigiano-Reggiano, Grana Padano is not nearly as grand an eating cheese; it is best as a grating cheese. Bear in mind that, though made in the same style as Parmesan, Grana Padano is less flavorful and less costly. On the other hand, all Grana Padano is well made and consistent. It is what it is—and because of this, there is no need to seek out specific brands.

TUSCANY, UMBRIA, AND THE MARCHES

(Toscano, Umbria, and Le Marche)

I have chosen to group Tuscany together with Umbria and the Marches because the cheeses and cuisine of these regions are so very similar. The cheeses are of one type only—sheep's milk, with a cooked, pressed curd which is molded and washed with brine—and are identical in all three regions.

Tuscany, like Piedmont and Lombardy, is an area of lovely physical diversity. The high Apennines in the northeast and west form almost a crescent of mountains that looms over the southeast. The landscape is forested, though rocky, with craggy peaks giving way to wooded glades. Curiously, I never see enough sheep in the grazeable pastureland to account for the plenitude of Tuscan cheeses that fill the shops. The roads twist and turn around the steep reaches of the rocky slopes, and in the summer Tuscany is every shade of green imaginable. The light is oddly diffused, though intense, as you continue on to the broad expanses

Tuscany, Umbria, and the Marches

The heart of Italy: Tuscany's gently sloping hills are dotted with tall cypresses, silvery centuries-old olive trees, and rustic, ancient farmhouses.

of wheat fields that give way to a sprawling, marshy area in the southwest called La Maremma, and then on to the rather anticlimactic coastline of the Mare di Tirreno, the Tyrrhenian Sea.

Though many travelers may disagree, whenever I arrive at the sea in Tuscany, I am disappointed. In such a land I expect crashing waves and towering pinnacles of immensely craggy rock. Instead, to me, it's like the Texas Gulf Coast or Barcelona's Catalan beaches—unexciting. However, this letdown is more than compensated for by the sheer beauty of the Chianti region. All in all, the rugged and remote wonderlands of the Apennines, the

mountainous areas around Florence all the way to Livorno and back again, are heart-stopping.

Tuscany's wines rank as global treasures. And, as if the numerous makers of fine Chianti and the often even finer Brunello di Montalcino weren't enough, many of these same wine-making estates bottle phenomenal extra-virgin olive oil from the ancient groves that are contiguous to the rows of grapevines.

Umbria is the rougher region, coarser, more mountainous, and less prosperous. Freshwater fish and small game prevail. There is less visible farmland and pastureland and the region is generally less smug and gentrified than Tuscany—

there's a refreshing paucity of expatriate Americans, British, and Germans. My impression of landlocked Umbria is one of vineyards, olive groves, summer camps, and deep, round lakes surrounded by hardwood forests. If it weren't for the olive trees, you'd think you were in Minnesota.

Umbria is home to Norcia, a pretty village famed for its pork products and *salumerie* (pork product shops). The fame of Norcia's cured sausages stretches back to the sixteenth century. Then—and now—pork shops throughout central Italy were referred to as *norcerie*. Umbria's wines, particularly the Lungarotti wines from Torgiano as well as superb whites from other winemakers, are also notable.

The Marches, whose name refers to the marshes found near the Adriatic coast, border Umbria to the east. Three times the size of Rhode Island, Le Marche is made up of four provinces which are named for the principal cities of Ascoli Piceno, Macerata, Ancona, and Pesaro. The western border is the spine of the Umbrian Apennines, where minor mountain ranges run perpendicular to the border creating long, narrow valleys that slope toward the coast, dissolving into a narrow coastal plain.

The Marches is a quiet, bucolic region,

wholly given over to agriculture inland and to fishing on the coast. Wheat, Chianina cattle, fruit, tobacco, and silkworms are the backbone of the local economy. The sheep that graze in the valleys of the Sibillini mountains just north of Norcia provide the milk for the region's Pecorino Le Marchigiano.

The Cheeses

PECORINO TOSCANO

Pecorino is the general name for any sheep's-milk cheese made in Italy, but I specifically adore name-controlled Pecorino Toscano (peh-koh-REE-noh-toh-SKAH-noh)

*This array of cheeses includes 100% sheep's-milk Pecorinos and an extravagant Caciotta Toscana made with truffle (*tartufo*) trimmings.*

IN PRAISE OF PECORINO TOSCANO

I must admit that Tuscany is among my favorite places on earth. There's something about the light, the air, the sky. Or maybe it's the olive oil . . . the Chianti . . . the Brunello . . . the Chianina beef.

And the cheese. Oh, the cheese! Every village is known for a certain style, shape, and size, and it's always "Ours is the best in all of Tuscany—ask anybody." But the delightful truth is, that of the six or eight completely different batches of Pecorino you have to choose from, whichever batch of whoever's cheese you are tempted by at any given moment—*that* is the finest in all of Tuscany, perhaps in all of Italy.

Pecorino Toscano is made all over Tuscany. I have sold Pecorino Toscano that comes from Arezzo in the east, from Pistoia and Prato in the north, from Livorno, from Prombino and Grossetto, and from scores of farms around Siena. My most prolific supplier is in Pienza. Their array of Pecorino includes the Marzolino and Pientino brands of young, unaged cheeses that are brimming with flavor. Smooth, practically melting—like ice cream—they are excellent.

Somewhat older than these young Pecorinos are Rossellino (Siena) and Il Palio (Siena) brand cheeses whose crusts have been rubbed with *doppo concentrato di pomodoro* (tomato paste), a hallmark of Pecorino from Siena. They have been aged for about six months, and the result is quintessential Tuscan Pecorino—firm, bone-colored paste, slightly flaky yet oily, and rich with huge nutty, herby, beefy flavor—not in the least sheepy-tasting. From Pienza comes Peperino, a brand of Pecorino flecked with dried, hot peppers—my choice as a perfect cocktail cheese to serve with dressed olives and *sopressata*.

Another of my favorite Pecorino Toscano cheeses is Corsignano, like the Rossellino and Peperino, a 3-pound (1¼-k) disk, but aged more than a year. The result is a bone-colored paste with a blackish crust that has been rubbed with olive oil. The cheese is immensely nutty, and on the exhale one tastes the grass, wild herbs, and the perfume of wildflowers, all of which abound in the Tuscan countryside from April through September. Most of all these cheeses are made from summer's milk when the pastures are at their most profuse.

Rossellino in Siena produces aged cheeses with a quintessential Pecorino flavor; name-controlled SOLP cheeses from Pienza are sold in a variety of styles.

and Pecorino dell'Umbria (del-OOM-bree-ah), and non-D.O.C. Pecorino Le Marchigiano (leh-MAR-kee-JAH-noh). They are among my favorite cheeses; I serve them more and more often with each passing year.

Before I began traveling extensively in Tuscany, Umbria, and the Marches, I was under the mistaken impression that the sheep's milk cheese there was universally referred to as Caciotta (kah-CHO-tah) or Casciotta (kah-SHO-tah). Naturally, that was the name under which I stocked them and all of my customers became familiar with those cheeses by those names. Imagine my chagrin when during several visits to the Tuscany area, no one responded to my requests for the cheese by those names. Some Tuscan cheese experts and chefs attest to the use of Caciotta, adding that it is also used as a term of endearment, literally meaning a "big little cheese." The consortium of Pecorino Toscano, which over-

sees production and marketing of this name-controlled cheese, takes a no-nonsense approach to protecting the name *they* want their cheeses to be known by, and is quick to suggest that Caciotta refers to "less good" Tuscan cheese, those that are made from a combination of sheep's milk and cow's milk rather than 100% sheep's milk.

In Umbria and the Marches, there is a predominance of mixed milk cheeses, while in Tuscany most of the cheeses—including Pecorino Toscano—are made of 100% sheep's milk. Umbria has not been awarded a D.O.C. for any of the region's many sheep's-milk or mixed-milk cheeses, but Le Marches has received the D.O.C. distinction for Casciotta d'Urbino, a mixed sheep- (70%) and cow's- (30%) milk cheese made by shepherds in Urbino. (It is not exported to the U.S.)

The Pecorino cheeses I have found in Tuscany, Umbria, and the Marches are made by small dairies. They are excellent—every single one of them. There is no merely average Pecorino from these regions available in the U.S.—it is all heavenly. For me these cheeses represent absolute perfection in terms of simplicity and rusticity. They can be young or aged or somewhere in between. (I think the best stage to eat all cheeses is somewhere in between—not too old, not too young, a little bit firm with good oiliness, beyond bland but just before reaching overly sharp.

Most Pecorinos are oily cheeses. Sheep's milk contains a very high percentage of butterfat (a main reason why these cheeses taste so good), and when a sheep's-milk cheese comes to room temperature, it has a tendency to weep—to cry some tears of this butterfat on the exposed face. There is abundant, luxurious flavor in this butterfat. If the cheese is half sheep's milk and half cow's as so many of the non-D.O.C. Pecorinos are, it will be less prone to weep. Such cheeses just won't be as flavorful as authentic pure sheep's milk cheese.

Tuscans, Umbrians, and the Marches people rarely use their Pecorino as an ingredient, although occasionally they'll add slivers of it to casseroles featuring greens and/or beans. In spring and summer they enjoy Pecorino for lunch with fresh, raw fava beans; at other times of the year it is eaten with thick slices of *salame,* thin slices of prosciutto, some fruit and bread, and red wine. Pecorino is a perfect meal accompaniment or salad-course cheese. It is very simple and charmingly, addictively raw and unrefined—so oily, olivey, and delicious!

In Umbria, several cheesemakers combine their sheep's milk curd with trimmings of the Umbrian black truffle (less flavorful, certainly, than Piedmont white truffles or black ones from Périgord). These truffled cheeses, known as Caciotta al Tartufo (kah-CHO-tah-ahl-tar-TOO-foh), are quite fine, and I frequently stock them, though they are expensive. Pecorino Nero (NEH-roh), a rare Tuscan Pecorino, is made only from the milk of black-fleeced sheep and is held in particularly high regard by Tuscans, but I can't detect any

PECORINO TOSCANO E FAGIOLI

Makes 4 servings

Evidence that the glorious Tuscan spring has arrived is the presence in the marketplaces of fresh, tender fava beans and new, tender, young Pecorino cheeses, referred to as Marzolino. Favas and young Pecorino are a delicious combination, whether eaten informally or as part of a composed salad.

½ pound (250 g) fresh fava beans
½ pound (250 g) young Pecorino, cut into ½-inch cubes
Extra-virgin olive oil, preferably Tuscan
Coarsely ground black pepper

1. Remove the favas from their pods. If you are serving them raw, peel the skin off the beans. If you'd like them lightly cooked, steam them for 3 minutes over simmering water. Allow them to cool slightly before peeling or rubbing off the skin.

2. In a medium-size bowl, combine the diced cheese and fava beans. Sprinkle with the olive oil and black pepper, and toss the salad with your hands, as they do in Tuscany.

difference in flavor from other Pecorinos. Though I was once able to stock it, it has been in very short supply in recent years.

Choosing and Serving Pecorino Toscano

Pecorino cheeses are nearly impossible to abuse, so you will rarely find an unacceptable example. Look for the words "100% pura percora," "tutti di latte di pecora," or "latte di pecora completo." For further verification, it helps to know the names of the cities and towns of Tuscany, Umbria, and coastal Le Marche because often the name of the village where the cheese is made is followed only by a two-letter abbreviation of the nearest major city or town. By consulting a map, you will be able to identify its place of origin and ensure you're buying an authentic Pecorino. For example, Pecorino Toscano may be made in a village you've never heard of, whose name is followed by GR (Grosetto) or SI (Siena) or LI (Livorno). Pecorino della Umbria may show PE (Perugia) or OR (Orvieto) or SP (Spoleto). Pecorino Le Marchigiano cheese labels will show PE (Pesaro) or AN (Ancona) or MA (Macerata). In the U.S., look for Tuscan cheeses

Miniature sheep perched atop a chunk of aged Pecorino are a whimsical reminder that this classic cheese is made from sheep's milk (pecora).

Straw-covered Chianti bottles are called fiaschi. For a perfect cheese and wine pairing, try Chianti Classico and Pecorino Toscano.

made by a Pienza company called SOLP. These name-controlled Pecorino Toscanos are sold in a number of variations—all grand. Currently only Pecorino Toscano is sold in the U.S., while Pecorino dell'Umbria and Pecorino Marchigiano are rarely found outside of central Italy. But this could change—and you'll be ready.

Pecorino cheeses come in disks and oblong shapes of varying sizes—usually 2 to 4 inches thick, 5 to 8 inches in diameter, weighing 1 to 4 pounds (500 g to 2 k), with either straight or convex sides. The color of the rind varies from pure white or beige (usually signifying a young cheese) to gray, orange, brown, or black. If the cheese is made from pure sheep's milk, the interior paste will be bone-colored; however, if the paste is more yellow, the cheese probably contains cow's milk.

Pecorino is best as part of a meal—either on the side with the salad course or with prosciutto, roasted peppers, salad, crusty bread, and Chianti for a simple supper. Served with a soup, stew, or pasta, Pecorino can linger on into dessert with fresh fruit and more Chianti, Brunello, Tignanello, or any wine made by the Lungarotti family in Umbria (especially their Rubesco Riserva). But the most memorable and truly exquisite way to serve Pecorino is in thin slices, fanned out on a plate and drizzled with some of Tuscany's cherished flower-scented acacia honey. For a more spectacular presentation, substitute white truffle paste from a tube for the honey. Simply squiggle a crooked line of this elegant paste onto each thin slice of cheese. Porcini mushroom paste also tastes marvelous with Pecorino Toscano. Look for the Brezzi, Urbani, or Boscovivo brands of porcini paste. The same companies also produce special "butters," combining white truffle and porcini mushroom slices with shards of Parmigiano-Reggiano and clarified butter. Their flavor is sumptuous beyond belief with these cheeses and some crusty bread.

THE SOUTH

(Abruzzio, Lazio, Molise, Campania, Apulia, Basilicata, and Calabria)

Combining all of the Italian provinces from Rome south and labeling them "The South" by no means implies that there is a lack of diversity among them. But for a cheesemonger's purposes, all of these beautiful areas—Abruzzi, Lazio (Latium), Molise, Campania, Apulia, Basilicata, and Calabria—must be grouped together because their cheeses are remarkably alike. The cheeses from these regions that you'll most likely find in the U.S. are the ones I've chosen to bring to your attention here. Many of this area's most exquisite cheeses are unfortunately too fresh and fragile to travel—for those you must visit Italy.

The north of Italy benefits from the alluvial plains of the Po river valley, the fertile detritus of the seabeds that once covered this large area. But as you get closer to Rome and head south of there, the topography becomes markedly infertile. (So many of the trees were cut down so long ago that whatever rich soil there was fell victim to erosion.) This infertility results in, among other things, a very different kind of cheese, made from the milk of the only animals that can subsist on this bleak type of terrain—sheep and goats. Though some goat's-milk cheeses do exist, they are strictly for local consumption. And though cow's-milk Provolone in all its myriad shapes and sizes is a major cash "crop" for Apulia, Lazio, and Cam-

Aged for over a year, Provolone piccante bears no resemblance to bland American Provolone. It's worth the wait at any cheese counter.

Teramo
Pescara
▲ Monte Corno
LAZIO (Latium)
ABRUZZI
Rome
Ternoli
San Severo
MOLISE
Isernia Campobasso
Foggia
CAMPANIA
Naples
Bay of Naples
Salerno
Potenza
APULIA
Gulf of Salerno
BASILICATA
Tyrrhenian Sea
Gulf of Taranto
The South
Cosenza
CALABRIA
Ionian Sea
Montalto ▲
Reggio di Calabria
SICILY
Adriatic Sea

The Cheeses

pania, it is sheep's-milk cheese that overwhelmingly dominates the business of cheesemaking throughout the South. Sheep reign here because they thrive where cattle cannot.

South of Naples, around Salerno, you begin to find a sprinkling of water buffalo and in the pastures the occasional herd of cattle (*caserta*), but then they are gone. There is an almost visible line in Italy, extending from Rome to Foggia, where crop farming and cattle grazing stops, and serious, productive pasturing of sheep begins.

Every region of southern Italy produces sheep's-milk cheeses known as Pecorino (peh-koh-REE-noh). Each of them is just the tiniest bit different from the other, but unquestionably the classic is Pecorino Romano, a cheese produced in the area around Rome (though the vast majority of it is now made in Sardinia).

The flavor of these hard cheeses is decidedly sheepy and usually piercingly sharp, with a flavor that is sensed on the exhale as well as on the tongue. Pecorino Romano is usually grated, although hard-core aficionados will whittle off shavings of it to eat with salami and bread and wine for lunch.

The poorest and most desolate parts of southern Italy produce Pecorino cheeses that you will never find north of Rome. For example, from Calabria there are Crotonese and Incanestrato, tall, barrel-shaped aged sheep's-milk cheeses that I find inordinately strong-flavored and overwhelmingly smelly.

Likewise, there are only a few cow's-milk cheeses produced south and east of Rome. Provolone, Caciocavallo, Scamorza, Burrata, and Gravina are all *pasta filata* (spun or pulled curd) cheeses that can be long-aged without fear of spoilage. They are straightforward, rather unrefined cheeses, with honest flavors that can be summed up in one word—sharp.

The area's few goats are generally kept for their meat and milk—very little of the milk is used for cheesemaking, and the fresh cheeses made from this milk must be consumed within a day or two.

PECORINO ROMANO

The most famous Pecorino in Italy is name-controlled Pecorino Romano (peh-koh-REE-noh-roh-MAH-noh), usually just called Romano. Only a few companies still make genuine Romano—genuine Romano being Romano made in the province of Rome. The shortage of *genuino* Romano is due to the cost of doing business on the Italian mainland. As a result only Locatelli, Fulvi, Brunelli, and Lopez produce the genuine article, and their cheeses are widely considered to be the finest. Most so-called Pecorino Romano should more accurately be called Pecorino Sardo (see page 255), since most is made in Sardinia, where sheep's milk is plentiful.

Pasta filata *(pulled or stretched curd) cheeses are made in a variety of sizes and shapes. From left to right: a small ball of Scamorza and gourd-shaped Caciocavallo, whose distinctive shape dates to the days when pairs of this Provolone-like cheese were suspended from a pole to ripen. In front are soft-ripened disks of Toma della Valcuvia, a wonderful cow's-milk cheese similar to French Brie and Camembert.*

Romano is a large, oily, cylinder of sharp-as-the-devil, aged sheep's-milk cheese—an irreplaceable cheese in the cu sine of southern Italy. Most weigh about 40 pounds (20 k) and are about 16 inches high, 12 inches in diameter. The thin, dry rind is the same bone-white color as the paste, though for no apparent reason some cheesemakers paint the rind black. The intense flavor is peppery, very sheepy, and, to me, overly salty. Romano is enjoyed all over Italy, but its most ardent devotees are southern Italians who know practically no other cheese. The people in southern Italy are resourceful, and cook with what's accessible—tomatoes, potatoes, olive oil, peppers, olives, anchovies, capers, artichokes, broccoli rabe, edible wild greens and countless varieties of chicory. Raised on Romano, they use it the same way northern Italians use Parmigiano-Reggiano. (It is still quite rare to encounter Parmesan south of Naples.) Romano is grated over pasta, combined with all manner of vegetables, and nibbled on its own.

Most makers of Pecorino Romano genuino emboss the top and sides of their cheeses' rinds with this D.O.C. symbol.

have never seen them served as such, except in southern Italy. Buy these cheeses in chunks and grate them yourself as needed to ensure freshness. You should be aware that much of the pre-grated Romano in the U.S. and Italy that purports to be *genuino* is not. By law Pecorino Romano *genuino*'s rind will be embossed with a sheep's-head logo and the words "Pecorino Romano." But some Pecorino Romano *genuino* will have a painted black rind that is not embossed, so you'll have to rely on the integrity of the cheesemonger. It is often difficult to tell if you are getting Pecorino Romano or Romano made in Sardinia.

Choosing and Serving Pecorino Romano and Other Pecorinos

In my opinion, Romano and the rest of the hard, southern sheep's-milk cheeses customarily used for grating make for rather overwhelming, overpower ng eating cheeses. I

MOZZARELLA

Since the second century A.D. water buffalo have lived in the area south and west of Naples, and the original Mozzarella (moh-tsah-REH- lah) cheese was made from their milk in the hills behind Salerno. This very important and singular cheese, Mozzarella *di bufala* (BOO-fah-lah), was made from water-buffalo milk until the 1940s, when the retreating Nazis destroyed all of the water buffalo. Not to be undone, after the war Italy brought in more animals from India. The herds have expanded and today there is a very healthy and thriving water buffalo–milk industry that ensures a plentiful supply of Mozzarella *di bufala.*

Cow's milk can also be used to make Mozzarella, and indeed, vast quantities of it are now made in Campania and Apulia (as well as throughout Italy)—at about half the price of the water buffalo type. But to me, Mozzarella made from buffalo milk is the finer of the two: It is sweeter and has an immediately recognizable depth of flavor that cow's-milk Mozzarella simply doesn't have. It also reveals a subtle, not immediately perceivable difference in color—a slightly greenish-yellow tint. Regardless of the milk used to make it, Mozzarella is a pulled-, or "spun-," curd cheese, known as *pasta filata.*

Mozzarella *di bufala* travels by truck from outside of Salerno and the plain of Battipaglia, where it is made, to Leonardo da Vinci airport in Rome. It is then flown to the U.S. so that it can be eaten within a day or two of being made. It is packed in 11-pound (5½ k) polystyrene cubes. Inside each cube are two layers of thick plastic bags filled with a whey and brine mixture so that, under refrigeration, the cheese is practically in suspended animation. The cheese itself is wrapped in very porous, thick paper inside the two plastic bags, and with the thermos effect of the polystyrene, it really does stay fresh. Actually, the cheese is stable enough to stay fresh for over a week, although no Italian would dream of eating two-day-old Mozzarella. They purchase and consume all of it daily and there are no leftovers. After a few days the texture does begin to break down, losing its resilience, and becomes "gloppy." It shouldn't be too creamy, and you should be able to slice it neatly.

Unsmoked Mozzarella *di bufala* comes in 8-ounce (250 g) balls, but the smoked variety is made in balls of over 1 pound (500 g plus) so that they won't fall apart during the smoking process. And they really are smoked: The cheeses are suspended in big, covered barrels, and hickory and chestnut chips are burned under them to produce a

very thick smoke. The effect is immediately evident when you open a package that contains these beautiful, lobed, nearly roasted balls of Mozzarella *di bufala affumicato*, charred brown to black. You can smell the woodsmoke—and what a wonderful thing it is!

Unsmoked *bocconcini* (baw-kawn-CHEE-nee, "little mouthfuls") are small, egg-shaped, 1½-ounce (45 g) balls of cow's-milk (common) or water buffalo–milk (rare) Mozzarella. You'll see them displayed floating in bowls of whey on countertops in Italy. They are sometimes called *ciliegini* (chee-lee-eh-GEE-nee; "little cherries"). At home we take them out of their whey and toss them with chopped parsley and garlic, a sprinkling of crushed red pepper flakes, and extra-virgin olive oil. This treatment makes for a truly memorable antipasto treat, especially if there's plenty of crusty bread on hand for sopping up the delicious marinade.

Fresh Mozzarella is, as it is often referred to in Italy, *il fiore di latte*, "the flower of the milk." It is an extremely satisfying cheese—moist, sweet, tender, milky, nutty, and buttery, with a springy, yielding texture unlike that of any other dairy product. In contrast, American supermarket-quality "pizza cheese" Mozzarella is rubbery and flavorless. It is meant to be melted into an amalgam of other ingredients, most of which are so assertive that a handmade cheese's subtle flavor would be eclipsed anyway. Its tastelessness is not even noticed; its presence only comes alive visually and texturally.

MOZZARELLA'S COUSIN

First made centuries ago in Basilicata, Scamorza (skah-MOOR-tsah) is a tender cow's-milk *pasta filata* cheese similar to Mozzarella, though a bit chewier and less moist. Made locally in small quantities, it is sold plain or smoked in 8-ounce (250 g), fern-wrapped balls. Scamorza makes a perfect appetizer, served thinly sliced with fresh or sun-dried tomatoes or sprinkled with freshly ground black pepper and extra-virgin olive oil. Considerable quantities of this cheese are made in Lombardy (see box, page 210), where it is formed into a myriad of amusing animal and bird shapes. Because Scamorza is produced on a small scale in southern Italy, most of the Scamorza sold in the U.S. is from Lombardy.

Choosing and Serving Mozzarella

Avoid fresh Mozzarella that smells sour, has yellowed, or looks dried out—it will have very little in common with truly fresh cheese. Real, fresh Mozzarella has a soft, yielding, pull-apart texture; it's never rubbery or hard. When cut, it will weep its own whey with a sweet, beckoning, lactic aroma. If you must

MAKING MOZZARELLA

To make Mozzarella, first 30-pound blocks of cow's-milk or water buffalo's–milk curd—they look like giant bed pillows—are cut into strips and passed through a *chitarra* ("guitar"), a boxlike contraption with sharp, taut, closely-strung wires that cut the curd into small pieces. Next, the pieces are immersed in very hot water to make the curd release its whey; the heavy curd falls to the bottom, where it re-amalgamates into a mass. This mass is then lifted, turned, and kneaded by hand, using a wooden paddle.

It is at this point the act of making fresh Mozzarella turns into an art. When the cheesemaker determines that the mass has achieved the proper consistency (the congealed curds will be rubbery in consistency), the actual "pulling" commences, a process that takes anywhere from 15 to 30 minutes. If the cheesemaker waits too long, the mass will release too much butterfat, robbing the finished product of much of its texture and flavor. (This is the fate that befalls machine-made Mozzarella.) If he ceases working the mass with the paddle too soon, the cheese will be cakey and/or crumbly.

The pulling is a process of twisting and knotting sections of the mass until the cheesemaker's instinct and sensitivity to the temperature of the water tells him to proceed with forming the cheese into balls. This trick of turning the elastic mass in on itself and tearing (*mozzare*) off handfuls inspired Mozzarella's name. Then each handful is repeatedly turned in on itself by hand until it reaches the desired shape and consistency. This part happens fast. If the cheese is meant to be salted, the balls are immersed in a brine solution. Unsalted balls of cheese are put into ice water to allow them to consolidate their shape and halt the cooking that the curd undergoes during its hot "bath." Salted Mozzarella will keep for about one week; unsalted, for just a couple of days.

buy your cheese in a supermarket, look for the passable, though marginal, fresh Mozzarella that is sold packed in water in small plastic tubs. While an improvement over pizza cheese, its quality still cannot approach that of imported fresh Mozzarella or the cheese made daily in small batches. Seek out your local cheese specialist for the real McCoy.

Eat up Mozzarella quickly—it loses its appeal after a day or two. Fresh cheeses such as Mozzarella and Ricotta should always be treated like, and considered no longer lived than, a carton of milk. The best way to keep Mozzarella—and never for longer than a week—is to begin by buying it salted. Immerse any leftover cheese in brine (lightly salted water—1 tablespoon of salt per pint of water) or in milk, and keep it in the refrigerator.

Generally, salted Mozzarella is best for eating by itself; unsalted Mozzarella is rather bland for eating (unless, of course, you prefer it that way) and is usually intended for cooking. (Unsalted Mozzarella is nearly sodium free, since most of the natural sodium is left behind in the liquid. Salted Mozzarella is higher in sodium due to its brine bath, but not overly so.)

Slice fresh Mozzarella and alternate it with ripe tomato slices, a few leaves of fresh basil, freshly ground black pepper, and extra-virgin olive oil (I like to roll up the basil leaves and julienne them into thin ribbons before strewing them about.) Sun-dried tomatoes are a delicious substitute for out-of-season, impossible-to-find, good, ripe tomatoes. Roasted peppers are also excellent with fresh Mozzarella, as are anchovies and olives. If the Mozzarella is fresh and hand-pulled, you really need nothing but a loaf of rustic crusty bread and some enjoyable wine. And perhaps that is the best way to enjoy it.

PROVOLONE

Essentially, if you take Mozzarella, hand-rub its surface with brine, bind it with rope, and hang it up to dry in a room with the proper temperature and humidity level, it will be transformed into an entirely different cheese—Provolone (proh-voh-LOH-neh). Although Provolone originated in Basilicata in southern Italy, today this name-controlled *pasta filata* (spun or pulled curd) cow's-milk cheese is made in every region of Italy and found in virtually every Italian home. Indeed, in southern Italy and in predominantly Italian neighborhoods found in many American cities, Provolone is more popular than Romano or Mozzarella.

Prova is Campanian dialect for a globular shape, and Provolones are created in a variety of these shapes in a range of sizes that run the gamut from half-pound (250 g) melons to 200-pound (100 k) torpedo shapes. Variations of Provolone—cheeses made from the same recipe, but each with its own name and unique shape—are also produced throughout the

WHEN IN THE SOUTH OF ITALY

Here are a few cheeses to seek out when traveling in the south of Italy:

• **Burrata** (boor-AH-tah): Cow's-milk cheese from Apulia and Basilicata, originally made from the milk of Podolian cattle. Essentially, Burrata is remnants of Mozzarella and cream enclosed in a "bag" of pulled curd, which, at the end of the process, is twisted closed. "Burrata" is a reference to the buttery cream inside. Burratas weigh from ½ to 1 pound (250 to 500 g) and are often wrapped in asphodel, a wild plant with a lovely flower that grows all over Apulia. Its gentle aroma permeates the cheese. Burratas rarely leave the region (principally Andria, Foggia, Cerignola, Martina Franca, and Torremaggiore) and are eaten on the day they are made.

• **Burrino, Butirro, Burrini, Burri, Manteche:** Local names in Calabria, Apulia, Basilicata, and Sicily for cheeses made from pieces ripped out of the curd being assembled for Provolone production. Often, these cheeses are stuffed with other edibles, such as nuggets of salami or lumps of sweet butter that is churned specifically for this purpose. They are ovoid in shape, weigh from 1 to 3 pounds (500 g to 1½ k), and are formed by hand with a topknot; frequently they are smoked. They are eaten either fresh or aged.

• **Raviggiolo** (rah-vee-JOH-loh): Commercial, noncommercial (local), and homemade; raw or pasteurized goat's or sheep's milk (sometimes with cow's milk added) cheese made in Campania, Naples, and the surrounding area. Raviggiolo is also made in Tuscany, Umbria, the Marches, Sardinia, and north of Rome. Essentially this is highly perishable fresh cheese, eaten after the whey has dripped away, at just one or two days old.

In Naples, the curd is placed in wicker baskets, like Ricotta, to make 1- to 3-pound (500 g to 1½ k) cheeses; in Tuscany, ferns or rushes are bound together for this purpose. This shaping and draining method makes salt unnecessary, and therefore the Raviggiolo, like Ricotta, remains sweet. (Ricotta is definitively from fatless whey, whereas Raviggiolo is from full-fat milk.) Raviggiolo is served as is, sugared or peppered, tossed with pasta, or fried with eggs *in tegame* (in a pan).

southern regions. These include name-controlled, bowling pin-shaped Caciocavallo (Basilicata, Calabria, Campania, Molise, Sicily); gourd-shaped Gravina (Molise); miniature, balloon-shaped Provola (Apulia); name-controlled rectangles of Ragusano (Sicily); and braided loaves of Scamorza (Abruzzi).

Provolone by any name is an oily, unsophisticated cheese that does not acquire much intensity of flavor until it has been aged for several months. Even so, it can be quite appealing in its simplicity when served at lunch with salami and a rough red wine or cold beer.

Choosing and Serving Provolone

Never believe that the soft, bland, rindless, factory-made American versions of Provolone that most of us grew up eating are real Provolone—they are far from it. Real Provolone is aromatic, with a yellowish rind and a firm, light-yellow interior that darkens with age and develops small fissures. Real Provolone, even if it has been precut and plastic-wrapped, is almost always sold in excellent shape. All

that need concern you is the age of the cheese, which will dictate the degree of sharpness. This sharpness is similar to that of an American aged Cheddar, though one that is augmented by a much more cheesy, jet-propelled sensation on the exhale. Provolone will be mildly piquant if aged for around three months, quite sharp after a year, and very sharp and hot on the tongue if it is aged for 18 months or more. (Provolones aged a year or more are often referred to as Provolone *piccante*.) The longer it is aged, the firmer and oilier the texture will become.

The natural rind of Provolone is the result of frequent rubbings with an oiled, brined cloth. On export Provolone, the rind and rope are coated with what is, in my opinion, a bothersome and unnecessary thin layer of paraffin to protect the cheese during shipping. It is inedible, but once the Provolone reaches room temperature in a shop, the waxy coating melts away and the rind once again becomes edible.

Serve Provolone with olives, peppers (pickled or raw, hot or sweet), raw vegetables, salami, crusty bread, and red wine or beer. You'll want to be aware that Provolone *piccante* will overwhelm almost any fruit, however.

SARDINIA AND SICILY

(Sardegna and Sicilia)

Sardinia and Sicily are, respectively, the second-largest and largest islands in the Mediterranean. And while not exactly within swimming distance of each other—Cagliari, Sardinia's capital, and Sicily's capital, Palermo, are separated by more than 250 miles—their hot, dry climates and chief dairy animal—sheep—are the same. Not surprisingly, their cheeses are similar, linked by their simplicity, their sturdiness, and their place in the lusty cuisine of these ancient islands. These cheeses also echo the style of those made on the southern Italian mainland (Pecorino Romano) and in the south of Spain (Murcia, Queso de Zuheros). Each island is the home of two D.O.C. cheeses—Sardinian cheesemakers produce name-controlled Fiore Sardo and Pecorino Sardo, while Sicilian cheesemakers make name-controlled Ragusano, one of the world's oldest cheeses, and Pecorino Siciliano.

SARDINIA

Sardinia sits due south of Corsica and due west of Naples. Though the land has been inhabited since the Stone Age, it was the Shardanes, a race from Asia Minor, who gave the island its name some 3,000 years ago.

Sardinia's population is concentrated largely in its practically treeless, relentlessly windswept interior—a rocky, mountainous, bar-

ren, wild land where even grass must be coaxed to grow. Though the beaches on much of Sardinia's coast are beautiful, for centuries Sardinians have chosen to live inland—partly for reasons of security and partly due to a once very real fear of rampant coastal malaria. The interior is a land of sheep and shepherds, game and wood fires. The cheeses made from the abundant sheep's milk are primitive and unvarying. They are good, honest cheeses whose forthright appeal has made them an important gastronomic contributor to Sardinia's economic success.

The Cheeses

FIORE SARDO

Also called Pecorino Sardo or Sardo

Pecorino is the generic name given to all Italian cheeses made from the milk of sheep (*pecora*). Fiore Sardo (fee-OH-reh-SAR-doh), which is also known as Pecorino Sardo or simply Sardo, is one of the best known Pecorinos. All Sardinian cheeses are merely variations on name-controlled Fiore Sardo. Confusion about this cheese is rife. The confusion arises—indeed, most people aren't even aware that they *should be* confused—because there are a number of fraudulent examples of so-called Sardo marketed in the U.S., Canada, *and,*

Near Alghero on Sardinia's western coast, local fishermen row past the caves that rise majestically above the area's famous coral beds. The island's 500 miles of rugged coastline are sprinkled with scores of these craggy formations.

yes, even in Europe. Argentina sells hundreds of tons yearly of a sharp, quite decent *cow's*-milk cheese which it brazenly markets as Sardo. More surprising still, even in Italy there are cheeses with names incorporating the word *fiore* (flower), which misleads consumers into believing they are buying Fiore Sardo. Though some of these cheese may indeed be made from sheep's milk, they are *not* Sardinian in origin. To top it all off, several larger Sardinian producers of Sardo further confuse the issue by marketing their cheeses *not* under one of the three authentic names, but instead under variatios on those names, inventing *new* names for their authentic Sardo cheese. Names such as Fiore Sardegna, Moliterno, Il Muflone d'Oro are all excellent examples of this cheese, despite the befuddling name game, and are worth looking for.

The name Fiore Sardo *is* theoretically protected under Italy's D.O.C. laws. The problem is that while Italian jurisdiction protects Italian cheesemakers from each other, it does not protect them from the rest of the world. It is toothless internationally, as are France's A.O.C. laws, which can't even protect French cheesemakers from themselves.

Fiore Sardo is a gently piquant, firm (but not rock-hard) sheep's-milk cheese that is usually made in 4-pound (2 k) disks, about 4 inches thick and 4 to 5 inches in diameter. At most ages (from three months to

between six and nine months), the rind will be buff-colored. The exterior of longer aged cheeses may be much darker because their firm but pliant rinds will have been frequently rubbed with olive oil. Sardo is an admirable table cheese in the tradition of the group of Tuscan sheep cheeses collectively called Pecorino Toscano. While I find the Tuscan cheeses to be markedly less sheepy than Sardo, with more enticing nuances and aftertastes, I must admit that over the last two decades, I've grown to like many of the Sardinian variations. Also, they can be a superb value, particularly when compared to the high prices asked for *anything* Tuscan.

Choosing and Serving Fiore Sardo

When buying Fiore Sardo, look for disks with natural, dry, brown- to buff-colored rinds and smooth, firm paste uninterrupted by holes or cracks. Be aware that any encased in *thick* plastic (as opposed to a film of thin plastic wrap) will most certainly have suffered in terms of flavor and texture because they will have been unable to breathe. Scrutinize the cheese's label, if possible. If you see any mention of the following towns of origin, you can be certain the cheese is an authentic one: Arborea, Arbus, Arzachena, Gesturi, Iglesias nel Caglianitano, Gardoni, Gavoi, Macomer Nuorese, Orgosolo Nuorese, Luogosanto, Ozieri, Pattada, Thiesi, or Villanova Monteleone nel Sassarese.

Identifying name-controlled Fiore Sardo, also called Sardo and Pecorino Sardo, can be difficult. Some authentic versions such as this one have fanciful new and confusing names.

SARDINIAN-MADE PECORINO ROMANO

Although Sardinia is the home of Pecorino Sardo, cheesemakers on the island have recently begun switching their focus to producing Pecorino Romano, a mainland cheese original to Lazio. In fact, curious as it may sound, there is a great deal more Romano produced now in Sardinia than on the Italian mainland. Note that I didn't call it Romano *genuino.*

Romano *genuino* comes only from Lazio in the province of Rome and is protected by the D.O.C. laws. Of course, that doesn't prevent tons of non-*genuino*, less expensive so-called Romano or Pecorino Romano from Sardinia and Sicily—often of inferior quality, from being sold as pricier *genuino* in both Italy and the U.S.

aluminum foil, in the vegetable compartment of the refrigerator.

I particularly enjoy a Sardo-type cheese called Peperdelizia, which features a liberal dose of chopped hot chiles (*peperoncino*) throughout it. It makes a marvelous appetizer on *bruschetta* or *fettunta*—slices of hot, crusty, garlic-rubbed bread that have been drizzled with extra-virgin olive oil. Serve it with freezer-cold vodka or your favorite red wine. I have found a delicious Sardinian wine called Cannonau di Sardegna and another, even better perhaps, called Giró di Cagliari, both of which are splendid with Sardo-type cheeses. The wines, and certainly the cheeses, of Sardinia have enormous potential.

Fiore Sardo is an excellent table cheese but it also shines in the kitchen, where it adds considerable flavor and richer texture to sauces. Think of pesto: Using a Sardo instead of Pecorino Romano won't overwhelm the sauce the way other grating cheeses, even Parmigiano-Reggiano can. Sardo is sturdy and long-lived, even after being cut. Store it, wrapped in waxed paper or

When shopping for Fiore Sardo, look for wheels of cheese with rustic, brown- to buff-colored rinds (bottom), rather than pale yellow ones (top) that are wrapped in plastic.

SICILY

Before the Greeks and the Arab Saracens left their indelible imprint on the island of Sicily, the largest region of Italy and largest island in the Mediterranean, it was home to three much older tribes—the Siculi, the Sicani, and the Elymians. As might be expected for an island set so directly in the path of Mediterranean conquerors, Sicily was beset at one time or another by almost any country or band of pirates that had ships. Today, 3,000 years later and despite an all-pervasive Saracen culture and cuisine, Sicilian food and cooking cannot be defined as a single unified tradition. Instead there are three distinctively different food legacies—eastern, central, and western—inspired by those three original tribes.

From its lush coast to its violently sun-baked, barren interior, Sicily is an island of uncommon beauty. Sheep's-milk cheeses predominate, along with considerable production of cow's-milk *pasta filata*–style (spun or pulled curd) cheese, specifically Caciocavallo and Mozzarella, the only cow's-milk cheeses made in the region. These markedly different, extraordinarily simple, unsophisticated cheese styles no doubt arose because of the hot climate, one not given to the cool and moist periods that instigate the variety of vegetation and bacterial interplay that result in the more complex cheeses found north of the Mediterranean.

The Cheeses

RICOTTA SALATA

One of the few cheeses of note that originated in Sicily is Ricotta Salata (ree-COH-tah-sah-LAH-tah), made from lightly salted sheep's-milk curd that is pressed and dried before its minimum of three months of aging. It takes the shape of a tall, 6-pound (3 k) wheel of soft and supple, pure white, rindless cheese, about 4 inches high and 6 to 7 inches across. Texturally, it is as smooth as a cheese can be, and its enticing flavor is mild and nutty.

Sicily, the largest island in the Mediterranean, flourished for centuries under Greek rule. Ancient ruins, such as these at Selinus, still dot the island.

Neither sheepy nor salty, it has a totally agreeable, sweetly milky flavor.

Not all Ricotta Salata is Sicilian. Some of it is Sardinian and some is made on the Italian mainland in Apulia, Lazio, and Campania. But the Sicilians go a step beyond other Ricottas to make a singular type of Ricotta Salata that is referred to as Ricotta Salata *per la grattugia* (for the grater). These special cheeses are tall, somewhat irregularly formed skinny cylinders—7 inches high and about 4 inches across—and are aged for a year or more to a crumbly rock-hardness. Uncut, the whole cheeses will last practically forever. Use them as you would other *grana*-type cheeses—grated onto pasta or used whenever a milder flavor than Romano is desired.

Choosing and Serving Ricotta Salata

Select any brand of young or aged Ricotta Salata (the Pinna and Mannoni brands are my favorites) that shows no mold. Store it in plastic wrap, in order to retain its moisture, in the vegetable compartment of the refrigerator. Serve it with fresh or grilled vegetables, fresh fava beans, or sweet, seasonal fruit, along with coarse salami or prosciutto, crusty bread or breadsticks, and whichever wine is handy.

Extremely versatile, Ricotta Salata makes a significant contribution diced into salads, sprinkled over garlicky sautéed vegetables or

WELL-DRESSED OLIVES

Cheese and olives have a natural affinity for each other and I enjoy serving my favorite sheep's-milk and goat's-milk cheeses alongside a bowl of marinated olives. Perhaps they taste so good together because olive groves, sheep, and goats all flourish in roughly the same climate. Whatever the reason, I almost never serve olives with cow's-milk cheeses because I just don't think they taste right together.

The olives used for the marinades described below can be found in any specialty food store. Steer clear of the olive types commonly found in supermarkets—cocktail olives, stuffed olives, black "ripe" olives.

Any style of high-quality, unpitted brine- or salt-cured olives can be made much more flavorful in practically no time at all. First, you'll want to debrine the olives: Set a colander in the sink, dump the olives into it, and allow them to drain for several minutes. Then run a vigorous flow of cold water over them, shaking the colander back and forth for a few minutes. Alternatively, simply drain the olives in a colander, transfer them to a saucepan, cover with fresh tap water, and simmer very gently for 10 minutes. Then, drain and cool.

Be sure the olives are well drained before combining them

---

tomato-based pasta sauces, bean dishes, or simply grated over *pasta all'olio*—freshly cooked pasta, topped with minced garlic that has been sizzled in good olive oil just until golden.

PECORINO SICILIANO

Incanestrato, Pepato

As noted earlier, Pecorino is the generic name given to all Italian cheeses made from the milk of sheep (*pecora*). The Pecorino cheeses of Sicily, which are name-controlled, are collectively known as Pecorino Siciliano. Of these, the most well known is Incanestrato (een-kah-neh-STRAH-toh), also called Canestrato, a sheep's-milk cheese made in Sicily as well as on the mainland in Calabria. (You'll want to note that I have used the mainland spellings of these cheeses, which are the ones used by U.S. retailers; on the island of Sicily they are often spelled somewhat differently.) Roughly translated, *incanestrato* means "basketed." The curds with any of the marinades below. Marinate for at least 4 hours at room temperature before serving, though 10 to 12 hours will give even more flavorful results. If the olives are refrigerated after the initial marinating, the olive oil will become cloudy and thick. Don't worry—allow them to sit for an hour or so at room temperature and the oil will once again be clear. Each of these marinades will transform 1 pound of olives and will taste delicious with Italian Pecorino Siciliano, Fiore Sardo, or Pecorino Toscano; French Brindamour or chèvre; Greek Kefalotyri and Kefalograviera; Spanish Idiazábal, Manchego, and Roncal.

French Niçoise: Combine 2 teaspoons *herbes de Provence* (a blend of dried herbs that usually includes basil, lavender, marjoram, rosemary, sage, summer savory, and thyme) with ¾ cup (175 ml.) extra-virgin olive oil, or enough to cover the olives.

Cracked Sicilian (or California Sicilian Style): Combine 4 large diced jalapeño peppers or 2 tablespoons dried red pepper flakes with 4 large peeled, crushed garlic cloves and ¾ cup (175 ml) extra-virgin olive oil, or enough to cover the olives.

Italian Gaeta or Greek Kalamata (Calamata): Combine the zest and juice of 1 large lemon with 4 large peeled, crushed garlic cloves and ¾ cup (175 ml) extra-virgin olive oil, or enough to cover the olives.

Moroccan Oil-Cured: Combine 4 large peeled, crushed garlic cloves with 2 sprigs bruised (not minced) fresh rosemary and ¾ cup (175 ml) extra-virgin olive oil, or enough to cover the olives.

---

are placed in woven straw or wire baskets, and when the whey has drained away, the cheese takes on the shape and ridged imprint of the basket.

Aged Incanestrato (ripened for up to nine months or a year) is a hard, strong, assertive, Pecorino-type cheese with a straw-colored interior and a powerful aroma. It is considered a delicacy—especially at Easter, when the sheep are giving the sweet spring milk from the first growth of grass. The younger cheeses (aged three to six months), which exhibit a very white, granular paste, are less aggressively strong and aromatic. All examples of Incanestrato will have a dry, off-white crust with ridged imprints. Ranging from 6 to 9 inches tall and 8 to 14 inches in diameter, their weight varies considerably, anywhere from 12 to 22 pounds (6 to 11 k).

Use Incanestrato as you would any Pecorino—as a grating cheese for pasta, or as a rustic table cheese served with fresh fruit, olives, salami, crusty bread, and a big, rough red wine such as Apulia's Salice Salentino or Sicilian Corvo.

Pepato (peh-PAH-toh) is another equally appreciated indige-

Fresh fava beans are harbingers of spring at markets here as well as in Italy. During fava season, bars set out plates of whole beans and patrons shell their own to nibble on along with bits of Pecorino and a glass of wine. (For a recipe using a Pecorino and favas, see page 241.)

nous Sicilian Pecorino. This 30-pound (15 k) wheel of cheese, 7 to 8 inches high and 16 inches in diameter, has liberal quantities of whole black peppercorns strewn horizontally throughout the middle. Like Incanestrato, its hard, white to off-white rind is ridged with the imprint of the "woven" molds (once made of straw, now of wire) in which it is formed. Pepato is available aged for at least a year (suitable for grating), and in a younger (aged about nine months), milder, less dense-textured version called Pepato *per la tavola*. The paste of older Pepato will be rock hard, a darkish straw color, and its flavor will be piquant and sheepy; the younger variety, which has a bone-white interior, will be less markedly sheepy. Both types are too salty

and sheepy for my taste, but you may feel otherwise. When sampling Pepato for the first time, I would certainly advise opting for the younger, milder, less rock hard examples.

Choosing and Serving Pecorino Siciliano

When shopping for any of the Pecorino Sicilianos, choose a cheese whose cut face is free of mold and not cracked. Lack of freshness is about the only defect you need concern yourself with, unless the cheese has been aged too long (more than a year), in which case it will be sharp and sheepy beyond belief.

PEPPERED PEPATO

A variation of Pepato, native to the town of Ragusa in southern Sicily, is Ragusano (rah-goo-ZAH-noh). Don't confuse this with another Sicilian cheese, name-controlled Ragusano Caciocavallo. Ragusono is a younger, softer, more elastic sheep's-milk cheese than its Pepato sibling. And instead of peppercorns strewn through its interior, there are shreds of dried, hot red chiles (*peperoncini*). Ragusano is not a particularly serious cheese, but it is assertively flavored and rather intriguing, making it a splendid choice for summer picnics. Make sure you have plenty of chilled wine, beer, or vodka on hand to extinguish the fire of the peppers.

Store the cheese in the vegetable compartment of the refrigerator wrapped in aluminum foil or plastic wrap.

Pecorino Sicilianos are excellent grating cheeses and Sicilians usually use them in place of Pecorino Romano. Like the Tuscans, Sicilians combine the diced cheese in a salad with fava beans, toss it with olive oil, and serve it as antipasto or for a light lunch. You'll also find these cheeses partnered with vegetables, olives, spicy salami, and other more highly flavorful fare such as hot peppers. Pepato in particular is incompatible with complex Italian wines, but like all Pecorino Sicilianos, is a good match for rougher, thick, rich reds such as Salice Salentino from Apulia or Amarone from Veneto.

Mainland versions of Incanestrato, a Pecorino Siciliano, are called Canestrato and often contain hot peppers. Aged examples of both are excellent grating cheeses.

Switzerland

Switzerland's lofty position as a titan of international finance, chemicals, and pharmaceuticals is a paean to "the industrious Swiss." Who else would have accomplished so much in a country dominated by such a fierce topography? The Alps *are* Switzerland—all 16,000 square miles of it. And while high Alps comprise a fourth of its total area, not all of Switzerland's terrain is as severe—fruit trees, flowers, and even

palm trees grow there in some places. There are thousands of secluded, picturesque villages rarely found by tourists. Switzerland's cheese production is almost as important a cash crop as tourism. I find it tremendously reassuring to note that the quality of these cheeses has not wavered in the 20 years I've been savoring and study-

A quintessential slope-roofed chalet in the canton of Bern, where Emmental and Tête de Moine have been made for hundreds of years.

ing them. Swiss cheeses are still as good as can be—rustic, full-flavored, and produced under immaculate conditions. Cheese and cattle are Switzerland's bread and butter. And Switzerland's reputation for cheese is unsurpassed, though the number of cheese types is more limited than in other important cheesemaking nations.

Each of Switzerland's 26 cantons (states of the Swiss Confederation), is ruled by its inhabitants, and everybody speaks at least two (if not four) languages—German and French, and often Italian and English as well. Swiss lifestyles, cooking, and dress reflect the border they are nearest: The Valais and Bern cantons are quite French in terms of language and cuisine. The canton of Ticino, on the border between Switzerland and Italy, is so decidedly Italianate that it is often difficult to remember which coun-

try you are in. While the residents in the north and northwest are as proud as any to be Swiss, they have considerably more in common culturally and gastronomically with their German and Austrian neighbors across the border than with fellow countrymen in far-flung cantons to the south.

Virtually all Swiss cheeses are "mountain cheeses," a term that usually refers to a physically large cheese that is made in the mountains from high-pasture (Alpine) milk. Mountain cheeses have certain common physical characteristics: They are nearly always firm, long-aged cheeses; they're rarely oozy, fresh cheeses—the only exception is Vacherin Mont d'Or, which is soft. Mountain cheeses are usually made from raw cow's milk and are characterized by an assertive flavor and firm texture. Their goodness is a result of the natural

GEOGRAPHY IS EVERYTHING

Unlike France, which offers a vast array of soft, fresh, perishable cheeses meant to be eaten very shortly after they are made, Switzerland's cheeses are big, hard-rinded, rugged ones that are much less fragile. Their physical configuration acknowledges the topography of the mountainous area where they originate. The most famous—Emmental and Gruyère—are dense-textured and massive in size, so large they must be hewn into smaller segments with double-handled knives. These sturdy cheeses evolved to meet the needs dictated by weather (long, cold winters) and terrain (remote pastures high in the Alps). They kept longer and in better condition throughout the long, cold winters than smaller, more perishable cheeses. And they were strong enough to survive undamaged on the long journeys from the remote mountain pastures where they were made to the lowlands where they were eventually sold.

resources the land provides: high elevation with lots of sunshine, pure air, delicious water, and remarkably lush pastures grazed by healthy, bountiful beasts. Though the number of varieties of Swiss cheese is relatively small, the cheeses are significant and their place in the world is great. Their recipes and production are strictly regulated, and as a result, one does not find regional quirks or local efforts to reinterpret the national cheesemaking tradition. The strict production controls may hinder originality, but the positive result is that you can count on the consistency of Switzerland's cheeses. Because cheese production is so regulated countrywide, it makes more sense to focus on Swiss cheeses by name, rather than by region.

The western part of Switzerland—the Emme Valley near Bern, Gruyère's canton of Valais, and Vacherin Mont d'Or's Vallée de Joux—produces by far the most important Swiss cheeses. This is the area that is home to Gruyère and Emmental, the legendary cheeses that everyone thinks of when they think of Swiss cheeses.

Most Swiss cheeses are enormous. They didn't start out that way, but as the techniques for making cheese were evolving and improving, it was discovered that the bigger the cheese, the better it kept.

The people who made the earliest Swiss cheeses over a thousand years ago were called Sennen, meaning "mountain people." (This term is still used today to describe the men and women who for cen-

SWISS I.D.

SCHWEIZ SUISSE SVIZZERA ® SWITZERLAND

Swiss cheeses are rarely marked by brand, but each type does bear an individual identification stamp. In addition, as further confirmation of authenticity, wheels of the largest Swiss cheeses— Emmental, Gruyère, and the hard mountain cheeses (Sbrinz, Spalen, Saanen)—are stamped on their rinds with the trademark symbol of the Switzerland Cheese Union. A Gruyère whose rind does not show this stamp is a copy, not the original Swiss cheese.

turies have owned the best pastures in the high Alps and have bred and developed the best cattle.) By the first half of the seventeenth century, their cheese came to have such tremendous export value—it traveled to France, Italy, and Germany, as well as other parts

THE NAME-CONTROLLED CHEESES OF SWITZERLAND

Switzerland produces cheese on a regionally controlled cooperative basis. The cheese factories are owned by the regional cooperatives, which control the cheese name and the recipe and process for making it. These syndicates are regulated by the national council that governs Switzerland. No region is allowed to make cheese other than those that are designated as native and original to that region.

The following is a complete list of the name-controlled cheeses of Switzerland, their canton or cantons of origin, and an idea of their availability in the U.S.

Appenzeller (also called **Appenzell**): Appenzell and other eastern cantons; widely available

Emmental (also called **Emmentaler**): Bern and other German-speaking lowlands cantons; widely available

Gruyère: Fribourg; widely available

Hard mountain cheeses: Sbrinz and **Spalen** (Bern Schwyz, Lucerne, Obwalden Uri, Unterwalden-Nidwalden,

Zug), **Saanen** (Fribourg): available, spotty

Raclette cheeses: Bagnes, Conches, Gomser, Orsières: Valais; rare (Bagnes is rarest)

Sapsago (also called **Glarner Schabzieger**): Glarus; widely available

Swiss Tilsit (formerly called **Royalp**): Saint Gallen, Thurgau, Zürich; available, spotty

Tête de Moine (also called **Bellelay**): Bern, Uri; available, spotty

Vacherin Fribourgeois (also called **Fribourgeois**): Fribourg; available, though very rare

In addition to the name-controlled cheeses above, **Vacherin Mont d'Or,** made in Vaud, is regionally controlled only and is overseen not by a cooperative but by a loosely organized group of cheesemakers within the canton of Vaud. Vacherin du Haut-Doubs, an identical cheese, is made in France (the French border skirts the Swiss pastures), and both countries enforce their own regional designations to preserve this cheese's integrity.

of Switzerland—that they were unable to keep up with the demand. The Sennen expanded and developed a unique cooperative system of cheesemaking that efficiently utilized the available labor, boundless pasturage, and ever-increasing herds. Today Swiss cheesemaking remains a regionally controlled, cooperative effort, with each area specializing in its own style of cheese.

The most important Swiss cheeses, which by law are made with raw Alpine milk are not marketed under brand names. If you see one of the few Swiss cheeses that is marketed under a brand name, you can assume that it is made with less desirable pasteurized milk from the lowlands.

The Cheeses

EMMENTAL

The valley of the Emme River in the canton of Bern is responsible for Emmental (EM-awn-TAHL), the classic big-eyed Swiss cheese that is I'm sure the world's most recognized cheese. (Keep in mind that a formidable Emmental is produced on the other side of the Jura mountains in France, and it is every bit as good as the Swiss version, and sometimes even better; see page 115.) There is no cheese more deserving of the adjectives sweet, nutty, and fruity.

HIGH PASTURE/ HIGH FLAVOR

High Alpine pastures yield a vaster, lusher, more flavorful profusion of plants and grasses than do lowland pastures. When cattle graze on these high pastures they produce rivers of luscious milk that is measurably higher in butterfat than the milk they give after grazing in the lowlands. For this reason, cheese made from milk of high-pasture origin has always commanded a premium price.

Emmentals weigh 175 to 220 pounds (87½ to 110 k) or more, and are as big as tractor tires. Each wheel is about 44 inches in diameter and 6 to 9 inches thick, with a smooth, beige to yellowish rind that, if the cheese will be exported, is stamped with the trademark symbol of the Switzerland Cheese Union. The edges are rounded and the top, bottom, and sides are relatively flat, unlike French Emmental, which is quite bulbous. The color of the interior is a pale, yellowish tan.

Both Swiss and French Emmental are famous for their random scattering of "eyes," or holes, which may be as small as olives or cherries, or as big as Ping-Pong balls. These holes are formed during the aging process, produced by bacteria that give off carbon dioxide, a result of the temperature that the cheese is stored at and the proportion of a specific starter used. The flavor is mild at first, but as it is absorbed on the palate, it builds in intensity to finish in a highly agreeable, savory nuttiness with a finishing bite.

Emmental is quite low in salt compared to other hard mountain cheeses. All milk naturally contains salt, but none is added to the curd. Only the rind is salted, a result of the brine bath in which the cheese floats for a few days before being put away to age. Also, the cow's milk used to make Emmental is partially skimmed, and as a result, the fat content is reduced enough so that it is also considered a "less-fat" cheese. But unlike most "diet" cheeses that are as low in flavor as they are in fat or salt, Emmental is, and always has been, made from the hallowed raw milk of Swiss cat-

At an open-air market, a vendor wraps a wedge of Swiss Emmental cut from an enormous half-wheel. The characteristic holes are created by pockets of natural carbon dioxide gases that expand in the interior of the cheese as it ripens.

tle that graze in Alpine pastures. The result is a cheese with big flavor.

In Switzerland no Emmental that is below par is marketed; all of it is virtually perfect cheese. Some critics claim that the ultrahygienic techniques of Swiss cheesemaking have caused the cheese to lose some of its flavor. I'm not so sure I agree. What is important to remember is that Emmental, like Swiss Gruyère, is made from raw milk. The complexities of raw milk cheesemaking include naturally occurring defects.

The Swiss won't compromise on the naturalness of the product; they would rather throw away the occasional off-batch. Their standards are the highest in the world. Raw-milk Emmental, whether French, Swiss, or from elsewhere, is consistently memorable. It is Emmental's pasteurized-milk imitators, such as Norwegian Jarlsberg and Wisconsin Alpine Lace, that have reduced the status of this fine cheese.

Choosing and Serving Swiss Emmental

The rind of all exported Emmental will have the word "Switzerland" imprinted on it in red, radiating out from the cheese's center. While it is preferable to purchase Emmental cut fresh from a section of the wheel, practically all Swiss Emmental in the U.S. will be

MAKING EMMENTAL

Rows of carefully tended Swiss Emmentals are aged in temperature-controlled curing rooms.

In making Emmental, starter and rennet are added to the raw cow's milk and the mixture curdles in about 30 minutes. Then the curd is cut until the pieces are tiny and the whey is released. Next, the curd is "cooked," actually heated to 127°F (53°C), in order to achieve a specific texture in the finished cheese. A piece of cheesecloth attached to a flexible frame is passed under and around the entire mass, then lifted, and the corners gathered with the help of a pulley to drain off more of the whey. It sounds simple. In reality, though, this step is a complex maneuver and the cheesemakers have to be deft at it—they do it thousands of times in their cheesemaking careers. (In Switzerland cheesemaking is a lifework. No part-timers here, and very few leave the industry to take on other careers.) The entire bag is then placed in a mold and the form is turned and pressed manually (and gently, so as not to disturb the starter bacteria) at regular intervals by a large, steel contraption.

Next, the Emmentals are taken from their molds and floated in a brine bath for several days. Then they are transferred to an aging room, where they are left to be turned and rubbed with a damp cloth at weekly intervals for several months. After an additional few months of curing, during which each cheese's rind is brushed frequently to cleanse, stimulate, and solidify the developing crust, the cheese is ready for consumption.

offered to you already cut, wrapped, and priced. This should not deter you, though, since Swiss Emmental and Gruyère are really quite sturdy, and if you are purchasing a piece cut even a day or two earlier, it will be sure to delight.

Emmental marries well with fruits and vegetables, meat, bread, and wine or beer. It is a key ingredient in fondue, Reuben sandwiches, and *croque monsieur* (a French-style ham and cheese sandwich that is dipped in beaten eggs and then grilled). Wine choices for Emmental are diverse, from whites such as Loire Muscadet to Rhône reds such as Saint-Joseph. For cooking, Emmental works best shredded. Be aware that it responds best to slow heating to achieve its creamiest consistency, but that no matter how low the heat or how long it has been cooked, it will effect a ropey, stretchy, less cohesive melt than high-butterfat Gruyère (which I much prefer for melting). Emmental is an excellent cheese-course choice.

Avoid any Emmental that shows mold and any that is pooling or has pooled its butterfat—evidence of retailer abuse. Particularly when sliced thin and stacked, Emmental has a tendency to dry out rather quickly, so it is advisable to buy it in quantities that you can finish in a few days. Store it in the vegetable

Gigantic wheels of Swiss Emmental are made at village cheese dairies in the verdant valley of the Emme River. Although the first documented mention of the name Emmental appeared in 1542, cheese was made here as early as 1293.

NOT THE REAL THING

Emmental is trimmed and cut down into big blocks so that it can fit into the omnipresent deli slicing machines, but Gruyère is very rarely treated this way. Some trimmed blocks of so-called Gruyère are marketed, but closer inspection reveals that these are a processed Gruyère-style product—a sort of Swiss version of processed "American" cheese with added emulsifiers. Avoid it at all costs. Processed Swiss, found on airplanes and in packages of premixed fondue, is a means of utilizing "mistakes" that sometimes occur in the cheesemaking process. The culprits include ineffective starter or rennet and faulty temperature gauges, defects which are revealed by the merciless system of Swiss quality control.

compartment of the refrigerator, wrapped in plastic so that it is airtight.

SWISS GRUYÈRE

Gruyère (grew-YAIR or gree-AIR) hails from the canton of Fribourg, an area north and east of Lake Geneva. Like Emmental, Gruyère is one of the truly great cheeses of the world. The longer I am in the business the more I realize the importance of Gruyère and the more forcefully I am struck by its supremacy, its majesty.

The raw cow's milk for Gruyère is not skimmed; otherwise it is made much the same way as Emmental but in smaller wheels. Gruyère has twice the flavor intensity of Emmental, with an abundance of sweet-saline beefiness and an undertone of fruit (apples, pears) and nuts.

Gruyère used to show a considerable distribution of pea-size holes due largely to happenstance. But you never find holes in Swiss Gruyère anymore, though you may find the occasional horizontal fissure (*lènure*) near the rind. Gruyère production has become so technologically controlled and so ultrahygienic that not enough raw milk bacteria survive long enough to produce the gas that causes the holes to form. Gruyère, which is aged at a higher temperature, has a much more assertive flavor than Emmental and requires a longer aging period. Emmental can be released after

TRADITIONAL FONDUE

Makes 4 servings

In Switzerland, fondue is made and served in a *caquelon,* a wide, shallow, flameproof, earthenware pot. Earthenware absorbs heat evenly and is the best choice, but a steel or cast-iron pot with an enameled interior will also work.

Diners spear chunks of crusty bread with foot-long, three-pronged fondue forks, swirl the bread around in the bubbling cheese a few times, then pop the morsel into their mouths. In Switzerland, fondue is usually accompanied by beer or black tea, though a glass of kirsch is also traditional.

Choosing the perfect combination of Swiss cheeses for fondue is considered something of an art in Switzerland and many Swiss dairy stores sell their own blends. Emmental and Gruyère are the most popular choices, used alone or in combination with other cheeses. Appenzeller adds a touch of piquancy to the mixture. Three classic French cheeses that also make a delicious fondue are Comté, Emmental, and Beaufort.

Instead of mopping the fondue pot clean with bread, leave a thin layer of fondue at the bottom, lower the heat of the flame, and allow a crust to form. This crust,

three to six months of aging; most Gruyère is kept for eight to ten months.

As a result of its longer aging, its cream content, and its dense texture, Gruyère's texture when melted is much softer and creamier than Emmental's. Choose Gruyère for gratins, soups, and grilled cheese sandwiches. The best Swiss fondues owe most of their savoriness to Gruyère; in fact, some fondue-lovers use *only* Gruyère. (If you like a sharp fondue, include a soupçon of Appenzeller—say, an ounce per person—to add a touch of piquancy to the mixture.)

A terrific aged Swiss Gruyère, called Fribourg, is a harder, sharper, older Gruyère that is usually aged two or more years. It is a great cheese—almost as good as the Savoie Beaufort d'Alpage from France—and a few of us American cheesemongers make a point of stocking this style of Swiss Gruyère.

called *la religieuse,* is considered a delicacy. Lift it out of the pan, break into pieces, and share it with your guests.

1½ cups (6 ounces; 180 g) grated Gruyère
1½ cups (6 ounces; 180 g) grated Emmental
½ cup (2 ounces; 60 g) grated Appenzeller
2 to 3 tablespoons cornstarch or all-purpose flour
1 clove garlic, halved
1 cup (¼ L) dry white wine, preferably Swiss Fendant, Neuchâtel, or Dézaley (Chablis or Riesling may also be used)
1 teaspoon fresh lemon juice
Splash of kirsch
Freshly ground black pepper, to taste
Pinch of nutmeg
Crusty bread cut into large cubes

1. In a medium-size bowl, combine the three cheeses and toss with the cornstarch.

2. Rub the inside of a fondue pot with the garlic halves. Add the wine and heat over medium heat until hot, but not boiling. Stir in the lemon juice and kirsch.

3. Add a handful of cheese at a time to the wine mixture, and stirring constantly with a wooden spoon, wait for each portion of cheese to melt before adding the next. Continue stirring until the cheese is completely melted, bubbling gently, and has the appearance of a light, creamy sauce. Season to taste with pepper and nutmeg.

4. Remove the pot from the heat and place over an alcohol safety burner set on a table. Adjust the burner flame so the fondue continues to bubble gently. Serve with plenty of crusty bread cubes.

Choosing and Serving Swiss Gruyère

As with Emmental, when possible, have your piece of Gruyère cut from a section of the whole wheel rather than purchasing it precut, wrapped, and priced, but don't worry if the cut kind is all you can get. Just try not to buy cut pieces with rind on three sides; otherwise, you'll be paying for rind rather than cheese. Gruyère is a sturdy cheese and likely will be fine. Avoid any that shows surface mold or that is pooling its butterfat into its plastic wrap. (As a cheese matures and its moisture evaporates, butterfat collects, or pools, in any hollow or hole.) Swiss Gruyère wheels are large—around 65 to 85 pounds (32½ to 42½ k), about 4 inches thick, and 38 inches in diameter—with a brown pebbled rind and interior color considerably whiter than that of Emmental. Its texture is almost immediately granular on the tongue, though it quickly dissolves to smooth and creamy, with enormous presence of flavor from start to finish. It tastes of grapey fruitiness and walnuttiness, aided and infused with an almost indescribable aromatic "air," a sort of release of all that is Alpine—soil, grass, cattle, and milk.

Gruyère is an admirable eating cheese that pairs nicely with pears and apples. Its inherent sweetness also makes it a fitting companion to salty *charcuterie*. Match Gruyère with red or white Burgundy, Rhône reds, or earthy Bandol. Gruyère is a superb choice for cooking because of its high butterfat-to-moisture ratio. It responds best to low heat, and leftovers remelt admirably. It resists becoming stale and dry surprisingly well, and I never hesitate to take home pieces larger than I really need. It should be stored in the

vegetable compartment of the refrigerator, wrapped as airtight as possible in plastic wrap.

THE RACLETTE CHEESES

Bagnes, Conches, Gomser, and Orsières

The word *raclette* comes from the French *racler,* to "scrape" or "scrape off," and is used to describe a number of cheeses that are used to make a Swiss melted cheese specialty called raclette.

Raclette (rack-LETT) cheeses are not nearly as large as Gruyère or Emmental. These are 13- to 17-pound (6½ to 8½ k) cheeses about the size of a big dinner plate and usually about 3 inches thick, with a rough dark-beige rind. All Raclette cheeses are made from whole, raw cow's milk, the better ones from the milk of cows that enjoy higher pasturage. They are mountain cheeses aged three to four months, with a creamy mouthfeel and semifirm paste that melts on your tongue with a terrific presence; an almost straight-from-the-tree fruitiness. The flavor is similar to but more pronounced than Gruyère and the texture is smoother, less granular, and more supple.

The different names of the Raclette cheeses reflect the origins of their pastures and/or the cheesemaking dairy. The name of the village nearest to where the cheese is

RACLETTE SANS FIREPLACE

D on't hesitate to serve raclette even if you have
neither a raclette machine nor
a fireplace. Cut 4-ounce (125 g)
portions of cheese, trim off
the rind, and arrange one on
each ovenproof dinner plate.
Set the plates in a preheated
450°F (232°C) oven and heat
the cheese for a few minutes
until thoroughly melted and
practically liquid. Serve with
boiled or pickled pearl onions,
boiled potatoes, cornichons,
and warm, crusty bread.

made will be molded convexly into
the edge of the rind, the raised letters formed by antique, hand-
carved wooden molds in which the
curd was pressed. The four best I
have tasted are made high in the
canton of Valais.

Choosing and Serving Raclette Cheeses

L ook for the village names of
Bagnes, Conches, Gomser, and
Orsières on Raclette. Make sure the
cheese has a healthy, dry, dark
beige rind with no cracks or reddening. Look for a creamy, firm texture and an ivory interior paste that
is not too hard, not granular, not
overbearingly salty, and not overly
sharp.

In addition to their superior
melting qualities, Raclette cheeses
are also absolutely splendid as table
cheeses, for snacks and lunchtime,
or after a fine meal, with fruit. *Bündnerfleisch*, the air-dried Swiss beef
from the canton of Graubünden,
goes very well with raclette, especially when sliced paper thin. Any
cured ham is also appropriate. The
Swiss rarely drink wine with raclette or fondue. Traditionally they
drink either beer, tea, or kirsch—
but I enjoy a big red wine with both.
Finish this meal with a salad.

Raclette cheese is also made in
France (see page 135).

THE HARD MOUNTAIN CHEESES

Sbrinz, Saanen, and Spalen

S wiss cheesemakers regionally regulate and market Sbrinz (SPRINZ)
and its smaller but otherwise identical counterparts, Saanen (SAH-
nen) and Spalen (SHPAH-len), under
the category name "hard mountain
cheeses." Little-known outside of
Switzerland, these are hard-rinded,
grainy cheeses that have been aged
for two years and are quite similar
to Italy's Parmigiano-Reggiano and
Grana Padano.

Sbrinz, the least obscure of the

hard mountain cheeses, is terrific; I always stock it at my cheese counters. Its name is an old spelling of the Swiss town, Brienz, in the canton of Bern. It is also made in the central Switzerland cantons of Schwyz, Lucerne, Obwalden, Uri, Unterwalden-Nidwalden, and Zug. Sbrinz is a raw cow's milk cheese that has been aged for two years to become amber colored, with a nutty, butterscotchy flavor. It comes in massive wheels that can run 80 pounds (40 k). The cheese is quite hard (ideal for grating), and its burnished-gold rind is even harder. But when thinly sliced or slivered, its true texture is discovered—Sbrinz literally melts on your tongue.

Sbrinz's identical, but smaller, counterparts differ only in size: They are Saanen, named for an area of the Fribourg canton, and Spalen, also called Sparen (SHPAR-ren) a corruption of a word that suggests the wheel-shape of the cheese. Like Sbrinz, Saanen and Spalen are very hard and very thick-rinded, but smaller in size—the wheels can be as small as 12 to 14 pounds (6 to 7 k). All of the hard mountain cheeses have been made the same way for centuries and are meant to last a long time without requiring refrigeration. (Saanen was so valuable and so long-keeping that it used to be included as part of a maiden's dowry.) All were created to ease the Swiss demand for Italian grating cheeses. This was centuries ago, but even then nationalist cheesemakers hated seeing money leave the region.

Choosing and Serving the Hard Mountain Cheeses

Despite their appeal, Switzerland's hard mountain cheeses have remained relatively unknown and underappreciated in the U.S. The reason seems to be no more than the fact that cheesemongers have not made a point of encouraging their customers to try them. They are much less sharp than Parmesan—ideal for people who desire a flavorful but mellow grating cheese. And they are superb for a simple lunch, as a salad cheese, and the perfect after-dinner cheese with fruit. Avoid any Sbrinz, Saanen, or Sparen that appears dry or cracked or that has developed a wealth of tiny white spots on the interior. These calcifications suggest that the cheese has been robbed of its butterfat and has dried out. Try to buy pieces cut directly from the wheel rather than settling for any that have been pre-cut and plastic-wrapped.

It may be difficult to find Sbrinz that hasn't already been pre-cut. Either way, I urge you to try this mellow grating cheese.

Sbrinz, one of Switzerland's hard-rinded mountain cheeses, is made near Brienz, a lovely lakeside resort that is also a famous center of Swiss wood-carving.

Hard mountain cheeses should not be considered only for grating. Their sweet, vaguely butterscotchy flavor and sturdiness recommend them as the perfect cheese to take outdoors when you are camping, fishing, or hiking, as they resist all manner of abuse (including not being refrigerated), while offering a gentle, immensely satisfying flavor that marries well with whatever is at hand. They are excellent with fruit, salami or ham, Dijon or honey mustard, crusty bread, and light, fruity red wines such as Beaujolais.

TETE DE MOINE

Also Called Bellelay

Tête de Moine (TET-duh-MWAHN), which means, literally, "monk's head," was originally an abbey cheese made by monks. It is now produced in cooperatives near the town of Bellelay in the canton of Bern, and often is referred to as Bellelay (bel-LAY).

Tête de Moine is a raw cow's milk mountain cheese about the

TETE DE MOINE'S FRENCH COUSIN

Girollin (zhir-oh-LAN) is a relatively new French cheese from Franche-Comté that is an unabashed knockoff of Tête de Moine, though a bit less firm-textured and not quite as assertively flavored. It is quite good—as are all the cheeses of Franche-Comté. Like Tête, it is made from raw cow's milk. Consider it an option if Tête de Moine is unavailable, or if you prefer a milder cheese.

size of a coffee can, only a little bit fatter and a little bit shorter. It is the single exception to the rule that all mountain cheeses are large. Each foil-wrapped drum weighs an average of 1¼ to 1¾ pounds (625 to 875 g) and is 4 to 5 inches high and 4 to 5 inches in diameter. Traditionally, it is sliced horizontally, rather than vertically, although it's fine to slice it either way. The slicing ritual probably contributed to the cheese's name—it is shaved across the top and down over the sides and thus resembles the tonsure of a monk.

Traditionally, the Swiss buy whole Têtes, remove the top rind, and store the cheese upside down in a dish of white wine, though sometimes they will merely cover the top with a cloth soaked in white wine. I don't like to macerate the cheese in any liquid. It is sufficient to wrap it in plastic wrap or aluminum foil. Not all Têtes come wrapped in silver foil, but most of those that are exported do. They have a brown, pebbly rind and are always made from superlative, unpasteurized cow's milk.

Tête has a pronounced, almost sharp flavor—very round and full with nothing missing. It will attempt to shoulder past anything that accompanies it—it really wants to take over. Like most mountain cheeses, Tête has a rather boastful exuberance, tasting fruity, nutty, and beefy, with a background of sweetness and saltiness. Tête is easily the strongest of the Swiss cheeses. Indeed, no other mountain cheese in the world possesses such intensity of flavor.

Intensely flavorful Tête de Moine was first made in monasteries. Always sliced horizontally rather than vertically, its name, which means "monk's head," is a reference to its appearance after the first slice of cheese has been shorn off the top.

Choosing and Serving Tête de Moine

Healthy Tête will have a dark-beige to brown dry, smooth rind. (This may be difficult to determine, as the majority of exported Tête is made by a cooperative that wraps its smooth-textured cheeses in silver foil. Another cooperative wraps their pebbled-rind Tête in loose-fitting plastic.) The interior of a healthy Tête will range from just off-white to straw-colored and will show the occasional pea-size hole and *lenures*, the horizontal fissures associated with similar mountain cheeses, such as Gruyère. The Tête's flavor will be sharply aromatic, huge and fruity, muscular and intense, but not at all unpleasant.

Should you find that you've purchased a too old Tête de Moine, its rancid flavor and overpowering odor will put you off its pleasures for a long time. The probability of its being in a refrigerated case at a low temperature can hide this fact, so be sure you taste it first. Watch out for a cracked, slimy rind and/or a graying, reddish interior.

Tête de Moine is extraordinarily delicious and is traditionally served with thin caraway-spiked crackers as a luncheon cheese or to accompany cocktails. It is terrific with apples, pears, and grapes, and marries well with any cured or dried meat, such as prosciutto, air-dried beef (*Bündnerfleisch*), or salami *(saucisson sec)*, as well as crudités, such as radishes, celery,

THE GIROLLE

The Swiss use an apparatus called a *girolle* to cut and serve a Tête. The cheese is "skewered" and held in place by a stainless-steel rod that juts up out of the center of a round cheese board. Then a dull vertical blade with a knob on its handle fits over the rod and rests on the bare top of the cheese. When you turn the handle round and round, the vertical "knife" scrapes off a thin ruffle of cheese—a morsel, a *coquille* (shell) or *girolle*—that you can pop into your mouth or use as a garnish. It's very indicative of the Swiss nature that this perfect little machine is made exclusively for Tête de Moine. I sell them, but they are pricey.

and carrots. It calls for a big red wine, a Rhône or Burgundy perhaps. Beer, ale, porter, and stout also go nicely with Tête.

Cheerily painted folk art motifs decorate the façades of buildings in the town of Appenzell, in the easternmost part of Switzerland.

APPENZELLER

Also Called Appenzell

The easternmost Swiss cantons produce a cheese called Appenzeller (AP-en-zeller) or Appenzell (AP-en-zell), though primarily it comes from the canton of Appenzell, close to Austria. It's a pressed, cooked-curd, brushed-rind cheese with the occasional scattering of pea- to cherry-size holes.

Appenzeller is a mountain cheese that is sharper than Gruyère, but not as sharp as Tête de Moine. It is a 3-inch-thick wheel, 12 to 14 inches in diameter, that generally weighs between 11 and 15 pounds (5½ to 7½ k), but I've seen them as

big as 20 pounds (10 k). The aging period is about three months. The standard cheese is made from whole, raw cow's milk, but a new lower-fat version—identified as "reduced fat"—is gaining favor here and abroad as a "diet" cheese—and a very good one it is. There are 75 Appenzell cheesemaking cooperatives that produce, under tight canton control, upward of 200,000 cheeses each year.

Appenzeller's most distinctive feature is its singular, fruity tang. This tanginess is characteristic of washed-rind cheeses. The new, just-formed Appenzeller is bathed in a once secret mixture of pepper, herbs, white wine (or cider), water, and brine that gives the cheese its decidedly spicy intensity.

There is another style of Appenzeller called Rässkäse (REHSS-kehz-eh), made in the cantons of Appenzell, Saint Gallen, Thurgau, and Zürich, which is aged much longer than the norm. It is very, very sharp, with a much darker interior and rind. Although I've never seen it in the U.S., I have sampled it in Switzerland. The Swiss in those cantons are so proud of this cheese that they have designed a specific black and gold foil label for it. The drawback is that since both styles of Appenzeller have grown so very expensive—even more expensive than Italy's Fontina—aged Appenzeller would be nearly impossible to retail here.

Choosing and Serving Appenzeller

Appenzeller is one of the cheeses that you will see in every good cheese shop. It is consistently good, as are all Swiss-made cheeses. Look for a healthy, brown rind with no cracks and no slime. The interior should be a uniform ivory color, not graying or reddish. Overripe, this cheese is awful, but there is no such thing as its being too young.

Appenzeller is an excellent snack or lunchtime cheese with bread or crackers, fruit—apples, pears, grapes—and a *cru* Beaujolais, a red Burgundy, or a sturdy beer. It's also a perfect melter for gratins, toast, or fondue and a splendid salad cheese, cubed, with walnuts, endive, watercress, grapes, and a light vinaigrette made with sherry vinegar and walnut oil.

SWISS TILSIT

Back in the 1800s, some Swiss cheesemakers traveled to Germany and "stole" the recipe for a cheese called Tilsiter. But, it should be pointed out, this was not an especially original crime since the Germans had previously "stolen" it from its Dutch originators, who at the time were living (for better pasturage) in Tilsit, East Prussia

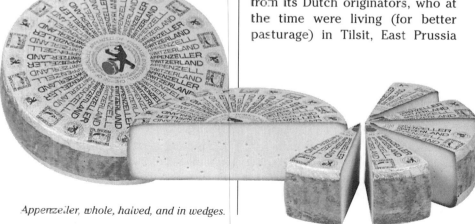

Appenzeller, whole, halved, and in wedges.

TAKE ME TO YOUR LEADER

In almost all parts of Switzerland, farmers make a great to-do over the changing of the seasons. In spring, the cattle emerging from the lowland pastures and barns are bedecked with flowers, and paraded about before they are led up into the high pastures to graze for the spring and summer. When summer is over the cattle must be led down again before the weather turns. So it is natural that there is a journey, a transhumance, to and from the pastures according to the seasons.

Each herd has one cow that is called the Herrkuh, the lead cow. This cow has a louder bell than any of the others, and with it she leads the cattle to and from the high Alpine pastures. The Herrkuh always has a thick, leather neck strap that identifies whose cow she is. These straps are beautiful examples of folk art, always with an evocative symbol etched into them—an anchor if the owner had always wished he were at sea, or a bell, or a religious symbol—and they always have a number on them, since each cow's performance is tracked and recorded by means of its assigned number. When the cow dies, the farmer retires her number with great reverence, and keeps either the decoration she wore, or a wooden plaque with the number, on the wall of his barn.

(now Sovetsk, Russia, just above Poland). Today the Swiss produce the definitive Tilsit (TILL-sit), having endowed it with a Swiss identity. (For some years, Tilsit was also called Royalp, but this name is no longer used.) It is a splendid cheese, similar to Appenzeller, though softer, made in 4-pound (2 k) wheels, 1½ inches thick and 7 inches in diameter. It, too, is made from whole, raw cow's milk and aged about three months, but it has a nuttier, earthier, more barnyardy flavor and aroma. Caution: When cut pieces of Swiss Tilsit have been stored for too long (a month or more), they lose freshness and become bitter. Just as less-than-fresh Gruyère tastes sickly fruity and sharp, Swiss Tilsit, too, has a terminal point in its life past which it's no longer enjoyable.

Choosing and Serving Swiss Tilsit

Swiss Tilsit is not easy to find, but if you do locate it, look for an aromatic cheese and avoid any that smells unhealthily strong. If the orange-brown rind is slimy and/or the paste is in any way pinkish or brownish, the cheese is past its prime. If it bears none of these defects, you're in for a very flavorful experience. Serve Swiss Tilsit with sweet fruit, crusty bread, and a strong, powerful red wine such as Côtes-du-Rhône. It's just as good with beer or ale, too.

VACHERIN MONT D'OR

There are two Vacherin cheeses made in Switzerland—Vacherin Mont d'Or and Vacherin Fribourgeois. The more important one is Vacherin Mont d'Or (vasher-ANN-moan-DOR), which is, without question, one of the greatest cheeses in the world. I love it because of its remarkable flavor, like woodsmoke, scrambled eggs, and butter, and its unique aroma—like that of new leather. A thin strip of resinous bark encircles the rind, adding balsamy flavor and aroma.

Swiss Vacherin Mont d'Or is made in the canton of Vaud in the area called Les Charbonnières or the Vallée de Joux. An identical A.O.C. cheese called Vacherin du Haut-Doubs is produced just across the border in France in Franche-Comté. The two cheeses further go to show you that, just as state lines blur in the U.S., so do country boundaries in Europe. Often people are very much the same on both sides of the border and that seems to be the case with cheeses as well. (For more about French Vacherin du Haut-Doubs and Swiss Vacherin Mont d'Or, including information on choosing and serving them, see page 120.) Do be aware that there has recently been a proliferation of Swiss Vacherin Mont d'Or made from pasteurized milk, which I urge you not to buy.

VACHERIN FRIBOURGEOIS

Switzerland's "other" Vacherin is not at all like Vacherin Mont d'Or. It is called Vacherin Fribourgeois (FREE-boor-ZHWAH), which means it's from the area around Fribourg in the canton of Valais. Think of it as a luscious Swiss version of Fontina. It has the same physical configuration and characteristics as Fontina d'Aosta—3-inch-thick

ACQUIRING A TASTE FOR SAPSAGO

Sapsago (sop-SAH-go), sometimes spelled Sap Sago, comes from the canton of Glarus in eastern Switzerland near Liechtenstein, where it was first made more than a thousand years ago by monks. Also called Glarner Schabzieger, it is a fat-free "novelty" cheese, made by turning skimmed cow's milk into curd. The curd is pressed, completely dried, ground into a powder, and then mixed with fenugreek and a local wild clover, which give it a unique flavor and pale green color. The mixture is then pressed into molds to become hard little 3-ounce (90 g) truncated cones (*stöckli*). The cones, meant to be used as a grating cheese, come wrapped in foil and are sold individually or in boxes of a dozen. They keep practically forever, even without refrigeration. Sapsago is also sold as a dried, fine powder, packaged in small, sprinkle-top containers and intended for use as a condiment. In this form, which is even more strongly flavored than the little cones, the cheese must be mixed with softened butter before using.

The taste of Sapsago is a bit strange—sharply herby and lettuce-like with flavor flashes reminiscent of sage. It is an interesting flavoring agent, especially since a little goes a long way. Try grating Sapsago into green salads or on noodle dishes. Blended with butter, cream cheese, Ricotta, or yogurt to lessen its herby sharpness, it makes an unusual spread for crackers. Thinned slightly, this same mixture can also be used as a dip with crudités.

wheels, about 14 inches in diameter, weighing around 17 pounds (8½ k)—and is a semifirm (though buttery and yielding), lightly pressed, raw cow's-milk cheese with a light-brown brushed, washed rind, aged for three to four months. Though it has been made in Switzerland for centuries (it predates its much more famous regional cousin, Gruyère), the Swiss have only put great export effort into it in the last several years, and they are really marketing it aggressively. Rightly so—it's a terrific cheese with a big, raw, nutty flavor that is a paean to the excellence of Switzerland's unpasteurized cow's milk.

Choosing and Serving Vacherin Fribourgeois

Once again, the only bugaboo to guard against with this particular cheese is retailer abuse, which mostly involves over-age. Drying or "dead" Vacherin Fribourgeois will look, taste, and smell horrible, with a mushy rind and gray interior. If the wheel is fresh it is one of the finest cheeses imaginable, in the same exalted class as Fontina d'Aosta and Morbier. This triumvirate makes up the three oldest, most desirable and most original semifirm cheeses.

Like the other two, Vacherin Fribourgeois is a great melter for soups, raclettes, gratins, and *tartines* (on toast!). It dices beautifully for green and fruit salads; and it is, of course, welcome always with seasonal fruit, crusty bread, and big reds from Burgundy, Bordeaux, the Rhône Valley, and Piedmont.

Nutty- flavored Vacherin Fribourgeois (left) and washed-rind Appenzeller (right), are great melting cheeses. Use either or both, along with Gruyère, for a mixed-cheese fondue known as moitié-moitié.

The British Isles

England, Scotland, Wales, Northern Ireland, the Republic of Ireland, and the adjacent islands comprise the British Isles. Though relatively small in area—roughly the size of New England—this territory endured Roman occupation, centuries of feudalism and almost continual wars, and, in time, became home to the British Empire, which at its height encompassed 25 percent of the world's area and population. The

Empire's expansion was mandatory and inevitable: even though half of the land was suitable for cultivation, the fact remained that the British Isles were too small to support any but the most basic way of life. The people needed to supplement their limited resources with products and goods that weren't available on home ground.

Practically all of the British Isles are, or were, pastureland—much of it extremely fertile, the rest fertile enough to provide the herbage necessary to support vast numbers of cattle and sheep. (Indeed, Ireland is said to be home to five times as many cattle as humans.) Unlike France, where each cheesemaking region is entirely different in terms

At London's most famous cheese shop owner/affineur *Randolph Hodgson*, one of the saviors of farmhouse cheeses, stocks nearly fifty new and traditional cheeses from England and Ireland.

ATLANTIC
OCEAN

Inverness

SCOTLAND

North
Sea

ENGLAND

IRELAND

Dublin

WALES

WEXFORD

TIPPERARY

Beechmount•

CORK

Blackwater

Lampeter•

Ffostrassol•

DYFED

Cardiff•

Wedmore•

SOMERSET

DEVON

CORNWALL

LANCA-
SHIRE

YORKSHIRE

•York

•Carnwath

CHESHIRE

NOTTINGHAM-
SHIRE

DERBY-
SHIRE

STAFFORD-
SHIRE

SHROP-
SHIRE

LEICESTER-
SHIRE

•Melton
•Mowbray

•Stilton

WORCESTERSHIRE

•Malvern

HEREFORD-
SHIRE

GLOUCESTERSHIRE

AVON
CORNWALL

*Mendip
Hills*

•Sturminster
Newton

DORSET

•London

English Channel

FRANCE

of terrain, and the United States, where subtropics, deserts, mountains, and plains exist, the British Isles are a dairy wonderland of common climate, temperature, elevation, and pasturage. Though differences in temperament and character exist among Welsh, Scottish, Irish, and English people, their diets, famines aside, historically have been similar. Food, for them, seems to have held less romance than it has for, say, the more agrarian, less industrial French and Italians.

In a land renowned for the high quality of its single and double cream, you would probably expect cheeses that reflect that richness—moist, fresh, elegant, diminutive cheeses, or glistening, smelly, washed-rind cheeses whose moist crusts foreshadow bursts of intense flavor. Not so. Generally speaking, the classic cheeses of the British Isles, the great ones such as Cheshire, Cheddar, and Wensleydale, are large, firm, dryish, and rather subdued in flavor. Interestingly, the recipes for many of the noblest English cheeses that survive today originated during the period of Roman occupation and influence. It was, in fact, because the Romans arrived with a history of cheesemaking, and shared it, that the English cheesemaking heritage took root.

For the next thousand years cheesemaking neither declined nor progressed; it was simply part of the daily routine and culture of farm life. But in the early seventeenth century, when the 300-year-long campaign to expand the United Kingdom coincided with the advent of the Industrial Revolution, the doors opened for larger scale production and prosperity. Trade increased, and as the Empire flourished, the citizens became less dependent on the land for sustenance. A transportation system was established that allowed commodities to be moved from where they were made, grown, or mined to distant areas. Milk was one of these commodities. In true Industrial Revolution style, the first cheese factories were opened in areas that had access to rail transportation. By providing work and income to a huge and hungry work force, the economic focus shifted away from self-sufficient, small farms and insular living to massive industrial growth and a population boom in the emerging cities and transportation centers.

World War I, not surprisingly, wreaked havoc on the whole of Europe's population and economy, and the resulting shortages and rationing, coupled with the loss of so much of the young male population, gravely wounded the British cheesemaking industry. Dairy farmers no longer enjoyed a sure market for their milk; sometimes it could

Holders of a Royal warrant, Paxton & Whitfield in London supplies Buckingham Palace with classic English cheeses such as Stilton and farmhouse Cheddar.

"The spirit of a country, if it is to be true to itself, needs continually to draw great breaths of inspiration from the simple realities of the country; from the smell of its soil, the pattern of its fields, the beauty of its scenery and from the men and women who dwell and toil in the rural areas."

Sir George Stapledon, as quoted in
***The Great British Cheese Book* by Patrick Rance**

be sold, but often, they were forced to quickly make cheese from the surplus. In most cases, standards slipped; cheesemaking became a chore geared toward preventing waste rather than perpetuating a valuable and tasty food tradition. Those farmers who could sell their fresh milk to creameries did so gladly; others were at a loss for a market, and many quit the dairy business, and by extension cheese-making, altogether.

The postwar economy was slow to recover, and finally, in 1933, the government took steps to bring order to the dairy industry, creating the Milk Marketing Board (MMB) to monitor and control milk sales throughout England. Dairy farmers were required to sell their milk to the MMB, for which they were paid a fair price. Milk destined to be bottled and sold on its own as milk, rather than a manufactured dairy product, was more costly; so-called "manufacturing" milk, which was used in the making of butter and cheese, powdered milk, etc., cost less. In some instances, the MMB arranged for the milk to be transported to dairy product manufac-

turers. In the case of cheesemakers, the milk bought by the MMB remained on the farm that had produced it, but the milk was sold back to the farmer/cheesemaker at a favorable price (essentially a paperwork transaction). The advantage of this system was that dairy farmers were assured of a steady, ready market for their milk and cheese.

In many ways the MMB was a noble endeavor as well as a clever idea. But along with the good came the bad. The MMB proceeded to impose controls on the cheesemaking process, setting rigid standards for the facilities and for hygiene. And it set very strict, textbook standards for cheese yield, processes (the cheeses' recipes), aging requirements, and grading. It also instituted a schedule of inspections conducted by pseudo experts, bureaucrats who were unfamiliar with traditional cheesemaking. The ironic result was that strict order was imposed upon a process that is as variable as anything ruled by nature. Naturally, most cheesemakers refused to alter their age-old ways and subsequently stopped making cheese altogether; the demise of farmhouse cheesemaking was well underway.

Eventually, the MMB found itself inundated with milk, much of it from producers in farflung locations. The few existing processing plants were widely spaced and the cost of moving the milk to these few, scattered facilities grew prohibitively high. The board began to finance construction of factories that could cope with receiving and pooling together this milk in central locations, in the process creating much-needed new jobs. Cheese made by the MMB factories (or dairies, as they were called), was made from milk gathered from thousands of herds scattered all over England. Once the milk was pooled and pasteurized, cheeses and other dairy products were produced in factories equipped with the latest technology. The end products were bland, lifeless, disk-shaped pasteurized cheeses with the same names and similar colors as the great cheeses of the British Isles. What these products lacked was the authentic flavor that results from using raw milk from specific herds and age-old production and ripening techniques.

The MMB also controlled distribution channels (and developed cozy relationships with the burgeoning supermarket industry), and as a result, small, traditional, artisanal cheesemakers found themselves simultaneously becoming unprofitable businesses and technological anachronisms. Eventually, inauthentic cheeses cornered the market.

Thus, the great cheeses of the British Isles came to be made in factories—their tried-and-true recipes altered to suit the machinery and technology of the day.

World War II and rationing policies contributed to the demise of the U.K.'s farm-made cheese industry. It was not until 1954 that rationing was lifted and cheesemakers experienced a freer hand in what they did to earn a living. By then, however, the MMB had crippled the cheese business by reducing the flavor of well-aged, handmade cheeses to nothing more than a faint memory. The outcome was the British cheese industry of today: Two clear and distinct types—not varieties—but *types* of cheese are made: factory cheeses, made by machines, and farmhouse cheeses, made by people.

Armed with portable milking equipment, a postwar dairy student heads for the herd.

With the emergence of a new generation that cares very much about what it eats and is fascinated by the notion of loving food from its own land and hands, honest, real farm-made cheeses are making a comeback. The movement begun in 1971 by activists in the Campaign for Real Ale (CAMRA), and a similar effort on behalf of bakers who wanted to return to Real British Bread inspired cheesemakers and cheese lovers to lobby for reinstituting and promoting farmhouse varieties of the classic British cheeses. Their persistence has begun to show results.

In 1994 the MMB was disbanded; dairy farmers were free to market their milk to whomever they wished and cheese production was deregulated. Today, farmhouse cheesemakers in Britain use milk from their own herds or milk purchased from a farmers' cooperative called Milk Marque, which also supplies large cheesemaking operations as well. Milk Marque, which collects and pools milk from farms throughout the U.K., is not directly involved in cheesemaking, but it is involved in encouraging the highest possible milk and cheese production standards in the British Isles. This group has shown support for the notion that fine, original cheese should, and can, exist, and it is a supporter and sponsor of the Specialist and Cheesemakers' Association's efforts to help the traditional cheeses of the British Isles reach a wider audience. Years ago, in order for a cheese to qualify as a farmhouse cheese, it had to be made in the legally delineated area from

which it derived its name; it was made from the milk of cattle pastured within that area; and it was handmade following recipe and aging requirements set down by local governing councils. Though there are no formal laws for farmhouse cheeses, since 1975, thanks in large part to the efforts of cheese authority Patrick Rance, many old and some new British and Irish cheesemaking artisans have voluntarily honored these guidelines and are producing fine cheeses. The demand for their product is strong and growing.

Informally, you can identify many farmhouse cheeses by their cloth-wrapped rinds, the most telling sign of farmhouse authenticity. (But keep in mind that some classic farmhouse varieties, specifically Stilton, Shropshire Blue, and Caerphilly, have natural rinds, so the absence of cloth is not a determiner for these types.) The cloth protects the "new," just-made cheese, enabling it to breathe during aging and ripening. Cheeses that are not cloth-wrapped are more prone to crack or dry out. No factory-made cheese is cloth-wrapped; it is covered with wax or thick plastic.

If it's flavor and memorability you're after, then the farmhouse cheeses of the British Isles are for you, and these are the cheeses I focus on here. You might not find every texture and flavor of cheese imaginable, but I can assure you, you'll have some enjoyable times set off by the flavor, aroma, and color of farmhouse Somerset Cheddar, Colston Bassett Stilton, Shropshire Blue, farmhouse Cheshire and Blue Cheshire, farmhouse Lancashire, and creamery Wensleydale.

A quarter-wheel of cloth-wrapped farmhouse Cheddar.

The Cheeses

CHEDDAR

Cheddar (CHEH-der), the world's most popular cheese, originated in England. But Cheddar, like Brie and Emmental, is made all over the world. The definition of Cheddar is a reflection of its recipe rather than the cheese's origin, though there is a town called Cheddar. The recipe that qualifies a cheese to call itself Cheddar involves scalding cow's-milk curd twice, followed by a "cheddaring," or milling process. Cheddaring is the repeated cutting and piling of the curd in order to remove the whey and break the curd into fine particles that are smooth and silky. It is this action, along with the double-scalding and subsequent aging, that gives Cheddar its taut texture and unique flavor. Though the method for English Cheshire, Gloucester, and Lancashire cheeses is similar, the finished cheeses have a slightly different texture and flavor. In France, the process for Cantal and Laguiole is comparable to that of Cheddar, producing a cheese that has the texture and flavor of good Cheddar.

The cheddaring process is exclusive to Cheddar and was "invented," probably through trial and error, in the southwestern county of Somerset. That is still where farmhouse English Cheddar is principally produced, though considerable quantities are also made in the flanking counties of Dorset, Devon, Avon, and Cornwall.

Farmhouse Cheddar is *always* a big, cylindrical drum (never a block shape), 14 to 16 inches high and 14 to 16 inches in diameter, weighing 56 to 66 pounds (28 to 33 k), with a gray-brown calico-wrapped rind.

True farmhouse English Cheddar has a full, deep-layered flavor, a firm, yet buttery texture, and a sweet, grassy aroma. I taste toffee,

THE QUEEN'S CHEDDAR

Among the thousands of wedding gifts presented to Queen Victoria during the 1840 celebration of her nuptials to Albert was a mammoth 1,250-pound, 9-foot-diameter Cheddar, produced at a cooperative by cheesemakers from two villages. Perhaps baffled by how to serve it, she sent the cheese off on a tour of England. When attempts were made to return it to her, she refused to take it back.

nuts, apples, hay, and hard-boiled eggs. The older the cheese, the more evident these flavors become. Most farmhouse Cheddars are aged for a minimum of six months, but the best will have been aged for a year or more. Cheddar is proof of one of my basic cheese precepts: The younger the cheese, the less flavor it will have. Older Cheddars are highly desirable: Two-year-old Cheddar is occasionally available, but three-year-olds are quite rare—usually the longer aging must be performed on the part of the retailer or not at all. My favorite farmhouse Cheddars are from Somerset—one made by George and Stephen Keen at Keen's Farm and the other made by the Montgomery family at Montgomery's Farm. Both stand as definitive, magnificent Cheddars that are head and shoulders above all other Cheddars.

Each drum or wheel varies—as do all artisanal cheeses—and I suggest that you open your mind and palate and try to articulate the flavors or sensations you detect.

The color of farmhouse English Cheddar is neither Wisconsin orange nor Vermont white, but rather a subtle, creamy, very natural straw-color, falling somewhere between yellow and beige. Though some cheesemakers use organic dyes in some other farmhouse cheeses and have for centuries, authentic farmhouse Cheddar is *never* orange in color.

Choosing and Serving Cheddar

Farmhouse English Cheddar is a cheese to adore. As long as the batch you have access to is not stale or dried out, you needn't worry about its vagaries—it is usually in fine condition.

Avoid any Cheddar (from anywhere) that has white patches or spots; both are indications that the cheese has been in storage too long, probably wrapped in plastic. If you come across an internal crack or blemish, don't worry, such things happen and shouldn't adversely affect the cheese's flavor. (Flaws are evidence of the wonderful handmade quality of farmhouse cheeses.) Avoid Cheddars that are referred to as "top hats" because they are usually undistinguished, mass-produced, factory Cheddars, made with milk from numerous herds, pasteurized into vapidity. The

CHEDDAR, THE TOWN THAT NAMED THE CHEESE THAT ISN'T MADE THERE

Cheddar is a village in the southwestern county of Somerset, about 100 miles from London. All in all, it is a beautiful area of green hills and Channel shoreline. But there is no Cheddar made in Cheddar anymore (and there hasn't been for ages), so there is no cheese-related reason to visit the town. The reason to visit is a geologic one. Cheddar is home to the famous and rather spectacular Cheddar Gorge, a dramatic and sudden canyon.

Beginning sometime in the sixteenth century, travelers who visited the gorge tasted the local cheese at inns and taverns. They liked it so much, they began taking home quantities of "cheese from Cheddar." Thus grew Cheddar's fame. The best Cheddar cheeses are made not far away by a number of small creameries (some of them located on farms) in Somerset, and what they produce is the genuine article, real Cheddar, made from the original recipe.

best Cheddars will always be cloth-wrapped and the classic size mentioned earlier.

Be wary of any cheese being touted as "farmhouse" if it is sold pre-cut, pre-wrapped, and/or pre-priced. English farmhouse cheeses should always be fresh cut, and you always should be able to see a portion of the cheese's cloth wrapping. Plastic wrap is fine for storing Cheddar at home. It needn't breathe as should, say, a traditional chèvre, where a loose, paper wrap is called for. Cheddar is sturdy and will be tasty and retain its texture for at least two weeks, if not more, when refrigerated. Should any surface mold develop, simply scrape it away.

Serve Cheddar anytime you feel like adding something wonderful to your life. Bread or crackers, wine or beer, fruit or not, it doesn't matter. This is a cheese that always satisfies. It is marvelous served with fruit pies, tarts, or cobblers, or shredded over salads or one-dish meals destined for the oven.

Cheddar's melting qualities are very agreeable, though different from those of Gruyère or Emmental. Once it has cooled slightly, Cheddar offers a more solid, toothsome melt with a decidedly different flavor, and if the cheese is aged more than six months, its flavor when melted will be considerably more evident than that of Gruyère or Emmental. Melted Cheddar has always

A cheesemaker at Chewton Dairy Farms in Somerset inspects a day-old farmhouse Cheddar that will eventually be aged for a minimum of six months.

been very popular in the U.S.—on basics, such as grilled cheese sandwiches, hamburgers, chili, or tuna melts or as a topping or filling for popular Mexican dishes. For melting purposes, Cheddar should be shredded, not finely grated or sliced. Taking into account the range of Cheddar's intensity of flavor, it is agreeable with light, fruity red wines and dark beers and ales.

STILTON

Stilton (STILL-tun) is England's only name-protected cheese. But there is no farmhouse Stilton produced anymore. All of it is made by Stilton specialists in largish facili-ties within Stilton's legal domain, the pastures of the beloved Shires—predominantly Leicestershire and Nottinghamshire, an area of rolling hills and dales separated by streams, rock fences, and hedges well known to generations of fox hunters and dairymen. Beneath the soil of these pastures are seams of coal and considerable deposits of iron, and many of us believe that this iron is a factor that contributes to the blueing of Stilton.

In addition to Leicestershire and Nottinghamshire, only the Dale of the Dove area, just westward in Derbyshire, is legally permitted to contribute milk or actually produce Stilton. The name-control law for the cheese stipulates that the milk and manufacture must occur in this specific area, and that the cheesemaker must follow the recipe and aging guidelines set down by The Stilton Cheese Makers' Association. Unfortunately, what is not protected by Stilton's name-control status is the quality of the finished product. Stilton may be, indeed too often is, far less than perfect—insufficiently blue due to inadequate or minimal aging; irregular in crust development; or texturally dry—mainly the fault of some manufacturers who release premature Stiltons from their aging rooms to fulfill high demand.

In 1967, the Stilton-makers rewrote the 1910 definition of their cheese in order to incorporate modern equipment and methods. The British High Court judgment defined Stilton as "a blue or white cheese made from full-cream cow's milk with no applied pressure, that

Cheesemakers in Leicestershire with cylinders of Stilton, England's only name-protected cheese.

could be pierced but not inoculated, that forms its own crust or coat, and that is made in a cylindrical form, the milk coming from English dairy herds in the district of Melton Mowbray and surrounding areas falling within the counties of Leicestershire [now including Rutland], Derbyshire, and Nottinghamshire." Sounds complete, doesn't it? But as noted British cheese authority Patrick Rance points out, the judgment includes no mention of the state of the milk used—neither raw nor pasteurized milk is specified. As a result of this oversight, all of today's Stilton production is from pasteurized milk. And while the definition of Stilton prohibits any variation in shape or size, it does not prevent shortcuts by the most pro-

lific, large-scale Stilton-makers. The result is plenty of inferior Stilton and a scarcity of the finest. Take care when buying it. Virtually all Stilton made today is blue. White Stilton is very good—sort of like a farmhouse Lancashire—but very rare. I haven't seen any for ages.

The flavor of a great Stilton cheese is full, rich, and creamy, as complex as that of any other great blue. It reveals layers and folds of the flavors of honey, leather, tobacco, and molasses. The finest Stilton must be well made from the best milk, turned often, aged properly, and "ironed." Ironing is a method of determining Stilton's readiness for eating. A cylindrical "plug" of cheese is removed, sometimes more than once, during a Stilton's aging period, by twisting an auguring tool, specifically designed for the cheese trade, into each form of Stilton. The cheese can then be sniffed, scrutinized for proper texture and blueing development, tasted, and the plug then reinserted into the cheese. The "scar" is minor and should be considered a testament to the care of its maker. According to the speed of each cheese's development, a Stilton can be aged for as little as six months or as long as 18 months. (Many Stiltons beg for more than the minimum six-month aging period in rooms, not caves, at or near each Stilton-making facility. The bacteria that provoke the blueing occur naturally in the milk as well as in the air that enters the cheese during the piercing process— long needles are used to aerate the interior to facilitate mold growth.)

Most Stiltons weigh 14 to 16 pounds (7 to 8 k), are 10 to 11 inches high, and 8 to 9 inches in diameter. The texture of well-aged Stilton should be crumbly, yet moist and creamy. Stilton's aroma is huge and spicy at room temperature, but merely pleasant when cold. Many lovers of

Stilton voraciously devour the natural crust. I love Stilton, but I never eat the rind. This is purely a matter of personal taste (Patrick Rance would never leave so much as a wisp of rind on his plate).

Excellent Stilton is made by four cheesemakers in the Melton Mowbray area of Leicestershire— Long Clawson Dairy, Millway Foods Ltd. (formerly St. Ivel), Tuxford & Tebbutt, and Webster's Dairy. Stiltons made in Derbyshire by J. M. Nuttall, and in Nottinghamshire by the Cropwell Bishop Creamery, are available in the United States, as is my favorite from Nottinghamshire, the harder-to-find Colston Bassett. Until 1992, Colston Bassett, located in Nottinghamshire, was the only brand that used unpasteurized milk. Alas, they no longer make their Stilton with raw milk, but no matter, theirs is still excellent—I consider it the best. When Long Clawson Dairy, which also turns out excellent Stilton, celebrated its seventy-fifth anniversary in 1990, I was proud to be one of the few cheesemongers in the world to be lucky enough to get my hands on not just one, but four of their mammoth, 60-pound (30 k) commemorative Stiltons. I'll never forget them, and, I warrant, neither will my customers.

Seventeen pounds (8½ k) of whole milk are used to make each 14- to 16-pound (7 to 8 k) Stilton.

Choosing and Serving Stilton

When Stilton is on your shopping list, my advice is to seek out a knowledgeable cheesemonger. Great Stilton can be purveyed properly only by someone who knows what he or she is doing. Look for a dry, brown, rough rind around a creamy, ivory paste with liberal blueing that spreads all the way to the edges and is uniform throughout the interior. The cheese should be crumbly, yet firm enough to cut without completely falling apart. The shape of the piece cut for you shouldn't make one bit of difference assuming it's from well-made, well-aged, well-kept Stilton.

To store 5 pounds (about 2½ k) of Stilton or more, cover the cheese with a clean, damp cotton cloth or cheesecloth and then wrap it in aluminum foil and refrigerate it for as long as a month in the vegetable compartment. Any fuzzy mold that develops can simply be scraped away. If you intend to consume a smaller piece within a week, waxed paper or aluminum foil alone will be fine.

Stilton is one of those mouthwatering cheeses that is perfect anytime. For entertaining, consider purchasing a layer of the entire round of Stilton rather than a wedge. A prettier sight you'll never see. Stilton's greatest glory comes at the end of a grand meal with a glass of Port or a fine red wine, good bread, and sweet fruit. On the other hand, Stilton marries well with celery at lunch or as a snack.

Leftover morsels can be blended together with crème fraîche or cream cheese for a tasty, informal spread. Never pour wine or Port over Stilton (or any cheese, for that matter)—modern refrigeration has made this practice unnecessary. The origin of this custom began 150 years ago (and won't die out) as a way of making palatable cheese that had dried to rock-hardness. And save the money you might spend on a Stilton scoop, they aren't necessary; any sharp knife will do the job beautifully.

CHESHIRE

Cheshire (CHESH-ur) is very likely England's oldest cheese. We can track mentions of it by name to the *Domesday Book,* and we believe that it predates Roman times, though doubtless the Romans in England's northwest contributed to its improvement and increased production. Authentic farmhouse Cheshire comes from the county of Cheshire and from parts of two neighboring counties—Shropshire and Staffordshire. This section of northwestern England is irrigated by the River Dee. In contrast to the

THE STILTON STORY

Our earliest recorded evidence of the existence of Stilton is prior to 1720, when Elizabeth Scarbrow, housekeeper to the Ashby family at Quenby Hall. Hungarton, in Leicestershire, is said to have pioneered its production. Scarbrow taught herself to make the local cheese, then known as Quenby, by using a recipe titled "Lady Beaumont's Cheese." Most of what was made then, not necessarily by Scarbrow, was sold at the Bell Inn at Stilton, a Great North Road coach house in adjacent Huntingdonshire. Though no cheese has ever been made in Stilton, this is where the cheese gained its fame and eventually its name, thanks to the many eighteenth-century travelers who passed through the inn and tasted the cheese there.

Having taught her daughter

The Bell Inn

and granddaughter to make the cheese, Elizabeth Scarbrow began a family dynasty, indeed a Stilton-making monopoly, and their dominance lasted about 50 years. By 1790, Stilton was being made in almost every village in the area, and it fetched a very pretty penny for its makers.

Stilton has always been the product of a rather troublesome and involved secret recipe. It used to require three separate curding processes (now two), and the curd had to be the result of the cream from an evening milking mixed with the full-fat milk from the next morning's milking. It is well known in cheese-making circles that 200 years ago, Mrs. Musson, a respected Stilton maker, rather pointedly observed, "Stiltons, with the exception that they make no noise, are more trouble than babies."

now-vanished sheep's-milk cheeses of the other northern counties and Scotland, which became cow's-milk cheeses in the seventeenth century, Cheshire has always been a cow's-milk cheese.

Today, all farmhouse Cheshire is made from raw milk. The classic

definition requires that the cheese be made from milk derived from the Cheshire area's pastures and made in that same locale, following the recipe requirements for this cheese-making process, as well as its aging. Color, size, shape, and extra aging are not controlled.

Until the first time I tasted Abbey Farm's farmhouse Cheshire cheese, I thought Cheshire had very little appeal. I had found previous examples (all factory-made) sour and crumbly, with no real discernible flavor. Now I know how ignorant I was. True Cheshire owes its savory, hint-of-salt-marsh flavor to the area's soil, which has a high concentration of underlying bedrock salt, delivered to the cheese via the milk of the Friesian cattle that graze there. Farmhouse examples of Cheshire, though not standardized, are usually tall, natural-rind, cloth-wrapped drums, 14 inches high and 7 to 8 inches in diameter, weighing 15 to 17 pounds (7½ to 8½ k).

Some farmhouse Cheshire is made in 4-pound (2 k) drums, and occasionally in cylinders the size and weight (56 to 66 pounds; 28 to 33 k) of Cheddar.

Genuine farmhouse Cheshire is stamped with the number of the farm, the date it was made, and "superfine" or "fine" quality gradings. Waxed cheeses (waxed over the cloth) not bearing these qualifiers cannot be marketed as farmhouse Cheshire. Some Cheshire cheesemakers wax their cloth-wrapped cheeses in an attempt to increase their shelf lives. Though I don't get in too much of a lather over it (since waxed farmhouse Cheshire is usually good), some people think

GETTING THE BLUES

Stilton, Blue Cheshire, Blue Wensleydale, and Shropshire Blue cheeses all achieve their color in the same way. The curd goes into a hoop or form and is wrapped with calico (fine-mesh cotton cloth) to bolster and promote the formation of the rind. The resulting shape is then put in a humid room, where it is pierced (the English say "pricked") with a long, slender needle to allow oxygen to enter the cheese and feed the natural bacteria in the cheese's interior. These bacteria would die without the oxygen, but with it, they live and thrive in such numbers that they manifest themselves by appearing bluish-green. In turn, they provide piquant flavor. The cheeses are rubbed and turned occasionally during the three to six months it takes for their flavor to develop.

This process is blue-cheese making the British way—a simpler cheese recipe there cannot be. Nothing is mixed into the curd to promote the blue as is the case with Roquefort. (For Roquefort the curds are mixed with powdered, mold-ridden rye bread crumbs—this is the much-touted *Penicillium roqueforti*—which feed the bacteria that trigger the blue mold.)

"Watching cows munching their way through the grasses of an English pasture, one can see why our British cheeses have a reputation for their sweet, creamy, rich, and complex scents and flavours. The characteristic sea spray freshness of Cheshire can only be obtained from the rich deposits lying just below the surface of the pastures while the distinct herby, slightly metallic blue taste of Stilton must surely be influenced by the mineral rich seams of coal and iron running through the rolling fields of Nottinghamshire, Leicestershire, and Derbyshire."

Julie Harbutt,
The Specialist Cheesemakers' Association Guide to the Finest Cheeses of Britain and Ireland

this practice induces injurious sweating between the cloth and the wax. My favorite Cheshire-maker, Lance Appleby of Abbey Farm, deplores this practice. His cloth-wrapped Cheshire is never waxed, and it is his Cheshire I pray you find (although other excellent choices are mentioned below).

Inside, a farmhouse Cheshire is a smooth, hole-less, dryish cheese the color of cantaloupe. The paste of real Cheshire is always orange, organically dyed with annatto (a harmless, flavorless coloring agent made from the pulp of annatto trees). It will have a raw, rustic, not too strong, tangy flavor, and its texture will be crumbly, like Cheddar, but drier. The flavor is slightly saline and beyond that difficult to articulate. Farmhouse Cheshire is neither nutty like Gruyère and Comté, nor fruity like Morbier and Saint-Nectaire. It is neither sharp like Parmesan, nor mellow like Cantal. The only description I can muster is that it has a sort of essential cheesiness that is slightly salty, pleasurably savory, and a bit like root beer or horehound candy with undertones of roasted chicken.

A tiny percentage of farmhouse Cheshire is sold as Blue Cheshire, a delicious and oddly mellow cheese. It is pierced, and then allowed to blue naturally with a month or two of extra aging. The blue in Blue Cheshire, and indeed sometimes the cheese itself, is referred to as "green fade," possibly because the blue mold takes on a greenish color in the orange cheese. Eventually all farmhouse English cheeses will blue naturally over time, with or without piercing or inoculation.

made with Cheshire cheese, is easy, fast, and tasty, Blue Cheshire is best enjoyed as is—with fruit, or at the end of a meal with vintage Port.

Farmhouse Cheshire like this one from the Bourne family (left) is wrapped in cloth that is sometimes waxed. It is natural for the moldy gray rind of a well-aged Red Leicester (right) to merge with its cloth covering, a sign it will taste rich and nutty.

Choosing and Serving Cheshire

Farmhouse Cheshire is a venerable cheese—take pains to find the real McCoy: unwaxed cheeses from the Appleby family's Abbey Farm and the Bourne family's farm called The Bank; waxed ones from Mollington Grange Farm and Chorlton Lodge Farm all are excellent choices. Some Cheshire is also produced by cheesemakers using "creamery" facilities that are larger than farmhouse operations, but not as large as most cheese factories. In terms of quality, creamery Cheshires are closer to the farmhouse types than to the factory-made ones. Avoid all factory Cheshires, many of which are sold as thin, 4-pound (2 k) wheels that are vacuum sealed in plastic. Buy only real, cloth-wrapped, farmhouse Cheshire—waxed or unwaxed.

Cheshire is a fine snack cheese to enjoy with fresh fruit, beer or light, fruity red or white wine, and crackers or bread. While Welsh rarebit (or rabbit), traditionally

WENSLEYDALE

Wensleydale, a few miles northwest of York in Yorkshire, one of England's northern counties, is one of the historic cheesemaking Dales. The cheeses of the area have Roman origins, and some of the more obscure ones—Cotherstone, Coverdale, and Swaledale—can be traced to Yorkshire's now defunct monastic orders, which came about as a result of the Norman Conquest of 1066. In the early days, all of the cheeses called Wensleydale (WENZ-lee-dale) were made from sheep's milk, and these fresh cheeses were brined briefly before aging into a pungent, soft, moist, blue cheese. But by the mid-seventeenth cen-

*Many's the long night
I've dreamed of cheese—
toasted, mostly.*

Robert Louis Stevenson

The medieval ruins of St. Mary's Abbey in York, near where Wensleydale is made, are a reminder that this cheese, a specialty since the thirteenth century, is as ancient as its surroundings.

tury, dairy cattle had replaced sheep as the source of milk for Wensleydale cheesemaking.

With the Industrial Revolution came standardization. Factories and creameries cropped up and the character and style of Wensleydale changed: The curd was salted, not brine-washed, and the cheese was pressed into a harder texture. The "new" Wensleydale was marketed in its young, still-white stage after only brief aging, and by the end of World War II less than a dozen farmhouse Wensleydale makers remained.

In 1954 the Milk Marketing Board (MMB) laid down technical requirements for the production of cheese in Yorkshire that subjected the cheeses to grading by outsiders who used moisture content standards that had no business being applied to the traditional methods of making this cheese. The last au-

thentic farmhouse Wensleydales were made in 1957. In complete and utter frustration, the traditional cheesemakers simply gave up.

No farmhouse Wensleydale exists today. What we think of as real Wensleydale, while not officially a "farmhouse" cheese, is now turned out by a small creamery called the Wensleydale Cheese Company. A creamery is a modern cheesemaking facility that, because of its relatively small size and output, is not (and should not) be considered or referred to as a factory or plant. Although not a farmhouse facility, creameries produce good Wensleydale, and indeed some is excellent.

If you want to sample some of the small-scale creamery production of Wensleydale, look for the cloth-wrapped, 12- to 14-pound (6 to 7 k), cylinders, 12 inches high and 10 inches in diameter, from the

Cows "at work" in Wensleydale.

Wensleydale Creamery at Hawes or from Kirkby Malzeard, both located in North Yorkshire. This Wensleydale is creamy yet crumbly, with a tart, nutty, buttermilk-like flavor and a mild aroma. The paste is always stark, bone-colored white—never dyed.

The original Wensleydale was blue. Today, a minuscule portion of the already tiny output of creamery Wensleydale is Blue Wensleydale, of the same weight and configuration as the white. Uncut Blue Wensleydale looks identical to white Wensleydale. Inside it is creamy though firm (softer than Stilton), with a marvelous flavor that is simultaneously peppery and honeyed. The dark blue veining is haphazard, resembling a roadmap striation effect in the otherwise bone-white paste. Aged for nine months to one year, Blue Wensleydale has a mild aroma, but tastes distinctly sharper than regular Wensleydale. The Kirkby Malzeard Dairy sends a few Wensleydales to the Unigate Dairy at Melton Mowbray to be blue-ripened alongside Unigate's Stiltons, and both blue cheeses are sold there. Tiny quantities of Blue Wensleydale occasionally reach the U.S. via either Unigate or J. M. Nuttall.

Choosing and Serving Wensleydale

When shopping for a good creamery Wensleydale, first look for a cloth-wrapped rind. If it has one, you are in the presence of the only good Wensleydale made

SEND IN THE SNAILS

Two centuries ago, British cheese-makers had difficulty maintaining regular sources of rennet to use for curdling milk. The handiest substitute was a lively black snail, a few of which they would toss into their vats. The snails did the trick, thanks to an enzyme these little gastopods excrete. How this handy substitution was discovered, we'll never know. I assume the creatures were fished out at some point, but then, who knows? Were their shells left on? Did they drown but add a distinctive crunch? Don't let this practice put you off British cheeses. It's not done anymore—truly.

tocay. Then, taste it. If that creamy, tangy-tart flavor and crumbly texture are pleasing to you, go right ahead and buy it. If you're offered Blue Wensleydale, remember it is quite rare—be sure to ask for a taste. But avoid any that shows fuzzy mold or tastes bitter.

Serve white or blue creamery Wensleydale as a snack or part of a simple repast with fruit, chutney, bread, and any wine, beer, ale, or cider. Either is a superb pie cheese. Store it as you would Cheddar or Cheshire—refrigerated, in waxed paper or aluminum foil. Wensleydale can be substituted for Cheshire or Cheddar when a shredding or melting cheese is desired.

SHROPSHIRE BLUE

Shropshire Blue (SHROP-shur-bloo) is a "new" cheese, still less than 25 years old, that was first commercially produced in Inverness, Scotland, but was marketed in England as having come from Shropshire. Now it is being made by three or four Shropshire creameries, as well as by Long Clawson, the Stilton-makers in Melton Mowbray, who recognized the potential of this striking wonder invented by Mrs. Hutchinson Smith in the 1970s.

Creamery Shropshire Blue has the same config-

Apple pie without cheese is like a kiss without a squeeze.

Old English saying

uration as Cheshire and Stilton—14- to 16-pound (7 to 8 k) cylinders, 11 to 12 inches high and 7 inches in diameter. It has Stilton's texture and rough, brown natural rind, but Shropshire Blue is considerably sharper and less perfumey tasting. Its paste, colored with annatto, is a brighter orange than Blue Cheshire's more muted tone, and its blue is an even brighter hue than that of Stilton. This cheese is one to welcome—its rustic qualities make it delicious to eat and gorgeous to behold—especially if you're a fan of Stilton. (If you closed your eyes and sampled both, you'd know which was which—Shropshire Blue offers all of Stilton's virtues and then some.)

Shropshire Blue is virtually identical to Stilton, but with an orange-colored interior and more vivid blueing. This example made by Long Clawson Dairy, a famous Stilton maker, is marketed as Blue Shropshire.

Choosing and Serving Shropshire Blue

Should you be able to find cream-ery Shropshire Blue, be con-cerned only with its freshness. Taste it—it should be sharp and winey with a lingering, spicy aftertaste. You'll know if it's good by looking at it. It will be bright orange, marked by liberal, blue-green mold—no fis-sures, no browning, no crumbling (Shropshire Blue is actually creamy!), with a rind that's neither slimy nor powdery. Old Shropshire Blue will have lost its bright orange luster and, with it, its remarkable flavor; instead, it will have been replaced by a bitter mustiness and a decid-edly granular texture.

Serve Shropshire Blue after dinner with the sweetest of fruits to meld with its sharpness, crusty bread, and big red wines, sweet dessert wines, Port, Madeira, or, yes, sherry. I prefer *fino* (dry) sherry from the source—Jerez de la Frontera.

LEICESTER

Leicester (LESS-ter), a cow's-milk cheese from Leicestershire, dates back to the eighteenth cen-tury when it was made on farms all over the shire. The only Leicester that is made in its native region today is a pasteurized one turned out by Tuxford & Tebbutt, a cream-ery-size facility in Melton Mowbray,

Stilton's domain. Leicester was originally made using milk left over from the production of Stilton, and thanks to the vigorous distribu-tion channels set up for Stilton in the eighteenth and nineteenth cen-turies, Leicester became quite pop-ular. Its deep orange hue and nutty, candy-like flavor are alluring and, amazingly, this flavor has survived despite pasteurization, a testament to the quality of the milk emanating from this lush county.

There is so little authentic Leicester made that its classic shape—a thick, broad wheel—has almost been forgotten. Almost all so-called Leicester is made in blocks, in factories outside of Leicester-shire. Tuxford & Tebbutt's cloth-wrapped Leicester cheeses are true to the classic form—45-pound (22½ k) wheels, 12 inches high and 20 inches in diameter (with some cheeses split horizontally so they are only 6 inches high), and aged for a minimum of three months (al-though they are much better after six or even nine months of aging). The rind is natural and thin be-neath the calico cloth covering.

I like Leicester because, be-sides having a great Cheddar-type flavor—although it's definitely not a Cheddar—it offers a red winey-ness, a sort of root beer or hore-hound-candy effect, but without being sweet. It is not at all like Cheshire or Wensleydale, except texturally, although it is, once again in the English mode of making cheese, a firm, rather dry, but not hard cheese. Leicester has a great dose of annatto (the dye also used to color Cheshires) added to it, so

Leicestershire, where Cheddar-like Leicester is made, lies in the heart of fox hunting and cheesemaking country.

that it has a deep orange color. (Some cheese experts believe the dye contributes to the cheese's flavor, but I don't agree.) Take care to find the authentic, cloth-wrapped, wheel-shaped examples of Leicester.

In the case of Leicester cheese, I am more concerned with *how* it is made than *where* and have found excellent Leicester produced by Chorlton Lodge Farm in Cheshire, Singleton's Dairy in Lancashire, and at North Leaze Farm in Somerset.

Choosing and Serving Leicester

Look for formidable, wide, 45-pound (22½ k), gray cloth-wrapped wheels, sheltering deep-red/orange interiors. A moldy, gray-brown rind that has essentially merged with the cloth is per-

fectly natural and desirable; it suggests the cheese was aged longer, at which point it will be harder, and the flavor will be richer, fuller, deeper, and nuttier. Its texture will be firm and smooth, without holes or fissures.

Next, taste it, being on the lookout for interior dryness, interior discoloration, and/or any hint of interior mold—all bad signs, signifying that the cheese should be avoided. Fine Leicester is a very satisfying cheese. It has a great presence and savoriness, slightly sharp, with a languorous, creamy mouthfeel. Store it refrigerated in plastic wrap or, better still, in aluminum foil. Leicester is prone to surface mold in the refrigerator (due to dampness); trim or scrape it away.

If you appreciate this straightforward style of English cheese, serve it at any meal. Fruit and light red wines or beer will thank you for it.

CAERPHILLY

Originally, Caerphilly (care-FILL-ee), a raw cow's milk cheese with a natural, not cloth-wrapped rind, was made on many farms all around Cardiff, Wales' principal city. It was a very simple, unsophisticated cheese, mild, semifirm, and slightly liquid around the edges nearest the crust. But by the beginning of the twentieth century, English demand had far outstripped Welsh supply. Welsh cheese merchants looked across the Bristol Channel to the lush pasturage of Somerset and easily persuaded the cheesemakers there to help fulfill their needs. And since Caerphilly matures rapidly (in around three weeks), enabling its maker to be paid months sooner than if he or she made Cheddar, it wasn't long before most of the Somerset Caerphilly being sold at London's Highbridge Market (the main wholesale cheese market of the era) was shipped back to Wales via the Burnham-to-Cardiff steamer.

When farmhouse cheese production in the British Isles waned between and after the wars, Caerphilly production in Wales ceased, too. The cheese then called Caerphilly became just another English factory-made knockoff with no resemblance whatsoever to the original. However, serious farmhouse Caerphilly—tangy, creamy, and savory—has reappeared, made in several English counties.

The Duckett family's farmhouse Caerphilly, made at Walnut

Small Caerphilly cheeses in a press at Felin Gernos Dairy Farm in Llandyssul, Dyfed, Wales.

Tree Farm, Wedmore, Somerset, is a marvel, and among the only worthy Caerphilly still available for export. Each 8- to 9-pound (4 to 4½ k) wheel, with its natural gray rind and creamy beige to yellow interior that's slightly oozy nearest the center, is a little more than 3 inches thick and 12 inches in diameter. Chris Duckett makes Caerphilly using the same method his family first followed a century ago. His cheeses are about three months old when I receive my monthly shipment of them, and they sell out quickly. The Ducketts' farmhouse Caerphilly is mild, but very pleasantly flavorful—creamy, buttery, and milky-tasting. The cheese is softer than Cheshire, Lancashire, or Wensleydale, and not nearly so dry. All Caerphilly, especially those made

STUFFED CABBAGE

Caerphilly was once consumed in great quantities by miners in southwestern England and Wales. They wrapped chunks of the cheese in cabbage leaves and ate the handy food parcels for lunch.

by Duckett, are a departure from the usual English idiom of firm, dry, fine-textured cheeses.

Choosing and Serving Caerphilly

Avoid any farmhouse Caerphilly whose interior appears stale, showing signs of obvious dryness or mold. The crust should be dry and grayish, rather than moist, mushy, and blackened.

In the idiom of British cheese, farmhouse Caerphilly is a perfect snack cheese. It goes well with fruit or bread, chutney or preserves. It melts nicely when shredded or sliced, laid atop slices of wholegrain bread, and passed under the broiler. I urge you to avoid any factory-made, rindless, plastic-wrapped Caerphilly, and instead seek out the fine Duckett cheese. Store this cheese in plastic wrap or aluminum foil in your refrigerator, but beware, it is more porous and less dense than, say, Cheddar or Cheshire, and will dry out and become stale after six or seven days. Buy only enough Caerphilly to last you for a week.

SINGLE AND DOUBLE GLOUCESTER

Now, while I have never been a huge fan of Gloucester (GLOSS-ter) cheese (it's simply too bland to be a personal favorite), its fame as a traditional English farmhouse cheese requires acknowledgment.

Either white or tinted pale orange in color with annatto, Cheddar-like Single Gloucester was originally made from the evening's skimmed, unpasteurized cow's milk combined with the whole milk from the morning milking. This supple, yet firm cheese, aged for two months, was intended to ripen quickly and was eaten young, as a "house" cheese on the farms where it was made. The tiny quantities of Single Gloucester made today follow a somewhat different recipe—one or both of the milkings is skimmed and the cheese is aged for nine months to a year. It is a rather dry, crumbly cheese with a bit of bite.

Double Gloucester was, and still is, made from the whole milk and cream of two milkings and then allowed to age for six to nine months. The same size and texture as Single Gloucester, it tastes just slightly creamier and less sharp than its lower-fat Single sibling. Some is white and some is dyed orange.

I'm pleased to be able to recommend two excellent sources. They are the farmhouse Single and Double Gloucester cheeses made by the Appleby family of Cheshire cheese fame (see page 307), as well as the fine, though quite subtly flavored cheeses made by Diana and Jamie Smart at Old Ley Farm, Vale of Gloucester, Gloucestershire. Both are marvelous choices for those who are looking for a mild, pleasant cheese, with a gentle, saline, slightly Cheddary quality.

The Smarts produce Single and Double Gloucesters, using their own unpasteurized Holstein milk to turn out 7- to 8-pound (3½ to 4 k) cylinders or wheels, 3 inches high and 8 inches in diameter. All of their cheeses are cloth-wrapped; the Singles have a clean, delicate flavor, while the Doubles are richer and more fully flavored. Their cheese is almost identical to a mild Cheddar.

Although made from pasteurized milk, the mellow-tasting Double Gloucester, from Quicke's is a fine tasting cheese.

QUICKE'S TRADITIONAL
DOUBLE GLOUCESTER
Made at Home Farm
Newton St. Cyres
Devon
J. G. Quicke & Partners

orange, not bright, which is an indicator of dryness. There should be no interior mold, cracks, or fissures. Avoid rindless, factory-made, plastic-encased 5-pound (2½ k) wheels of so-called Double Gloucester, which are mild and banal.

Serve Single or Double Gloucester as a simple snack, with fruit and crackers and just about any beverage. Don't hesitate to shred or slice it thin for grilled cheese sandwiches, or use it anytime a mild, Cheddary melt is desired.

Choosing and Serving Single and Double Gloucester

Choose any cloth-wrapped Gloucester (signifying farmhouse origin and quality) that appears fresh. It should be a pastel

SAGE DERBY AND DERBY

Those of us who have been aware of English Sage Derby (DAR-bee) over the years know of rindless, plastic-wrapped disks featuring a surface and interior that appear to be some form of man-made, green and white marble—a firm cow's-milk cheese overwhelmingly imbued with the flavor of sage. In reality, the stark green hue is the result of the chlorophyll in spinach juice. Colorless, dried, powdered sage is mixed nto the milk before the curding process to instill the sage flavor, without which this so-called Sage Derby is quite characterless, owing to its pasteurized milk and mass production.

However, to be fair, a small industry has sprung up that does make a more authentic sage cheese, and they really do chop up sage leaves and mix them with the curd—a rather bizarre duo. (If you've ever had the sage stuffing that the British adore so much, you'll understand their predilection for a similarly flavored cheese—maybe.) This "real" sage cheese is made by the Kirkby Malzeard Dairy, which sells it to other exporters, such as Tuxford & Tebbutt, who label it as their own.

Derby cheese, without the sage, does exist, from farmhouse origin (cloth-wrapped) as well as from factories (pre-cut and plastic-wrapped). Derby is a dense, off-white cow's-milk cheese with a texture neither as dry as farmhouse Cheshire, nor as moist as farmhouse Double Gloucester. The flavor is only nominally beyond bland.

Choosing and Serving Sage Derby and Derby

If sage mixed with cheese appeals to you, choose any that doesn't look like Irish Spring soap. Instead,

The Peak District, near Beeley, Derbyshire.

look for examples with pastel green paste that features flecks of real sage instead of the green and white mottling.

Look for cloth-wrapped wheels of either Derby weighing from 14 to 22 pounds (7 to 11 k). Be sure of freshness by checking for dryness, interior or exterior mold, or discoloration in the form of whitish patches. Avoid the factory versions that are 5-pound (2½ k), rindless, plastic-wrapped disks. Serve Derby any time a mild, firm cheese is desirable.

I advise you not to partner Sage Derby with other cheeses, as the sage will overwhelm their flavors. Also be aware that this flavor will affect any foods and wines, regardless of whether they precede or follow the cheese.

Lesser-Known Cheeses

I purchase almost all of my English and Irish cheeses from Randolph Hodgson, the owner of Neal's Yard Dairy, a wholesale supplier and retail shop located near London's Covent Garden. Mr. Hodgson specializes in English and Irish farmhouse cheeses, and as a result my counters are blessed with the more or less constant presence of cheeses worthy of worship. Each cheese is chosen by Hodgson himself or his knowledge-

IT WAS THE FIRST

In 1870, Derby became the first English cheese to be produced in a factory.

able employee Jason Hinds, and are selected to reflect the best from each batch. So, in addition to remarkable Cheddar and Cheshire, these discerning cheesemongers make Stilton, Irish Cashel Blue, Lancashire, Gloucester, and even Caerphilly available to U.S. cheese specialists. In farmhouse form, all of these cheeses are rare, though most can be found on our shores at serious cheese counters in large cities.

It is a tribute to the quality and unique flavor of some of the lesser-known cheeses that four of them are not only my personal favorites, I also consider them to be among the world's greatest cheeses (see page 34).

Blue Vinney (BLOO-vinny): I think of Blue Vinney as a phantom cheese since for years its very existence has been the subject of considerable debate. "Vinney" was derived from the Old English *vinew,* a word for mold. But the original Blue Vinney died out by the beginning of World War II. If it truly exists now at all, Blue Vinney is said to be a Dorset cow's-milk cheese made on just one farm between Dorchester and Puddletown. And supposedly, it was originally made only for family and friends. Over the last 20 years reports of its availability at this or that shop created an occasional clamor in the press. What was available was not the hard, sharp, Stilton-like blue cheese born out of the idiosyncratic dairy life of Dorset in the eighteenth century, but inferior Stilton "seconds," sold to unsuspecting cheese merchants (so they said) as the much-talked-about-and-sought-after phantom Blue Vinney.

Jason Hinds of Neal's Yard Dairy in London tells me that a true example of Blue Vinney *is* being made, in tiny quantities, by Michael Davies on his Woodbridge Farm, Stock Gaylard, Sturminster Newtown, in Dorset. It is an unpressed cheese made with skimmed raw cow's milk, and Jason says it is very strong and piercing, with a very distinctive, rather bitter taste. Perhaps Blue Vinney won't remain a phantom after all. I'd like to take part in its revival.

Cashel Blue (KASH-ul-BLOO): The Grubb family has lived in Ireland since the seventeenth century, when they fled England for religious reasons. Ever since, family members have been millers and buttermakers on the family's farm at Beechmount (near Cashel) in the valley of the Suir River, County Tipperary. About ten years ago, Jane and Louis Grubb began making a raw cow's milk blue cheese, the only one in Ireland, from their herd of Friesian cattle. It quickly won an enthusiastic audience, of which I am an ardent member. Grubb's herd is a rarity, a "closed" herd, meaning that new stock is acquired only from existing animals within that specific herd. Now *that's* a farm cheese! Each fat, foil-wrapped,

4-pound (2 k) cheese, 5 inches high, 6 inches in diameter, aged two to three months, is so creamy that at room temperature—anywhere from 65° to 85° F (18° to 29° C)—it becomes practically liquid—runs and oozes like Vacherin Mont d'Or. But, to my mind, what Cashel Blue most resembles is the world's finest Gorgonzola. I'm rarely out of it.

Coolea (KOO-lee): A Gouda-type cheese made from unpasteurized cow's milk. After selling their restaurants in Holland, Hélène and Dick Willems moved to a farm at Coolea, County Cork, in the Irish countryside. With their son, Dick, Jr., they produce over 18 tons (about 16,000 k) of excellent Coolea per year on the 60-acre farm. Their cheese is available young (three months) or aged (one year), and is as fine as any farmer's Gouda I have ever tasted.

Made by Helena Willems in Macroom Co. Cork from Raw Cow's Milk, Cheese Cultures, Rennet, Salt.

Coolea

Selected and matured by Neal's Yard Dairy
More than 60 days old
Product of Eire

Cornish Yarg: From Cornwall, the county at the "toe" of England's "boot," this is a unique, pasteurized cow's-milk cheese, vegetable renneted and aged for about two months. It is slightly softer and creamier than the Ducketts' Caerphilly, but just as flavorful and satisfying. What makes it unique is that its natural rind is covered with the aromatic leaves of an indigenous Cornish nettle. This practice was once common in Cornwall, but has died out entirely, except in the instance of this Yarg made by Mike Horrell at Lynher Valley Dairy. The effect of these nettle leaves is such a unique sensation on the exhale that it is difficult to describe—pleasantly peppery, grassy, lemony, herby, and, above all, aromatic.

Croghan (KRO-gun): A supple, succulent, raw goat's milk cheese originated and made at Croghan Goat Farm by Luc and Anne van Kampen, Blackwater, County Wexford, Ireland. This is another of my favorite cheeses, as perfect a cheese as I have ever encountered—soft, bulging, two-month-old cheese, made from unpasteurized milk taken from the van Kampen's own herd of 50 or so British Saanens, which graze in pastures overlooking the Irish Sea. The brine-washed rind is a pinkish tan and its surface seems to undulate so that each 2- to 3-pound (1 to 1½ k) disk looks more like a gland or some potter's failure. The flavor is a triumph—full, a bit goaty, and effusive of nuts, herbs, and garlic. The texture is bulgy and satiny. It is seasonal and expensive—I have them only from spring until Christmas.

Farmhouse Lancashire (LANK-uh-shur): From the county north of Cheshire and west of Yorkshire, this is a big, rustic, crumbly (yet buttery), white, raw cow's milk cheese, similar to Cheshire. The Lancashire I love most (actually one of my very favorite cheeses) comes from John and Ruth Kirkham's 40-acre Beesley Farm in Goosnargh (Lancashire), near the Forest of Bowland, one of the deepest, darkest, most magically beautiful areas in all of England. Ruth is the cheesemaker, and she uses traditional techniques that include mixing the curd of two or three days' milkings from the Kirkhams' Friesian cows. The result is a very white, tangy, and milky-flavored cheese, cloth-wrapped, with a texture described locally as a "buttery-crumble." The cheeses are made in cylinders of various sizes. I stock the 3-pound (115 k) size, about 12 inches high and 9 to 10 inches in diameter. Lancashire is the classic "toasting" cheese, a good melter that is ideal for making cheese toast or Welsh rarebit.

Gubbeen (goo-BEAN): A 2- to 3-pound (1 to 1½ k) wheel of tender, pungent, raw cow's milk cheese, on the order of French Reblochon or Saint-Nectaire, made by Giana and Tom Ferguson in County Cork in the south of Ireland. Gubbeen is Gaelic for "small mouth." The cheeses are aged for two months, the rinds are

Gubbeen

Cheesemaker Leon Downey "irons" a Llangloffan, using a special instrument to remove a "plug" of cheese to determine if the cheese is ripening properly.

brine-washed and orange in color, and the aroma and flavor are pronounced and full. Gubbeen tastes intensely nutty (imagine an omelet with Munster or Gruyère), with a beefy, faintly smoky undertone. As a fan of Gubbeen, I count it among my favorite cheeses.

Hereford Hop (HER-furd-HOP): Made in Herefordshire by Charles Martell of Laurel Farm, Gloucestershire, from pasteurized cow's milk. What makes this cheese singular is the medieval tradition of rubbing each 3- to 4-pound (1½ to 2 k) disk with ground, toasted hops, the same bitter flavoring agent and preservative used in the brewing of beer. The cheese, 1½ inches thick and 8 inches in diameter, is firm, though tender and buttery, and the aroma of the buff-colored hops adhering to the rind is immediately discernible and welcome in the flavor of the cheese. Now, while Patrick Rance would joyously consume the cheese's natural rind en-

crusted with hops, I trim it away, as I find the rind a bit bitter. I enjoy Hereford Hop with a good, cold beer—a rather obvious choice, wouldn't you say?

Lanark Blue (LAN-ark-BLOO): The only exported farmhouse Scottish cheese, an excellent-quality, unpasteurized sheep's milk blue cheese from H. G. Errington. Lanark Blue is quite similar to Roquefort in flavor, texture, and configuration, though mellower and slightly firmer. Cheesemaker Humphrey Errington, who has a degree in history from Cambridge, tends his cross-bred Friesian sheep deep in the Scottish Lowlands in Ogscastle, Carnwath, Lanarkshire, milking them twice daily and making the cheese in between using vegetable rennet.

Llangloffan (LANG-loff-un): A cow's-milk cheese, rather like Caerphilly, made by Joan and Leon Downey of Llangloffan Farmhouse on the Pembrokeshire coast of Wales from their original recipe. Llanglof-

Famous cheesemonger Patrick Rance, an ardent crusader for the preservation of farmhouse cheeses and author of The Great British Cheese Book, surveys a collection of favorite cheeses.

fan, which has a natural rind and is aged for two to six months, is made from the Downeys' own Jersey cattle's unpasteurized milk. Its configuration is the same as Caerphilly—9-pound (4½ k) wheels, 4 inches thick and 12 inches in diameter. It is semifirm, flaky, and full-flavored, dry, yet buttery, with big creamy flavor. The Downeys' farm is certified organic, and they milk only 20 cows, but the milk they give is very high in butterfat. Llangloffan is an excellent snacking cheese.

Malvern: A handmade, unpasteurized sheep's milk cheese made in 3- to 4-pound (1½ to 2 k) disks by Nick Hodgetts of the Malvern Cheesewrights in Worcestershire in the shadows of Worcester Cathedral in the Severn Valley. It is firm and mild, on the order of Spanish Manchego, though less salty. Made using vegetable rennet, Malvern is aged from two to four months.

Milleens (mih-LEENS): A remarkable, creamy, washed-rind, raw cow's milk cheese, aged for about three weeks, made by its originators Veronica and Norman Steele on their farm in County Cork, Ireland. Veronica is the founder of Cáis, the Irish cheesemaking association. The Steeles began making small quantities of Milleens in 1978; these days their annual production is around 22 tons (about 22,000 k). Milleens is soft, smelly, and rich, with enormous flavor—a cheese I'd love to make if I were a cheesemaker. Alas, as a raw-milk cheese aged less than 60 days, it is illegal for U.S. import, which is a shame since I count it among my own best-liked cheeses.

Scottish Cheddar and Dunlop: Farmhouse and creamery production of Scottish Cheddar and Dunlop—once Scotland's two most revered cheeses—ceased in the 1950s. All of the product currently exported is factory-made. However, in Scotland, an assortment of wonderful, delicious, traditional unpasteurized cow's and ewe's milk cheeses can be had—even some good Cheddar. Also, the revival of Crowdie (KRAOW-dee), Scotland's oldest cheese (a moist, cottage cheese-type), and Caboc (KAB-bok), a buttery double-cream cheese that is covered with toasted oatmeal, is a thumb-your-nose gesture at the Scottish Milk Marketing Board (the Scottish incarnation of England's MMB), which bought up all the traditional creameries and

POETIC CHEESE

Dunlop, Scotland's most famous hard cheese, was once made on farms owned by Scotland's national poet, Robert Burns.

turned them into Dunlop and Cheddar factories.

Somerset Blue: A wonderfully creamy (Jersey cattle are synonymous with super-high butterfat) unpasteurized cow's milk blue cheese that is aged for about three months in a traditional Exmoor cowshed made of rocks and logs. It has a rough, natural rind just like Stilton's, but each cylinder is about half as big. An absolutely stunning cheese, it is made by Alan Duffield at Exmoor Blue Cheese in Somerset. Its flavor is considerably stronger than that of Stilton, more peppery and sharper.

Teifi (TIE-fee): Made by Patrice and John Savage, Glynhynod, Ffostrassol, Llansyssul, Dyfed, Wales, this is an unpasteurized, 16-pound (8 k) Gouda-type cheese, with a natural, brushed rind, aged for four to 12 weeks. Patrice was apprenticed to Boerenkaas, one of the best makers of farmer's Gouda in Holland, and the cheese she makes is excellent. The Savages use vegetable rennet to curdle the cow's milk, all of which comes from a neighboring farm. When aged about one year, the flavor multiplies considerably.

T'yn Grug (TIN-GREEG): A creamy Welsh Cheddar-type cheese made in the mountains of central Wales on a small farm at Goetre Isaf,

Lampeter, Dyfed, which is owned by Dougal Campbell, a guiding light in the Welsh dairy industry and in the U.K. organic foods movement. He and his co-cheesemaker, Martin Trethowan, use the unpasteurized milk from Campbell's own herd of organically raised cattle. Each natural–rind, cloth-wrapped, coffee can-shaped cheese weighs either 18 or 36 pounds (9 or 18 k) and offers a splendid cheese experience, one that is every bit as memorable as the taste of farmhouse Cheddar from Somerset. T'yn Grug is texturally creamier, though, and markedly sweeter. Serve it with crackers or bread, fruit and cold meat, with whatever beverage is at hand.

Tyning (TY-ning): A cheese made from raw sheep's milk, with a light-gray, natural rind that is made in the Mendip Hills of Somerset by Mary Holbrook of Sleight Farm following a recipe for Italian Pecorino Toscano. Tyning is Mary's sheep's-milk counterpart to Mendip. Amber-colored, hard, and piquant, it is aged for about three months, resulting in a firm cheese that is as perfect as any hard sheep's milk cheese in existence.

Spain

I t wasn't until my third trip to Spain that I truly became acquainted with this beautiful country and its diverse spectrum of cheeses. I'm usually not so slow, but the truth is I've always had help in the form of a book or a tip from an enthusiastic customer, importer, or native export consolidator. Not until 1991, when I came upon a detailed poster devoted to regional Span-

ish cheeses, did I realize I had some work to do. Prior to that, no one was talking about Spain, no one was writing about it, and outside of sherry wine vinegar and olive oil, none of us in the specialty food trade did much business with it.

Well, all that has changed. My breakthrough was aided by a number of people: Mariano Sanz Pech and Enric Canut, both of whom must be honored as scribes, prophets, and saviors of Spanish regional cheeses; Monica Lavery, a brilliant young British woman, whose business is supplying English shops and restaurants with Spanish cheeses and other foodstuffs; and American Gerd Stern, a cheese importer, whose knowledge of and devotion to cheese are unparalleled.

Separately and in tandem, Mariano and Enric have documented

An artisanal Spanish cheesemaker kneads curd by hand to expel the whey.

the magnificent realm of existing Spanish cheeses: Enric, with his books (published only in Spanish), and Mariano, as a representative of the Spanish Ministry of Agriculture, Fish, and Food. Though both men urged me to follow my instincts and intensify my efforts to locate exceptional Spanish cheeses, neither suggested that it would be easy. I knew that if I could get these cheeses, I would have no problem selling them in the U.S.

The difficulties became apparent when I discovered that convincing Spanish cheesemakers to part with their goods was easier for them to agree to than do. In effect, what I perceived as a windfall for them, would, in reality, complicate and transform their way of life and their way of doing business, not only by adding to their workload but by altering their routine. And though we would pay more—much more—than the locals for the cheeses, Spanish cheesemakers are accustomed to being paid in advance whereas the export market is such that payment comes much later, often subject to delays and maddening variables such as the weight and condition of the cheeses upon arrival.

Nonetheless, I want you to know about many of the Spanish cheeses that have so enthralled me. A number of them have made it to cheese counters and I see no problems with subsequent shipments. A much larger number are pending from Spain's spectrum of more than 60 cheeses. And I'll wager they'll become as well known as many other imported cheeses from better-known cheesemaking countries.

QUESOS CON DENOMINACION DE ORIGEN (D.O.)— THE NAME-CONTROLLED CHEESES OF SPAIN

Name-control, or denomination of origin, is a means by which France, Italy, Switzerland, and Spain are able to ensure that their best and most traditional wines, cheeses, and other foodstuffs (French Périgord truffles, Italian *prosciutto di Parma,* Swiss *grisons,* Spanish *serrano* ham) are protected by law from being copied or misrepresented. In France there are 32 name-controlled (*appellation d'origine contrôlée*) cheeses, in Italy there are 26 name-controlled cheeses (*denominazion di origine controllata*), and in Switzerland all cheeses are rigidly controlled by name.

Spain's efforts to establish protection laws for its cheeses may have come late—the first cheese to be name-controlled was Roncal in 1981—but they were still in plenty of time to protect the authenticity of many of the country's traditional cheeses. In addition, the *denominación de origen* (D.O.) designation has served to encourage the perception of added value in the minds of the Spanish cheese-buying public. The designation lends unequivocal respectability to these cheeses, without which they would merely be also-rans alongside the classic, well-known Manchego and/or the new, highly commercial, state-subsidized Spanish cheeses such as Iberico, which are being made for export and do not exhibit any regional integrity beyond the fact that they are indeed made in Spain.

The following is a complete list of the name-controlled cheeses of Spain, their places of origin, and an idea of their availability in the U.S. It is worth noting that, with the exception of Manchego, until recently most Spanish cheeses were rather rare in the U.S. This situation is beginning to change, and while only

Sheep and goats graze on the vast, harsh, and often craggy expanses of Spain's interior, which is known as the Meseta. Bordered by mountain ranges, the climate is blazing hot in the summer and freezing cold in the winter. While a few of Spain's cow's-milk cheeses are name-controlled, most of those that have earned the protection of denominación de origen *are made from sheep's or goat's milk, or mixed milk*

two of Spain's name-controlled cheeses—Cabrales and Manchego—are widely available at this writing, others are becoming increasingly available, particularly in larger specialty food stores. And I anticipate that some of the others not yet exported to this country will very likely be available in small quantities in the near future.

Cabrales: Asturias; widely available

Cantabria: Cantabria; available, though rare

Idiazábal: Basque Country; available, though rare

La Serena: Extremadura; not exported (rare even in Spain)

Manchego: Castile–La Mancha; widely available

Mahón: Minorca; available, spotty

Quesos de Liébana: Cantabria; a generic denomination that groups together the following name-controlled Cantabrian cheeses: **Ahumado de Aliva:** available, though rare; **Pido:** not exported (rare even in Spain): **Picón:** available, spotty; **Quesuco:** available, though rare

Roncal: Navarre; available, spotty

Tetilla: Galicia; available, spotty

Zamorano: Castile–León; available, though rare

THE NORTHERN COAST OF SPAIN

Spain's economy along the Atlantic's Bay of Biscay—from Galicia's La Coruña east for 250 miles through Asturias to Cantabria's Santander—has always been based on the fishing industry. But just beyond the beaches, a very different culture begins and agriculture rules. This long coastline is seemingly impregnable—fenced by rugged mountains that appear more austere and foreboding from a distance than they actually are up close. And the winters are rough—cold, gray, windy, and rainy. But during spring, summer, and fall, the interiors of these three regions beckon, and beyond the rocky beaches and across the first tier of mountains, the land opens up, offering forests, pastures, glades, valleys, lakes, rivers, and streams, a wealth of hardwood trees for shade, and lush pastures that provide nourishment for cows, sheep, and goats.

GALICIA

Galicia is the north-westernmost region of the Iberian Peninsula, the area north of Portugal, surrounded on the west and north by the Atlantic Ocean. It is an area steeped in history, occupied at various points by the Romans, Vandals, Muslims, and Moors.

Name-controlled Manchego (bottom), from Castile–La Mancha, is Spain's most popular cheese. Torpedo-shaped San Simón (top), made in Galicia, is smoked over hardwood to achieve its unique flavor.

Northern Coast of Spain

The Cheeses

TETILLA AND SAN SIMON

W hat is immediately remark-able about Galicia's Tetilla (teh-TEE-yah) and San Simón (SAN-see-MOHN) is not their flavor, but their shape. Name-controlled Tetilla, made from pasteurized cow's milk and weighing about 2 to 3 pounds (1 to 1½ k), is shaped like a woman's breast—hence its name. (Actually, it looks like a gigantic Hershey's Kiss made of white chocolate.) It is 5 to 6 inches in diameter at the base and 4 to 5 inches tall, with a greenish-beige rind and a semisoft, white interior. Though at one time this cheese was shaped by hand, today the curd is placed in plastic molds to achieve its form. The texture is soft and supple but the cheese is easily cut into wedges.

Tetilla has no hole structure and its flavor is rather similar to that of Monterey Jack—mild and tangy.

San Simón, though also breast-shaped or pineapple-shaped, is a taller, more conical, 2½- to 3-pound (1¼ to 1½ k) cheese made from pasteurized cow's milk and always smoked to a rich, burnished, walnut brown. San Simón's shape is sometimes referred to as *bufone* (dunce cap).

Upon leaving its *bufone* mold, San Simón is hardwood-smoked for two weeks or so, creating a flavor rather like Italian Scamorza—a mild, aged, smoky Mozzarella-type cheese. As it is allowed to cure, becoming firmer and drier, its flavor begins to take on a piercing, aged Provolone-like sharpness.

Though as well-known as Tetilla, which is made in large quantities at commercial cheesemaking facilities all over Galicia, San Simón's produc-tion is about one-tenth of that of Tetilla and centers mainly around the town of Villalba. Recently, San Simón has also been produced at

Savoring the tidbits called tapas *is a culinary national pastime in Spain. At big-city bars* (tascas) *like this one, as many as 50 types of tapas are served as accompaniments to sherry or beer. The array may include* jamón (ham), *marinated olives or mussels, grilled mushrooms, and cheeses such as Manchego, Cabrales, or Tetilla.*

some of the larger Galician facilities. And though Tetilla's flavor remains mild no matter how long I hold onto it, I have discovered San Simón becomes a much more interesting, more intensely flavored cheese when I age it under temperature- and humidity-controlled refrigeration for several months.

Choosing and Serving Tetilla and San Simón

Choose Tetilla and San Simón that appear alive and healthy. If less than fresh, their exterior colors will have very obviously faded: Tetilla's greenish-beige will have become gray, and San Simón will be a dull, earth color rather than a rich, walnut brown. Their interior paste should look lively, not dry or cracked, faded or old. The flavor of both cheeses will be mild and creamy, with San Simón decidedly smoky. Aged San Simón will be markedly sharper than younger examples, but old, as opposed to aged, Tetilla will simply taste dry and woody.

Tetilla and San Simón make fine accompaniments to fruits and raw vegetables. They are superb served alongside fruit-based pastries—pies, cobblers, and tarts—as well as with cured or smoked ham and *salchichón* (salami). They are mild enough to warrant white wines, particularly sparkling Spanish *cava* or another *méthode champenoise* sparkler.

ASTURIAS AND CANTABRIA

Asturias, just east of Galicia, is one of the most breathtakingly beautiful regions in all of Europe, with its Bay of Biscay coastline, alternately rocky and sandy, and its rugged, mountainous interior. This is a region largely given over to agriculture (sheep, cattle, and goats) and tourism. Summer campers make a beeline for Asturias and the national parks that cater to them. Oviedo is its ancient capital.

To the east of Asturias lies Cantabria, the region surrounding the major port city of Santander, which is the area between the Basque Country and Asturias. Its beaches are clean and sandy and *very* popular. The inland parts of Cantabria, though, are as mountainous as Asturias—wild, gorgeous, and remote—and it is these highlands that separate the region from the plains of Castile.

Santander is a wonderful spot—elegant, with a Belle Epoque ambience evoked by ornate palaces perched on cliffs overlooking the sea, lush flower gardens palm trees, and regal old hotels. Before he was deposed and exiled in 1931, King Alfonso XIII and his family spent summers at the royal palace of Magdalena, Santander's most fa-

On Spain's north-central coast, cows graze on the mountain-rimmed rolling pastures of Cantabria. Their milk is used to make loaf-shaped Cantabria, the region's mild and buttery namesake cheese.

mous landmark, perched high on a hill overlooking the ocean. Golf is hugely popular in Cantabria; indeed, this is the home of professional golfer and two-time Masters champion Severiano "Seve" Ballesteros.

Seafood is understandably a Cantabrian treasure. Hake (*merluza*) reigns supreme, along with tuna, exquisite anchovies (*anchoas*), crab, lobsters, langoustines, sardines, and mussels, as well as inland freshwater fish, such as trout and salmon. Other regional specialties such as *cocido montañés*, a stew of pork and sausages, have the mountains as their origin and inspiration. *Quesada* is the famous regional cheesecake made of soft cheese curds, lemon juice and peel, and eggs

The Cheeses

....

CABRALES AND PICON

Two of the most remarkable cheeses I ever have tasted, cheeses that I rate among Spain's best, are from contiguous areas separated by the Asturias-Cantabria border. Cabrales (kah-BRAH-lace), made in Asturias, and Picón (pee-KONE), made in Cantabria, are virtually identical 5- to 9-pound (2½ to 4½ k) wheels of blue cheese, made from a mixture of cow's, sheep's, and goat's milk. (Often, though, Picón is made solely from cow's milk.) Although these name-controlled cheeses are made year-round, the very best of them are made with unpasteurized spring and summer milk, making winter the best time to buy and enjoy them.

What makes Cabrales and Picón (which is also called Picos de Europa) so remarkable is, of course, their flavor, and almost as striking, their vivid, nearly purple veining. Like Roquefort in style, size (around 3 inches high, 7 to 8 inches in diameter), and shape, the cheeses are crumbly and fragile, but unlike most Roquefort, they are not wet and sticky, and salt does not predominate. Instead, their flavor immediately electrifies the tongue with a variety of sensations and layers of flavor—blackberries and currants, bittersweet chocolate, grass and hay, leather and woodsmoke, walnuts and, yes, beef. These flavors linger long after a chunk of bread and a swig of wine have followed the cheese, and as you exhale through your nose, you yearn to try just one more bite.

Understanding Cabrales's and Picón's complexity is easy once you know the purity of their origin. The milk comes from animals that graze on extremely high and remote pastures—a testament to the hardiness of the artisans who raise the cattle, goats, and sheep and gather their milk, and to the other artisans who turn that milk into cheese. Mother Nature helps out by providing the mile-high atmosphere, the natural limestone caves that provide the ideal temperature and humidity required for the aging process as well as the natural, airborne bacteria that "blue out" the cheese.

While Cabrales and Picón are blue cheeses by type, their color is

One of the world's most striking cheeses, Cabrales from Asturias is a memorably flavored blue, made from a mixture of cow's, sheep's, and goat's milk.

not. Just as Roquefort's blue color is more of a green (hence the French predilection for terming it *persillée*—"pars eyed"), Cabrales's and Picón's blues are so intense, they are closer to purple. Both are renneted by enzymes from the lining of the stomachs of young goats, and the milk is allowed to "settle" for three or four hours prior to the curding process.

Once made, the wheels are pierced with long needles to allow in oxygen to feed the bacteria picked up during the settling process. Finally the cheeses age in the caves of their respective regions for three to six months. Once deemed ready for market, both Cabrales and Picón may be wrapped first in huge maple, oak, or sycamore leaves, then in heavy aluminum foil or plastic.

Choosing and Serving Cabrales and Picón

When shopping for Cabrales and Picón, avoid any examples whose interior paste is turning gray. Underneath their heavy foil or plastic wrappers, the cheeses will appear truly fresh, with intense, not murky, purple veining. Store Cabrales and Picón wrapped in waxed paper in the vegetable compartment of the refrigerator.

Cabrales and Picón are cheeses that demand one's full attention. Despite this, I am guilty of enjoying these extraordinary cheeses as an accompaniment to salad or as part of a cheese tray with two or three

QUESOS DE LIEBANA

The regions of Asturias and Cantabria are home to a profusion of cheeses, including a group of Cantabrian cheeses so important that they have been awarded a generic denomination by the Spanish government and grouped together as Quesos de Liébana, named for the *comarca* (district) of Liébana. The group designation assures *denominación de origen* (D.O.) protect on to Ahumado de Aliva, Picón, Fido, and Quesuco.

However, it also creates some confusion. Given that several of the cheeses are nearly identical to others from the same or neigh-

boring regions and that they are sometimes shipped unlabeled to the U.S., correctly identifying them is very difficult—even for me.

Of the four Quesos de Liébana only Picón, also called Picos de Europa, is currently exported to the U.S. in any significant quantities. Of the other three, Ahumado de Aliva and Quesuco are so obscure that they are seldom available outside of the region in which they are made. I consider myself lucky if I get a small shipment. Pido, should you come across it, is basically an unripened Quesuco.

other choices. But as an introduction, I suggest you let one or the other introduce itself to you solo, accompanied only by bread, walnuts, fruit, and red wine. If you enjoy strong cheese, these are for you (and me).

Serve Cabrales and/or Picón with sweet fruit, raw vegetables, or salad—as a meal or a snack, with strong Spanish reds from regions such as El Bierzo, Rioja, Ribera del Duero, or Navarra. They are also very special after-dinner cheeses, excellent with Spanish sherries, sweet or dry.

QUESUCO AND AHUMADO DE ALIVA

Name-controlled Quesuco (kay-SOO-koh), another cheese from the high mountain pastures of the Picos de Europa in Cantabria, is also worthy of note. It is a 1-pound (500 g) disk, 2 inches thick, 4 inches in diameter, made of a mixture of goat's, cow's, and sheep's milk. Actually, Quesuco is known by several names—a decidedly confusing situation. In its equally prevalent smoked (usually with green juniper wood) version, it is name-controlled as Ahumado de Aliva (ah-hoo-MAH-doh-day-ah-LEE-vah). Ahumado de Aliva is made in Los Puertos de Aliva, a historic zone of high mountain pastures in the Picos de Europa region, not to be confused with Avila, the town west

of Madrid. Bear with me here—it's simply a fact that nearly everything and every place in much of Spain goes by more than one name.

The Quesuco confusion increases further since diminutive cheeses of this type—mixed milks, disk-shaped—are referred to as Quesucos in areas as far west as central Asturias. But Quesuco and Ahumado de Aliva are principally Cantabrian and are part of the group of Cantabrian cheeses that are combined under the generic denomination of name-controlled cheeses identified as Quesos de Liébana (see box, page 335).

Unsmoked or smoked, these cheeses are sold in a range of ages from just a few weeks old, when they are soft, mild, and slightly sour, to several months old, with rough, firm crusts, a much drier interior, and, naturally, a more concentrated flavor. But even rock hard at about four months old, as I sell them at my

*With a nut-like flavor and firm texture, Quesuco is ideal to tuck into a picnic basket. Serve it with cured ham (*jamón*) and olives.*

counter (when I can get them), they are still by no means strong cheeses—rather, they resemble my oldest Pecorino Toscano. Whereas Provolone and Cheddar become markedly sharper with age, Quesuco and Ahumado de Aliva become nuttier. These are splendid little cheeses to travel with, easily tucked into a tote and sturdy enough to withstand high temperatures.

Choosing and Serving Quesuco and Ahumado de Aliva

If you have the option, select Quesuco or Ahumado de Aliva while it is still soft and young, then "graduate" up the scale to those that are rock hard.

Typically, Quesuco and Ahumado de Aliva are not served at any particular time or with any specific accompaniments. Instead, they seem to appear anytime, with any meal or snack, served with whatever is at hand, be it vegetables or fruit, ham or sausage, cold, pickled, or smoked fish, and usually wine. Store them indefinitely, wrapped in aluminum foil or waxed paper in the vegetable compartment of the refrigerator.

AFUEGA'L PITU

Afuega'l Pitu (ah-FWAY-gahl pee-TOO)—what a joy! Any cheese whose name in Asturian dialect—

babel—translates as "sets fire to your gullet" is a cheese I've got to know. Though definitely piquant, Afuega'l Pitu is intensely nutty rather than ferocious, with hints in its texture and color that would suggest it is made from goat's milk. But unpasteurized cow's milk it is— a cheese totally artisanal in production. It is sold in a range of ages (from 2 to 8 weeks), plain or in a paprika version called *rojo, roxo,* or *roxo del Aramo* (a reference to the more mountainous section of Asturias). The paprika imparts a bit of its sweetness and a delayed fiery bite, in addition to the reddish color, inside and out. Afuega'l Pitu is the Spanish version of charming beggar's purse–shaped cheeses—rustic, buff-colored, squatty bundles, each weighing about 1 pound (500 g).

In 1980, a festival celebrating Afuega'l Pitu was established in the district of Morcín y Riosa, just south of Cudillero. This annual festival, scheduled for the last Sunday in February, is publicized all over Spain and has contributed to the success of this cheese, one of Asturias's oldest. But while its

Rustic looking Afuega'l Pitu is one of the nearly 30 cheeses made in Asturias, an area of only 3,861 square miles (10,000 km). Although made from unpasteurized cow's milk, it tastes a bit like a goat's-milk cheese.

success has resulted in increased production, Afuega'l is still rarely found outside of Asturias. (In fact, with the exception of Manchego, regional Spanish cheeses are rarely found outside their particular regions.) It is Afuega'l's tradition and simplicity that make it so alluring— as far removed from modernity, commerciality, and mass production as a woodfire is from a microwave oven.

Choosing and Serving Afuega'l Pitu

Afuega'l Pitu is as rustic in appearance as any cheese I can think of, and should you come across it, here or in Spain, jump on it. It will be superb. You'll want it as young as possible, at which point it is meltingly soft at room temperature, though even if it is hard and dry from aging, it is wonderful. Do not store it in plastic, just shroud it loosely in aluminum foil or in a paper bag. It must breathe.

Afuega'l Pitu marries perfectly with fruits, cured or smoked pork products, and your favorite red wines. Crusty, coarse bread is a must. The wines of El Bierzo, made in the highlands of León, just south of Asturias, are perfect with this cheese. Their grape is the Mencía, one that falls between the Tempranillo of Rioja and Cabernet Sauvignon in terms of tannin, creating wines that are meaty and taste of blackberries, celery, and licorice, and with aromas of dates and raisins.

PEÑAMELLERA

Another notable cheese of Asturias is Peñamellera (PAIN-yah-may-YAIR-ah), named after a high peak that rises like a tent from the valley of the Río Cares, at the extreme eastern end of Asturias. The capital of the Peñamellera Alta district is the village of Alles. Although the valley is small, its cheese is known throughout northern Spain.

Peñamellera is a mix of goat's, cow's, and sheep's milk, a 4- to 7-ounce (125 to 210 g) disk, 1 inch thick and 3½ inches in diameter, with a yellowish-beige crust, slightly less yellowish interior, and a considerable sprinkling of tiny holes. Its brassy, meaty flavor is not strong, but lingering and buttery, reflecting an artisanal touch. Aging is a minimum of two weeks and as much as three months, at which point the rind is drier, the interior softer, and the flavor more expansive.

Choosing and Serving Peñamellera

Select Peñamellera that is slightly yielding to the squeeze rather than rock hard, at which point salt may predominate. I recently received a batch that was as perfect as any cheese in my experience. Having been air-shipped, the Peñamelleras were young and tender, with a light yellow interior that flowed at room temperature and a wrinkled beige crust that was nutty and chewy rather than bitter and salty. At room temperature, the aroma expands and you'll certainly be aware there's a special cheese in the house. The presence of goat's and sheep's milk is always deliciously present in the taste and visible in the whiteness of the paste. If allowed to age another month or so, Peñamellera will have become slightly shrunken, the crust darkened with mold, and the interior will have turned firm and chewy. At this stage the flavor will have intensified, tending toward light saltiness. The rind should be trimmed away.

Serve this excellent cheese with all manner of fruits, ham, *salchichón* (salami), and have a crusty loaf of bread close at hand. Partner it with any big Spanish red from the north of Spain.

CANTABRIA, VIDIAGO, QUESO DE NATA

Cantabria's cheeses are as homely and appealing as the mild, buttery cheeses from Asturias, although not nearly as varied. To date, I have rarely been able to import the two originals, name-controlled Cantabria (cahn-TAH-bree-uh), and its Asturian twin, Vidiago (vid-ee-AH-go). Both are rectangular, loaf-shaped,

pasteurized cow's milk cheeses, weighing 1 to 4½ pounds (500 g to 2¼ k), about 2 inches thick, 4 inches across, and 8 inches long. Occasionally they are made in wheels of the same weight. They owe their soft, supple texture to the moist, ambient air of the humid coastal area where they are made.

Recently both of these cheeses have been dressed up a bit into a "new" commercial cheese that is made in large quantities for export. And this new cheese, called Queso de Nata (KAY-soh-day-NAH-tah)—*nata* meaning "cream," or *crème de la crème*—is one that is available to us in the U.S. While I decry this sort of development and would prefer access to the originals, I must admit that Nata, made in 4½-pound (2¼ k) wheels, is just as mild, buttery, and pleasant as its artisanal forebears.

Choosing and Serving Cantabria, Vidiago, and Queso de Nata

Cantabria, Vidiago, and Queso de Nata are sturdy cheeses and selecting a good one should present no problem. They are so mild and unassuming, yet so buttery and pleasant, that they will enhance nearly anything you serve with them. Use them as you would any mild cheese that is a good melter—in an omelet or a quesadilla, or melted on a grilled tomato sandwich. White wines are the best companions.

THE SPANISH PYRENEES

(The Basque Country, Navarre, Northern Aragón, and Northern Catalonia)

The coastal area, where Spain's Basque Country (País Vasco) abuts France, is very busy, noisy, traffic-ridden, and not so charming. But inland (south) and east, into the Pyrenees mountains themselves, you will find yourself in a place you have sought all your life. The Basques are among the most welcoming people I have ever met, and they're living in paradise—at least *my* idea of paradise.

The Basque Country is a completely agricultural society, one that begs to be recognized as one of the oldest, most cohesive, and individualistic clans found anywhere, a tribe bound to and defined by this gorgeous land they have occupied for millennia. Their language is ancient and unlike any other. To the traveler, it is seemingly indecipherable, rife with consonant combinations that defy pronunciation. Basque cooking is among the best in Spain, making use of all the foodstuffs the area is known for—seafood, hams, sweet and hot peppers, fine wines, and excellent breads. Olive oil is the primary fat used for cooking and dressing vegetables.

Cheese is an important staple, both for cooking and eating out of

For nearly 3,000 years olivey, nutty Roncal cheese has been made in the seven bucolic villages that dot the Roncal valley of Navarre.

hand. Sheep's-milk cheeses are the only type made in this area, whereas in the French Pyrénées—an area as Basque as the Spanish Pyrenees—some cow's-milk cheeses are also made. Despite the Spanish political divisions of this area, which sprawls easterly all the way to Catalonia, from the coastal Basque Country to Navarre and the northern tip of Aragón, the region is largely considered to be a unit—or at least unified—an area of breathtaking beauty. You simply must visit—to feast your eyes on the ancient Pyrenean villages, taste the artisanal cheeses, and revel in the magnificent Navarra wines, including the world-class reds.

The Cheeses

IDIAZABAL

One of the most important cheeses of the Basque Country and Navarre is name-controlled Idiazábal (ee-dee-ah-ZAH-bahl), a 5- to 6-inch-thick wheel of raw sheep's milk cheese, about 5 to 7 inches in diameter and weighing 5 to 9 pounds (2½ to 4½ k). Idiazábal, named for a village in the País Vasco area, is most often found smoked, and it gets that way in the most serendipitous manner.

For many generations, Basque shepherds pastured their flocks of Lata breed sheep high in the Pyrenees above Pamplona throughout the spring and summer. In late September or early October, forced down by the first snows, the shepherds would appear laden with the summer's cheeses, rich in fat and flavor thanks to the lush diet enjoyed by their sheep in these luxurious high pastures. The cheeses were already aged and smoked—due to the shepherds' habit of storing them in the stone chimneys of their cramped mountain *chabolas* (huts). Over the years these wonderful, handmade smoked sheep's-milk cheeses became readily recognizable and found themselves in great favor and demand all over the Basque Country and, today, throughout Spain.

Idiazábal richly deserves its name-controlled status and is one of Spain's most well-crafted, highest-quality cheeses. Having almost always (at least for export purposes) been treated to hardwood smoking, the exterior of these cheeses varies from orange to a rich walnut brown, and though the smoking colors only the hard rind, its flavor permeates the interior gently but unmistakably, resulting in an effect that is both balsamy and smoky. The interior is a pale, yellowish beige with an even proliferation of tiny holes throughout. Though the rind is hard, nearly too hard to chew, the interior is firm yet supple and easily cut with any sharp knife. Idiazábal is, blessedly, always made from raw milk, another reason why it tastes so splendidly nutty. It un-

dergoes an aging period of two to four months, the longer-aged cheeses resulting in considerably stronger, sharper flavor (which makes older versions good for use as a grating cheese). But no matter how strong or sharp, it is Idiazábal's mountain perfume and butteriness that rule the taste experience.

Choosing and Serving Idiazábal

If the Idiazábal you find has a moldy exterior (*enmohecido*), do not be alarmed. This condition is natural, indeed, a plus—evidence that the cheese has been treated to long and patient aging. Interior mold, however, is an obvious sign of a lack of freshness.

The perfume and butter of Idiazábal marry beautifully with all manner of fruits and pork products—ham and salami (*salchichón*)—with crusty breads and red Navarra wines. This is cheese that begs to be taken outdoors and enjoyed under the sky. Store Idiazábal in the vegetable compartment of the refrigerator, wrapped in aluminum foil or waxed paper so that it can continue to breathe without drying out. It will keep a long time—a month or more—before becoming stale.

RONCAL

Across the river Esca, in the Navarre region, lies the Roncal

The first cheese to be awarded a Spanish denomination, Roncal is made from the rich milk of Latcha or Aragonese Rasa sheep.

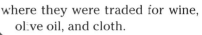

where they were traded for wine, olive oil, and cloth.

Roncal became so famous that in 1981 it was honored with the very first *denominación de origen* distinction given by Spain to one of its cheeses. This cheese, to this day a product of fresh mountain air, is one that, through several months of slow, patient ripening, gains a delicious, moist, smooth, olivey, and nutty flavor that I find so rustically appealing. I am selling ever-increasing quantities of Roncal. I believe it has all the merit of Manchego (see page 351).

Roncal cheeses are thickish wheels, about 4 to 4½ inches high and 6 to 7 inches in diameter, weighing from 5 to 7 pounds (2½ to 3½ k). They are quite firm, with smooth, beige to dark gray rinds, and look slightly imperfect or handmade (mold may occasionally be present).

valley. This valley is made up of the seven villages that figure in the production and marketing of the famed name-controlled cheese called Roncal (roan-KAHL), which enjoys specific recordings and registries of Pyrenean sheep herds that date to the thirteenth century. Literally all the residents of these Roncal villages became a formal *junta* way back then—a society that worked as one, surviving and prospering on the raising of sheep for wool, milk, cheese, and meat; lambs for meat and skins; forestry (lumber, firewood); and horses. The bulk of serious labor occurred between the periods of *transhumancia*, the twice-yearly trek of animals and their shepherds to (in mid-May) and from (in mid-October) the high pastures. During the spring and summer, the citizens of the valley roamed all over the Pyrenees, tending their flocks. Their products found a ready market in Pamplona,

Choosing and Serving Roncal

As with Idiazábal, Roncal's sturdiness practically eliminates the necessity for careful inspection when buying it. Be watchful for the obvious defects—cracks, discoloration, surface mold on the cut face of the interior—that suggest a loss of freshness.

Roncal is a highly agreeable partner to fruits and raw vegetables, cured or smoked pork products, crusty bread, and Navarra wines. It is superb for use as a grating cheese for soups, casseroles, and pasta.

THE EASTERN AND SOUTHEASTERN COAST

(Catalonia, Southern Aragón, Valencia, Murcia, Andalusia, and Minorca)

The Mediterranean coast of eastern Spain is an enticing mixture of places and things and foods I love—Barcelona in toto, anything by Gaudí, and fresh-caught fish and seafood—as well as some I don't love, say, the teeming resorts between Tarragona and Alicante. But if you stick to the roller-coaster coastal highway and continue farther south and west, eventually you'll get to Andalusia, a place for me—especially in the central and western part, where the glories of Córdoba, Granada, Jérez de la Frontera, Huelva, Seville, and Cádiz lie.

The Cheeses

GARROTXA

Garrotxa (gar-ROACH-uh), a north-central province within Catalonia, and twenty miles north

Now a national monument, Catalan architect Antoni Gaudí's famous Casa Milá in Barcelona was built in 1905. The façade's undulating stone pillars are characteristic of Gaudí's free use of form.

East and Southeast Coast of Spain

of Girona, gives its name to a relatively new cheese that has become very popular in Spain over the past decade. It is delicious, made from pasteurized goat's milk, and as unique a cheese as any I have experienced. Garrotxa is a gray-rinded, felt-textured disk that weighs about 2 pounds (1 k). Inside is a bone-white, tight-textured cheese (the rind is super-thin), firm yet supple, with a mild, very satisfying flavor—nutty and herbal with hints of thyme and rosemary (reflecting the goats' Mediterranean diet). Obviously a considerable marketing effort is afoot, as this stunning cheese has been met with great favor throughout Spain, and I welcome it to the United States. There is simply no other goat cheese like it from anywhere. If I made cheese, this is certainly one I'd be proud to call my own.

Choosing and Serving Garrotxa

Garrotxa's three weeks of aging are enough to rid the cheese of excess moisture, giving it a slightly dry though cohesive texture that immediately transfers its herby nuttiness to the palate. Avoid any Garrotxa that is cracked or shows interior mold—the obvious signs of a lack of freshness. Store leftovers in the vegetable compartment of the refrigerator, tightly wrapped in aluminum foil or waxed paper.

Garrotxa is a perfect accompaniment to all that I love—olives, sweet summer fruits, cured ham or coarse salami, rough, crusty multi-grain bread, and strong red wines, certainly those from Spain's Rioja or Ribera del Duero.

TRONCHON

Tronchón, a village in the Maestrazgo area just south of coastal Tarragona in southern Aragón, gives its name to a famous Spanish mixed-milk cheese. As with many Spanish cheeses, Tronchón (trone-CHONE) is made at a number of facilities, some with considerable production and some contributing very minor quantities. Those cheesemakers able to produce larger quantities tend to use pasteurized sheep's milk; those that are more artisanal use raw sheep's or goat's milk, usually a mixture of the two.

The unique shape of Tronchón makes it easily recognizable: Each 4½-pound (about 2¼ k) form is dome-shaped, about 6 inches in diameter, with a deep indentation in the top. This indented dome is the result of the olivewood molds that are used by commercial and small producers alike. I'm delighted that all of the makers of this Spanish cheese have continued to adhere to the old ways and the old tools as much as possible. Cervantes speaks lovingly of Tronchón in *Don Quixote,* and it is recorded that Marie Antoinette became an avid consumer of Tronchón after

Dome-shaped Tronchón is formed in a mold that leaves behind a characteristic dimple in the top.

she was introduced to it at a banquet honoring the Spanish ambassador, the Count of Aranda.

Tronchón is a firm, mild cheese with considerable tiny hole distribution throughout. Its natural buff-colored rind is dry, not quite smooth, and a bit more yellowish than the interior. Tronchón impresses me—its flavor is so fine, reminiscent of tiny, precious, greenishly iridescent Tomme d'Arles from Provence and similar to my best pure sheep Pecorino from coastal Grossetto in Tuscany. Tronchón lets you taste the wild herbs—thyme, lavender, and rosemary—that figure so importantly in the diet of these animals.

Choosing and Serving Tronchón

Tronchón is another sturdy cheese that suffers only if abused—check for signs of dryness and a general lack of freshness. Store Tronchón in the vegetable compartment of the refrigerator, wrapped in aluminum foil or waxed paper. Serve it with cracked green olives dressed with extra-virgin olive oil and crushed garlic and make the wines white or red, as long as they are light, fruity, fresh, and full of bounce. Tronchón is also a perfect cocktail or appetizer cheese.

QUESO DE MURCIA AND QUESO DE MURCIA AL VINO

Queso de Murcia (KAY-soh-day-moor-SEE-ah), while mild, is a very agreeable, moist, smooth goat's-milk cheese, as are practically all of the cheeses from this part of Spain's southeast coast. The region is hot, arid, and barren, with marshy areas made productive by copious irrigation for rice crops. In 1986, the autonomous Murcian government put their cheesemakers' feet to the fire by insisting they come up with a cheese unique to the area that could be awarded regional commercial status and distinction. The idea was to give Murcia a measure of prestige as well as considerable revenue, both of which the area needed and richly deserved.

The result was Queso de Murcia al Vino (KAY-soh-day-moor-SEE-ah-al-VEE-noh), a reinterpretation of the region's Queso de Murcia, which they cleverly chose to wash with the local *vino tinto* (red wine). This wine, heavy with tannin and rich in color not only gives the exterior of the cheese a dramatic visual effect, it also enhances the cheese's otherwise blandish character with its fruitiness and lusciously grapey aroma. By 1987, Queso de Murcia al Vino had become a huge commercial hit regionally, and today it is available in other parts of Spain as well. Both versions of this disk-shaped cheese weigh between 2 and 3½ pounds (1 and 1¾ k) and are 2 inches thick and 5 inches in diameter. For now, you'll have to look for Queso de Murcia and Queso de Murcia al Vino in Spain; I have not yet managed to import either cheese, though I suspect it will happen in the not too distant future.

Choosing and Serving Queso de Murcia and Queso de Murcia al Vino

Queso de Murcia and Queso de Murcia al Vino are soft, moist cheeses that must be sold in a very fresh state. If not absolutely fresh, they will taste sour rather than fruity. Airtight plastic wrap and refrigeration are necessary to keep them at their best, and your portion should really be consumed within a week of purchase. This style of cheese lends itself best to sweet, summer fruits and red or white light, fruity wines.

QUESO DE ZUHEROS

The sprawling region of Andalusia harbors only a nominal cheese-making effort. Although a few goat's-milk cheeses (Queso de la Calahorra, Queso de Alhama de Granada, Queso de Málaga, Queso Grazalema, Queso de Cádiz) are indigenous to the area, they are scarce. It is more likely you will find only Spain's countrywide favorites such as Manchego and Mahón in the shops of Andalusia. An exception, however, is Queso de Zuheros (KAY-soh-day-zoo-HAIR-ohs), a hard, piquant, fruity goat cheese made near Córdoba. It is the only Andalusian goat's-milk cheese that I bring to the U.S. Queso de Zuheros is a 2-pound (1 k) cylinder, 4 inches high and 4 inches in diameter. Its reddish-orange rind is the result of having been rubbed with tomato paste, and the Manchego-like cross-hatching impressions on the surface are left by the cheese's molds, which are woven of *esparto* grass.

Choosing and Serving Queso de Zuheros

Queso de Zuheros is quite firm and stark white inside with enormous, fruity-sharp flavor. It is a cheese that marries well with fruit. And it is delicious served with olives and almonds, alongside a glass of cold, dry, white Andalusian sherry (*fino*), a wine you can start out on as a cocktail, savor with an appetizer, and stay with through the end of a meal.

Zuheros is sturdy enough to withstand a great deal of abuse—still extremely palatable even after a few weeks. Store it in the vegetable compartment of the refrigerator, wrapped in aluminum foil or waxed paper.

MAHON

Minorca (Menorca), the outermost of the three Spanish Balearic Islands is, by far, the least affected by tourism. It is an island almost completely given over to agriculture. Over the centuries, it became renowned for its cheese, which is very popular on the mainland of Spain and in the U.K. Today it is home to one of the most advanced and respected dairy plants in all of Europe. It is surprising that an island this small (only 300 square miles) produces so much cheese.

Mahón is the major town on Minorca and also the name of Spain's second most popular cheese next to Manchego. Name-controlled Mahón (mah-HONE) is unique in its production and distribution. A century or so ago, *los recoge-dores-afinadores* (gatherer-ripeners) emerged, a class of island society that still exists. In addition to providing Minorcan agriculture with seed, fertilizer, and a variety of agrarian tools, these people are responsible for collecting the young *quesos,* storing them in underground facilities to ripen, and then distributing them to the mainland and Majorca. Majorca consumes a great deal of Mahón, despite the production of its own Mahón-type cheese called Mallorquín (mah-yor-KEEN). It is, I believe, the gatherer-ripeners' talent for aging these cheeses that has made Mahón so famous. In its youth Mahón is just another cow's-milk cheese. But ripened for six months, a full year, or even

To make Mahón, chopped curd is gathered into a square of cloth and the corners are tied together tautly and anchored with a peg. After draining and pressing, the cheeses ripen on wooden shelves for at least 60 days.

as long as two years, Mahón becomes as magnificent as Dutch Boerenkaas (farmer's Gouda), which is aged twice as long! With the exception of Parmigiano-Reggiano and California Dry Jack, no other extra-aged cow's-milk cheese is Mahón's equal.

The Mahón I sell are round-edged, 8-inch squares about 2 inches thick, weighing about 5 or 6 pounds (2½ to 3 k) each. The flavor is buttery sharp, slightly salty, and lightly aromatic, the aroma sweet and nutty. Farm-made *artesano* (artisanal) Mahón will usually be quite young *(fresco)*—no more than three months old—and is considerably softer, with a much more evident barnyardy aroma, which is a real plus from my point of view.

Choosing and Serving Mahón

Avoid any Mahón that is mushy or discolored (graying, reddening) or, conversely, is cracked or dried out. Young or *fresco* (aged about two weeks) Mahón will have a burnished, bright orangey-gold rind and a white, chalky-textured interior. *Curado* or *semi-curado* (aged about two months) Mahón will have a paler, buff-colored rind and a much whiter inner paste than will *duro* (aged six months) or *añejo* (aged 18 months to two years) Mahón, whose rind will be an almost chocolate brown with a straw- or amber-colored interior. As would be expected, Mahón *duro* and *añejo* will be much sharper and fruitier in flavor than younger examples, which are nutty and considerably more aromatic. All aged Mahón has a proliferation of tiny holes.

Young Mahón should be kept in the vegetable compartment of the refrigerator, wrapped airtight in plastic wrap; the harder, longer-aged variety should be wrapped in aluminum foil or waxed paper.

Mahón is agreeable with cold beer and, in fact, is a splendid sandwich cheese. Or eat it the traditional way, sliced, then sprinkled with olive oil, black pepper, and tarragon.

THE INTERIOR OF SPAIN

(Castile–La Mancha, Castile–León, and Extremadura)

S pain's interior has it all—great contrast in topography and climate, along with enormous touristic beauty. From the barren, forbidding expanse of Castile–La Mancha, to the wild, ruggedly beautiful, mountainous Extremadura, to the rolling plains and plateaus of Castile-León, "inner" Spain is impossible to characterize with any sense of unity. Likewise, the cheeses are dissimilar—most never leaving their particular areas. Name-controlled Manchego is an exception.

La Mancha was named by the Arabs, who ruled this area from the eighth to the eleventh century and referred to it as *manyá,* meaning "waterless." And a fierce, monotonous, windy, dry, and seemingly barren land it is, a high, flat plateau rising to more than 2,600 feet above sea level. With its constant, buffeting winds, its unrelenting winters, and its crazy temperature swings from season to season, it is obvious that the only creatures who could withstand the climatic pain would be thick-fleeced sheep. The cities ringing Castile–La Mancha's perimeter—Toledo, Ciudad Real, Albacete, and Cuenca—encircle a near-empty expanse, populated primarily by sheep and shepherds. And today, after the wine industry, cheese rules.

The magnificent frescoes adorning the ceiling of the royal mausoleum of the Basilica de San Isidoro in León have been called the Sistine Chapel of Romanesque art.

The Cheeses

MANCHEGO

Name-controlled Manchego (mon-CHAY-goh), Spain's most popular cheese, is available in a range of ages and corresponding textures—from the young and mild *fresco* (aged for two months), to semi-aged, slightly piquant *curado* (aged one year), to *añejo* or *viejo* (extra-aged—two years), to pre-cut 8-ounce (250 g) wedges, bathed in extra-virgin olive oil, tinned, and aged indefinitely. Each thickish sheep's-milk wheel is 4 to 5 inches thick and 8 to 9 inches in diameter, weighing 6 to 7 pounds (3 to 3½ k).

At any age Manchego's flavor is mild, with a slight briny nuttiness, and rather dry on the palate, making me wonder what the fuss is all about. I can only surmise its appeal lies in its simplicity and its ability to enhance the flavors of its accompaniments.

The traditional, zigzagging cross-hatch pattern found on Manchego's rounded edge was formed by its original molds or presses, made from hand-plaited strands of a tough grass called *esparto,* which is found all over Spain. Today the molds are made of plastic, though they leave behind the familiar pattern. According to each maker's whim (and there are several dozen), Manchego cheeses will have rinds of beige, gray, or black. The interior paste, with an even distribution of small holes, ranges from stark white to off-white to slightly yellowish, according to age.

MORE THAN MANCHEGO

Manchego owes its fame to La Mancha's contiguousness with Madrid, Spain's populous capital. Over the last century its popularity has been simply a matter of its being the cheese that is the most familiar to the most people.

Now, while I like Manchego, under no circumstances can I recommend it over similar, but more flavorful, cheeses, such as Roncal (see page 342), Zamorano, or its Castilian counterpart, Queso Castellano (see page 354 for both). The fame of Manchego is such that unless Spain mounts a campaign to promote the rest of its cheeses, all its cheeses, *including* Manchego, will suffer.

Great quantities of cheese are consumed in restaurants. Spanish restaurateurs are so awed by Manchego's dominance that they are holding back other, even more honest cheeses. And the worst part of it is that Spain is subsidizing brand-new factories that are turning out mass-production cheeses of "adequate" quality under new, made-up names. This country has a remarkable wealth of rustic, traditional cheeses of extraordinary quality, regionality, and significance, and the makers of these cheeses would jump at the chance to be recognized. We need the opportunity to get to know them better. It would be a shame if Spain turned its back on its past, as if tradition were like an old pair of shoes. Spain is going to lose some of her gastronomic majesty, just like France and Italy have, all in the name of modernity.

Choosing and Serving Manchego

Buy Manchego at a busy shop where you are sure of frequent turnover and try to taste it before choosing. It is difficult to tell by looking whether or not the Manchego is good, particularly if it is an aged example. Stale Manchego will simply taste sheepy, with few hints of its usually mild, but pleasantly saline nuttiness.

In Spain, Manchego is omnipresent in markets and on restaurant menus, where it usually appears as *tapas,* as an appetizer all by itself, or perhaps with a few cracked or split green Andalusian olives, cured in olive oil with garlic and lemon or fennel. As for wines, with a young Manchego, serve Catalonian sparkling whites (*cava*), a light Navarra red, or *fino* sherry; with an aged cheese, opt for a well-knit Spanish red, such as one from Ribera del Duero or Rioja. In some restaurants Manchego is offered as a dessert choice, served with either fresh fruit or honey. And it is also used frequently as a grating cheese, usually for baked vegetable dishes.

Manchego is always plated in a very particular way—I've never, ever seen it done in any other manner. Here's the classic method: The Manchego is cut into ⅛-inch-thick finger-food size triangular wafers (obviously cut from a wedge, taken from the whole wheel.) The top, side, and bottom edges of rind are trimmed off and the triangles of cheese are fanned out on a small plate. (Accompaniments usually are served on separate plates.) The triangles of Manchego are nibbled using one's fingers or a knife and fork. I have never seen a big hunk of Manchego with a knife stuck into it come out of any Spanish

kitchen—or from behind a bar— only these dainty little wafers. Such an agreeably delicate means of handling a decidedly sturdy cheese!

QUESO IBORES

Extremadura is the most rugged, least developed, and most economically distressed region in Spain. Its cheeses reflect these conditions in their rusticity and lack of recognition. Queso Ibores (KAY-soh-ee-BORE-ace), also called Sierra Ibores (see-AIR-ah-ee-BORE-ace), is a hard, dense raw goat's milk cheese that becomes sharper with age. It is a very agreeable, peasanty Spanish regional cheese that holds for me all the allure, simplicity, and richness of flavor that I find so lacking in the "new" commercial factory cheeses.

Choosing and Serving Queso Ibores

Queso Ibores (or Sierra Ibores) is an orange-rinded disk about 4 inches thick and 5 inches in diameter, weighing about 1 pound (500 g). The cheeses are rubbed during their aging period of up to two months with a mixture of olive oil and sweet paprika. Their flavor is strong and a bit goaty but very enjoyable, one that marries well with all manner of fruits and raw vegetables (peppers, cucumbers, radishes), pork products (cured or smoked), crusty breads, and strong red wines. Not much can go wrong with this sturdy, dense, very firm cheese that quite likely will splinter or crack unevenly when cut. It will remain tasty, for at least a month, when wrapped in aluminum foil or waxed paper and stored in the vegetable compartment of the refrigerator. Shavings of Ibores work miracles on a green salad or ripe tomatoes.

ZAMORANO AND CASTELLANO

Castile–León is the name of a sprawling region of Spain that skirts Portugal's northeastern border. It is made up of nine provinces, each a rather famous historical city-state—León, Palencia, Burgos, Zamora, Valladolid, Segovia, Soria, and Avila. The entire area is a relatively treeless plain broken up by rugged plateaus, deep gorges, and Extremadura's rugged mountains at its southern border.

In addition to Avila's famous goat's milk cheese, Queso del Tiétar (named for a valley), and Burgos's equally famous fresh, white, moist, soft

Zamorano

sheep's milk cheese, Queso de Burgos, Castilla y León is well known for two other cheeses: name-controlled Zamorano (zah-moh-RAH-noh), an artisanal cheese made only in the province of Zamora, and Castellano (kahss-tay-YAH-noh), which is highly commercial and made in all nine provinces. Both are made of pasteurized and unpasteurized sheep's milk, and in Zamorano's case, specifically from the Churra breed of sheep, which give particularly high-quality milk. Castellano and Zamorano are identical in recipe, configuration, and appearance to La Mancha's Manchego, and can be considered in every regard its equal—or better.

Choosing and Serving Zamorano and Castellano

Should you find one or both of these sturdy cheeses, ask for a taste. Since they are nearly impervious to abuse, staleness is the only threat. Stale examples will appear dull, fading to gray, and the flavor will have become lifeless and dull. Fresh Zamorano and Castellano should have a dry, ungummy texture and distinctly nutty flavor. Serve them as you would Roncal or Manchego—with ham, melon, pears, tomatoes, crusty bread, and a solid red wine.

THE JOYS OF JAMON

Spaniards from all regions are fanatical about their country's cured pork products. And whether it's the more common *serrano* (mountain) variety or the rare super-expensive, longer-aged Jabugo from near Andalucia's port city of Huelva, Spanish ham (*jamón*) is as much a passion with me as it is with Spaniards. Spanish restaurateurs serve thin, hand-hewn shards of these miraculous hams with Manchego, Zamorano, Castellano, and the other similar Spanish sheep's-milk cheeses. They are extraordinarily flavorful and sweet, owing to the craftsmanship involved in their production—a style of butchering (*matanza*) and curing that has been going on for centuries—and a so to the pig's diet. Acorns, chestnuts, and molasses make up a major part of the feed for the *cerdo iberico*, a unique species of Spanish pig.

As a rule, Spanish hams are smaller than Italian hams, much firmer, and their flesh is darker—a burgundy color rather than prosciutto-pink. The fat in ham is where the flavor is, and while Spanish ham is no more or less fatty than prosciutto, the remarkable thing is its marbling. Somehow, the flesh delivers huge flavor—even more than prosciutto. While I admire Spanish hams completely, they are not a replacement for other types of ham. They are more properly finger foods, while prosciutto tends to be draped, rolled, and on occasion eaten with a knife and fork.

Jabugo ham comes from a sub-species of the *cerdo iberico,* a black-hoofed breed of pig called *pata negra.* Jabugo—as exalted a foodstuff as foie gras with truffles (and as costly)—has a flavor that is at once red-winey, intensely nutty, and sweet, without a trace of the saltiness that too often pervades hams of a lesser pedigree. The texture of Jabugo is like silk, with a mouth-feel that is sublime—at first resistant to teeth and tongue, but gradually yielding, becoming more and more pliant, soon literally melting, drenching the palate with an intensity of flavor I can describe only as perfect.

LESSER-KNOWN CHEESES OF SPAIN

Although you'll have a next-to-impossible time locating any of these cheeses outside of Spain, do look for them when traveling in the country.

Mató (mah-TOH): found in the southern part of Catalonia, roughly from Barcelona west and well into Lérida and Tarragona provinces. It is a fresh cheese made from a combination of goat's milk and cow's milk. This cheese is very popular with Spaniards, much as Ricotta is with Italians. Mató is very white, very fresh, soft and moist, completely mild and unsalty, almost sweet, served with honey poured over it at breakfast or as a dessert. Its size and shape vary, but this 2- to 4-pound (1 to 2 k) cheese is

Mató

usually hemispherical and flat-bottomed, with the top slightly domed, as though its mold were a salad or soup bowl. It can also be served with a wide variety of fruits and vegetables. You will see Mató at markets throughout Catalonia. I urge you to try it.

Queso Ansó-Hecho (KAY-soh-on-SOH-AY-choh): made between the Pamplona district of Roncal and that of Huesca, where Navarre fades into northernmost Aragón. It is a raw sheep's milk cheese similar in configuration, size, and flavor to Roncal—firm, buttery, and olivey, but more yellowish in color. Ansó and Hecho are villages united under auspices similar to those of the Roncal valley whereby an independent community manages to be self-sufficient by virtue of its produce—chiefly cheese. This artisanal Pyrenean triumph is a perfect examp.e of uncommercial Pyrenees cheese, one that is completely authentic and delicious.

Queso de Arzúa (KAY-soh-day-ar-ZCO-ah); also called **Queso Gallego** (KAY-soh-guy-YAY-goh), **Queso de Ulla** (KAY-soh-day-ooh-YAH), or **Queso de Ulloa** (KAY-soh-day-ooh-yoe-ah): I must be mellowing because recently I actually reveled in one of the other mild Galician cheeses. It was at a spectacular seafood restaurant called La Trainera in Madrid. As we entered, I saw the cheese prominently displayed behind glass on a countertop. This cow's-milk cheese, Queso de Arzúa, was the only cheese offered. It was served as dessert with *membrillo* (mem-BREE-yoh), a loaf of firm, golden to deep red quince paste with a spicy, sweet chewiness that is just perfect with the flavor of a mild, tangy, slightly saline cheese such as Queso de Arzúa. As with Cheddar and apple pie, mild Spanish cheeses such as this really find a home next to your favorite homemade, fruit-based pastries. If it ever comes to these shores, try it with a fruit cobbler.

Queso de Burgos

Queso de Benasque (KAY-soh-day-bay-NAH-skay): Made in the extreme northeast corner of Huesco province, right on the border with France, this is a 3-pound (1½ k), firm-textured wheel of raw cow's-milk cheese, with a full, round, buttery flavor. It is not currently exported. When in Spain, try it with red Navarra wines and cured ham. It is a wonderful, rustic cheese made in small quantities.

Queso de los Beyos (KAY-soh-day-los-BAY-ohs); also called **Queso Beyos** or **Queso Beyusco** (BAY-ohs-coh): A firm, yet tender, 1-pound (500 g) natural-rind cylinder of unpasteurized cow's milk or goat's milk cheese that is very lightly smoked. Its flavor is pronounced, though smooth. Very rare.

Queso de Buelles (KAY-soh-day-boo-AY-yace): A firm, natural-rind, unpasteurized Asturian goat cheese that I may just get my hands on for export. Its flavor is light and buttery, and each cheese weighs about 2¼ pounds (2 k). Made in infinitesimal quantities.

Queso de Burgos (KAY-soh-day-BOOR-gose): A commercially distributed pasteurized sheep's-milk cheese now sold fresh, though it was once more popular in its aged state. The cylindrical size varies from 2½ to 6½ pounds (1¼ to 3¼ k). While I sell aged Burgos, a very Manchego-like cheese, Burgos is now predominantly sold in a very fresh, white, rindless stage and is increasingly being made from a mixture of cow's milk and sheep's milk. (Some is also made of 100 percent cow's milk.) Made in Castile–León, it is very popular in Spain, eaten at breakfast with fruit or preserves.

Queso Casín (KAY-soh-kah-SEEN): From the Asturian region of Concejo de Caso, this is a flat, 2¼-pound (about 1 k) disk of raw cow's milk cheese. This cheese has ancient roots, as evidenced by the traditional, hand-carved wooden molds used to emboss a purportedly magical hieroglyph upon each cheese's face. The exact meaning of this mystical mark has been lost to the ages, though it continues to carry great significance and symbolism to the herdsmen who are its makers.

Queso de Cebreiro

Queso Casín is a strong-flavored cheese that starts out with a slightly granular feel on the palate and then smooths out. Very rare.

Queso Cassoleta (KAY-soh-KOSS-oh-LAY-tah): A 1-pound (500 g) unaged version of Tronchón (see page 346), that is made and featured prominently farther down the coast, in the provinces of Castellón and Valencia. Cassoleta refers to the olive-wood molds used to give sheep's milk Tronchón and Cassoleta their indented dome shape. Though not exported, Cassoleta is extremely well known throughout this area,

where it is served fried with sweet peppers and tomatoes, as an appetizer tidbit with apéritifs, and as part of the *tapas* assortment served in local bars.

Queso de Cebreiro (KAY-soh-day-seh-BRAIR-oh): From Los Puertos del Cebreiro, near Lugo and the Portuguese border, this is an ancient Galician raw cow's milk cheese you are unlikely to encounter outside the area. As of this writing it is not exported. It is thought that this cheese has survived because of its remote origin—as far from the sea as one can get in Galicia—and because its recipe is completely original, guarded fiercely, and handed down from mother to daughter.

Aside from its peculiar but alluring flavor—at once sour like yogurt and slightly bitter like Sicilian almonds—and buttery aroma (both of which intensify with age), Cebreiro has a most remarkable shape. Weighing 2 to 4 pounds (1 to 2 k), it looks exactly like a squashed chef's toque, and it's the same size, too. The curd is placed in cheesecloth, the corners gathered and knotted on top, and the bottom encircled by a wooden belt. The cheesecloth forms the pouf of the toque, while the belt shapes the brim. Young Cebreiro's crust is beige and the interior paste is unctuous and white with yellow, sort of buttery striations. Older Cebreiro is firmer and more pronounced in flavor.

Queso Cassoleta

Queso Gamonedo

Queso Gamonedo (KAY-soh-gam-oh-NAY-doh); also called **Gamoneú** (gam-oh-NAY-oo): The most expensive cheese of Asturias and worth every extra *peseta*. Classically t is made from a mixture of goat's, sheep's, and, predominantly, cow's milk. It is practically identical to Cabrales (see page 334), but slightly firmer and taller and without the leaf wrapping. Though it is produced year-round, the best is made from summer milk and transported to the valley for cave aging. Gamonedo has a dry, gray-mold rind with sharply defined edges. Each 5-pound (2½ k) wheel is 7 inches high and 7 inches in diameter. Gamonedo is considerably firmer than Cabrales or Picón, but its flavor is equally stunning—complex, earthy, and sharp. Gamonedo, which offers all of the layers of flavor of Cabrales, takes its name from a lovely wild mountain lily.

Queso Genestoso (KAY-soh-hay-nay-STO-soh); also called **Queso Xenestoso** (pronounced same as Genestoso): Named after its southern Asturian village of origin (just south of Cangas de Nar-

cea), it is a hard cylinder of unpasteurized cow's milk cheese that weighs under 2 pounds (less than 1 k). Its woven *esparto* grass molds make it appear to have been cinched by a belt, sort of gathered at the waist. The flavor is slightly strong and a little bit salty; the texture, chewy and smooth. Very rare.

Queso Genestoso

Queso Pasiego (KAY-soh-pah-see-AY-goh): A Cantabrian cheese, made in such minuscule quantities and so very fragile that you'll simply have to seek it out on a visit to Vega de Pas or any of the villages along the valley of the river Pas in Cantabria. A stunning cheese that is as flat as a pancake in the same fashion as the Paglia-style cheeses from Italy's Piedmont region. The white-beige crust bears the marks of the rush or reed used to separate the stacked cheeses during their open-air ripening and developing stages. It is much like perfect Brie, Camembert, or Pagliola—a lush, creamy, yellow, flowing interior sur-

Queso Pasiego

rounded by a thin, chewy, edible rind sprinkled with white *Penicillium* growth. The flat disks are irregular in shape and size; most are round and weigh about 1 pound (500 g). The flavor is mushroomy and garlicky and completely wonderful.

Queso Porrúa (KAY-soh-por-OOH-ah): Made in extreme eastern Asturias, across the Sierra del Cuera to the north and within sight of the sea, Porrúa is practically identical to Peñamellera (see page 338) in size and shape. In my experience it has always been presented in its fresh state, that is, crustless and white, mild (unlike Peñamellera), and with that lactic tang so noticeable in cheeses this young (from a few hours to a couple of days out of its mold). Though Porrúa is a full-fat cheese, it is exactly like Italian Ricotta—gelatinous in texture with a sweet and nutty flavor that lends itself to informality. Eat it with a spoon with all types of fruit as a breakfast cheese.

Queso del Tiétar (KAY-soh-dell-tee-AY-tar): Named for a valley in Avila, this is a 3- to 4-pound (1½ to 2 k), firm-textured disk of raw goat's milk cheese with an off-white interior and a pronounced nutty flavor. It is rarely found in the U.S. When in Spain, try it with olives and *fino* (sherry) or one of the big reds such as Pesquera or Rioja.

Queso de Tupí (KAY-soh-day-too-PEE): Found all over Catalonia, principally in the northern (Pyrenean) part, where it is

Queso de Tupí

sold in earthenware pots of varying shapes and sizes. Tupí is an ancient cheese, a potted mixture related to French versions such as *mattons* from Lorraine and *metton* and Cancoillotte, both from Franche-Comté. Shepherds once carried Tupí with them as they roved with their flocks to distant pastures far from home.

Whereas its French counterparts are made up of curdled whey and herbs or spices, Catalonia's Tupí is made using sheep's milk curd and a shredded sheep's milk cheese called Serrat (sair-ROTT), a hard cheese from the Catalan Pyrenees valley of Arán. (Serrat derives its name from the word *cerrado,* meaning "closed," referring to the cheese's closed, or compact, texture.) Rum or brandy is added to the mixture, which is left to ferment and ripen into a very strong, lactic, aromatic cheese. The flavor is similar to Italian Romano.

Today, Tupí is found rarely at market, though it remains a staple in the diet of those in this area whose lives are spent raising sheep or cattle. It is spread on bread as a high-energy snack to be enjoyed whenever hunger strikes. If you find it at farmers' markets in Catalonia, be sure to try it.

Queso de Urbiés (KAY-soh-day-oor-bee-ACE): A most singular Asturian cheese and the Spanish cheese least likely to show up on American counters. It is sold in an earthenware crock, and the uncovered top of the cheese is charmingly embossed with a wooden, hand-carved stamp that imprints the name of its particular maker—for example, Urbiés Dominica. It is actually a fermented spread, made from raw cow's milk curd that is ripened to a smooth, golden consistency, subsequently acquiring a penetrating sharpness that belies its buttery, mild appearance. There are similar fermented cheese spreads made on farms all over the north of Spain, but Queso de Urbiés predates them all. Practically all of it is produced for their own home use by farm families who want something extraordinarily flavorful and simple to go with lots of homemade bread and red wine as sustenance against the winter cold. The one family whose production of Queso de Urbiés is sold retail in Asturias is that of Dominica Fernandez. I recommend it.

Queso del Valle de Arán (KAY-soh-dell-VAH-yay-day-ah-RON): A raw cow's milk cheese that comes from an area, near Benasque, that is completely insulated by the Pyrenees. The valley of Arán is another community of Spanish Pyreneans much more influenced by French Gascon and Spanish Catalan culture and history than by purely Spanish influences. About 40 years ago, the Aranese made cattle, rather than sheep, their principal source of income. The cheese they make is notable for its unusual, slightly smoky flavor, a result of exterior washings with a mixture of vinegar, rum, and Armagnac—obviously French Gascon influenced, as I have known no other Spanish cheeses to undergo this felicitous treatment. This 3-pound (1½ k), irregularly shaped, roughish, yellowish-beige disk of cheese has a rather strong flavor and tastes of licorice. Though completely artisanal in production, you will find it at local farmers' markets.

Torta del Casar (TOR-tah-dell-kah-SAR): I predict this cheese, made in Extremadura and currently known only to cheese connoisseurs in Spain, will emerge over the next few years as one of the superstars of European cheeses. It resembles a perfectly ripened French and Swiss Vacherin Mont d'Or, except that it is made from unpasteurized sheep's milk, rather than cow's milk. Each buttery, nutty, full-flavored disk weighs from 3 to 4 pounds (1½ to 2 k), and is 2 to 3 inches thick, 8 inches in diameter. The bone-white interior is enclosed in a rough, buff- to russet-colored washed rind, the circumference of which is wrapped with a band of burlap-like cloth. It is presented at the table whole—with either the entire top rind removed or a portion of the center of the rind cut away—and the glistening, pudding-soft interior is scooped up and eaten with a spoon.

Torta del Casar

U.S.A.

The spectrum of America's cheese types is actually a global microcosm. In the beginning, this country of ours grew so fast there simply wasn't time for native cheeses to evolve. Since we had all come from somewhere else, the cheeses first made here were the ones our forebears were familiar with, the ones they had grown up eating in England, Holland, Germany, France, and elsewhere. As a consequence,

we have virtually no original cheese heritage; ours is a borrowed one. With the exception of Jack cheese, which originated in California, and Brick and Colby, which originated in Wisconsin, American cheeses are imitations or adaptations of the European originals.

Despite the recent—and very welcome—artisanal cheesemaking revolution now taking place across this country, for better or worse, the cheeses that Americans are most familiar with are the products of large factories, most of which are located in California, Wisconsin, Michigan, Ohio, Pennsylvania, and New York State. And as is often the case with so much in life, familiarity is a mixed blessing. Just because we are used to them in their all too

often bland, characterless, plastic-wrapped, mass-produced incarnations in the supermarket dairy case, just because we have all been eating these cheeses since we were lit-

The milk of Holsteins, the most common U.S. dairy cow, is rich and sweet.

In 1910, Tillamook cheesemakers in Oregon posed proudly with a power curd mill, one of the first pieces of modern machinery at the factory.

tle children, does not mean they are actually good things to eat.

The American food industry is geared toward mass production. It produces edibles on a vast scale, and cheese is no exception—the United States is the world's largest producer of cheese. But bigger is seldom better, or even good, and regardless of how delicious some of these cheeses may have been long ago, today most of them have become waxy, cheeselike dairy substances that fuel the food service and fast food industries. Profits rather than palatability and gastronomic pleasure are the corporate goals that stand between Americans and good cheese.

The American cheese types I outline in the first section of this chapter are primarily what you will encounter at the supermarket. I would be less than candid if I failed to point out that in most cases these are also the very same factory-made cheeses that I hope you steer clear of whenever possible.

But don't think that everything in the supermarket is less than it could be; several supermarket cheeses successfully straddle the line that separates the mass-produced from the artisanal. One of them is Auricchio brand Provolone (see page 431), a cheese that is identical to the Italian original. Another is Tillamook (a word the Native Americans of the Pacific Northwest used to describe a "land of many waters") Cheddar (see page 419) from Oregon, a cheese that ranks with the finest Cheddar made anywhere.

The second section of this chapter is a guide to some of the wonderful domestic artisanal—handmade—cheeses that cannot be found in supermarkets—not yet anyway. My fondest hope is that it will happen—and soon. Until then, practically all of the cheesemakers listed here will be happy to ship directly to you or direct you to the nearest cheese specialist they sell to. And I further urge you to seek out a dedicated cheesemonger near you.

AMERICAN CHEESE TYPES

American, or pasteurized process(ed) cheese, is the cheese that most of us, and indeed the world, identifies as the quintessential American cheese, so its name is surely apt. It begins as young, pasteurized cow's-milk Cheddar, and often ends up machine-sliced and plastic-separated into hamburger-friendly slices. In the process, the Cheddar is milled into shreds, then "cooked" with added dyes, emulsifiers, and assorted other "modern technology" dairy ingredients in order to achieve a smooth, mild (yet cheesy), orange or white, odorless, meltable, stable (long shelf life) commodity that virtually no American doesn't like. Its popularity is undeniable—over half of all cheese consumed in the U.S. is American Process(ed) Cheese.

CHEESE FOOD AND PROCESS CHEESE PRODUCTS

Other legal classifications for processed cheese (based on their quantity of natural cheese content) include "cheese food" and "pasteurized process cheese product." Cheese food (Cheez Whiz and other jarred products) and pasteurized process cheese products (Velveeta,

Although supermarket cheese selections have improved in recent years, many Americans still make a beeline for good old American Process(ed) Cheese.

for example) have a lower natural cheese content than American Cheese, which results in a longer shelf life and makes them a less "troublesome" cheese to stock.

COLD PACK CHEESE

"Cold pack cheese" is a mixture of natural cheese, usually Cheddar, and other ingredients that are blended without the use of heat. Spices and artificial flavorings such as "port wine" are often added to a Cheddar base. The Hickory Farms stores across the U.S. specialize in cold pack cheese, usually marketed in hinged earthenware crocks.

IMITATION CHEESE

"Imitation cheese" is essentially pasteurized process(ed) cheese from which butterfat has been removed in favor of nonfat milk or whey solids and water in order to create a "cheese" with a shelf life that is practically limitless, a food product that requires little or no refrigeration.

Imitation cheeses are identical in characteristics to substitute cheese (see page 368), but are not nutritionally equivalent. They are often touted as having healthful benefits because they are fat-free.

CHEESE SPREADS

Cheese spread may be homemade from fresh ingredients, or store-made as a means of utilizing otherwise useless cheese scraps or ends of cheese that have exceeded the "sell-by" date stamped on the label. Often, cream cheese is the medium and other cheese or cheeses are grated, shredded, or melted and blended in. Flavoring ingredients may be added as well, such as garlic, herbs, vegetables, "caviar," or horseradish.

Commercial, factory-made cheese spreads start with cream cheese and contain additional gums and emulsifiers as well as flavorings or other cheeses such as Roquefort or Cheddar. These commercial, pasteurized, process(ed) cheese spreads are similar to cheese food, but they have an even lower milk fat content and higher moisture content. Stabilizers are usually added to make the substance spreadable at room temperature. Fleur de Lait is a popular brand.

*Clifton Fadiman wrote that
cheese is milk's leap towards
immortality, which is witty,
but untrue. Velveeta is
immortal, but it is not
cheese; cheese is milk's leap
toward a life of its own.*

John Thorne,
Serious Pig

SUBSTITUTE CHEESE

"Substitute cheese" is manufactured by using various milk- or soy-based ingredients to produce a substance that can be reduced-fat or lactose-free and that supposedly has all of the "characteristics" of real cheese. Vegetable oil replaces the butterfat, and a milk- or soy-based protein solid called casein stands in for curd. The Swiss cheesemaking industry recently created and began exporting Fitt-Frei, a wheel-shaped, 3-inch-thick cheese, averaging 12 pounds (6 k), that has had all of its butterfat replaced with Simplesse, a trademarked fat substitute that is just a margarine made from vegetable oil. Like other products in this category, Fitt-Frei offers some cheese-like flavor, but is rubbery in texture. The purported benefit of substitute cheeses is that they are nutritionally equivalent to the natural or processed cheeses for which they substitute, but they are far removed from real cheese in terms of flavor and texture. Cheeses of this ilk usually identify themselves in fine print on the label or wrapper.

ASIAGO

In Veneto and Friuli, Italy, Asiago (ah-zee-AH-goh) has for centuries existed as a much-loved cheese available in a range of ages (and therefore varying degrees of firmness and flavor intensity). Originally made of unpasteurized sheep's milk, but made from unpasteurized cow's milk for the last 200 years, Italian Asiago is a cheese that has yet to find a universal following in the U.S. However, for at least 60 years, American-made Asiago has been very popular with Italian-Americans, as well as with anyone who simply enjoys a hard, sharp cheese. As with American Provolone and the Italian original, the differences between American Asiago and the Italian original are rather marked. Curiously, the American variety, even the lesser-aged, brown paraffin–rinded version, is considerably sharper than aged Italian Asiago. Also, the American cheese does not exhibit the Italian one's proliferation of tiny apertures, featuring instead a smooth, usually hole-less interior. It is my feeling that American Asiago is an immensely desirable and satisfying cheese, particularly the aged Vella and Auricchio brand versions. This cheese is rock hard and almost piercingly sharp, and of the three or four other American-made versions, I recommend these above all others. American Asiago is a delicious table cheese that is also suitable for grating.

BEL PAESE

Bel Paese (BEL-pie-EH-zeh), which means "beautiful country," was invented in Lombardy, Italy, by the Galbani cheese company in 1929 to appeal to those who preferred soft, mild, cow's milk cheese over the hard, sharp varieties that proliferated in Italy. Though an essentially undistinguished cheese, Bel Paese became internationally famous in a relatively short time. Today a version identical to the Italian-made Galbani brand is produced in New Jersey. The New Jersey factory offers the cheese plain or flavored with basil or sun-dried tomatoes. Each 3-inch thick wheel weighs 4½ pounds (2¼ k), though it is usually sold in supermarkets in plastic-wrapped wedges.

BLUE

American-made blue cheeses represent one of the brightest aspects of American cheese production. While Danish Blue (made from cow's milk) and French Roquefort (made from sheep's milk) together command more than three quarters of the American market for blue cheese, U.S. production is growing at an encouraging rate and should command a 50% share in the near future. Basic American blue cheese, most of which is made from pasteurized cow's milk, is a very decent and sharp, if one-dimensional, cheese. Its peppery flavor does its job in salad dressings, spreads and/or dips, or crumbled over salads or pasta. Production is centered primarily in Wisconsin, Iowa, and Illinois, where the cheese is usually down-sized from 6-pound (3 k) wheels and packaged in wedges, disks, or "crumbles" (for use in salads).

Wisconsin, the number-one cheese-producing state, makes more than 80% of all domestic blue cheese. "Cheesehead" souvenirs and local cheese are sold at this shop in Madison.

In addition to the usual American blues found in supermarkets, there are also three absolutely terrific artisanal American-made blues from small producers. Look for Dietrich's sheep's-milk Pur Chèvre Bleu from Illinois, cow's-milk Maytag Blue from Iowa, and Northland Sheep Dairy's Bergère Bleue from New York State, each of which is as memorable as any famous European blue.

BRICK

B rick is one of the few cheeses that originated in the U.S. This popular Midwestern cheese, practically unknown in other regions of America, was invented around 1877 by John Jossi, a Wisconsin cheesemaker of Swiss descent. Jossi discovered that if his curd for Limburger was adjusted to have a low moisture content and was then squeezed between two bricks, the resulting cheese would be almost as strong and aromatic as Limburger, but texturally much firmer. Like Cheddar, Brick ranges in flavor from very mild (young) to sharp and piquant (aged). Many people think of it as a cross between Limburger and Cheddar, but it is really more like Danish Tilsit than anything else. Brick is usually a pungent, tangy, semi-soft, rindless cheese dotted with numerous small holes. It is sold in vacuum-packed rectangular chunks that weigh about 1 pound (500 g). Most often it is eaten with crackers or in sandwiches, but Brick is occasionally an ingredient in macaroni and cheese.

BRIE

A few of France's largest cheese-making companies (Besnier, Bresse, Reny Picot) have built factories in the U.S. in order to meet the ever-growing demand for Brie and to take advantage of our high-quality milk, top-notch distribution channels, and currency fluctuations. The cheese they produce is identical to the pasteurized-milk, soft-ripened cheese these companies manufacture in France and Canada, and, it must be stressed, it bears little resemblance, except visually, to raw-milk, name-controlled Brie de Meaux or Coulommiers (see page 70), both of which have enormous flavor. This factory-made Brie is a very accessible, uncomplicated cheese, crafted for a wide audience.

CAMEMBERT

A merican Camembert is, for the most part, made by French-owned (Besnier, Reny Picot) factories in the Midwest. The cheeses are mild and tender, with a slightly mushroomy aroma. They are identical to their very commercial, French factory-made counterparts,

none of which bear much resemblance in terms of authentic flavor or rustic, ripened appearance to the famous name-controlled original—Véritable Camembert de Normandy. However, Blythedale Farm's Vermont Camembert and Brie (see page 422) are good examples of well-crafted, small-production American Camembert and Brie.

CHEDDAR

The "big cheese" of American cheeses is Cheddar, and much of the 9.1 pounds (4½ k) per year of it that Americans consume is quite good, though few examples are in the same league as the original Cheddar still made in some parts of the United Kingdom. Although cheddaring, the unique process of milling and piling curds prior to pressing that gives Cheddar its name, is the technique used in both countries, there are enormous differences between factory-made American versions and authentic English farmhouse Cheddar. Real Cheddar is cloth-wrapped and aged at a higher temperature than the mass-produced, plastic-wrapped American examples that cannot breathe as they ripen. American Cheddar, almost always made from pasteurized milk, is sort of one-dimensionally sharp, while real, raw-milk Cheddar offers infinitely more complexity and depth of flavor.

Most American-made Cheddar is organically dyed orange with annatto and is processed into a number of other types of cheeses, most of which are sold in supermarkets. These include cold pack varieties (usually with added flavorings), brands like Velveeta and Cheez Whiz, American Cheese, cheese food, and cheese spread. But there is also top-quality, aged Cheddar made in a number of states, including Oregon (Rogue River Valley Creamery, Tillamook County Creamery Association) and Vermont (Grafton Village, Shelburne Farms). Descriptions of these highly desirable American Cheddars can be found later in the chapter, in the "American Cheesemakers" section.

American Coon cheese, a Cheddar hybrid, is no longer produced much except in the Midwest.

A MOUNTAIN OF CHEESE

The United States is not only the world's largest *producer* of cheese, it is also the world's largest *importer* of cheese. In 1993, the most recent year for which there are statistics, 264,172,146 pounds (123,086 tons) of cheese were imported into the U.S.

COLBY

Colby is a cheese invented in Colby, Wisconsin, in the late nineteenth or early twentieth century. It is similar in flavor to Cheddar, as is its process, though Colby is softer and more open in texture (almost lacy), with a higher moisture content and subsequently shorter shelf life. While even the mildest examples of Cheddar require some aging, Colby does not. Mild and tender, Colby is used by Americans in many dishes that call for an all-purpose cheese. Longhorn is the designation for whole Colbys made in an elongated conical shape. These are usually cut into half-moons and wrapped in plastic for sale in super-markets and delis.

COTTAGE CHEESE, POT CHEESE, FARMER CHEESE

These are fresh, relatively bland cheeses made from pasteurized cow's milk, with varying regional differences, and are found in the dairy sections of supermarkets. Low in fat and very nutritious, they are excellent sources of calcium. Farmer cheese is curdless, grainy and firm enough to cut, whereas spoonable pot and cottage cheeses feature noticeable curds of variable size. These cheeses are usually consumed along with fresh fruits or vegetables, but also find their place in recipes for lasagna, dips, and desserts such as cheesecake as a replacement for higher-fat cream cheese.

CREAM CHEESE, NEUFCHATEL, CREAM CHEESE SPREAD

Cream cheese is perhaps best known as a branded dairy product called Philadelphia, or just "Philly." Made from pasteurized whole cow's milk with extra cream added, it is used primarily as a spread or a cooking ingredient (especially in cheesecake and dips). In the Northeast and Midwest, cream cheese is marketed as Neufchâtel, for no particular reason other than it has a nice ring to it; the cheese bears no resemblance to the soft-ripened Neufchâtel cheese from Normandy, France (see page 54). Practically all of the cream cheese on the market today contains flavorless organic thickeners such as carrageenan, xanthan, or guar gums. Reduced-fat cream cheeses, which have all but commandeered the entire market, have been whipped to inflate them with air. There are a few traditional cream cheese producers left, in New York (Ben's Fresh Cream Cheese in New York City) and California (Pauly brand Gina Marie Cream Cheese in San Francisco), who make fresh, gum-free cream cheese, a product with a nuttier flavor and a far more elegant texture than supermarket versions.

Rondelé and Alouette are brand-name cheese spreads—herb- or pepper-flavored spreads with a white, bland, cream cheese base—that have less textural heft than the Philadelphia brand flavored cream cheeses. These lighter, frothier cheeses are American versions of Boursin, a famous brand of flavored French cream cheese. All such spreads are informal, highly commercial, very popular, and nothing that any cheese enthusiast should treat very seriously.

EDAM

As is also true of Gouda, considerable quantities of factory-made Edam are produced in the U.S., principally in Wisconsin and New York State. Edam is made from pasteurized partially skimmed cow's milk and is sold in traditional red paraffin–coated oblong spheres, oval-shaped balls, and 6-pound (3 k) loaves. The cheese is mild and slightly salty, with a pronounced finishing tang, and is virtually indiscernible from the rather blah Dutch original.

FETA

Most American-made Feta is from Wisconsin, where it is made from cow's milk instead of sheep's milk. The result is remarkably similar to Greek Feta, though less flavorful. Some very small artisanal American producers make Feta from sheep's and goat's milk. If you can find these cheeses, their quality will be excellent.

GOAT CHEESE (CHEVRE)

In the past decade, widespread enthusiasm for American goat's-milk cheese made in the French tradition (*fromage de chèvre*), has created a considerable growth industry for this now-fashionable food. While the overwhelming majority of its production is cottage-industry size, ever increasing quantities are being turned out by several large U.S. concerns in Wisconsin and Michigan, using imported frozen curd from Israel. Very little of any of the goat's-milk cheese made in the U.S., whether artisanal or commercial, is marketed as aged or ripened. Most is sold as "fresh" chèvre because it is widely believed, though in my opinion erroneously, that American palates are too timid for the more pronounced flavor of the aged type. Some fine cheesemakers such as Capriole, Inc., Coach Farm, Belle Chèvre, and Westfield Farm stress the versatility of fresh, creamy, mild, spreadable, unripened chèvre. Much of the fresh chèvre made in the U.S. has added flavorings—herbs, spices, even edible flowers—an attempt to make its blandness more compelling. Makers of chèvre exist in nearly every state. Most are members of the American Cheese Society and/or The American Dairy Goat Association, both of which have been instrumental in promoting artisanal American goat's-milk cheeses and products.

GORGONZOLA

While completely acceptable as a blue cheese, domestic Gorgonzola (Wisconsin) has little, in terms of flavor and texture, in common with Italian Gorgonzola (Lombardy). The U.S.-made version is usually a crumbly, white cheese with blue striations, while the real thing is a soft-textured, beige cheese with profuse greenish-blue striations. As for flavor—the difference is readily apparent: Domestic Gorgonzola is pleasantly sharp and peppery, while the best Italian Gorgonzola has more nuance, more spice, and a considerably more powerful aroma. In a nutshell, domestic Gorgonzola is an acceptable, albeit rather ordinary cheese (with the exception of Auricchio's very good BelGioioso brand), while the Italian original is a majestic example of the cheesemakers' art.

GOUDA

American examples of this famous Dutch cow's-milk cheese are made in Wisconsin and New York and are virtually identical to the original, a relatively unexciting, smooth-textured cheese that is mellow and a bit salty. Aside from the fact that Gouda is made in thick, round-edged wheels, weighing about 8 pounds (4 k), Gouda and Edam are nearly identical in terms of recipe, flavor, and texture. Both cheeses are

Hidden under bright red paraffin—U.S.-made gouda.

encased in a protective red paraffin coating.

HAVARTI

This ever-popular, mild, and versatile Danish sandwich and omelet cheese has only recently (over the past decade) been copied and made by several American cheesemakers with large-scale facilities in Wisconsin and New York State. The domestic version is virtually indistinguishable from the Danish original, a mild-flavored, rindless cow's-milk cheese with tiny "eyes." Like the Danish original, it is made in 9-pound (4½k) loaves about the size of a loaf of sandwich bread. Made with and without added flavorings such as caraway, dill, herbs, and jalapeño peppers, it is also sold in a reduced-fat version.

JACK CHEESE

Also Called Monterey Jack, Sonoma Jack, or Jack

This extremely popular American original was created by a Scotsman named David Jacks, near Monterey, California, in the 1890s. Made of pasteurized cow's milk, it is very soft, white, and gentle, with an acidic tang. Authentic Jack, which ripens for only about a week, is a curved-edge, practically rindless, 8- to 10-pound (4 to 5 k) round. Wisconsin Jack, made in 40-pound (20 k) blocks, is firmer and does not have the tiny eye structure found in authentic California Jack. Chopped jalapeño peppers are often added to the curd during the cheesemaking process. Two of the finest examples of Monterey Jack are the California-based Vella family's Bear Flag brand (see page 397), and the Viviani family's Sonoma Jack (see page 396). Teleme (see page 383), another California-made cheese, is similar to Jack.

A related cheese, Dry Jack, is made by aging Monterey Jack for seven to ten months. Hard, pale yellow, and with a sharp, nutty flavor, Dry Jack can be used as an eating and grating cheese.

LIEDERKRANZ

Produced for the past 75 years in a factory in Van Weit, Ohio, Liederkranz was "invented" around 1892 by Emil Frey. He experimented with recipes for years until the Manhattan delicatessen-owner who had commissioned his efforts accepted his creation as a much-desired exact replica of German Schlosskäse—a washed-rind cow's-milk cheese that is sold in a ½-pound (250 g), foil-wrapped brick. It is creamy, slightly salty, and strong, with a detectable fried-egg taste and pronounced aroma. Liederkranz was named for a German-American choral group in Yorkville, a once predominantly German neighborhood on Manhattan's Upper East Side. The group assumed the role of the cheese's largest consumer, greatest admirer, and most ardent promoter. Today, Liederkranz is greatly underappreciated, a circumstance you might say is inevitable since it is virtually unavailable in most parts of the country. Along with the equally smelly and hard-to-find Limburger, Liederkranz is something of an anachronism.

LIMBURGER

This cousin of Liederkranz originated in Belgium, near Liège. Great quantities, though, have long been produced in Bavaria—to the extent that for all intents and purposes, it is now considered a German cheese. Today, American Limburger is made in Wisconsin, though overall production of this once-popular beer cheese has waned considerably over the last few decades. Still it remains ever popular and ever aromatic in the German enclaves of the Midwest and Northeast U.S. Limburger produced domestically from pasteurized cow's milk is undistinguishable from the German version of the Belgian original, and shares its configuration, an 8-ounce (250 g) rectangular block. It is the several rind-washings in brine that account for Limburger's notoriously powerful smell. It is a very flavorful cheese, very soft and a bit salty. Limburger's powerful odor has rendered this delicious cheese a laughingstock, except among those few brave Americans who have been savoring it for years. It can be found in supermarkets—mostly in areas settled by Germans, such as upper New York State, Pennsylvania, Ohio, Michigan, Illinois, Wisconsin, and Minnesota. Beware overripeness— evidenced by a wrinkled foil-wrap in which the cheese has obviously shrunken; its rind will be grayish. Look for a moist, buff-colored rind that is neither slimy nor dry. The best way to store this odoriferous cheese as it ripens is in the refrigerator in a jar with a tightly closed screw cap.

MASCARPONE

E ssentially full-fat cream that has been acidulated to release all of its moisture, Mascarpone made in the U.S. is every bit as delicious as that from Italy. In fact, Mascarpone is such an uncomplicated,

straightforward product that even I can't taste the difference between U.S.-made examples and the Italian original. Usually packed in 4- or 8-ounce (125 or 250 g) plastic containers or sold by weight from 5-pound (2½ k) tubs, Mascarpone has reached an enormous American audience since I brought the Italian original to the U.S. back in 1979. Here and in Italy, it is made from pasteurized cow's-milk cream, and once opened should be used within a few days. Mascarpone can be frozen but will separate somewhat, even if thawed at low temperatures (For more about Mascarpone, see page 215.)

THE LAST LIMBURGER IN AMERICA

V irtually all Limburger produced in the U.S. today is made at the Chalet Cheese Co-op located near the village of Monroe, Wisconsin. Established in 1885, the co-op transforms the milk provided by its 35 dairy-farm members into approximately a million pounds of cheese annually. The best way to eat this powerful cheese is to pair it with a thick slice of onion, tuck it between slices of rye or dark bread, and wash it down with an icy cold beer.

MOZZARELLA

Also Called "Pizza Cheese"

T he most commonly sold American Mozzarella is stocked in the dairy section of supermarkets. It is very different in terms of taste, texture, and manufacture from fresh, handmade Italian Mozzarella. The American version is much denser, drier, less perishable, and has neither the nutty, milky-sweet flavor of the Italian cheese, nor its tenderness and springy texture. While the Italian original may be made from cow's milk or water buffalo milk (Mozzarella *di bufala*), the American one is always made from

AND IN SECOND PLACE

Mozzarella is second only to Cheddar in terms of per capita consumption in the U.S.

cow's milk. Fresh Italian Mozzarella is often eaten as a table cheese but most Americans ignore this virtue of Mozzarella, preferring to utilize it melted, chiefly for pizza, lasagna, and the like. Indeed, mass-produced American Mozzarella fuels the food service industry to the tune of well over a billion dollars each year, a figure that is on the increase.

On the bright side, however, and outside of the supermarkets, there are pockets of artisanal Mozzarella production in America. For example, excellent American-made Mozzarella can be found in small Italian specialty food shops located in the major urban areas of the Northeast and West where there are significant concentrations of Italian-Americans. These shops, which purchase cow's-milk curd in 40-pound (20 k), plastic-wrapped bundles, use

it to make fresh, hand-pulled Mozzarella daily. This is real Mozzarella, every bit as splendid as the Italian-made kind—truly delicious. And if all you've ever known is the supermarket variety, with its supernaturally long shelf life, you're in for a treat. In New York City, for instance, fresh, handmade Mozzarella, the kind that is best eaten within a day or two of its creation, is a staple whose ready availability is taken for granted by thousands of New Yorkers, each of whom has a favorite source—Joe's Dairy on Sullivan Street, Alleva Dairy on Delancey Street in Little Italy, and Todaro Brothers in Kip's Bay. Philadelphia residents seek out Claudio's Mozzarella; in Boston a favorite brand is Gigi Mozzarella; Dallas residents look for examples from The Mozzarella Company, and in the San Francisco area residents check their neighborhood stores for the Mozzarella Fresca brand.

MUENSTER

Mild, soft, white, rindless (a tasteless sprinkling of sweet paprika coats the exterior), and atypically odorless, American-made Muenster is meant to echo the Danish and German versions of this French original. Danish and German Munsters—without an "e"—are very different (blander) from the French one, whose hallmarks are a huge, beefy, nutty flavor and a wonderfully smelly rind. To further confuse

HOW HIGH WILL IT BOUNCE?

U.S. shoppers spend more than $3 billion annually on Mozzarella. The reason is the pizza industry, and what they're calling Mozzarella is a machine-folded, -bent, -kneaded, -spindled, -mutilated curd that is supposed to result in the *pasta filata* cheese we know as Mozzarella. But after this processing, what's left is an absolutely characterless piece of white rubber. To begin with, this cheese is made

from "dead" milk (meaning over-pasteurized cow's milk, which is turned into curd, then kneaded and pulled by a stainless-steel machine until all of the butterfat is driven out and what's left is a rubbery "cheese" that can be held under refrigeration for a long time. Why not? There's little in it to spoil. Finally it is shredded or sliced for the pizza industry.

matters, the American version is different from all three European styles. While Danish and German Munsters are typically round, the domestic cheese is usually formed into a loaf shape in order to adapt more easily to its sandwich destination. While the Danish and German varieties are not nearly as pronounced in flavor as the French original they are nevertheless considerably more flavorful than American Muenster, a cheese whose utter mildness and smooth, soft texture are its greatest appeal. American Muenster melts readily, and legions of American home cooks use it in recipes that call for cheese with good melting capabilities.

PARMESAN

I am considerably less than enthusiastic about American versions of Italy's venerable Parmigiano-Reggiano because of my complete adoration for the original, and because the American examples are so bland. Nonetheless, Auricchio, one of Italy's premier cheesemakers, also has facilities in Wisconsin (see page 431), and its U.S.-made Parmesan won first prize in 1993 at an international competition, so perhaps my opinions are too traditionalist. Most American Parmesan is made in Wisconsin, though consid-

DON'T EVEN THINK ABOUT IT

The American Parmesan most of us were raised sprinkling over Mom's spaghetti and meatballs still lurks on supermarket shelves in those ubiquitous cylindrical containers with the holes in the top. It is cheese in only the loosest sense of the word, having been pulverized, dried, blended with other cheeses, and treated with an anti-caking agent that discourages lumps. It has a  nearly limitless shelf life and is a far cry from Parmigiano-Reggiano or Grana Padano, which are artisanal Italian cheeses. Authentic Italian Parmesan was created over centuries and even the most carefully made domestic versions don't come close to its splendor. To choose an American Parmesan over the real thing from Italy is really an exercise in gastronomic futility.

erable quantities also come from New York State. The 15-pound (7½ k) American cheeses, which are usually coated with paraffin, are much smaller than the Italian originals, which weigh 53 to 88 pounds (26½ to 44 k).

PROVOLONE

Although authentic, firm, sharp, Italian-style Provolone has been made in the U.S. since 1979 by Italy-based Auricchio, the world's largest producer of Provolone, at its factories in Wisconsin, at least a generation of Americans have been raised on a Provolone that is quite different from the Italian original. American Provolone is featured in delis and supermarkets only as a 9- to 12-pound (4½ to 6 k) tube-shaped cheese meant to be sliced for sandwiches. Beige in color, pliant, and quite mild in flavor, it resembles Mozzarella much more than true Italian Provolone. The enormous differences between these two versions of a cheese sharing the same name is in keeping with the American preference for mild rather than forcefully flavored cheeses.

RICOTTA

American Ricotta is made from whole or partially skimmed cow's milk, rather than from the sheep's-milk whey used to make the Italian original (for more about Ital-

Like the Italian original, domestic Provolone is made in a variety of sizes and shapes. These cheeses will bear the indentation marks of the cord or rope from which they were suspended during the curing or ripening process.

ian Ricotta, see page 214). It is much blander, sweeter, moister, smoother, and creamier. The point here is that once you have tasted authentic Italian ricotta (whether made from sheep's milk, water buffalo milk, or goat's milk), American Ricotta reveals itself to be significantly lacking the sweet, nutty flavor and drier, more substantial texture of the sheep's-milk original. American-made Ricotta is sold in plastic tubs marked with a freshness expiration date; Italian-made Ricotta will be enclosed in thick paper, occasionally overwrapped with plastic wrap.

ROMANO

R omano, justly famous and long a staple foodstuff in Italian cuisine, and indeed across the world, is a rock-hard, super-sharp sheep's-milk cheese used mainly for grating over pasta. But the American version, also hard and used mainly for grating, is the Elvis impersonator of cheeses. Made from cow's milk, not sheep's, it looks sort of like Italian Pecorino Romano, but it certainly doesn't taste the same. The flavor is entirely different, albeit sharp, but definitely not true Romano-sharp. Authentic Italian Romano has an aggressive flavor that unmistakably reveals it is an aged sheep's-milk cheese. Aged cow's-milk cheeses, made from recipes similar to Romano's, are not nearly so pungent or aromatic. That said, American Romano is generally a well-crafted, perfectly acceptable grating cheese for those who cannot find imported Romano, or who simply prefer the domestic version's less acrid flavor. As is also the case with American Parmesan, supermarkets carry cylindrical containers of dried, pre-grated Romano that contains added salt

THE AMERICAN CHEESE SOCIETY

Founded by a small group of East Coast cheesemakers in the early 1970s, the American Cheese Society (ACS) is a grassroots organization that strives to foster communications between cheesemakers, cheese sellers, and cheese enthusiasts. Dedicated to celebrating and perpetuating fine farmstead and specialty American cheeses, the society holds an annual conference each August that features panels, workshops, tastings, and a comprehensive competition in which cheeses from across America are evaluated by an international panel of judges. In contrast to many other American and European competitions, this one takes into consideration both the aesthetic *and* technical aspects of the competing cheeses, which are entered in a wide range of categories based on milk type (cow, goat, etc.) and "recipe." A number of the artisanal cheeses mentioned in the primer have won awards at this important annual judging. For more information, I urge you to contact: The American Cheese Society, 1523 Judah Street, San Francisco, California 94122; phone (415) 661-3844.

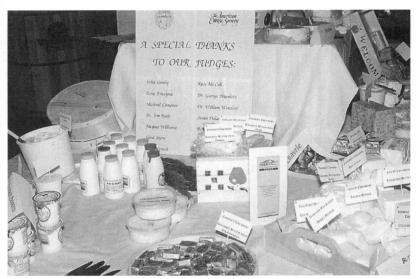

In addition to artisanal cheeses, butter and yogurt are also evaluated at the American Cheese Society's yearly conference. The judging panel, made up of cheesemakers and dairy scientists, awards points for aroma, taste, texture, and overall appearance.

and an anti-caking ingredient to ensure limitless shelf life. This is not Romano, this is not cheese, this is cheesy sawdust that should be avoided at all costs.

STRING CHEESE

Rope or Braided Cheese; Also Called Armenian-Style String Cheese

This is essentially Mozzarella that has been pulled into strands, braided, and encased in plastic. It is a "fun" cheese that counts children as its primary consumers and fans. Often black sesame or caraway seeds have been sparingly insinuated into the cheese, which usually comes in 8-ounce (250 g) packages.

SWISS- OR EMMENTAL- STYLE

Very decent Swiss-type or Emmental-style cheese is made in the U.S., mostly in Wisconsin and New York State. Dotted with cherry-to walnut-size holes, its flavor is milder and sweeter than Swiss-made versions. Rindless, it is cut down from large blocks and shipped in loaves ready to be machine sliced for sandwiches at supermarket delis. Baby Swiss, thickish round wheels with paraffined rinds, can be found in most supermarket cheese cases. American Swiss/Emmental cheese offers shoppers great value, fetching about half the price of imported Swiss or French Emmental. American Swiss/Emmental is made from pasteurized, partially skimmed cow's milk, and while very popular in the U.S., it is more expensive than so-called Swiss cheeses imported from Finland, Austria, Germany, Hungary, and New Zealand, which are often offered at lower prices.

TELEME

This California cheese has Greece as its inspiration, having first been made by Greek immigrants in that state more than a century ago. It is based on a Cretan goat cheese called Touloumi, but it is made from cow's milk. Similar to Monterey Jack (see page 375), Teleme (TELL-uh-me) is even softer and its fresh tanginess becomes deeper and more nut-like as it ages. The finest example of this American treasure, made by the Peluso family of Los Banos, California, features a novel rice flour–dusted rind. Each 3- to 4-inch-thick, square loaf weighs about 10 pounds (5 k).

AMERICAN TREASURES: THE BEST AMERICAN CHEESES

In today's burgeoning parade of artisanal American cheeses, there are some that rise head and shoulders above the rest, brilliantly made cheeses with such unique flavor and texture that they will take your breath away. Some of these cheeses are derivative of classic European ones; others are completely unique American originals. Each is an American Treasure and is identified in the text by a star symbol.

What these cheeses represent and reflect is enlightenment, both on the part of the cheesemaker and the consumer. They are delicious proof that the business of food need not be controlled by faceless corporate entities. Fine cheese requires a communion between the seasons, the animals, soil and water, the farm and the family. The cheeses I consider American Treasures are the result of such a communion, elevated to the highest level by the creativity and hard work of their makers. Some of the cheesemakers are carrying on hallowed family traditions, making the same cheeses produced by their fathers and grandfathers. Others are building new traditions. And, miraculously, several larger cheesemaking concerns, like Auricchio Cheese, Inc., in Wisconsin and Maytag Dairy Farms in Iowa,

are making American Treasure cheeses of great integrity on a large scale. What these artisans and companies share is a passionate connection to their art and a love of good things to eat combined with the extraordinary levels of patience, dedication, and expertise that transform milk into a miracle of flavor.

Auricchio Provolone, BelGioioso Gorgonzola
Errico Auricchio
BelGioioso/Auricchio Cheese, Inc.
Denmark, Wisconsin

Brier Run Farm Aged Chèvre, Fromage Blanc
Greg and Verena Sava
Brier Run Farm
Birch River, West Virginia

Capriole Banon, Mont St. Francis, Old Kentucky Tomme, Wabash Cannonball
Judy Schad
Capriole, Inc.
Greenville, Indiana

Coach Farm Green Peppercorn Goat Cheese Pyramids
Miles, Lillian, and Susan Cahn
Coach Farm
Pine Plains, New York

Crowley Cheese
Kent Smith
Crowley Cheese Company
Healdville, Vermont

Cypress Grove Aged Chèvre
Mary Keehn
Cypress Grove Chèvre
McKinleyville, California

Dietrich's Pur Chèvre Blu
Tom Dietrich
Dietrich's Dairy
Fowler, Illinois

Fantôme Boulot
Anne Topham
Fantôme Farm
Ridgeway, Wisconsin

**Fromagerie Belle Chèvre
Fromage Blanc, Chèvre de
Provence**
Elizabeth Parnell
Fromagerie Belle Chèvre
Elkmont, Alabama

**Grafton Village Classic Reserve
Vermont Cheddar**
Scott Fletcher
Grafton Village Cheese Company
Grafton, Vermont

**Hollow Road Farms Soft-Ripened
Sheep's-Milk Cheese, Ricotta**
Joan Snyder and Ken Klienpeter
Hollow Road Farms
Stuyvesant, New York

Hubbardston Blue, Classic Blue
Bob and Letitia Kilmoyer
Westfield Farm
Hubbardston, Massachusetts

**Laura Chenel's Aged
California Chèvre**
Laura Chenel
Laura Chenel's Chèvre, Inc.
Sonoma, California

**Major Farm Vermont
Shepherd Cheese**
Cynthia and David Major
Major Farm
Putney, Vermont

Maytag Blue
Jim Stevens
Maytag Dairy Farms
Newton, Iowa

Mossholder Cheese
The Mossholder family
Mossholder Farm
Appleton, Wisconsin

Peluso's Tomales Bay Teleme
Franklin Peluso
Peluso Cheese, Inc.
Los Baños, California

**Rollingstone Idaho Goatster,
Bleu Agé Chèvre**
Karen and Chuck Evans
Parma, Idaho

**Sally Jackson's Aged
Sheep's-Milk and
Goat's-Milk Cheeses**
Sally and Roger Jackson
Sally Jackson Cheeses
Oroville, Washington

**Shelburne Farms Raw-Milk
Farmhouse Cheddar**
Mariano Gonzales
Shelburne Farms
Shelburne, Vermont

Vella's Bear Flag Dry Jack
Ignazio Vella
Vella Cheese Company
of California, Inc.
Sonoma, California

**Wieninger's Raw-Milk Aged
Goat Cheese**
Sally and Ted Wieninger
Wieninger's Goat Products
Hunter, New York

**Yerba Santa Alpine
Shepherd's Cheese**
Chris and Jan Twohy
Yerba Santa Goat Dairy
Lakeport, California

AMERICAN CHEESEMAKERS

My genuine enthusiasm for many of the American artisanal cheeses that follow is not mere jingoism. Regardless of origin, these cheeses are brilliant. And though today interest in them is growing, their brilliance is not yet noticed by enough of us. But I am encouraged by signs that fine American cheeses are beginning to emerge and assume their rightful status as American Treasures (see box page 384) in much the way that fine American wines did several decades ago.

I have purposefully excluded a number of companies whose operations must be described as factories and their cheeses as mass-produced, with few redeeming qualities. At the same time, I am sure I've failed to include more than one artisan completely deserving of praise. For this I apologize in

advance my only excuse being that significant American cheesemaking has entered a period of rebirth and renewal at a pace that makes it nearly impossible to keep up. And I'm in the thick of it! Also, bear in mind that while every effort has been made to ensure this list of cheesemakers is up-to-date, most of the firms are small, very hands on operations subject to the usual vagaries of any small business. That said, practically all of these cheesemakers will ship to you, or if they can't, they'll tell you where you can obtain their cheese in your area.

While some of the cheesemakers that follow are old-timers—Grafton (Grafton Village Cheddar), Maytag (Maytag Blue), Peluso (Teleme), and Vella (Bear Flag Dry Jack)—most are newer ones whose cheeses are enjoying success at shops all over the country. The reason for this is simple—American artisanal cheeses are reaching an ever-increasing audience that cares about flavor. The fact is that many types of imported cheeses are boring, bland, and lifeless, and these artisan-made American ones are anything but. Americans who care deeply about what they eat and drink are being won over to the realization that there are now some very serious cheeses being made right here at home. I urge you to give this chapter a close look—use it as a field guide for your exploration of the best of both new and classic American-made cheeses. Seek them out at your local cheese shop or specialty food store or place an order with the cheesemaker. Your curiosity will be well rewarded.

Alabama

FROMAGERIE BELLE ☆
CHEVRE
**Leone Asbury and
Elizabeth Parnell**

26910 Bethel Road
Elkmont, Alabama 35620
(205) 423-2238; (800) 735-2238

Goat's-milk cheeses

This north Alabama company makes excellent fresh chèvre in *bûches* (logs), fromage blanc, and stunningly delicious Chèvre de Provence, which are little 2-ounce (60 g) disks of chèvre, marinated in olive oil and herbs and packed two to a jar. Liz Parnell's cheeses are highly commendable and I can say without hesitation that her fromage blanc and Chèvre de Provence are American Treasures (see her pasta recipe on page 389). They have also won multiple awards from the American Dairy Goat Association and the American Cheese Society. In fact, both cheeses walked off with first

place honors at 1994 and 1995 American Cheese Society judgings. Liz's fromage blanc, which freezes well, is not just a tastier low-fat substitute for sour cream or cream cheese, it's a magnificent addition to lasagna or sautéed greens. At my home, we also use it crumbled into salads, tossed with pasta, spread on bagels, or served with fresh fruit.

favorite is a creamy invention they call Elberta, which is a cross between French Munster and Italian Bel Paese. They also make heart-shaped fresh goat's-milk cheeses (available from February to October) and a goat's milk version of Gouda. I have a particular fondness for their efforts because they live just up the road from my mom and dad, who live nearby in Gulf Shores.

SWEET HOME FARMS
Alyce Birchenough and Doug Wolbert

27107 Schoen Road
Elberta, Alabama 36530
(334) 986-5663

Cow's-milk cheeses, fresh and aged goat's-milk cheeses

To my knowledge, Alyce and her husband Doug run the only organic farmstead cheese operation in Alabama. Since 1986, Alyce and Doug have made and sold almost 12,000 pounds (6,000 k) of raw-milk cheese right on the farm. All the milk comes from their own Guernsey cattle and Nubian goats. They use no pesticides or chemical fertilizers on the pastures or crops they grow to feed the herds.

All of Sweet Home's output—Swiss, Jack, Blue, Edam, Gouda, Cajun Spice Gouda, cow's-milk "Romano," cottage cheese, cream cheese, Mascarpone, Montabella, Mozzarella, Peppered Asiago, cheese fudge, and butter—is first class. My

California

BULK FARMS/OAKDALE
**Cheese and Specialities
Walter and Lenneke Bulk**

10040 Highway 120
Oakdale, California 95361
(209) 848-3139

Gouda, Edam, quark

Bulk Farms is the home of the Bulks, fourth-generation Dutch cheesemakers who for the past 15 years have specialized in Gouda and Edam cheeses, made using starter that comes directly from the Netherlands. Their Gouda is available plain, with cumin (like Leyden) or garlic. Some of their Gouda is aged, and although it's always in short supply, it is wonderful. The Bulks also make quark and European-style yogurt. All of their products are for sale at the small retail store on their four-acre farm.

OUR FAVORITE PASTA WITH SPINACH AND FROMAGE BLANC

Makes 4 servings

2 bunches (1¼ to 1½ pounds; 625 to 750 g) fresh spinach
4 tablespoons extra-virgin olive oil
1 medium onion, chopped
2 to 3 cloves garlic, minced
1 pound (500 g) pasta, such as fusilli, conchiglie, rotelle, or radiatore, cooked al dente and drained
1 pound (500 g) fromage blanc
8 ounces (250 g) freshly grated Parmigiano-Reggiano
Crusty bread

1. Stem the spinach, wash the leaves thoroughly, and set aside to drain.

2 Heat the olive oil in a large skillet or stockpot over medium-high heat. Add the onion and garlic and sauté until the onion is translucent, 2 minutes. Add half the spinach, using a wooden spoon to push it down into the pot, and let it wilt for about 10 seconds before adding the second batch. Stir the spinach until wilted but still bright green, 2 to 3 minutes.

3. To serve, divide the cooked pasta among 4 plates. Top each serving with spinach, then the fromage blanc. Build each serving so it resembles a snow-topped mountain. Sprinkle with grated Parmigiano-Reggiano. Serve with plenty of hot, crusty bread.

CYPRESS GROVE CHEVRE
Mary Keehn

4600 Dows Prairie Road
McKinleyville, California 95521
(707) 839-3168; fax (707) 839-2322

Fresh and aged goat's-milk cheeses

I first met Mary Keehn when I was a judge at an American Dairy Goat Product Association (ADGPA) cheese competition. The association, of which Mary is past chair, is

an extraordinarily tight-knit, ardent, and loyal organization of wonderful people, totally devoted to raising goats and making the most of their milk. Mary, a legend within the group, certainly does both. Her farm, situated within the far north coastal redwood area near the Oregon border, is an absolute paradise.

Cypress Grove's cheeses, which are all excellent, include fresh and aged chèvre, fromage blanc, goat's-milk Cheddar, and Feta. Mary's talent for bringing her traditional French-style chèvres to middle age is what distinguishes her cheeses from the plethora of fresh chèvre that is so ubiquitous these days. And it is what makes them American Treasures. Her disks, pyramids, and logs reach cheese counters wrapped in porous waxed paper that allows them to breathe and continue to develop. At this delectable middle age, these chèvres are flaky and firm, yet moist and mouthwateringly piquant with an edible rind. Their nutty, spicy flavor has earned my rapt attention.

Also excellent is Fromage à Trois, a cheese torta she and fellow ADGPA member Judy Schad, of Capriole, Inc., in Indiana (see page

401), created together and each makes on her respective farm. It is a layered blend of fresh goat cheese partnered with basil pesto, pine nuts, and sun-dried tomatoes.

LAURA CHENEL'S CHEVRE, INC.
Laura Chenel

4310 Fremont Drive
Sonoma, California 95476
(707) 996-4477; fax (707) 996-1816

Fresh and aged goat's-milk cheeses

Laura Chenel is a pioneer in the art of American-made goat's-milk cheeses in the French style, having begun commercial production back in 1981. A desire to create a self-sufficient, back-to-the-land life had prompted the purchase of her first goats in the 1970s, and as is so often the case, their abundant milk inspired her first small-scale cheesemaking efforts. Laura's growing interest in developing the finest-tasting cheese prompted her to spend four months in France living with farm families in various regions to learn the secrets of chèvre-making. Today her 9-ounce (270 g) classic *taupinières* and diminutive 3-ounce (90 g) *crottins* are as perfect as goat's-milk cheese can be. Her cheeses are made with hand-ladled curd, but what sets Laura apart from so many cheesemakers is that she possesses the taste and skill to age her cheeses to that mystical, imprecise point where they take on the mantle of magic that separates rather banal fresh cheeses from the infinitely more memorable aged ones.

SADIE KENDALL'S CREME FRAICHE CORN CHOWDER

Makes 4 servings

For centuries crème fraîche, acidulated (thickened) cow's-milk cream that has been allowed to "incubate" briefly until it achieves a velvety thickness, was a dairy farm staple throughout France, principally in Normandy and Brittany. Crème fraîche is so much a part of Norman life that it is expected to exude personality, just like cheese. Sadie Kendall, a former cheesemaker, now devotes her skill to making excellent Normandy-style crème fraîche that is indescribably nutty and tangy with a lactic sweetness that begs to be a part of any recipe that simply calls for cream. Her Kendall Farms crème fraîche is distributed throughout California, where the most discriminating chefs use it. It adds velvety body to sauces, makes a superb topping for fruits and pastries, and stars in each of the nearly 200 recipes in Sadie's book, *The Crème Fraîche Cookbook* (262 pages; $12, plus shipping): Kendall Farms, Box 686, Atascadero, California 93423; (805) 466-7252.

1 slice smoked bacon, cut into 1-inch pieces
½ medium onion, finely diced
1 medium potato, peeled and finely diced

2 cans (16 ounces; 500 g each) niblet corn
4 cups (1 l) chicken stock
½ cup (120 ml) milk
1 tablespoon dried dill
1 cup (¼ l) crème fraîche
4 ounces (125 g) fresh goat cheese
Sourdough bread, sliced and toasted

1. In a medium-size saucepan render the fat from the bacon over medium-high heat. When the bacon is golden and crisp, remove it from the pan. Drain on a paper towel; set aside.

2. Add the chopped onion and potato to the bacon fat and sauté over medium-high heat until the onion turns translucent, 2 to 3 minutes. Stir in the corn along with its liquid. Add the chicken stock. Reduce the heat to medium and simmer, covered, stirring occasionally, until the potatoes are nearly soft, 10 minutes. Stir in the milk and dill and cook for 5 minutes, taking care not to let the chowder boil. Add the crème fraîche, 1 tablespoon at a time, stirring well after each addition.

3. Pour the chowder into 4 warmed soup bowls. Garnish with the bacon and walnut-size pieces of fresh goat cheese. Serve with sourdough toast.

Thin-rinded, paper-wrapped (then swathed in cellophane), Laura's chèvres are as close to the French originals as you will find—flaky, barely moist, bone-white, and extraordinarily delicious.

In the early days of her business, Laura shipped her then hard-to-find chèvres to customers direct from her cheesemaking facility. These days her popular chèvres, which like all soft cheeses are not really

QUESO FRESCO AND OTHER MEXICAN CHEESES

A s Mexican and Latin cuisines have grown in popularity across America, demand for once hard-to-find authentic ingredients has increased. As a result, a range of *quesos* (cheeses), is now making its way into mainstream supermarkets, especially on the West Coast. Most often made from cow's milk, these cheeses are usually white or cream color with a mild, fresh taste (aged versions are more pungent), and can be used both for eating and cooking. There is currently little standardization among the commercial makers; you'll find the cheeses sold under a wide variety of names—some generic, some trademarked brands.

• **Asadero:** Drained, heated curds molded into a long log, then sliced; firm and smooth; buttery and a bit tangy in flavor; many brands similar to Provolone; a terrific melter for nachos, fondue, quesadillas.

• **Cotija** (also called **Queso Anejado,** or "aged cheese"): Aged curd in small rounds or large blocks; crumbly, pungent, salty; soft like Feta or very firm like Parmesan, depending on the brand; used to add flavor; crumble or grate over pizza, tacos, beans, pasta, soups, salads, and casseroles.

• **Queso Blanco Fresco** (also called **Queso Para Freir,** or "cheese for frying"): Fresh, pressed curds sold in blocks; mild flavor, firm texture; holds shape and softens when heated; can be sliced and pan-fried.

• **Queso Fresco:** Fresh curds pressed in round molds; soft, crumbly, slightly grainy and salty; similar in flavor to Ricotta or farmer cheese; softens but does not melt when heated; crumble, slice, or dice to top or fill tacos, chiles rellenos, enchiladas, burritos, etc.

• **Requeson:** Fresh; similar to Ricotta; soft and spreadable with a fresh, milky taste; use as a filling for enchiladas and pasta or with jam as a spread for crackers or bread.

sturdy enough to bang about in boxes stacked in warehouses or to be jostled about in delivery trucks, are more difficult to find at their peak of perfection. But when a gently handled Laura Chenel–made and -ripened goat cheese finds its way to your table, it will be an American Treasure without question.

LOLETA CHEESE FACTORY
Carol and Robert Laffranchi

252 Loleta Drive
P.O. Box 607
Loleta, California 95551
(707) 733-5470; (800) 995-0453

Cheddar, Jack

Carol and Bob Laffranchi make more than a million and a half pounds of cheese annually at their 12-year-old cheese business located in the picturesque dairy community of Loleta. The Laffranchis' interest in cheesemaking was sparked during Bob's previous career as a teacher of agriculture and dairy methods. Although they also make Havarti, Fontina, and queso fresco, the Laffranchis specialize in plain or flavored Cheddar and Jack cheeses that run the seasoning gamut from salami and salmon to caraway seeds and jalapeño peppers. Milk for the cheeses comes from cattle that graze on lush, fertile pastures situated only a mile or two from the Pacific Ocean. Visitors are welcome at the remodeled turn-of-the-century factory, which has a tasting room with a large observation window overlooking the cheesemaking facility.

PELUSO CHEESE INC.
Franklin Peluso

429 H Street
Los Baños, California 93635
(209) 826-3744; (800) 253-6668;
fax (209) 826-6782

Teleme, Haloumi, String Cheese, Queso Crema

Californian Franklin Peluso and his antecedents have been turning out Peluso's Teleme (TELL-uh-me) for more than 80 years. Though Franklin and his father, Frank, also produce a range of other cheeses that includes Haloumi and queso crema, as well as several cheeses that are similar to those made in Nicaragua and El Salvador, it is the Peluso's sublime Teleme, made from pasteurized cow's milk, that is famous among cheese aficionados.

Teleme has as its root a Cretan goat cheese called Touloumi that is made strictly for local consumption in Greece. I have read that Teleme is related to a quite different, brined, Feta-like northern Greek/southern Bulgarian cheese called Telemea, but to me, Teleme resembles the Cretan cheese much more. Teleme's originators emigrated to this part of northern California, Merced County, more than a century ago. They came by ship from Crete, across the Atlantic,

HOW TO RIPEN AND SERVE TELEME AT HOME

I do urge you to try my "scientific" Teleme ripening technique in your own refrigerator. Start with a whole 10-pound (5 k) Teleme in its box. Leave it undisturbed for two months (or three if you're particularly daring) at the back of the bottom shelf of the refrigerator. After the minimum aging time, bring it out once or twice a week, open the box flaps, and inspect the top rind. Poke it with your finger—if it feels like a water bed, it's ready to eat. If not, allow it to age for another week and test the cheese again.

Once ripened, the enticing, chewy rice-flour rind turns to a gray, greenish-black sludge that must be skimmed off, while the inner cheese becomes liquescent, bone-colored, and extraordinarily flavorful—similar to Vacherin Mont d'Or, but more intense and not nearly so delicate—nutty, beefy, and woody, with hints of peat, like a single malt Scotch from Islay. The cheese is tumescent, glistening—so much so that it must remain constrained by the four sides of its box and be served with a ladle.

If you invite a few friends over, it may be fun to unveil the ripened wonder right before their incredulous eyes: Remove the four cardboard flaps from the top of the box and cut down the sides of the box so that the cheese extends above them by about a half inch. Using a long, sharp carving knife, saw off the top of the cheese, cutting right across the top, parallel to the tabletop. If it comes off intact, you may want to scrape the cheese away from the underside to within a few millimeters of the sludgy rind. If it gets messy, just do the best you can—the cheese will be delicious no matter how many bits of rind remain. My advice is to ignore them, they're harmless. Bring the cheese to room temperature and then simply spoon it out onto plates or into shallow bowls. Have plenty of bite-size hunks of crusty bread on hand for scooping up this incredibly delicious cheese fondue-style. I like to accompany it with garlicky salami, cured or smoked ham, pieces of honeydew or cantaloupe, and raw or blanched cold vegetables. The wine should be a California red—a Cabernet or Merlot. Teleme at this stage of ripeness is also delicious incorporated into hot mashed potatoes or used as a topping for baked potatoes.

around Cape Horn, and up the western coast of the Americas, dropping sail and finding shelter at Tomales Bay, where they homesteaded. They had found heaven—the land was lush, the soil fertile, and cattle thrived there, in contrast to the hardscrabble existence of goats and sheep on Crete, where cattle couldn't survive. Altering Touloumi's recipe to accommodate the less-delicate cow's milk was a cinch, and the logical result was a cheese resembling one from the old country.

Today, Peluso's Tomales Bay Teleme, which was singled out as "Best of Show" at the 1992 American Cheese Society judging, must be praised as an American Treasure. Each square cheese, 3 to 4 inches thick and about 12 inches across, weighing about 10 pounds (5 k), nestles inside its own cardboard box that bears a portrait of Frank Peluso's grandfather, Giovanni. The rind is coated with rice flour and, in its youth, when the soft, bone-white, tart cheese visibly bulges following a vertical cut, this rind is scrumptiously edible—nutty, chewy, compelling. At this stage the cheese has undergone minimum aging, about two weeks. Should you find Teleme for sale in this young stage, buy it—it's delicious and far more interesting than the best young Monterey Jack, which it resembles. It is good as a breakfast cheese with pastry, fruit, and coffee.

Now, while I am more than happy to sell young Teleme (and indeed to enjoy it myself), its truest, most memorable stage occurs after

it has been subjected to a very sophisticated ripening technique of my own invention, perfected after two decades of trial and error (see "How to Ripen and Serve Teleme at Home," facing page).

REDWOOD HILL FARM AND GRADE A GOAT DAIRY
Jennifer Bice and Steven Schack

10855 Occidental Road
Sebastopol, California 95472
(707) 823-8250; fax (707) 823-6976

Goat's-milk cheeses

I first met Jennifer Bice in 1988 when I was judging the annual cheese competition of the American Dairy Goat Association, of which Jennifer is an active and highly respected member. Using only non-animal (vegetable) enzymes for starter and rennet, Jennifer and Steven make a delightful soft-ripened goat's-milk "Camembert," Feta, chèvre, Teleme, and

both sharp and smoked goat's milk Cheddar, all from the milk of their herd of 250 purebread dairy goats at Redwood Hill. In 1995, realizing a longtime dream, they opened a cheesemaking facility five miles from the farm. It is located near Iron Horse Vineyards in western Sonoma County in what is known in winemaker circles as the Green Valley appellation. Goat's-milk yogurt and soaps are also made at the factory. Jennifer and Steven are developing a new series of small, mold-ripened cheeses that have been a hit at the local farmers' market. Some day soon they'll think of names for them.

SEA STARS GOAT CHEESE
Nancy Gaffney

5407 Old Coast Road
Santa Cruz, California 95060
(408) 423-7200

Fresh goat's-milk cheeses

A t her idyllic locale within earshot of the Pacific Ocean, Nancy Gaffney produces fresh, creamy, mild goat cheeses of pristine quality that are as delicious as any I've tasted, here or abroad. Lately, she has managed to further imbue them with nature's touch by decorating their surfaces with home-grown edible flowers—brilliantly colorful, peppery nasturtiums and marigolds. Though the flowers contribute little discernible flavor, they do make her tiny chèvre disks even more irresistible, and it's no wonder that they're met with such favor from her

many devotees across the country.

Nancy also turns out tangy, low-fat fromage blanc, plain or flavored with dill, parsley, chives, and garlic, or with sun-dried tomatoes. Several Sea Stars Tortes are also offered—layers of fresh goat cheese incorporating either fresh basil and sun-dried tomatoes, or pistachios and dried California apricots. Nancy's chèvre logs and fromage blanc have both earned first place rankings at American Cheese Society judgings.

SONOMA CHEESE FACTORY
Pete and David Viviani

2 Spain Street
Sonoma, California 95476
(707) 996-1000; fax (707) 935-3535

Sonoma Jack, Dry Jack, Teleme, Havarti, Cheddar

G enerations ago David Viviani's grandfather, Celso, was a big deal in the California cheese industry. The Sonoma Cheese Factory dates back to 1931 when Celso Viviani and the Vellas, another famous Jack cheesemaking family (see next listing), were partners.

And though the partnership dissolved in the 1950s, the cheesemaking traditions established during those years continue to survive in both families.

Although the word "factory" suggests a product that has expanded beyond its artisanal origin—and the Sonoma Cheese Factory does indeed produce great quantities of cheese by any standard—its cheeses nonetheless qualify as artisanal, reflecting a heritage of hands-on attention. David and his father, Pete, make the best fresh, mild, high-moisture Jack cheese anywhere—they call it Sonoma Jack. Keeping it company, you'll also find great Teleme, Dry Jack, Cheddar, and Havarti, as well as a line of reduced-fat cheeses.

VELLA CHEESE COMPANY OF CALIFORNIA, INC.
Ignazio Vella

315 Second Street East
P.O. Box 191
Sonoma, California 95476
(707) 938-3232; (800) 848-0505;
fax (707) 938-4307

Jack, Dry Jack, Asiago,
raw-milk Cheddar

L et there be a visible aura around this text, because elder statesman Ig Vella and his magnificent cheeses are driving forces behind the emergence of American-made cheeses that must be ranked among the world's finest. Ig's Bear Flag Brand Dry Jack is a rock-hard, unpasteur-

The Vella Cheese Company was founded in 1931 by Tom Vella (left), shown here at the age of 94 with his son Ignazio, who carries on the family cheesemaking tradition today.

ized cow's-milk cheese that rivals Parmigiano-Reggiano in its magnificent depth of flavor and visual appeal.

In 1931, the Vella family decided to make Jack, a cheese that was already famous in northern California. But they took it a crucial step further, deciding to age some of their Jack so that it would appeal to the then expanding influx of Italian immigrants. The result was Dry Jack, an 8-pound (4 k) round-sided, flat-bottomed wheel, its rind coated with a mixture of vegetable oil, cocoa, and pepper, and aged for two years. The Vellas kept the name "Jack" given to the cheese by its originator, a Scot named David Jacks who ended up in California during the Gold Rush. But to convey its texture and aging time they added the word "dry." Whether splintered from the wheel in tasty shards to be eaten by itself, or grated over pasta, soups, salads, or stews, Vella's Dry Jack, with its colorful bear-bedecked California state flag label, stands out as a cheese with extraordinary flavor—truly an American Treasure.

Ig's newest cheese is a sharp Asiago that is so toothsomely rich and fruity, so completely alluring, that I can barely restrain myself from eating too much of it at one sitting. I find it somewhat sweeter than the Wisconsin-made Auricchio brand Asiago (see page 431), of which I am also an ardent fan. Each Vella Asiago weighs around 16 pounds (8 k) and is aged from six months to a year. The Vella cheesemakers also produce young Jack (plain or flavored) and a quite fine aged, raw-milk Cheddar.

YERBA SANTA GOAT DAIRY ☆
Chris and Jan Twohy

6850 Scotts Valley Road
Lakeport, California 95453
(707) 263-8131; (800) 499-8131
(California only)

Fresh and aged goat's-milk cheeses

Although the Twohys make fresh, French-style chèvres, I most appreciate their gorgeous, amorphous, khaki-colored ovoid wheels of rock-hard, aged goat cheese that is flinty-textured and pungently butterscotchy in flavor. The Twohys

call this Alpine Chèvre Shepherd's Cheese and it is so special, with such rustic depth of flavor, that I am delighted to single it out as an American Treasure. Only in Spain, in Andalusia and Extremadura, have I tasted cheeses made in this style—visually and texturally neolithic. It is excellent flaked or grated into salads, pasta, and cooked vegetables, and is delicious with fruit. It also stands up well at room temperature, making it a welcome fellow traveler aboard automobile, train, boat, or plane—all you need is a good loaf of bread or some decent crackers and a sharp knife. Chris and Jan's cheeses have consistently placed first in the "hard aged" (shepherd's cheese) category at judgings sponsored by the American Cheese Society and the American Dairy Goat Association. Milk from the couple's goats is also used to make 14-ounce (420 g) mini-wheels of Chevito, a unique, crumbly, Feta-like cheese, as well as quark.

Florida

TURTLE CREEK DAIRY
James Berke

P.O. Box 326
Loxahatchee, Florida 33470
(407) 798-GOAT

Fresh goat's-milk cheeses

Jim Berke is doing superb work at Turtle Creek Dairy. I see his goat cheeses in shops and on restaurant menus all over Florida. While sales

continue to grow, Jim is patiently and assiduously increasing the size of his herd to accommodate increased demand for his simply delicious fresh chèvre, sold plain, ashed, peppered, or herbed; Tomme la Floride (six to eight times bigger than his diminutive chèvre disks and logs); goat's-milk Camembert; and a fresh, white goat cheese that he calls Casio Blanco, a sort of Italian-style queso blanco that has found favor with Latin American patrons. His versatile, low-fat Ricotta is nutty and sweet.

Idaho

ROLLINGSTONE CHEVRE
Karen and Chuck Evans

27349 Shelton Road
P.O. Box 683
Parma, Idaho 83660
(208) 722-6460

Fresh and aged goat's-milk cheeses

On their farm along a bend in the Snake River, artists/potters Karen and Chuck Evans turn out remarkably fine cheeses that have garnered top honors at American Cheese Society and American Dairy Goat Association judgings. Since 1977 Karen has been making chèvres that taste and look like they must have come from southwestern France, surely not from Idaho's Treasure Valley near the Oregon border. The more than two dozen cheeses (made with milk from the couple's purebred Saanen goats),

exude such grace and style that it quickly becomes apparent that the Evanses infuse each with an artist's aesthetic.

They produce two American Treasures—Idaho Goatster, an excellent 4-pound (2 k) wheel of firm, aged cheese similar to Italian sheep's-milk Pecorino Toscano, and my favorite, the award-winning Bleu Agé, a surface-ripened aged chèvre round that offers a hint of mild Stilton tones. There is a diminutive fresh chèvre featuring sweet, nutty roasted garlic worked into the curd, each cheese topped with a whole clove of roasted garlic, then wrapped in a grape leaf, as well as Fleur, fresh chèvre rounds decorated with edible flowers, which are tiny pastiches of great beauty.

In addition to a delicious fromage blanc (plain or herbed), Karen has also been experimenting with a variety of flavored, layered, torta-style concoctions, including a walnut-sprinkled one in which layers of plain chèvre are combined with a layer of chèvre blended with dried cranberries and a bit of orange zest.

Illinois

DIETRICH'S DAIRY
Tom Dietrich

Route 1, Box 83
Fowler, Illinois 62338
(217) 434-8460; fax (217) 434-8401

Fresh and aged goat's-milk cheeses, blue goat cheese

Dietrich makes a Danish Blue–style goat cheese, which he calls Dietrich's Pur Chèvre Bleu, that is completely unique and completely delicious—an American Treasure. It is stark white with jet-black blueing—a gorgeous effect. The flavor is intense—peppery hot, with that unmistakable piney goat-cheese undertone. This is excellent cheese to serve with tender young salad greens, for dessert with ultra-sweet fresh fruits, or to use as a marvelous base for a raw vegetable dip (just blend sour cream with the cheese to the desired consistency). Dietrich also makes Fleur du Prairie, a French-style unrenneted *crottin* with a white and blue mold exterior, as well as an ashed variation called Fleur de Nuit.

Indiana

CAPRIOLE, INC.
Judy Schad

P.O. Box 117
Greenville, Indiana 47124
(812) 923-9408; (800) 448-4628

Fresh and aged goat's-milk cheeses

To create her array of outstanding farmstead cheeses, Judy Schad uses milk from her own Alpine herd that grazes on a 150-year-old family farm in the rolling hills of the Ohio River valley Judy's cheeses are outstanding because of their style and flavor, most particularly her hand-ladled disks of chèvre called Banon. Named after the chestnut leaf-wrapped French Dauphiné disks, Judy's recipe is nearly the same as the French original, but there's a rewarding difference: hers are much, much better than any I've tasted in France. Furthermore, at 6 ounces (180 g), Judy's are bigger than the 3½ to 5-ounce (105 to 150 g) French Banons. And she goes another step further, macerating the lovely chestnut leaves in a mixture of brandy and white wine. Allowed to breath and mature to the stage I like best, I have found the Banons to be stunningly delicious as they ripen, becoming more substantial, sharper, and drier after a month of aging. Equally stunning are her perfect little 1-ounce (30 g) ashed and aged Wabash Cannonballs, which took "Best of Show" honors at the 1995 American Cheese Society judging held in Indiana.

Judy also makes fresh chèvre logs and pyramids (plain, ashed, peppered, and herbed); fig-shaped, paprika-dusted Crocodile Tears; and a delectable 4-pound (2 k) torta called Fromage à Trois that involves layers of chèvre, basil pesto, toasted pine nuts, and sun-dried tomatoes. Fromage à Trois is the joint creation of Judy and fellow American Dairy Goat Product Association member Mary Keehn of Cypress Grove Chevre in California (see page 389). The two cheesemakers collaborated on developing the recipe, name, and distinctive label, and each makes the tortas on her respective farm.

Judy's farmstead cheesemaking expertise has grown increasingly more refined over the years I've known her. I am especially impressed with her newer cheeses, presented *affiné*, or ripened. My biggest criticism of many American cheesemakers is that they not only misread the American palate as a timid one (it is

At the American Cheese Society's 1995 judging, Ricki Carroll of the New England Cheesemaking Supply Company (left) congratulates cheesemaker Judy Schad of Capriole, Inc., on winning the Best of Show ribbon for her Wabash Cannonball.

Iowa

MAYTAG DAIRY FARMS
Jim Stevens

Box 806
Newton, Iowa 50208
(800) 247-2458; (800) 258-2437
(Iowa only); fax (515) 792-1567

Maytag Blue, Cheddar, Edam

not nearly so timid as supposed), but they also miss the point of cheese as a gastronomic experience. Food must be memorable. And, to my mind, fresh, unripened cheeses are good, but far from memorable as a category. Judy's *affiné* cheeses are memorable. Her unique 3-pound (1½ k) wheels of Livarot-like Mont St. Francis are ripened, washed-rind, cooked-curd goat's-milk cheeses—perfectly delicious. Her wittily named Jack-style Old Kentucky Tomme, aged for four months, is incredibly rustic and satisfying and makes a terrific grating cheese. Not surprisingly, Judy consistently wins medals at American Cheese Society and American Dairy Goat Products Association judgings. Certainly I consider her Banon, Mont St. Francis, Old Kentucky Tomme, and Wabash Cannonballs to be American Treasures.

Maytag appliances are world-famous. They are made in Newton, Iowa, in an enormous facility about an hour east of Des Moines. Here, too, down a lovely country road, is the Maytag family farm where Maytag Blue is made. It is an American Treasure. Each 4-pound (2 k) wheel is handmade from unpasteurized cow's milk, the curd hand-seeded with *Penicillium roqueforti,* then hand-ladled into hoops, hand-salted, and aged for six months, twice as long as most commercially produced American blue cheese, in cellars carved directly into the side of a hill on the farm. To understand how this marvelous cheese came about, I traveled to the farm and took in the whole process. Why are they making

For generations the rich milk from Maytag Dairy Farms' blue-ribbon herd of cows has made this justifiably famous midwestern blue cheese an American Treasure.

FRAN LOZANO'S MAYTAG BLUE CHEESE DRESSING

Makes 1½ cups

Cookbook author Susan Hermann Loomis, who discovered this zesty recipe on a visit to Maytag Dairy Farms, points out that "its use isn't limited to a salad dressing . . . it makes a good dip for fresh vegetables, crackers, or toast. Try it first with just one clove of garlic, then add the other if you really want a garlicky zing." It is absolutely sublime tossed with mixed salad greens and bits of fresh pear.

2 ounces (60 g) Maytag Blue, crumbled (⅔ cup)
¼ cup (120 ml) mild vegetable oil such as canola or safflower

1 teaspoon grated lemon zest
1 tablespoon freshly squeezed lemon juice
1 cup (¼ l) sour cream
½ teaspoon salt
1 to 2 cloves garlic, peeled and minced

Place all the ingredients in a food processor. Process, using short pulses, until the ingredients are thoroughly mixed but there are still some lumps of cheese. Refrigerate for at least 1 hour to mellow the flavors before serving. Remove the dressing from the refrigerator 30 minutes before you plan to use it. Leftover dressing will keep, covered, for 3 to 4 days in the refrigerator.

Adapted from *Farmhouse Cookbook* by Susan Herrmann Loomis.

cheese instead of simply marketing milk? How did they determine that blue cheese was a viable alternative to something simpler like Cheddar or Colby? Well, the answer is that, indeed, the sons of Elmer Maytag, whose father founded the appliance company, did try the milk business. Not much fun or profit there. So after their father died in 1940, Frederick and Robert enlisted the services of an Iowa State University dairy professor who advised them that a premium blue cheese might be the way to go. That was it. From 1941 to the present, Maytag Blue has established itself, purely by word of mouth, as the intelligentsia's American blue cheese—no advertising, no national marketing, no modernization—and a whopping 80 percent of it is sold via mail-order. The rest passes directly over the counters of the front office shop that is filled with a time-warp panoply of antique cheese-making equipment, old milk bottles and *bidons* (milk cannisters), butter churns, pictures of 1930s milk trucks, and photos of old Elmer's prize cattle festooned with blue ribbons. Maytag's famous Holstein-Friesian cows, which graze on 1,600 acres of the surrounding countryside, have won hundreds of awards.

Maytag Blue has a marvelous peppery flavor with a creamy fondant texture that coats your palate and finishes with a lingering, creamy aftertaste that beckons you to succumb to just one more portion slathered onto a bite-size piece of bread. I, too, buy it mail-order, and have for years, in order to supply my own customers' demand. May-

tag Blue is very stable, becoming increasingly piquant with age. I recommend it to my most discerning customers with the same reverence I attach to my other stellar blues—Spanish Cabrales and Gamonedo, French Papillon or Coulet Roquefort, English Colston Bassett Stilton, and Italian Gorgonzola *naturale*.

The Maytag family's board chairman and spokesman is fourth-generation Fritz Maytag, who also owns the Anchor Steam Brewing Company in San Francisco, makers of a beer I adore. As you might expect, it's a beverage I enjoy serving with Maytag Blue.

Maytag also makes an Edam and a terrific white Cheddar.

Visitors are welcome at the dairy's cheese shop, which overlooks the cheese plant and farm.

Visitors to the Squire Tarbox Inn are invited to join innkeeper Karen Mitman in the barn as she feeds the Inn's small herd of Nubian goats.

The Squire Tarbox Inn's Chevre Pound Cake

Makes 12 to 16 servings

This pound cake is luxurious on its own, but Karen and Bill Mitman recommend serving it with fresh strawberries and whipped cream.

½ pound (250 g) soft goat cheese,
  at room temperature
3 sticks (¾ pound; 375 g)
  unsalted butter, at room
  temperature
2 cups (400 g) sugar
Pinch of salt
1½ teaspoons lemon extract or
  grated lemon zest
2 teaspoons vanilla extract
6 eggs, at room temperature
3 cups (450 g) all-purpose flour

1. Preheat the oven to 325°F. Heavily butter a 10-inch tube pan and dust it with flour.

2. Place the goat cheese and butter in a large bowl and cream with a mixer on high until well blended. Add the sugar, salt, and lemon and vanilla extracts, and beat the mixture until it is very light. Add the eggs one at a time, beating well after each addition. Continue beating until the mixture is light and fluffy. Reduce the mixer speed to low and add the flour. Beat just until the batter is mixed in.

3. Spoon the batter into the prepared pan. Bake until a toothpick inserted into the center of the cake comes out clean, 1¼ hours. Let the cake stand for 5 minutes, then invert it onto a wire rack and cool completely before serving.

Maine

The Squire Tarbox Inn
Karen and Bill Mitman

Box 620
Wiscasset, Maine 04578
(207) 882-7693

Fresh and aged goat's-milk cheeses

Karen and Bill Mitman have created a life for themselves on the coast of Maine that I can only aspire to. All of their cheeses—fresh chèvre with chives and garlic, a hard, wax-covered aged goat's-milk Caerphilly with a smooth texture and mellow flavor, and a drum-shaped Tellicherry Crottin, aged several days and rolled in cracked Tellicherry peppercorns—are excellent, as is their inn. The inn's cheeses are offered at a cheese buffet before dinner. After dinner, guests are invited to the barn to milk and feed the inn's small herd of Nubian goats.

The original house was built in 1763 (it's on the National Register of Historic Places), and if you love Maine and cheese as I do, I highly recommend that you pay them a visit. Send their award-winning Caerphilly to someone as a gift. It is versatile—for grating onto pasta, salads, and soups, or for eating as is.

YORK HILL FARM
Penny and John Duncan

York Hill Road
New Sharon, Maine 04955
(207) 778-9741

Fresh and aged goat's-milk cheeses

The Duncans run a small family farm on ten acres in central

Maine where the milk comes from their own herd of primarily French Alpine dairy goats. Their Capriano is an excellent hard, Parmesan-like goat cheese that is aged for more than a year. You'll also find fresh goat cheeses (plain, herbed, or peppered) and the Duncans' newest specialty, Roulé, 3-pound (1½ k) jellyroll-shaped chèvres flavored with a hint of garlic and rolled in either dill or black or green peppercorns.

Massachusetts

MANNY'S DAIRY
Maria and Manny Moreira

267 Brockelman Road
Lancaster, Massachusetts 01523
(508) 534-5411

Fresh cow's-milk cheese

Manny and Maria Moreira met each other in a Dunkin' Donuts in Massachusetts but both grew up on those tiny specks of land off the coast of Portugal called the Azores. Maria grew up without electricity or plumbing, but speaks of a childhood where everyone had a bit of land and a cow and the village was made up of pristine stone houses cheerily filled with Portuguese lace and fresh flowers. "We were almost entirely self-sufficient," Maria recalls. The islanders' diet primarily consisted of milk, fish, and vegetables. And with the leftover milk they made fresh cheese. It is this soft, white, unaged cheese—made with just salt, rennet, and milk from the dairy's 200 Holsteins—that the Moreiras' dairy sells under the name Fresh Portuguese. Manny gets up every morning at 3:30 A.M to make milk deliveries, while Maria gets to sleep in until 4:00 A.M., and then personally delivers the cheeses to the large Portuguese community around Lancaster. These are cheesemakers to keep an eye on.

SMITH'S COUNTRY CHEESE
Carol and David Smith

20 Otter River Road
Winchendon, Massachusetts 01475
(508) 939-5738

Farmstead Gouda, Gouda spreads, diet Gouda, Farmstead Cheddar

Since the Smiths started making cheese back in 1985, their reputation and output have grown admirably. Their raw-milk Gouda—plain or smoked, with caraway or cumin, or in a low-cholesterol, low-sodium version—is made from the milk of

their own Holstein cattle. They sell their cheeses, which also include raw-milk medium and sharp Cheddar, from the store located on their farm in north-central Massachusetts.

WESTFIELD FARM ☆
Bob and Letitia Kilmoyer

28 Worcester Road
Hubbardston, Massachusetts 01452
(508) 928-5110

Fresh and aged goat's-milk cheeses

Since 1981 the Kilmoyers have made three distinctly different styles of goat cheese on their 20-acre farm. One is the traditional French style in rounds and logs. Its texture is a bit fluffier than that of Laura Chenel's rather flinty aged chèvre and the Kilmoyer examples have more of a goaty tang. The Kilmoyers call this style "blue," but rest assured, the name applies to the light-blue exterior, not to any internal veining. Their second style of cheese is a soft-ripened goat's-milk, white-mold "Camembert" with admirable flavor and texture. Lastly,

there's Westfield Farm fresh chèvre, in 5-ounce (150 g) rounds, that are as good as can be. I consider the Hubbardston Blue rounds (5 ounces; 150 g) and the Classic Blue log (about 7 ounces; 210 g), two of the finest cheeses made anywhere in the world, and definitely American Treasures. The Hubbardston Blue took "Best of Show" honors at the American Cheese Society's 1993 judging and placed first in its category in 1995. And the Classic Blue earned top honors at the 1993 judging.

WINDY HAMLET FARM
Dorothy Benedict

29 Hunt Road
West Brookfield,
   Massachusetts 01585
(508) 867-6111

Fresh and aged goat's-milk cheeses

Windy Hamlet was meant to be the retirement home of Dorothy Benedict's fancy show horse. A pet pygmy goat was meant to be the horse's companion, but as so often happens with humans who start out with one goat, the farm is now

home to a sizable herd of 200 Nubians, Saanens, and Toggenburgs. Dorothy is adept at cheesemaking. Her fresh Capriole cheeses are 6-ounce (180 g) or 2½-pound (1¼ k) logs, her well-ripened *crottins* (named after the classic French Crottin de Chavignol) weigh around 3 ounces (90 g), and she also makes a variety of herbed logs and pyramids.

Minnesota

DANCING WINDS FARM
Mary Doerr

6863 County 12 Boulevard
Kenyon, Minnesota 55946
(507) 789-6606

Fresh goat's-milk cheeses

Since 1987 Mary Doerr has devoted her cheesemaking skills to those who, like herself, are lactose intolerant (allergic to cow's milk). On her 20-acre Grade A goat dairy farm located in the prairie area of Minnesota, she practices sustainable farming methods, including rotational grazing of her mixed herd of Saanen, French Alpine, and Swiss Oberhasli goats. She's done well with her goat's milk cheeses and serendipitously discovered that they could be just as delicious without adding the custom-

ary salt. Her fresh chèvre (plain or in any of 12 herb-coated versions), fromage blanc (flavored with black peppercorns or jalapeño peppers), and ow-salt Feta are also low in fat and cholesterol.

LA PAYSANNE, INC.
Lucie and Roger Steinkamp

Route 3, Box 27
Hayward, Minnesota 56043
(507) 256-4788

Fresh and aged sheep's-milk cheeses, cow's-milk Swede Alley

Lucie and Roger Steinkamp traveled around France and Italy gleaning the wisdom and ways of artisanal farmstead cheesemakers before settling in Minnesota to establish La Paysanne, Inc., where they now make more than 10,000 pounds of cheese annually.

The Steinkamps, who were awarded membership in the prestigious French Guide de Fromagers et Compagnons de Saint-Uguzon in 1994, produce impressive sheep's-milk cheeses in a range of ages and textures. Their wheels of natural-rind Pecorino range from semisoft and mild (aged 40 to 70 days) to a hard, sharp, Romano-style grating cheese that is aged for more than a year. A golden-colored, buttery-flavored version is smoked over hardwood chips. Other aged sheep's-milk cheeses include a classic Feta and loaves of smoked Ocszypek, a *pasta filata* cheese that originated in Poland's Tatra Mountains where shepherds made the cheese in their huts at night, then tucked it up in the eaves to smoke overnight. The couple's fresh sheep's-milk cheeses include a Recuite (the French name for Ricotta), Ricotta Salata, Labneh (a tart, refreshing low-fat Middle East–style fresh cheese), and La Fraiche, tiny wheels of basket-weave imprinted brined farmer cheese based on a recipe from Lucie's Burgundian grandmother. La Fraiche is sold plain and sprinkled with either chives or hot pepper; it is splendid melted on pizza or atop a baked potato. Bonasai, named after a town in Sardinia, is a 4-inch square of robust soft-ripened cheese that Roger describes as having "the creamy texture of Brie with a mild blue taste."

The last time I spoke with Lucie and Roger they were negotiating to buy a parcel of land with an old cheese factory, built in the 1930s, that has two miles of sandstone aging caves, one of only two such sites in the U.S. Obviously, both the Steinkamps and their cheeses are quite special.

New Mexico

COON RIDGE GOAT CHEESE
Andy and Nancy Coonridge

Star Route, Box 47
Pie Town, New Mexico 87827
(505) 224-8393

Fresh and aged goat's-milk cheeses

Coon Ridge goat cheeses are produced in the western part of New Mexico (near the Continental Divide), at an elevation of 8,000 feet. The Coonridges chose this remote area so that their herd of Alpine goats could graze "free range" as naturally as possible. This area is indeed remote—residents point out that "there are more elk than people here," and when you contact the Coonridges, the call goes through a mobile operator hundreds of miles from their home. Among their cheeses are fromage blanc, a fresh goat cheese in olive oil with herbs, and another that is slightly aged and coated with Southwestern herbs.

New York

COACH FARM
Miles, Lillian, and Susan Cahn

105 Mill Hill Road
Pine Plains, New York 12567
(518) 398-5325; fax (518) 398-5329

Fresh and aged goat's-milk cheeses, yogurt, Yo-goat

Miles, Lillian, and daughter Susan Cahn's cheeses and yogurt, made from the milk of their own enormous herd of around 800 Alpine goats, have set an almost unattainable standard for America's cheesemakers. If I can put aside my own prejudice for a moment (the Cahns are very good friends of mine), perhaps I can explain why.

The Cahns are successful business people, having founded, run, and eventually sold the famous Coach leather company, manufacturers of prestigious, highest-quality handmade leather goods. Instead of retiring, they chose to build another business, this time one whose revenues focus on the inside of the animal rather than the outside. They have spent the last decade watching their Columbia County farm grow into the largest goat farm and creamery in the U.S., producing not only a top-notch array of cheeses but also a delicious yogurt and a goat's-milk yogurt drink called Yo-goat.

Feeding time at Coach Farm: A herd of 800 lovingly tended Alpine goats provides the milk for a range of American Treasure cheeses made at the largest goat farm and creamery in the U.S.

Their cheese is superb. From the very beginning, Miles, Lillian, Susan and I (as their consultant) agreed it should be de-Frenchified—this from three avowed Francophiles! Instead of chèvres, *bûches, pavés, crottins,* etc., Coach offers farmstead goat's-milk cheeses with understandable "American" names for the shapes: buttons, disks, cones, logs, sticks, pyramids, bricks, and wheels. Buttons, disks, logs, and some bricks are marketed fresh, that is, unaged in the style that Americans (excluding me) seem to enjoy most. (As you have already figured out, I am not a major fan of fresh cheeses, preferring instead the more complex and assertive flavors of ripened cheeses.) But with the help of a *Penicillium* mold added in the curding process, the rest of the line is aged until the various shapes grow the fuzzy, white rind found on soft-ripened cheeses such as Brie. But there the similarity ends. Aged Coach cheeses are not allowed to ripen to a Brie-like texture; they are meant to be moist and flaky.

The flavor of Coach Farm cheese reigns supreme. To me, it's like ice cream without sugar. It cries out for olives, olive oil, sweet peppers, hot peppers, cucumbers, summer tomatoes, fresh corn, lettuce salads, vinaigrettes, potatoes—boiled, roasted, mashed, or gratinéed—leeks, garlic, wild mushrooms. It commands a setting of the sweetest of fruits and fine, crusty bread. It brings the outdoors inside.

Miles has a penchant for green peppercorns and for caraway seeds,

both of which make appearances in several of the Coach shapes. Initially, I gave him a pretty hard time about these as I have a problem with the idea of stuff in stuff, but Miles prevailed, and I was proven wrong—both flavors are delicious melded with Coach Farm cheese, and I consider the green peppercorn version an American Treasure. Aged pyramids, cones, and disks are available in this style. Coach's reduced-fat log is creamy, sweet, and as close to fat-free as you're likely to encounter, delicious spread on bread in place of butter.

To see Coach Farm and to realize the complexities involved in its operation, not to mention the capital risk, is to understand how grand a world this can be when people who mix heart and soul with vision, taste, and consummate business skill are turned loose on a project. Indeed, the farm provokes complete awe in most people. There are beatific, frolicking baby goats, high on the list of the world's most adorable crea-

tures. There is a carousel milker, which is like a merry-go-round for goats. The females (does) walk onto it, rotate slowly around as they're milked, then stroll off to the immaculate cheesemaking salon and the breezeway rock piles, where they display atavistic agility.

EGG FARM DAIRY
Jonathan White

2 John Walsh Boulevard
Peekskill, New York 10566
(914) 734-7343; (800) CREAMERY;
fax (914) 734-9287

Fresh and aged sheep's-milk and goat's-milk cheeses

One summer afternoon at an American Cheese Society judging held several years ago at Shelburne Farm in Vermont I was collared by a bespectacled computer engineer named Jonathan White, who

was clearly fascinated by dairy science, cheesemaking, and anything that had to do with milk. He wanted to talk about cheese, mainly his first attempts. White and Charles Palmer, the gifted chef/owner of several Manhattan restaurants including the famous Aureole, had just formed a partnership to establish Egg Farm Dairy in the verdant farming community of Peekskill, New York. A year later, White had officially become an ACS member and in 1994 won second prize at the Society's annual judging for his soft-ripened Muscoot, a cream-added cow's-milk cheese. In 1995 Egg Farm's Mascarpone earned first place honors in the unripened cow's-milk cheese category.

In addition to the award-winning Muscoot, the dairy also makes unusual, slightly chewy, aged cow's-milk Peekskill Pyramids that taste more like butter than cheese; a rich, dense-textured ripened cow's-milk cheese called Anawalk; and robust Limburger-like Hollis. Another specialty is Cheddar that is "wild ripened"—the name White gives to the process by which a Vermont Cheddar from an unnamed source (I would guess Grafton), is aged 12 to 18 months at its source and then ripened further at Egg Farm Dairy. Certainly it becomes a delicious Cheddar, as good as any I have tasted, though very expensive.

Jonathan not only makes his own cheese, he air-freights in a selection of Portuguese cheeses that are ripened at the Dairy. Portuguese Jaime (HI-may) is a sheep and goat cheese that, after ripening for around three months, develops a smoky, hazelnut-and-chocolate flavor and a rough, rustic grayish rind; Amelia are small nutty, fragrant buttons of Portuguese goat's-milk cheeses that develop a pale gray, downy rind. The Dairy also makes low-moisture, cultured sweet butter churned from clabbered cream; little Chocolate Butter Hearts from this butter flavored with extra bittersweet chocolate; and thick clabber ("the New World's crème fraîche") with a distinctive raw-cream flavor.

HAWTHORNE VALLEY FARM
Robert Roman

RD 2, Box 225A
Ghent, New York 12075
(518) 672-4465 or 672-7500;
fax (518) 672-4887

Hawthorne Valley Cheese

Hawthorne Valley Farm is an organic farm lying in the rolling hills of the Hudson Valley, about two hours up the river from New York City. It is owned and operated by the famous Rudolf Steiner Educational and Farming Association, a pioneer in biodynamic farming. Cheesemaker Robert Roman is responsible for a sort of Tilsit/Appenzeller cheese made from raw cow's milk. It is semifirm when aged for about ten months, considerably softer and milder at six months. It has extraordinary flavor. Each wheel weighs about 10 pounds (5 k) and there is a choice of mild, medium, sharp, or extra-sharp. The cheese is also available flavored with caraway, garlic, or hot peppers. In late 1994, the farm began producing Monterey Jack. Certified biodynamic organic milk is also available.

HOLLOW ROAD FARMS ☆
**Joan Snyder and
Ken Klienpeter**

Route 1, Box 93
Stuyvesant, New York 12173
(518) 758-7214; fax (518) 758-1899

***Sheep's-milk cheeses, mixed
sheep's- and cow's-milk cheeses***

Joan Snyder and Ken Klienpeter are farming dairy sheep. From this milk they are producing fresh cheeses, soft-ripened cheeses in the style of Camembert and

Hollow Road Farms

Saint-André, yogurt, and Ricotta. All are so fine I can't adequately express my admiration.

Sheep's milk is unique in terms of the texture and flavor qualities it imparts to cheese. Yet while many of the world's greatest cheeses—Roquefort, Pecorino Romano, Manchego—are made from sheep's milk, only a handful of American cheesemakers have chosen sheep's milk as their medium. The reason America has not fostered a sheep dairying tradition is twofold. First, sheep are most desirable in unfertile grazing areas because they can subsist on much less vegetation than cattle. (This is also true of goats, but goats are notoriously finicky about what they will and won't eat.) Since much of New York State is lush, most people don't even consider raising sheep. Cows eat 12 times as much as sheep, but if they can feed themselves (as they certainly can in this region), they will deliver 20 times as much milk as sheep. The second reason is that most Americans came here from countries where sheep mean wool and meat, not milk and cheese. As yet, we have no tradition for Feta, Ricotta, yogurt, Romano, or Roquefort.

I urge you to become acquainted with Joan and Ken's products. The Ricotta, an American Treasure that took second place honors in its category at the 1995 American Cheese Society judging, and the yogurt are equally good eaten as is or used in cooking.

The cylinders and squares of fresh cheese—dusted with dried herbs or freshly ground peppercorns—are a delight. The glorious soft-ripened Camembert-style cheese placed first in its category at the 1995 ACS judging. And Hollow Road Farms' 4-pound (2 k) round of soft-ripened Saint-André-style cheese is also an American Treasure deserving of a place of honor on your cheeseboard. In 1995 it placed first in its category at the ACS judging. This cheese is as lush, creamy, and rich as ice cream.

LITTLE RAINBOW CHEVRE
Tom and Barbara Reed

15 Doe Hill Road
Hillsdale, New York 12529
(518) 325-3351; fax (518) 325-4409

Fresh and aged
goat's-milk cheeses

T om and Barbara Reed are among the most talented cheesemakers in the U.S. The Reeds and their Toggenburg and La Mancha herd live in a lovely area, lush

Cheesemaker Barbara Reed with a tray of ripening crottins.

and rolling, barely an hour north of New York City. Cheesemakers for more than 15 years, they sell most of their products at New York City's famous Greenmarket at Union Square. From their fresh logs to their Berkshire Blue, each Little Rainbow cheese possesses an innate flavor and panache that is unsurpassed—even in France. There are also Crottin "Mediterraneen," a cheese that they call Chèvre de Ferme (with or without peppercorns), triple-crème Chèvre d'Amour. Feta, an aged raw-milk goat cheese, and a few others.

NORTHLAND SHEEP DAIRY
Jane North

RD#1, Box 107B
Marathon, New York 13803
(607) 849-3328

Aged sheep's-milk cheeses

J ane North spent ten years in France's eastern Pyrénées to perfect her cheesemaking prowess and in preparation for building a farm in New York's gorgeous Finger Lakes region. Her cheeses are magnificent—one in the firm, olivey, high butterfat style of the Pyrénées called Tomme Bergère, and another in the style of Roquefort, called Bergère Bleue, for which Jane uses a *Penicillium roqueforti* spore mixture from Canada. The result is a sheep's-milk blue cheese that offers a flavor sensation that is as multilayered as that of France's finest Roquefort or Spain's Cabrales. Both are very serious, exquisite cheeses.

TODARO BROTHERS
Lucian Todaro

555 Second Avenue
New York, New York 10016
(212) 532-0654

Mozzarella, Caciocavallo,
Manteca, Scamorza,
Smoked Provola

Lou Todaro is an importer of fine cheeses and European foodstuffs first, a retailer second, and a cheesemaker third. He and his wife Mary own one of America's finest and most fascinating Italian specialty food stores. Founded in 1917 by Lou's father, Pellegrino, and uncles Paolo and Giuseppe, the store is a treasure to its neighborhood and a virtual prototype for the ever-proliferating "gourmet" food shops and upscale supermarkets now found across the country. Lou literally grew up in his father's store, spending the slow times playing baseball—using huge green Sicilian olives as balls and paddle-shaped lengths of *bottarga* (dried roe sacs of mullet or tuna) as bats—and the busy times behind the counter. A run was scored when an olive rocketed through the shop's open doors. Lou's father was the original importer of an Italian cheese called Montasio, one of

todaro®
bros.

Imported and Domestic Gourmet Foods
Since 1917

555 Second Avenue
New York City 532-0633

the countless Italian specialties he won a solid reputation providing.

Lou Todaro's Mozzarella and other *pasta filata* cheeses represent a dying art that is still thriving in Manhattan. In addition to his hand-pulled Mozzarella made fresh daily on the premises, he and his cheesemakers fashion Caciocavallo, Manteca (stuffed with butter and other delicacies), Scamorza (aged, dried Mozzarella), smoked Provola (a sort of diminutive Provolone), and a variety of fresh-curd, basket cheeses.

WIENINGER'S GOAT ☆
PRODUCTS
Sally and Ted Wieninger

Star Route, Box 106
Hunter, New York 12442
(518) 263-4772

Aged raw goat's-milk cheese,
low-sodium goat cheese

One day in 1984 a woman appeared at my counter at Fairway Market in New York City. Her shopping cart held not Fairway fruits and vegetables but two blue-eyed babes nestled between three or four brown paper grocery sacks bulging with what appeared to be buff-colored, 10-pound (5 k) wheels of cheese. She proceeded to tell me that she and her husband Ted made the cheeses on their homestead near Hunter, New York, in the northern Catskill Mountains. They kept goats, and in an attempt to have them earn their keep, Sally had taught herself to make cheese.

She used a Gouda recipe and through much trial and error had finally perfected a process that resulted in the cheeses she brought with her. Aside from the substitution of goat's milk for cow's milk, she told me, the only difference between her cheese and Dutch Gouda was that hers turned out to be quite palatable without adding salt to the curd, or at least with very little added. Fine, I said, but let's taste and see.

By now, you have probably figured out that few cheeses excite me less than a young Gouda. I love Dutch aged Gouda—rock hard and super-sharp—but nothing younger has ever pleased me. I had already formulated a prediction regarding what I was about to taste before Sally had even mentioned a "Gouda recipe." So many well-intentioned people burdened with a surplus of good, clean milk decide to make cheese. They write away for a cheesemaking booklet; invariably it urges them to make Gouda. Nine times out of ten the results are bland, narcoleptic cheeses with no prospect of delighting anyone but their maker.

Sally hoisted a wheel with one hand, and to show her my forearms were no slouches either, I deftly grasped another one, single-handed, rapidly maneuvering it to a clear counter space. I knew this cheese was the one out of ten that has exceptional merit even before I tasted it. As I split the wheel with a double-handled knife the cheese inside released an aroma of outdoorsy, lactic herbiness. The hewn face was gran-

THE BIG CHEESE

In 1802 a publicity-minded cheesemaker delivered a 1,235-pound wheel of cheese to President Thomas Jefferson in Washington. Amazed citizens called it "the big cheese," a phrase that has been used ever since to describe someone of importance. Another theory regarding the origin of this term is that it is derived from *chiz*, the Hindi word for "thing."

ite-like, though bone-colored, with a sort of pearly iridescence. The aroma and visual effect so excited me that I would have been quite surprised had the cheese tasted any less good than I expected. It tasted a lot like a Tuscan sheep cheese and sort of like a Spanish Pyrenean sheep cheese, but it was nothing like any goat's-milk cheese I had ever tasted before. Owing to the complete absence of added salt, its sweetness allowed nuances of other flavors to come through more fully—nuts, pine, rosemary, and toffee. What a great day it was!

Wieninger's goat cheese became a fixture at my counter. Customers were urged to snack on it with crackers and beer, in keeping with its simplicity. Many found its grating advantages appealing, especially those who desired something milder than Parmigiano-Reggiano or a cheese low in sodium. Others enjoyed its counterpoint qualities when partnered with just about any other cheese. It seems to contrast excellently, providing a dramatic bridge between, say, a washed-rind cow's-milk cheese such as Taleggio, and a moist, fresh cheese such as Robiola Piemonte, and it fits perfectly between a blue such as Stilton, and a soft-ripened type such as Gratte-Paille.

The Wieninger cheese is admirably full-flavored without being overly strong. Sally ages her cheeses in a temperature- and humidity-controlled shed for between four and six months (export Dutch Gouda is aged for only around two months). The textural difference between ordinary, young, cow's-milk Gouda and Sally's rock-hard goat's-milk cheese is immense. This is a very satisfying cheese, an American Treasure—a cheese I hope Sally keeps making forever.

North Carolina

YELLOW BRANCH FARM
Karen Mickler and Bruce DeGrott

Route 2, Box 176E
Robbinsville, North Carolina 28771
(704) 479-6710

Cow's-milk cheese

At Yellow Branch Farm, nestled in the sylvan Great Smoky Mountains, cheesemaking is a multi-generational effort. Karen Mickler, who studied cheesemaking at Ontario's University of Guelph, as well as at the University of Wisconsin, makes Yellow Branch Cheese with her husband Bruce DeGrott and Bruce's siblings and parents. The cheese is high in butterfat for extra flavor, aged for 60 days, and is hard enough to grate yet soft enough to slice. It resembles a cross between a cow's-milk Cheddar and a Jack, and comes plain or flecked with organically grown jalapeño peppers.

Ohio

MINERVA CHEESE FACTORY
Phil and Polly Mueller

Box 60
Minerva, Ohio 44657
(216) 868-4196; fax (216) 868-7947

Cow's-milk cheeses

Phil Mueller and his wife Polly are fourth-generation cheesemakers whose ancestors first made cheese in Wisconsin back in 1890. Not surprisingly, their certified organic cow's-milk cheeses represent the pride and joy of Wisconsin, except

that they're made in Ohio, 75 miles south of Cleveland. Their roster includes Cheddar, Colby, Jack, Swiss, Marble (Swiss and Jack combined), Baby Swiss, queso blanco, low-fat yogurt cheese, a full line of "diet" cheeses, and butter.

Oregon

ROGUE RIVER VALLEY CREAMERY
Thomas and Ignazio Vella

311 North Front Street
Central Point, Oregon 97502
(503) 664-2233

Blue, Jack, Cheddar, Mozzarella

Ignazio Vella's dad Tom is ninety-something years old and has been a giant in the cheesemaking industry on the West Coast for 60 years, having spent a lifetime as a cheesemaker and consultant to commercial giants such as Kraft and Borden. While Ig's Vella Cheese Company in Sonoma, California, is noted for its Bear Flag Dry Jack (see page 397), his father's Oregon operation, overseen by cheesemaker Steve O'Brien, features Rogue River Blue, made from cow's milk, as its stellar attraction. His raw-milk Cheddar is marvelous, too, as are the Jack and Mozzarella. These Oregon pastures are lush and the result is milk of extraordinary quality. I highly recommend the cheeses from this creamery without reservation. Indeed, you may want to enjoy them while you still can—Ig's mother wants to sell the place. Ig, however, is adamant about preserving it, not only because of the wonderful cheeses but also because Rogue River is one of only three remaining cheese factories in this state that once supported a thriving cheese industry.

TILLAMOOK COUNTY CREAMERY ASSOCIATION
Harold Schild

4175 Highway 101 North
P.O. Box 3B
Tillamook, Oregon 97141
(503) 842-4481; (503) 842-6039

Cheddar, Colby, Jack

This is a big outfit, a cooperative that dates back to 1909. Its founding dairy farmers and cheesemakers were Swiss and they were simply confounded by their failed attempts to reproduce their beloved Swiss cheeses in a climate atypical of Switzerland's. This lush Oregon coastal area is so influenced by the weather—almost constantly cloudy

In 1913 the Tillamook Country Creamery Association won first prize for its exhibit at the Oregon State Fair.

and very humid—and the ocean that Swiss-style cheeses were just not to be. So the early members of the confederation enlisted a Scottish-Canadian named Peter McIntosh and he advised them to turn their sights to Cheddar, a cheese more suited to the climate. Thanks to his expertise, Tillamook became, and remains, a premium Cheddar, one I highly recommend and often enjoy myself. Today, the Tillamook plant processes one million pounds of milk every day, seven days a week, and plays host to 600,000 visitors a year. I love most their oldest cheese, extra-sharp Vintage White Cheddar, aged for 18 months.

Pennsylvania

GREYSTONE NUBIANS
Douglass Newbold

764 Hillview Road
Malvern, Pennsylvania 19355
(610) 296-0463

Fresh goat's-milk cheeses

Douglass Newbold raises a herd of Nubian goats that are among the top ten milkers in the U.S. on her farm in Pennsylvania. Located about 30 minutes west of Philadelphia, the lush rolling hills of Chester County is an area dotted with expensive horse farms. Like many "goat people" who also make cheese, Douglass is as interested in her purebred Nubians ("very individualistic, with more personality than other breeds") as she is in the cheese she has been making from their milk for the past 15 years. Her slightly tart and creamy *fromages de chèvre,* which she calls Greystone Chèvratel, are the result of kiln-dried alfalfa, hand milking, hand-ladled curd, and extra-gentle pasteurization. Most of her cheese production is sold to well-known Philadelphia restaurants. Just how fresh is the delicious Chèvratel? "It's four days from the goat to the restaurant," says Douglass.

GREYSTONE CHÈVRATEL
Fresh Goat Cheese
Ingredients: Goat Milk, Culture, Rennet, Salt.
Greystone Nubians, Inc., Malvern, PA 19355

South Carolina

SPLIT CREEK FARM
Evin J. Evans

3806 Centerville Road
Anderson, South Carolina 29625
(803) 287-3921

Goat's-milk cheeses

This Nubian goat herd, the only one in this predominantly dairy-agricultural county, supplies the milk that results in extra-high-protein, high-butterfat, extra-creamy cheeses, many of which are fruit-flavored (blueberry, raspberry, peach). Split Creek Farm's cheeses include fromage blanc, *crottins,* logs, pyramids, and Feta.

Texas

LARSEN FARMS, INC.
Bud Larsen

HC01, Box 98B
Dripping Springs, Texas 78620
(512) 858-7680

Fresh goat's-milk cheeses

In the Texas hill country between Austin and San Antonio, Bud Larsen uses goat's milk from his herd of five different breeds to make fresh chèvre, available plain, peppered, with herbs or jalapeños, or marinated in olive oil. He also makes a pinwheel "pesto roll" com-

bining his cheese with basil and sun-dried tomatoes.

THE MOZZARELLA COMPANY
Paula Lambert

2944 Elm Street
Dallas, Texas 75226
(214) 741-4072; (800) 798-2954;
fax (214) 741-4076

Cow's-milk cheeses, goat's-milk cheeses, water buffalo-milk Mozzarella

Since 1982 Paula Lambert has tirelessly and aggressively built a reputation for quality, creating a demand not only for domestic Mozzarella but also for her line of more than 25 specialty cheeses and dairy products with a Texas twist. Using cow's milk, goat's milk, or a combination of the two, The Mozzarella Company makes Ricotta, Mascarpone, Crescenza, cream cheese, fromage blanc, crème fraîche, smoked Scamorza, a Texas chèvre, and Montasio. The Scamorza, a dense-textured Mozzarella that has been lightly smoked over pecan shells, was rated number one in the *pasta filata* category at 1995, 1994, and

Mozzarella Company owner Paula Lambert (fourth from left) and her cheesemakers re-create this classic Italian cheese, handmaking it daily in a small factory in downtown Dallas.

1992 American Cheese Society judgings.

Paula's latest endeavor is producing the first commercially made buffalo-milk Mozzarella in America, using milk supplied by a firm in Texarkana, Arkansas. It is quite delicious and indistinguishable from Italian Mozzarella *di bufala*. My only lament is that it is just as expensive as the Italian original.

Vermont

BLYTHEDALE FARM
Karen Galayda and Tom Gilbert

HCR 82, Box 100
Corinth, Vermont 05039
(802) 439-6575

Cow's-milk cheeses

What was once simply a 50-acre Jersey cattle farm has now blossomed into a dairy and cheesemaking operation where Karen Galayda and Tom Gilbert create Vermont Brie and Camembert that are as good as any French Brie or Camembert that has been legally imported to the United States for decades. They also make wheels of Gruyère-like "aged mountain cheese."

Jersey cattle are known for giving superior milk but with fat globules that are so large the milk doesn't readily lend itself to cheesemaking. Karen and Tom overcome this problem, pasteurizing the milk so very gently that it consistently results in soft-ripened cheese with raw-milk flavor. Nuance-packed raw-milk flavor is essential to a soft-ripened cheese, and it simply doesn't exist in imported, factory-made French Brie or Camembert.

For eight years Karen and Tom were the cheesemakers at the now defunct Craigston Cheese Company in Massachusetts, where they made America's first farmstead mold-

ripened cheese. They moved to this 65-acre former dairy farm and founded their own operation in 1992.

CABOT CREAMERY COOPERATIVE

Box 128
Main Street
Cabot, Vermont 05647
(802) 563-2231; (802) 563-2604

Cheddar, Jack

Cabot Creamery Cooperative, owned by Agri-mark, is the largest dairy cooperative in the Northeast, made up of 2,100 farm families. It has been making cheese for more than 65 years. The distinctive two-year-old Private Stock Cheddar is excellent, a tribute to the co-op's commitment to

flavor through patient aging. Cabot butter is also superb. Though I've never been much of a fan of young Jack cheese, the Cabot version is just fine. Lately I've seen their nonfat yogurt and cottage cheese in stores as well. It sounds a little busy up there at Cabot Creamery, so let's hope that the fine Cheddar is receiving its fair share of attention.

CROWLEY CHEESE COMPANY ☆

Healdville Road
Healdville, Vermont 05758
(802) 259-2340; (800) 683-2606;
fax (802) 259-2347

Colby

It's a tribute to the timeless taste of Crowley cheese, one of America's most important cheeses, that it is still made by hand at this country's oldest cheesemaking facility. Founder A. Winfield Crowley made his first cheese back in 1882 and his recipe for this American Treasure has remained unchanged for more than a century, perpetuated first by his son and grandson, then honored by the Randolph Smith family, which acquired the small firm in 1967. Today Randolph's lawyer/ cheesemaker son Kent, who assumed ownership a decade ago, continues to produce this unique American cheese at a facility tucked away in the lovely rural hamlet of Healdville, Vermont.

According to the USFDA "standards of identity" established at the turn of the century, Crowley cheese is classified as a Colby, although in

OLD-FASHIONED MACARONI AND CHEESE

Makes 4 servings

*10 ounces (285 g) small elbow
　macaroni
2 tablespoons unsalted butter
1½ tablespoons all-purpose
　flour
¾ cup (180 ml) milk
1½ cups (6 ounces; 180 g) grated
　Crowley cheese*

1. Bring a large saucepan of water to boil over high heat. Add the elbow macaroni, lower the heat to medium, and cook, stirring occasionally, for 7 to 10 minutes. Drain.

2. While the macaroni is cooking, melt the butter in a medium-size skillet over medium-low heat. Whisk the flour into the butter, and continue cooking, whisking constantly until the mixture reaches the consistency of a thick paste, about 2 minutes.

3. Raise the heat to medium, add the milk, and continue cooking, whisking constantly, until the mixture thickens, about 5 minutes. Add the grated cheese and stir with a wooden spoon until the cheese is melted, about 2 minutes.

4. Stir the drained macaroni into the cheese sauce and serve.

my opinion it is neither a Colby nor a Cheddar, occupying a delicious spot somewhere in between. Whether aged two months (mild) or a year or more (sharp), it is markedly more flavorful than any Colby I have ever tasted and possesses a much smoother mouthfeel. Its taste is decidedly Cheddar-like, but with more of a richer, deeper flavor of cream than a Cheddar. It is at its best served with crackers and beer, slices of ham and salami, and some chutney. Crowley also melts beautifully in cooking, making it the perfect primary ingredient for a comforting dish of good old macaroni and cheese.

Made in a range of ages, shapes (blocks, wheels, oblong bars), and sizes, Crowley cheese is available at cheese and specialty food shops in most states. Kent Smith also makes versions flavored with sage, caraway, dill, garlic, onion, or hot

pepper, but I feel this venerable American Treasure is best savored for its simplicity, so I would opt for an unflavored Crowley cheese that has been aged for a year or more.

GRAFTON VILLAGE CHEESE ☆ COMPANY, INC.
Scott Fletcher

P.O. Box 87
Townshend Road
Grafton, Vermont 05146
(802) 843-2221/(800) 472-3866;
fax (802) 843-2210

Cheddar

Grafton Village Cheddar, made since 1890, is definitely one of my favorites. This raw-milk Vermont Cheddar is in the same superior league as Shelburne Farms' Farmhouse Cheddar—and sometimes even better. Only a few Vermont Cheddar-makers do everything the old way, making their cheeses in small batches, and Grafton follows this tradition. They commit themselves to the aging process, which takes time and ties up money. The re-

sult is more flavor for us. Insist on Grafton's raw-milk, white (undyed) Classic Reserve Extra Sharp Vermont Cheddar, aged at least two years. It is magnificent, an authentic American Treasure. Under the direction of head cheesemaker Scott Fletcher, Grafton also makes applewood-corn cob smoked Cheddar and Cheddars flavored with sage, dill, or garlic.

MAJOR FARM ☆
Cynthia and David Major

RFD 3, Box 265
Putney, Vermont 05346
(802) 387-4473

Aged sheep's-milk cheese

This spectacular raw sheep's-milk cheese is the Majors' version of the cheese made in the French Pyrénées, name-controlled Ossaulraty (from Béarn in the Eastern Pyrénées, near Pau; see page 171). Ossau-Iraty is a perfect example of the French Pyrénées idiom—a firm, buttery, Gouda-shaped sheep's-milk cheese with wondrous grassy, herby, nutty flavor.

The Majors' Vermont Shepherd Cheese, an American Treasure, is considerably less firm, with a more rustic shape (discus-like) and rind (ribbed and rough). The cheeses are also slightly larger than their French counterparts. Typical French Pyrénées cheeses, at least those that are exported, weigh about 10 pounds (about 5 k); the Majors' cheeses are a bit heavier. Cynthia and David must be regarded as two of the finest cheesemakers in America, a fact that the experts at the American Cheese Society's 1995 judging recognized by honoring Vermont Shepherd Cheese as the best aged sheep's-milk cheese.

PLYMOUTH CHEESE CORPORATION

P.O. Box 1
Plymouth, Vermont 05056
(802) 672-3650

Cow's-milk cheese

"The business of America is business," President Calvin Coolidge once observed. The business of the Plymouth Cheese Corporation is cheese. The company was founded in 1890 by the President's father, Col. John C. Coolidge, and remained in operation until 1934, when it closed during the Great Depression. In 1960 it was reopened in the same location by Calvin's son, John. The original recipe is still used to make raw cow's milk Plymouth Cheese, which is a "granular" (large) curd style once typical of New England farmhouse cheesemaking. The tangy, rich cheeses, which are aged from six months up to two years, are available in 3-pound (1½ k) and 5-pound (2½ k) wheels, and 40-pound (20 k) blocks, either plain (mild, medium, extra-sharp) or in a variety of flavors (sage, garlic, caraway). This is a moist cheese with a network of apertures and levels of tanginess that are more pronounced in the older cheeses. It's a tasty, old-fashioned, uncomplicated cheese that I find most enjoyable plain rather than flavored.

The factory is a four-story white frame building located in the Plymouth Notch Historic District, which is the birthplace and boyhood home of Calvin Coolidge. Time has stood still in this rural Vermont village where the homes of Coolidge's family and neighbors, the church, one-room schoolhouse, general store, and cheese factory have been carefully preserved and are open to the public.

Shelburne Farms' head cheesemaker, Mariano Gonzales, and his staff make more than 500 pounds of award-winning Cheddar every day.

SHELBURNE FARMS
Mariano Gonzales

102 Harbor Road
Shelburne, Vermont 05482
(802) 985-8686; fax (802) 985-8123

Cheddar

Shelburne is one of my three favorite American Cheddarmakers, a triumvirate of taste that includes Grafton Village Cheese Company and Cabot Creamery Co-operative, which are also in Vermont. Shelburne is located on Lake Champlain in a gorgeous setting and, lucky for us, their cheesemaking expertise is as exhilarating as the views are scenic. Raw-milk Shelburne Farmhouse Cheddar is an American Treasure made entirely by hand under the supervision of cheesemaker Mariano Gonzales, using only fresh milk from an award-winning herd of 60 purebred Brown Swiss cows (all born and raised at Shelburne) who are fed hay and silage produced on the farm. Rich and savory, this superior Cheddar is available in a range of ages from six months (smooth and mellow in texture and flavor) to two years (crumbly in texture with a real bite).

Shelburne's cheeses have consistently garnered the American Cheese Society's highest awards, including "Best of Show" in 1990 (scoring a perfect 30 points) and "Best Farmhouse Cheese" in 1994. The Smoked Cheddar, which is smoked to perfection by the monks of New Skete, New York, was judged best in its category in 1993.

Shelburne Farms' dairy and cheese facilities are actually one part of an unusual nonprofit environmental educational organization whose mission is to teach and demonstrate the wise use of natural and agricultural resources on more than 1,000 acres of farmland, meadows, and forests. In the late 1800s the site was created as the elegant country estate of William Seward Webb and his wife, Lila. Showing an abundance of good taste, Webb hired Frederick Law Olmsted, famed designer of New York City's Central Park, to create the farm and its landscape as an agricultural experiment. Today, more than 60,000 visitors (children are especially welcome) tour this historic property, which also includes a famous inn and restaurant.

long as she deems necessary, usually at least two years. Using hickory and maple chips, some of the cheeses are smoked for three days and nights, which imbues them with an unmistakably outdoorsy quality that is highly appealing. In addition to aged and smoked Cheddar, Betsy ships Green Mountain Jack, Green Mountain Blue, and Vermont Sage cheeses, each dipped in three protective coats of special microcrystalline cheese-coating wax. The Luce family also sells their own pure Vermont maple syrup, made by Larry, who taps the farm's 3,500 hardrock maple trees.

SUGARBUSH FARM
Betsy and Larry Luce

RR1, Box 568
Woodstock, Vermont 05091
(802) 457-1757; (800) 281-1757;
fax (802) 457-3269

Aged and smoked cheeses

B etsy Luce is not a cheesemaker, but an *affineur et fumeur,* a ripener and smoker. She selects the finest available cheeses from the numerous Vermont producers and ages them at the Luce family's 580-acre hilltop farm in climate-controlled artificial caves for as

VERMONT BUTTER & CHEESE COMPANY
Allison Hooper and Bob Reese

Pitman Road, Box 95
Websterville, Vermont 05678
(802) 479-9371; (800) 884-6287

Goat's-milk and cow's-milk cheeses

A s if their fresh Vermont Chèvre weren't good enough (which it most assuredly is, with blue ribbons from the American Cheese Society judgings to prove it), Allison and Bob recently expanded their efforts to include a goat's-milk Cheddar, two tortas (one with salmon,

which earned top honors at the American Cheese Society's 1995 judging, the other with basil), and quark. The quality of their crème fraîche, fromage blanc, and Mascarpone, each made without stabilizers or preservatives, has guaranteed them an exalted place on the dairy shelves of the finest shops.

Washington

SALLY JACKSON CHEESES ☆
Sally and Roger Jackson

Star Route, Box 106
Oroville, Washington 98844
(509) 485-3722

Aged sheep's-milk and goat's-milk cheeses

A few years ago when I asked Sally Jackson why an archrival New York shop was carrying her cheese when I didn't even know it existed, she laconically replied, "Well, they pay their bills fast. And they told me your store didn't." She called me not so long ago from the Okanogan Valley highland forest where she and Roger cleared a glade for their sheep to graze. Thinking she was calling because my accountant had somehow slipped up, I said, "What? Sally, I'll pay, I'll pay!" She replied. "It's okay—you're not due yet. It's just that last night I lost a ewe during labor and I need you to pay in advance so I can buy a new one."

Sally's sheep's-milk cheeses are like something you loved, long lost, out of their place in time, a re-apparition. Their flavor is sort of a pilgrimage for me, as if I've discovered that my father was really a Corsican and I'm standing in his closet and when I inhale and close my eyes I'm nestled in a thicket of the *maquis* breathing in thyme and rosemary, breathing out savory and coriander. Sally uses no herbs—just raw sheep's- or goat's-milk cheese, chestnut leaves, and her astonishing technique. Her American Treasures will knock you out and wake up your tastebuds.

WASHINGTON STATE UNIVERSITY
Marc Bates

University Creamery
Department of Food Science
  and Nutrition
Food Quality Building 101
Pullman, Washington 99164-6392
(509) 335-4014; fax (509) 335-7525

Cow's-milk cheeses

W hen I was a kid in the 1950s and 1960s, the University of Missouri had an on-campus creamery. This one at W.S.U. has been operating since 1948, teaching students the business of dairy manufacturing. But while the one in my hometown, Columbia, offered 15-cent ice cream cones featuring fresh, made-on-the-premises ice cream in portions as big as your head, W.S.U.'s creamery has long been famous for a unique cheese made from Washington State cow's milk.

Their Cougar Gold cheese comes in a can! And it's delicious—rich, soft, nutty, and cheesy. The cans, which contain nearly 2 pounds (about 1 k) of cheese, are fashionably retro in design, and make a memorable gift. The creamery also produces a milder cheese called Viking that's variously flavored with olives, basil, dill, and garlic, jalapeño peppers, oregano and basil, or rosemary. The oregano and basil version of Viking was rated number one in the "Spiced, Herbed, and Flavored Cow's Milk Cheese" category at a 1993 American Cheese Society judging. There is also excellent aged Cheddar and smoked Cheddar.

West Virginia

BRIER RUN FARM ☆
Greg and Verena Sava

Birch River, West Virginia 26610
(304) 649-2975

Fresh and aged goat's-milk cheeses

Former schoolteachers Greg and Verena Sava produce a fine array of goat's-milk cheeses on their 160-acre farm northeast of Charleston, West Virginia, in the Appalachian

Cheesemaker Verena Sava hand ladles curd into molds for Brier Run Farm's American Treasure aged chèvre.

foothills. The location is perfect "goat country," with steep mountains, rocky land, lush forests, pastures, and brush, and the Savas' goats forage freely over the hillsides, nibbling on the mountain herbs that imbue their milk. The couple takes pride in the fact that their farm is certified organic by the International Organic Crop Improvement Association, a guarantee that their cheeses contain no residues from herbicides, pesticides, or antibiotics since none are used in any of the feed consumed by the Brier Run goats.

I love Brier Run Farm's cheeses, which have repeatedly won recognition at American Cheese Society judgings, and I recommend them to you very highly as American Treasures. I especially like their rindless aged chèvre, which I believe is a far more satisfying cheese than fresh chèvre. The Savas also make an excellent quark that is similar to whole-milk yogurt, but less thick and more tart. Their fromage blanc, which I also salute as an American Treasure, is less tart than the quark and a bit thicker, but I use the two interchangeably—in salad dressings and in some soups, including borscht.

Wisconsin

BELGIOIOSO AURICCHIO ☆ CHEESE, INC.
Errico Auricchio

5810 Highway NN
Denmark, Wisconsin 54208
(414) 863-2123; fax (414) 863-8791

Provolone, Gorgonzola

Errico Auricchio's family started their cheesemaking company in Naples, Italy, in 1877. It has since grown to become the world's largest producer of Provolone, a fact which should not mislead you into assuming that this is not a premium-quality cheese to be reckoned with and enjoyed. Embossed in red with the Auricchio name, their cheeses hang in shops throughout the world.

In 1979, the family decided it would be prudent to produce their cheese in the U.S. for a variety of reasons involving export costs, currency fluctuations, marketing issues, and because, as Errico once told me, Wisconsin "offers the finest pasturage and livestock in the world." I never thought I'd hear a European cheesemaker admit that, but it's a fact—Wisconsin does. And by 1984, Errico, who oversees the Wisconsin facility, discovered that it was running to capacity while demand continued to grow, so another plant was built nearby in Pulaski, and a third was opened soon afterward.

The Auricchio Provolone made in Wisconsin is

identical to the company's Italian-made Provolone, which is available primarily in Italian specialty food shops. Auricchio's aged Provolone is the most enjoyable to me because it is sharp and filled with character, having lost the waxy chewiness of unaged versions. It crumbles on the palate and almost simultaneously melts into an onrush of mouthwatering flavor. Their aged Provolone, an American Treasure, is a cheese that is sure to grab your attention. Auricchio sells aged Provolone in several shapes and two ages, both enjoyable. The version labeled "sharp" is aged for seven months and has won first prize in its category at American Cheese Society judgings; the "extrasharp" cheeses are aged for a year or more.

In addition to their famous Provolone, Auricchio makes a superb Gorgonzola, marketed under the brand name BelGioioso, which I also consider to be an American Treasure. Recognized as best in its class at the 1995 American Cheese Society judging, it is much milder and less aromatic than Italian-made Gorgonzola, but considerably fresher tasting and pleasantly creamy, even oozy. The company's Mascarpone is also excellent.

While I am an ardent fan of the company's Provolone and Gorgonzola, I am less enamored of their other cheeses, which include Par-

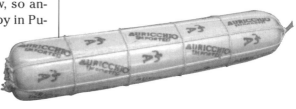

mesan, Asiago, cow's-milk Romano, and a mild Italian table cheese called Toscanello. But what do I know? Auricchio Parmesan has garnered a number of top honors including the grand prize in 1986 at the Sixteenth Biennial World Championship Natural Cheese Contest in Europe.

FANTOME FARM
Anne Topham

Route 1, Box 158
Ridgeway, Wisconsin 53582
(608) 924-1266

Fresh and aged goat's-milk cheeses

F antôme Farm produces some of the truest, most evocative French-style, farm-made chèvre made in the U.S. Anne Topham's farm, about 30 minutes west of lovely Madison, is home to 25 Alpine goats who freely roam the acreage, grazing on the vegetation that springs from the rich limestone soil. Anne's cheeses, as a result, offer fascinating permutations of flavor as wildflowers come and go, replaced by wild leeks and onions that give way to field mushrooms as the seasons roll by.

Anne taught herself how to make goat cheese from French textbooks but also spent considerable time in France as well. Her cheeses are really, really wonderful—nutty, herby, and toothsome. The football-shaped, aged Boulot (each about 2 ounces; 60 g), an American Treasure, is buff-colored and chewy, sometimes packed several to the glass jar, with Provençal herbs and

extra-virgin olive oil. The aged chèvre is usually disk-shaped in varying sizes, and the fresh, unaged chèvre can be had plain or herbed. Anne sells virtually all of the cheese she makes to local restaurants and to her many fans who frequent Madison's Dane County Farmer's Market. I sure hope there will be some left for you.

MOSSHOLDER FARM
The Mossholder Family

4017 North Richmond Street
Appleton, Wisconsin 54915
(414) 734-7575

Cow's-milk cheese

S eventy years ago, Grandfather Otto Mossholder "invented" delicious Mossholder Cheese on a stove in the family kitchen and gave it the family's name. The milk comes from their own cattle. The cheese is a hybrid involving recipes for Colby and Swiss-style Brick, with a bit of Trappist cheese-curing technique thrown in for a more pronounced flavor and more buttery texture. The 5-pound (2½ k) loaves, paper-wrapped and tied with string, are virtually rindless, with a firm, supple, light yellow paste containing numerous tiny eyes. The cheese is boldly aromatic, spicy, and full-flavored—nutty and fruity. It reminds me of Danish Esrom, though it is firmer. Enjoy it with black bread, smoked country sausage (for which Wisconsin is famous), hot mustard, and cold beer. Mossholder cheese is sold mild, medium, aged (nine months to a year), and extra-aged (one to three years old). Versions flavored with caraway seeds or crushed red pepper are also available. No amount of praise can overstate the merit of this fine, utterly original American Treasure.

ROTH KASE U.S.A., LTD.
Fermo Jaeckle

657 2nd Street
Monroe, Wisconsin 53566
(608) 328-2122; (800) ALP-DELL

Cow's-milk cheeses

American Fermo Jaeckle had been a manufacturer and importer of cheeses all of his adult life until his family sold their German plants and famous New Jersey importing company, Otto Roth, a few years ago. In 1991, Jaeckle bought a defunct cheese plant in Wisconsin and set out to become the first American producer of European mountain cheeses, Gruyère and Fontina.

The state-of-the-art Roth Käse plant features subterranean temperature- and humidity-controlled rooms for aging as well as some of America's largest-magnitude copper vats (15,000-pound/7,500 kg milk capacity), copper being a crucial material in terms of finished flavor. The vats are used to cook the curd, a prerequisite to producing the venerable cheeses of this type. The milk, which comes from select southwestern Wisconsin herds, is heat-treated at the plant, a technique that falls short of pasteurization, which would rob the cheeses of much of their flavor, while providing the cheesemaker with more control over this tricky process. In addition to the 18-pound (9 k) Gruyère (4½ inches thick, 18 inches diameter) and the 22-pound (11 k) Italian-style Fontina (slightly larger), Roth Käse features a sort of Trappist/Esrom-style, 5-pound (2½ k) loaf called St. Bernard, which is mild and buttery. A glass-enclosed viewing gallery runs right down the center of the plant, where some 3,000 people each month visit to watch the impressive process.

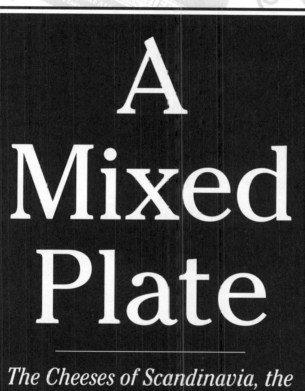

A Mixed Plate

The Cheeses of Scandinavia, the Netherlands, Belgium, Germany and Austria, the Balkans, and Canada

This chapter includes those cheese-producing countries whose cheeses, I am sorry to say, largely fall short of the joys contained within the natural, rustic rinds of the cheeses I admire from other countries. On the whole, the cheeses from the countries included— all of Scandinavia, Austria, Germany, the Netherlands, Belgium, the Balkans, and Canada—tend to imitate, approximate, and generally fall short of the great cheeses discussed at length earlier in the primer. But don't misunderstand me, some of these cheeses are important, especially the refined and original ones from the Netherlands and Greece, which loom head and shoulders above their chaptermates.

My standards are strict because I stubbornly insist on holding all cheeses up to comparison with the world's greatest—those from France, Italy, Switzerland, and Spain, and England's farmhouse cheeses. I demand that any cheese match the grace, tradition, regionality, rusticity, depth of flavor, and visual perfection found in the great cheeses, the overwhelming majority of which come from this handful of countries. My attitude may strike

High in the Bavarian Alps, cows garlanded with flowers make their annual descent, or transhumance, from the high mountains to the summer pastures in the valleys.

At Holland's famous Alkmaar cheese market, workers wearing colorful hats load Edam and Gouda onto wooden sleds and transport them to warehouses. The hat colors identify the various warehouses.

you as a bit mean-spirited, but my job, in and out of this book, is to share my excitement, enthusiasm, and respect for cheeses, as well as my knowledge, experience, and opinion. So I would be less than honest if I were to soft-pedal my feelings about these cheeses. My major problem with most of them is that they are ordinary. And the culprit is the desire for export dollars. To garner and hold fast to an export share, cheeses must be made in huge quantities that are utterly inconsistent with quality. Such quantities mean cheeses must be made in factories that employ scientific technology and, of course, pasteurization. This combination of pasteurization and mass production

negates rusticity. It is the antithesis of the art of cheesemaking. The absence of authenticity and artisanal care in cheesemaking invariably leads to lack of character in the final product, a void in which the memorable quirks of flavor and texture have no room to breathe. For me, the big business of cheese typified by most of the following countries results in completely forgettable cheeses. Taste and treasure the memorable ones singled out here, and forget the rest. Life is too short to spend it eating uninspired cheeses.

Due to the limited number of significant cheeses in the aforementioned countries, I have grouped the countries together in one chapter.

THE SCANDINAVIAN COUNTRIES

Scandinavia—Denmark, Norway, Sweden, and Finland—exports enormous quantities of cheese to the United States. Indeed, sales of Scandinavian cheeses in the U.S. account for 50% of all cheeses imported from Europe. Practically all of these cheeses are made from pasteurized cow's milk; most are mild in flavor, semisoft in texture, and often feature as their main attraction some added ingredient, such as caraway seeds or mustard seeds. Some are made from partially skimmed milk, which not only lowers the retail price, it also makes the cheeses more appealing to people who limit butterfat in their diets. As a group, these cheeses are simple and economical, and there's always something positive to be said for any food that is neither complicated nor expensive.

While I personally characterize most Scandinavian cheeses as mild and "versatile" (not strong positives from my point of view), I'm aware that many people love them specifically for these traits. Like most factory-produced cheeses, their quality is constant, varying little from batch to batch—the result of modern facilities and scientific technology, much of which is actually "imported" from the U.S. The cheeses are as nutri-

Charming houses dot the narrow cobble-stone streets of Denmark's cities.

tious and healthful as any others, and children respond avidly to their smooth textures and mild, often tame, flavors. Many of these cheeses lend themselves to recipe applications as substitutes for stronger or more expensive cheeses.

The Cheeses of Denmark

Danbo: (DAN-boh); also called **King Christian** or **Christian IX**: Widely available in the U.S.; a mild, semisoft cheese, made from partially skimmed cow's milk: usually it's flavored with caraway seeds. It comes in 12-pound (6 k), round-edged squares, about 4 inches thick, with a soft, smooth, beige interior. The thin, natural rind (usually waxed), is the same color as the inner paste. Were it not for the caraway seeds, you might easily assume you were eating processed American cheese.

Esrom (ESS-rum); also called **Danish Port-Salut**: Widely available in the U.S. My favorite Scandinavian cheese, it is a full-flavored, semisoft, big-aroma, Trappist-style cheese, made from partially skimmed cow's milk. It comes in foil-wrapped, 3-pound (1½ k) rectangles, about 2 inches thick. Under the foil the rind is orange, the result of periodic rubbings with brine over several months—a process essential to this singular Danish cheese's

recipe. Esrom exhibits a tiny hole structure throughout its yellow paste and is mercifully free of any added flavorings such as caraway seeds, pepper, or dill. Its flavor has been so heightened thanks to the rind washings and curing time that no flavor enhancer is necessary. I have found great pleasure in partnering Esrom with raw onions, sardines, crackers, and beer. It is also a lovely melter—the heat provokes great billows of flavor.

Danish Fontina

Danish Fontina (fawn-TEE-nah): So-called to differentiate it from the Swedish or the Italian versions; available in the U.S. A semisoft, smooth-textured, partially skimmed cow's milk cheese with a pleasant but bland flavor. It comes in 3½-inch-thick, 12-pound (6 k) wheels, coated with red paraffin. Danish Fontina is a perfect illustration of the type of cheese that I call flabby and glossy. It's okay, but you can surely do better.

Fontal (fawn-TAL), a variety of Danish Fontina, is brown-rinded and slightly stronger due to longer aging. The qualitative differences between real Fontina and Fontina-type cheeses are readily apparent, but can only be judged once you have come to know both. Real Fontina is discussed at length on page 191.

Havarti (huh-VAR-tee): Widely available in the U.S.; made from whole cow's milk; has tiny "eyes" or apertures throughout. This classic sandwich cheese is similar to Montery Jack—mild, and often flavored with herbs, spices, or peppers. It comes in 9-pound (4½ k), oblong, sandwich bread–size rindless blocks or loaves and is almost white to faintly yellow in color. Havarti is the least offensive cheese in the world—so simple that it would be curmudgeonly to say anything even slightly negative about it.

Havarti

Danish Tilsit (TILL-sit); also called **Tilsit Havarti**: Not widely available in the U.S.; made from partially skimmed cow's milk. Tilsit has a much fuller flavor than Havarti—I think of it as Havarti with a kick and an aroma to match. It comes in 9-pound (4½ k), oblong loaves. Though flavorful, I find Danish Tilsit rather one-dimensional—intense in flavor, but lacking nuance.

Danish Tilsit, though honest, is milder than big-flavored German Tilsiter and is made in loaves, rather than the wheels characteristic of Tilsiter and Swiss Tilsit (see page 442 for more on Tilsit). Danish Tilsit, like the German and Swiss versions, is semifirm, with a foil-covered, brownish-orange washed rind. The interior is yellowish—considerably darker in color than Havarti, but with the identical tiny hole structure. It slices easily and melts nicely.

Samsoe (SAM-soh): Rare in the U.S.; made from partially skimmed cow's milk. Samsoe is similar to Swiss Emmental, but moister, sweeter, and less flavorful. It comes in 40-pound (20 k) slabs. Samsoe has a white interior, tending toward yellow, and a thin, natural rind that is usually coated with a thin layer of wax. Softer than Emmental and Gruyère, it is shiny and moist with the flabby texture typical of many Scandinavian cheeses. Samsoe will occasionally sport the odd eye, round and walnut-sized or flattened, with smaller eyes nearby. **Tybo** (TIE-boh), very similar to Samsoe, is even milder, without eyes, and marketed in smaller blocks. I find both cheeses uninterestingly mild.

Blue (or **Blå**) **Castello** (BLAH-cass-TELL-oh): Widely available in the U.S.; a Brie-like (though richer in butterfat) cow's-milk blue made by Tholstrup, a large, commercial producer that also makes Saga blue cheese at its factory in Wisconsin. The Blue Castello, however, is richer than Saga and is made only

Denmark's cooperative farming system has made it one of the world's largest producers of cheese and butter.

in Denmark. Similar to U.S.-made Saga and Bresse Blue and distantly derivative of Italy's Gorgonzola, this cheese is marketed in boxed, 2.2-pound (1 k) half-wheels. The flavor is mild and forgettable, with distant hints of blue intensity. A very popular cheese, but give me Gorgonzola every time.

Crema Danica (KREH-mah DAN-ick-ah); also called **Crema Dania**. Rare in the U.S. These boxed, 6-ounce (180 g) rectangles of soft-ripened, double-cream (72% butterfat), cow's-milk cheese are also made by Tholstrup, in an admirable imitation of France's soft-ripened Brie and Camembert. Though once extremely popular as a dessert cheese, Crema Danica is rarely marketed in the U.S. anymore—hard to find, but worth seeking out if you favor a rich, mild, cream-added cheese.

Danish Blue: Widely available in the U.S.; sold under a variety of brand names. The best, in my opinion, is Flora Danica. I appreciate this rindless cow's-milk cheese because of its creaminess, consistency, and craftsmanship. I find it represents one of the few instances in which technology and mass production result in something that's actually interesting to eat. Consistent quality and excellent value are Danish Blue's greatest virtues. While the flavor is not complex, it is big and hearty. Its smooth texture is moist and marvelous—unlike any other blue except aged Gorgonzola—and it can be sliced, spread, crumbled, or diced.

THE FIRST TILSIT

Tilsit was originally made in a village of the same name, by Dutch cheesemakers who had emigrated to what was then East Prussia (Sovetsk), a part of U.S.S.R. Today, the town of Tilsit is officially in Lithuania, where its link to a namesake cheese is all but forgotten. However the cheese has definitely survived; in addition to the Danish version, it is also made and consumed in great quantities in Germany. The definitive Tilsit, however, is the well-crafted Swiss version—now known as Swiss Tilsit but formerly called Royalp—which is exported in small quantities.

Each foil-wrapped 6-pound (3 k) wheel of Danish Blue is from 4½ to 5½ inches thick and about 8 inches in diameter. The stark white interior is copiously stippled with dark navy, almost ultraviolet blueing, which should extend right up to the surface. Danish Blue is best cut with a wire, but a hot, wet knife will also do the trick.

Avoid any Danish Blue that shows butterfat or is oily—this suggests a lack of freshness or that the cheese has not been kept refrigerated. Danish Blue is sturdy—not much can go wrong with it. It will be welcome on any cheeseboard and valued in any kitchen where the cook is serious about quality ingredients. As with any blue, it calls for a wine with equal power and presence, usually a big red.

The Cheeses of Finland

Finlandia Swiss: Widely available in the U.S.; made from partially skimmed cow's milk, resulting in a cheese identical to Emmental in every respect *except* it's pasteurized, and therefore slightly less flavorful. It comes in machine-sliceable blocks. A very decent Swiss type that is acceptable as an everyday sandwich cheese. **Finnish Lappi** (LAP-pee) which is widely available in the U.S. is similar to Finlandia Swiss but

firmer. Also made in blocks, it is usually found pre-cut and wrapped for sale in supermarkets, where it sells well because of its mild flavor and low price.

Turunmaa (too-roon-MAH): Widely available in the U.S.; similar to Danish Havarti, but made from partially skimmed cow's milk. It comes in Fontina-size wheels (about 4 inches thick and 14 inches in diameter), ranging from 14 to 17 pounds (7 to 8½ k). It is mild and semifirm; rather bland but with a slight tang; imminently forgettable, eminently ordinary. **Masurkaa** (mah-ZER-kah) is a similar cheese.

The Cheeses of Norway

Jarlsberg (YARLS-burg): Widely available in the U.S.; made from partially skimmed cow's milk. An Emmental-type cheese, though sweeter and softer, Jarlsberg is America's largest-selling imported cheese. With its striking yellow paraffin coating and dramatic, large-eyed hole structure, 22-pound (11 k) wheels of Jarlsberg, 6 inches thick, have found a loyal U.S. audience.

Compared to the flavor and texture of Swiss or French Emmental, though, it falls disappointingly short, lacking the nutty intensity created by the raw milk found in the authentic cheeses.

Gjetost (YEAY-toast): Widely available in the U.S.; a sweet, brown, firm cheese, made from pure goat's milk, or a cow-goat mix, that is cooked until caramelized (hence its color), then curded and pressed. The typical 1-pound (500 g) blocks of this cheese gained popularity as a Scandinavian skiers' snack. The designation "Ekte Gjetost" on the label signifies that the cheese is made solely from goat's milk—*gjet* means "goat" in Norwegian.

Gjetost is much loved by many people in Scandinavia as well as in the U.S. Children are drawn to it for its sweetness, but it's much too sweet for my taste. It is served in the U.S. and abroad at breakfast with toast, and in Norway as a sandwich or snack cheese. The mixed-milk version can be found in supermarkets in a red box, while the Ekte Gjetost is sold in rectangular 1-pound (500 g), cellophane-wrapped blocks. Mixed-milk Gjetost is also exported in 9-pound (4½ k) blocks.

Ridder (RID-duhr): Rare in the U.S.; made from partially skimmed cow's milk. This semifirm, washed-rind cheese has a rich, buttery taste and texture. It comes in 3-pound (1½ k) wheels. Ridder is not disagreeable in any way, merely a simple, rather ordinary cheese, similar to Trappist-style cheeses such as Saint-Paulin from France and Austria, and Canadian Oka.

Nökkelost (NAW-kul-loast); also called **Kuminost** (KOO-min-ohst): Widely available in the U.S.; made from partially skimmed cow's milk. This is a semifirm cheese that is usually spiced with caraway, cumin, and cloves. It is derivative of Dutch Leyden, but much softer, with a thin, natural rind, thickly coated with red paraffin.

Gammelost (GAM-ul-ohst): Very rare in the U.S. It's not likely you'll find this cheese in the U.S. because it is not made in sufficient enough quantities to export. The enigma is that this is by far the most traditional and least derivative Scandinavian cheese. Though its name means "old cheese," old refers not to the length of its aging but to its traditional fabrication—soured, rather than fresh, skimmed cow's milk curd is used, which beneficially affects the finished flavor. As the cylinders of Gammelost ripen, the fluffy tufts of mold that sprout from them are worked into the surface of the cheese by hand. The result is a very rustic, honest, blue-green crust and interior mold that contributes to its big, genuine flavor. It is a firm, extremely low-fat, unpasteurized, bone-colored cheese with irregular blue veins and enormously pronounced pungency and aroma.

These days very little authentic Gammelost is made, and none, to my knowledge, is exported to the U.S. Unfortunately, the technique of encouraging spontaneous mold growth, followed by hand-rubbings, is labor intensive and therefore out of step with today's modern, briskly efficient, Scandinavian dairy technology. Most Gammelost is a fresh rather than aged cheese, ready in four or five weeks, and marketed with seemingly no link to the barely extant original other than its name and slightly pungent flavor. Do seek it out if you're in Norway, though I doubt you'll be lucky enough to find any.

The Cheeses of Sweden

Ambrosia (am-BROH-zha): Scattered availability in the U.S.; made from whole cow's milk. This cheese is Havarti-like in texture and color but much bigger in flavor. It comes in 10-pound (5 k) wheels. Ambrosia is an invented name; the cheese is produced in several of Sweden's largest dairy plants. There's nothing bad about it, but certainly nothing good or special.

Swedish Fontina: So-called to

Although most cheese in Sweden is produced in large factories, traditional "household cheese," called hushållsost, *is made on farms such as this one in Småland, one of Sweden's largest southern provinces.*

differentiate it from the Danish, French, and Italian versions; widely available in the U.S. Smooth-textured, with occasional small eyes, Swedish Fontina can be identified by its mild flavor and red paraffin rind. The thick, 10-pound (5 k) wheels are made from partially skimmed cow's milk. The qualitative differences between Swedish Fontina and Italian Fontina d'Aosta are immense: The Swedish version lacks the depth of flavor and fruity aroma of the Italian original. Swedish Fontina is mellow and ordinary, *very* ordinary. It is, though, as good a cheese "substance" as its Danish cousin or the minimally less banal French-made "Fontinas."

THE NETHERLANDS

Recently I have begun to specialize in some of the lesser known but worthy cheeses of the Netherlands. For years the only cheeses exported from the Netherlands were Gouda and Edam. However, at my counters we have begun to celebrate the Netherlands by showing off its underappreciated cheesemaking prowess, presenting cheeses that are much more interesting than that factory-made twosome—although I'll lead off with them.

The Cheeses

Gouda (GAOW-duh) and **Edam** (EH-dam): Both widely available in the U.S. Gouda and Edam are two towns that for centuries have been the commerce centers for cheeses produced in the Netherlands. Mellow Gouda is a whole-milk cow's-milk cheese. Slightly tangier Edam is made with partially skimmed milk. They are two of the most unexciting cheeses imaginable, offering little depth of flavor. Rather blah, they are slightly salty, cheesy, smooth, and filling, and taste best accompanied by beer.

Gouda and Edam are exported to the U.S. encased in ⅛-inch-thick red paraffin with an overwrap of transparent, ruby-red cellophane. (This is not the way you will see them presented for Dutch and European consumption. The natural, buff-colored rinds of those cheeses are left alone and stickered with the bright labels and logos of the cheeses' maker.) Our export Gouda cheeses are thick, round-edged wheels, about 4 inches thick and 10 inches in diameter, each weighing about 8 pounds (4 k). Edam cheeses are made in sandwich bread–size loaves of about 6 pounds (3 k) and in oval or oblongish spheres that range from 1 to 5 pounds (500 g to 2½ k).

Keep in mind that Gouda and Edam are very similar cheeses in terms of flavor and texture. But, before the production of Gouda and Edam became so automated in the

Gouda accounts for more than half of the Netherlands' cheese production. Here, at a small-scale cheesemaking facility, carefully tended farmhouse Goudas ripen on wooden planks.

1960s, these cheeses had recognizable identities and exhibited palpable differences. Edam, for example, was a much sharper cheese than it is now. These days the manufacture of both cheeses is on such a vast scale that their individual merits have become completely blurred and they are now virtually interchangeable. The cheeses for export share identical, uncomplicated recipes, save the fact that Edam is made from partially skimmed milk whereas Gouda is always made from whole milk. Their minimal aging periods of about two months under identical conditions further serve to negate any detectable differences between them.

Clearly there is little sense in purchasing examples of Gouda or Edam encased in red paraffin and cellophane. Ignore as well a Gouda called **Roomkaas** (ROME-kahss), a cream-added cheese that looks like ordinary Gouda, without the paraffin. What I recommend is that you look for either aged Gouda (page 448) or farmer's Gouda, also called Boerenkaas (also page 448), which is occasionally available in serious U.S. cheese shops. And as for Edam—simply consider it lost to us for all time.

OINK IF YOU LOVE PIGS

Largely because of its enormous cheese output, the Netherlands has more hogs per square mile than anywhere else in the world. Why? The result of cheesemaking is an overabundance of whey, and it is well known that pigs love and are nourished by whey. As a result, the Netherlands has a considerable problem—getting rid of pig manure.

Pig manure is overwhelming the country, finding its way into the canals and water sources, polluting the water. The Dutch are spending tens of millions of dollars in an attempt to control this problem.

You'll find pigs near cheese facilities not only in the Netherlands but also in Italy, England, and the U.S. Though you might expect that France, what with its massive cheese output, would have the most, it doesn't—whey is a product of cheese factories, not of small, artisanal producers.

Aged Gouda: Widely available in the U.S. Early in the last century, owing to the Europe-wide fame of Parmigiano-Reggiano, it was discovered that if Gouda was stored at the right temperature and humidity and turned frequently over two or more years, the cheese became a miracle of flavor. Aged Gouda is very hard and amber-colored, and has a perfumy, Scotch-whisky kind of aroma—both sharp and sweet at the same time, like molten honey or butterscotch. An aged Gouda is a truly delicious thing, almost totally divorced from the blandness of its youth. Edam is also aged the same way, but every example I've tasted has been overwhelmingly salty—I've yet to taste good aged Edam.

When choosing aged Gouda, look for sufficient aging—at least two years. Much of what's available simply hasn't been aged long enough. I have experimented with it as a substitute for Parmigiano-Reggiano, and though my allegiance is, of course, with Parmesan, I would have to say that it is an admirable grating cheese in most respects. When it comes to pasta, however, aged Gouda's honeyed perfumyness is inappropriate. Instead, try it grated over baked potatoes or a potato gratin. Serve it with your favorite fruits, good bread, and any wine or beer. Despite aged Gouda's sharpness, I find it goes very well with light reds and even fruity whites.

Boerenkaas (BORE-en-kahss) and **aged Boerenkaas:** Rare in the U.S.; occasionally found in specialty food shops. Boerenkaas, which means "farmer's cheese," is a farmhouse Gouda that is much larger than the ordinary, red-waxed Goudas that are exported.

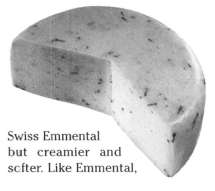

Boerenkaas is usually a round-edged, flat-topped wheel, weighing 18 to 28 pounds (9 to 14 k), made from raw cow's milk, and meant to be eaten young—at about four months—or aged for as long as six or seven years. Young or aged, it is simply a delight—intensely flavorful and imbued with an impressive, rustic presence.

The difference between red-rind export Gouda and Boerenkaas is most evident when you taste them side by side. In Boerenkaas I sense a complexity of flavors, the first of which reminds me of nuts and perhaps olives. But on the back of my tongue I pick up the sweetness and fruitiness, which when I exhale through my nose, brings out the perfume of the milk, the grass, and the soil. With red-waxed export Gouda I chomp, swallow, and that's the end of it—there is nothing to savor.

Boerenkaas is completely unlike ordinary, young, export Gouda. When you see red plastic or red paraffin around Goudas and Edams, it tells you the milk has been pasteurized, and they've been made for export by some huge factory in the Netherlands. But if you see a burnished golden rind that hasn't been trapped in plastic, a hard, gigantic wheel with rounded edges in the classic Gouda shape, what you have come across is Boerenkaas, and it is a cheese to cherish and take home. It's terrific.

Both young and aged Boerenkass are perfect choices for lunch or a snack with fruit and bread, a light, fruity red wine or beer. Aged Boerenkaas is robust enough to stand up to cocktails before dinner, and it is an excellent grating cheese. It has a perfumy, piquant sharpness that is very satisfying with sweet, fruit-based drinks. Parmigiano-Reggiano and Ignazio Vella's Bear Flag Dry Jack (see page 397) fall within the same idiom as aged Boerenkaas.

Texelaar (TECKS-uh-lar) and **Friesian Clove Cheese** (FREE-zhun): Both rare in the U.S. Not long ago, I attended a big food show in Barcelona. That's where I discovered a cheese called Texelaar, made on Texel, an island situated off the coast of the Netherlands and West Germany in the Frisian Islands chain. Texel is famous for its excellent dairy cattle, and Westland, the company that produces Texelaar, apparently buys up all of the Texel milk to make it. Texelaar is very much like Swiss Emmental but creamier and softer. Like Emmental, it is unpasteurized and has a sweet and nutty flavor. Texelaar cheeses are big-eyed, coated with yellow wax, and, like Jarlsberg, weigh 17 to 22 pounds (8½ to 11 k). They are round-edged, flat-topped wheels.

Also from the Frisian Islands is Friesian Clove Cheese, a dried, clove-spiked, Gouda/Leyden-style cheese much appreciated by the Dutch. I find it quite enjoyable (you might not, if you don't adore cloves) and like to partner it with ham, fruit, rye crackers or bread, and beer.

Leyden (LIE-den or LAY-den), also called Leidsekaas (LEED-zuh-kahss), widely available in the U.S.; and **aged Leyden,** rare in the U.S.:

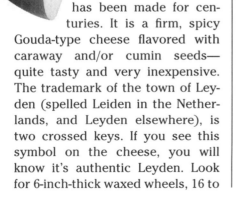

Leyden is a very good cow's-milk cheese that has been made for centuries. It is a firm, spicy Gouda-type cheese flavored with caraway and/or cumin seeds—quite tasty and very inexpensive. The trademark of the town of Leyden (spelled Leiden in the Netherlands, and Leyden elsewhere), is two crossed keys. If you see this symbol on the cheese, you will know it's authentic Leyden. Look for 6-inch-thick waxed wheels, 16 to 18 inches in diameter, weighing about 16 pounds (8 k).

Aged Leyden is quite remarkable and to date rare in the U.S. The batches I sell are very old, aged for about six years. While young Leyden is a light yellow, almost beige cheese, aged Leyden is creamy, brown-orange in color, and very hard in texture. To cut it, I have to put all of my weight on the double-handled knife. But no matter: The flavor of this cheese, a bit spicy and mysterious, is so alluring, what matters is not how the cheese looks, but that it is in your possession. I serve it as an extra-special treat along with country ham, crackers or bread, and a good beer. Chip off little morsels and let them melt in your mouth. No other cheese is anything like aged Leyden.

Kernhem (KER-num): Rare in the U.S. The story goes that about 25 years ago, Kernhem was "invented" by a Dutch cheesemaker who inadvertently cured a sizable batch of Roomkaas cheeses (cream-added Gouda) at too high a temperature. In testing one of them, he found that it literally stuck to his knife—hence the name Kernhem, which means "knife-sticker." This odd batch of imperfectly cured cheeses met with such favor among the rest of the staff that they decided to re-create the cheese

in all its serendipitous glory. Instead of a firm, rather ordinary Gouda, the cheese that resulted was almost gooey, with a much more pronounced, memorable flavor.

Kernhem is a very pleasurable, rich, nutty cheese. Look for orange-rinded wheels about 2 inches thick, weighing about 4 pounds (2 k), with an obviously healthy, cheesy aroma. Taste it. It should be full-flavored, but not piercing or bitter.

Serve Kernhem with fruit and crusty bread, fruity or coarse red wines, or beer. Don't hesitate to use it in sandwiches, or even better, melt it over slices of crusty bread, maybe with ham.

Maasdam Leerdammer (MAHSS-dahm-LEER-dahm-ur), **Maasdammer** (MAHSS-dahm-ur), and **Aalsdammer** (AHLS-dahm-ur): All widely available in the U.S. Three large cheese manufacturers in Holland make these Swiss-style cheeses. Though not particularly serious, these are

acceptable, well made, and a good value besides. All are Emmental types with the configuration of over-sized Goudas (round-edged, convex-topped, flat-bottomed wheels) weighing about 22 pounds (11 k) each, ranging from about 5 inches thick at the outer edge to 8 inches at the center, with a proliferation of large holes. If you want a simple

cheese to go with your ham sandwich, buy one of these, but remember, Dutch "Swiss" is merely an imitation of the excellent Swiss or French Emmental, though the Dutch cheese industry would like you to believe these are original Dutch cheeses.

Other Dutch Cheeses

There are goat's milk cheeses made in Holland that, other than the milk they are made from, are exactly like cow's-milk Goudas and resemble regular Gouda in terms of texture and physical configuration. The difference is in color (these goat's-milk "Goudas" are whiter) and in flavor. While mild, these cheeses have the typical almost peppery goat's milk finish with a pronounced tanginess. These are honest and straightforward cheeses—decent enough choices to accompany a glass of wine or beer—but by no means very exciting ones. The three brands to look for, each from a highly respected Dutch cheesemaker, are Benning, Arina, and Darcy. I am aware of no exported cheeses from the Netherlands made of sheep's milk, nor, to my knowledge, is there any dairying of sheep there at all.

BELGIUM

Belgium has a thriving and aggressive cheese industry. Most outstanding of its original or traditional cheeses are the true Trappist and Trappist-style varieties, principally from Chimay, that I find highly admirable. These semisoft, cow's-milk cheeses are long on aroma and flavor. Their production is modest, however, and the cheeses aren't exported. Unfortunately, the majority of Belgian cheeses are workman-like, bulky, and without much finesse or variety. The original Limburger, a Trappist cheese, came from Belgium, but the Germans copied Belgium's Limburger and adopted it as their own; these days German cheesemakers produce it by the ton. Today's most popular Belgian cheeses include a number of soft, strong, smelly cow's-milk cheeses in the Herve (AIR-vuh) style, named for a farming region in the province of Liège. Herve cheeses, which are also considered to be made in the Trappist idiom, are ubiquitous, sold in 4- to 5-pound (2 to 2½ k) wedges, cut from 3-inch-thick wheels, and in rectangular blocks *à la* Limburger and 6-ounce (180 g) cubes.

*Some of Belgium's finest soft cheeses (*pâte molle*) are difficult to find unless you are traveling abroad.*

Traditional Belgian cheesemaking nearly died out in the postwar years. But in the 1960s, scholars visited farms and abbeys seeking out historic recipes and techniques, many of which are used today.

The Cheeses

R emoudjou (REH-moh-joo): Not available in the U.S.; a very tasty Herve-style Belgian cheese that takes its name from the Belgian word *remoud,* which means "after-milk," the very rich milk that cows produce after lactation. Since modern technology has seen to it that cows are milking all the time and never become completely dry, there is really no such thing as commercial aftermilk. But Remoudjou it is called nonetheless, a Munster-like, soft, smelly cheese with strong flavor, sold in hunks cut from rectangular, 2-inch-thick, 3-pound (1½ k)

blocks. It is not exported, but if you're visiting Belgium, try some with any of the marvelous, fruity Belgian beers like Duvel.

Maredsous (MAH-red-soo): Rare in the U.S. This cheese is an old-time original—more than a century old—a basic, semisoft cow's-milk Trappist cheese with a pronounced cheesy flavor and aroma. It has a natural, dark-orange, usually waxed and painted rind, and is made in 2-inch-thick rectangular bricks of 3 or 4 pounds (1½ or 2 k). Smooth textured with occasional eye structure and a straw-colored interior, it is supple yet firm.

Fagnar (FAHN-yar): Rare in the U.S. A semifirm, reasonably flavorful cow's milk cheese, it is made in 3-

Belgium, one of the world's great brewing regions, produces nearly as many cheeses as it does beers.

pound (1½ k) disks, about 2½ inches thick, with a painted blackish-brown rind, and a yellowish, smooth interior. Rather unsensational overall. Fagnar has Trappist-style cheese as its root, and it is this idiom to which it adheres: smooth and supple texture with a slightly pronounced flavor and aroma on the order of Canadian Oka or French Port-Salut.

Passendale (PASS-sen-dale): Rare in the U.S. A soft cow's-milk cheese housed in an attractive, dome-shaped, futuristically "nat-

ural" looking rough, gray rind. This has got to be factory-technology's attempt to make a rustic-looking cheese! The cheese is buttery and pleasantly tangy, albeit rather ordinary. It has a proliferation of tiny eyes throughout and is made in squarish, domed loaves about 5 inches thick at the center and weighing around 6 pounds (3 k) each.

Damme (DOM-uh): Rare in the U.S. An orange-rinded, semisoft, rather flabby and shiny but tasty Belgian cow's-milk cheese that is almost identical in flavor to Fagnar.

Père Joseph (PAIR-jo-SEFF): Not widely available in the U.S. This is another semisoft, supple Trappist-style Belgian cheese that is somewhat milder than others, with a "painted" black rind. In typical Trappist configuration, this cow's-milk cheese is made in 2-inch-thick disks, 7 inches n diameter, weighing about 3 pounds (1½ k). Père Joseph's most distinguishing feature is that it is considerably less costly than any other exported Belgian cheese. For what it is—a well-made, serviceable, everyday cheese—it's a good value.

Wynendale (WY-nun-dale): Rare in the U.S.; the best of the exported Belgian cheeses. It is full-flavored, soft and creamy, with a nutty, lingering flavor and buttery mouthfeel. Wynendale is made in rather flat, 8-pound (4 k) disks, 1¾ inches thick and 9 to 10 inches in diameter, that resemble serious, rustic, traditional, handcrafted cheeses, which—as it happens—they're not. They are made from pasteurized cow's milk and come from ultramodern Belgian cheese factories that are capable of enormous output by anyone's standards.

Rond Artois (ROND-ar-TWAH): Not available in the U.S.; made in 1-pound (500 g) disks, 1½ inches thick and 5½ inches in diameter with a natural, dry, brown, washed rind, on the order of France's Savoyard Reblochon. But whereas Reblochon is one of the great cheeses, Belgium's Rond Artois suffers from a lack of hands-on human attention. It's just another factory cheese.

GERMANY AND AUSTRIA

Many of the original cheeses of Germany and Austria are just that—true originals. Generally speaking, though, to my mind German cheeses, while standing tall in aroma and flavor intensity, fall short when it comes to depth and nuance of flavor and are only somewhat less disappointing in terms of texture and visual effect. Strong German and Austrian cheeses are often only that—*strong*.

Texturally, the German cheeses are flabbier and more rubbery than Austrian ones, owing partly to their mass-production and partly to the fact that pasteurization has rendered the flavor-lending organisms nonexistent. Ultrafiltration, a very modern homogenizing technique, results in fat globules that are so uniform in size that the cheeses have no textural diversity.

The entire range of European cheese types are made in Germany and Austria and most are exported. Those cheeses that are most original are the washed-rind cow's-milk ones, which are soft, strong, and smelly. The Bries and Camemberts, the Swiss types, the Brie-like blues, and those flavored with herbs, mushrooms, pepper, bacon, or salami, are merely mass-market cheeses that offer nothing of special interest.

The towering Munster cathedral in Freiburg has been a landmark for more than seven centuries. At the Munsterplatz outdoor market nearby, local cheeses, meats, and produce from the Black Forest area are bountifully displayed for sale.

At Dallmayr, Munich's legendary food emporium, counters filled with an international array of cheeses, specialty meats, and other delicacies border the store's famous cherub-bedecked fountain

Austria and Germany produce prodigious quantities of Emmental and Gruyère that enjoy brisk sales domestically and are exported all over the world as well. While it is a fact that these examples of two of the world's greatest cheeses (both France and Switzerland qualify as their countries of origin) are completely decent and honest, it is also a fact that neither measures up to the originals on any level.

The Cheeses of Germany

Allgäuer Emmenthaler (AWL-gow-ur-EMM-en-TAH-lur): Widely available in the U.S.; like Swiss or French Emmental, but usually it's made from pasteurized cow's milk. Allgäuer Emmenthaler is a decent cheese, but with markedly less flavor and cachet than the originals. German Emmenthaler cheese is typically made in large wheels but is subsequently downsized into blocks or 20-pound (10 k) loaves. Avoid any that appears less than "just cut," that is, any that looks dry or shows surface mold or obvious cracks. Serve and enjoy as you would any Emmental or Emmental-style mountain cheese—with sandwiches, as a table cheese with fruit and bread or crackers, as a canapé or hot hors d'oeuvre ingredient, melted for gratins, soups, fondues, and Reuben sandwiches, or cubed in salads.

Bruder Basil (BREW-der-BAH-zul), **Rauchkase** (RAOWSH-kase), **Sebastian,** and **Caram** (KARE-um): All widely available in U.S. specialty

Cheese and bread make the cheeks red.

German proverb

food shops; made from partially skimmed cow's milk. These four cheeses are nearly identical, simple, mild, smoked Trappist-style cheeses—some rectangular, some round, each 2 inches thick and weighing in the neighborhood of 2½ to 3 pounds (1¼ to 1½ k). Popular as

snack cheeses to serve with beer and sandwiches, raw vegetables and dips, their inedible paraffin covering must be removed to expose the edible, smoked rind beneath. Under this thin, chewy rind is a yellowish, semisoft cheese, usually showing even distribution of tiny apertures (not rounded holes). All slice neatly and melt readily.

Limburger (LIM-ber-guhr): Regionally available in the U.S. Originally a Belgian Trappist cheese. Limburger is now predominantly a German cow's-milk cheese that in

QUARK AND TOPFEN

Two important dairy substances—I hesitate to refer to them as cheese, since they are fresh dairy products—that are original to Germany (especially Bavaria) and western Austria are quark and topfen. These fresh, bright white "cheeses" are consumed in vast quantities by Germans and Austrians who relish their tanginess, simplicity, and versatility.

Quark can best be described as a cross between yogurt and American curdless or small-curd cottage cheese. Topfen is also like cottage cheese, leaning more toward what we on the East Coast of the U.S. refer to as pot cheese, a drier form of cottage cheese. Like yogurt and cottage cheese, topfen and quark are very low in fat because they

are mostly water, with very little butterfat. Both are sold in small tubs in the dairy sections of supermarkets and shops in Germany and Austria in the same manner cottage cheese and yogurt are merchandised in the U.S.

Quark and topfen are staple ingredients in countless recipes, both sweet and savory, and they are also mixed with seasonings for use as spreads and toppings. In the region of the Harz mountains they are mixed with caraway seeds, packed into crocks, and allowed to "ripen" until very strong and highly aromatic—in other words, smelly. In Saxony, quark or topfen is blended with scallions, chives, or onions, or all three, and mixed with sour cream to be used as a topping on potatoes.

LIMBURGER HIGH JINKS

I remember when I was a kid, before the hoods of cars became impossible to open, the most popular application for Limburger was to place a hunk of it on the engine block of someone's car. As the motor heated up, the cheese melted and released its pungent aroma as the unsuspecting motorist tooled down the highway. Ah, youth!

my opinion has a great deal more aroma than flavor—give me Alsatian Munster any day. Healthy Limburger will have considerable aroma but should not smell rancid. Beneath the thin, light brown, edible rind is a soft, smooth, whitish paste, with a rather one-dimensional taste—salty, cheesy, sharp, and devoid of nuance. Choose unwrinkled, foil-wrapped packages that surround an 8-ounce (250 g) rectangular cheese that hasn't begun to sag on top or bulge at the sides (evidence of having sat on the shelf too long). Serve Limburger with beer, crackers, raw vegetables, or fruit. I also like it with sardines and raw onions, a few crackers, and a tasty beer.

Romadur (roh-mah-DOOR): Rare in the U.S.; a cow's-milk cheese very similar to Limburger, though softer. It is sold in a variety of shapes, usually 8-ounce (250 g) squares that are 1½ inches thick.

German Münster or **Muenster** (MUN-ster): Rare in the U.S. Three villages in Germany go by the name of Münster, but ironically none is

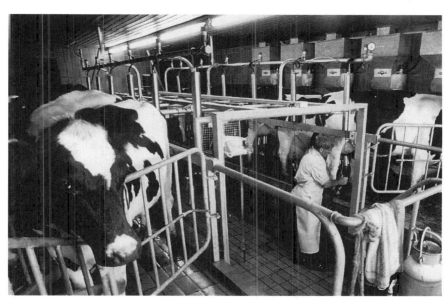

These Holstein-Friesian cows, patiently awaiting milking time at a mechanized dairy farm near Bonn, were crossbred to produce prodigious amounts of milk.

Tradition meets technology: An old Bavarian farmhouse sports TV antennae.

the home of this cheese—Munster is a corruption of the German and French words that once meant "monastery." Munster, the cheese, is first and foremost the pride of Alsace (see page 82). German Münster (with an umlaut) came about as an attempt to imitate this cheese, but while it is certainly decent, there is no way it can be considered more than remotely similar to Munster d'Alsace. German Münster is considerably firmer, and the 6-pound (3 k), foil-wrapped disks are more than twice the height of Munster d'Alsace. It is a factory cheese that clearly suffers from the requirements of large-scale production. Look for any example that appears to be fresh. If the interior face of a cut wheel is grayish or whitish, it's old; look for the paste in its natural straw color. German Münster

will have strong flavor that is neither piercingly sharp nor overwhelming. Serve it as a snack, luncheon, or dessert cheese with fruit, raw vegetables, bread, ham or salami, and beer or spicy white or rough red wine. Remove the foil wrap before cutting and serving.

Tilsiter (TILL-situr): Rare in the U.S.; a simple, very typical German cheese made from partially skimmed, pasteurized cow's milk. Semifirm with numerous tiny apertures (not quite holes), a brownish-orange washed rind, and a big briny, spicy flavor, it is versatile for cooking (melted or cubed) and good sliced for sandwiches. When buying Tilsiter, be aware that piercing flavor is evidence that the batch has sat on the shelf too long. The flavor should be strong, but not overpowering. Tilsiter is made in wheels ranging from 6 to 9 pounds (3 to 4½ k), 3 to 5 inches thick, and like Danish Tilsit, can also be found in block form.

Cambozola (kam-bo-ZO-lah): Widely available in the U.S.; a very popular brand-name German factory-made cheese (produced by a company called Champignon) that imitates both Brie and Gorgonzola. Indeed, its name is a combination of Camembert and Gorgonzola. This cheese has little character and goes against everything I believe in—it is the result of successful

marketing, not cheesemaking. Made in thick wheels of about 4 pounds (2 k) each, Cambozola has a white, Brie-like, soft-ripened rind, and is sold plastic- or foil-wrapped.

The Cheeses of Austria

A**ustrian Emmenthaler** (EM-awn-TAHL-ur); also called **Austrian Swiss**: Widely available in the U.S.

Austrian versions are indistinguishable from all of the other Emmental Swiss types that have holes and are made from pasteurized milk. I find them flabby, rubbery, bland versions of the real articles from France and Switzerland. It is sold in 15-pound (7½ k) blocks that are cut to the size of sandwich bread, for which it is principally intended. Not a bad cheese, just not special.

Austrian Gruyère (grew-YAIR or gree-AIR): See Austrian Emmenthaler above. This cheese is much less flavorful than Swiss Gruyère or French Comté. It is sold in blocks for the sandwich and restaurant food-service trade.

Mondseer (MOND-sear): Not widely available in the U.S.; very decent, plastic-wrapped, round-edged, 2-pound (1 k) disks of inexpensive, soft, strong, smelly, full-flavored, partially skimmed, pasteurized cow's milk cheese. Similar to Danish Esrom (see page 439) in color and flavor, but with a slightly firmer texture. Avoid any that smells too strong. Serve with beer and crackers.

Saint Michael (SAINT-MY-kul): Not widely available in the U.S. A Tilsit-style Austrian cheese, though smoother in texture and without apertures. Saint Michael has a big, pleasant flavor, but not much character. Still, it is a very decent, very inexpensive cheese, which gives it a certain appeal. Choose any that appears fresh when cut from the 8- to 10-pound (4 to 5 k) wheels. Trim away the brown rind. Serve this cheese simply—for lunches and snacks, with beer and crackers.

THE BALKAN COUNTRIES

The Balkan countries—Greece, Bulgaria, Romania, parts of the former Yugoslavia, and, for these immediate purposes only, Turkey and Cyprus—offer little of the cheese variety and romance of Western Europe. Most Balkan cheeses are brined, fresh cheeses made from sheep's milk, goat's milk, or a combination of the two milks. This area of Eastern Europe is predominantly mountainous, rough, rocky, and not very fertile, not by a long shot.

Technologically underdeveloped, the Balkan countries face two major problems: They are undertooled in their ability to compete for export dollars, and they face tremendous obstacles in finding widespread acceptance of the unique flavors of their cheeses. Were it not for Feta, this area wouldn't figure on the cheese front at all, except in the not inconsiderable ethnic markets.

The Cheeses

Feta (FET-uh): Widely available in the U.S. Greece is best known for Feta, a young, crumbly sheep's-milk cheese that is pickled in brine. I sell tons of it. Feta is made in big, irregular cylinders and blocks with flat tops and bottoms, and each cheese weighs from 10 to 30 pounds

Sheep supply wool, meat, and milk for cheesemaking.

An idyllic Mediterranean afternoon: sunshine, friends, Feta to nibble on, and retsina to sip.

(5 to 15 k). These large cheeses are then cut or sliced (*feta* means "slice" in Greek) into wedges and cubes that fit into 100-pound (50 k) wooden barrels, or into blocks that fit into a 30-pound (15 k) tin can. A brine solution of water and salt is poured over the pieces to arrest the ripening process, and the virtually "pickled" cheese is immersed in the brine to keep it young, fresh, and full of savor. (Before serving, you might want to rinse Feta under tap water to remove this brine, as it has a tendency to make the cheese overly salty.)

Feta is a cheese that, while not offering the complexity and fascination of so many cheeses I hold dear, is eminently agreeable in its simplicity when served simply with olives, bread, and wine. It is frequently used in the classic Greek dishes of *pastitsio* and *spanakopita,* and it is also served as an appetizer or table cheese accompanied by vegetables, ham, salami, pickled or dried fish, salad, or fruit.

In New York City, I find that my Feta customers, many of whom are Greek, are exceptionally demanding. As a result, I stock several varieties of top-quality Feta. People raised on Feta—not just Greeks, but also Slavs, Romanians, Bulgarians, and Turks—are extremely opinionated about this cheese. I constantly hear, "This is the best Feta!" or "This is not very good Feta, you got it from . . ." Personal preferences for one Feta over another seem to

THE GREEK GIFT

In early Greek mythology, the ability to make cheese was referred to as "a gift of everlasting value."

be inflexible. To me, if it's good Feta, it's good Feta. But to my many "Fetaphiles" much more matters: One may be (or seem to be) slightly creamier than another, or less salty, or have an herbier flavor. But whatever the perceived difference, it is a difference which renders all other Fetas inferior to "this one." I'm always surprised that this simple, straightforward cheese inspires such fervency. But Feta buyers have an emotional attachment to their favorite . . . and that's that! I have learned to go with the flow rather than attempt to be a Feta tastemaker. It is the one cheese my customers continue to force me to jump through hoops over.

I carry one Greek Feta (widely available in the U.S.) that is shipped across the ocean in gorgeous wooden barrels that fall completely to pieces once they are opened. This breaks my heart every time. I handle them as carefully as I can in an attempt to preserve these lovely

Traditional Feta is cut into wedges, then ripened and shipped in parchment-lined wooden barrels.

GOAT'S MILK FETA

Some Feta made in Greece and the United States is made from goat's milk. In my experience, it is very similar to the more traditional sheep's-milk Feta and is commendable.

things (they're big enough for a tumble over Niagara Falls). This Feta goes by no particular brand name, and several Greek importers, including Fantis and Boboris, handle it.

My other favorite "Greek" Feta of barrel-aged Peloponnese origin is something of a puzzle. Just under the wooden lid is a circle of white, brine-soaked paper printed in red and blue insoluble ink. Amidst a riot of Greek language announcing the brand name, is just a bit of English. It reads: "100% sheep's milk, product of Italy." Wherever its roots, it's great Feta. It, too, goes by no particular name other than that of the importer, Krinos, the largest importer of Greek foodstuffs in the U.S. Most likely, it comes from Sardinia, where sheep's milk flows like a river. I assume it's shipped to Greece, where it is put in tins or barrels and in turn exported throughout the world, ostensibly as a Greek product. And there's no deception intended. The Greek importer I buy it from was completely unabashed when I asked him about it. His reply was: "You asked me for my best Greek Feta. That's what I sent you." He was right. It was, and continues to be, excellent Feta. And it does come from Greece—sort of.

Bulgarian Feta: My Bulgarian Feta also has an enormous following. As Feta goes I would say that this is less sheepy-tasting, not quite as salty (owing to the weaker salt-to-water ratio of the brine it is packed in), and has a creamier flavor and texture than much of the exported Greek Feta.

Besides Greek, Bulgarian, French, Israeli American (made from cow's or goat's milk), and Italian Feta, you may also come across examples from the former Yugoslavia, Hungary, Romania, Turkey, and Lebanon. Quality? You be the judge. I prefer stronger ones to blander versions, but in the end, it's best to taste and then buy what you like best.

Kasseri (kah-SAIR-ri), **Kefalotyri** (KEF-ah-oh-TEER-r), **Kefalograviera** (KEF-ah-loh-grahv-YAIR-ah): Available in specialty food shops and ethnic markets in the U.S. The roots of these three cheeses are the same, as evidenced by their similar names. In Greece the most basic sheep cheeses are called Kasseri.

They are big, 20-pound (10 k) wheels of fairly firm, supple cheese. They are usually well aged—six months to one year—and are made from uncooked curd. Kasseri has obvious similarities to those basic cheeses usually referred to as Kashkaval (KASH-kah-vahl), found in Turkey, Bulgaria, and the former Yugoslavia. Kasseri isn't over-assertive and doesn't even have an overtly sheepy flavor, it just doesn't have much flavor at all, and is best when dressed up before serving (see page 467). What flavor there is could be described as a waxy, oily tang with a hint of olives.

After emerging from their molding and pressing stage, these cheeses are given a simple brine bath to arrest their development. They are then set aside to dry and age for six months to one year, during which time they are turned frequently. The cheeses are encased in thick plastic before a crust is allowed to form. The dryish rind that covers the off-white interior is usually trimmed away before the cheese is served.

FRENCH FETA

I can usually correctly identify the country of origin of most Fetas by observing and tasting. French (and Israeli) Feta, for example, are, in my opinion, rather neutral in flavor if not altogether characterless. A few years ago when France reduced the legal boundaries permissible for the gathering of sheep's milk for Roquefort production, many cheesemakers chose to turn the resulting glut of milk into enormous quantities of Feta geared toward the lucrative export market for this popular cheese.

Less easily found in the U.S., though common in most parts of Greece, is Kefalotyri, essentially an extra-aged Kasseri. (*Kefalo* means "head" in Greek and refers to cheeses of the size of, or bigger than, your head.) Kefalotyri is rather like Italian Romano, though slightly less salty and less rock hard. Grated or shredded, it is used frequently in cooking. It is also eaten as a table cheese with dried sausage, raw vegetables, and bread. Like Kasseri, Kefalotyri are rather thick and cumbersome cheeses, which are never precisely uniform in weight; they may weigh from 18 to 23 pounds (9 to 11½ k). They are usually about 6 inches thick and 17 inches in diameter, and often have one flat side, an indicator that the cheese was dried on its side rather than lying flat, a process that has no particular advantage worthy of note.

Kefalograviera cheeses are much smaller than either Kasseri or Kefalotyri—just as thick, but usually roundish 12- to 14-pound (6 to 7 k) shapes, about 8 to 12 inches in diameter. Kefalograviera is a sort of sheep's-milk Gruyère, featuring small, random holes, and is considerably less aged than Kefalotyri (one year as opposed to Kefalotyri's two or more). It is a cheese that I relish for its rusticity and its honest raw-milk goodness and stolidity. I particularly enjoy the application of the Alpine Gruyère style to a sheep's-milk cheese. If from a commendable batch (and consistency is a serious problem with Greek cheeses), Kefalograviera offers a rich, robustly nutty flavor and a

A Greek shepherd tends his flock under a sweltering sun. Goats and sheep abound in Greece, where mountains comprise nearly three-quarters of the country's terrain.

Similar to Italian Pecorino Romano, though less salty, extra-aged sheep's-milk Kefalotyri is often used as a grating cheese.

smooth mouthfeel. It is sort of a middle-ground cheese, falling between Kasseri and Kefalotyri in terms of texture and flavor intensity.

Fundamentally similar, Kasseri, Kefalotyri, and Kefalograviera are the result of cheesemaking recipes that diverge only slightly in the curing stage; both temperature and humidity are lower for the longer-aged Kefalotyri. All three are made in smallish facilities throughout Greece, principally in Larissa, the Peloponnese, and Crete. The best I've found come from a facility in Crete, where the work is done by hand and on a smaller scale than in the Peloponnese. The milk is left unpasteurized, resulting in a more flavorful cheese.

You should be advised that while all three of these Greek cheeses are available in the U.S., unless your town is home to a sizeable Greek community, you are not likely to find Kefalotyri or Kefalograviera available. Kasseri, on the other hand, is much more common, although I find it to be a far less interesting

cheese than Kefalotyri or Kefalograviera.

When shopping for Kasseri, Kefalotyri, or Kefalograviera look for smooth, white or off-white interiors that are free of pooling butterfat between the plastic wrap and the cheese. Owing to its 100% sheep's milk content, Kasseri may give off a slight greenish glow, which is completely natural and appropriate. You'll want to be aware that Greeks rarely purchase less than 2 pounds (1 k) of Kasseri at a time, so prepare yourself for a disbelieving stare if you request a measly ½ pound (250 g) in

SAUTEED KASSERI

Makes 4 appetizer or first-course servings

½ pound (250 g) Kasseri
3 tablespoons extra-virgin
  olive oil
2 cloves garlic, minced
Fresh lemon juice

Cut the Kasseri into strips 4 inches long and ¼ inch thick. In a medium-size skillet over medium heat, sauté the Kasseri strips and garlic until lightly browned on both sides, about 2 minutes per side. Remove from the skillet, sprinkle with fresh lemon juice, and serve immediately.

the store. Avoid any cheese that shows obvious defects such as dryness, interior mold, cracks, or mushiness. I enjoy Kasseri sautéed or grilled, served as an appetizer or first course along with raw vegetables, fresh fruits, olives, cured ham, dry sausage, crusty bread, and any wine you enjoy. Kefalotyri and Kefalograviera are a little too firm for frying, grilling, or sautéing. Consider them, instead, as superior cheeses for grating or shredding over beans, soups, and stews, or onto slices of garlic-rubbed bread. Drizzle a little extra-virgin olive oil over the bread and cheese and place it under the broiler until the surface turns golden. Serve as an appetizer along with olives.

Manouri (mah-NOOR-ree): Available only in ethnic markets in the U.S.; another staple Greek sheep's-milk cheese. I like Manouri very much because its flavor reminds me of Italy's nutty Ricotta Salata, though its texture is different. It is rich, with a marked, buttery mouthfeel. Manouri comes in plastic-wrapped 6- to 8-pound (3 to 4 k) cylinders (sort of like white artillery shells).

Thin slices of velvety-textured Manouri are delicious paired with peppers.

> ## AWAITING A COMEBACK
>
> In the Balkan countries, Bryndza (BRIN-dza) is a Hungarian-style spread made from odds and ends of leftover sheep's-milk cheese that are mashed and combined with sweet or hot paprika. It used to be exported to the U.S. in the 1970s, but I haven't seen it since then.

It is rindless, stark white, buttery soft, and slightly crumbly. Choose any Manouri that is free of exterior mold. It is superb shredded into salads and pasta or thinly sliced and eaten with raw or pickled vegetables, especially hot or sweet peppers.

Myzithra (mih-ZEE-thra) and **Anthotiro** (an-THO-tee-roh): Both available only in ethnic markets in the U.S. Fresh sheep's-milk cheeses that are very much like real Italian sheep's-milk Ricotta are common throughout Greece. Every region has a different name for this fresh curd: One region calls it Myzithra, another calls it Anthotiro, but it's the same terrific-tasting cheese. It has such a good nutty flavor, much better than the bland Ricotta you get in the U.S. Imported Ricottas from Greece and Italy aren't just wiggling blobs, they're cottony and drier, with a wonderful texture in the mouth—not gritty, but not creamy either. You really should try them. In the Czech language, this fresh sheep's-milk cheese is called Urdu (ER-dew) or Urda (ER-dah). In the Czech republic, in Slavic communities, and in Hungary, it is used in casseroles as well as in desserts made with pastry. It is also eaten as a table cheese with fruits or vegetables.

Dried Myzithra is used for grating; fresh, it's delicious mixed with a bit of honey.

Myzithra and Anthotiro both lend themselves beautifully to cooking—they are terrific blended into pasta dishes. A pressed and dried version of Myzithra, similar to Italian Ricotta Salata, is a popular grating cheese in Greece.

Anari (ON-ah-ree): Available primarily in ethnic markets in the U.S.; a fresh, soft, mild sheep's-milk cheese produced in Cyprus. Should Anari find its way out of the ethnic market, it would be a big hit with dieters because it has only 20% butterfat. It has the sweet, nutty flavor of sheep's-milk Ricotta, but it is a tighter-textured, denser, drier, more substantial cheese than Myzithra, Anthotiro, or Italian Ricotta. It is sold by the slab or hunk, cut from rather amorphous loaves of about 20 pounds (10 k) each. You might want to try warming slices of Anari in the oven and serving them with shredded radicchio and freshly ground black pepper. This "salad" is delightful as a first course. Anari is also served at breakfast and lunch with whatever is at hand, chiefly fruits and vegetables.

Haloumi (hah-LOO-mee; also pronounced ha-LOOM): Available primarily in ethnic markets in the U.S.; a very popular cheese in Turkey and Cyprus as well as throughout the Arab world. This sheep's-milk cheese is flavored with shreds of fresh mint and is sold in little blocks or squares of about 8 ounces (250 g) each, encased in vacuum-packed plastic, usually with a bit of brine. Haloumi is semifirm though supple, easily sliced, and rather mild, with an unmistakable aftertaste of mint. It is eaten as a snack, usually sliced and stuffed into pita bread, with whatever else is at hand, often hot or sweet peppers or bottled hot chili sauce, and black or green olives. Haloumi sort of squeaks as your teeth break it down. All of it is good—choose any. In a certain light, sheep's-milk cheeses such as Amari and Haloumi will appear to have a slight greenish glow which has nothing to do with the mint—it is the nature of sheep's milk and sheep's-milk cheese.

CANADA

Though one would expect that a country as big as Canada would be home to a great many cheesemaking facilities and a prodigious quantity of cheese, it is not. Curiously, Canadians are not big consumers of cheese. I find that baffling. Their ancestors—Scots, Scandinavians, and certainly the French—all came from decidedly cheese-eating cultures. And while it is a fact that the more western provinces are largely unpopulated—enormous tracts of land given over to the raising of beef cattle—dairy cattle abound in southern Ontario and Quebec. Where does all the milk go? Apparently, if not transformed into Cheddar, it winds up in dairy cases simply as milk or cream. Most of the cheeses Canadians eat are imported, which suggests they prefer the originals made by their European and Scandinavian ancestors over the Canadian versions.

The Cheeses

Oka (OH-kuh): Widely available in the U.S., Oka was once a Trappist cheese made by monks who emigrated in the 1880s from Brittany to Canada and continued to make their Port-Salut–type cheese at a monastery in the village of Oka, near Montreal. Nowadays, it is a slightly smelly, semisoft, pasteurized cow's-milk cheese made in modest quantities by Agropur, the largest dairy cooperative in Canada, at a modern plant in Oka. The cheese is still aged in the monastery's cellars, which are adjacent to

Agropur's cheesemaking facility. A very honest cheese, Oka has a good, full flavor. Each brown-crusted, creamy, 1½-inch-thick wheel weighs about 4 pounds (2 k), and has been aged for around two months before it is marketed. Oka is neither as cloying nor as flabby and glossy as French Port-Salut. Its dry, brown crust is the result of several rind brushings, or washings, in a weak brine solution.

Canadian Cheddar: Widely available in the U.S., Canadian Cheddar is uniformly excellent. But beware—the most popular, Black Diamond Cheddar, is overpriced and no better than Cheddars from smaller, less-famous makers in Ontario and Quebec.

The Forfar Dairy in Ontario produces a tiny amount of truly excellent Cheddar—one of the finest examples of North American Cheddar I've encountered. I have sold nine-year-old Forfar Cheddar—quite an experience—that has tiny, white, granular crystals that crunch when you bite into the cheese. This Cheddar is so sharp it makes your tongue smart with pleasure. You can be sure I have my order in for more.

In general, though, there is no earthly reason to eschew American Cheddar in favor of Canadian. They are identical, according to age, but the Canadian cheeses are usually more expensive—my advice is to buy the one that is the better value.

Fromagerie Tournevent in Chesterville, Quebec, makes a range of goat cheeses (fresh, aged, in olive

oil), of which two are goat's-milk Cheddars. All of their cheeses are excellent. The fresh cheeses, weighing about 3 ounces (90 g), are cylindrical and encased in soft paraffin with a nifty zip-strip that is hygienic, efficacious, and novel—I like it. And I like the creamy, nutty, savory cheese inside, too. The Cheddars—mild Chevrino (aged for up to three months) and Le Chèvre Noir (aged for a minimum of six months)—are made in 2-pound (1 k) black wax–covered blocks. The cheese is stark white, flinty hard, yet moist and pleasantly sharp. Tournevent has been exporting to the U.S. for eight years, so keep an eye out for their cheeses—they are quite good.

The Great Cheeses

Ready Reference

T hese alphabetical thumbnail sketches of what I consider to be the world's most important cheeses are designed to be used as a quick reference source. You should find them especially helpful to consult before shopping for cheese. Each includes the cheese's "vital statistics," everything from how to pronounce its name and what brands (or makers) to look for in the shops, to its type, size, weight, and characteristics.

I also give an idea of the cheese's availability in the U.S. (excellent, good, rare, etc.). General information about appropriate wines is provided, though I have chosen not to be too specific, usually offering instead overall recommendations about certain styles or groups of wines.

Should you not find a cheese profiled here, it most likely is either because it is unavailable in the U.S. or because I feel it simply doesn't deserve to be considered an important cheese. For example, despite the fact that French Brie de Melun is a name-controlled cheese, I do not consider it an important one. And although I respect them greatly, you will not find Swedish Vasterbotten or Norwegian Gammelost, which are so rare they are nearly

To savor the great cheeses of the world is to taste history.

impossible to locate outside of Sweden or Norway. The monastery-style cheeses of Belgium are good, but they, too, don't qualify in my eyes for any list of the world's finest cheeses. At the other end of the spectrum, there is a handful of important cheeses which, though I believe they are overrated (Asiago d'allevo, for example), must be acknowledged as significant.

American cheeses and cheesemakers are not listed here, since as of this writing, you are more likely to locate them by contacting the cheesemaker or small producer directly than to find them in your local cheese shop or specialty food source. They are discussed in depth in their own section (see page 401).

One last word before you go shopping—always remember that if there is a choice between a pasteurized and an unpasteurized cheese, there is no question you should choose the unpasteurized one. Raw-milk cheeses always have the most flavor and character.

ABONDANCE

(ah-oone-DAHNCE); A.O.C.; also called Tomme d'Abondance (tum-DAH-bone-DAHNCE)

Origin: France—Savoie
Type: Partially skimmed cow's milk, unpasteurized; semi-firm; pressed curd; natural, brushed rind (inedible)
Availability: Rare
Form: Wheels
Dimensions: 3 inches thick, 14 to 13 inches in diameter
Weight: 15 to 20 lbs. (7½ to 10 k)

Fat Content: 40%
Best Brands: All excellent
Characteristics: Firm, yet supple, creamy-brown crust; light yellow interior; enormous presence, yet not too strong; buttery, intensely fruity and nutty flavor; fruity aroma
Appropriate Wines: All light and fruity reds; big whites
Related Cheeses: French Beaufort, Comté, Morbier, Le Brouère; Swiss Gruyère, Raclette cheeses (Bagnes, Conches, Gomser, Orsières), Vacherin Fribourgeois; Italian Fontina d'Aosta
The Bottom Line: Magnificent; an excellent melting cheese (think raclette and fondue).

APPENZELLER

(AP-en-zeller); also called Appenzell (AP-en-zell)

Origin: Switzerland—Appenzell, Saint Gallen
Type: Cow's milk, unpasteurized; firm; pressed curd; natural, brushed rind (inedible)
Availability: Good
Form: Wheels
Dimensions: 3 to 4 inches thick, 12 to 14 inches in diameter
Weight: 11 to 15 lbs. (5½ to 7½ k)
Fat Content: 45%
Best Brands: All excellent; not marketed by brand
Characteristics: Brown, pebbled rind ivory-colored, smooth interior with occasional scattering of pea- to cherry-size holes; pronounced spicy, fruity, tangy flavor; strong aroma
Appropriate Wines: *Cru* Beaujolais, such as Château de la Chaize

(Brouilly); red Burgundies (the Swiss are the world's largest importers of Burgundy)

Related Cheeses: Swiss Gruyère, Vacherin Fribourgeois, Raclette cheeses (Bagnes, Conches, Gomser, Orsières); French Abondance, Raclette; Italian Fontina d'Aosta

The Bottom Line: A horrendously expensive Swiss classic.

ASIAGO D'ALLEVO

(ah-zee-AH-goh-dah-LEH-voh); D.O.C.

Origin: Italy—Veneto, Friuli–Venezia Giulia

Type: Partially skimmed cow's milk, unpasteurized; firm; cooked curd; brushed rind (inedible)

Availability: Good

Form: Wheels

Dimensions: 7 to 9 inches high, 14 to 16 inches in diameter

Weight: 18 to 24 lbs. (9 to 12 k)

Fat Content: 45%; also available 30%

Best Brands: All excellent; not marketed by brand

Characteristics: Light beige interior and exterior with small-hole distribution throughout, mild, tangy flavor and aroma (young); very dry, grayish rind, bone to amber interior, bland, sharp flavor (aged). Available *fresco* (fresh, aged 2 to 3 months); *mezzano* (medium-ripe, semi-hard, and mild, aged 3 to 5 months); and *vecchio* (hard and a bit sharper, aged 9 months or longer)

Appropriate Wines: Any light, fruity reds, such as Grave del Friuli, Dolcetto d'Alba; bigger, coarser Italian reds, such as Barolo, Brunello di Montalcino, Chianti Riserva

Related Cheeses: Italian Montasio;

Danish Havarti, Graddost; Finnish Masurkaa, Lappi; Swedish Vasterbotten. *Note:* American Asiago is related only by name—it is a completely different cheese that more closely resembles Provolone

The Bottom Line: A vastly overrated cheese—I believe—although it does have an appreciative audience.

BANON

(BAN-awh)

Origin: France—Dauphiné (Isère, Drôme), Provence (Vaucluse)

Type: Cow's or goat's milk, pasteurized and unpasteurized; soft; rindless; usually wrapped in chestnut or grape leaves that have been dipped in white wine, *eau-de-vie,* or *marc* (tied with ribbon or raffia)*;* sometimes without leaves, but sprinkled with herbs or spices

Availability: Rare

Form: Disks; usually wrapped in chestnut leaves and tied with raffia or ribbon

Dimensions: 1 inch thick, 3 inches in diameter

Weight: 3½ to 5 oz. (105 to 150 g)

Fat Content: 45%

Best Brands: Fromagerie Royannais-Teche is the only producer that exports to the U.S.; their factory-made (*laitier*) examples are adequate, although somewhat vapid. In France, look for leaf-wrapped *fermier* examples. Interestingly, U.S.-made Capriole Banon from Indiana (page 401) is as delicious as any *fermier* versions to be found in France

Characteristics: Beige or blue-mold-covered crust; soft, runny beige

interior; intensely rustic, nutty, and fruity (slightly winey) flavor
Appropriate Wines: With young cheese, whites, rosés, and reds from the Côtes de Provence; with ripe cheese any Rhône red
Related Cheeses: French Picodon, Saint-Marcellin
The Bottom Line: Not nearly as interesting as it looks.

BEAUFORT

(bo-FORE); A.O.C.

Origin: France—Savoie
Type: Cow's milk, unpasteurized; firm; pressed, cooked curd; natural, brushed rind (inedible)
Availability: Rare
Form: Wheels
Dimensions: 8 inches thick, 36 inches in diameter
Weight: About 80 lbs. (40 k)
Fat Content: 50%
Best Brands: All excellent; look for Beaufort d'Alpage, made from the lush, rich, end-of-summer milk from high Alpine pastures (*alpages*)
Characteristics: Smooth, beige rind and paste; firm, creamy texture with occasional *lèrures* (horizontal fissures); mild, fruity, sweet flavor. Extraordinary melting capacity—terrific for fondue
Appropriate Wines: All big reds. This is an example of an especially fine cheese that elevates the rough and simple reds, such as some Côtes-du-Rhône and everyday Bordeaux. Also good with Châteauneuf-du-Pape, Cornas, Gigondas, Hermitage, St. Joseph
Related Cheeses: French Comté; Swiss Gruyère

The Bottom Line: Superb mountain cheese; equally fine for eating or melting; price is its only drawback—costs at least twice as much as French Comté and Swiss Gruyère.

BEAUMONT

(bo-MAWH)

Origin: France—Savoie
Type: Cow's milk, unpasteurized; semisoft; pressed; washed rind (inedible)
Availability: Illegal for export to U.S. (raw cow's milk cheese aged less than 60 days)
Form: Disks
Dimensions: 1½ to 2 inches thick, 8 inches in diameter
Weight: 3½ lbs. (about 1¾ k)
Fat Content: 50%
Best Brands: This is a trademarked cheese made by Girod, an excellent commercial producer located in Beaumont
Characteristics: Smooth, dark tan rind ivory-to-straw interior; pronounced, not unpleasant, barnyardy aroma; full, rich, earthy flavor; smooth, creamy texture; this is an oversize bulk version of the splendid Reblochon
Appropriate Wines: Well-knit Rhône reds
Related Cheeses: French Murol, Munster, Reblochon, Saint-Nectaire, Le Pavin, Tamié; Italian Taleggio, Robiola Lombardia
The Bottom Line: Highly recommended; one of the all-too-seldom seen examples of excellent factory-made cheese.

BLEU D'AUVERGNE

(bluh-doe-VAIRN); A.O.C.

Origin: France—Auvergne
Type: Cow's-milk blue, pasteurized; soft; rindless (edible, salty exterior)
Availability: Good
Form: Foil-wrapped wheels
Dimensions: 4 inches high, 8 inches in diameter
Weight: 6 lbs. (3 k)
Fat Content: 45%
Best Brands: All good; seek out La Memée and Roussel (my favorite)
Characteristics: Rindless, salty exterior; white- to beige-colored interior with liberal blue veining; more gently flavored than Bleu des Causses
Appropriate Wines: Big, chewy Rhône reds, especially Châteauneuf-du-Pape, Comas, Hermitage; Sauternes; red Bordeaux
Related Cheeses: American Maytag Blue, Dietrich Pur Chèvre Blu, French Bleu des Causses, Bleu de Laqueuille, Fourme d'Ambert, Roquefort; Scottish Lanark Blue; Spanish Cabrales, Gamonedo, Picón
The Bottom Line: Uncomplicated but admirable basic blue; excellent value.

BLEU DE BRESSE

(BLUH-duh-BRESS)

Origin: France—Burgundy (Bresse)
Type: Cow's-milk blue, pasteurized; soft-ripened; bloomy rind (edible)
Availability: Good
Form: Foil-wrapped wheels, cylinders, and small medallions
Dimensions: Three sizes
Weight: Wheels: 4 lbs. (2 k); cylinders:

3 lbs. (1½ k); small medallions: 8 oz. (250 g)
Fat Content: 50%
Best Brands: All imported brands excellent; look for Pipo 'Crem. A widely available American-made version—called Bresse Bleu—is vapid and no match for imported brands.
Characteristics: Off-white, fuzzy crust; creamy-white, slightly bulging interior with blue veining; buttery, one-dimensional Brie-like flavor
Appropriate Wines: Light, fruity reds, such as Beaujolais; stronger reds, such as Côtes-du-Rhône, Burgundy
Related Cheeses: American Saga Blue; Danish Saga Blue, Blue Castello; French Pipo 'Crem; Italian Gorgonzola; German Cambozola, Montagnolo
The Bottom Line: The real thing from France is an acceptable alternative to Italian Gorgonzola, but forget about U.S.-made versions.

BLEU DE GEX, BLEU DE SEPTMONCEL

(BLUH-duh-JECKS, BLUH-duh-SETmoan-sell); A.O.C.

Note: These two virtually identical name-controlled cheeses are grouped together under the A.O.C. designation of Bleu de Gex-Haut-Jura. This A.O.C. name, however, is not used by retailers. In shops, these two cheeses will be identified by their individual names.

Origin: France—Franche-Comté
Type: Cow's-milk blue, unpasteurized; soft; slightly pressed curd; natural, brushed rind (inedible)
Availability: Rare

Form: Convex, flat-topped wheels
Dimensions: 3 to 3½ inches high,
14 to 16 inches in diameter
Weight: 12 to 14 lbs (6 to 7 k)
Fat Content: 45%
Best Brands: All excellent
Characteristics: Dry, pebbled, grayish-beige rind yellowish-ivory paste with liberal, light sky blue veining; gently saline nutty, fruity flavor; piquant but not overpowering; creamy texture
Appropriate Wines: Young, fruity reds, such as *cru* Beaujolais, or stronger reds, such as Burgundy, Côtes-du-Rhône; Arbois
Related Cheeses: French Fourme d'Ambert, Sassenage
The Bottom Line: Divinely gentle blue cheeses.

BLEU DE HAUT-JURA

(BLUH-duh-hoh-zhura); see Bleu de Gex, Bleu de Septmoncel, above.

BLEU DES CAUSSES

(bluh-duh-KOSE); A.O.C.

Origin: France—Rouergue
Type: Cow's-milk blue, unpasteurized; soft; rindless (edible, salty exterior)
Availability: Rare
Form: Foil-wrapped wheels
Dimensions: 4 inches high, 8 inches in diameter
Weight: 5 to 5¼ lbs. (2½ to 2¾ k)
Fat Content: 45%
Best Brands: All excellent
Characteristics: Rindless, salty exterior; bone-white interior with liberal blue veining; moist and slightly crumbly; stronger flavor

and aroma than Bleu d'Auvergne
Appropriate Wines: Big, chewy Rhône reds, especially Châteauneuf-du-Pape, Cornas, Hermitage; Sauternes; red Bordeaux
Related Cheeses: American Maytag Blue, Dietrich Pur Chèvre Blu; Danish Blue; French Bleu d'Auvergne, Bleu de Laqueuille, Fourme d'Ambert, Roquefort; Scottish Lanark Blue; Spanish Cabrales, Gamonedo, Picón
The Bottom Line: A scrumptious cheese; differs from French Roquefort only in that it is made from raw cow's milk rather than raw sheep's milk.

BOERENKAAS

(BORE-en-kahss); also called Farmer's Gouda

Origin: The Netherlands
Type: Cow's milk, unpasteurized; semi-firm to rock hard (according to age); pressed, cooked curd; natural rind, painted or waxed (inedible)
Availability: Rare; occasionally found in specialty food shops
Form: Wheels with rounded sides
Dimensions: 4 to 5 inches thick, 14 to 16 inches in diameter
Weight: 18 to 28 lbs. (9 to 14 k)
Fat Content: 45% to 50%
Best Brands: All excellent
Characteristics: Natural burnished golden rind; beige-yellow interior; rich, sharp, complex flavor (young and aged); piquant and perfumy (aged); pleasant, nutty aroma
Appropriate Wines: All light, fruity reds; beer
Related Cheeses: Markedly less tasty relatives—Dutch Gouda and Leyden (although it's spiced); French Mimolette

The Bottom Line: The Gouda the Dutch save for themselves.

BOULETTE D'AVESNES

(boo-LETT-dah-VANE)

Origin: France—Flanders (Thiérache, Hainaut), Artois, Picardy
Type: Cow's milk, pasteurized and unpasteurized; soft; spiked with paprika, parsley, tarragon, crushed pepper, and cloves; washed rind (edible)
Availability: Rare
Form: Irregular cones
Dimensions: 4 to 6 inches high
Weight: 7 to 9 oz. (210 to 270 g)
Fat Content: 50%
Best Brands: All excellent; in France and U.S., look for Fouquet
Characteristics: Red, paprika-dusted rind; beige- to straw-colored interior flecked with seasonings; strong, spicy flavor; beware of overripeness
Appropriate Wines: Any coarse, strong, rough reds (Cahors); often accompanied by a glass of beer or gin!
Related Cheeses: Any strong, spiced cheese, such as French Dauphin (an identical cheese in the shape of a dolphin or porpoise), Géromé au Cumin, Maroilles, flavored Munster; Dutch Leyden
The Bottom Line: Visually striking and completely unique.

BOURSAULT

(boor-SO)

Origin: France—Ile-de-France (Brie)
Type: Cow's milk, pasteurized and unpasteurized; triple-crème; natural, bloomy rind (edible)
Availability: Rare
Form: Cardboard-boxed, paper-wrapped drums
Dimensions: 3 by 3 inches
Weight: About 8 oz. (250 g)
Fat Content: 75%
Best Brands: Boursault is both the cheese name and proprietary brand name. Gold label signifies raw milk production; silver, pasteurized. If you have a choice, opt for the more flavorful gold. Ignore "Consommer Avant" (date) on box bottom; instead, open box and examine paper-wrapped cheese. If too hard or too soft, shrunken, or if the paper is sodden or moldy, do not purchase
Characteristics: Thin soft, edible rind; light-yellow paste; nutty, rich, creamy flavor
Appropriate Wines: Light, fruity wines, white or red; Champagne; Vouvray
Related Cheeses: All French triple-crèmes, especially Brillat-Savarin, Explorateur, Gratte-Paille, Pierre Robert, Saint-André
The Bottom Line: Excellent factory-made cheese, whether pasteurized or unpasteurized.

BRIE DE MEAUX

(BREE-duh-MOH); A.O.C.

Origin: France—Ile-de-France (Brie)
Type: Cow's milk, pasteurized and unpasteurized; soft-ripened; bloomy rind (edible)
Availability: Rare; only version sold in U.S. is Rouzaire (pasteurized)
Form: Flat, platter-sized wheels;

always wrapped in waxed paper and
enclosed in a lidded wooden box
Dimensions: 1½ inches thick,
14 inches in diameter
Weight: About 5 lbs. (2¼ k)
Fat Content: 45% (unpasteurized),
60% (pasteurized)
Best Brands: Both pasteurized and
unpasteurized are A.O.C. In France,
look for San Simeon and Rouzaire; in
U.S., only Rouzaire (pasteurized) is
available
Characteristics: White, bloomy rind
with beige mottling; buttery, golden
paste (if it is *à point,* it will bulge but
not run); beefy, nutty, garlicky flavor;
mushroomy aroma
Appropriate Wines: Any big red
Bordeaux or Burgundy
Related Cheeses: French soft-
ripened cow's-milk cheeses such as
Camembert and Roucoulons, as well
as other Bries (Brie de Melun, Brie
de Montereau, Fontainebleau,
Coulommiers); Italian Paglia-style
and Toma cheeses
The Bottom Line: If you can find this
in the U.S., I guarantee it will be very
expensive and probably nowhere
near properly ripened.

BRINDAMOUR

*(BRAN-Jah-MORE); also called Brin
d'Amour or Fleur du Maquis
(FLUR-doo-MAH-KEY)*

Origin: France—Corsica
Type: Sheep's (usually) or goat's
(rare) milk (or mixture of the two),
pasteurized and unpasteurized; soft;
rindless, herb-coated exterior crust
(theoretically edible but coating will
be bitter)
Availability: Good (pasteurized)

Form: Pillow-shaped squares
Dimensions: 2 to 2½ inches high, 4 to
5 inches square
Weight: 1¼ to 1¾ lbs. (625 to 875 g)
Fat Content: 45%
Best Brands: All excellent; examples
labeled Fleur du Maquis are more
than likely made from unpasteurized
milk
Characteristics: Unique presentation, texture, and flavor; exterior
crust coated with dried rosemary,
powdered thyme, and savory, with
coriander seeds, juniper berries, and
the occasional tiny, whole red chile
pepper; according to age, paste color
and texture range from snow-white,
creamy, moist, and soft (young), to
bone-white and almost runny (aged)
Appropriate Wines: All rough, sharp,
earthy reds and whites; Corsican
wines, especially Sciacarello and
Patrimonio
Related Cheeses: Other Corsican
cheeses, including Fium'orbu, Golo,
Niolo, Venaco
The Bottom Line: One of my
favorites; if you like herbs, you'll
adore this.

CABECOU

(CAB-bay-koo)

Origin: France—Quercy, Périgord,
Languedoc, Rouergue
Type: Goat's or sheep's milk (usually)
or mixture of the two (rarer), unpasteurized; soft to hard (according to
age); rindless
Availability: Illegal for export to U.S.
(raw goat or sheep's milk cheese
aged less than 60 days)
Form: Small, flat disks; sometimes
wrapped in chestnut leaves

Dimensions: About the size of a silver dollar or a 50-cent piece, but twice as thick

Weight: About 1 oz. (30 g)

Fat Content: 45%, but varies

Best Brands: All excellent; the most famous are made in Rocamadour

Characteristics: White, soft, creamy interior (young); hard and brown (aged); flavor varies according to age from creamy and sweet (young) to acrid and unpleasantly goaty (very aged or overripe)

Appropriate Wines: Loire Valley white; red Bordeaux; Bourgueil, Cahors, Madiran

Related Cheeses: All traditional French goat cheeses, including Bouton de Culotte, Crottin de Chavignol, Pélardon, Picodon, Rocamadour

The Bottom Line: A joy; after Roquefort, *the* cheese of southwest France.

CABRALES

(kah-BRAH-lace); D.O.

Origin: Spain—Asturias

Type: Mix of goat's, cow's, and sheep's milk, pasteurized and unpasteurized (artisanal); blue; semi-firm; cave-aged for minimum of 3 months; natural rind (usually too salty to eat)

Availability: Good

Form: Wheels, inside heavy aluminum or plastic wrapping

Dimensions: 3 to 3½ inches high, 7 to 8 inches in diameter

Weight: 5 to 9 lbs. (2½ to 4½ k)

Fat Content: 45% to 48%

Best Brands: All excellent

Characteristics: Salty, inedible, buff-colored rind; fragile, moist, crumbly

interior with intense purple veining; rich, intense flavor

Appropriate Wines: All strong Spanish reds, including those from Bierzo, Ribera del Duero, Rioja, Navarra; Spanish sherries, sweet or dry

Related Cheeses: Spanish Picón, Gamonedo; French Roquefort; all blue cheeses

The Bottom Line: One of the world's most remarkable cheeses; striking appearance and flavor; you *must* try this.

CAERPHILLY

(care-FILL-ee)

Origin: Wales (Dyfed), England (Somerset)

Type: Cow's milk, pasteurized and unpasteurized; semi-firm; pressed curd; natural, brushed rind (inedible)

Availability: Rare, farmhouse production; good, factory-made

Form: Wheels (usually); also spheres (like squashed cricket balls)

Dimensions: 3 to 3½ inches thick, 10 to 12 inches in diameter

Weight: 8 to 9 lbs. (4 to 4½ k)

Fat Content: 45%

Best Brands: Farmhouse examples, especially Caws Cenarth Caerffili (Wales); Duckett's Caerphilly (England); Glynhynod Cerphilly (Wales); Welsh Farmhouse Caerphilly (Wales)

Characteristics: Dry, gray crust; ivory, dryish, crumbly paste (runny around edges near crust if aged); creamy throughout; mild, lemony flavor

Appropriate Wines: Dry whites, such as California or Australian Chardonnay, French Muscadet,

German Riesling, Sylvaner, Gewürz-traminer

Related Cheeses: English Cheddar, Cheshire, Derby, Gloucester, Lancashire, Leicester, Wensleydale; Italian Bra; Welsh T'yn Grug, Llangloffan; Cornish Yarg

The Bottom Line: A nearly extinct buttery dream of a cheese.

CAMEMBERT DE NORMANDIE

(kam-um-BARE-duh-nor-mahn-DEE); A.O.C.

Origin: France—Normandy (Pays d'Auge)

Type: Cow's milk, pasteurized (non-A.O.C.) and unpasteurized (A.O.C.); soft-ripened bloomy rind (edible)

Availability: Unpasteurized A.O.C. versions illegal for export to U.S. (raw cow's milk cheese aged less than 60 days); good availability pasteurized Camembert, but most are not recommended

Form: Small disks in wooden or cardboard boxes

Dimensions: 1 inch thick, 4 inches in diameter

Weight: 8 oz. (250 g)

Fat Content: 45% to 50%

Best Brands: In France, look for "V.C.N." (Véritable Camembert de Normandie) on label affixed to top of box, as well as the notation *au lait cru* (made with raw milk); Véritable Camembert de Normandie by Moulin de Carel (the best), Artisan Fromager, Etendard, Grand Béron, Henri Voy's Camembert de Paris, Isigny Sainte-Mère, La Ferme d'Antignac, Lanquetôt, Féo. In U.S. few non-A.O.C. pasteurized versions are worth buy-

ing; look for Vallée, Lescure, Isigny Sainte-Mère brands. Better yet, seek out Italian Toma di Carmagnola, Toma di Valcuvia, and Paglia-style cheeses, all of which are vastly superior to pasteurized French Camembert; also seek out the French-made brand called Roucoulons (not a Camembert) made by Milleret (Franche-Comté)

Characteristics: Bloomy rind with slight beige mottling (unpasteurized); bloomy rind with considerable reddish mottling (pasteurized); straw-colored interior (uniformly ripe and not chalky) huge flavor of mushroom, garlic, and truffle with strong mushroomy aroma (unpasteurized); mild flavor with slightly mushroomy aroma (pasteurized)

Appropriate Wines: Burgundy's Vougeot; all Gamay and Pinot Noir reds

Related Cheeses: All French soft-ripened cow's milk cheeses, including Brie; Italian Paglia-style and Toma cheeses, especially Toma di Carmagnola, Toma della Valcuvia; American Blythedale Vermont Brie

The Bottom Line: A once superb classic, now those available here are mostly banal. The examples really worth eating are unpasteurized and available only in France.

CANTAL

(kahn-TAHL); A.O.C.; also called Cantal de Salers (kahn-TAHL-duh-sah-LAIR); Fourme du Cantal (FORM-doo-kahn-TAHL)

Note: Name-controlled Salers (sah-LAIR), also called Fourme du Salers (Form-doo-sah-LAIR), is a nearly identical cheese made only from unpasteurized milk.

Origin: France—Auvergne
Type: Cow's milk, pasteurized and unpasteurized; semi-firm; pressed; natural, brushed rind (inedible)
Availability: Good
Form: Tall, cylindrical drums
Dimensions: 18 inches high, 20 inches in diameter
Weight: About 80 pounds (40 k)
Fat Content: 45%
Best Brands: All excellent; most Cantal is factory-made from pasteurized milk and therefore rather mild; if possible, opt for more flavorful Salers, made only from unpasteurized milk
Characteristics: Grayish-brown exterior; moist, straw-colored paste; very prone to blue mold (*fleurs de bleu*) that can be trimmed away (not a negative); almost crumbly texture; mild, buttery flavor
Appropriate Wines: Any light, fruity red or white; Beaujolais; Côte d'Auvergne
Related Cheeses: French Laguiole; English Cheddar (slight similarity)
The Bottom Line: One of the world's oldest cheeses; honest, workmanlike, and straightforward.

CAPRINI

(kah-PREE-nee)

Origin: Italy—Piedmont, Lombardy
Type: Goat's or cow's milk, pasteurized; fresh; unripened; rindless
Availability: Rare
Form: Paper-wrapped cylinders
Dimensions: 4 inches long, 1 inch in diameter
Weight: About 2 oz. (60 g)
Fat Content: 40% to 50%
Best Brands: All excellent; in U. S. and Italy, look for Mauri or Cademartori. Goat's-milk version is sold in green wrapper, cow's-milk in blue wrapper
Characteristics: Snow-white, moist interior and exterior; soft texture; tart, sweet-cream flavor
Appropriate Wines: Crisp white wines, such as Orvieto, Pinot Grigio
Related Cheeses: All fresh, unripened Italian cheeses, especially Robiola Piemonte, Mascarpone; French Petit-Suisse
The Bottom Line: Absolutely *delizioso!* Nothing like it is made outside of Italy. I am astounded that no American cheesemakers produce a domestic version.

CHABICHOU DU POITOU

(SHAH-bee-shew-due-pwah-TOO); A.O.C.

Origin: France—Poitou, Berry, Périgord
Type: Goat's milk, pasteurized and unpasteurized; soft to firm (according to age); natural rind (edible)
Availability: In France, A.O.C. version is artisanal and rare even in its areas of production; in U.S., unpasteurized version is unavailable due to USFDA restrictions on raw goat's milk cheeses aged less than 60 days; good availability of Chabichou-type cheeses
Form: Small cylinders
Dimensions: 3 to 4 inches high
Weight: 6 oz. (180 g)
Fat Content: 45%
Best Brands: In France and U.S., look for Le Chevrot made at Sèvre-et-Belle Coopérative (Poitou), Jacquin's Cornilly (Berry), Chabis made by Desport or Soreda (Périgord), Chabichou made by Chèvrechard (Poitou).

In France, look for examples made by La Chèvrerie Authon (Poitou)
Characteristics: Natural beige rind (if aged, occasional mottling of blue mold); white interior (all ages); fresh, sweet, mild flavor (young); piquant and intensely nutty flavor (aged); soft, moist, spreadable texture (young); firm, flinty, chewy texture (older)
Appropriate Wines: If cheese is young, dry whites such as Sauvignon Blanc, Fumé Blanc, Chardonnay; if cheese is riper, heavier reds such as Bordeaux, Bourgueil, Cahors, Chinon
Related Cheeses: All traditional French goat cheeses, especially Crottin de Chavignol. Pouligny-Saint-Pierre, Sainte-Maure de Touraine, Selles-sur-Cher, Valençay
The Bottom Line: Unsurpassedly scrumptious, surprisingly scarce.

CHAOURCE

(shah-OORSE); A.O.C.

Origin: France—Champagne (near the Langres plateau where the Burgundy/Champagne border blurs)
Type: Cow's milk, pasteurized and unpasteurized; soft-ripened; bloomy rind (edible)
Availability: Good (pasteurized)
Form: Short, fat drums
Dimensions: 3 to 4 inches high, 3 to 4 inches in diameter
Weight: 8 oz. (250 g) to just over 1 lb. (500 g)
Fat Content: 50%
Best Brands: All excellent; in France, look for Hugerot or Rouzaire; in U.S., look for Lincet (pasteurized)
Characteristics: Identical in recipe and similar in fat content to Brie, but flavor is richer and more acidic; bloomy, white crust (aged shows red mottling); ivory to light-yellow paste (according to age); three stages of ripeness—young (rather bland, very white, chalky), aged (creamy, runny around the edges), fully ripe (reddish mottling, soft, nutty, very runny); all stages rich, tart, moist
Appropriate Wines: Champagne or Bouzy, a still (nonsparkling) red from the Champagne region; light, fruity wines; Sancerre rosés
Related Cheeses: French Ervy-le-Châtel (identical, but always made from raw milk); half-ripened Epoisses and Langres, Saint-Florentin, all double-crèmes
The Bottom Line: So fragile that U.S. importers shy away from bringing them in—a pity.

CHEDDAR

(CHEH-der)

Origin: England—Somerset, Dorset, Cornwall, Devon, Avon
Type: Cow's milk, pasteurized (factory-made) and unpasteurized (farmhouse production); firm; pressed; cloth-covered rind (inedible)
Availability: Good, both farmhouse production and factory-made
Form: Varies—cloth-wrapped high, cylindrical drums (farmhouse production); also rectangles and less desirable smaller wheels
Dimensions: 14 to 16 inches high, 14 to 16 inches in diameter
Weight: 56 to 66 lbs. (28 to 33 k)
Fat Content: 45%
Best Brands: Keen's Farm (Somerset) and Montgomery's Farm (Somerset)—

outstanding; Quicke's Farm (Somerset)—excellent

Characteristics: Gray-brown, calico-wrapped rind; straw-colored interior; firm, buttery, rich texture; full, layered flavor; sweet, grassy aroma

Appropriate Wines: All light, fruity reds; dark beers and ales

Related Cheeses: English Cheshire, Gloucester, Lancashire, Leicester, Wensleydale; French Cantal; all other Cheddars, including American examples

The Bottom Line: English farmhouse Cheddar is an eye-opening taste experience for everyone raised on American Cheddar; grace, complexity, and history in every bite.

CHESHIRE

(CHESH-ur)

Origin: England—Cheshire, parts of Shropshire and Staffordshire

Type: Cow's milk, pasteurized and unpasteurized (farmhouse production); firm; pressed; organically dyed orange; natural, waxed or unwaxed, cloth-covered rind (edible)

Availability: Good, both farmhouse production and factory-made

Form: Tall drums

Dimensions: 14 inches high, 7 to 8 inches in diameter

Weight: 15 to 17 lbs. (7½ to 8½ k); also available in 4-lb. (2 k) drums

Fat Content: 45%

Best Brands: Any cloth-wrapped, traditional farmhouse examples (waxed or unwaxed); look for Abbey Farm (my favorite), The Bank, Mollington Grange Farm. Avoid vapid factory-made, plastic-wrapped varieties in wheels and blocks. Creamery-pro-

duced examples are acceptable but are also sold in blocks and may be confused with factory-made examples; look for creamery versions in the traditional drum shape

Characteristics: Cloth-wrapped rind (farmhouse); firm, yet crumbly, tender texture; light orange (dyed) or white (undyed) interior; slightly saline, tangy, mild, savory flavor

Appropriate Wines: All light, fruity reds or whites

Related Cheeses: English Cheddar, Leicester, Wensleydale, Caerphilly

The Bottom Line: England's oldest cheese; a rustic, savory beauty.

COMTÉ

(cone-TAY); A.O.C.; also called Gruyère de Comté (grew-YAIR or gree-AIR-duh-cone-TAY)

Origin: France—Franche-Comté

Type: Cow's milk, unpasteurized; firm; pressed, cooked curd; natural, brushed rind (inedible)

Availability: Good

Form: Large, flat wheels

Dimensions: 4 inches thick, about 3 feet in diameter

Weight: About 80 lbs. (40 k)

Fat Content: 45%

Best Brands: All excellent; in France and U.S., look for Maxim's and Jura-Gruyère (both Lons-le-Saulniers) and Girod (Beaumont-en-Savoie), brands which indicate Haut-Jura Comté origin on their labels, an assurance cheese is made with Alpine milk. Finest grade examples have a bell symbol and the word "Comté" stamped in green on rind

Characteristics: Gray-brown, pebbled rind; yellowish-ivory paste; pea- to

cherry-size eye structure, along with occasional *lenures* (horizontal fissures near rind); smooth flavor with hints of fruit, hazelnuts and toffee
Appropriate Wines: Big reds, such as Côtes-du-Rhône, Châteauneuf-du-Pape red Burgundies; fruity reds, such as Beaujolais
Related Cheeses: French Beaufort, Emmental; Swiss Gruyère, Emmental
The Bottom Line: One of the world's greatest cheeses; marvelous melted.

COULOMMIERS

(koo-LOAM-yay); A.O.C.

Origin: France—Ile-de-France (Brie)
Type: Cow's milk, pasteurized and unpasteurized; soft-ripened, bloomy rind (edible)
Availability: Good (pasteurized); unpasteurized illegal for export to U.S. (raw cow's milk cheese aged less than 60 days)
Form: Flat disks
Dimensions: 1½ to 2 inches thick, saucer- to dinner-plate size in diameter
Weight: 1½ lbs. (750 g)
Fat Content: 45%
Best Brands: In France, look for Le Fougéru (unpasteurized) made by Rouzaire; in U.S., look for Le Fougéru (pasteurized) made by Rouzaire; Coulommiers de Gaye (pasteurized) made by Lincet, is less good, but more widely available
Characteristics: A "rougher" Brie; soft, uneven exterior with brown mottling; bulging, straw-colored interior; full, rich, buttery flavor dominated by mushroom, truffle, garlic
Appropriate Wines: Any big red Bordeaux or Burgundy

Related Cheeses: French soft-ripened cow's-milk cheeses such as Camembert and Roucoulons, as well as other Bries (Brie de Meaux, Brie de Melun, Brie de Montereau, Fontainebleau); Italian Paglia-style and Toma cheeses
The Bottom Line: If it's not Le Fougéru made by Rouzaire, forget it.

CROTTIN DE CHAVIGNOL

(crow-TAH-duh-shah-veen-YOLE); A.O.C.

Origin: France—Berry
Type: Goat's milk, pasteurized and unpasteurized; soft to firm (according to age); natural rind (edible)
Availability: Only exported name-controlled version, a factory-made one produced by Denizot, is not widely available; however, very good non-A.O.C. *crottins* made outside Chavignol are more available
Form: Little barrels with flat tops and bottoms
Dimensions: 1½ inches high, 2 inches in diameter
Weight: 2 to 3 oz. (60 to 90 g)
Fat Content: 45%
Best Brands: In France, look for excellent A.O.C. examples by Chamaillard, Crochet, Dubois-Boulay, or Triballat. In U.S., avoid the only exported A.O.C. example, factory-made Denizot brand; look for excellent non-A.O.C. examples by Anjouin and Jacquin (both Berry), Desport and Soreda (both Périgord), Bougon (Poitou)
Characteristics: Stark white exterior, snow-white, soft interior with mild flavor (fresh or young); beige exterior, firm, bone-white interior with

flinty, nutty flavor (middle-aged); brownish or blue mold-covered exterior, firm, bone-white interior with spicy, nutty flavor (extra-aged)
Appropriate Wines: Red or white Sancerre with cheeses of any age; with riper cheeses, any good red, especially Côtes-du-Rhône, Morgon
Related Cheeses: All traditional French goat cheeses, especially Chabichou du Poitou, Pouligny-Saint-Pierre, Sainte-Maure de Touraine, Selles-sur-Cher, Valençay
The Bottom Line: *The* tastiest little chèvres.

EMMENTAL

(EM-awn-TAHL); French

Origin: France—Franche-Comté, Savoie, Haute-Savoie, Burgundy, Alsace
Type: Partially skimmed cow's milk, unpasteurized; semi-firm; pressed, cooked curd; brushed, oiled, natural rind (edible and inedible)
Availability: Rare
Form: Huge, convex wheels
Dimensions: 6 to 12 inches thick (outer edge to epicenter), 40 to 44 inches in diameter
Weight: 175 to 220 lbs. (87½ to 110 k)
Fat Content: 45%
Best Brands: All excellent; look for "Emmental Français Grand Cru" stamped in red on the rind, confirmation the cheese is made with Alpine milk; avoid pasteurized imitators
Characteristics: Yellowish-beige rind, with origin stamped in red; tender, yielding, slightly chewy texture; well-spaced proliferation of large, walnut-size holes; light straw–colored paste; sweet, buttery, nutty, fruity flavor

with satiny mouthfeel
Appropriate Wines: Light, fruity reds, such as Beaujolais, Chinon, Corbières, Côte-de-Lubéron or any Côtes-du-Rhône (though strong); light, spicy whites, such as Alsace Sylvaner or Traminer; dry Vouvray
Related Cheeses: Swiss Emmental; all Swiss-style Emmentals, including American Swiss, Dutch Leerdammer, Finlandia Swiss, New Zealand Swiss, Norwegian Jarlsberg
The Bottom Line: Rare in the U.S. but often superior to Swiss Emmental.

EMMENTAL

(EM-awn-TAHL); Swiss

Origin: Switzerland—Bern (valley of the Emme river)
Type: Partially skimmed cow's milk, unpasteurized; semi-firm; pressed, cooked curd; brushed, oiled, natural rind (edible or inedible)
Availability: Excellent
Form: Huge, convex wheels
Dimensions: 6 to 9 inches thick (outer edge to epicenter), 40 to 44 inches in diameter
Weight: 175 to 220 lbs. (87½ to 110 k)
Fat Content: 45%
Best Brands: All excellent; not marketed by brand. Widely copied; avoid mass-market imitations from other countries (made with non-Alpine, pasteurized milk); the rinds of Emmental made for export are imprinted with the word "Switzerland"
Characteristics: Smooth, beige to yellowish rind; pale, yellowish-tan paste; random proliferation of large, walnut-size holes; mild, yet full, nutty, fruity flavor with characteristic finishing savory bite

Appropriate Wines: Light, fruity reds, such as Swiss Dôle, French Eandol, Beaujolais, Corbières; more substantial reds, such as Côtes-du-Rhône or Saint-Joseph; light, fruity whites, such as Swiss Fendant, French Aligoté, Muscadet
Related Cheeses: French Emmental (Emmental Français Grand Cru); all Swiss-style Emmentals, including American Swiss, Dutch Leerdammer, Finlandia Swiss, New Zealand Swiss, Norwegian Jarlsberg
The Bottom Line: All those holes! The world's most recognizable cheese.

EPOISSES DE BOURGOGNE

(ay-PWOSS-duh-boor-GOYNE); A.O.C.

Origin: France—Burgundy (around the village of Epoisses)
Type: Cow's milk, pasteurized and unpasteurized; soft; washed (*marc de Bourgogne*) rind (edible)
Availability: Illegal for export to U.S. (raw cow's milk cheese aged less than 60 days); good availability of non-A.O.C. version made with pasteurized milk, but it is not recommended
Form: Small disks in wooden boxes
Dimensions: 1 to 1¼ inches thick, 4 inches in diameter
Weight: 9-oz. (270 g) disk; also 1-lb. (500 g) wheels of same diameter
Fat Content: 45%
Best Brands: In France, Berthaut (the sole A.O.C. version), Ami du Chambertin (made in Brochon, a small town outside of the designated name-controlled region); in U.S., avoid the tasteless Lincet brand made with pasteurized milk

Characteristics: Smooth, reddish-brown rind; rich, huge flavor; delightfully smelly, barnyardy aroma
Appropriate Wines: Red Burgundies; any big red
Related Cheeses: French Ami du Chambertin, Langres, Livarot, Maroilles, Munster, Pont l'Evêque
The Bottom Line: Absolutely my favorite French cheese. Everything you know about eating will be redefined with your first taste.

EXPLORATEUR

(ex-plore-ah-TOOR)

Origin: France—Ile-de-France
Type: Cow's milk, pasteurized; soft-ripened; triple-crème; bloomy rind (edible)
Availability: Good
Form: Barrels, disks, wheels
Dimensions: 3½ inches high, 3 inches in diameter (barrels); 1½ inches thick, 4½ inches in diameter (disks); 1¾ inches thick, 9 inches in diameter (wheels)
Weight: 8-oz. (250 g) barrels; 14-oz. (420 g) disks; 4 lb. (12 k) wheels
Fat Content: 75%
Best Brands: One maker—Fromagerie du Petit Morin, the originator
Characteristics: Bloomy Brie-like crust; bone-colored paste; buttery texture; very rich, very smooth, very big flavor
Appropriate Wines: Champagne
Related Cheeses: All French double- and triple-crèmes, especially triple-crèmes such as Boursault, Brillat-Savarin, Gratte-Paille, Pierre Robert, Saint-André
The Bottom Line: Explorateur is to cheese as Champagne is to wine.

FONTINA D'AOSTA

(fawn-TEE-nah-DAOW-stah); D.O.C.

Origin: Italy—Piedmont
Type: Cow's milk, unpasteurized; semi-firm; pressed, cooked curd; brushed rind (inedible)
Availability: Good
Form: Large wheels
Dimensions: 4 inches thick, 18 inches in diameter
Weight: 17 to 22 lbs. (8½ to 11 k)
Fat Content: 45% to 50%
Best Brands: All excellent; look on rind for stenciled purple circle with a mountain in the center and the word "Fontina"
Characteristics: Reddish-brown, brushed rind; beige interior; firm, supple texture; earthy, herby flavor; delicate, fruity, perfumed aroma
Appropriate Wines: Piedmont's big reds—Barolo, Barbaresco, Spanna, Gattinara
Related Cheeses: Swiss Raclette cheeses (Bagnes, Conches, Gomser, Orsières), Vacherin Fribourgeois; French Morbier, Raclette
The Bottom Line: One of the world's greatest cheeses.

FOURME D'AMBERT

(FORM-dom-BAIR or FORM-uh-dom-BAIR); A.O.C.

Origin: France—Auvergne
Type: Cow's-milk blue, unpasteurized (rare) and pasteurized (usually); semisoft; slightly pressed curd; natural rind (inedible)
Availability: Good
Form: Cylinders
Dimensions: 8 to 9 inches high, 4 to 5 inches in diameter
Weight: 5 lbs. (2½ k)
Fat Content: 45%
Best Brands: Most excellent; look for my favorite brands, La Memée and Roussel; avoid mass-produced brands such as Cantorel, Auvergnat, and Centro-lait
Characteristics: Gray-brown rind; firm, creamy, beige paste with liberal navy-blue veining; pronounced but not overly sharp flavor
Appropriate Wines: When in France, drink the light, chewy Auvergne reds or the white Condrieu (Rhône); all big reds, especially Bordeaux, Burgundy, and Beaujolais
Related Cheeses: French Bleu d'Auvergne, Bleu des Causses, Bleu de Gex, Bleu de Septmoncel, Fourme de Montbrison, Persillé d'Aravis; English Stilton
The Bottom Line: Not nearly as good as it once was—industrialization is the culprit.

GAPERON

(gah-PAIR-ohn)

Origin: France—Auvergne
Type: Partially skimmed cow's milk or buttermilk, pasteurized and unpasteurized; soft; pressed curd mixed with chunks of garlic and cracked peppercorns; white, bloomy rind (edible)
Availability: Good
Form: Flat-bottomed domes; usually tied with raffia or yellow ribbon
Dimensions: About the size of a baseball
Weight: 12 oz. (375 g)

Fat Content: Varies, about 30% to 45%
Best Brands: All excellent; in U.S. and France, seek out those made by Garmy (Ponte-Astier)
Characteristics: Bloomy, snow-white exterior, firm, chalky interior, and tart flavor (young, underripe); fuzzy, gray-mottled white exterior, blondish, soft, bulging interior (runny around edge of rind), and buttery, Brie-like flavor with an almost overwhelming garlic and pepper presence (ripened)
Appropriate Wines: All coarse and robust reds, such as Côtes-du-Rhône, specifically Corbières
Related Cheeses: None
The Bottom Line: The first flavored cheese—in a class by itself.

GORGONZOLA

(gor-gohn-ZOH-lah)

Origin: Italy—Lombardy
Type: Cow's-milk blue, pasteurized; soft; inoculated curd; washed rind (edible or inedible)
Availability: Good
Form: Foil-wrapped wheels or hatbox shapes
Dimensions: 3 to 4 inches thick, 12 to 14 inches in diameter
Weight: 18 to 26 lbs. (9 to 13 k); original thickness and weight is double that given, but the cheese is shipped to retailers in half-wheels that are horizontally split in half
Fat Content: 48%
Best Brands: All excellent; in Italy and U.S.. look for Galbani, Klin, Lodigiani, Mauri
Characteristics: Thin, reddish-brown, slightly sticky rind; creamy-

beige interior with profuse greenish-blue striations; pronounced spicy, earthy flavor; powerful, cheesy aroma. Marketed in two styles: sweet (*dolce*), which is soft, mild, and odoriferous, and aged (*naturale*), which is firmer, more assertive in flavor and aroma
Appropriate Wines: Big Italian reds such as Amarone, Barbaresco, Barolo, Brunello di Montalcino, Chianti Riserva, Gattinara, Salice Salentino, Taurasi, Tignanello; also dessert wines, such as Marsala, Picolit
Related Cheeses: French Fourme d'Ambert, Roquefort; English Stilton; Spanish Cabrales, Picón. Popular, but less flavorful, imitations include French Bleu de Bresse; German Cambozola, Montagnolo; Danish Saga
The Bottom Line: Awesome; I am constantly grateful a cheese this good exists.

GRATTE-PAILLÉ

(GROTT-PIE)

Origin: France—Ile-de-France (Brie)
Type: Cow's milk, pasteurized and unpasteurized; soft-ripened; double-crème; bloomy rind (edible)
Availability: Good, pasteurized
Form: Brick shapes with slightly concave sides; wrapped in waxed paper with open ends; sometimes placed on a plastic tray
Dimensions: 3 inches high, 5 inches long, 3 inches wide
Weight: 12 oz. (375 g); also available in half-size
Fat Content: 70%
Best Brands: In France, Rouzaire (unpasteurized); in U.S., Rouzaire (pasteurized)
Characteristics: Beige-mottled,

white, bloomy rind; buttery texture; extraordinary triple-crème flavor with irresistible raw-milk taste; over-ripe examples can be bitter and salty
Appropriate Wines: Champagne or Bouzy, a still (nonsparkling) red from the Champagne region; Sauternes
Related Cheeses: All French double- and triple-crèmes, especially Boursault, Brillat-Savarin, Explorateur, Pierre Robert, Saint-André
The Bottom Line: Robert Rouzaire's triple-crèmes define the idiom; sweet and sumptuous.

GRUYERE

See Swiss Gruyère, page 511; Comté, page 486.

IDIAZABAL

(ee-dee-ah-ZAH-bahl); D.O.

Origin: Spain—País Vasco (the Basque Country), Navarre
Type: Sheep's milk, unpasteurized; quite firm; pressed, cooked curd; smoked (usually); natural rind (inedible)
Availability: Rare
Form: High-sided wheels
Dimensions: 5 to 6 inches high, 5 to 7 inches in diameter
Weight: 5 to 9 lbs. (2½ to 4½ k)
Fat Content: 45% to 50%
Best Brands: All excellent
Characteristics: Hard, orange to rich walnut brown exterior; yellowish-beige paste with a proliferation of tiny holes throughout; firm yet supple texture; rich, buttery, nutty flavor with overtones of smoke and balsam
Appropriate Wines: All Navarra reds

Related Cheeses: Spanish Roncal, Manchego, San Simón, Zamorano; French Pyrénées cheeses
The Bottom Line: A vastly under-sung cheese.

LAGUIOLE

(lah-YOLE or lie-YULL); A.O.C.; also called Laguiole-Aubrac (lah-YOLE-oh-BROCK or lie-YULL-oh-BROCK)

Origin: France—Rouergue
Type: Cow's milk, unpasteurized; semi-firm; pressed; natural, brushed rind (inedible)
Availability: Rare
Form: Fat barrel shapes with slightly swollen sides
Dimensions: 16 inches high, 16 inches in diameter
Weight: 70 to 80 lbs. (35 to 40 k)
Fat Content: 45%
Best Brands: All excellent
Characteristics: Dry, grayish-brown rind; crumbly, straw-colored, very moist interior; sharp, complex flavor with a hint of grassiness
Appropriate Wines: Hermitage, other Rhône reds and rare Madiran; any young, fresh, fruity reds
Related Cheeses: French Cantal, Salers; slightly related to all Cheddars
The Bottom Line: A towering cheese in every regard.

LANCASHIRE

(LANK-uh-shur)

Origin: England—Lancashire
Type: Cow's milk, unpasteurized; firm; pressed; natural, cloth-covered

rind (inedible)
Availability: Rare
Form: Cloth-wrapped cylindrical
drums with straight (not convex)
sides
Dimensions: 11 to 13 inches high, 9
to 10 inches in diameter
Weight: 20 lbs. (10 k)
Fat Content: 45%
Best Brands: Avoid factory-made
blocks; in U.K. and U.S., look for
farmhouse examples made by John
and Ruth Kirkham at Beesley Farm
(Lancashire)
Characteristics: Gray exterior; snow-
white paste; tightly compacted
crumbly texture; mild, milky, and
nutty flavor with lactic tang
Appropriate Wines: Superb with any
wine you happen to enjoy, especially
a Chardonnay or Muscadet
Related Cheeses: Cow's-milk farmhouse English cheeses, including
Caerphilly, Cheddar, Cheshire,
Gloucester, Leicester, Wensleydale
The Bottom Line: A reemerging
classic—subtle and sophisticated.

LANGRES

(LAHNG-gruh); A.O.C.

Origin: France—Champagne (area
around the village of Langres)
Type: Cow's-milk, unpasteurized;
soft; washed rind (edible)
Availability: Illegal for export to U.S.
(raw cow's milk cheese aged less
than 60 days)
Form: Small drums, concave tops;
usually not wrapped
Dimensions: 3 inches high, 3 inches
in diameter
Weight: 5 oz. to 1½ lbs. (180 to 750 g)

Fat Content: 45%
Best Brands: All excellent; look for
Germain and Schertenleib
Characteristics: Concave top; red-
orange rind; blond-colored interior;
rich, soft texture; huge flavor—spicy,
intense, delightfully smelly
Appropriate Wines: Gigondas,
Châteauneuf-du-Pape, other big
Rhône reds
Related Cheeses: French Epoisses de
Bourgogne, Munster; Italian Robiola
Lombardia
The Bottom Line: Stunningly
delicious.

LE BROUERE

(luh-broo-AIR)

Origin: France—Alsace
Type: Cow's milk, pasteurized; firm;
pressed, cooked curd; natural,
brushed rind (inedible)
Availability: Good
Form: Imperfectly round, lopsided,
wheel-shaped disks
Dimensions: 4 inches thick, 10 to
20 inches in diameter
Weight: From 14 to 20 lbs. (7 to 10 k)
Fat Content: 45%
Best Brands: Ermitage is both the
originator of the trademark and the
only producer.
Characteristics: Milk chocolate–
brown rind bears a bas-relief design
of trees and grouse; creamy texture;
smooth mouthfeel; bright yellow
interior; buttery, nutty, and sweet-
tasting; each cheese is numbered
and signed
Appropriate Wines: Red Burgundies;
red Côtes-du-Rhônes; beer or hard
cider

Related Cheeses: French Abondance, Beaufort, Comté; Swiss Gruyère
The Bottom Line: A brilliant new version of Gruyère, though why they've chosen to make it from pasteurized milk is beyond me.

LEICESTER

(LESS-ter)

Origin: England—Cheshire, Lancashire, Leicestershire, Somerset
Type: Cow's milk, pasteurized; firm; pressed; organically dyed orange; natural, cloth-covered rind (inedible)
Availability: Rare
Form: Cloth-wrapped wheels
Dimensions: 12 inches thick, 20 inches in diameter
Weight: 45 lbs. (22½ k)
Fat Content: 45%
Best Brands: All cloth-wrapped, creamery-produced examples are good; in U.K. and U.S., look for Tuxford & Tebbutt
Characteristics: Gray-brown rind; deep red-orange interior; rich, nutty, candy-like flavor with a hint of sharpness; creamy mouthfeel
Appropriate Wines: Light reds; beer
Related Cheeses: English Caerphilly, Cheddar, Cheshire, Gloucester, Lancashire
The Bottom Line: A once-great cheese, now practically extinct.

LEYDEN

(LIE-den or LAY-den); spelling may vary—Leiden, Leyde; also called Leidsekaas (LEED-zuh-KAHSS)

Origin: The Netherlands
Type: Cow's milk, pasteurized and unpasteurized (rare); firm (young) or splintery and rock-hard (aged); pressed, cooked curd; flavored throughout with caraway and/or cumin seeds; natural rind (inedible)
Availability: Good (young); rare (aged)
Form: Thick, waxed wheels
Dimensions: 6 inches thick, 16 to 18 inches in diameter
Weight: Average 16 lbs. (about 8 k)
Fat Content: 40%
Best Brands: All excellent; authentic versions bear the two crossed keys, trademark symbol of the town of Leyden; seek out rare aged examples, which are magnificent and taste like toffee
Characteristics: Very firm; light-yellow interior (young), creamy, brown-orange interior (aged); Gouda-like but spicy; flavored with caraway and/or cumin seeds; spicy aroma
Appropriate Wines: Spicy reds such as Zinfandel; beer
Related Cheeses: All other Dutch cheeses
The Bottom Line: Bring on the ham, onions, mustard, crackers, and cold beer!

LIVAROT

(LEE-vah-roe); A.O.C.

Origin: France—Normandy
Type: Partially skimmed cow's milk, pasteurized and unpasteurized; soft; washed rind (inedible)
Availability: Good (non-A.O.C., pasteurized only)
Form: Disks, wrapped in orange

paper, always packed in a wooden box
Dimensions: 2 inches thick, 3 to
4½ inches in diameter
Weight: 8 oz. to 1 lb. (250 to 500 g)
Fat Content: 40% to 45%
Best Brands: In France all excellent,
look for La Ferme de la Viette; in U.S.,
look for Graindorge or Levasseur
(pasteurized, excellent)
Characteristics: Orange crust with
five narrow strips of red raffia encircling sides; straw-colored interior;
strong, beefy, nutty flavor; wonderfully smelly
Appropriate Wines: Big reds,
preferably Burgundy or Bordeaux;
Calvados (cider brandy); hard apple
ciders; beer
Related Cheeses: French Epoisses,
Langres Pont-l'Evêque, Munster;
Italian Robiola Lombardia, Taleggio
The Bottom Line: The next best
thing to raw-milk Camembert.

MAHON

(mah-HONE); D.O.

Origin: Spain—Minorca
Type: Cow's milk, pasteurized
(factory-made) and unpasteurized
(farm-made, *artesano*); semifirm to
firm (according to age); pressed;
range of ages—young or *fresco* (aged
about 2 weeks), middle-aged or *semi-
curado* (aged about 2 to 3 months),
viejo or *duro* (aged 6 months), *añejo*
(aged 18 months to 2 years or more);
natural rind (inedible)
Availability: Rare
Form: Thickish, round-edged
squares
Dimensions: 8 inches square,
2 inches thick

Weight: 5 to 6½ lbs. (2½ to 3¼ k)
Fat Content: 45%
Best Brands: All excellent; in Spain,
farm-made *fresco* examples made
with unpasteurized milk are the best;
in U.S., virtually all Mahón is *semi-
curado* (aged about 2 months), made
with pasteurized milk
Characteristics: Hard, smooth, burnished orangey-gold rind (darkens
with age); paste ranges from very
pale amber (young) to dark gold
(aged); hard, chewy texture that
melts on the palate (all ages); rich,
creamy mouthfeel; all but young
cheeses show a proliferation of
tiny holes; flavor ranges from
intensely nutty with a full aroma
(young) to sharp, salty, buttery, and
fruity with a lightly nutty aroma
(aged)
Appropriate Wines: All Spanish
reds; beer
Related Cheeses: Dutch Boerenkaas,
Edam, Gouda
The Bottom Line: The way Gouda
wishes it could taste.

MANCHEGO

(mon-CHAY-goh); D.O.

Origin: Spain—La Mancha
Type: Sheep's milk, pasteurized
(primarily) and unpasteurized (rare);
firm; pressed; aged a minimum of
60 days to more than 3 years; natural
rind (inedible)
Availability: Good, but watch for
imitations; look for La Mancha origin
on label
Form: Wheels
Dimensions: 4 to 5 inches high, 8 to
9 inches in diameter

Weight: About 6 to 7 lbs. (3 to 3½ k)
Fat Content: 45% to 57%
Best Brands: All excellent, but price varies widely based on age—very rare, artisanal examples will be quite expensive (my favorite is Pasamontes)
Characteristics: Black, gray, or buff-colored rind with a crosshatch pattern; interior ranges from stark white to slightly yellowish (according to age), with even distribution of holes; mild, slightly briny, nutty flavor
Appropriate Wines: With young cheese, fruity Spanish reds and whites, such as Catalonian sparkling whites (*cava*), a light Navarra, or dry sherry (Andalusian *fino*); with aged cheese, big, well-knit Spanish reds, such as those from Pèndes, Ribera del Duero, Rioja
Related Cheeses: Spanish Castellano, Idiazábal, Zamorano, Roncal
The Bottom Line: Receives far more attention than it deserves. You would do better to explore Spain's less well-known treasures.

MAROILLES

(mah-WAHL); A.O.C.

Origin: France—Picardy, Flanders (Hainaut, Avesnois, Thiérache), Artois
Type: Cow's milk, pasteurized and unpasteurized; soft; washed rind (usually inedible)
Availability: Rare
Form: Boxed squares
Dimensions: 1¼ to 1½ inches thick
Weight: About 1 lb. (500 g); 4- and 8-oz. (125 and 250 g) sizes also made
Fat Content: 45% to 50%

Best Brands: All excellent
Characteristics: Very similar in recipe, form, appearance, and flavor to Pont-l'Evêque (and Gris de Lille), though less refined and considerably stronger; ridged, rough, brown crust, usually inedible (gritty and bitter); soft, bulging texture; often salty; very smelly
Appropriate Wines: Burgundy's red (not white) Corton, a forceful, lingering wine for a cheese of the same effect; beer; gin
Related Cheeses: French Gris de Lille, Limburger, Livarot, Pont-l'Evêque; Italian Taleggio; Belgian Herve
The Bottom Line: About as subtle as a bolt of lightning—get out a clothespin.

MASCARPONE

(mahs-kar-POH-neh); also called Mascherpone

Origin: Italy—Lombardy
Type: Cow's cream, pasteurized (not actually a cheese—no starter or rennet is used in its production)
Availability: Good
Form: Formless
Dimensions: Formless
Weight: Sold in bulk; also in 8-oz. (250 g) and 1-lb. (500 g) containers
Fat Content: 70% to 75%
Best Brands: All excellent; interestingly, U.S.-made versions are also excellent. In Italy, seek out rare and expensive examples made in Campania with water buffalo milk
Characteristics: Pale-blond color; soft, smooth, cake icing–like texture; sweet, rich, creamlike flavor
Appropriate Wines: With berries or

other fruit, a sweetish dessert wine such as Marsala or Picolit.
Related Cheeses: French crème fraîche, triple-crèmes; English Devonshire cream, clotted cream; American Mascarpone, heavy whipping cream, cream cheese
The Bottom Line: An Italian staple that deserves to be universally adored.

MIMOLETTE

(MEE-moh-LETT)

Origin: France—Flanders, Normandy
Type: Cow's milk, pasteurized; firm; pressed curd; dyed (organically) orange inside and out; natural, brushed rind (usually inedible)
Availability: Good
Form: Spheres, slightly flat on top and bottom
Dimensions: 7 to 8 inches in diameter (about the size of a medium honeydew melon)
Weight: Average 7 to 8 lbs. (3½ to 4 k)
Fat Content: 45%
Best Brands: In France and U.S., look for examples from the Normandy producers Besnier Isigny-Sainte-Mère, and Valco.
Characteristics: Orange rind and paste; firm texture with occasional cracks and small holes; bland, mild flavor
Appropriate Wines: Any light wine; beer is a better choice
Related Cheeses: Dutch Edam, Gouda
The Bottom Line: French General Charles de Gaulle's favorite cheese. Obviously the General ate too much army food.

MONTASIO

(mohn-TAH-zee-yoh); D.O.C.

Origin: Italy—Friuli–Venezia Giulia, parts of Veneto
Type: Cow's milk, partially skimmed, unpasteurized; hard; unpressed, cooked curd; natural, brushed rind (inedible)
Availability: Spotty
Form: Wheels
Dimensions: 3 inches thick, 12 to 14 inches in diameter
Weight: 15 to 23 lbs. (7½ to 11½ k)
Fat Content: 45%; 30% also available
Best Brands: All excellent
Characteristics: Light grayish-beige rind; beige interior with small apertures throughout; mild, tangy, butterscotch flavor and aroma
Appropriate Wines: With young cheese, light, fruity reds such as Grave del Friuli, Dolcetta d'Alba; with aged cheese, coarser, more robust reds, such as Amarone, Gattinara, Ghemme
Related Cheeses: Italian Asiago *d'allevo*, Bra, Bitto
The Bottom Line: Think of this as "Casper the Friendly Cheese"—nice but nearly indiscernible flavor.

MORBIER

(MORE-bee-yay)

Origin: France—Franche-Comté (Jura, Doubs)
Type: Cow's milk, pasteurized and unpasteurized; semisoft; pressed; natural, brushed rind (inedible)
Availability: Good
Form: Wheels
Dimensions: 3 to 4 inches thick,

10 to 18 inches in diameter
Weight: 13 to 16 lbs. (6½ to 8 k)
Fat Content: 45%
Best Brands: In France and U.S., look for Brunnerois (Franche-Comté); also any examples made in the *départements* of Jura or Doubs with labels stating *lait cru* (raw milk). Labels of imitation Morbiers will state "Fabriqué en Poitou" or "Fabriqué en Auvergne;" flavorless Livradois is an example of a phony Morbier made in the Auvergne region.
Characteristics: Creamy-brown crust; interior is two layers of glossy, yellowish-ivory paste separated by thin, flavorless layer of ash; compelling flavor of nuts and fruit; fresh hay aroma
Appropriate Wines: Light, fruity reds, such as *cru* Beaujolais
Related Cheeses: Swiss Raclette cheeses (Bagnes, Conches, Gomser, Orsières), Vacherin Fribourgeois; French Saint-Nectaire; Italian Fontina d'Aosta
The Bottom Line: The most seductive of all semisoft cheeses.

MUNSTER

(moon-STAIR or MUN-ster); A.O.C.

Origin: France—Alsace
Type: Cow's milk, pasteurized (*laitier*) and unpasteurized (*fermier*); soft; washed rind (edible)
Availability: Good to spotty; only pasteurized (*laitier*) available in U.S.
Form: Disks
Dimensions: 1¼ inches thick, 7 inches in diameter; smaller sizes also made
Weight: boxed-1¼ lbs. (625 g)

Fat Content: 45% to 50%
Best Brands: All excellent; in France, look for *fermier* examples from numerous small producers, including Remy-Rudler; in U.S., look for *laitier* examples made by Avid, l'Ermitage, or Marcillat
Characteristics: Firm, dry, russet-colored rind and white chalk interior (young); dark russet rind and straw-colored interior (ripe); soft, supple, creamy texture; huge, beefy, nutty flavor; wonderfully smelly rind
Appropriate Wines: Alsatian wines are perfect—Gewürztraminers, Reislings; Muscadet; fresh, fruity reds, such as Beaujolais; most big reds, such as Burgundy and Bordeau; beer
Related Cheeses: Danish Esrom; French Epoisses, Chaumes, Géromé, Langres, Reblochon; Italian Robiola Lombardia, Taleggio
The Bottom Line: A triumph of cheesemaking, even when made from pasteurized milk.

OSSAU-IRATY

(OH-soh-ear-ah-TEE); A.O.C.

Note: *The A.O.C. granted to Pyrénées sheep's-milk cheeses in 1980 designated the protected name as Ossau-Iraty brebis Pyrénées, which is usually known simply as Ossau-Iraty. Somewhat confusingly, however, the A.O.C. also applies to other brebis Pyrénées. They are: Abbaye de Bellocq (AB-BAY-duh-bel-AWK), Etcheria (etch-eh-REE-ah), Larceveau (larse-VOE), Laruns (la-ROON), and Matocq (mah-TOKE).*

Origin: France—Western Pyrénées (Pays Basque, Béarn, parts of Bigorre)

Type Sheep's milk, unpasteurized; firm; pressed; natural, brushed rind (ined..ble)
Availability: Rare; good availability of non-A.O.C. pasteurized versions
Form: Wheels with rounded sides
Dimensions: 4 inches thick, 12 inches in diameter
Weight: 8 to 10 lbs. (4 to 5 k)
Fat Content: 45%
Best Brands: All excellent; in U.S., look for excellent non-A.O.C. pasteurized versions, such as Esbareich, Etorki, Onetik, Prince de Claverolle, Prince de Navarre, Yolo
Characteristics: Brownish rind; ivory interior; firm, oily texture; nutty, olivey, fruity flavor
Appropriate Wines: Bordeaux; Madiran, Cahors; all Rhône reds
Related Cheeses: All other Pyrénées sheep's-milk cheeses; American Major Farm Vermont Shepherd Cheese, Northland Sheep Dairy Tomme Bergère; Spanish Idiazábal, Roncal
The Bottom Line: Among the world's oldest and most heavenly cheeses; probably as good today as they were 4,000 years ago.

PAGLIA-STYLE CHEESES

(PAHL-yah)

Note: This is an overall designation for a specific style of soft-ripened cow's-milk cheeses, which are sold under various proprietary names.

Origin: Italy—Piedmont, parts of Lombardy
Type: Cow's milk, pasteurized; soft-ripened; bloomy rind (edible)
Availability: Rare

Form: Flat disks, paper-wrapped
Dimensions: ½ inch thick, 4 inches in diameter
Weight: 6 to 8 oz. (180 to 250 g)
Fat Content: 45%
Best Brands: All excellent; in Italy and U.S., look for Paglierino made by Quaglia, Paglietta made by Cademartori, and Pagliola made by Mauri.
Characteristics: White, bloomy rind that becomes beige-mottled when ripe; soft and supple; straw-colored interior; depending upon age, texture ranges from chalky (underripe) to bulgy (ripe) to runny (overripe); mushroomy, garlicky aroma and flavor
Appropriate Wines: Big Piedmont reds—Barolo, Barbaresco, Spanna, Ghemme, Barbera, Gattinara
Related Cheeses: Italian Toma; French Brie, Camembert
The Bottom Line: Italy's answer to France's Brie and Camembert. Terrific, but an endangered species.

PARMIGIANO-REGGIANO

(par-mee-JAH-noh-reh-JAH-noh); D.O.C.

Origin: Italy—Emilia-Romagna
Type: Partially skimmed cow's milk, unpasteurized; hard; pressed, cooked curd; brushed, oiled rind (inedible)
Availability: Good
Form: Convex-sided, flat-topped drums
Dimensions: 12 inches thick, 18 to 20 inches in diameter
Weight: 66 to 88 lbs. (33 to 44 k)
Fat Content: 28% to 32%
Best Brands: All excellent; the words "Parmigiano-Reggiano" are always

stamped very closely together around the side of the rind, along with a plant code number and the date of production

Characteristics: Burnished, golden rind; yellowish-white interior (young, 18 months old), splintery, straw-colored interior (aged, 2 years old); enormous, piquant, slightly salty flavor

Appropriate Wines: Big Italian reds such as Barbaresco, Barbera, Barolo, Brunello di Montalcino, Chianti Riserva, Salice Salentino, Taurasi, Tignanello

Related Cheeses: Italian Grana Padano, Pecorino Romano, all *grana* cheeses; Swiss Sbrinz; American Dry Jack; Dutch aged Gouda; Parmesan derivatives such as Argentinian Reggianito, American Parmesan

The Bottom Line: *Il formaggio migliore nel mondo*—the world's greatest cheese.

PECORINO ROMANO

(peh-koh-REE-noh-roh-MAH-noh); D.O.C.

Origin: Italy—Lazio, Sardinia
Type: Sheep's milk, unpasteurized; hard; pressed; natural rind, often "painted" black (inedible)
Availability: Widely available; sold grated and in chunks
Form: Tall, broad cylinders
Dimensions: 16 inches high, 12 inches in diameter
Weight: 40 lbs. (20 k)
Fat Content: 45%
Best Brands: All excellent; by law, rind of authentic (*genuino*) versions will be embossed with a sheep's-head logo and the words "Pecorino Romano." In Italy and U. S., look for

genuino made by Brunelli, Fulvi, Locatelli, Lopez

Characteristics: Thin, dry rind (often "painted" with nontoxic black coloring); bone-white inner paste; hard and granular with occasional interior fissures; intensely peppery, sheepy flavor; often quite salty

Appropriate Wines: All full-bodied reds

Related Cheeses: All Italian sheep's-milk cheeses, including Fiore Sardo, Incanestrato; also *grana* cheeses such as Parmigiano-Reggiano, Grana Padano

The Bottom Line: Italy's most famous Pecorino; the grating cheese of choice in southern Italy.

PECORINO TOSCANO

(peh-koh-REE-noh-toh-SKAH-noh); D.O.

Note: *Pecorino is the generic name given to all sheep's-milk cheeses made in Italy. Pecorino Toscano is the name of the sheep's-milk cheeses made in Tuscany.*

Origin: Italy—Tuscany
Type: Sheep's milk, pasteurized and unpasteurized; firm; pressed; natural rind (inedible unless very fresh, i.e., unaged)
Availability: Rare
Form: Varies; usually disks and oblong shapes
Dimensions: 2 to 4 inches thick, 5 to 8 inches in diameter
Weight: 1 to 4 pounds (500 g to 2 k)
Fat Content: 45% to 50%
Best Brands: In Italy and U.S., look for the following brands all labeled *pura pecora* ("pure sheep")—Corsignano, Marzolino, Peperino (flavored with crushed, dried hot red peppers),

Pientino and Rossellino, made by SOLP; Dolce Siena, Il Palio, Manciano, Scansano, and Val d'Elsa, from various makers

Characteristics: Variously colored rinds depending on maker (Il Palio and Rossellino are rubbed with tomato paste to set them apart visually from other brands); ivory interior (darker and oilier with age); texture varies, depending upon age, from semisoft to semi-hard; flavor and aroma similarly vary from mild to piquant, though all have olivey, nutty flavor

Appropriate Wines: Orvieto or Lungarotti whites with young Pecorinos; Chianti, Brunello, or Lungarotti reds with aged ones

Related Cheeses: Italian Casciotta d'Urbino, Pecorino dell'Umbria, Pecorino Le Marchigiano, Pecorino Sardo; French sheep's-milk Pyrénées cheeses; Spanish Manchego

The Bottom Line: My second favorite cheese in the world.

PETIT-SUISSE

(PEH-tee-SWEES)

Origin: France—Normandy

Type: Cow's milk, pasteurized; fresh; soft (almost fluid); acidulated cream-added curd; unsalted; rindless

Availability: Rare

Form: Small cylinders—in 6-packs; also available mixed with fruit compotes

Dimensions: Each cylinder 2 inches high, 1 inch in diameter

Weight: Each cylinder 1 to 2 oz. (30 to 60 g)

Fat Content: 60% to 75%

Best Brands: All excellent

Characteristics: Snowy white; pudding-soft texture; sweet, tart, and fresh tasting

Appropriate Wines: None

Related Cheeses: All fresh, white, smooth-textured cheeses

The Bottom Line: Further proof that the French have more fun with their food than we do.

PICODON DE LA DROME

(pee-koh-DAW-duh-lah-DROHM). D.O.C.

Note: *Picodon de l'Ardèche (pee-koh-DAW-duh-lar-DESH), an identical chèvre made in Languedoc, shares A.O.C. status with Picodon de la Drôme.*

Origin: France—Dauphiné, Provence

Type: Goat's milk, unpasteurized; natural rind (edible), often soaked in spirits (*eau-de-vie,* brandy, wine)

Availability: A.O.C. version unavailable in U.S.; only factory-made cow's-milk versions are exported

Form: Thickish disks

Dimensions: ¾ inch thick, 2½ inches in diameter

Weight: 3 to 4 oz. (90 to 125 g)

Fat Content: 45%

Best Brands: A.O.C. examples not exported to U.S.; only inauthentic, factory-made, plastic-wrapped cow's-milk versions available in U.S.; avoid them. In France, farm-produced (*fermier*) examples are excellent; look for J. Ramade (Nyons) and Cavet Frères Dieulefit

Characteristics: Off-white, slightly wrinkled exterior, soft, creamy white interior, and very sweet, mild flavor (young, unmarinated); if aged in spirits, dark-golden exterior, buff-colored

interior, with strong, nutty, balsamy flavor; often sold herbed, peppered with garlic, or packed in jars with olive oil and herbs (excellent)
Appropriate Wines: Red or white Côtes-du-Rhône
Related Cheeses: French Pélardon, all traditional French goat cheeses
The Bottom Line: An exquisite chèvre with flavor that is pure poetry; as much a part of the south of France as olive trees and wild herbs.

PICON

(pee-KONE); D.O.

Origin: Spain—Cantabria
Type: Usually cow's milk only, sometimes a mix of cow's, goat's, and sheep's milk, pasteurized and unpasteurized (artisanal); semi-firm; blue; cave-aged for minimum of 3 months; natural rind (usually too salty to eat)
Availability: Spotty
Form: Wheels, usually leaf-wrapped (oak, maple, sycamore), then covered with foil or plastic
Dimensions: 3 to 3½ inches high, 5 to 7 inches in diameter
Weight: 5 to 9 lbs. (2½ to 4½ k)
Fat Content: 45% to 48%
Best Brands: All excellent
Characteristics: Salty, inedible, buff-colored rind; moist, fragile, crumbly interior with intense purple veining; rich, intense flavor
Appropriate Wines: All strong Spanish reds, including Bierzo, Rioja, Ribera del Duero, Navarra; Spanish sherries, sweet or dry
Related Cheeses: Spanish Cabrales, Gamonedo; French Roquefort; all blue cheeses

The Bottom Line: A rising-star Spanish cheese; the equal of Roquefort and Gorgonzola.

PONT-L'EVEQUE

(PAWNH-leh-VECK); A.O.C.

Origin: France—Normandy (Pays d'Auge)
Type: Cow's milk, pasteurized and unpasteurized; soft; washed rind, occasionally only brushed (edible or inedible)
Availability: Good (pasteurized only)
Form: Squares, always packed in wooden boxes
Dimensions: 1 to 1½ inches thick, 3½-by 5-inch rectangle
Weight: Standard sizes are about 8 oz. (250 g) and 13 oz. (390 g), although some brands offer versions weighing 4 to 5 lbs. (2 to 2½ k)
Fat Content: 50%
Best Brands: In France, Bisson et fils, La Varinière, Lanquetôt, Lepeudry, Levasseur; in U.S., pasteurized versions by Graindorge (excellent) and Levasseur (very good)
Characteristics: Beige to reddish-golden crust with crosshatching impressions; ivory- to straw-colored paste; supple texture; Camembert-like flavor, but bigger and more intense; pleasantly smelly
Appropriate Wines: Any full-bodied red Bordeaux, Rhône, Burgundy
Related Cheeses: French Epoisses, Langres, Livarot, Maroilles, Munster, Reblochon; Italian Taleggio
The Bottom Line: After Roquefort, Brie, and Camembert, this is the most popular cheese in France.

POULIGNY-SAINT-PIERRE

(POO-'een-yee-SAHN-pee-AIR); A.O.C.

Origin: France—Berry
Type: Goat's milk, unpasteurized; soft to hard (according to age); natural rind (edible)
Availability: A.O.C. is rare; limited availability of non-A.O.C. versions
Form: Truncated tallish, four-sided pyramids
Dimensions: 4 to 5 inches high
Weight: 7 to 9 oz. (210 to 270 g)
Fat Content: 45%
Best Brands: In France and U.S., look for Courthial Père et Fils and Couturier; Couturier primarily exports character-less, mass-produced, plastic-wrapped versions with blue and silver foil labels, but they also produce and export a much scarcer A.O.C. version with a red and gold foil label that is well worth seeking out. Also look for Jacquin's La Pointe de Bique ("nannygoat's horn"), which is identical to the Couturier A.O.C. version, but is made just outside of the name-controlled area for Pouligny; highly recommended
Characteristics: Very white exterior, fragile, moist, and creamy interior (fresh or young); beige crust with blueing (middle-age); dark beige crust with extensive blueing, hard, dry interior and exterior (extra-aged); all have piquant flavor, goaty aroma
Appropriate Wines: Loire and Burgundy whites such as Sauvignon and Mercurey
Related Cheeses: Its identical neighbors pyramid-shaped Tournon-Saint-Martin and Tournon-Saint-Pierre; all

traditional French goat cheeses, especially Chabichou du Poitou, Crottin de Chavignol, Sainte-Maure de Touraine, Selles-sur-Cher, Valençay
The Bottom Line: A visually dramatic classic chèvre.

PROVOLONE

(proh-voh-LOH-neh); D.O.C

Origin: Throughout Italy, chiefly Basilicata, Lombardy, Veneto
Type: Cow's milk, pasteurized and unpasteurized; firm; *pasta filata;* natural rind, lightly coated with paraffin (edible or inedible)
Availability: Good
Form: Wide variety of shapes and sizes, always bound with rope: balls, torpedoes, squash shapes (*mandarini*), salami shapes (*salamini*), *giganti,* etc.
Dimensions: Vast range, depending on shape and weight
Weight: Balls—1 to 3 lbs. (500 g to 1½ k); torpedoes—10 to 200 lbs. (5 to 100 k); *mandarini*—40 lbs. (20 k); *salamini*—1 to 5 lbs. (500 g to 2½ k)
Fat Content: 45%
Best Brands: All excellent; the premium brand is Auricchio, which is made in Italy and U.S.; also look for Cabre, Il Giardino, Soresina
Characteristics: Yellowish-beige rind (darkens with age); firm, yellowish-white interior (darkens with age); firm, waxy texture (young), firm, oily, crumbly texture (aged); sharp flavor at all ages; sharpest version, aged a year or more, called Provolone *piccante*
Appropriate Wines: All big Italian reds; simple, inexpensive Italian reds such as Chianti Classico; beer

Related Cheeses: All Italian *pasta fi-lata* cheeses, such as Burrato, Caciocavallo, Gravina, Provola, Ragusano, Scamorza
The Bottom Line: An unsophisticated, workmanlike antipasto cheese whose chief virtue is sharpness.

RACLETTE

(rack-LETT); French

Origin: France—Franche-Comté, Savoie, Haute-Savoie
Type: Cow's milk, pasteurized and unpasteurized; semi-firm; pressed, cooked curd; natural, brushed rind (inedible)
Availability: Good
Form: Wheels
Dimensions: About 3 inches thick, 13 to 17 inches in diameter
Weight: 13 to 17 lbs. (6½ to 8½ k)
Fat Content: 45%
Best Brands: Look for raw milk examples produced by Brunnerois (Franche-Comté) and Perrin (Savoie); avoid the commercial examples made by Livradois from pasteurized milk; Perrin also makes a pasteurized version
Characteristics: Brownish-beige rind (meant to be trimmed away); buff-colored inner paste; firm, supple texture; full, beefy flavor (unmelted) that intensifies when heated (Raclette is the basis for a traditional melted cheese dish in France and Switzerland called *raclette*); big, sweet, fruity aroma
Appropriate Wines: Light, fresh, fruity reds such as Fleurie, Juliénas, Saint-Amour (all Beaujolais)
Related Cheeses: Swiss Raclette cheeses (Bagnes, Conches, Gomser,

Orsières), Vacherin Fribourgeois; French Morbier, Abondance, Tomme *de chèvre pour raclette;* Italian Fontina d'Aosta
The Bottom Line: Made to be melted, it's as simple as that.

RACLETTE

(rack-LETT); Swiss

Note: *This is a group of cheeses whose names reflect the name of the village closest to where they are made: Bagnes (BAHN-yuh), Conches (KONCH), Gomser (goam-ZAY), Orsières (oar-see-AIR).*

Origin: Switzerland—Valais
Type: Cow's milk, pasteurized and unpasteurized; semi-firm; pressed, cooked curd; natural, brushed rind (inedible)
Availability: Rare
Form: Wheels
Dimensions: About 3 inches thick, 13 to 17 inches in diameter
Weight: 13 to 17 lbs. (6½ to 8½ k)
Fat Content: 45%
Best Brands: All unpasteurized examples excellent; not marketed by brand; look for Valais origin (the name of the village where the cheese is made is molded into the edge of the rind); avoid pasteurized examples
Characteristics: Dark-beige rind (meant to be trimmed away); buff-colored inner paste; firm, supple texture; full, beefy flavor (unmelted) that intensifies when heated; creamy mouthfeel; big, sweet, fruity aroma
Appropriate Wines: Swiss Fendant (white) or Dôle (red); all light, fruity reds; Beaujolais
Related Cheeses: French Raclette, Morbier; Italian Fontina d'Aosta;

Swiss Vacherin Fribourgeois
The Bottom Line: The ultimate melting cheese.

REBLOCHON

(ruh-bloe-CHAW); A.O.C.

Origin: France—Savoie, Haute-Savoie (best areas are Aravis, Haute-Tarantaise)
Type: Cow's milk, unpasteurized; soft; slightly pressed curd; washed rind (edible or inedible)
Availability: Most illegal for U.S. import (raw cow's milk cheese aged less than 60 days). *Note:* Reblochon is aged 50 to 55 days. Recently a few U.S. importers have asked their French suppliers to age the cheese a few extra days to meet USFDA requirements. This cheese is now occasionally available in the U.S.
Form: Disks, tucked between two paper-thin wafers of wood, then wrapped in paper
Dimensions: 1 inch thick, 5½ inches in diameter
Weight: 1 lb. (500 g)
Fat Content: 50%
Best Brands: All excellent; numerous small producers in France, especially in the villages of Thônes, La Clusaz, Le Grand-Bornand
Characteristics: Velvety café au lait—colored rind; bone-colored paste; Brie-like texture; very sweet, beefy, nutty flavor; deliciously smelly
Appropriate Wines: Fruity, white Savoie wines; fresh, young, fruity reds, such as Fleurie, Saint-Amour, Juliénas
Related Cheeses: French Beaumont, Tamié. Tavaillon, Vacherin Mont d'Or
The Bottom Line: A triumph of

cheesemaking—its rind is like the velvet on a deer's antler, its flavor like filet mignon.

RICOTTA SALATA

(ree-COH-tah-sah-LAH-tah)

Origin: Italy—Apulia, Campania, Lazio, Sardinia, Sicily
Type: Sheep's milk whey, or whey and whole milk, pasteurized; pressed curd; rindless
Availability: Good
Form: Plastic-wrapped wheels
Dimensions: 4 inches thick, 6 to 7 inches in diameter
Weight: About 6 lbs. (3 k)
Fat Content: 45% (though whey content suggests less fat, this cheese is pressed and therefore very dense)
Best Brands: All excellent; in Italy and U.S., look for Pinna or Mannoni, which are often sweeter and moister than others
Characteristics: Firm, yet tender, smooth-textured, pure white interior; mild, sweet (usually), nutty, milky flavor
Appropriate Wines: Any
Related Cheeses: Cypriot Haloumi; Greek Feta, Manouri
The Bottom Line: Versatile and a great value. Give me Ricotta Salata over Feta any day.

ROBIOLA LOMBARDIA

(roh-bee-OH-lah-lom-bar-DEE-ah).

Note: Do not confuse with Robiola Piemonte. Robiola Lombardia is a generic name given to a group of Lombardy cheeses that are essentially diminutive Taleggios.

Origin: Italy—Lombardy
Type: Cow's milk, pasteurized or unpasteurized; soft; washed rind (edible or inedible)
Availability: Rare
Form: Various paper- or foil-wrapped shapes, usually small cubes, rectangles, half-moons, or disks
Dimensions: Vary with shape
Weight: Varies with shape; most from 6 oz. to 1½ lbs. (180 to 750 g)
Fat Content: 45%
Best Brands: In Italy and U.S., seek out Acquistapace's Robiola; Cademartori's Baitella, Tartufella, and Introbiola; Gigli's Robiola; Lodigiani's La Baita; Mauri's d'Artavaggio and Maurella; Merlo's Antica Cascina
Characteristics: Rough, reddish-brown rind, often touched with blue mold, occasionally moist to the touch; off-white to faintly yellow interior; bulging form; meaty, nutty, slightly salty flavor with nuances of fruit; very cheesy aroma
Appropriate Wines: Big Italian reds such as Amarone, Barbaresco, Barbera, Barolo, Brunello di Montalcino, Chianti Riserva, Salice Salentino, Taurasi
Related Cheeses: Italian Taleggio; French Beaumont Pont-l'Evêque, Reblochon
The Bottom Line: An undersung treasure—the equal of far more famous French washed-rind cheeses.

ROBIOLA PIEMONTE

(roh-bee-OH-lah-pyeh-MAWN-teh).

Note: *Do not confuse with Robiola Lombardia. Robiola Piemonte is the generic name of a group of fresh, rind-less, cream-added Piedmont cheeses. Included in the group are two D.O.C. cheeses—Robiola di Roccaverano (roh-kah-vehr-AH-noh) and Murazzano (moor-ah-TZAH-noh).*

Origin: Piedmont
Type: Unripened cow's-, goat's-, or sheep's-milk (or a mixture of the three), pasteurized or unpasteurized; almost always cream-added; soft; rindless
Availability: Rare
Form: Waxed or plastic paper-wrapped units in a variety of shapes, usually somewhat amorphous cubes or disks; sometimes sold in tubs
Dimensions: Various
Weight: Varies with shape; about 6 to 14 oz. (180 to 420 g)
Fat Content: 50%
Best Brands: Osella's Annabella La Morbida and Robiola Osella
Characteristics: Snowy white throughout; soft, moist, and creamy texture; slightly tart, mild, lactose-sweet flavor; fruity aroma
Appropriate Wines: Dry or sweet whites from Piedmont; *spumanti;* Gavi, Cinqueterre, Moscato
Related Cheeses: Italian Caprini, Mascarpone; French Saint-Florentin, Brie de Melun *frais,* Petit-Suisse
The Bottom Line: A superb breakfast or brunch cheese to serve with a fresh fruit salad.

RONCAL

(roan-KAHL); D.O.

Origin: Spain—Navarre
Type: Sheep's milk, pasteurized and unpasteurized; hard; pressed; aged for a minimum of 3 months; hard natural rind (inedible)
Availability: Rare
Form: Thick wheels
Dimensions: 4 to 4½ inches high, 6 to 7 inches in diameter
Weight: 5 to 7 lbs. (2¼ to 3½ k)
Fat Content: 50%
Best Brands: All excellent
Characteristics: Hard, beige-to-gray rind; beige paste (turns amber with age); rich, olivey, nutty flavor
Appropriate Wines: Navarra reds
Related Cheeses: Spanish Manchego, Idiazábal, Zamorano; French Pyrénées cheeses; Italian Pecorino Sardo
The Bottom Line: They've been making this fabulous cheese in Spain for nearly 3,000 years—isn't it about time you tasted it?

ROQUEFORT

(roke-FORE); A.O.C.

Origin: France—Rouergue
Type: Sheep's-milk blue, unpasteurized soft; rindless (outside of cheese is edible, though salty)
Availability: Excellent
Form: Foil-wrapped wheels
Dimensions: 3¾ inches high, 8 inches in diameter
Weight: 5½ to 6½ lbs. (2¾ to 3¼ k)
Fat Content: 45%
Best Brands: All excellent; I strongly prefer Gabriel Coulet and Le Papil-

lon, but Carles and Constans-Crouzat also excellent
Characteristics: Foil-wrapped (rindless); soft, but crumbly and moist; ivory-colored interior with profuse green-blue veining; intense, complex, spicy flavor
Appropriate Wines: Strong reds such as Châteauneuf-du-Pape; sweet whites such as Sauternes
Related Cheeses: French Bleu des Causses, Bleu d'Auvergne (both cow's milk); Danish Blue; Scottish Lanark; Spanish Cabrales, Gamonedo, Picón
The Bottom Line: The reason God created caves.

SAINTE-MAURE DE TOURAINE

(SAHNT-MORE-duh-ter-RAN); A.O.C.

Origin: France—Touraine (A.O.C.); neighboring regions of Berry and Poitou (non-A.O.C.)
Type: Goat's milk, pasteurized and unpasteurized; soft to hard (according to age); natural rind, ashed or unashed (edible)
Availability: A.O.C. is rare; limited availability of non-A.O.C. versions
Form: Log-shaped; authentic versions have a piece of straw or a stick stuck through from end to end
Dimensions: 1½ to 2 inches thick, 5 to 8 inches long
Weight: 11 to 14 oz. (330 to 420 g)
Fat Content: 45% to 50%
Best Brands: All A.O.C. examples made in Touraine are excellent, but production is quite limited. However, versions made outside of name-controlled area are also excellent, every bit as good as A.O.C. version.

In France, look for Saint-Christophe-en-Bazelle made by Anjouin in Berry (excellent); in U.S., best available A.O.C. versions are by Courthial Père et Fils, Couturier, or Jacquin; also look for non-A.O.C. examples made by Coopérative Sèvre-et-Belle (Poitou) and Jacquin and Desport (both Périgord)

Characteristics: Very white exterior, fragile, moist, and creamy (fresh or young); beige crust with blueing (middle-aged); dark beige crust with extensive blueing, hard, dry interior and exterior (extra-aged); all have piquant flavor, goaty aroma; all ages skewered with a dowel or piece of straw piercing cheese from end to end

Appropriate Wines: All reds and whites of the Touraine region; if the cheese is young, Vouvray, Champigny, Mont Louis, Saumur; if an older, riper cheese, Bourgueil, Chinon

Related Cheeses: All traditional French goat cheeses, especially Chabichou du Poitou, Crottin de Chavignol, Pouligny-Saint-Pierre, Selles-sur-Cher, Valençay

The Bottom Line: A classic, traditional French chèvre.

SAINT-MARCELLIN

(SAN-mar-sell-AN)

Origin: France—Dauphiné (Isère)
Type: Cow's milk, pasteurized and unpasteurized; soft; rindless (usually wrapped in chestnut leaves dipped in wine, *eau-de-vie,* or *marc*)
Availability: Rare
Form: Disks, usually wrapped in chestnut leaves and tied with raffia or ribbon
Dimensions: ¾ inch thick, 3 inches in diameter
Weight: About 3 oz. (90 g)
Fat Content: 50%
Best Brands: In U.S., look for Fromagerie Royannais-Teche versions (not leaf-wrapped); labels will indicate *crèmier* (small dairy) and *affiné* (ripened). In France, seek out *fermier* (farm-made) examples
Characteristics: Beige crust covered with blue mold; soft, beige, creamy interior; intensely rustic, nutty, fruity flavor
Appropriate Wines: All Rhône reds
Related Cheeses: Banon
The Bottom Line: In its *crèmier* version, no finer cheese exists; a cheese to worship.

SAINT-NECTAIRE

(SAN-neck-TARE); A.O.C.

Origin: France—Auvergne
Type: Cow's milk, pasteurized and unpasteurized; semisoft; pressed; natural rind (inedible)
Availability: Good (pasteurized); unpasteurized illegal for export to U.S. (raw cow's milk cheese aged less than 60 days)
Form: Disk
Dimensions: 1½ inches thick, 8 inches in diameter
Weight: About 3½ lbs. (1¾ k)
Fat Content: 45%
Best Brands: In France and U.S., look for examples from small producers such as Babut (my favorite), Allayrangue, Prugne; Roussel is best factory-made brand; in France, look for

an oval green stamp on the rind identifying *fermier* (farm-made) examples
Characteristics: Smooth, reddish rind; ivory- to straw-colored interior, with occasional tiny holes; soft, supple texture; earthy, fruity flavor; pleasantly grassy aroma
Appropriate Wines: Rhône reds; Beaujolais; Chanturgue (a big, beefy red from Auvergne)
Related Cheeses: French Beaumont, Le Pavin, Munster, Port-Salut, Reblochon, Saint-Paulin; Canadian Oka; Irish Gubbeen; Swiss Tilsit
The Bottom Line: Ironically, despite its name-controlled status, this cheese is a victim of industrialization.

SAN SIMON

(SAN-see-MOHN)

Origin: Spain—Galicia
Type: Cow's milk, pasteurized and unpasteurized; soft to very firm (according to age); smoked; natural rind (edible or inedible)
Availability: Rare
Form: Tall, conical shape—looks like a dunce cap (*bufone*)
Dimensions: 6 to 7 inches high, 4 to 6 inches in diameter at base
Weight: 2½ to 3 lbs. (1¼ to 1½ k)
Fat Content: 45%
Best Brands: All good
Characteristics: Burnished, walnut-brown rind; light yellow to golden paste (according to age); creamy, decidedly smoky flavor, ranging from mild (young) to slightly piquant (aged)
Appropriate Wines: All Spanish whites, especially Catalonia sparkling whites (*cava*); Andalusian dry sherry (*fino*)
Related Cheeses: Spanish Cantabria,

Queso de Nata, Tetilla, Vidiago
The Bottom Line: Intriguing shape, but no big deal.

SBRINZ

(SPRINZ)

Origin: Switzerland—Bern, Lucerne, Obwalden, Schwyz, Uri, Unterwalden-Midwalden, and Zug
Type: Cow's milk, unpasteurized; hard; pressed curd; aged from 6 months to more than 3 years; brushed, oiled rind (inedible)
Availability: Rare
Form: Large wheels
Dimensions: 5 inches thick, 32 to 33 inches in diameter
Weight: 60 to 80 lbs. (30 to 40 k)
Fat Content: 45%
Best Brands: All excellent; not marketed by brand
Characteristics: Burnished-gold rind; firm to rock-hard texture; amber, melt-in-your-mouth interior; mild, nutty, butterscotchy flavor
Appropriate Wines: Spicy, dry Swiss or Alsatian whites; light, fruity reds such as Beaujolais
Related Cheeses: Swiss Saanen and Spalen (also called Sparen), both identical to Sbrinz but smaller; Italian Bitto, Grana Padano, Parmigiano-Reggiano; Dutch aged Gouda
The Bottom Line: A real find and a terrific value—think of it as a milder version of Parmigiano-Reggiano.

SELLES-SUR-CHER

(SELL-sir-SHAIR); A.O.C.

Origin: France (Loire River Valley)—Berry, Orléanais (Sologne)

Type: Goat's milk, pasteurized and unpasteurized; soft to firm (according to age); natural rind, usually ashed (edible)
Availability: Available (pasteurized)
Form: Thickish, flat-sided disks, tending toward conical
Dimensions: 1 to 1½ inches thick, 3 to 3½ inches in diameter
Weight: 4 to 6 oz. (125 to 180 g)
Fat Content: 45%
Best Brands: In U.S., the best example available is Jacquin, which is excellent; Anjouin, a brand found only occasionally in U.S., is also excellent
Characteristics: Stark black (ashed) exterior; perfectly white interior; firm, yet soft, moist, and fragile to the touch; sweet, nutty flavor; light, goaty aroma
Appropriate Wines: All whites and reds of the Loire Valley
Related Cheeses: All traditional French goat cheeses, especially Crottin de Chavignol, Chabichou du Poitou, Pouligny-Saint-Pierre, Sainte-Maure de Touraine, Valençay
The Bottom Line: The prototypical black-as-coal ashed chèvre.

SHROPSHIRE BLUE

(SHROP-shur-bloo)

Origin: England—Shropshire
Type: Cow's-milk blue, pasteurized; firm; natural, brushed rind (inedible)
Availability: Good
Form: Tall cylinders
Dimensions: 11 to 12 inches high, 7 inches in diameter
Weight: 14 to 16 lbs. (7 to 8 k)
Fat Content: 45%

Best Brands: All excellent
Characteristics: Rough, brown rind; crumbly, yet firm and creamy texture; bright orange, liberally blued interior; sharp, rustic, slightly tannic flavor
Appropriate Wines: All big reds; Bordeaux, Côtes-du-Rhône; sherry, port, Madeira, Sauternes; beer
Related Cheeses: English Blue Cheshire, Blue Vinney, Blue Wensleydale, Dorset Blue, Stilton; Irish Cashel Blue; Scottish Lanark Blue
The Bottom Line: A glorious blue cheese identical to Stilton, but orange rather than ivory in color.

STILTON

(STILL-tun); England's only name-protected cheese

Origin: England—Leicestershire (Melton Mowbray), Nottinghamshire, part of Derbyshire (Dale of the Dove)
Type: Cow's milk blue, pasteurized; firm; natural, brushed rind (inedible)
Availability: Good
Form: Top hat–shaped cylinders
Dimensions: 10 to 11 inches high, 8 to 9 inches in diameter
Weight: About 14 to 16 lbs. (7 to 8 k); also available in smaller cylinders and in earthenware crocks
Fat Content: 55%
Best Brands: Colston Bassett (best); Long Clawson Dairy, J. M. Nuttall, Millway Foods Ltd., Tuxford & Tebbutt (all excellent)
Characteristics: Dry, rough, brownish rind; ivory-colored paste with liberal greenish-blue veining; pronounced full, rich, cheesy flavor; moist, firm yet crumbly texture; huge, spicy aroma

Appropriate Wines: All robust reds; excellent with sherry and port
Related Cheeses: English Blue Cheshire, Blue Vinney, Blue Wensleydale, Dorset Blue, Shropshire Blue; Irish Cashel Blue; Scottish Lanark Blue; French Fourme d'Ambert; Italian Gorgonzola *naturale* (aged)
The Bottom Line: A magnificent blue cheese all too often sold in below-par condition.

STRACCHINO

(strah-KEE-noh); also called Crescenza (kreh-SHEN-tsah) or Stracchino di Crescenza (strah-KEE-no-dee-kreh-SHEN-tsah)

Origin: Italy—Lombardy
Type: Cow's milk, pasteurized; soft; pressed curd; natural rind, washed once (edible)
Availability: Spotty
Form: Waxed paper-wrapped slabs or loaves
Dimensions: About 2 inches thick
Weight: 4 to 8 oz. (125 to 250 g); 2 to 3 lbs. (1 to 1½ k)
Fat Content: 48%
Best Brands: All excellent
Characteristics: Very thin, smooth, supple, nearly undetectable bone-white rind over a soft, white paste (young); beige, dry, rind dusted with *Penicillium candidum* mold over oozy, satiny, white paste (ripened); flavor ranges from faintly tart (young) to very tart and quite fruity (ripened); fruity aroma (aged)
Appropriate Wines: Light, fruity Italian whites such as Grave del Friuli
Related Cheeses: Italian Gorgonzola
The Bottom Line: Unique and provocative—an acquired taste.

SWISS GRUYERE

(SWISS-grew-YAIR or gree-AIR); Swiss

Origin: Switzerland—Fribourg
Type: Cow's milk, unpasteurized; firm; pressed, cooked curd; natural, brushed rind (inedible)
Availability: Good
Form: Large, flat wheels
Dimensions: 4 inches thick, about 38 inches in diameter
Weight: 65 to 85 lbs. (32½ to 42½ k)
Fat Content: 45%
Best Brands: All excellent; not marketed by brand
Characteristics: Brown, pebbled rind; smooth, creamy-beige interior with occasional *lènures* (horizontal fissures near rind); assertive flavor with hints of fruit and nuts; pleasantly fruity aroma
Appropriate Wines: Red or white Burgundies; a range of Rhône reds from Côte Rôtie to Châteauneuf-du-Pâpe; Bandol; Alsatian reds and whites
Related Cheeses: French Abondance, Beaufort, Comté (Gruyère de Comté), Emmental; Swiss Emmental, Fribourg, aged Gruyère, Vacherin Fribourgeois; Greek Kefalograviera
The Bottom Line: Everything Swiss Emmental isn't and wishes it were.

SWISS TILSIT

(SWISS-TILL-sit)

Note: Formerly called Royalp.

Origin: Switzerland—Zurich, Saint Gallen, Thurgau
Type: Cow's milk, unpasteurized; semi-firm; pressed, cooked curd;

natural, washed, brushed rind
(inedible)
Availability: Rare
Form: Wheels
Dimensions: 1½ inches thick,
7 inches in diameter
Weight: About 4 lbs. (2 k)
Fat Content: 45%
Best Brands: All excellent; not
marketed by brand
Characteristics: Orange-brown rind;
smooth texture; occasional scattering of pea- to cherry-size holes;
pronounced nutty, earthy, barnyardy
flavor and aroma
Appropriate Wines: Strong, powerful
reds, such as Côtes-du-Rhône; beer,
ale
Related Cheeses: Swiss Appenzeller;
not very similar to Tilsit types made
in other countries
The Bottom Line: The best of all
Tilsits.

TALEGGIO

(tah-LEDGE-oh); D.O.C.

Origin: Italy—Lombardy (Valtellina,
Valsassina)
Type: Cow's milk, pasteurized and
unpasteurized; soft; pressed curd;
washed rind (edible or inedible)
Availability: Good
Form: Thick squares
Dimensions: 2 inches thick, 8 inches
square
Weight: About 5 lbs. (2½ k)
Fat Content: 48% or more
Best Brands: In Italy and U.S., look
for Acquistapace, Buonacasa, Cade-
martori, Lodigiani, Mauri, Oreum.
Characteristics: Rough, reddish-
brown rind; off-white, faintly yellow

interior; meaty, nutty, slightly salty
flavor, with nuances of fruit; very
cheesy aroma
Appropriate Wines: Big Italian reds,
such as Barbaresco, Barolo, Brunello
di Montalcino, Chianti Riserva, Salice
Salentino, Taurasi
Related Cheeses: Italian Robiola
Lombardia; French Beaumont,
Livarot, Pont-l'Evêque, Reblochon,
Saint-Nectaire, Tavaillon; Spanish
Mahón
The Bottom Line: Northern Italy's
best-kept secret—the most refined
and sophisticated of all Italian
cheeses.

TETE DE MOINE

*(TET-duh-MWAHN); also called Bellelay
(bel-LAY)*

Origin: Switzerland—Bern (Bellelay)
Type: Cow's milk, unpasteurized;
semi-firm; pressed curd; natural,
washed, brushed rind (inedible)
Availability: Good
Form: Small drums, usually foil-
wrapped
Dimensions: 4 to 5 inches high, 4 to
5 inches in diameter
Weight: Average 1¼ to 1¾ lbs. (625 to
875 g)
Fat Content: 45% to 50%
Best Brands: All excellent; not marketed by brand
Characteristics: Light-brown to
brown, dry, pebbled or smooth rind;
straw-colored interior with occasional fissures (*lènures*); strong
fruity, nutty, beefy flavor; strong
aroma
Appropriate Wines: Big reds, such
as Châteauneuf-du-Pape, Hermitage,

Saint-Blaise (a Swiss red, much-appreciated, but rare in the U.S).; beer, ale, porter, stout
Related Cheeses: Swiss Raclette cheeses (Bagnes, Conches, Gomser, Crsières) and Gruyère (although all are milder in flavor), Appenzeller; French Abondance, Girollin
The Bottom Line: No other mountain cheese in the world possesses such intensity of flavor—stunning and memorable.

TETILLA

(teh-TEE-yah)

Origin: Spain—Galicia
Type: Cow's milk, pasteurized and unpasteurized (artisanal); semisoft; pressed curd; natural rind (edible or inedible)
Availability: Good (pasteurized only)
Form: Squat cone shapes (look like giant Hershey's Kisses)
Dimensions: 4 to 5 inches high, 5 to 6 inches in diameter at base
Weight: About 2 to 3 lbs. (1 to 1½ k)
Fat Content: 45%
Best Brands: All good
Characteristics: Greenish-beige rind; soft (young), white interior; mild and tangy flavor, similar to Monterey Jack; firm (aged) but supple texture
Appropriate Wines: All Spanish whites, especially Catalonia sparkling whites (*cava*); Andalusian dry sherry (*fino*)
Related Cheeses: Spanish Cantabria, Queso de Nata, San Simón, Vidiago
The Bottom Line: Like San Simón, an intriguing shape for a forgettable cheese.

TOMA

(TOH-mah)

Note: *This is an overall designation for a specific style of soft-ripened cow's-milk cheeses, which are sold under various proprietary names.*

Origin: Italy—Piedmont, parts of Lombardy
Type: Cow's milk (occasionally goat's milk), pasteurized and unpasteurized; soft-ripened; bloomy rind (edible)
Availability: Rare
Form: Thickish disks, paper-wrapped
Dimensions: 2 inches thick, 4 inches in diameter
Weight: 8 to 12 oz. (250 to 375 g)
Fat Content: 50%
Best Brands: All excellent; in Italy and U.S., look for Toma della Valcuvia, Toma di Carmagnola, Caprella (a version of Carmagnola made with goat's milk bolstered with the addition of cow's-milk cream)
Characteristics: White, bloomy rind that becomes beige-mottled when ripe; soft and supple; straw-colored interior (Caprella is ivory); depending upon age, texture ranges from chalky (ripe) to bulgy (perfect) to runny (overripe); haunting, white-truffle flavor: mushroomy, garlicky aroma
Appropriate Wines: Big Piedmont reds—Barolo, Barbaresco, Spanna, Ghemme, Barbera, Gattinara
Related Cheeses: Italian Paglia-style cheeses; French Brie, Camembert
The Bottom Line: An Italian cheese that's good news for lovers of real French Brie and Camembert—as

good or better than the finest raw-milk versions of those two cheeses.

TOMME DE SAVOIE

(TUM-duh-sav-WAH)

Origin: France—Savoie, Haute-Savoie
Type: Cow's milk, pasteurized and unpasteurized; semi-firm; pressed curd; natural rind (inedible)
Availability: Good, but beware of similarly named look-alike imitators. Read the label: It must say "Fabriqué en Savoie," not "Affiné en Savoie." Often these imitators are made elsewhere (Poitou, Auvergne), then trucked to Savoie where they are "aged" (or so they tell us); these cheeses are without flavor or merit.
Form: Medium-size disks; also over-size-disks and barrel shapes
Dimensions: 2 inches thick, 8 inches in diameter
Weight: 3½ lbs. (1¾ k), regular disks; 4 to 12 lbs. (2 to 6 k), oversize disks; 1½ lbs. (750 g), barrel shapes
Fat Content: 20% to 40%
Best Brands: Numerous producers, all excellent; in France and U.S., seek out my favorite made by Perrin (Haute-Savoie); in France, look for examples made in Bauges (Haute-Savoie) and Les Bellevilles (Savoie)
Characteristics: Unmistakable fuzzy, thick, gray-brown rind; beige- or straw-colored paste, usually with tiny hole structure; slightly saline, mild but savory (beefy) flavor; very mild aroma
Appropriate Wines: Any light, fruity red or white. If you're in Savoie, drink the local wines (which don't travel well), especially Mondeuse and Abymes
Related Cheeses: French Saint-Nectaire
The Bottom Line: A personal favorite—rustic, simple, delicious.

TRONCHON

(trone-CHONE)

Origin: Spain—Southern Aragón, parts of Catalonia, Valencia
Type: Sheep's or goat's milk, or a combination of the two, pasteurized and unpasteurized artisanal; firm; pressed curd; usually slightly aged (3 to 4 months); natural rind (edible or inedible)
Availability: Rare
Form: Dome shapes, with deep indentation on top
Dimensions: About 6 inches in diameter at base
Weight: 4½ lbs. (2¼ k)
Fat Content: 45% to 50%
Best Brands: All excellent
Characteristics: Buff-colored rind; bone-colored interior with a proliferation of tiny holes; mild, distinctly herby flavor, firm yet melting texture
Appropriate Wines: All Spanish whites, especially Catalonian sparkling whites *(cava)*; Andalusian dry sherry *(fino)*
Related Cheeses: None
The Bottom Line: A delicious oddball with a romantic herbiness; there's no other cheese like it. You owe it to yourself to try some.

VACHERIN DU HAUT-DOUBS

(vasher-ANN-doo-oh-DOO); A.O.C.;
also called Vacherin Mont d'Or
(vasher-ANN-moan-DOR)

Origin: France—Franche-Comté
Type: Cow's milk, unpasteurized;
very soft; washed rind (edible)
Availability: Illegal for export to U.S.
(raw cow's milk cheese aged less
than 60 days)
Form: Varies from dinner plate– to
saucer-size rounds; always banded
with a strip of bark and packed in a
lidded wooden box
Dimensions: 1 to 1¼ inches thick,
9 inches in diameter; also 1½ to
2 inches thick, 4 to 5 inches in
diameter
Weight: 5 to 7 lbs. (2½ to 3½ k); also
smaller rounds, 1 lb. (500 g)
Fat Content: 45%
Best Brands: All excellent in France;
look for examples made by the
Badoz family in Pontarlier (Franche-
Comté); in U.S., seek out my favorite
faux Vacherins, Edel de Cléron and
the identical (but with a different
label) Ecorcé de Sapin, made by
Perrin (Franche-Comté), which are
easily as good as the finest raw-milk
Vacherin Mont d'Or; also look for the
slightly less desirable Tourrée de
l'Aubier made by Prédor (Dauphiné)
and Tavaillon made by Girod
(Savoie)
Characteristics: Wavy, reddish-
brown, velvety rind; supple texture;
big, fruity, faintly raw, woodsy, nutty
flavor with slight bite; strong aroma
Appropriate Wines: French and
Swiss Vacherins improve the flavor
of many less-than-big wines; choose
fruity and/or light red wines (Beaujolais) or big whites (Chardonnay)
Related Cheeses: Swiss Vacherin
Mont d'Or; beyond this, no cheese is
quite like it, although French Reblochon is similar; there are also excellent French *faux* Vacherins made
with pasteurized milk
The Bottom Line: Ambrosial; part of
the Holy Trinity of cheeses, along
with Parmigiano-Reggiano and
Roquefort.

VACHERIN FRIBOURGEOIS

(vasher-ANN-FREE-boor-ZHWAH)

Origin: Switzerland—Valais
Type: Cow's milk, unpasteurized;
semi-firm; lightly pressed curd;
natural, brushed, washed rind
(inedible)
Availability: Spotty
Form: Wheels
Dimensions: 3 inches thick, 12 to
14 inches in diameter
Weight: 16 to 18 lbs. (8 to 9 k)
Fat Content: 45%
Best Brands: All excellent; not
marketed by brand
Characteristics: Light-brown rind;
straw-colored interior; occasional
fissure/aperture and tiny hole struc-
ture; big, raw, nutty flavor
Appropriate Wines: Big reds from
Burgundy, Bordeaux, the Rhône
Valley, and Piedmont
Related Cheeses: Italian Fontina
d'Aosta; French Abondance, Comté,
Morbier, Raclette; Swiss Raclette
cheeses (Bagnes, Conches, Gomser,
Orsières), Gruyère
The Bottom Line: One of Switzer-
land's finest cheeses; so luscious

you'll want to eat it with a knife and fork.

VACHERIN MONT D'OR

(vasher-ANN-moan-DOR)

Origin: Switzerland—Vaud
Type: Cow's milk, pasteurized and unpasteurized; very soft; washed rind (edible)
Availability: Illegal for export to U.S. (raw cow's-milk cheese aged less than 60 days); pasteurized versions are exported to U.S., but rare
Form: Varies from saucer-size to dinner plate–size rounds; always in lidded wooden box
Dimensions: 1 to 1¼ inches thick, 9 inches in diameter; also 1½ to 2 inches thick, 4 to 5 inches in diameter
Weight: 5 to 7 lbs. (2½ to 3½ k); also smaller rounds, 1 lb. (500 g)
Fat Content: 45%
Best Brands: All unpasteurized examples are excellent; not marketed by brand
Characteristics: Wavy, reddish-beige, velvety rind; supple texture; big, fruity, faintly raw, woodsy, buttery flavor with slight bite; unique aroma (smells like new leather); thin strip of resinous bark encircling rind contibutes balsamy flavor and aroma
Appropriate Wines: Swiss and French Vacherins improve the flavor of many less-than-big light, fruity wines, such as Beaujolais, Swiss Fendant, Dôle; Alsatian Riesling, Tokay, or Muscat
Related Cheeses: French Vacherin du Haut-Doubs (also called Vacherin Mont d'Or); no other cheese is quite like it, although French Reblochon is similar

The Bottom Line: One of the highest achievements of human civilization.

VALENCAY

(VAL-awn-SAY)

Origin: France—Berry
Type: Goat's milk, pasteurized and unpasteurized; soft to firm (according to age); natural rind, sometimes ashed (edible)
Availability: Good
Form: Four-sided, truncated pyramids (shorter than Pouligny-Saint-Pierre)
Dimensions: 3½ inches high
Weight: about 8 oz. (250 g)
Fat Content: 45%
Best Brands: In France, look for Anjouin or Jacquin (both Berry); in U.S., look for Jacquin (excellent) or Anjouin (rare, but excellent); also, excellent non-A.O.C. examples by Chèvrechard and Coopérative Sèvre-et-Belle (both Poitou), Desport (Périgord). If these are unavailable, look for the more commercial, plastic-wrapped Couturier brand (Berry)
Characteristics: Natural beige rind (unless ashed); white interior; best stage of ripeness is a matter of taste (hard, brown, highly aged examples too strongly flavored for most tastes)
Appropriate Wines: If the cheese is young, dry, flinty whites like Sancerre and Pouilly-Fuissé; also, Alsatian whites, California Chardonnay; if the cheese is riper, serve with light, fruity reds
Related Cheeses: All traditional French goat cheeses, especially Chabichou du Poitou, Crottin de Chavignol, Pouligny-Saint-Pierre,

Sainte-Maure de Touraine, Selles-sur-Cher

The Bottom Line: Napoleon loved it, so will you; one of France's most distinctive cheeses.

WENSLEYDALE

(WENZ-lee-dale)

Origin: England—Yorkshire
Type: Cow's milk, pasteurized; firm; pressed curd; natural, cloth-wrapped rind (inedible)
Availability: Good, creamery-made
Form: Cloth-covered cylinders and wheels; factory-made is plastic-wrapped, rectangular blocks or 3-inch-thick wheels
Dimensions: 12 inches high, 10 inches in diameter
Weight: About 12 to 14 lbs. (6 to 7 k)

Fat Content: 40% to 45%
Best Brands: Kirkby Malzeard Dairy, The Wensleydale Cheese Company (both North Yorkshire)—if these are unavailable, wait until you visit England; in England, look for the limited production of Ashes Farm, Redesdale Dairy, Shepherd's Purse
Characteristics: Bone-white paste; crumbly, fine-grained texture; very mild, slightly sour, nutty flavor, often described as "refreshing"; mild aroma
Appropriate Wines: Dry white wines, such as California or Australian Chardonnay; beer, ale; cider
Related Cheeses: English Caerphilly, Cheddar, Cheshire, Cornish Yarg, Lancashire, Stilton; Italian Bra; Welsh Tyn Grug, Llangloffan
The Bottom Line: A historic English cheese that's as much a part of English life as ale or fish and chips.

Bibliography

Androuët, Pierre. *Guide du Fromage: The Complete Encyclopedia of French Cheese*. New York: Harper & Row, 1973.

Anifantakis, Emmanuel. *Greek Cheeses: A Tradition for Centuries*. Athens: National Dairy Committee of Greece, 1991.

Brillat-Savarin, Anthelme. *The Physiology of Taste*. Translated by M. F. K. Fisher. New York: Harcourt Brace, 1978.

Brown, Bob. *The Complete Book of Cheese*. New York: Gramercy, 1955.

Canut, E. and Navarro, F. *Catálogo de Quesos de España*. Madrid: Ministerio de Agricultura, Pesca y Alimentacion, 1990.

Canut, E. *Manual de Quesos, Queseros y Quesomanos*. Madrid: Ediciones Temas de Hoy, 1988.

Courtine, Robert J. *Larousse des Fromages*. Paris: Librairie Larousse, 1973.

Domingo, Xavier. *The Taste of Spain*. Paris: Flammarion, 1992.

Eekhof-Stork, Nancy. *The World Atlas of Cheese*. London: Paddington Press Ltd., 1976.

Gray, Patience. *Honey from a Weed: Fasting & Feasting in Tuscany, Catalonia, the Cyclades & Apulia*. New York: Harper & Row, 1987.

Harbutt, Juliet. *The Specialist Cheesemakers' Association Guide to the Finest Cheeses of Britain and Ireland*. Staffordshire: Specialist Cheesemakers' Association, 1994.

Il Mio Formaggio. Rome: Librex, 1982.

Layton, T. A. *Cheese and Cheese Cookery*. New York: Crown (Bonanza Books), 1967.

Lindon, Raymond. *Le Livre de l'Amateur de Fromages*. Paris: Robert Laffont, 1961.

Loomis, Susan Herrmann. *Farmhouse Cookbook*. New York:

Workman Publishing Company, Inc., 1991.

Marquis, Vivienne, and Haskell, Patricia. *The Cheese Book.* New York: Simon & Schuster, 1964.

Martin, Arturo. *Los Quesos Artsanales Asturianos.* Madrid: SADEL,1985.

McGee, Harold. *On Food and Cooking: The Science and Lore of the Kitchen.* New York: Charles Scribner's Sons, 1984.

Michael-Degner, Rotraud. *The Cheeses of Italy.* Rome: The Italian Institute of Foreign Trade, n.d.

Ministero Agricoltura e Foreste, UNALAT in collaboration with INSOR, eds. *DOC Cheeses of Italy: A Great Heritage.* Milan: FrancoAngeli, 1990.

Pourrat. *The Roquefort Adventure.* Roquefort: Société Anonyme des Caves et des Producteurs Réunis de Roquefort, 1956.

Rance, Patrick. *The French Cheese Book.* London: Macmillan, 1982.

Rance, Patrick. *The Great British Cheese Book.* London: Macmillan, 1982.

Root, Waverley. *The Food of France.* New York: Vintage, 1977.

Root, Waverley. *The Food of Italy.* New York: Vintage, 1977.

Root, Waverley, and de Rochemont, Richard. *Eating in America.* New York: William Morrow, 1976.

Sevilla, María José. *Life and Food in the Basque Country.* New York: New Amsterdam Books, 1989.

Signanini, Sergio. *Form and Substance—Il Pecorino Toscano.* Grosseto: The Agricultural Department of the Tuscany Region, 1992.

Stobbs, William. *Guide to Cheeses of France.* London: Apple Press Ltd., 1984.

Squire, John, ed. *Cheddar Gorge.* London and Glasgow: Collins Clear-Type Press, 1937.

Stamm, Eunice R. *The History of Cheese Making in New York State.* New York: The Lewis Group Ltd., 1991.

Vernus, Michel. *Le Comte.* Lyon: Textel, 1988.

Wells, Patricia. *The Food Lover's Guide to France.* New York: Workman Publishing Company, Inc., 1987.

Wells, Patricia. *The Food Lover's Guide to Paris.* New York: Workman Publishing Company, Inc., 1984.

Photo Credits

TITLE PAGE/CONTENTS

Title page: John Bean. Page ix: (left) courtesy of the Wisconsin Milk Marketing Board; (lower right) John Bean. Page x: (top left) Sheilah Scully; (bottom left) courtesy of Rouzaire; (bottom right) John Bean. Page xi: (left) John Bean; (lower right) courtesy of the Milk and Fontina Manufacturers of the Valley of Aosta. Page xii: (lower left) Sheilah Scully. Page xiii: (upper right) courtesy of the Swiss National Tourist Office; (middle left) John Bean; (lower left) Walt Chrynwski; (upper right) BTA/ETB; (lower right) John Bean. Page xiv: (left) Ministry of Agriculture, courtesy of ICEX Foods from Spain; (top right) Pablo Neustadt/Sobremesa, courtesy of ICEX Foods from Spain. Page xvi: (right) Joel Gardner, courtesy of Shelburne Farms. Page xvii: (left) Walt Chrynwski; (right) courtesy of the National Dairy Committee of Greece and the Greek Trade Commission.

INTRODUCTION: SAY CHEESE!

Page xix: Michelle Sims. Page xx: Walt Chrynwski. Page xxi: Michelle Sims. Page xxii: Walt Chrynwski. Page xxiv: Steve Jenkins. Page xxvi: Sara Matthews. Page xxvii: (top left) John Bean; (bottom left) Walt Chrynwski. Page xxviii: (right) John Bean; (left) Sheilah Scully.

ABOUT CHEESE

Page 3: New York Public Library Picture Collection. Page 4: courtesy of the Wisconsin Milk Marketing Board. Page 5: courtesy of the Comté Cheese Association. Page 7: courtesy of the Wisconsin Milk Marketing Board. Page 8: courtesy of the Wisconsin Milk and Marketing Board. Page 10: (top) Walt Chrynwski; (bottom) Sheilah Scully. Page 11: (top) Sheilah Scully; (bottom) courtesy of Roucoutons. Page 12: courtesy of Sweet Home Farm. Page 13: (top) courtesy of the Stilton Cheesemakers Association and Osborne Publicity Services. Page 14: courtesy of the Vermont Butter & Cheese Company. Page 15: courtesy of Rouzaire.

IN STORE AND AT TABLE

Page 18: Steve Jenkins. Page 19: Joe Viesti/Viesti Associates. Page 20: Sara Matthews. Page 24: Sheilah Scully. Page 27: Louis Monier. Page 28: Michelle Sims. Page 29: Michelle Sims. Page 30: Joe Viesti/Viesti Associates. Page 32: Walt Chrynwski.

FRANCE

Page 39: Maryland CartoGraphics. Page 40: courtesy of Food and Wines from France. Page 41: Steven Rothfeld. Page 44: Sheilah Scully. Page 45: Maryland Carto-Graphics. Page 47: courtesy of the New

York Public Library Picture Collection. Page 50: John Bean. Page 51: Steven Rothfeld. Page 52: John Bean. Page 53: Sheilah Scully. Page 56: Sheilah Scully. Page 57: Steven Rothfeld. Page 58: A. DeBenito/Sobremesa, courtesy of ICEX Foods from Spain. Page 60: Steven Rothfeld. Page 61: Maryland CartoGraphics. Page 63: New York Public Library Picture Collection. Page 65: John Bean. Page 66: John Bean. Page 67: Maryland CartoGraphics. Page 72: John Bean. Page 73: Sara Matthews. Page 74: John Bean. Page 76: courtesy of Rouzaire. Page 78: Sheilah Scully. Page 79: Steven Rothfeld. Page 80: Steven Rothfeld. Page 81: Maryland CartoGraphics. Page 82: courtesy of the French Government Tourist Office. Page 84: John Bean. Page 88: Steven Rothfeld. Page 89: Maryland CartoGraphics. Page 93: courtesy of the French Government Tourist Office. Page 94: John Bean. Page 98: courtesy of Food and Wines from France. Page 99: The Bettmann Archive. Page 102: Gea Koenig, courtesy of the French Government Tourist Office. Page 104: Maryland CartoGraphics. Page 105: courtesy of the French Government Tourist Office. Page 107: Michel Guillard/Scope, courtesy of Food and Wines from France. Page 109: courtesy of the French Government Tourist Office. Page 112: Maryland CartoGraphics. Page 113: J. Guillard/Scope, courtesy of the Comté Cheese Association. Page 114: C.I.G.C., courtesy of the Comté Cheese Association. Page 116: Sheilah Scully. Page 118: C.I.G.C., courtesy of the Comté Cheese Association. Page 119: John Bean. Page 120: J. Guillard/Scope, courtesy of the Comté Cheese Association. Page 121: John Bean. Page 123: courtesy of the French Government Tourist Office. Page 126: The Bettmann Archive. Page 127: Maryland CartoGraphics. Page 128: courtesy of the French Government Tourist Office. Page 133: John Bean. Page 136: courtesy of the French Government Tourist Office. Page 137: Maryland CartoGraphics. Page 138: courtesy of the French Government Tourist Office. Page 139:

Steven Rothfeld. Page 142: Maryland CartoGraphics. Page 143: Sheilah Scully. Page 145: Sheilah Scully. Page 150: Steven Rothfeld. Page 153: courtesy of Société des Caves, Roquefort, France. Page 155: John Bean. Page 156: courtesy of Société des Caves, Roquefort, France. Page 157: courtesy of Société des Caves, Roquefort, France. Page 159: John Bean. Page 162: Sara Matthews. Page 163: Maryland CartoGraphics. Page 164: Steven Rothfeld. Page 168: Steven Rothfeld. Page 169: Maryland CartoGraphics. Page 173: Steven Rothfeld. Page 174: Maryland CartoGraphics. Page 175: courtesy of the French Government Tourist Office. Page 176: John Bean. Page 178: Steven Rothfeld.

ITALY

Page 182: Sara Matthews. Pages 183: Maryland CartoGraphics. Page 184: Sheilah Scully. Page 188: Maryland CartoGraphics. Page 189: Sheilah Scully. Page 192: courtesy of Milk and Fontina Manufacturers of the Valley of Aosta. Page 199: Sheilah Scully. Page 202: Maryland CartoGraphics. Page 203: Sheilah Scully. Page 204: John Bean. Page 206: John Bean. Page 209: Sheilah Scully. Page 211: John Bean. Page 213: Sheilah Scully. Page 214: Sheilah Scully. Page 217: Sheilah Scully. Page 218: Sheilah Scully. Page 220: Maryland CartoGraphics. Page 221: Sheilah Scully. Page 222: John Bean. Page 224: Sheilah Scully. Page 225: Thomas Kanzler/Viesti Associates. Page 226: Maryland CartoGraphics. Page 227: Sheilah Scully. Page 228: Sheilah Scully. Page 232: Sheilah Scully. Page 234: Sheilah Scully. Page 236: Maryland CartoGraphics. Page 237: Sheilah Scully. Page 238: John Bean. Page 242: Sheilah Scully. Page 243: Sheilah Scully. Page 244: Sheilah Scully. Page 245: Maryland CartoGraphics. Page 246: John Bean. Page 251: courtesy of BelGioioso Aurucchio Cheese, Inc. Page 254: Maryland CartoGraphics. Page 255: Joseph F. Viesti/Viesti Associates. Page 257: Sheilah Scully. Page 258: Maryland

CartoGraphics. Page 259: Steven Rothfeld. Page 262: Sheilah Scully.

SWITZERLAND

Page 266: Maryland CartoGraphics. Page 267: courtesy of the Swiss National Tourist Office. Page 268: Photo by SVZ/F. Pfenniger, courtesy of the Swiss National Tourist Office. Page 269: courtesy of the Switzerland Cheese Association. Page 272: The Bettman Archive. Page 273: courtesy of the Swiss National Tourist Office. Page 274: courtesy of the Swiss National Tourist Office. Page 275: courtesy of the Switzerland Cheese Association. Page 276: courtesy of the Switzerland Cheese Association. Page 277: courtesy of the Switzerland Cheese Association. Page 278: courtesy of the Switzerland Cheese Association. Page 280: Walt Chrynwski. Page 281: courtesy of the Swiss National Tourist Office. Page 283: courtesy of the Switzerland Cheese Association. Page 284 Photo by SVZ, courtesy of the Swiss National Tourist Office. Page 285: courtesy of the Switzerland Cheese Association. Page 286: courtesy of the Swiss National Tourist Office. Page 288: Walt Chrynwski. Page 289: John Bean.

THE BRITISH ISLES

Page 292: Susan Lund/Mirror Syndication International. Page 293: Maryland Carto-Graphics. Page 294: Julian Nieman/Mirror Syndication International. Page 296: E.C. Chapman/Mirror Syndication International. Page 298: John Bean. Page 301: John Melville/Mirror Syndication International. Page 302: Anthony Blake/Mirror Syndication International. Page 303: John Bean. Page 304 and page 305: courtesy of the Stilton Cheesemakers Association and Osborne Publicity Services. Page 308: John Bean Page 309: Lori S. Malkin. Page 310: David Hughes/Mirror Syndication International. Page 311 John Bean. Page 313: David Hughes/Mirror Syndication In-

ternational. Page 314: John Melville/Mirror Syndication International. Page 317: Mirror Syndication International. Page 320: John Bean. Page 321: John Melville/Mirror Syndication International. Page 322: ETA/ETB.

SPAIN

Page 326: Pablo Neustadt/Sobremesa, courtesy of ICEX Foods from Spain. Page 327: Maryland CartoGraphics. Page 329: Antonio de Benito/Sobremesa, courtesy of ICEX Foods from Spain. Page 330: John Bean. Page 331: Maryland CartoGraphics. Page 332: Joe Viesti/Viesti Associates. Page 333: M.A. Taborga, courtesy of ICEX Foods from Spain. Page 334: John Bean. Page 336: Ministry of Agriculture, courtesy of ICEX Foods from Spain. Page 337: Ministry of Agriculture, courtesy of ICEX Foods from Spain. Page 340: Pablo Neustadt/Sobremesa, courtesy of ICEX Foods from Spain. Page 341: Maryland CartoGraphics. Page 344: Hollander/Sherwin. Page 345: Maryland CartoGraphics. Page 346: Ministry of Agriculture, courtesy of ICEX Foods from Spain. Page 349: Enric Canut, courtesy of ICEX Foods from Spain. Page 350: Oronz, courtesy of ICEX Foods from Spain. Page 351: Maryland Carto-Graphics. Page 352: Ministry of Agriculture, courtesy of ICEX Foods from Spain. Page 354: Ministry of Agriculture, courtesy of ICEX Foods from Spain. Page 355: Carlos Navajas, courtesy of ICEX Foods from Spain. Pages 356–361: Ministry of Agriculture, ICEX Foods from Spain.

U.S.A

Page 364: courtesy of Tillamook County Creamery. Page 365: courtesy of Tillamook County Creamery. Page 366: Sheilah Scully. Page 369: Elizabeth Mackin. Page 371: courtesy of Vermont Butter & Cheese Company. Page 372: Sheilah Scully. Page 375: Joan Dark. Page 377: courtesy of Vermont Butter & Cheese Company. Page 379: Sheilah Scully. Page 380: Joanna Maria Ciccolini Mankiewicz. Page 381: courtesy of Wisconsin Milk Marketing Board. Page 382: courtesy of Deborah K. Haws, DKH Marketing Services. Page 383: Sheilah Scully. Page 386: Maryland CartoGraphics. Page 397: courtesy of Vella Cheese Company. Page 401: courtesy of Capriole, Inc. Page: 402: courtesy of Maytag Dairy Farms. Page 403: courtesy of Maytag Dairy Farms. Page 404: Photo by Karen Mitman, courtesy of The Squire Tarbox Inn. Page 411: Photo by David Jennings, courtesy of Coach Dairy Farm. Page 415: Jonathan Atkin. Page 420: courtesy of Tillamook County Creamery. Page 422: courtesy of The Mozzarella Company. Page 427: Joel Gardner, courtesy of Shelburne Farms. Page 430: courtesy of Brier Run Farm. Page 431: courtesy of BelGioioso Auricchio Cheese, Inc.

A MIXED PLATE/
THE GREAT CHEESES

Page 436: courtesy of the German Information Center. Page 437: courtesy of the Dutch Dairy Bureau. Page 438: courtesy of The Danish Tourist Board. Page 439: (top) Walt Chrynwski; (bottom) Michelle Sims. Page 440: Michelle Sims. Page 441: courtesy of The Danish Tourist Board. Page 443: (left) Sheilah Scully. Page 445: Chad Ehlers/Tony Stone Images. Page 447: courtesy of The Dutch Dairy Bureau. Page 449: courtesy of The Dutch Dairy Bureau. Page 450: courtesy of The Dutch Dairy Bureau. Page 451: courtesy of The Dutch Dairy Bureau. Page 452: courtesy of the Belgian National Tourist Office. Page 453: Michael M. Fairchild, courtesy of the Belgian National Tourist Board. Page 454: (top) Michael M. Fairchild, courtesy of the Belgian National Tourist Office; (bottom) courtesy of Passendale. Page 456: courtesy of the German Information Center. Page 457: courtesy of Alois Dallmayr. Page 459: courtesy of the German Information Center. Page 460: (top) courtesy of the the German Information Center; (bottom) Michelle Sims. Page 461: Michelle Sims. Page 462: National Dairy Committee of Greece, courtesy of the Greek Trade Commission. Page 463: courtesy of the Greek National Tourist Organization. Page 464: National Dairy Committee of Greece, courtesy of the Greek Trade Commission. Page 466: National Dairy Committee of Greece, courtesy of the Greek Trade Commission. Page 467: National Dairy Committee of Greece, courtesy of the Greek Trade Commission. Page 468: National Dairy Committee of Greece, courtesy of the Greek Trade Commission. Page 469: National Dairy Committee of Greece, courtesy of the Greek Trade Commission. Page 470: courtesy of Agropur. Page 471: courtesy of Fromagerie Tournevent.